The HERITAGE OF WORLD CIVILIZATIONS

The HERITAGE OF WORLD CIVILIZATIONS

TEACHING AND LEARNING CLASSROOM EDITION

BRIEF FOURTH EDITION

VOLUME TWO

Albert M. Craig
HARVARD UNIVERSITY

William A. Graham
HARVARD UNIVERSITY

Donald Kagan
YALE UNIVERSITY

Steven Ozment
HARVARD UNIVERSITY

Frank M. Turner
YALE UNIVERSITY

Prentice Hall
Upper Saddle River London Singapore
Toronto Tokyo Sydney Hong Kong Mexico City

Executive Editor: Charles Cavaliere
Editorial Assistant: Lauren Aylward
Editor in Chief, History: Priscilla McGeehon
Production Project Manager: Lynn Savino Wendel
Associate Editor: Emsal Hasan
Director of Marketing: Brandy Dawson
Senior Marketing Manager: Laura Lee Manley
Marketing Assistant: Athena Moore
AV Project Manager: Mirella Signoretto
Manager, Rights and Permissions: Zina Arabia
Manager, Visual Research: Beth Brenzel
Image Permission Coordinator: Michelina Viscusi
Cover Image Specialist: Karan Sanatar

Composition/Full Service Project Management: Rebecca Dunn, Prepare, Inc.
Director, Media & Assessment: Brian Hyland
Media Editor: Sarah Kinney
Media Project Manager: Tina Rudowski
Senior Operations Specialist: Mary Ann Gloriande
Senior Art Director: Maria Lange
Interior Designers: IDesign, Frubilicious Design Group, John Christiana
Cover Designer: John Christiana
Printer/Binder: Courier Kendallville
Cover Printer: Lehigh-Phoenix Color/Hagerstown

This book set in 10/13 Goudy.

Credits and acknowledgments borrowed from other sources and reproduced, with permission, in this texbook appear on appropiate page within text (or on page C-1).

Library of Congress Cataloging-in-Publication Data
The heritage of world civilizations / Albert M. Craig [et al.].—Teaching and learning classroom ed., 4th ed.
   p. m.
   Includes index.
   ISBN 978-0-205-66104-6 (combined)—ISBN 978-0-205-66103-9 (v. 1)—ISBN 978-0-205-66097-1 (v. 2)
   1. Civilization—History—Textbooks.   I. Craig, Albert M.
   CB69.H45 2010
   909—dc22
                               2008043472

10 9 8 7 6 5 4 3 2 1

Prentice Hall
is an imprint of

ISBN 13: 978-0-205-66104-6
ISBN 10:   0-205-66104-1
ISBN 13: 978-0-205-66097-1
ISBN 10:   0-205-66097-5

www.pearsonhighered.com

BRIEF CONTENTS

v

PART 6 Into the Modern World, 1815–1949

25 Northern Transatlantic Economy and Society, 1815–1914 612

26 Latin America from Independence to the 1940s 640

27 India, The Islamic Heartlands, and Africa, 1800–1945 664

MAPS

The response of the United States to the events of September 11, 2001, including the war in Iraq and Afghanistan, have brought upon the world a new awareness of human history in a global context. Prior to the attacks on New York and Washington and the subsequent U.S. intervention in the Middle East, readers in North America generally understood world history and globalism as academic concepts. They now understand them as realities shaping their daily lives and experience. The immediate pressures of the present and of the foreseeable future draw us to seek a more certain and extensive understanding of the past.

The idea of globalization is now a pressing reality on the lives of nations, affecting the domestic security of their citizens, the deployment of armed forces, their standard of living, and, increasingly, the environment. We have certainly entered a new era in which no active citizen or educated person can escape the necessity of understanding the past in global terms. Both the historical experience and the moral, political, and religious values of the different world civilizations now demand our attention and our understanding. It is our hope that in these new, challenging times *The Heritage of World Civilizations* will provide one path to such knowledge.

THE ROOTS OF GLOBALIZATION

Globalization—that is, the increasing interaction and interdependency of the various regions of the world—has resulted from two major historical developments: the closing of the European era of world history and the rise of technology.

From approximately 1500 C.E. to the middle of the twentieth century, Europeans gradually came to dominate the world through colonization (most particularly in North and South America), state-building, economic productivity, and military power. That era of European dominance ended during the third quarter of the twentieth century after Europe brought unprecedented destruction on itself during World War II and as the nations of Asia, the Near East, and Africa achieved new positions on the world scene. Their new political independence, their control over strategic natural resources, the expansion of their economies (especially those of the nations of the Pacific Rim of Asia), and in some cases their access to nuclear weapons have changed the shape of world affairs.

Further changing the world political and social situation has been a growing discrepancy in the economic development of different regions that is often portrayed as a problem between the northern and southern hemispheres. Beyond the emergence of this economic disparity has been the remarkable advance of radical political Islamism during the past forty years. In the midst of all these developments, as a result of the political collapse of the former Soviet Union, the United States has emerged as the single major world power, though its position is increasingly being challenged by China, whose growing economic might now rivals that of the United States and whose military has embarked on a rapid buildup of its forces.

The second historical development that continues to fuel the pace of globalization is the advance of technology, associated most importantly with transportation, military weapons, and electronic communication. The advances in transportation over the past two centuries including ships, railways, and airplanes have made more parts of the world and its resources accessible to more people in ever shorter spans of time. Over the past century and a half, military weapons of increasingly destructive power enabled Europe and then later the United States to dominate other regions of the globe. Now the spread of these weapons means that any nation with sophisticated military technology can threaten other nations, no matter how far away. Furthermore, technologies that originated in the West from the early twentieth century to the present have been turned against the West. More recently, the electronic revolution associated with computer technology and most particularly the Internet has sparked unprecedented speed and complexity in global communications. It is astonishing to recall that personal computers have been generally available for less than twenty-five years and the rapid personal communication associated with them has existed for less than fifteen years.

Why not, then, focus only on new factors in the modern world, such as the impact of technology and the end of the European era? To do so would ignore the very deep roots that these developments have in the past. More important, the events of recent years demonstrate, as the authors of this book have long contended, that the major religious traditions continue to shape and drive the modern world as well as the world of the past. The religious traditions link today's civilizations to their most ancient roots. We believe this emphasis on the great religious traditions recognizes not only a factor that has shaped the past but also one that is profoundly and dynamically alive in our world today.

STRENGTHS OF THE TEACHING AND LEARNING CLASSROOM EDITION

ACCESSIBILITY

Acclaimed by instructors and students for its exciting new approach to learning history, the Teaching and Learning Classroom Edition of *The Heritage of World Civilizations* provides a concise narrative enriched by abundant illustrations, focused study tools, and critical-thinking questions that make the past come alive. This new edition of *The Heritage of World Civilizations*, TLC Edition, incorporates even more learning support for students and additional teaching resources for history instructors.

BALANCED AND FLEXIBLE PRESENTATION

In this edition, as in past editions, we have sought to present world history fairly, accurately, and in a way that does justice to its great variety. History has many facets, no one of which can account for the others. Any attempt to tell the story of civilization from a single perspective, no matter how timely, is bound to neglect or suppress some important part of that story.

Historians have recently brought a vast array of new tools and concepts to bear on the study of history. Our coverage introduces students to various aspects of social and intellectual history as well as to the more traditional political, diplomatic, and military coverage. We firmly believe that only through an appreciation of all pathways to understanding of the past can the real heritage of world civilizations be claimed.

The Teaching and Learning Classroom (TLC) Edition of *The Heritage of World Civilizations* is designed to accommodate a variety of approaches to a course in world history, allowing teachers to stress what is most important to them. Some teachers will ask students to read all the chapters. Others will select among them to reinforce assigned readings and lectures.

CURRENT SCHOLARSHIP

As in previous editions, changes in this edition reflect our determination to incorporate the most recent developments in historical scholarship and the expanding concerns of professional historians. To better highlight the dynamic processes of world history, significant new and expanded coverage of prehistory, Africa, East Asia, Southeast Asia, the Atlantic World, and the Middle East has been added to the TLC edition.

CONTENT AND ORGANIZATION

The many changes in content and organization in this TLC edition of *The Heritage of World Civilizations* reflect our ongoing effort to present a truly global survey of world civilizations that at the same time gives a rich picture of the history of individual regions:

- **Global Approach.** This TLC Edition continues to explicitly highlight the connections and parallels in global history among regions of the world. Each chapter begins with a "Global Perspective" essay that succinctly places in a wider global framework the regions and topics that are to be discussed with an emphasis on the connections, parallels, and comparisons between and among different cultures.

- **Expanded Map Program.** As in previous editions, great attention has been paid to extending and refining the map program for *The Heritage of World Civilizations*. The TLC Edition includes many new maps that graphically illustrate key developments in global history. In addition, when appropriate, existing maps in the text have been redesigned and modified for greater visual appeal and accuracy. Many maps are now accompanied by a global locator that helps students situate the main map in a wider geographical setting.

    Maps new to this TLC Edition:

    Centers of Greek Philosophy

    Early Korean States

    Vietnam and Neighboring Southeast Asia

    Great Zimbabwe

    Origins of African Slaves Sent to the Americas

    Subscriptions to the *Encyclopedia*

    The Languages of Europe, ca. 1850

    British India, 1820 and 1856

    West Asia, Central Asia, and the Mediterranean, ca. 1850

    Nineteenth-Century Reform Movements in Africa and Arabia

    The Long March

    The Colonial Economy of Africa, 1880–1914

    The Growth of European Union

    Distribution of HIV in Africa

A listing of all the maps in the text can be found on pp. xv-xvi.

- **Improved Organization and New Scholarship.** Though the number of chapters remains unchanged in the Teaching and Learning Classroom Edition, the organization of several chapters has been revised to improve narrative flow and highlight important topics more clearly. Chapter 5, on the early history of Africa, now includes extensive discussion of the sources and tools used by anthropologists and historians in their work. Chapter 9, formerly devoted to the early history of Japan, now takes a wider perspective in examining early state formation and cultural developments in Korea and Vietnam as well. Chapter 10 now includes discussion of Nestorian Christianity. The coverage of African history from 1000 to 1700 has been moved to Chapter 14 to more fully integrate the discussion of crucial African developments in this period with developments in Europe and the Americas during this time. Chapter 18, on the formation of an Atlantic World in the sixteenth to eighteenth centuries, now includes extensive treatment of the Columbian exchange and the most recent data on the slave trade. Chapter 27, on India, the Islamic world, and Africa in the nineteenth and early twentieth centuries, has been extensively revised to sharpen the perspective of native peoples on the experience of imperialism. Chapter 32's discussion of the West since World War II now presents coverage of climate change and the tensions this has caused between the United States and Europe. Chapter 34, the final chapter, has been extensively revised to highlight important recent events in Africa, Latin America, South Asia, and the Middle East.

- **New Design and Photo Program.** The entire text has been set in a crisp and engaging new design. Each of the thirty-four chapters includes photos never before included in previous editions of the text. New graphs and tables have also been added to the text to help students visualize important data.

PEDAGOGICAL FEATURES OF THE TLC EDITION

This TLC edition retains many of the pedagogical features of previous editions while providing increased assessment opportunities.

- **NEW Interpreting the Past** feature, found at the end of each chapter, presents students with MyHistoryLab which, sheds light on a significant problem in world history. Problems include the nature of kingship in early societies, Islam's encounter with the "other," perspectives on the Atlantic slave trade, Japan's relations with the outside world during the Tokugawa shogunate, and feminism and civil rights after World War II. Students are asked to consider how the sources relate to each other and how they shed light on the problems historians face in interpreting the past.

- **NEW Global Perspective Essays** introduce the key problems of each chapter and place them in a global and historical context. Focus Questions prompt students to consider the causes, connections, and consequences of the topics they will encounter in the main narrative.

- **Religions of the World** essays examine the historical impact of each of the world's great religious traditions: Judaism, Christianity, Islam, Buddhism, and Hinduism.

- **Focus Questions** organized by key subtopics open each chapter and help students think about important topics for study and review. The focus questions are repeated at the appropriate sections in each chapter.

- **Overview Tables** summarize key concepts and reinforce material presented in the main narrative.

- **Chronologies** within each chapter help students situate key events in time.

- **Documents,** including selections from sacred books, poems, philosophical tracts, political manifestos, letters, and travel accounts, expose students to the raw material of history, providing an intimate contact with peoples of the past. Questions accompanying the source documents direct students toward important, thought-provoking issues and help them relate the documents to the main narrative.

- **NEW Visual Analysis Questions** ask students to consider photographs, fine art, and other illustrations as visual evidence.

- **Key Terms** are boldfaced in the text and are defined in the margin of the page.

- **Chapter Summaries** conclude each chapter, organized by subtopic, and recap important points.

- **Chapter Review Questions,** organized by key subtopics, help students interpret the broad themes of each chapter.

A Note on Dates and Transliteration

We have used B.C.E. (before the common era) and C.E. (common era) instead of B.C. (before Christ) and A.D. (*anno domini*, the year of our Lord) to designate dates.

Until recently, most scholarship on China used the Wade-Giles system of romanization for Chinese names and terms. China, today, however, uses another system known as pinyin. Virtually all Western newspapers have adopted it. In order that students may move easily from the present text to the existing body of advanced scholarship on Chinese history, we now use the pinyin system throughout the text.

Also, we have followed the currently accepted English transliterations of Arabic words. For example, today Koran is being replaced by the more accurate Qur'an; similarly Muhammad is preferable to Mohammed and Muslim to Moslem. We have not tried to distinguish the letters '*ayn* and *hamza*; both are rendered by a simple apostrophe (') as in Shi'ite. With regard to Sanskritic transliteration, we have not distinguished linguals and dentals, and both palatal and lingual *s* are rendered *sh*, as in Shiva and Upanishad.

Support Materials

The Heritage of World Civilizations, TLC Edition, comes with an extensive package of support materials for teachers and students.

For Instructors

- **The Instructor's Manual/Test Item File** includes chapter outlines, overviews, key concepts, discussion questions, suggestions for useful audiovisual resources, and approximately 1,500 test items (essay, multiple choice, true/false, and matching).

- **My Test** is a computerized test management program for Windows and Macintosh environments. The program allows instructors to select items from the test item file to create tests. It also allows for online testing.

- **The Instructor's Resource Center** (www.prenhall. com) Text-specific materials, such as the instructor's manual, the test item file, map files, and PowerPoint™ presentations, are available for downloading by adopters.

- **MyHistoryLab** (www.myhistorylab.com) With the best of Prentice Hall's multimedia solutions in one easy-to-use place, MyHistoryLab for *The Heritage of World Civilizations*, TLC Edition, offers students and instructors a state-of-the-art, interactive solution for world history. Organized by the main subtopics of *The Heritage of World Civilizations*, TLC Edition, and delivered within a course-management platform, MyHistoryLab supplements and enriches the classroom experience and can form the basis for an online course.

For the Student

- Extensively revised and updated, the **Primary Source: Documents in Global History DVD** is both an immense collection of textual and visual documents in world history and an indispensable tool for working with sources. Extensively developed with the guidance of historians and teachers, the revised and updated DVD version includes over 800 sources in world history—from cave art to satellite images of the Earth from space. More sources from Africa, Latin America, and Southeast Asia have been added to this revised and updated DVD version. All sources are accompanied by headnotes, and focus questions and are searchable by topic, region, or time period.

- **World History Study Site** (www.pearsonhighered. com) This course-based, open-access online companion provides a wealth of resources for both students and professors, including test questions, flash cards, links for further research, and Web-based assignments.

- Titles from the renowned **Penguin Classics** series can be bundled with *The Heritage of World Civilizations* for a nominal charge. Please contact your Pearson Arts and Sciences sales representative for details.

- *The Prentice Hall Atlas of World History*, **Second Edition**, includes over 100 full-color maps in world history, drawn by Dorling Kindersley, one of the world's most respected cartographic publishers. Copies of the atlas can be bundled with *The Heritage of World Civilizations*, TLC Edition, for a nominal charge. Contact your Pearson Arts and Sciences sales representative for details.

Pearson Prentice Hall is pleased to serve as a sponsor of the the World History Association Teaching Prize and the World History Association and Phi Alpha Theta Student Paper Prize (undergraduate and graduate divisions). Both of these prizes are awarded annually. For more information, contact thewha@hawaii.edu.

ACKNOWLEDGMENTS

We are grateful to the many scholars and teachers whose thoughtful and often detailed comments helped shape this as well as previous editions of *The Heritage of World Civilizations*. The advice and guidance provided by Katie Janssen on the coverage of African history and Thomas M. Ricks on the coverage of Islam and the Middle East are especially appreciated.

REVIEWERS

Wayne Ackerson, *Salisbury State University*
W. Nathan Alexander, *Troy University*
Jack Martin Balcer, *Ohio State University*
Charmarie J. Blaisdell, *Northeastern University*
Deborah Buffton, *University of Wisconsin at La Crosse*
Loretta Burns, *Mankato State University*
Gayle K. Brunelle, *California State University, Fullerton*
Douglas Chambers, *University of Southern Mississippi*
Chun-shu Chang, *University of Michigan, Ann Arbor*
Mark Chavalas, *University of Wisconsin at La Crosse*
Anthony Cheeseboro, *Southern Illinois University at Edwardsville*
William J. Courteney, *University of Wisconsin*
Samuel Willard Crompton, *Holyoke Community College*
James B. Crowley, *Yale University*
Bruce Cummings, *University of Chicago*
Stephen F. Dale, *Ohio State University, Columbus*
Clarence B. Davis, *Marian College*
Raymond Van Dam, *University of Michigan, Ann Arbor*
Bill Donovan, *Loyola University of Maryland*
Wayne Farris, *University of Tennessee*
Anita Fisher, *Clark College*
Suzanne Gay, *Oberlin College*
Katrina A. Glass, *United States Military Academy*
Robert Gerlich, *Loyola University*
Samuel Robert Goldberger, *Capital Community-Technical College*
Andrew Gow, *University of Alberta*
Katheryn L. Green, *University of Wisconsin, Madison*
David Griffiths, *University of North Carolina, Chapel Hill*
Louis Haas, *Duquesne University*
Barry Hankins, *Baylor University*
Joseph T. Hapak, *Moraine Valley Community College*
Hue-Tam Ho Tai, *Harvard University*
David Kieft, *University of Minnesota*
Don Knox, *Wayland Baptist University*
Frederick Krome, *Northern Kentucky University*
Lisa M. Lane, *Mira Costa College*
Richard Law, *Washington State University*
David Lelyveld, *Columbia University*
Jan Lewis, *Rutgers University, Newark*

James C. Livingston, *College of William and Mary*
Garth Montgomery, *Radford University*
Richard L. Moore Jr., *St. Augustine's College*
Beth Nachison, *Southern Connecticut State University*
Robin S. Oggins, *Binghamton University*
George S. Pabis, *Georgia Perimeter College*
Louis A. Perez Jr., *University of South Florida*
Jonathan Perry, *University of South Florida*
Cora Ann Presley, *Tulane University*
Norman Raiford, *Greenville Technical College*
Norman Ravitch, *University of California, Riverside*
Thomas M. Ricks, *University of Pennsylvania*
Philip F. Riley, *James Madison University*
Thomas Robisheaux, *Duke University*
William S. Rodner, *Tidewater Community College*
David Ruffley, *United States Air Force Academy*
Dankwart A. Rustow, *City University of New York*
James J. Sack, *University of Illinois at Chicago*
Anthony R. Santoro, *Christopher Newport University*
William Schell, *Murray State University*
Marvin Slind, *Washington State University*
Daniel Scavone, *University of Southern Indiana*
Linda B. Scherr, *Mercer County Community College*
Roger Schlesinger, *Washington State University*
Charles C. Stewart, *University of Illinois*
Nancy L. Stockdale, *University of Central Florida*
Carson Tavenner, *United States Air Force Academy*
Truong-bu Lam, *University of Hawaii*
Harry L. Watson, *Loyola College of Maryland*
William B. Whisenhunt, *College of DuPage*
Paul Varley, *Columbia University*
Deborah Vess, *Georgia College and State University*
Gilmar Visoni, *Queensborough Community College*

Finally, we would like to thank the dedicated people who helped produce this revision: our editor, Charles Cavaliere; Maria Lange, who created the handsome new design for this edition; Lynn Savino Wendel, our project manager; Mary Ann Gloriande, our senior operations specialist, and Rebecca Dunn, our production editor. We also owe a special thanks to Katie Janssen for her invaluable help in preparing this TLC edition.

A.M.C.

W.A.G.

D.K.

S.O.

F.M.T.

Albert M. Craig is the Harvard-Yenching Research Professor of History Emeritus at Harvard University, where he has taught since 1959. A graduate of Northwestern University, he received his Ph.D. at Harvard University. He has studied at Strasbourg University and at Kyoto, Keio, and Tokyo universities in Japan. He is the author of *Choshu in the Meiji Restoration* (1961), *The Heritage of Chinese Civilization* (2001), and, with others, of *East Asia, Tradition and Transformation* (1989). He is the editor of *Japan, A Comparative View* (1973) and co-editor of *Personality in Japanese History* (1970). At present he is engaged in research on the thought of Fukuzawa Yukichi. For eleven years (1976–1987) he was the director of the Harvard-Yenching Institute. He has also been a visiting professor at Kyoto and Tokyo universities. He has received Guggenheim, Fulbright, and Japan Foundation Fellowships. In 1988 he was awarded the Order of the Rising Sun by the Japanese government.

William A. Graham is Albertson Professor of Middle Eastern Studies in the Faculty of Arts and Sciences and O'Brian Professor of Divinity and Dean in the Faculty of Divinity at Harvard University, where he has taught for thirty-four years. He has directed the Center for Middle Eastern Studies and chaired the Department of Near Eastern Languages and Civilizations, the Committee on the Study of Religion, and the Core Curriculum Committee on Foreign Cultures. He received his B.A. in Comparative Literature from the University of North Carolina, Chapel Hill, an A.M. and Ph.D. in History of Religion from Harvard, and studied also in Göttingen, Tübingen, Lebanon, and London. He is former chair of the Council on Graduate Studies in Religion (U.S. and Canada). In 2000 he received the quinquennial Award for Excellence in Research in Islamic History and Culture from the Research Centre for Islamic History, Art and Culture (IRCICA) of the Organisation of the Islamic Conference. He has held John Simon Guggenheim and Alexander von Humboldt research fellowships and is a fellow of the American Academy of Arts and Sciences. Among his publications are *Beyond the Written Word: Oral Aspects of Scripture in the History of Religion* (1987); *Divine Word and Prophetic Word in Early Islam* (1977—ACLS History of Religions Prize, 1978); and *Three Faiths, One God* (coauthored, 2003).

Donald Kagan is Sterling Professor of History and Classics at Yale University, where he has taught since 1969. He received the A.B. degree in history from Brooklyn College, the M.A. in classics from Brown University, and the Ph.D. in history from Ohio State University. From 1958 to 1959 he studied at the American School of Classical Studies as a Fulbright Scholar. He has received three awards for undergraduate teaching at Cornell and Yale. He is the author of a history of Greek political thought, *The Great Dialogue* (1965); a four-volume history of the Peloponnesian war, *The Origins of the Peloponnesian War* (1969); *The Archidamian War* (1974); *The Peace of Nicias and the Sicilian Expedition* (1981); *The Fall of the Athenian Empire* (1987); a biography of Pericles, *Pericles of Athens and the Birth of Democracy* (1991); *On the Origins of War* (1995), and *The Peloponnesian War* (2003). He is coauthor, with Frederick W. Kagan, of *While America Sleeps* (2000). With Brian Tierney and L. Pearce Williams, he is the editor of *Great Issues in Western Civilization*, a collection of readings. He was awarded the National Humanities Medal for 2002.

Steven Ozment is McLean Professor of Ancient and Modern History at Harvard University. He has taught Western Civilization at Yale, Stanford, and Harvard. He is the author of nine books. *The Age of Reform, 1250–1550* (1980) won the Schaff Prize and was nominated for the 1981 National Book Award. Five of his books have been selections of the History Book Club: *Magdalena and Balthasar: An Intimate Portrait of Life in Sixteenth Century Europe* (1986), *Three Behaim Boys: Growing Up in Early Modern Germany* (1990), *Protestants: The Birth of a Revolution* (1992), *The Burgermeister's Daughter: Scandal in a Sixteenth Century German Town* (1996), and *Flesh and Spirit: Private Life in Early Modern Germany* (1999). His most recent book is *Ancestors: The Loving Family of Old Europe* (2001). *A Mighty Fortress: A New History of the German People* was published in January 2004.

Frank M. Turner is John Hay Whitney Professor of History at Yale University and Director of the Beinecke Rare Book and Manuscript Library at Yale University, where he served as University Provost from 1988 to 1992. He received his B.A. degree from the College of William and Mary and his Ph.D. from Yale. He has received the Yale College Award for Distinguished Undergraduate Teaching. He has directed a National Endowment for the Humanities Summer Institute. His scholarly research has received the support of fellowships from the National Endowment for the Humanities, the Guggenheim Foundation, and the Woodrow

Wilson Center. He is the author of *Between Science and Religion: The Reaction to Scientific Naturalism in Late Victorian England* (1974), *The Greek Heritage in Victorian Britain* (1981), which received the British Council Prize of the Conference on British Studies and the Yale Press Governors Award, *Contesting Cultural Authority: Essays in Victorian Intellectual Life* (1993), and *John Henry Newman: The Challenge to Evangelical Religion* (2002). He has also contributed numerous articles to journals and has served on the editorial advisory boards of *The Journal of Modern History, Isis,* and *Victorian Studies.* He edited *The Idea of a University,* by John Henry Newman (1996), *Reflections on the Revolution in France by Edmund Burke* (2003), and *Apologia Pro Vita Sua and Six Sermons* by John Henry Newman (2008). He served as a Trustee of Connecticut College from 1996 to 2006. In 2003, Professor Turner was appointed Director of the Beinecke Rare Book and Manuscript Library at Yale University.

15

Africa ca. 1000–1700

Benin Plaque.
Some of the world's finest works of art were made by the artists of Benin and Ife, though much is still unknown about them. Rarely found elsewhere in Africa, bronze panels like the plaque shown here adorned the royal palace and are considered examples of "court art." The figures are typical of the Benin style in their proportions of head to body—about one to four—perhaps emphasizing the head's importance as a symbol of life and behavior.

Benin Plaque. Brass. Lost wax. W. Africa 16th–17th century C.E. Hillel Burger/Peabody Museum, Harvard University © President and Fellows of Harvard College. All rights reserved.

What details do you notice in this plaque?

NORTH AFRICA AND EGYPT *page 362*

HOW DID the Ottomans govern North Africa and Egypt?

THE SPREAD OF ISLAM SOUTH OF THE SAHARA *page 363*

HOW DID Islam spread south of the Sahara?

SAHELIAN EMPIRES OF THE WESTERN AND CENTRAL SUDAN *page 364*

WHAT WERE the four most important states in the Sahel between 1000 and 1600?

THE EASTERN SUDAN *page 370*

WHY DID Christianity gradually disappear in Nubia?

THE FORESTLANDS: COASTAL WEST AND CENTRAL AFRICA *page 370*

HOW DID the arrival of Europeans affect the peoples of West and Central Africa?

EAST AFRICA *page 373*

HOW DID Swahili language and culture develop?

SOUTHERN AFRICA *page 376*

HOW DID slavery affect race relations in Cape Colony?

GLOBAL PERSPECTIVE

AFRICA, 1000–1700

Long-distance trade—the movement of goods, people, and, inevitably, cultural practices and ideas in patterns driven by supply and demand—is typically an engine of historical change. This was as true in Africa in the early centuries of the second millennium as it was in the Americas, Europe, Asia, or anywhere in the world. Different regions in Africa were oriented differently in relation to trade routes and trading partners, and these regions developed in markedly different ways between 1000 and 1700.

The North African coast and the Sahel were situated amidst trading networks that linked the Mediterranean world, the growing *Dar al-Islam* (the "House of Submission," or Islamic world), and the rich kingdoms of West Africa. The East African coast was integrated into the trading and cultural networks of the Indian Ocean basin and was firmly engaged with the Muslim world there. The rest of sub-Saharan Africa was culturally diverse; people here engaged primarily in intra-African trade with cultures that occupied other ecological niches. It is important to remember that Africa is a continent that is home to many societies with different histories, languages, religions, and cultures. In this way it is similar to Europe, but Africa is also much larger than Europe and more ethnically and culturally diverse.

Along the Mediterranean, the key new factor in African history at this time was the Ottomans' imperial expansion into Egypt and the **Maghreb.** The long Ottoman hegemony altered the political configuration of the Mediterranean world. Merchants and missionaries carried Islam and Arabian cultural influences across the Sahara from North Africa and the Middle East to the western, central, and Nilotic Sudan, where Muslim conversion played a growing social and political role, especially among the ruling elites who profited most from brokering trade between their lands and the Islamic north. Islam provided a shared arena of expression for at least some classes and groups in societies over a vast area from Egypt to Senegambia. In Africa as elsewhere, new converts modified Islam through a process of syncretism. Distinctively African forms of Islam emerged, faithful to the central tenets of the religion, but differing in observances and customs from those of the Arabian cultural sphere, especially in attitudes toward women and relationships between the sexes.

Dar al-Islam In Arabic, the "House of Submission," or Islamic world. There are many shades of meaning, ranging from a place where the government is under Muslim control, to a place where individuals are free to practice Islamic beliefs.

Maghreb Literally, in Arabic, "place of sunset," or the west; refers to the northwest of Africa, and specifically what is now Morocco.

Different parts of the African continent had very different histories early in the second millennium C.E. Many regions in Africa had substantial interactions with the Islamic and European worlds, while others engaged in trade and cultural exchanges within the continent. Although the Atlantic slave trade is treated in Chapter 18, its importance must be kept in mind as we review the period's other developments. We begin with Africa above the equator, where the influence of Islam increased and where substantial empires and kingdoms developed. Then we discuss West, East, Central, and South Africa and the effects of first Arab-Islamic and then European influence in these regions. ■

NORTH AFRICA AND EGYPT

HOW DID the Ottomans govern North Africa and Egypt?

As we saw in Chapter 13, Egypt and other North African societies played a central role in Islamic and Mediterranean history after 1000 C.E. From Tunisia to Egypt, Sunni religious and political leaders and their Shi'ite (especially Isma'ili) counterparts struggled for the minds of the masses. In general, a feisty regionalism characterized states, city-states, and tribal groups north of the Sahara and along the lower Nile. No single power controlled them for long. Regionalism persisted even after 1500, when most of North Africa came under the influence—and often direct control—of the Ottoman Empire.

By 1800 the nominally Ottoman domains from Egypt to Algeria were effectively independent. In Egypt the Ottomans had established direct rule after their defeat of the Mamluks in 1517, but by the seventeenth and eighteenth centuries, power had passed to Egyptian governors descended from the earlier Mamluks. The Mediterranean coastlands between Egypt and Morocco were officially Ottoman provinces, or regencies, but by the eighteenth century, Algiers, Tripoli (in modern Libya), and Tunisia had institutionalized their own political structures.

South of the Sahara, dynamic processes of state-building and trade were the main forces for cultural change. In Central and South Africa, except along the eastern coast, and in the West African forests, older African traditions held sway, and there was little or no evidence of Islam beyond individual Muslims involved in trade. On the eastern coast, however, Islam influenced the development of the Swahili culture and language, a unique blend of African, Indian, and Arabian traditions, and Islamic traders linked the region to India, China, and the Indies. In sub-Saharan Africa, the spread of Islam took place almost entirely through peaceful means.

Along the Atlantic and Indian Ocean coasts of Africa, the key development of the fifteenth century was the arrival of ships carrying traders and missionaries from Christian Europe. The strength of African societies and the biological dangers to Europeans venturing into the interior meant that most of the trade between the African interior and Europeans on both coasts remained under the control of Africans for generations. Even before Europeans themselves reached the interior, however, the trade in slaves, weapons, and gold that they fostered greatly altered African political and social structures not only along the coasts but also in regions untouched by the outsiders. The European voyages of discovery of the fifteenth and sixteenth centuries presaged the African continent's involvement in a new, expanding, and, by the eighteenth century, European-dominated global trading system. This system generally exploited rather than bolstered African development, as the infamous Atlantic slave trade (see Chapter 18) and the South African experience illustrate.

Focus Questions

◆ Where in Africa was Islamic influence concentrated? How did Islam spread? What does this reveal about the relationship between commerce and cultural diffusion?

◆ Why did different regions in Africa develop in different ways between 1000 and 1700?

Morocco, ruled by a succession of **Sharifs** (leaders claiming descent from the family of the Prophet Muhammad), was the only North African sultanate to remain fully independent after 1700. The most important *Sharifian* dynasty was that of the Sa'dis (1554–1659). One major reason for Morocco's independence was that its Arab and Berber populations united after 1500 to oppose the Portuguese and the Spaniards.

Sharifs A term for leaders who are direct descendants of the prophet Muhammad through his first grandson, Hasan ibn Ali.

THE SPREAD OF ISLAM SOUTH OF THE SAHARA

Islamic influence in sub-Saharan Africa began as early as the eighth century. By 1800 it affected most of the Sudanic belt and the coast of East Africa as far south as modern Zimbabwe. The process was mostly peaceful, gradual, and partial. Conversion to Islam was rare beyond the ruling or commercial classes, and Islamic faith tended to coexist or blend with indigenous beliefs. Agents of Islam brought commercial and political changes as well as the Qur'an, new religious practices, and literate culture.

HOW DID Islam spread south of the Sahara?

In East Africa, Muslim traders moving down the coastline with the ancient monsoon trade routes had begun to "Islamize" ports and coastal regions even before 800 C.E. From the thirteenth century on, Islamic trading communities and city-states developed along the coast from Mogadishu to Kilwa.

In the western and central parts of the continent, Islam was introduced south of the Sahara primarily by traders from North Africa and the Nile valley. Berbers who plied the desert routes (see Chapter 5) to trading towns such as Awdaghast on the edge of the Sahel as early as the eighth century were Islam's chief agents. From there Islam spread south to centers such as Kumbi Saleh and beyond, southeast across the Niger, and west into Senegambia. Emigrants from Egypt and the Nilotic Sudan helped spread Islam; migrating Arab tribal groups in search of new land came west to settle in the central sub-Saharan Sahel.

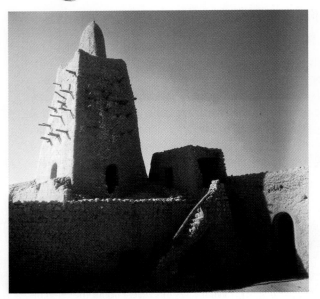

The Great Mosque in Timbuktu. This mud and wood building is typical of western Sudanese mosques. The distinctive minaret was a symbol of the presence of Islam, which came to places like Timbuktu in Central and West Africa by way of overland trade routes.

How widely was Islam adopted in western Sudan?

The year 985 marks the first time a West African royal court—that of the kingdom of Gao, east of the Niger bend—officially became Muslim (see Chapter 5). The Gao rulers did not try to convert their subjects. By contrast, as we shall see later in the chapter, the rulers of the later kingdom of Ghana long maintained their indigenous traditions even though they traded with Muslims and had Muslim advisers.

Starting in the 1030s zealous militants known as Almoravids (see Chapter 13) began a conversion campaign that eventually swept into Ghana's territory, taking first Awdaghast and later, in 1076, Kumbi Saleh. Thereafter, the forcibly converted Soninke ruling group of Ghana spread Islam among their own populace and farther south in the savanna. They converted Mande-speaking traders, who brought Islam south into the forests. Farther west, the Fulbe rulers of Takrur became Muslim in the 1030s and propagated their new faith among their subjects. The Fulbe, or Fulani, remained important carriers of Islam over the next eight centuries as they migrated gradually into new regions as far east as Lake Chad, where some rulers were Muslim as early as 1100.

Major groups in West Africa strongly resisted Islamization, especially the Mossi kingdoms founded in the Volta region at Wagadugu around 1050 and Yatenga about 1170.

SAHELIAN EMPIRES OF THE WESTERN AND CENTRAL SUDAN

WHAT WERE the four most important states in the Sahel between 1000 and 1600?

As we noted in Chapter 5, substantial states had risen in the first millennium C.E. in the Sahel regions just south of the Sahara proper. From about 1000 to 1600, four of these developed into relatively long-lived empires: Ghana, Mali, and Songhai in the western Sudan, and Kanem-Bornu in the central Sudan.

GHANA

Ghana established the model for later empires of the Sahel region of the western Sudan. It was located well north of modern Ghana (and unrelated to it except by name) in the region between the inland Niger Delta and the upper Senegal to the north. Ghana emerged as a regional power near the end of the first millennium and flourished for about two centuries. Its capital, Kumbi Saleh, was on the desert's edge, well sited for the Saharan and Sahelian trade networks. Ghana's major population group was the Soninke; *Ghana* is the Soninke term for "ruler."

The Ghanaian rulers were descended matrilineally (through the previous king's sister). They ruled through a council of ministers. The king was supreme judge and held court regularly to hear grievances. The king was held to be divinely blessed, if not semidivine, and royal ceremonies in Kumbi Saleh highlighted regal wealth and power.

Slaves were at the bottom of Ghana's hierarchical society; farmers and draftsmen above them; merchants above them; and the king, his court, and the nobility on top. Ghana's power rested on a solid economic base. Tribute from the empire's many chieftaincies and taxes on royal lands and crops supplemented duties levied on all incoming and outgoing trade. This trade—north–south between the Sahara and the savanna, and especially east–west through the Sahel between Senegambia and more easterly trading towns like Gao on the Niger Bend—involved a variety of goods. Imported salt, cloth, and metal goods such as copper from the north were probably exchanged for gold and perhaps kola nuts from the south. The regime apparently also controlled the gold (and, presumably, the slave) trade that originated in the savanna to the south and west.

Although the king and court of Ghana did not convert to Islam, they made elaborate arrangements to accommodate Muslim traders and government servants in their own settlement a few miles from the royal preserve in Kumbi Saleh. Muslim traders were prominent in the court, literate Muslims administered the government, and Muslim legists advised the ruler.

A huge, well-trained army secured royal control and enabled the kings to extend their sway in the late tenth century to the Atlantic shore and to the south (see Map 15–1). Ghanaian troops captured Awdaghast, the important southern terminus of the trans-Saharan trade route to Morocco, from the Berbers in 992. The empire was, however, vulnerable to attack from the desert fringe, as Almoravid Berber forces proved in 1054 when they took Awdaghast in a single raid.

MAP EXPLORATION

To explore this map further, go to **http://www.prenhall.com/craig_maps**

MAP 15–1 Africa ca. 900–1500.   Shown are major cities and states referred to in the text. The main map shows the region of West Africa occupied by the empire of Ghana from about 990 to about 1180. The inset shows the region occupied by Mali between 1230 and 1450.

Why was Ghana's location important for its prosperity?

Ghana's empire was probably destroyed in the late twelfth century by the anti-Muslim Soso people from the mountains southeast of Kumbi Saleh; they were a Malinke clan who had long been part of the Ghanaian Empire. Their brief ascendancy between 1180 and 1230 apparently spelled the end of the once great transregional power centered at Kumbi Saleh.[1]

MALI

With Ghana's collapse and the Almoravids' focus on North Africa, the western Sudan broke up into smaller kingdoms. The former Ghanaian provinces of Mande and Takrur were already independent before 1076, and in the early twelfth century Takrur's control of the Senegal valley and the gold-producing region of Galam made it briefly the strongest state in the western Sudan. Like Ghana, however, it was soon eclipsed, first by the brief Soso ascendancy and then by the rise of Mali.

In the mid-thirteenth century, the Keita ruling clan of Mali forged a new and lasting empire, built on monoplization of the lucrative north–south gold trade. The Keita kings dominated enough of the Sahel to control the flow of West African gold from the Senegal regions and the forestlands south of the Niger to the trans-Saharan trade routes and the influx of copper and salt in exchange. Based south of their Ghanaian predecessors, in the fertile land along the Niger, they controlled all trade on the upper Niger, as well as the Gambia and Senegal trade to the west. They also used captives for plantation labor in the Niger inland delta to produce surplus food for trade.

Agriculture and cattle farming were the primary occupations of Mali's population and, together with the gold trade, the mainstays of the economy. Rice was grown in the river valleys and millet in the drier parts of the Sahel. Together with beans, yams, and other agricultural products, this made for a plentiful food supply. Fishing flourished along the Niger and elsewhere. Cattle, sheep, and goats were plentiful. The chief craft specialties were metalworking (iron and gold) and weaving of cotton grown within the empire.

The Malinke, a southern Mande-speaking people of the upper Niger region, formed the core population of the new state. They apparently lived in walled urban settlements typical of the western savanna region. Each walled town held 1,000 to 15,000 people, and was linked to neighboring cities by trade and intermarriage.

The Keita dynasty had converted to Islam around 1100 C.E. Keita's rulers even claimed descent from Muhammad's famous *muezzin* Bilal ibn Ribah, a former black slave from Abyssinia whose son was said to have settled in the Mande-speaking region. During Mali's heyday in the thirteenth and fourteenth centuries, its kings often made the pilgrimage to Mecca, bringing back with them military aids, such as Barbary war horses, and new ideas about political and military organization. Through Muslim traders' networks, Mali was connected to other areas of Africa, especially to the east.

Mali's imperial power was built largely by the Keita King Sundiata (or Sunjaata, r. 1230–1255). Sundiata and his successors exploited their agricultural resources, significant population growth, and Malinke commercial skills to build an empire even more powerful than that of Ghana. Sundiata extended his control west to the Atlantic coast and east beyond Timbuktu. By controlling the commercial entrepôts of Gao, Walata, and Jenne, he dominated the Saharan as well as the Niger trade. He built his capital, Niani, into a major city. Niani was located on a tributary of the Niger in the savanna at the edge of the forest in a gold- and iron-rich region. It had access to the forest trade products of gold, kola nuts, and palm oil; it was easily defended by virtue of its surrounding hills; and it was readily reached by river.

[1]D. Conrad and H. Fisher, "The Conquest That Never Was: Ghana and the Almoravids, 1076," *History in Africa* 9 (1982): 1–59; 10 (1983): 53–78.

QUICK REVIEW

Mali

- Keita clan forged Mali in mid-thirteenth century
- Keita kings controlled the flow of West African gold
- Agriculture and cattle farming were primary occupations of Mali's people

muezzin The leader of a mosque's call to prayers.

The empire that Sundiata and his successors built ultimately encompassed three major regions and language groups of Sudanic West Africa: (1) the Senegal region (including Takrur), occupied by speakers of the West Atlantic Niger-Kongo language group (including Fulbe, Tukulor, Wolof, Serer); (2) the central Mande states between Senegal and Niger, occupied by the Niger-Kongo-speaking Soninke and Mandinke peoples; and (3) the peoples of the Niger in the Gao region who spoke Songhai, a Nilo-Saharan language. Mali was less a centralized bureaucratic state than the center of a vast sphere of influence that included provinces and tribute-paying kingdoms. Many individual chieftaincies were independent but recognized the sovereignty of the supreme, sacred *mansa*, or "emperor," of the Malian realms.

The greatest Keita king proved to be Mansa Musa (r. 1312–1337), whose pilgrimage through Mamluk Cairo to Mecca in 1324 became famous. He paid out or gave away so much gold in Cairo alone that he started massive inflation lasting over a decade. He returned with many Muslim scholars, artists, and architects. At home, he consolidated Mali's power, securing peace for most of his reign throughout his vast dominions. Musa's devoutness fostered the spread of Islam in the empire and beyond. Under his rule, Timbuktu became the leading intellectual center of sub-Saharan Islam—famous for its *madrasas* and libraries as well as its poets, scientists, and architects—and a major trading city of the Sahel, roles it retained long after Mali's imperial sway ended.[2] Mali's dominance waned after Musa, evidently as the result of rivalries for the throne.

SONGHAI

There was a Songhai kingdom around Gao, on the eastern arc of the great bend of the Niger, as early as the eleventh or twelfth century. In 1325 Mansa Musa brought this kingdom and the Gao region under the control of Mali and the Malinke. Mali's domination ended with the rise of a dynasty in Gao known as the Sunni or Sonni around 1375. The kingdom became an imperial power under the greatest Sunni ruler, Sonni Ali (r. 1464–1492). For more than a century the Songhai Empire was arguably the most powerful state in Africa (see Map 15–2). With a strong military built around a riverboat flotilla and cavalry, Sonni Ali took Jenne and Timbuktu. He pushed the Tuareg Berbers back into the northern Sahel and Sahara and stifled threats from the southern forestland.

His successor Askia Muhammad al-Turi (r. 1493–1528) continued Sonni Ali's expansionist policies. Between them, Sonni Ali and Askia Muhammad built an empire that stretched west nearly to the Atlantic, northwest into the Sahara, and east into the central Sudan. Like their Ghanaian predecessors, they took advantage of their control of access to the gold and other desirable commodities of West Africa to cultivate and expand the caravan trade to the North African coast. This provided their major source of wealth.

Unlike Sonni Ali, who held to the traditional religious faith of his people, Muhammad al-Turi was an enthusiastic Muslim. He built up the Songhai state after the model of the Islamic

[2] For more on Mali, especially its wealth and Timbuktu's role as a center of scholarship, see E. Gilbert and J. T. Reynolds, *Africa in World History: From Prehistory to the Present* (Upper Saddle River, NJ: Prentice Hall, 2004), pp. 91–93.

QUICK REVIEW

King Sundiata (r. 1230–1255)

◆ Built Mali's imperial power

◆ Mali's empire was more powerful than its Ghanaian predecessor

◆ Empire encompassed three major regions: Senegal, the central Mande states, and the peoples of Niger in the Gao region

mansa Malian emperor, from Mandinka word meaning "king of kings."

Mansa Musa, King of Mali. The fourteenth-century Catalan Atlas shows King Mansa Musa of Mali, seated on a throne holding a nugget of gold. A rider on a camel approaches him.

Why would a fourteenth-century European atlas show Mansa Musa?

MAP EXPLORATION

To explore this map further, go to http://www.prenhall.com/craig_maps

MAP 15–2 **Africa ca. 1500–1700.** Important towns, regions, peoples, and states. The inset shows the empire of Songhai at its greatest extent in the early sixteenth century.

What was Songhai's major source of wealth?

marabout In Sunni Islam as practiced in West Africa, a *marabout* is a spiritual leader, versed in the Koran, who often guides the personal lives of his followers.

empire of Mali. During his reign, many Muslim scholars came to Gao, Timbuktu, and Jenne. He appointed Muslim judges (*qadis*) in towns throughout the empire and made Timbuktu a major intellectual and legal training center for the whole Sudan. He also replaced native Songhais with Arab Muslim immigrants as government officials to strengthen his centralized power. Like Mansa Musa before him, Muhammad made a triumphal pilgrimage to Mecca, where he was hailed as "Caliph of the western Sahara." From his vast royal treasury he supported the poor and the Sufi leaders, or *marabouts*, and built mosques throughout the realm. Nevertheless, he failed to Islamize the empire or to ensure a strong central state for his successors.

The last powerful Askia leader was Askia Dawud (r. 1549–1583), under whom Songhai economic prosperity and intellectual life achieved its apogee. The trans-Saharan trade reached new heights, and royal patronage of the arts rose to new levels. Still, difficulties mounted. The Askia battled the Mossi to the south and Berber forces from the north. Civil war broke out over succession to the throne in 1586, and the empire was divided. In 1591 an assay sent by the Sa'dis of Morocco used superior gunpowder weapons, coupled with the aid of disaffected Songhai princes, to defeat the last Askia of Gao at Tondibi, and the Gao Empire collapsed.

KANEM AND KANEM-BORNU

A fourth sizable Sahelian empire—in the central Sudan—arose after 1100. Called Kanem, it began as a southern Saharan confederation of the nomadic tribes known as Zaghawah. By the twelfth century a Zaghawah group known as the Kanuri had apparently settled in Kanem. From there they began a campaign of military expansion during the thirteenth century. Their leader, Mai Dunama Dibbalemi (r. ca. 1221–1259), was a contemporary of Sundiata in Mali. Dibbalemi was a Muslim, and he used a synthesis of Islam and African traditions of sacred kingship to sanction his rule. Islam provided a rationale for expansion through *jihad*, or holy "struggle" against polytheists.

Dibbalemi and his successors expanded Kanuri power north into the desert to include the Fezzan in modern Libya and northeast along the Sahel-Sahara fringe toward Nilotic Africa. In both directions they controlled important trade routes—north to Libya and east to the Nile and Egypt. The next two centuries saw the mixing of Kanuri and local Kanembu peoples, primarily those known as the So. There was a corresponding transformation of the Kanuri leader from a nomadic **shaykh** to a Sudanic king, and a shift of Kanem from a nomadic to a largely sedentary kingdom with quasi-feudal institutions. Like Mali to the west, Kanem's dominion was of two kinds: direct rule over and taxation of core territories and groups, and indirect control over and collection of tribute from a wider region of vassal chieftaincies. Islamic acculturation progressed most rapidly in the core territories under direct rule.

Civil strife, largely over the royal succession, weakened the Kanuri state. After 1400 the locus of power shifted westward to the land of Bornu, southwest of Lake Chad. Here, at the end of the fifteenth century, a new Kanuri empire arose almost simultaneously with the collapse of the Askia dynasty of the Songhai Empire at Gao. Near the end of the sixteenth century firearms and Turkish military instructors enabled the Kanuri leader Idris Alawma (r. ca. 1575–1610) to unify Kanem and Bornu. He set up an avowedly Islamic state and extended his rule as far as Hausaland, between Bornu and the Niger River. The center of trading activity, political power, and security shifted from the Niger bend east to the territory under Kanuri control.

Deriving its prosperity from the trans-Saharan trade, Idris Alawma's regional empire survived for nearly a century. It was broken up by a long famine, Tuareg attacks, weak leadership, and loss of control over trade to smaller, better-organized Hausa states to the west. The ruling dynasty held out until 1846, but by 1700 its power had been sharply reduced.

CHRONOLOGY

SAHELIAN EMPIRES OF THE WESTERN SUDAN

ca. 990–ca. 1180?	Empire of Ghana
1076	Ghana loses Awdaghast to Almoravids
1180–1230	Soso clan briefly controls the old Ghanaian territories
ca. 1230–1450	Empire of Mali, founded by Sundiata
1230–1255	Reign of Sundiata
1312–1337	Reign of Mansa Musa
1374	Independent Songhai state emerges in Gao after throwing off Malian rule
ca. 1450–1600	Songhai Empire at Gao
1464–1492	Reign of Sonni Ali
1464–1591	Askia dynasty
1493–1528	Reign of Askia Muhammad al-Turi
1549–1583	Reign of Askia Dawud
1590s	Collapse of the Songhai Empire

shaykh Arabic word for a tribal elder or Islamic scholar; can also be rendered as sheikh, sheik, or cheikh.

CHRONOLOGY

CENTRAL SUDANIC EMPIRES

ca. 1100–1500	Kanuri empire of Kanem
ca. 1220s–1400	Height of empire of Kanem
ca. 1221–1259	Reign of Mai Dunama Dibbalemi
ca. 1575–1610	Reign of Idris Alawma, major architect of the state
ca. 1575–1846	Kanuri empire of Kanem-Bornu

THE EASTERN SUDAN

WHY DID Christianity gradually disappear in Nubia?

The Christian states of Maqurra and Alwa in the Nilotic Sudan, or Nubia, lasted for more than six hundred years, beginning in the early seventh century. They maintained political, religious, and commercial contact with Egypt, the Red Sea world, and much of the Sudan.

After 1000 C.E. Maqurra and Alwa continued treaty relations with their more powerful northern Egyptian neighbors. However, the Mamluks intervened repeatedly in Nubian affairs, and Arab nomads constantly threatened the Nubian states. Both Maqurra and Alwa were subject to immigrating Muslim Arab tribesmen and to traders and growing Muslim minorities. Long-term intermingling of Arabic and Nubian cultures created a new Nilotic Sudanese people and culture.

A significant factor in the gradual disappearance of Christianity in Nubia was its elite character there and its association with the Egyptian world of Coptic Christianity. Maqurra became officially Muslim at the beginning of the fourteenth century, although Christianity survived there briefly. The Islamization of Alwa came later, under the long-lived Funj sultanate that replaced the Alwa state.

The Funj state flourished between the Blue and White Niles and to the north along the main Nile from just after 1500 until 1762. The Funj were originally cattle nomads who apparently adopted Islam soon after setting up their kingdom. During the late sixteenth and seventeenth centuries, the Funj developed an Islamic society whose Arabized character was unique in sub-Saharan Africa. A much reduced Funj state held out until an Ottoman Egyptian invasion in 1821.

THE FORESTLANDS: COASTAL WEST AND CENTRAL AFRICA

HOW DID the arrival of the Europeans affect the people of West and Central Africa?

WEST AFRICAN FOREST KINGDOMS: THE EXAMPLE OF BENIN

Many states with distinct political, religious, and cultural traditions had developed in the southern and coastal regions of West Africa. The forest kingdom of Benin reflects the sophistication of West African culture before 1500; its art, in particular, is renowned for its enduring beauty.

The Edo speakers of Benin have occupied the southern Nigerian region between Yorubaland and the Ibo peoples east of the lower Niger for millennia. Traditional Edo society is organized according to a patrilineal system emphasizing primogeniture. The village is the fundamental political unit, and authority is built around the organization of males into age-grade units.[3]

Traditional Edo culture was closely linked to that of Ife, one of the most prominent Yoruba states northwest of Benin. A distinct kingdom of Benin likely existed as early as the twelfth century, and traditional accounts of both Ife and Edo agree that an Ife prince was sent to rule in Benin around 1300. The power of the *oba*, or king, at this time was sharply limited by the Edo leaders who invited the foreign ruler. These leaders were known as the *uzama*, an order of hereditary chiefs. According to tradition, the fourth *oba* managed to wrest more control from these chiefs and expanded his ceremonial authority. In the fifteenth century, with King Ewuare, Benin became a royal autocracy and a large state of regional importance.

oba   Title of the king of Benin.

uzama   An order of hereditary chiefs in Benin.

---

[3]A. F. C. Ryder, *Benin and the Europeans, 1485–1897* (New York: Longman, 1969), p. 1. Ryder's work is a basic reference for the following brief summary about Benin.

Ewuare rebuilt the capital—known today as Benin City—and named it and his kingdom Edo. He exercised his sweeping authority in light of the deliberations of a royal council. Ewuare formed this council not only from the palace *uzama* but also from the townspeople. He gave each chief specific administrative responsibilities and rank in the government hierarchy. Ewuare and his successors developed a tradition of military kingship and engaged in major wars of expansion, into Yorubaland to the west and Ibo country to the east, across the Niger River. They claimed for the office of *oba* an increasing ritual authority that presaged more radical developments in the king's role.

In the seventeenth century the *oba* was transformed from a military leader into a religious figure with supernatural powers. Human sacrifice, specifically of slaves, seems to have accompanied the cult of deceased kings and became even more frequent later in the nineteenth century. Succession by primogeniture was discontinued, and the *uzama* chose *obas* from any branch of the royal family.

The global significance of Benin lies in its court art, especially its famous brass sculptures. The splendid terra-cotta, ivory, and brass statuary sculpture of Ife-Benin is among the glories of human creativity. Some scholars trace the artistic and technical lineage of these magnificent works to the sculptures of the Nok culture of ancient West Africa (see Chapter 5). Cast bronze plaques depicting legendary and historical scenes were mounted in the royal palace in Benin City before the sixteenth century. There are also brass heads, apparently of royalty, that resemble the many life-size terra-cotta and brass heads found at Ife. Similar sculptures have been found both to the north and in the Niger Delta.

EUROPEAN ARRIVALS ON THE COASTLANDS: SENEGAMBIA AND THE GOLD COAST

Along the coasts of West and Central Africa, between 1500 and 1800, the changes wrought by the burgeoning Atlantic slave trade are the most notorious (see Chapter 18). But there were other important changes. The introduction of food crops from the Americas—maize, peanuts, squash, sweet potatoes, cocoa, and cassava (manioc)—had significant impacts. Africa's gradual involvement in the emerging global economic system paved the way for European colonial domination. The European names for segments of the coastline—the Grain (or Pepper) Coast, the Ivory Coast, the Gold Coast, and the Slave Coast—identify the main exports that could be extracted by ship.

In West Africa, Senegambia—which takes its name from the Senegal and Gambia Rivers—was one of the earliest regions affected by European trade. Its interior had long been involved in long-distance trade. Senegambia's maritime trade with European powers, like the older overland trade, was primarily in gold and products such as salt, cotton goods, hides, and copper. For roughly a century Senegambian states also provided slaves for European purchase; perhaps a third of all African slaves exported during the sixteenth century came from Senegambia. Thereafter, however, the focus of the slave trade shifted south and east along the coast (see Chapter 18). Over time, Portuguese-African mulattos and the British came to control the Gambia River trade, while the French won the Senegal River markets.

The Gold Coast was another West African coastal district heavily affected by the arrival of international maritime trade. As the name suggests, after 1500 the region served as the outlet for the gold fields in the forestland of Akan. Beginning with the Portuguese at Elmina in 1481, but primarily after 1600, European states and companies built coastal forts to protect their trade and to serve as depots for inland goods. The trade in gold, kola nuts, and other commodities seems to have encouraged the growth of larger states in the region, perhaps because they could better handle and control the overland commerce.

CHRONOLOGY

BENIN

ca. 1100–1897	Benin state
ca. 1300	First Ife king of Benin state
1440–1475	Reign of Ewuare

QUICK REVIEW

Changing Roles of Edo Kings

- Edo leaders invited limited rule by Ife prince around 1300
- King Ewuare developed military and ceremonial authority in fifiteenth century
- Kings became religious figures with supernatural powers in seventeenth century
- Deceased kings honored by human sacrifice in nineteenth century

Head of a King, from Ife, ca. thirteenth century C.E. The serene classicism of Ife art is equaled only by that of ancient Greece.

What other artistic traditions seem to be linked to Ife?

Benin Bronze Plaque. From the palace of the *obas* of Benin, it dates to the Edo period of Benin culture (1575–1625). It depicts two Portuguese males, perhaps a father and son, holding hands. The figures probably represent the traders or government officials who came to the African coasts in increasing numbers from the end of the fifteenth century on. **Why would Europeans be depicted in Benin bronzeworks?**

The intensive contact of the Gold Coast with Europeans also led to the importation and spread of American crops, notably maize and cassava. The success of these crops in West and Central Africa likely contributed to substantial population growth in the sixteenth and seventeenth centuries. The Gold Coast was an importer of slaves until long after 1500. Slaves became major exports in the late seventeenth century, especially in the Accra region. The economy was so disrupted by the slave trade that gold mining declined sharply. Eventually more gold came into the Gold Coast from the sale of slaves than went out from its mines (see Chapter 18).

CENTRAL AFRICA: THE KONGO KINGDOM AND ANGOLA

Before 1500 natural barriers, including swamps in the north, coastal rain forests to the west, highlands to the east, and deserts in the south, impeded international contact and trade with the vast center of the continent. Bantu peoples and languages moved, over many centuries, from western and west-central Africa south into the Zaire basin and east around the equatorial forest into the highlands of East Africa. In the tropical central area, there were regional interactions in movements of peoples and in trade and culture. Political, economic, and social units varied in size. Peoples such as the Lunda and the Luba, for example, on the southern savanna below the rain forest, carved out sizable kingdoms by the fifteenth century and expanded their control over neighboring areas into the eighteenth century.

The Portuguese came to the western coastal regions looking for gold and silver but found none. Ultimately, their main export was slaves. These slaves were taken first for gang labor to the Portuguese sugar plantations on Sao Thomé island in the Gulf of Guinea and then, in vast numbers, to perform similar plantation labor in Brazil. In the 1640s the Dutch briefly succeeded the Portuguese as the major suppliers of African slaves to English and French plantations in the Caribbean.

The Kongo kingdom was located on a fertile, well-watered plateau south of the lower Zaïre River valley. Astride the border between forest and grassland, the Kongo kings had built a central government based on a pyramid structure of tax or tribute collection, dating from probably the fourteenth century. The king's authority was tied to acceptance of him as a kind of spiritual spokesman of the gods or ancestors. By 1600 Kongo was half the size of England and boasted a high state of specialization in weaving and pottery, salt production, fishing, and metalworking.

When the Portuguese came to Central Africa in 1483, Kongo was the major state with which they dealt. The Portuguese brought Mediterranean goods, preeminently luxury textiles from North Africa, to trade for Central African goods. Slaves became the primary export. Although imported luxuries augmented the prestige and wealth of the ruler and his elites, they did nothing to replace the labor pool lost to slavery. At first the Portuguese put time and effort into education and Christian proselytizing, but the desire for more slaves eventually outweighed these concerns. As the demand grew, local rulers increasingly attacked neighbors to garner slaves for Portuguese traders (see Chapter 18).

The Kongo ruler Affonso I (r. ca. 1506–1543) was a Christian convert who initially welcomed Jesuit missionaries and supported conversion. But in time he broke with the Jesuits. Affonso had constant difficulty curbing the more exploitative slaving practices and independent-minded provincial governors, who undermined royal authority by dealing directly with the Portuguese (see Document, "Affonso I of Kongo Writes to the King of Portugal.") Affonso's successor finally restricted Portuguese activity to Mpinda harbor and the Kongo capital of Mbanza Kongo

CHRONOLOGY

CENTRAL AFRICA

1300s	Kongo kingdom founded
1483	Portuguese come to Central African coast
ca. 1506–1543	Reign of Affonso I as king of Kongo
1571	Angola becomes Portuguese proprietary colony

(São Salvador). A few years later, Portuguese attempts to name the Kongo royal successor caused a bloody uprising against them that led in turn to a Portuguese boycott on trade with the kingdom.

Thereafter, disastrous internal wars shattered the Kongo state. Slavery contributed to provincial unrest. Independent Portuguese traders and adventurers soon did their business outside government channels and tried to manipulate the Kongo kings.

Kongo, however, enjoyed renewed vigor in the seventeenth century. The Kongo kings ruled as divine-right monarchs at the apex of a complex sociopolitical pyramid. Royal power came to depend on musket-armed hired soldiers. The financial base of the kingdom rested on tribute from officials and taxes and tolls on commerce. Christianity, the state religion, was accommodated to traditional beliefs. Sculpture, iron and copper technology, dance, and music flourished.

To the south, in Portuguese Angola, the experience was even worse than in Kongo. The Ndongo kingdom flourished among the Mbundu people during the sixteenth century, though the Portuguese controlled parts of Angola as a proprietary colony (the first white colonial enterprise in black Africa). By the end of the 1500s Angola was exporting thousands of slaves yearly through the port of Luanda. In less than a century the hinterland had been depopulated. New internal trade in salt and the spread of American food crops such as maize and cassava (which became part of the staple diet of the populace) produced some positive changes in the interior, but in the coastal region the Portuguese brought catastrophe.

Queen Nzinga of Ndongo, who ruled from 1615 to 1660. This contemporary engraving shows her negotiating a treaty with the Portuguese. She is seated on the back of a slave. **Who seems to have the most power in this scene?**

EAST AFRICA

SWAHILI CULTURE AND COMMERCE

The participation of East African port towns in the lucrative South Seas trade was ancient. Arabs, Indonesians, and even some Indians had been absorbed into what had become, during the first millennium C.E., a predominantly Bantu-speaking population from Somalia south. From the eighth century onward Islam traveled with Arab and Persian sailors and merchants to these southerly trading centers of what the Arabs called the land of the *Zanj*, or "Blacks" (hence "Zanzibar"). Conversion to Islam, however, occurred only along the coast. In the thirteenth century Muslim traders from Arabia and Iran began to dominate coastal cities from Mogadishu to Kilwa. By 1331 the traveler Ibn Battuta wrote of Islamic rulers, inhabitants, and mosques all along the coast.

A shared language called **Swahili**, or Kiswahili (from the Arabic plural *sawahil*, "coastlands"), developed along the coast. Its structure is Bantu; its vocabulary is largely Bantu but incorporates many words with Arabic roots, and it is written in Arabic script. Like the language, Swahili culture is basically African with a large contribution by Arab, Persian, and other extra-African elements. This admixture created a new consciousness and identity. Today, many coastal peoples who share the Swahili language join African to Persian, Indian, Arab, and other ancestries.

Like the Swahili language and culture, the spread of Islam was largely limited to the coastal civilization, with the possible exception of the Zambezi valley, where Muslim traders penetrated upriver. This contrasts with the Horn of Africa, where Islamic kingdoms developed both in the Somali hinterland and on the coast.

Swahili civilization reached its apogee in the fourteenth and fifteenth centuries. The harbor trading towns were the administrative centers of the local Swahili states,

HOW DID Swahili language and culture develop?

Swahili A language and culture that developed from the interaction of Africans and Arabs along the East African coast.

DOCUMENT

Affonso I of Kongo Writes to the King of Portugal

*I*n 1526 Affonso, the Christian African king of Kongo, wrote to the Portuguese monarch ostensibly to complain about the effects of slaving on the Kongo people and economy. But the real issue was that the Portuguese were circumventing his own royal monopoly on the inland slave trade. One of the insidious effects of the massive demand of the Atlantic trade for slaves was the ever-increasing engagement in it of African monarchs, chieftains, and merchants.

- **How** had the introduction of Portuguese merchants and European goods upset the social and political situation in Kongo? How had these goods tempted Affonso's subjects into the slave trade? How did Affonso wish to change the relationship of his people to Portugal? Was the king more worried about human rights or his economic losses?

Sir, Your Highness [of Portugal] should know how our Kingdom is being lost in so many ways that it is convenient to provide for the necessary remedy, since this is caused by the excessive freedom given by your factors and officials to the men and merchants who are allowed to come to this Kingdom to set up shops with goods and many things which have been prohibited by us, and which they spread throughout our Kingdoms and Domains in such an abundance that many of our vassals, whom we had in obedience, do not comply because they have the things in greater abundance than we ourselves; and it was with these things that we had them content and subjected under our vassalage and jurisdiction, so it is doing a great harm not only to the service of God, but the security and peace of our Kingdoms and State as well.

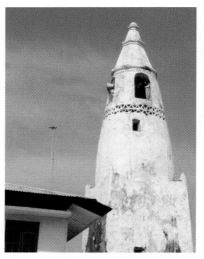

The Malindi Mosque on Zanzibar Island is an example of the influence of Islam on Swahili culture.

What are some other examples of Islamic influence on Swahili culture?

QUICK REVIEW

East African Port Towns
- Part of trade with Middle East, Asia, and India
- Tied together by common language, Swahili
- Swahili civilization reached its peak in the fourteenth and fifteenth centuries

and most of them were sited on coastal islands or easily defended peninsulas. Merchants came from abroad and from the African hinterlands. These towns were impressive, with stone mosques, fortress-palaces, harbor fortifications, fancy residences, and commercial buildings combining African and Arabo-Persian elements.

The Swahili states' ruling dynasties were probably African in origin, though elite families often included Arab or Persian members. Swahili coastal centers boasted an advanced, cosmopolitan culture; by comparison, most of the populace in the small villages lived in mud and sometimes stone houses and earned their living by farming or fishing. Society's principal groups were the local nobility, the commoners, resident foreigners engaged in commerce, and slaves (although their local extent—as opposed to their sale—is disputed.)

The flourishing trade of the coastal centers was based on inland ivory. Other exports included gold, slaves, turtle shells, ambergris, leopard skins, pearls, fish, sandalwood, ebony, and cotton cloth. The chief imports were cloth, porcelain, glassware, glass beads, and glazed pottery. Cowrie shells were a common currency in the inland trade, but coins minted at Mogadishu and Kilwa from the fourteenth century on were increasingly used in the major trading centers.

THE PORTUGUESE AND THE OMANIS OF ZANZIBAR

The original Swahili civilization declined in the sixteenth century. Trade waned with the arrival of the Portuguese, who destroyed both the Islamic commercial monopoly on the oceanic trade and the main Islamic city-states along the coast. Decreases in rainfall or invasions of Zimba peoples from inland regions may also have contributed to the decline.

The Portuguese undoubtedly intended to gain control of the South Seas trade (see Chapter 18). In Africa, as everywhere, they saw the **Moors** (the Spanish and Portuguese term for Muslims) as their implacable enemies; they viewed the struggle to wrest the commerce and the ports of Africa and Asia from Islamic control as a Christian crusade.

And we cannot reckon how great the damage is, since the mentioned merchants are taking every day our natives, sons of the land and the sons of our noblemen and vassals and our relatives, because the thieves and men of bad conscience grab them wishing to have the things and wares of this Kingdom which they are ambitious of; they grab them and get them to be sold; and so great, Sir, is the corruption and licentiousness that our country is being completely depopulated, and Your Highness should not agree with this nor accept it as in your service. And to avoid it we need from those [your] Kingdoms no more than some priests and a few people to teach in schools, and no other goods except wine and flour for the holy sacrament. That is why we beg of Your Highness to help and assist us in this matter, commanding your factors that they should not send here either merchants or wares, because it is *our will that in these Kingdoms there should not be any trade of slaves nor outlet for them.**

Concerning what is referred above, again we beg of Your Highness to agree with it, since otherwise we cannot . . . remedy such an obvious damage. Pray Our Lord in His mercy to have Your Highness under His guard and let you do for ever the things of His service. I kiss your hands many times . . . .

Source: From *The African Past*, trans. by J. O. Hunwick, reprinted in Basil Davidson (Grosset and Dunlap, The Universal Library), pp. 191–193. Reprinted by permission of Curtis Brown Ltd., New York on behalf of Basil Davidson. Copyright © 1964 by Basil Davidson.

*Emphasis in the original

After the initial Portuguese victories along the African coast, there was no concerted effort to spread Christianity beyond fortified coastal settlements. Thus the long-term cultural and religious consequences of the Portuguese presence were slight. The Portuguese did, however, cause widespread economic decline. Inland Africans refused to cooperate with them, and Muslim coastal shipping from India and Arabia was reduced sharply. Ottoman efforts in the late sixteenth century failed to defeat the Portuguese, but after 1660 the strong eastern Arabian state of Oman raided the African coast with impunity. In 1698 the Omanis took Mombasa and ejected the Portuguese everywhere north of Mozambique.

Under the Omanis, Zanzibar became a new and major power center in East Africa. Control of the coastal ivory and slave trade fueled prosperity by the later eighteenth century. Zanzibar itself benefited from the introduction of clove cultivation in the 1830s; cloves became its staple export. (The clove plantations became also the chief market for a new internal slave trade.) Omani African sultans dominated the east coast until 1856, when Zanzibar and its coastal holdings became independent under a branch of the same family that ruled in Oman. Zanzibar passed eventually to the British in the late 1880s. Still, the Islamic imprint on the whole coast survives today.

CHRONOLOGY

EAST AND SOUTHEAST AFRICA

900–1500	"Great Zimbabwe" civilization
ca. 1200–1400	Development of Bantu Kiswahili language
ca. 1300–1600	Height of Swahili culture
1698	Omani forces take Mombasa, oust Portuguese from East Africa north of the port of Mozambique
1741–1856	United sultanate of Oman and Zanzibar

Moors The Spanish and Portuguese term for Muslims.

Great Zimbabwe. Ruins of a stone wall called "The Great Enclosure" and other structures are part of the Great Zimbabwe site.

What were some probable sources of Great Zimbabwe's power?

SOUTHERN AFRICA

HOW DID slavery affect race relations in Cape Colony?

prazeros Portuguese and mixed-race owners of large estates in the Zambezi valley.

SOUTHEASTERN AFRICA: "GREAT ZIMBABWE"

About the same time that the east-coast trading centers were beginning to flourish, a different kind of civilization was thriving farther south, in the rocky, savanna-woodland watershed between the Limpopo and Zambezi Rivers, in modern southern Zimbabwe. This civilization was sited far enough inland never to have felt the impact of Islam. It was founded in the tenth or eleventh century by a Bantu-speaking Shona people, and became a large and prosperous state between the late thirteenth and late fifteenth centuries. We know it only through the archaeological remains of an estimated 150 settlements in the Zambezi-Limpopo region.

The most impressive of these ruins is the apparent capital known today as "Great Zimbabwe," a huge site encompassing two major building complexes. One, called the "acropolis," is a series of stone enclosures on a high hill. It overlooks a larger enclosure that contains many ruins and a circular tower, all surrounded by a massive wall some thirty-two feet high and up to seventeen feet thick. The acropolis complex may have contained a shrine, whereas the larger enclosure was apparently the royal palace and fort. The stonework reflects a wealthy and sophisticated society. Artifacts from the site include gold and copper ornaments, soapstone carvings, and imported beads, as well as glass and porcelain of Chinese, Syrian, and Persian origins.

The state seems to have partially controlled the gold trade between inland areas and the east-coast port of Sofala. Its territory lay east and south of substantial gold-mining enterprises. This large settlement was probably home to the ruling elite of a prosperous empire. Its wider domain was made up mostly of smaller settlements whose inhabitants lived by subsistence agriculture and cattle raising.

Earlier Iron Age sites farther south suggest that other large state entities may have preceded Great Zimbabwe. The specific impetus for Great Zimbabwe may have been a significant immigration around 1000 C.E. of Late Iron Age Shona speakers who brought with them mining techniques and farming innovations, along with their ancestor cults. Improved farming and animal husbandry could have led to substantial population growth. The expanding gold trade linked the flourishing of Zimbabwe to that of the East African coast from about the thirteenth century.

Without new sources, we may never know why this impressive civilization declined after dominating its region for nearly two hundred years. It appears that the northern and southern sectors of the state split up, and people moved away from Great Zimbabwe, probably because the farming and grazing land there was exhausted. The southern successor kingdom, Changamire, was powerful from the late 1600s until about 1830. The northern successor state, which stretched along the Zambezi, was known to the first Portuguese sources as the kingdom ruled by the Mwene Mutapa, or "Master Pillager," the title of its sixteenth-century ruler, Mutota, and his successors.

THE PORTUGUESE IN SOUTHEASTERN AFRICA

Portuguese attempts to obtain gold from the Zambezi region of the interior by controlling trade on the Swahili coast were failures. The Portuguese then established fortified posts up the Zambezi and meddled in Shona politics. In the 1690s the Changamire Shona dynasty conquered the northern Shona territory and pushed the Portuguese out of gold country.

All along the Zambezi, a lasting and destabilizing consequence of Portuguese intrusion was the creation of quasi-tribal chiefdoms. These were led by mixed-blood Portuguese landholders, or ***prazeros***, descended from the area's first Portuguese estate holders. Their descendants eventually formed a few clanlike groups of mixed-blood members (from unions with Africans, Indian immigrants, or other estate families). By the end of the eighteenth century, they controlled vast landholdings, commanded armies (often made up

Carving from Great Zimbabwe. This carving (steatite, 40.5 cm high) is thought to represent a mythical eagle that carries messages from man to the gods. It dates to about 1200 to 1400 C.E.

What is known about the culture at Great Zimbabwe?

largely of slaves), and were a disruptive force in the region because they were too strong for either the Portuguese or the regional African rulers to control.

SOUTH AFRICA: THE CAPE COLONY

In South Africa the Dutch planted the first European colonials almost inadvertently, yet the consequences were grave and far-reaching. The first Cape settlement was built in 1652 by the Dutch East India Company as a resupply point for Dutch vessels on their way back and forth between the Netherlands and the East Indies. The support station grew gradually, becoming by century's end a large settler community (the population of the colony in 1662, including slaves, was 392; by 1714 it had reached 3,878).[4] These settlers were the forebears of the Afrikaners of modern South Africa.

Local Khoikhoi people were gradually incorporated into the new colonial economy. The Khoikhoi (see Chapter 5) were mostly pastoralists; they had neither traditions of strong political organization nor an economic base beyond their herds. At first they freely bartered livestock for iron, copper, and tobacco. However, when settlers began to displace the Khoikhoi in the southwestern Cape, conflicts ensued. The results were the consolidation of European landholdings and a breakdown of Khoikhoi society. Dutch military success led to even greater control over the Khoikhoi by the 1670s. Treated as free persons, they became the chief source of colonial wage labor—labor in ever-greater demand as the colony grew.

The colony also imported slaves from all along the South Seas trade routes, including India, East Africa, and Madagascar. Slavery set the tone for relations between the emergent, and ostensibly "white," Afrikaner population and the "coloreds" of other races. Free or not, the latter were eventually all too easily identified with slave peoples.

After the first settlers spread out around the company station, nomadic white livestock farmers, or **Trekboers**, moved more widely afield, leaving the richer but limited farming lands of the coast for the drier interior tableland. There they contested still wider groups of Khoikhoi cattle herders for the best grazing lands. The Trekboers developed military techniques—notably the "commando," a collective civilian punitive raid—to secure their way of life by force where necessary. Again the Khoikhoi were the losers. By 1700 they were stripped almost completely of their own pasturages, and their way of life was destroyed. Increasing numbers of Khoikhoi took up employment in the colonial economy. Others moved north to join with other refugees from Cape society (slaves, mixed bloods, and some freedmen) to form raiding bands operating along the frontiers of Trekboer territory close to the Orange River. The disintegration of Khoikhoi society continued in the eighteenth century, accelerated sharply by smallpox—a European import against which this previously isolated group had no immunity.

Cape society in this period was diverse. The Dutch East India Company officials (including Dutch Reformed ministers), the emerging Afrikaners (both settled colonists and Trekboers), the Khoikhoi, and the slaves played differing roles. Intermarriage and cohabitation of masters and slaves added to the social complexity, despite laws designed to check such mixing. Accommodation of nonwhite minority groups within Cape society proceeded; the emergence of *Afrikaans*, a new vernacular language of the colonials, shows that the Dutch immigrants themselves were subject to acculturation. By the time of English domination after 1795, the sociopolitical foundations of modern South Africa—and the bases of *apartheid*—were firmly laid.

CHRONOLOGY

SOUTHERN AFRICA

1652	First Cape Colony settlement of Dutch East India Company
1795	British replace Dutch as masters of Cape Colony

Trekboers   White livestock farmers in Cape Colony.

Afrikaans   The new language, derived from Dutch, that evolved in the seventeenth- and eighteenth-century Cape Colony.

apartheid   "Apartness," the term referring to racist policies enforced by the white-dominated regime that existed in South Africa from 1948 to 1992.

---

[4]R. Elphick and H. Giliomee, *The Shaping of South African Society, 1652–1820* (Cape Town: Longman, 1979), p. 4.

SUMMARY

HOW DID the Ottomans govern North Africa and Egypt?

North Africa and Egypt. Developments in African history from 1000 to 1700 varied from region to region. In North Africa, the key new factor was the imperial expansion of the Ottoman Empire as far west as Morocco. But the development of independent regional rulers soon rendered Ottoman authority in North Africa purely nominal. *page 362*

HOW DID Islam spread south of the Sahara?

The Spread of Islam South of the Sahara. Between the eighth century and 1800, Islam was introduced. In most cases, the process was slow, peaceful, and partial; ruling elites and traders were more likely to practice Islam, whereas most commoners followed traditional practices. *page 363*

WHAT WERE the four most important states in the Sahel between 1000 and 1600?

Sahelian Empires of the Western and Central Sudan. Several substantial states arose south of the Sahara: Ghana, Mali, Songhai, and Kanem. The ruling elites of these states converted to or were heavily influenced by Islam, although most of their populations practiced local religions or engaged in syncretism. Much of the wealth of these states was tied to their control of the trans-Saharan trade routes. *page 364*

WHY DID Christianity gradually disappear in Nubia?

The Eastern Sudan. The Nubian Christian states of Maqurra and Alwa were gradually Islamized. *page 370*

HOW DID the arrival of Europeans affect the peoples of West and Central Africa?

The Forestlands: Coastal West and Central Africa. In the coastal forestlands of West Africa, a substantial kingdom arose in Benin, famous for its brass sculptures. Senegambia and the Gold Coast were influenced by contact with European traders and the introduction of food crops from the Americas. Social, political, and economic structures in Kongo and Angola were disrupted by Portuguese slave trading. *page 370*

HOW DID Swahili language and culture develop?

East Africa. On the east coast, Islam influenced the development of the distinctive Swahili culture and language, and Islamic traders linked the region to India and East Asia. Omanis gained control of Zanzibar. *page 373*

HOW DID slavery affect race relations in Cape Colony?

Southern Africa. The ruins at Great Zimbabwe leave many questions unanswered. The Portuguese followed the Zambezi to the gold fields that fed the trade at the Swahili coast, but they were unable to profit much. In southernmost Africa, Trekboers displaced Khoikhoi. The Trekboers imported slaves from India and other parts of Africa, and soon the master-slave relationship became their model for all interactions with non-whites. *page 376*

INTERPRETING THE PAST

Africa and Islam

Sources from MyHistoryLab for Chapter 15

1) Ibn Battuta in Mali
2) Al-Umari describes Mansa Musa of Mali

Source from Chapter 15

1) Great Mosque at Timbuktu (p. 364)

The primary source documents and image listed above chronicle the interaction of African and Islamic cultures in sub-Saharan Africa from the tenth to the fourteenth centuries. As the text sources indicate, Islam coexisted with indigenous ideas and practices, which are usually characterized as "pagan" by these Muslim writers and in later centuries by Christians. Paganism in

REVIEW QUESTIONS

1. Why did Islam succeed in sub-Saharan and East Africa? What role did warfare play in its success? What role did trade have in it?

2. What is the importance of the empires of Ghana, Mali, and Songhai to world history? Why was the control of the trans-Saharan trade so important to these kingdoms? What was the importance of Islamic culture to them? Why did each of these empires break up?

3. What was the impact of the introduction of food crops from the Americas on various regions of Africa during this period?

4. How did Swahili culture form? Describe its defining characteristics. Why has its impact on the East African coast endured?

5. What was the impact of the Portuguese on East Africa and Central Africa? How did European coastal activities affect the African interior?

6. Why did Ottoman influence decline in northern Africa in the eighteenth century?

7. How did the Portuguese and Dutch differ from or resemble the Arabs and other Muslims who came as outsiders to sub-Saharan Africa?

8. What is known about Great Zimbabwe? What questions remain? How might the remaining questions be answered?

9. Discuss the diversity of Cape society in South Africa before 1700. Who were the Trekboers and what was their conflict with the Khoikhoi? How was the basis for apartheid formed in this period?

KEY TERMS

Afrikaans (AF-rih-KAHNS) (p. 377)
apartheid (a-PART-HAYT) (p. 377)
Dar al-Islam (DAR-ahl-his-LAHM) (p. 362)
Maghreb (MUHG-RUHB) (p. 362)
mansa (MAHN-SAH) (p. 367)
marabout (MAYR-uh-BOOZ) (p. 368)

Moors (p. 375)
muezzin (myoo-EHZ-ihn) (p. 366)
oba (OH-bah) (p. 370)
prazeros (p. 376)
Sharifs (shuh-REEFS) (p. 363)
shaykh (SHAYK) (p. 369)
Swahili (swah-HEE-lee) (p. 373)
Trekboers (TREHK-BOR) (p. 377)
uzama (p. 370)

Note: To learn more about the topics in this chapter, please turn to the Suggested Readings at the end of the book.

Africa can be more accurately defined as *animism*, the belief that souls or spirits inhabit inanimate aspects of the natural world (the stars, sea, rivers, mountains) as well as plants and nonhuman animals.

The Ibn Battuta text documents his visit to West Africa (Mali), noting how indigenous African customs coexisted with Islamic practices. Al-Umari's description of Mansa Musa, the great fourteenth century king of Mali, and his *hajj* (pilgrimage) to Mecca, also includes valuable information about indigenous customs, which predate the introduction of Islam.

Use the source documents along with the photo of Timbuktu Mosque to address the following thematic questions focusing on the spread of Islam and the reasons for the continuation of indigenous customs and animistic beliefs. Use specific examples from the documents to support your assertions.

Questions

What indigenous African customs and spiritual beliefs are recorded by Ibn Battuta and al-Umari in their accounts? Carefully note and assess each writer's attitudes (both writers are Muslims). Do they seem impartial, positive, or negative in these descriptions? How would you characterize the nature of these customs and beliefs (religious/social/economic)?

How are Islamic beliefs and customs revealed in Mali? What are the writers' attitudes toward each ruler and their adherence to the Islamic faith?

Are there any indications of Islam being modified through the process of syncretism (combining elements of several spiritual traditions)? When and where are they most apparent?

16

Europe to the Early 1500s: Revival, Decline, and Renaissance

The Medieval Universe. In medieval Europe, the traditional geocentric or earth-centered universe was usually depicted by concentric circles. In this popular German work on natural history, medicine, and science, Konrad von Megenberg (1309–1374) depicted the universe in a most unusual but effective manner. The seven known planets are contained within straight horizontal bands that separate the earth below from heaven, populated by the saints, above.

Which realm seems more important to the artist, heaven or earth?

REVIEW OF EMPIRE, CHURCH, AND TOWNS *page 382*

WHAT IMPACT did the Crusades have on Medieval European Society?

MEDIEVAL SOCIETY *page 389*

WHAT NEW group was added to the three traditional groups in medieval society?

GROWTH OF NATIONAL MONARCHIES *page 391*

HOW DID England and France develop strong royal governments by the thirteenth century?

POLITICAL AND SOCIAL BREAKDOWN *page 393*

WHAT WERE the consequences of the Black Death?

ECCLESIASTICAL BREAKDOWN AND REVIVAL: THE LATE MEDIEVAL CHURCH *page 396*

WHY DID France's king support the Great Schism?

THE RENAISSANCE IN ITALY (1375–1527) *page 397*

WHY WAS the Renaissance a transition from the medieval to the modern world?

REVIVAL OF MONARCHY: NATION BUILDING IN THE FIFTEENTH CENTURY *page 399*

WHAT WERE the bases for the rise of the modern sovereign state in the fifteenth century?

THE HIGH MIDDLE AGES IN WESTERN EUROPE

With its borders finally secured, western Europe during the High Middle Ages was able to concentrate on its political institutions and cultural development, which had been ignored during the early Middle Ages. For western Europe, the High Middle Ages was a period of clearer self-definition during which individual lands gained much of the geographic shape we recognize today. Europe also began to escape its relative isolation from the rest of the world, which had prevailed since the early Middle Ages. Two factors contributed to this increased engagement: the Crusades and renewed trade along the Silk Road linking China and Europe, made possible by the Mongol conquests in Asia.

Under the Song dynasty (960–1279), before Mongol rule, China continued its technological advance. In addition to the printing press, the Chinese invented the abacus and gunpowder. They also enjoyed a money economy unknown in the West. But culturally, these centuries between 1000 and 1300 were closed and narrow by comparison with those of the Tang dynasty. Politically, the Song were far more autocratic. This was also an era of

expansion for Chinese trade, and one of the few in Chinese history in which merchants as a group were able to advance in wealth and status. Although the imperial reach of the Song was limited, Chinese culture in this period was more open to outside influences than in any previous era.

In the late twelfth century Japan shifted from civilian to military rule; the Kamakura *bakufu* governed by mounted warriors who were paid with rights to income from land in exchange for their military services. This rise of a military aristocracy marked the beginning of Japan's "medieval," as distinct from its "classical," period. Three Mongol invasions in the thirteenth century also fostered a strong military to resist them. With a civilian court also in existence, Japan actually had a dual government (that is, two emperors and two courts) until the fourteenth century. However, this situation differed greatly from the deep and permanent national divisions developing at this time among the emerging states and autonomous principalities of western Europe.

T he high Middle Ages (from the eleventh through the thirteenth centuries) was a period of political expansion and consolidation and of intellectual flowering and synthesis. The Latin, or Western, church established itself as a spiritual authority independent of secular monarchies, which became more powerful and self-aggrandizing. The parliaments and popular assemblies that accompanied the rise of these monarchies laid the foundations of modern representative institutions.

An agricultural revolution increased food supplies and populations. Trade and commerce revived, towns expanded, banking and credit developed, and a "new rich" merchant class rose to power in Europe's cities. Universities were established. Contact with the Arab world gave access to the writings of the ancient Greek philosophers, which stimulated the great expansion of Western culture during the late Middle Ages and the Renaissance.

The late Middle Ages and the Renaissance, roughly from 1300 to 1500, were a time of both unprecedented calamity and bold new beginnings in Europe. France and England grappled with each other in a bitter conflict known as the Hundred Years' War (1337–1453). Bubonic plague killed as much as one third of the population in many regions between 1348 and 1350. A schism divided the church (1378–1417). And in 1453 the Turks captured Constantinople. But at the same time, the late Middle Ages witnessed a rebirth that would continue into the seventeenth century. Scholars began criticizing medieval assumptions about the nature of God, humankind, and society. Patriotism and incipient nationalism became major forces in the independent nation-states of Europe. ■

WHAT IMPACT did the Crusades have on Medieval European Society?

REVIVAL OF EMPIRE, CHURCH, AND TOWNS

OTTO I AND THE REVIVAL OF THE EMPIRE

The fortunes of both the old empire and the papacy began to revive in 918, when the Saxon Henry I ("the Fowler," d. 936) became the first non-Frankish king of Germany. Henry rebuilt royal power. His son Otto I (r. 936–973) maneuvered his relatives into power in Bavaria, Swabia, and Franconia and then invaded Italy and proclaimed him-

Within the many developing autonomous Islamic lands at this time, the teachings of Muhammad created an international culture. Religious identity enabled Muslims to transcend their new and often very deep regional divisions. Similarly, Christianity allowed Englishmen, Frenchmen, Germans, and Italians to think of themselves as one people and to unite in Crusades to the Holy Land. As these Crusades got under way in the late eleventh century, Islam too was on the march, penetrating Anatolia and Afghanistan and impinging upon India, where it met a new challenge in Hinduism.

The legacy of the Crusades was mixed. They accomplished few of the goals that originally motivated the European Crusaders; the Holy Land remained under Islamic control, the Crusader kingdoms there collapsed within a few generations of their founding, and the animosity toward Christians fostered by the Crusades resonates even today in the Middle East. Still, the Crusades brought Europeans into more direct and frequent contact with the non-European world than they had known since the heyday of the Roman Empire. Crusaders sampled and sent home products from the Middle East, Asia, and North Africa, creating new tastes in food, art, and even fashion. The resulting growth in demand impelled rising numbers of European merchants to seek these products beyond Europe. Eventually Europeans sought to bypass the Islamic world entirely and secure supplies of Eastern products, especially spices, by going directly to the sources in India and East Asia. By such development, European isolation was ended.

Focus Questions

◆ How did the High Middle Ages in Europe differ from the early Middle Ages?

◆ What was the legacy of the Crusades for Europe? In what ways did they signal the start of new relationships between Europe and the wider world?

self its king in 951. In 955 he defeated the Hungarians at Lechfeld, securing German borders against new barbarian attacks and earning the title "the Great."

Otto enlisted the help of the church in rebuilding his realm. He appointed bishops and abbots to administer his land, since these men possessed a sense of universal empire but they could not marry and found families to compete with his own. In 961, Otto responded to a call for help from Pope John XII (955–964), and on February 2, 962, Otto received in return an imperial coronation. The church was brought ever more under royal control, but it was increasingly determined to assert its independence.

THE REVIVING CATHOLIC CHURCH: THE CLUNY REFORM MOVEMENT AND THE INVESTITURE STRUGGLE

Otto's successors became so preoccupied with Italy that they allowed their German base to disintegrate. As the German empire began to crumble in the eleventh century, the church, unhappy under imperial domination, declared its independence by embracing the Cluny reform.

The great monastery at Cluny had been founded in 910 in east-central France. The Cluny reformers maintained that clergy should not be subservient to kings and that all clergy should come directly under the authority of the pope. They denounced "secular" parish clergy, who lived with concubines in a relationship akin to marriage. Distinctive features of Western religion—separation of church and state, and the celibacy of the Catholic clergy—had their origins in the Cluny reform movement. From Cluny, reformers were dispatched throughout France and Italy, and in the late eleventh century the papacy embraced their reforms.

Pope Gregory VII (r. 1073–1085) advocated other reforms, too. In 1075, he condemned under penalty of excommunication the well-established custom of a king appointing bishops to administer his estates, "investing" them with the ring and staff that symbolized their ecclesiastical office. Emperor Henry IV of Germany considered Gregory's action a direct challenge to his authority. Germany's territorial princes, on

A Black Crusader Saint. St. Maurice was a third-century Egyptian Christian who commanded an Egyptian legion of the Roman army in Gaul. The Romans executed him in 286 C.E. for refusing to worship their gods. Thereafter his Christian cult grew. He was a favorite saint of Charlemagne and other warring medieval German kings. In the era of the Crusades, Western rulers believed that the dark-skinned, patron saint of Magdeburg, Germany would help them win trust in the Eastern lands they occupied and traded in—for which reason artists painted him ever darker.

How do you imagine Middle Easterners would have reacted to this portrayal of St. Maurice?

the other hand, were inclined to support the pope, for they believed that anything that weakened the emperor strengthened them.

The lines of battle were quickly drawn. Henry assembled his loyal German bishops at Worms in January 1076 and had them proclaim their independence from Gregory. Gregory promptly excommunicated Henry and absolved all Henry's subjects from loyalty to him. The German princes were delighted, and Henry faced a general revolt. He had no choice but to come to terms with Gregory. In a famous scene, he prostrated himself outside the pope's castle retreat in northern Italy in January 1077, reportedly standing barefoot in the snow off and on for three days before the pope gave him absolution. Papal power seemed to triumph, but the struggle was not yet over.

The Investiture Controversy was finally settled in 1122 with the Concordat of Worms in which the new Emperor Henry V (r. 1106–1125) agreed not to invest bishops with the ring and staff, and Pope Calixtus II (r. 1119–1124) recognized the emperor's right to grant bishops their secular fiefs. The emperor effectively retained the right to nominate or veto a candidate. The settlement had the effect of separating spheres of ecclesiastical and secular authority; it also set the stage for future conflicts between church and state.

THE CRUSADES

What the Cluny reform was to the clergy, the **Crusades** to the Holy Land were to the laity: an outlet for the heightened religiosity of the late eleventh and twelfth centuries.

Late in the eleventh century, the Byzantine Empire was under severe pressure from the Seljuk Turks, and the Eastern emperor, Alexius I Comnenus, appealed for Western aid. At the Council of Clermont in 1095, Pope Urban II responded by launching the First Crusade. (See Document, "Pope Urban II (r. 1088–1099) Preaches the First Crusade.") Scholars debate the motives of the Crusaders. Genuine religious piety played a major part. The papacy promised Crusaders forgiveness for all their sins should they die in battle, and a crusade to the Holy Land was the ultimate religious pilgrimage. But the pope and others may also have hoped to stabilize the West by sending large numbers of restless, feuding young nobles off to foreign lands. (About 100,000 took part in the First Crusade.) Younger sons of noblemen, for whom there were no estates at home, may have hoped that a crusade would make their fortunes. Urban also saw the Crusades as an opportunity to reconcile Eastern and Western Christianity.

Drawn by the dream of liberating the holy city of Jerusalem, which the Seljuk Turks had held since the seventh century, three great armies gathered in France, Germany, and Italy. As the Crusaders marched by different overland routes toward Constantinople, they seized the opportunity to rid Europe of Jews as well as Muslims. Jewish communities, especially in the Rhineland, suffered bloody pogroms (see Map 16–1).

The eastern emperor was suspicious of the uncouth, spirited soldiers who gathered at his capital, and his subjects, whose villages the Europeans plundered, were openly hostile. Nevertheless, the Crusaders succeeded in doing what Byzantine armies had failed to do. They routed the Seljuks and on July 15, 1099, took the city of Jerusalem. They owed their success to their superior military discipline and weaponry and to the fact that the Muslims failed to unite to oppose them.

The victorious Crusaders set up a "kingdom of Jerusalem" composed of a number of tiny feudal states. These were tenuously held islands in a sea of Muslims intent on their destruction. As the Crusaders built castles for the defense of their new territories, their focus shifted from conquest to economic development. Some, like the military-religious order of the Knights Templar, acquired vast fortunes.

After about forty years, the Crusader states began to fall. The Second Crusade, preached by the Cistercian monk Bernard of Clairvaux (1091–1153), attempted a rescue but met with dismal failure. In October 1187, Saladin (r. 1138–1193), king of

MAP 16–1   The Early Crusades.   Routes and several leaders of the Crusades during the first century of the movement are shown. The names on this map do not exhaust the list of great nobles who went on the First Crusade. The even showier array of monarchs on the Second and Third Crusades still left the Crusades, on balance, ineffective in achieving their goals.

What obstacles did the Crusaders encounter?

Egypt and Syria, reconquered Jerusalem, a victory so brilliant and unexpected that Pope Urban III was said to have dropped dead upon hearing about it. Save for a brief interlude in the thirteenth century, the holiest of cities remained in Islamic hands until the twentieth century.

The Third Crusade in the twelfth century (1189–1192) attempted to reclaim Jerusalem, under three of Europe's greatest rulers: Richard the Lion-Hearted of England, Frederick Barbarossa of the Holy Roman Empire, and Philip Augustus of France. Barbarossa died in an accident en route to the front, and Philip Augustus returned to France to prey on Richard's lands. Left alone, Richard could do little. On his way home, Richard was captured by Emperor Henry VI. England paid a huge ransom to win his release. Popular resentment at the failed, costly venture contributed to the events that produced the Magna Carta in 1215, an effort to curb the power of England's kings.

Crusades   Religious wars directed by the church against "infidels" and "heretics."

CHRONOLOGY

THE CRUSADES

1095	Pope Urban II launches First Crusade
1099	Crusaders take Jerusalem
1147–1149	Second Crusade
1187	Jerusalem retaken by the Muslims under Saladin
1189–1192	Third Crusade
1202–1204	Fourth Crusade

Pope Urban II (r. 1088–1099) Preaches the First Crusade

When Pope Urban II summoned the First Crusade in a sermon at the Council of Clermont on November 26, 1095, he painted a savage picture of the Muslims who controlled Jerusalem. Urban promised the Crusaders, who responded by the tens of thousands, remission of their unrepented sins and assurance of heaven. Robert the Monk is one of four witnesses who left a summary of the sermon, which exists in five different accounts, a sign of its wide reporting and dissemination.

- **Is** the pope engaging in a propaganda and smear campaign? What images of the enemy does he create, and how accurate and fair are they? Did the Christian church have a greater claim to Jerusalem than the people then living there? Does a religious connection with the past entitle one group to confiscate the land of another?

From the confines of Jerusalem and the city of Constantinople a horrible tale has gone forth and very frequently has been brought to our ears, namely, that a race from the kingdom of the Persians [that is, the Seljuk Turks], an accursed race, a race utterly alienated from God, a generation forsooth which has not directed its heart and has not entrusted its spirit to God, has invaded the lands of those Christians and has depopulated them by the sword, pillage and fire; it has led away a part of the captives into its own country, and a part it has destroyed by cruel tortures; it has either entirely destroyed the churches of God or appropriated them for the rites of its own religion. They destroy the altars, after having defiled them with their uncleanness. They circumcise the Christians, and the blood of the circumcision they either spread upon the altars or pour into the vases of the baptismal font. When they wish to torture people by a base death, they perforate

Foundry in Florence. Skilled workers were an integral component of the commerce of medieval towns. This scene shows the manufacture of cannons in a foundry in Florence.

What parts of this image are most detailed? Why?

Politically and religiously the first three Crusades were a failure. But they stimulated Western trade with the East, as Venetian, Pisan, and Genoan merchants followed the Crusaders across Byzantium to lucrative new markets.

Venetian commercial ambitions shaped the Fourth Crusade. Thirty thousand Crusaders gathered in Venice in 1202, intending to sail to Egypt. When they could not raise the money to pay for their transport, they negotiated: In exchange for passage, they agreed to take the rival Christian port of Zara for Venice. Europe was stunned, but worse was to come. The Crusaders were next diverted to Constantinople, which fell to their assault in 1204. A Latin ascended the Byzantine throne, and Venice became the dominant commercial power in the eastern Mediterranean.

Pope Innocent III was chagrined by the misdirection of a Crusade he had authorized, but once Constantinople was in Latin hands, he changed his mind. The opportunity to bring Greek Christians under the control of the Latin church was too tempting. The Greeks, however, could not be reconciled to Latin rule, and in 1261 the man they recognized as their legitimate emperor, Michael Paleologus, recaptured the city. He had help from Venice's rival, Genoa. The Fourth Crusade did nothing to heal the political and religious divisions that separated East and West.

TOWNS AND TOWNSPEOPLE

In the eleventh and twelfth centuries, most towns were small. Only about 5 percent of western Europe's population were urban dwellers, but they were some of the most creative members of medieval society.

Towns were dominated at first by feudal lords, whose charters guaranteed the towns' safety and gave their inhabitants relative independence. The purpose of towns was originally to concentrate skilled laborers who could manufacture the finished goods desired by lords and bishops. As towns grew, they attracted serfs who used their

their navels, and dragging forth the extremity of the intestines, bind it to a stake; then with flogging they lead the victim around until the viscera having gushed forth and the victim falls prostrate upon the ground. Others they bind to a post and pierce with arrows. Others they compel to extend their necks and then, attacking them with naked swords, attempt to cut through the neck with a single blow. What shall I say of the abominable rape of the women? The kingdom of the Greeks is now dismembered by them and deprived of territory so vast in extent that it can not be traversed in a march of two months. On whom therefore is the labor of avenging these wrongs and of recovering this territory incumbent, if not upon you? ...

Jerusalem is the navel of the world; the land is fruitful above others, like another paradise of delights. This the Redeemer of the human race has made illustrious by His advent, has beautified by residence, has consecrated by suffering, has redeemed by death, has glorified by burial. This royal city, therefore, situated at the centre of the world, is now held captive by His enemies, and is in subjection to those who do not know God, to the worship of the heathens. She seeks therefore and desires to be liberated, and does not cease to implore you to come to her aid. From you especially she asks succor, because, as we have already said, God has conferred upon you above all nations great glory in arms.

Accordingly undertake this journey for the remission of your sins, with the assurance of the imperishable glory of the kingdom of heaven.

Source: Translations and reprints from *Original Sources of European History*, Vol. 1 (Philadelphia: Department of History, University of Pennsylvania, 1910), pp. 5–7.

skills and industriousness to raise themselves into higher social ranks. Lords in the countryside had to offer serfs better terms of tenure to keep them on the land, so the growth of towns improved the lot of all serfs.

The first merchants may have been enterprising serfs. Long-distance traders were often people who had nothing to lose and everything to gain from the enormous risks of foreign trade. They traveled together in armed caravans and convoys, buying goods and products as cheaply as possible at the source and selling them for all they could get in Western ports (see Map 16–2). Merchants were outside the traditional social groups of nobility, clergy, and peasantry, but as they gained wealth, they gained respect and imitators. They also challenged traditional seigneurial authority.

Townspeople needed simple, uniform laws and a government sympathetic to new forms of business activity. Commerce was incompatible with the fortress mentality of the lords of the countryside. Merchants especially wanted to end the arbitrary tolls and tariffs imposed by regional magnates. Small shopkeepers and artisans identified far more with merchants than with aloof lords and bishops. The lesser nobility (small knights) outside the towns also supported the new mercantile economy. During the eleventh and twelfth centuries, the burgher upper classes successfully challenged the old noble urban lords. Struggle often led towns in the High and late Middle Ages to form their own independent communes. Towns allied with kings against the nobility in the countryside, rearranging the centers of power in medieval Europe and dissolving classic feudal government.

With urban autonomy came new models of self-government. Around 1100 the old urban nobility and the new burgher upper class merged into an urban patriciate. From this new ruling class was born the aristocratic town council. Enriching and complicating the situation, small artisans and craftspeople also slowly developed their own protective associations or **guilds** and began to gain a voice in government. The towns' opportunities for the "little person" had created the slogan "Town air brings freedom." Townspeople thought of themselves as citizens with basic rights, not subjects at the mercy of their masters' whim.

The University of Bologna in central Italy was distinguished as the center for the revival of Roman law. This carving on the tomb of a Bolognese professor of law shows students attending one of his lectures.

Why were universities important in medieval history?

guild An association of merchants or craftsmen that offered protection to its members and set rules for their work and products.

MAP EXPLORATION

To explore this map further, go to http://www.prenhall.com/craig_maps

MAP 16–2 **Medieval Trade Routes and Regional Products.** Trade in Europe varied in intensity and geographical extent in different periods during the Middle Ages. The map shows some of the channels that came to be used in interregional commerce. Labels tell part of what was carried in that commerce.

How strong were the connections among Europe, the Middle East, and Africa at this time?

Towns became a major force in the transition from feudal societies to national governments and were a ready source of educated bureaucrats and lawyers who knew Roman law, the tool for running the state. Money earned by townspeople enabled kings to hire their own armies, freeing them from dependence on the nobility. Towns, in turn, won royal political recognition and had their constitutions guaranteed. In France, towns became integrated early into royal government. In Germany, they fell under ever tighter control by the princes. In Italy, uniquely, towns became genuine city-states during the Renaissance.

Towns attracted Jews, who plied trades in small businesses. Many became wealthy as moneylenders to kings, popes, and businesspeople. Jewish intellectual and religious culture both dazzled and threatened Christians. These factors encouraged suspicion and distrust among Christians and led to an unprecedented surge in anti-Jewish sentiment in the late twelfth and early thirteenth centuries.

In the twelfth century, translations and commentaries by Byzantine and Spanish Islamic scholars introduced western Europeans to the philosophical works of Aristotle, the writings of Euclid and Ptolemy, the texts of Greek physicians and Arab mathematicians, and the corpus of Roman law. The resulting intellectual ferment gave rise to modern Western universities such as Bologna (established 1158) and the University of Paris.

In the High Middle Ages, people assumed that truth was already known and only needed to be properly organized, elucidated, and defended. Under this model of learning, known as **Scholasticism**, students summarized and compared the traditional authorities in their field, elaborated their arguments pro and con, and drew the logical conclusions. After Aristotle's works were popularized in the West, logic and dialectic became the new tools for disciplining thought and knowledge. Dialectic was the art of discovering a truth by pondering the arguments against it. Together with aspiring philosophers, theologians, and lawyers, even medical students learned their vocation by debating the authoritative texts in their field, not by clinical medical practice.

Peter Abelard (1079–1142) was the boldest and most controversial of the advocates for the new Aristotelian learning. The leading philosopher and theologian of his day, he became Master of Students at Notre Dame. His thinking was unique in its appreciation of subjectivity. He claimed, for instance, that a person's motives determined whether the person's actions were good or evil, not the acts themselves. He also said that an individual's feeling of repentance was a more important factor in receiving God's forgiveness than the church's sacrament of penance.

His audacious logical critique of religious doctrine earned him powerful enemies. Abelard, as he laments in his autobiography, played into their hands by seducing Heloise, a young woman he was hired to tutor. She was the niece of a powerful church leader. After she became pregnant, Abelard wed her—but kept the marriage secret, for university teachers, like clergy, were required to be celibate. Her uncle hired men to castrate Abelard. Thereafter he became a monk, and she entered a convent. They exchanged letters in which he denigrated his love for her as wretched desire. Repentance failed to ingratiate him with the church authorities. In 1121, his works were burned, and in 1140, nineteen propositions that he had taught were condemned as heresies. Heloise outlived him by twenty years and won renown for her efforts to improve conditions for cloistered women.

Scholasticism Method of study based on logic and dialectic that dominated the medieval schools. It assumed that truth already existed; students had only to organize, elucidate, and defend knowledge learned from authoritative texts, especially those of Aristotle and the Church Fathers.

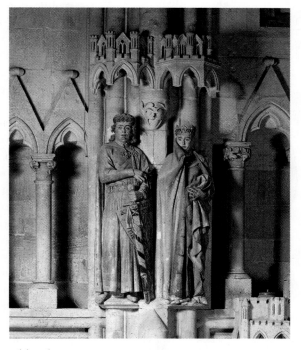

Ekkehard and Uta, ca. 1240–1250. This famous noble pair founded Naumburg Cathedral in Germany in the middle of the thirteenth century and are exemplars of medieval nobility.

What can you guess about these individuals' roles and personalities based on these carvings?

MEDIEVAL SOCIETY

THE ORDER OF LIFE

In the art and literature of the Middle Ages, three basic social groups were represented: the landed nobility, the clergy, and the peasantry and village artisans. After the eleventh century, long-distance traders and merchants emerged as a fourth social group.

No medieval social group was absolutely uniform. Noblemen formed a broad spectrum. Dignity and status within the nobility were directly related to the exercise of authority over others. By the late Middle Ages, separate classes of higher and lower nobility had evolved in both town and country. The higher were the great landowners and territorial magnates, long the dominant powers in their regions; the lower were petty landlords, the descendants of minor knights, newly rich merchants, or wealthy farmers.

Arms were the nobleman's profession, waging war his sole occupation. In the eighth century, the adoption of stirrups made mounted warriors Europe's most valued military assets. The chief virtues of these knights were physical strength, courage, and belligerency.

WHAT NEW group was added to the three traditional groups in medieval society?

regular clergy   Monks and nuns who belong to religious orders.

secular clergy   Parish clergy who did not belong to a religious order.

Dominicans (top) and Franciscans (bottom). Unlike the other religious orders, the Dominicans and Franciscans did not live in cloisters but wandered about preaching and combating heresy. They depended for support on their own labor and the kindness of the laity.

Cliche Bibliothèque Nationale de France, Paris.

Why are books so prominent in both these images?

QUICK REVIEW

Peasant Life

- Peasants were the largest and lowest social group
- Many peasants worked on manors
- Serfs were not chattel slaves

By the late Middle Ages, several factors forced the landed nobility into a steep economic and political decline from which it never recovered. Climatic changes and agricultural failures created large famines, while the great plague (discussed later) brought about unprecedented population losses. Changing military tactics (the use of infantry and heavy artillery during the Hundred Years' War) made the noble cavalry nearly obsolete. And the alliance of wealthy towns with the king weakened the nobility. After the fourteenth century, land and wealth counted for far more than lineage as qualification for entrance into the highest social class.

Unlike the nobility or peasantry, one was not born into the clerical estate. It was acquired by religious training and ordination and was, in theory, open to anyone. There were two fundamental categories of clergy. The **regular clergy** were the monks who lived according to a special ascetic rule (*regula*) in cloisters apart from the world. In the thirteenth century, two new orders were sanctioned, the Franciscans and the Dominicans, whose members went out into the world to preach the church's mission and to combat heresy. The **secular clergy**, who lived and worked directly among the laity in the world (*saeculum*), formed a vast hierarchy. At the top were the wealthy cardinals, archbishops, and bishops who were drawn almost exclusively from the nobility. Below them were the urban priests, the cathedral canons, and the court clerks. Finally, there was the great mass of poor parish priests, who were neither financially nor intellectually much above the common people they served.

During most of the Middle Ages, the clergy were honored as the first estate, and theology was the queen of the sciences. There was great popular respect and reverence for the clergy's function as mediators between God and humanity. The priest brought the Son of God down to earth when he celebrated the sacrament of the Eucharist, and his absolution released penitents from punishment for sin. Mere laypeople did not presume to judge priests.

The largest and lowest social group in medieval society was one on whose labor the welfare of all others depended: the agrarian peasantry. Many peasants lived and worked on the manors of the nobility. The lord of the manor required a certain amount of produce (grain, eggs, and the like) and services from the peasant families, and he held judicial and police authority over them. The lord owned and operated the machines that processed their crops into food and drink, and he had the right to subject his tenants to exactions known as *banalities*. He could, for example, force them to breed their cows with his bull, and pay for the privilege, or make their wine in his wine press. The lord also collected as an inheritance tax a serf's best animal. Without the lord's permission, a serf could neither travel nor marry outside the manor in which he served. Serfs were not chattel slaves, however. It was to a lord's advantage to keep his serfs healthy and happy; his welfare, like theirs, depended on a successful harvest. Serfs had their own dwellings and modest strips of land, and they lived off the produce of their own labor and organization. They could market for their own profit any surpluses, and serfs could pass their property on to their children.

Two basic changes transformed the peasantry during the Middle Ages. The first was the increasing importance of single-family holdings: As families retained property from generation to generation, family farms replaced manorial units. The second was the conversion of the serf's dues into money payments, a change made possible by the revival of trade and the return of a monetary economy. By the thirteenth century, many peasants held their land as rent-paying tenants and no longer had servile status.

In the mid-fourteenth century, when the great plague and the Hundred Years' War created a labor shortage, nobles in England and France tried to turn back the clock by increasing taxes on the peasantry and restricting their migration to the cities. Their efforts triggered rebellions, which were brutally crushed. As growing national sentiment would break European society's political unity, and heretical movements end its nominal religious unity, the peasantry's revolts revealed the absence of medieval social unity.

MEDIEVAL WOMEN

The image of women and the reality of their lives were quite different in the Middle Ages. The image was sketched by celibate male clergy who viewed virginity as morally superior to marriage and claimed that women were physically, mentally, and morally inferior to men. They defined only two respectable roles for women: subjugated housewife or confined nun. Many medieval women were neither.

The clerical view of women was contradicted both within the church itself and in secular society. During the twelfth and thirteenth centuries, the burgeoning popularity of the cult of the Virgin Mary, of chivalric romances, and of courtly love literature celebrated women as natural moral superiors of men. Peter Lombard (1100–1169), an influential theologian, taught that God created Eve from Adam's rib because God intended woman neither to rule nor to be ruled but to be at man's side as his partner in a mutual relationship.

Germanic law treated women better than Roman law had done, recognizing basic rights that forbade their treatment as chattel. German women married husbands of similar age, and a German bride was entitled to a gift of property from her husband that she retained in case of his death. German law gave women the right to inherit, administer, dispose of, and confer property, and it allowed women to take men to court and sue for bodily injury and rape.

The nunnery was an option for single women who could afford it: Entrance required a dowry. Within a nunnery a woman could rise to a position of leadership and exercise authority, but even cloistered women had to submit to supervision by male clergy. The number of women in cloisters was never very large; in late medieval England no more than 3,500 women entered the cloister.

In the ninth century, the Carolingian monarchs obeyed the church and began to enforce monogamy. This was both a gain and a loss for women. Wives were accorded greater dignity and legal security, but their burdens as household managers and bearers of children multiplied. The mortality rates of Frankish women increased and their longevity decreased in the ninth century.

The vast majority of medieval women worked for income. Between the ages of ten and fifteen, girls and boys were apprenticed to learn productive trades. Married women often operated their own shops or became partners in the shops of their husbands. Women appeared in virtually every "blue-collar" trade, from butcher to goldsmith, but mostly worked in the food and clothing industries. Women belonged to guilds, just like men, and they could become craftmasters, but working women were paid less than men who did the same jobs. In the late Middle Ages, townswomen had opportunities to get some schooling and acquire **vernacular** literacy, but they were excluded from the learned professions of scholarship, medicine, and law.

Medieval Marketplace. A fifteenth-century rendering of an eleventh- or twelfth-century marketplace. Medieval women were active in all trades, but especially in the food and clothing industries.

Scala/Art Resource, N.Y.

How did the realities of women's lives compare to the images put forward by Christian clergy?

vernacular The everyday language spoken by the people, as opposed to Latin.

GROWTH OF NATIONAL MONARCHIES

ENGLAND: HASTINGS (1066) TO MAGNA CARTA (1215)

Medieval England's political destiny was determined by the response to the death of the childless Anglo-Saxon ruler Edward the Confessor (r. 1042–1066). Through a connection with Edward's mother, a Norman princess, Duke William of Normandy (d. 1087) laid claim to the vacant English throne. The Anglo-Saxon assembly preferred a native nobleman, Harold Godwinsson (ca. 1022–1066). William invaded England, defeating Harold's army at Hastings on October 14, 1066. William I "the Conqueror" was crowned king of England in Westminster Abbey.

HOW DID England and France develop strong royal governments by the thirteenth century?

Battle of Hastings. William the Conqueror on horseback urging his troops into combat with the English at the Battle of Hastings (October 14, 1066). From the Bayeux Tapestry, about 1073–1083.

William haranguing his troups for combat with the English army. Detail from the Bayeux tapestry, scene 51. Musee de la Tapisserie, Bayeux, France. Photograph copyright Bridgeman-Giraudon/Art Resource, N.Y.

How did changes in military tactics influence relationships between monarchs and nobles in the Middle Ages?

Magna Carta The "Great Charter" limiting royal power that the English nobility forced King John to sign in 1215.

William established a strong monarchy but kept the Anglo-Saxon tax system, the practice of court writs (legal warnings) as a flexible form of central control over localities, and the Anglo-Saxon quasi-democratic tradition of frequent *parleying*—that is, the holding of conferences between the king and lesser powers who had vested interests in royal decisions. The result was a balancing of monarchical and parliamentary elements that continues to characterize English government today.

William's grandson, Henry II (r. 1154–1189), had large French holdings through inheritance and his marriage to Eleanor of Aquitaine (1122–1204). Henry II's increasing autocracy was met with strong political resistance from both the nobility and the clergy. Under Henry's successors, the brothers Richard the Lion-Hearted (r. 1189–1199) and John (r. 1199–1216), burdensome taxation turned resistance into outright rebellion. With the full support of the clergy and the townspeople, the barons forced King John to recognize the **Magna Carta** ("Great Charter") in 1215, a document that reaffirmed traditional rights and personal liberties still enshrined in English law. This famous cornerstone of modern English law put limits on royal power and secured the right of representation in government to the privileged. The Great Charter enabled the English to avoid both dissolution of the monarchy by the nobility and the abridgment of the rights of the nobility by the monarchy.

FRANCE: BOUVINES (1214) TO THE REIGN OF LOUIS IX

Powerful feudal princes dominated France from the beginning of the Capetian dynasty (987) until the reign of Philip II Augustus (1180–1223). During this period, the Capetian kings wisely concentrated their limited resources on securing the territory surrounding Paris, which by the time of Philip II had become the center of French government and culture.

The Duke of Normandy, who after 1066 was master of England, was also a vassal of the French king in Paris. Philip Augustus acted decisively to maintain control over his Norman vassal: His armies occupied all the English territories on the French coast except for Aquitaine. At Bouvines on July 27, 1214, the French won handily over the English and their German allies. The victory unified France around the monarchy and thereby laid the foundation for French ascendancy in the late Middle Ages.

Louis IX (r. 1226–1270), the grandson of Philip Augustus, embodied the medieval view of the perfect ruler. He inherited a unified and secure kingdom. Under him, the efficient French bureaucracy became an instrument of order and fair play in local government. He sent royal commissioners to monitor the local officials and act as champions of the people. Louis abolished private wars and serfdom within his own royal domain, gave his subjects the right of appeal from local to higher courts, and made the tax system more equitable. The French people came to associate their king with justice, and a unifying national identity grew strong.

During Louis's reign, French society and culture became an example to all of Europe, a pattern that continued into the modern period. Northern France became the showcase of monastic reform, chivalry, and Gothic art and architecture. It was the golden age of Scholasticism, and Europe's greatest thinkers converged on Paris.

MAP 16–3   **Germany and Italy in the Middle Ages.**   Medieval Germany and Italy were divided lands. The Holy Roman Empire (Germany) embraced hundreds of independent territories that the emperor ruled only in name. The papacy controlled Rome and tried to enforce its will in central Italy. Under the Hohenstaufens (mid-twelfth to mid-thirteenth centuries), internal German divisions and papal conflict reached new heights; German rulers sought to extend their power to southern Italy and Sicily.

Why were emperors unable to unite Germany and Italy in the Middle Ages?

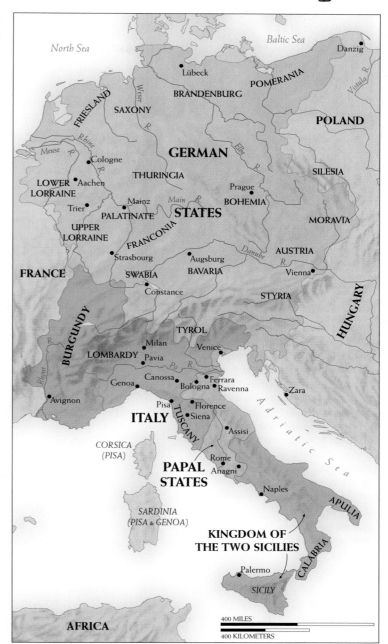

THE HOHENSTAUFEN EMPIRE (1152–1272)

While stable governments developed in both England and France during the Middle Ages, the Holy Roman Empire fragmented (see Map 16–3). Frederick I Barbarossa (1152–1190), the first of the Hohenstaufens, reestablished imperial authority but also initiated a new phase in the contest between popes and emperors. In 1186 his son—the future Henry VI (r. 1190–1197)—married Constance, heiress to the kingdom of Sicily. The Papal States were now encircled, which turned the popes into determined opponents of the German emperor. When Henry VI died in September 1197, Germany was thrown into civil war. Henry VI's four-year-old son, Frederick, had for his own safety been made a ward of Pope Innocent III (r. 1198–1215). Innocent had both the will and the means to challenge the Hohenstaufens.

In December 1212, the pope supported his ward's coronation as Emperor Frederick II. But Frederick soon disappointed his papal sponsor by giving the German princes what they wanted—undisputed authority over their territories. Germany was fragmenting into petty kingdoms. The papacy punished Frederick by excommunicating him (four times) and leading German princes in revolt against him. This transformation of the papacy into a formidable political and military power made the church highly vulnerable to criticism from religious reformers and royal apologists.

When Frederick died in 1250, the German monarchy died with him. The princes established an electoral college in 1257 to pick the emperor, and the "king of the Romans" became their puppet.

POLITICAL AND SOCIAL BREAKDOWN

HUNDRED YEARS' WAR

The Hundred Years' War (May 1337 to October 1453) started when the English king Edward III (r. 1327–1377), grandson of Philip the Fair of France (r. 1285–1314), claimed the French throne. But the war was more than a dynastic quarrel. England and France were territorial and economic rivals with a long history of prejudice and animosity between them, making the Hundred Years' War a struggle for national identity.

 WHAT WERE the consequences of the Black Death?

Gothic Cathedral. The portal of Reims Cathedral, where the kings of France were crowned. The cathedral was built in the Gothic style—emblematic of the High Middle Ages—that originated in France in the mid-twelfth century. The earlier Romanesque (Roman-like) style from which it evolved is characterized by fortress-like buildings with thick stone walls, rounded arches and vaults, and few windows. The Gothic style, in contrast, is characterized by soaring structures, their interiors flooded with colored light from vast expanses of stained glass.

How did the Christian church change as an institution during the medieval period?

Black Death The bubonic plague that killed millions of Europeans in the fourteenth century.

France had three times the population of England, was far wealthier, and fought on its own soil. But most major battles were stunning English victories. Unlike England, France was still struggling to make the transition from a fragmented feudal society to a centralized modern state. France's defeats also resulted from incompetent leadership and English military superiority. The English infantry was more disciplined than the French, and English archers could fire six arrows a minute with enough force to pierce an inch of wood or the armor of a knight at 200 yards. Eventually, thanks in part to the inspiring leadership of Joan of Arc (1412–1431) and a sense of national identity and self-confidence, the French were able to expel the English. By 1453, all that remained to the English was their coastal enclave of Calais.

The Hundred Years' War had lasting political and social consequences. It devastated France, but it also awakened French nationalism and hastened the country's transition from a feudal monarchy to a centralized state. In both France and England the burden of the war fell most heavily on the peasantry, who were forced to support it with taxes and services.

THE BLACK DEATH

Agricultural improvements spurred population growth in the late Middle Ages. Europe's population roughly doubled between the years 1000 and 1300. There were more people than there was food to feed them or jobs to employ them, and the average European faced the probability of extreme hunger at least once during his or her expected thirty-five-year life span. Between 1315 and 1317, for example, cold weather and crop failures produced a great famine. Decades of overpopulation, economic depression, famine, and bad health made Europeans vulnerable to a virulent plague that struck with full force in 1348.

The **Black Death**, so called because it discolored the body, followed the trade routes from Asia into Europe. Appearing in Sicily in late 1347, it entered Europe through the port cities of Venice, Genoa, and Pisa in 1348, and from there swept rapidly through Spain and southern France and into northern Europe. Areas outside the major trade routes, like Bohemia, remained virtually unaffected. Bubonic plague made numerous reappearances in succeeding decades. It is estimated that western Europe had lost as much as two fifths of its population by the early fifteenth century (see Map 16–4).

The plague was transmitted by fleas and rats, but it also entered the lungs and could be spread by sneezes. Contemporary physicians had little understanding of how diseases worked. Popular wisdom held that bad air caused the disease. Some thought that earthquakes had released poisonous fumes. Psychological reactions sometimes went to extremes. Some hoped that moderation and temperance would save them; some indulged in sexual promiscuity; some fled in panic, and some developed a morbid religiosity. Parades of flagellants whipped themselves, hoping to induce God to show mercy and intervene. Jews were baselessly accused of spreading the disease, and pogroms flared. The church tried to maintain order, but across western Europe people developed an obsession with death and dying and a deep pessimism that endured for decades.

Whole villages vanished. The labor supply shrank, so wages increased and those of skilled artisans soared. Many serfs substituted money payments for their labor services and pursued more rewarding jobs in the cities. Agricultural prices fell because of lowered demand, and the price of luxury and manufactured goods—the work of skilled artisans—rose. The noble landholders suffered the greatest decline in power. They were forced to pay more for finished products and for farm labor, while receiving a smaller return on their agricultural produce. Rents declined everywhere.

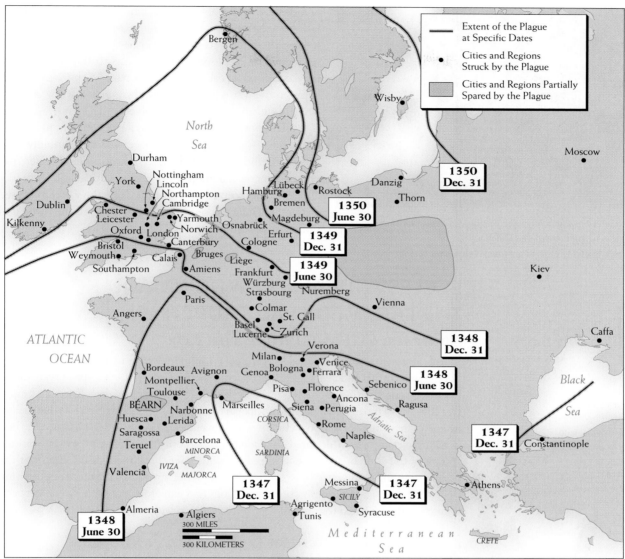

MAP 16–4   Spread of the Black Death.   Apparently introduced by sea-borne rats from areas around the Black Sea, where plague-infested rodents have long been known, the Black Death had great human, social, and economic consequences. According to one of the lower estimates, it killed 25 million in Europe. The map charts the spread of the plague in the mid-fourteenth century. Generally following trade routes, it reached Scandinavia by 1350, and some believe it then went on to Iceland and even Greenland. Areas off the main trade routes were largely spared.

What were some social and economic consequences of the plague?

Some landowners converted arable land to sheep pasture, substituting more profitable wool production for labor-intensive grain crops. The propertied classes also used their political influence to pass repressive legislation that forced peasants to stay on their farms and froze wages at low levels. The result was an eruption of peasant rebellions in France and England.

Although the plague hit urban populations hard, cities recovered relatively quickly. Cities had always protected their interests by regulating competition and immigration from rural areas. After the plague the reach of such laws was extended to include the lands of nobles and landlords, many of whom were now integrated into urban life.

Black Death. Men and women carrying plague victims in coffins to the burial ground in Tournai, Belgium, 1349.

How did the high mortality rates of the Black Death alter socioeconomic relationships?

Guilds used their political influence to pass restrictive legislation that protected their markets. Master artisans wanted to keep their numbers low to limit competition, but the journeymen they employed wanted access to the guild so that they could set up shops of their own. To the old conflict between the urban patriciate and the guilds was now added a struggle within the guilds themselves.

There was gain as well as loss for the church, too. Many clergy died—up to one third in places—as they dutifully ministered to the sick and dying. As a great landholder, the church's income and, therefore, its political influence declined. But it received new revenues from the vastly increased demand for religious services for the dead and the dying and from new gifts and bequests.

ECCLESIASTICAL BREAKDOWN AND REVIVAL: THE LATE MEDIEVAL CHURCH

WHY DID France's king support the Great Schism?

BONIFACE VIII AND PHILIP THE FAIR

By the fourteenth century popes faced rulers far more powerful than themselves. When Pope Boniface VIII (r. 1294–1303) issued a bull, *Clericis Laicos*, which forbade lay taxation of the clergy without prior papal approval, King Philip the Fair of France (r. 1285–1314) unleashed a ruthless antipapal campaign. Boniface made a last-ditch stand against state control of national churches on November 18, 1302, when he issued the bull *Unam Sanctam*, which declared that temporal authority was "subject" to the spiritual power of the church. The French responded with force. Philip sent troops that beat the pope badly and might even have executed him had not an aroused populace rescued him. No pope ever again seriously threatened kings and emperors. Future relations between church and state tilted toward state control of religion within particular monarchies.

Papal Authority. Pope Boniface VIII (r. 1294–1303), who opposed the taxation of the clergy by the kings of France and England, issued one of the strongest declarations of papal authority, the bull *Unam Sanctam*. This statue is in the Museo Civico, Bologna, Italy.

Statue of Pope Boniface VIII. Museo Civico, Bologna. Scala/Art Resource, N.Y.

Why did royal power grow relative to papal power in this period?

THE GREAT SCHISM (1378–1417) AND THE CONCILIAR MOVEMENT TO 1449

Boniface VIII's successor, Clement V (r. 1305–1314), moved the papal court to Avignon on the southeastern border with France, where it remained until Pope Gregory XI (r. 1370–1378) reestablished the papacy in Rome in January 1377. When Pope Urban VI (r. 1378– 1389) proclaimed his intention to reform the papal government in the **Curia**, France's Charles V (r. 1364–1380) feared a loss of influence. Charles V supported the **Great Schism**, which began on September 20, 1378, when thirteen cardinals (all but one of whom were French) elected a cousin of the French king as Pope Clement VII (r. 1378–1397). Clement returned to Avignon. Allegiance to the competing papal courts divided along political lines England and its allies—the **Holy Roman Empire** (based on the old Roman Empire, mostly Germany and northern Italy), Hungary, Bohemia, and Poland retained their allegiance to Urban VI. France and its orbit—Naples, Scotland, Castile, and Aragon—supported Clement VII. (Only the Roman line is now recognized as official by the church.) In 1409 a council at Pisa deposed both the Roman and the Avignon popes and elected yet another pope, recognized by neither Rome nor Avignon. This intolerable situation lasted until November 1417, when a church legal council elected a new pope, Martin V (r. 1417–1431), and reunited the church.

The papacy regained much of its prestige and authority, and in 1460 the papal bull *Execrabilis* condemned all appeals to councils as "completely null and void." But the conciliar movement had planted deep within the conscience of Western peoples the conviction that the leader of an institution must be responsive to its members.

THE RENAISSANCE IN ITALY (1375–1527)

The **Renaissance** is the term used to describe fourteenth- and fifteenth-century efforts to revive ancient learning. It marked a transition from the medieval to the modern world. Medieval Europe, especially before the twelfth century, had been a fragmented feudal society with an agricultural economy, its thought and culture dominated by the church. Renaissance Europe, especially after the fourteenth century, was characterized by growing national consciousness and political centralization, an urban economy based on organized commerce and capitalism, and ever greater lay and secular control of thought and culture.

The distinctive features and achievements of the Renaissance are most striking in Italy from roughly 1375 to 1527, the year of the infamous sack of Rome by imperial soldiers. What was achieved in Italy during these centuries deeply influenced northern Europe.

THE ITALIAN CITY-STATE: SOCIAL CONFLICT AND DESPOTISM

The Renaissance began in the cities of late medieval Italy. Italy was the natural gateway between East and West; Venice, Genoa, and Pisa traded with the Middle East throughout the Middle Ages. During the thirteenth and fourteenth centuries, the trade-rich Italian cities became powerful city-states, dominating the political and economic life of their regions. By the fifteenth century, the great Italian cities had become the bankers for much of Europe. There were five major competing states in Italy: the duchy of Milan, the republics of Florence and Venice, the Papal States, and the kingdom of Naples.

Social strife and competition for political power were so intense within the cities that most had evolved into despotisms by the fifteenth century. Venice, ruled by a successful merchant oligarchy, was the notable exception. Elsewhere, the new social classes and divisions within society produced by rapid urban growth fueled chronic, near-anarchic conflict. In Florence, true stability was not established until the ascent to power in 1434 of the wealthy Cosimo de' Medici (1389–1464), who controlled the city from behind the scenes. His grandson Lorenzo the Magnificent (1449–1492, r. 1478–1492) ruled Florence in an almost totalitarian fashion.

Despotism was less subtle elsewhere in Italy. Dominant groups in many cities cooperated in the hiring of a strongman, known as a *podesta*, to maintain law and order. Political turbulence and warfare also fostered diplomacy. City-states strove to stay abreast of foreign military developments and, if shrewd enough, gained power and advantage without actually going to war.

HUMANISM

Humanism was the scholarly study of the Latin and Greek classics and the ancient Church Fathers, both for their own sake and to promote a rebirth of ancient norms and values. Humanists advocated the *studia humanitatis*, a liberal arts program that embraced grammar, rhetoric, poetry, history, politics, and moral philosophy. The first humanists were orators and poets. They wrote original literature inspired by the newly discovered works of the ancients, and they taught rhetoric within the universities. They were sought as secretaries, speech writers, and diplomats in princely and papal courts.

Classical and Christian antiquity had been studied before, but the Italian Renaissance of the late Middle Ages was more secular and lay dominated, had broader interests, recovered more manuscripts, and possessed far superior technical skills than

WHY WAS the Renaissance a transition from the medieval to the modern world?

Curia The papal government.

Great Schism The appearance of two, and at times three, rival popes between 1378 and 1415.

Holy Roman Empire The revival of the old Roman Empire, based mainly in Germany and northern Italy, that endured from 870 to 1806.

Renaissance The revival of ancient learning and the supplanting of traditional religious beliefs by new secular and scientific values that began in Italy in the fourteenth and fifteenth centuries.

humanism The study of the Latin and Greek classics and of the Church Fathers both for their own sake and to promote a rebirth of ancient norms and values.

studia humanitatis During the Renaissance, a liberal arts program of study that embraced grammar, rhetoric, poetry, history, philosophy, and politics.

chiaroscuro The use of shading to enhance naturalness in painting and drawing.

Mannerism A style of art in the mid to late sixteenth century that permitted artists to express their own "manner" or feelings in contrast to the symmetry and simplicity of the art of the High Renaissance.

Jan van Eyck, "Adam and Eve" (1432). In the wings of the Dutch painter Jan van Eyck's earliest work, the Ghent Altarpiece, Adam and Eve appear after their fall. Unlike the Italian Renaissance masters, the Netherlandish master portrays them as true-to-life humans, not heroic, idealized figures. Above their heads their son Cain kills his brother Abel, a commentary on humankind after the Fall.

Why would church paintings be important during this period?

earlier rebirths of antiquity. Unlike their Scholastic rivals, humanists drew their own conclusions after reading original sources in Latin or Greek.

Francesco Petrarch (1304–1374), the father of humanism, celebrated ancient Rome in his writings and tirelessly collected ancient manuscripts. His critical textual studies, elitism, and contempt for the allegedly useless learning of the Scholastics were shared by many later humanists. Dante Alighieri's (1265–1321) *Vita Nuova* and *Divine Comedy*—together with Petrarch's sonnets—form the cornerstones of Italian vernacular literature. Petrarch's student and friend Giovanni Boccaccio (1313–1375) wrote the *Decameron*, a hundred bawdy tales told in various voices, and assembled an encyclopedia of Greek and Roman mythology.

The classical ideal of a useful education that produces well-rounded, effective people inspired far-reaching reforms. The most influential Italian Renaissance tract on education, Pietro Paolo Vergerio's (1349–1420) *On the Morals That Befit a Free Man*, was written directly from classical models. Vittorino da Feltre (d. 1446) directed his students to a highly disciplined reading of ancient authors, together with vigorous physical exercise.

Educated and cultured noblewomen had a prominent place at Renaissance courts, among them Christine de Pisan (1363?–1434). She was an expert in classical, French, and Italian languages and literature whose most famous work, *The City of Ladies*, describes the accomplishments of history's great women.

RENAISSANCE ART IN AND BEYOND ITALY

Throughout Renaissance Europe, the values and interests of the laity were less subordinated to those of the clergy than in previous centuries. In education, culture, and religion, the secular world's many purely human pursuits were appreciated as ends in themselves.

This perspective on life is especially prominent in the painting and sculpture of the High Renaissance (late fifteenth and early sixteenth centuries), when Renaissance art reached its maturity. In imitation of Greek and Roman art, painters and sculptors created well-proportioned and even heroic figures. Whereas Byzantine and Gothic art had been religious and idealized, Renaissance art, especially in the fifteenth century, reproduced nature and human nature realistically in both its physical beauty and grotesqueness.

Italian artists led the way, taking advantage of new technical skills and materials developed during the fifteenth century: oil paints, the technique of shading to enhance realism (**chiaroscuro**), and sizing figures to convey to the viewer a feeling of continuity with a painting (linear perspective). Compared with their flat Byzantine and Gothic counterparts, Renaissance paintings seem filled with energy and life. The great masters of the High Renaissance include Leonardo da Vinci (1452–1519), Raphael (1483–1520), and Michelangelo Buonarroti (1475–1564). A modernizing, experimental style known as **Mannerism** followed, reaching its peak in the late sixteenth and early seventeenth centuries. Tintoretto (d. 1594) and the Spaniard El Greco (d. 1614) were Mannerism's supreme representatives.

ITALY'S POLITICAL DECLINE: THE FRENCH INVASIONS (1494–1527)

Italy's autonomous city-states had always cooperated to oppose foreign invaders. In 1494, however, Naples, supported by Florence and the Borgia pope Alexander VI (1492–1503), prepared to attack Milan. The Milanese despot Ludovico il Moro (r. 1476–1499) invited the French to revive their dynastic claim to Naples. Within five months the French king Charles VIII (r. 1483–1498) had crossed the Alps (August 1495) and raced as conqueror through Florence and the Papal States into Naples. Ferdinand of Aragon (r. 1479–1516), who was also king of Sicily, helped create a counteralliance, the League of Venice, which forced Charles to retreat. The French returned to Italy under Louis XII (r. 1498–1515), this time assisted by the Borgia pope Alexander VI

(1492–1503). Alexander, probably the most corrupt pope in history, sought to secure a political base in Romagna, officially part of the Papal States, for his son Cesare. Seeing that a French alliance could allow him to reestablish control over the region, Alexander abandoned the League of Venice. Louis successfully invaded Milan in August 1499. In 1500 he and Ferdinand of Aragon divided Naples between themselves, while the pope and Cesare Borgia conquered the Romagna without opposition.

In 1503 Cardinal Giuliano della Rovere became Pope Julius II (1503–1513). He suppressed the Borgias and placed their newly conquered lands in Romagna under papal jurisdiction. After securing the Papal States with French aid, Julius changed sides and sought to rid Italy of the French invaders. Julius, Ferdinand of Aragon, and Venice formed a Holy League in October 1511, and soon Emperor Maximilian I (r. 1493–1519) and the Swiss joined them. By 1512 the French were in full retreat.

The French invaded Italy again under Francis I (r. 1515–1547). French armies massacred Swiss soldiers of the Holy League in September 1515. That victory won from the Medici pope Leo X (r. 1513–1521) an agreement known as the Concordat of Bologna (August 1516), which gave the French king control over the French clergy and the right to collect taxes from them in exchange for French recognition of the pope's superiority over church councils. This helped keep France Catholic after the outbreak of the Protestant Reformation. But the new French entry into Italy also led to the first of four major wars with Spain in the first half of the sixteenth century, the Habsburg-Valois wars, none of which France won.

NICCOLÒ MACHIAVELLI

These invasions made a shambles of Italy. Niccolò Machiavelli (1469–1527) became convinced that Italian political unity and independence were ends that justified any means. Machiavelli admired the heroic acts of ancient Roman rulers, what Renaissance people called their *Virtù*. Juxtaposing the strengths of idealized ancient Romans with the failures of his contemporaries, Machiavelli became famously cynical. Only an unscrupulous strongman, he concluded, could impose order on so divided and selfish a people. Machiavelli hoped to see a strong ruler emerge from the Medici family. But the second Medici pope, Clement VII (r. 1523–1534), watched helplessly as Rome was sacked by the army of Emperor Charles V (r. 1519–1556) in 1527, the year of Machiavelli's death.

Niccolò Machiavelli. Santi di Tito's portrait of Machiavelli, the Italian political theorist who advised Renaissance princes to practice artful deception and inspire fear in their subjects if they wished to succeed.

Scala/Art Resource, N.Y.

Is Machiavelli's advice still relevant today?

REVIVAL OF MONARCHY: NATION BUILDING IN THE FIFTEENTH CENTURY

After 1450, unified national monarchies progressively replaced fragmented and divisive feudal governance. The dynastic and chivalric ideals of feudalism did not disappear: Minor territorial princes survived, and representative assemblies even gained influence in some regions. But by the late fifteenth and early sixteenth centuries, the old problem of the one and the many was being decided in favor of monarchy.

In the feudal monarchy of the High Middle Ages, the basic powers of government were divided between the king and his semiautonomous vassals. The nobility and the towns acted with varying degrees of success through such evolving representative bodies as the English Parliament, the French Estates General, and the Spanish Cortes to thwart the centralization of royal power. As a result of the Hundred Years' War and the schism in the church, however, the landed nobility and the clergy were in decline in the late Middle Ages. Towns began to ally with the king, and townspeople staffed the royal offices. This new alliance between king and town slowly broke the bonds of feudal society and made possible the rise of the modern sovereign state.

In a sovereign state, the powers of taxation, war making, and law enforcement are concentrated in the monarch and exercised by his chosen agents. Taxes, wars, and laws

WHAT WERE the bases for the rise of the modern sovereign state in the fifteenth century?

CHRONOLOGY

MAJOR POLITICAL EVENTS OF THE ITALIAN RENAISSANCE (1375–1527)

1434	Medici rule in Florence established by Cosimo de' Medici
1454–1455	Treaty of Lodi allies Milan, Naples, and Florence (in effect until 1494)
1494	Charles VIII of France invades Italy
1495	League of Venice unites Venice, Milan, the Papal States, the Holy Roman Empire, and Spain against France
1499	Louis XII invades Milan (the second French invasion of Italy)
1500	The Borgias conquer Romagna
1512–1513	The Holy League (Pope Julius II, Ferdinand of Aragon, Emperor Maximilian I, and Venice) defeat the French
1513	Machiavelli writes *The Prince*
1515	Francis I leads the third French invasion of Italy
1516	Concordat of Bologna between France and the papacy
1527	Sack of Rome by imperial soldiers

become national matters. Monarchies began to create standing national armies in the fifteenth century. As the noble cavalry receded and the infantry and the artillery became the backbone of armies, mercenary soldiers were recruited from Switzerland and Germany to form the mainstay of the "king's army." The growing cost of warfare increased the need to develop new national sources of royal income. The highest classes stubbornly believed they were immune from government taxation, so royal revenue grew at the expense of those least able to resist and least able to pay. Monarchs had several options. As feudal lords they could collect rents from their royal domain. They might also levy national taxes on basic food and clothing, such as the *gabelle* or salt tax in France and the *alcabala* or 10 percent sales tax on commercial transactions in Spain. Kings could also levy direct taxes on the peasantry and on commercial transactions in towns under royal protection. The French *taille* was such a tax. Sale of public offices and the issuance of high-interest government bonds were innovative fund-raising devices. Kings turned for loans to rich nobles and to the great bankers of Italy and Germany.

MEDIEVAL RUSSIA

Golden Horde Name given to the Mongol rulers of Russia from 1240 to 1480.

In the late tenth century Prince Vladimir of Kiev (r. 972–1015), then Russia's dominant city, received delegations of Muslims, Roman Catholics, Jews, and Greek Orthodox Christians, each group hoping to win the Russians to its religion. Prince Vladimir chose Greek Orthodoxy, which became the religion of Russia, adding a new cultural bond to the long-standing commercial ties the Russians had with the Byzantine Empire.

Vladimir's successor, Yaroslav the Wise (r. 1016–1054), developed Kiev into a magnificent political and cultural center, but after his death, rivalry among princes challenged Kiev's dominance, and it became just one of several national centers.

Mongol (or Tatar) armies (see Chapters 8 and 13) invaded Russia in 1223, and Kiev fell in 1240. Russian cities became tribute-paying principalities of the segment of the Mongol Empire called the **Golden Horde**, which had its capital on the lower Volga. Mongol rule further separated Russia from the West but left Russian political institutions and religion largely intact. Thanks to their far-flung trade, the Mongolians brought most Russians greater peace and prosperity than they had enjoyed before. The princes of Moscow grew wealthy

A **painting** of the Kremlin in the fifteenth century showing the warren of wooden houses that surrounded the palaces and churches.

What factors contributed to Moscow's growth?

and expanded the principality. Ivan III, called Ivan the Great (d. 1505) brought all of northern Russia under Moscow's control and ended Mongol rule in 1480. By the last quarter of the fifteenth century, Moscow had replaced Kiev as the political and religious center of Russia. In Russian eyes it was destined to become the "third Rome" after the fall of Constantinople to the Turks in 1453.

FRANCE

There were two cornerstones of French nation building in the fifteenth century: England's retreat from the continent following its loss of the Hundred Years' War, and the defeat of Charles the Bold (r. 1467–1477) and his duchy of Burgundy. The dukes of Burgundy were probably Europe's strongest rulers in the mid-fifteenth century, and they hoped to build a dominant middle kingdom between France and the Holy Roman

Empire. Continental powers joined forces to oppose them, and Charles the Bold was killed in battle at Nancy in 1477.

The dissolution of Burgundy left Louis XI (r. 1461–1483) free to secure the monarchy in his expanded kingdom. Louis harnessed the nobility and expanded trade and industry. It was because Louis's successors inherited such a secure and efficient government that France was able to pursue Italian conquests in the 1490s and to fight a long series of losing wars with the Habsburgs in the first half of the sixteenth century. By the mid-sixteenth century France was again a defeated nation, almost as divided as it had been during the Hundred Years' War.

SPAIN

Spain, too, became a strong country in the late fifteenth century. Both Castile and Aragon had been poorly ruled, divided kingdoms until the 1469 marriage of Isabella of Castile (r. 1474–1504) and Ferdinand of Aragon (r. 1479–1516). Castile was by far the richer and more populous of the two. Each retained its own government agencies and cultural traditions. Together, Isabella and Ferdinand were able to subdue their realms, secure their borders, and venture abroad militarily. Townspeople allied themselves with the crown and progressively replaced the nobility within the royal administration. The crown also extended its authority over the wealthy chivalric orders.

Spain had long been remarkable as a place where Islam, Judaism, and Christianity coexisted with a certain degree of toleration. This ended decisively. Ferdinand and Isabella exercised almost total control over the Spanish church as they placed religion in the service of national unity. They appointed the higher clergy and the officers of the Inquisition. Spanish spiritual life became uniform and regimented, which is a major reason Spain became a base for Europe's Counter-Reformation in the sixteenth century.

The anti-French marriage alliances Isabella and Ferdinand arranged for their children determined much of European history in the sixteenth century. Their patronage of the Genoese adventurer Christopher Columbus (1451–1506) led to the creation of the Spanish Empire in the New World. Gold and silver from mines in Mexico and Peru helped make Spain Europe's dominant power in the sixteenth century.

ENGLAND

The last half of the fifteenth century was especially difficult for the English. Following the Hundred Years' War, civil war broke out in England between two rival branches of the royal family, the House of York and the House of Lancaster. This conflict, named the Wars of the Roses (York's symbol, according to legend, was a white rose, and Lancaster's a red rose), kept England in turmoil from 1455 to 1485.

The Lancastrian monarchy of Henry VI (r. 1422–1461) was consistently challenged by the Duke of York and his supporters in the prosperous southern towns. In 1461 Edward IV (r. 1461–1483), son of the Duke of York, seized power. His brother and successor was Richard III (r. 1483–1485), whose reign saw the growth of support for the exiled Lancastrian Henry Tudor. Henry returned to England to defeat Richard in August 1485 and became King Henry VII (r. 1485–1509), founder of a Tudor dynasty that endured until 1603.

To bring the rival royal families together and give his offspring an incontestable hereditary claim to the throne, Henry married Edward IV's daughter, Elizabeth of York. With the aid of a much-feared instrument of royal power, the Court of Star Chamber, he imposed discipline on the English nobility. He shrewdly construed legal precedents to the advantage of the crown and used English law to further his own ends. He confiscated so much noble land and so many fortunes that he was able to govern without depending on Parliament for grants. Henry constructed a powerful monarchy that became one of early modern Europe's most exemplary governments during the reign of his granddaughter, Elizabeth I (r. 1558–1603).

SUMMARY

WHAT IMPACT did the Crusades have on Medieval European Society?

Revival of Empire, Church, and Towns. Germany's Otto I breathed new life into both empire and papacy. In the tenth century, the Cluny reform movement increased popular respect for the church and strengthened the clergy. In the Investiture Controversy, the papacy secured the independence of the clergy by enlisting the support of the German princes against the Holy Roman Emperors, thus weakening imperial power in Germany. The Crusades were based on the intense passions of popular piety. The rise of merchants, self-governing towns, and universities helped restructure power. By supporting rulers against the nobility, towns gave kings the resources to build national governments. *page 382*

WHAT NEW group was added to the three traditional groups in medieval society?

Medieval Society. In theory, medieval society was divided into three main groups: clergy (those who prayed), nobility (those who fought as mounted warriors), and laborers (peasants and artisans). But merchants became a fourth group. Women faced constraints, but their lives were far richer and more varied than Christian imagery suggested. *page 389*

HOW DID England and France develop strong royal governments by the thirteenth century?

Growth of National Monarchies. Much of medieval history involved the struggle by rulers to assert their authority over powerful local lords and the church. In England and France, monarchs and nobles reached accommodation, and national identity was strengthened. The Holy Roman Empire, however, disintegrated. *page 391*

WHAT WERE the consequences of the Black Death?

Political and Social Breakdown. Both the Hundred Years' War and the Black Death weakened the nobility. Bubonic plague devastated areas surrounding trade routes. Population loss had many consequences, including a shortage of labor and high demand for luxury goods leading to a rise in status for artisans. Cities and kings were, on balance, strengthened. *page 393*

WHY DID France's king support the Great Schism?

Ecclesiastical Breakdown and Revival: The Late Medieval Church. By the end of the thirteenth century, kings had become more powerful than popes, and the French king, Philip the Fair, was able to defy the papacy. In the fourteenth century, the Great Schism further weakened papal prestige. The papacy never recovered its authority over national rulers. *page 396*

WHY WAS the Renaissance a transition from the medieval to the modern world?

The Renaissance in Italy (1375–1527). The Renaissance, which began in the Italian city-states in the late fourteenth century, marks the transition from the medieval to the modern world. Humanism promoted a rebirth of ancient norms and values and the classical ideal of an educated, well-rounded person. The growth of secular values led to a great burst of artistic activity by artists such as Leonardo da Vinci, Raphael, and Michelangelo. The political weakness of the Italian states invited foreign intervention. The sack of Rome in 1527 marks the end of the Renaissance. *page 397*

WHAT WERE the bases for the rise of the modern sovereign state in the fifteenth century?

Revival of Monarchy: Nation Building in the Fifteenth Century. By the fifteenth century, England, France, and Spain had developed into strong national monarchies with centralized bureaucracies and professional armies. Although medieval institutions, such as the English Parliament, limited royal power in theory, in practice monarchs in these countries held unchallenged authority. In previous centuries, the Great Schism, the Hundred Years' War, and the Black Death weakened the church and the nobility. Townspeople supported the kings. A similar process was beginning in Russia, where the rulers of Moscow were extending their authority after throwing off Mongol rule. *page 399*

REVIEW QUESTIONS

1. How do you account for the success of the Cluny reform movement? Can major features of the modern Catholic Church be found in the Cluny reforms?

2. Was the Investiture Controversy a political or religious conflict? Summarize the respective arguments of Gregory VII and Henry IV. Is the conflict a precedent for the modern doctrine of the separation of church and state?

3. What was the legacy of the Crusades for Europe? In what ways did they signal the start of new relationships between Europe and the wider world?

4. Why did Germany remain divided while France and England began to coalesce into reasonably strong states during the High Middle Ages?

5. How did the responsibilities of the nobility differ from those of the clergy and the peasantry during the High Middle Ages? How did each social class contribute to the stability of society?

6. Describe the circumstances that gave rise to towns. How did towns change traditional medieval society?

7. How did the Hundred Years' War, the Black Death, and the Great Schism in the church affect the course of history? Which had the most lasting effects on the institutions it touched?

8. Was the church an aggressor or a victim in the late Middle Ages and the Renaissance? How successful was it in its confrontations with Europe's emerging dynastic states?

9. What was "reborn" in the Renaissance? Were the humanists the forerunners of modern secular education and culture or eloquent defenders of a still medieval Christian view of the world against the church's secular and pagan critics?

10. Historians find features of modern states developing in Europe during the late Middle Ages and Renaissance. What modern features can you identify in the governments of the Italian city-states, the northern monarchies, and in Russia?

KEY TERMS

Black Death (p. 394)
chiaroscuro (KEY-ahr-uh-SKYOOR-oh) (p. 398)
Crusades (p. 385)
Curia (p. 397)
Golden Horde (p. 400)
Great Schism (p. 397)
guild (p. 387)
Holy Roman Empire (p. 397)

humanism (p. 397)
Magna Carta (p. 392)
Mannerism (p. 397)
regular clergy (p. 390)
Renaissance (p. 397)
Scholasticism (p. 389)
secular clergy (p. 390)
studia humanitatis (p. 397)
vernacular (p. 391)

Note: To learn more about the topics in this chapter, please turn to the Suggested Readings at the end of the book.

INTERPRETING THE PAST

Struggles for Authority in Medieval and Early Modern Europe

Sources from MyHistoryLab for Chapter 16

myhistorylab

1) Magna Carta, 1215

2) Behâ ed-Din: Richard I Massacres Prisoners

3) Peter Abelard Defends Himself

Source from Chapter 16

1) Pope Urban II Preaches the First Crusade (p. 386)

Visual Sources from MyHistoryLab

1) Albrecht Dürer, woodcut showing use of perspective

2) Leonardo da Vinci, sketches and drawings

As he recalled the episode in his *History of My Calamities*, the professor Peter Abelard (1079–1142) claimed to have been a victim of ignorance and intolerance during a debate over one of his books. Refuting a charge that he had made heretical arguments about the Christian Trinity, Abelard attempted to reason with his opponents, but they merely exclaimed, "We don't care about rational argument or any interpretation you might have. The only thing that matters is the word of authority."

In the period 1000–1500, however, the nature and claims of "authority" were in flux in many specific respects. The period was characterized by a series of ongoing debates about where and how the line between various powers and institutions could be drawn. Using the documents and images here, demonstrate how Europeans debated the following issues:

◆ Kings v. Nobles—the Magna Carta excerpts

◆ Christians v. Muslims—Urban II's call for a crusade and Behâ ed-Din on the Massacre at Acre in 1191

◆ Reason v. Authority—document by Peter Abelard on reason and religion

◆ Tradition v. Innovation—specifically in the arts, as reflected in the images created by Dürer and Leonardo.

Questions

Did the proponents of each position need their opponents?

How did people in this period construct their identities in terms of "the Other"?

17

Europe 1500–1650: Expansion, Reformation, and Religious Wars

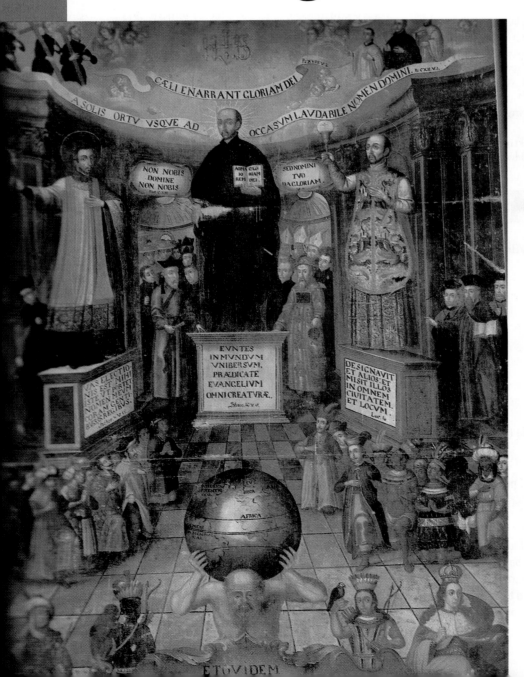

Allegory of the Jesuits and their missions in the four continents from the church of San Pedro, Lima, Peru. Anonymous painter (eighteenth century). St. Ignatius is flanked on his left by Francis Xavier, sporting a chasuble with Asian motifs. In the background, Jesuits living all over the world and occupying a variety of hierarchies within the church, including those wearing Chinese costumes and prelate robes, preside over the conversion of the faithful in India, China, Africa, and the Americas. Like Atlas, the Jesuits carry the globe on their shoulders.

Why do you think the peoples of India, China, Africa, and the Americas are shown smaller than the European missionaries in this painting?

THE DISCOVERY OF A NEW WORLD *page 406*

WHY DID western Europeans start exploring, trading, and settling around the world in the fifteenth century?

THE REFORMATION *page 410*

WHO WERE the early Protestant leaders?

THE REFORMATION AND DAILY LIFE *page 419*

HOW DID family life change during the Reformation era?

THE WARS OF RELIGION *page 421*

WHY DID religious divisions lead to war?

SUPERSTITION AND ENLIGHTENMENT: THE BATTLE WITHIN *page 424*

WHO WERE some of the most significant writers and thinkers between 1500 and 1700?

EUROPEAN EXPANSION

The European turn to the Atlantic was a consequence of its weakness in the East due to Muslim domination there. However, a recovering Europe was now able to compete for access to valuable goods in Eastern markets by navigating the high seas. In the late fifteenth and sixteenth centuries, Europeans sailed far from their own shores to Africa, southern and eastern Asia, and the New World of the Americas. From Japan to Peru, they directly confronted civilizations other than their own and that of Islam, with which they already had contact in the form of trade and, more often, by force of arms. A major motivation for the voyages, which began with a reconnaissance of the West African coast, was to circumvent the Muslim monopoly on the movement of spices from the Indian Ocean into Europe, a grip that had only strengthened with the rise of the Ottomans. A wealthier, more self-confident Europe, now recovered from the great plague-induced population decline of the fourteenth century—its taste for Asian spices long since whetted during the Crusades—was ready to take those spices at their sources.

For much the same reasons (trade and self-aggrandizement) voyages of exploration also set forth from Ming China—especially between 1405 and 1433—reaching India, the Arabian Gulf, and East Africa. Had those voyages been followed up, they might have prevented Europeans from establishing a presence in the Indian Ocean. But the Chinese now faced both serious pressures on their northern and western borders and the problem of administrating a vast, multicultural empire stretching into Central Asia, where non-Chinese rivals had to be kept under control. Moreover, the dominant Neo-Confucian philosophy espoused by the scholar-bureaucrats in the imperial court disdained merchants and commerce, extolling instead a peasant agrarian economy.

These factors led the Chinese to turn inward and abandon overseas trade and exploration precisely at the moment when Europeans were exploring the coast of Africa on their way to the Indian Ocean. It was a fateful choice, because it meant that the Asian power best able to resist the establishment of European commercial and colonial empires in the Indian Ocean had abdicated that role, leaving a vacuum of power for Europeans to fill. Still, Chinese merchants continued to ply ocean trade routes and

F or Europe the late fifteenth and sixteenth centuries were a period of unprecedented territorial expansion. Permanent colonies were established in the Americas, and the exploitation of the New World's human and mineral resources began.

Starting in the second decade of the sixteenth century, a powerful religious movement spread rapidly throughout northern Europe, altering society and politics as well as the spiritual lives of men and women. Attacking what they believed to be burdensome superstitions and corrupt practices, Protestant reformers led a revolt against the medieval church. Hundreds of thousands of people from all social classes set aside the beliefs of centuries and adopted a simplified religious practice.

The Protestant Reformation challenged aspects of the Renaissance, especially its tendency to follow classical sources in glorifying human nature and its loyalty to traditional religion. Protestants were more impressed by the human potential for evil than by the inclination to do good. But Protestants also embraced many Renaissance values, especially humanist educational reforms and the study of ancient languages, which gave them tools to master Scripture and challenge the papacy. Reform within the church (Counter-Reformation) gave birth to new religious orders, rebutted Protestantism, and won back many of its converts.

As different groups identified their political and social goals with either Protestantism or Catholicism, bloody confrontation began in central Europe, then shifted to western Europe. During the Thirty Years' War (1618–1648), international armies of varying religious persuasions clashed in central and northern Europe. ■

THE DISCOVERY OF A NEW WORLD

WHY DID western Europeans start exploring, trading and settling around the world in the fifteenth century?

The discovery of the Americas dramatically expanded the geographical and intellectual horizons of Europeans. Knowledge of the New World's inhabitants and exploitation of its vast wealth set new cultural and economic forces in motion. Beginning with the successful voyages of the Portuguese and Spanish in the fifteenth century, commercial settle as far from home as the Philippines and, in later centuries, the west coasts of North and South America. Wherever there was commerce in Chinese goods, there were Chinese merchants, albeit now operating without support from their government.

Although parallels may be drawn between the court culture of the Forbidden Palace in Beijing and that of King Louis XIV in seventeenth-century France, the Chinese government, with its philosophy of Confucianism, remained more unified and patriarchal than its counterparts in the West. The Chinese, at first, tolerated other religions, warmly embracing Jesuit missionaries, doing so in part because political power in China was not bound to a particular religion. The Japanese were also admirers of the Jesuits, who arrived in Japan with the Portuguese in 1543. The admiration was mutual, leading to three hundred thousand Christian converts by 1600. Tolerance of Christianity did not last as long in Japan as in China. Hideyoshi, in his drive for internal unity, banned Christianity in the late sixteenth century. Nonetheless China and Japan, as well as many Islamic societies, including the Ottomans and the Mughals, demonstrated more tolerance for foreign religions, such as Christianity, than did the West for Islam or Asian religious traditions.

Focus Questions

◆ Why did western Europeans launch voyages of exploration in the fifteenth and sixteenth centuries? What role did the Crusades and the rise of the Ottoman Empire play in this enterprise?

◆ Why did the Chinese voyages of exploration under the Ming come to a halt? What were the consequences for world history?

◆ What was the biological impact of the European discovery of America?

supremacy shifted from the Mediterranean and Baltic Seas to the Atlantic seaboard, and western Europe's global expansion began in earnest (see Map 17–1).

THE PORTUGUESE CHART THE COURSE

Seventy-seven years before Columbus sailed under Spain's flag, Portugal's Prince Henry the Navigator (1394–1460) began exploration of Africa's Atlantic coast. The Portuguese first sought gold and slaves. During the second half of the fifteenth century, the Portuguese delivered 150,000 slaves to Europe. By the end of that century, they were hoping to find a sea route around Africa to spice markets in Asia.

Overland routes to India and China had long existed, but they were difficult, expensive, and monopolized by Venetians and Turks. The first exploratory voyages were slow and tentative, but the experience they provided taught sailors the skills needed to cross the oceans to the Americas and the Orient.

In 1455, the pope gave the Portuguese rights to all the lands, goods, and slaves they might discover from the coast of Guinea to the Indies. The church hoped that conquests would be followed by mass conversions. The explorers also kept an eye out for "Prester John," rumored to be a potential Christian ally against the Muslim infidel. Bartholomew Dias (d. 1500) opened the Portuguese Empire in the East when he rounded the Cape of Good Hope at the tip of Africa in 1487. A decade later, in 1498, Vasco da Gama (d. 1524) stood on the shores of India. When he returned to Portugal, his cargo was worth sixty times the cost of the voyage. Later, the Portuguese established colonies in Goa and Calcutta and successfully challenged the Arabs and the Venetians for control of the European spice trade.

While the Portuguese concentrated on the Indian Ocean, the Spanish set sail across the Atlantic, hoping to establish a shorter route to the East Indies. Rather than beat the Portuguese at their own game, however, Columbus unwittingly discovered the Americas.

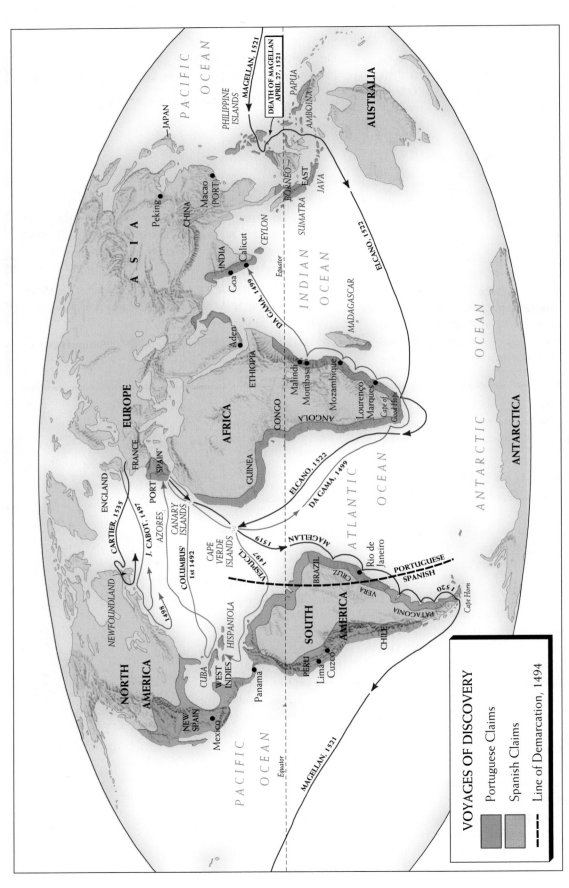

MAP 17–1 European Voyages of Discovery and the Colonial Claims of Spain and Portugal in the Fifteenth and Sixteenth Centuries. The map dramatizes Europe's global expansion in the fifteenth and sixteenth centuries.

Why did western Europeans want to find a sea route to Asia?

MAP 17–2 **Martin Behaim's "Globe Apple."** What Columbus knew of the world in 1492 was contained in this map by Nuremberg geographer Martin Behaim (1440–1507), creator of the first spherical globe of the earth. The ocean section of Behaim's globe is reproduced here. Departing the Canary Islands (in the second section from the right), Columbus expected his first major landfall to be Japan, or what he calls Cipangu (in the second section from the left). When he landed at San Salvador, he thought he was on an outer island of Japan; after reaching Cuba, he believed it to be Japan. Only slowly did it dawn on him that these new lands had never before been seen by Europeans.

From *Admiral of the Ocean Sea* by Samuel Eliot Morison. Copyright 1942 © renewed 1970 by Samuel Eliot Morison. By permission of Little, Brown and Company, Boston, MA.

How did this map influence Columbus's world view?

THE SPANISH VOYAGES OF CHRISTOPHER COLUMBUS

On October 12, 1492, after a thirty-three-day voyage from the Canary Islands, Columbus landed in San Salvador (Watlings Island) in the eastern Bahamas. He thought San Salvador was an outer island of Japan, for his knowledge of geography was based on Marco Polo's account of his years in China during the thirteenth century and a global map by Martin Behaim, a Nuremberg map-maker, which showed only ocean between the west coast of Europe and the east coast of Asia (see Map 17–2).

Naked, friendly natives met Columbus and his crew. They were Taino Indians, who spoke a variant of the Arawak language. Believing he had landed in the East Indies, Columbus called the native people Indians. The natives' generosity amazed Columbus, as they freely gave his men all the corn and yams they desired, along with many sexual favors. "They never say no," Columbus marveled, observing how easily they could be enslaved.

Soon Amerigo Vespucci (1451–1512), after whom America is named, and Ferdinand Magellan (1480–1521) carefully explored the coastline of South America. Their travels proved that the new lands were an entirely unknown continent that opened on the great Pacific Ocean. Magellan, in search of a westward route to the East Indies, sailed on to the Philippines, where he died.

IMPACT ON EUROPE AND AMERICA

Unbeknownst to those who undertook and financed it, Columbus's first voyage marked the beginning of more than three centuries of Spanish conquest, exploitation, and administration of a vast American empire. The wars Christian Aragon and Castile waged against the Islamic Moors had just ended, and the early Spanish explorers retained their zeal for converting non-Christians.

The voyages to the New World had important consequences for both Europe and America. They created Europe's largest and longest-surviving trading bloc and

Christopher Columbus in old age (d. 1506) by Sebastiano del Piombo.

What did Columbus intend to do when he sailed west across the Atlantic?

QUICK REVIEW

Impact of Columbus's First Voyage on Europe and America

◆ Spurred other European nations to colonial expansion

◆ Financed Spain's role in the age's political and religious conflicts

◆ Brought disease, war, and destruction to native peoples

yielded great wealth for Spain. This wealth fueled European-wide economic expansion and spurred other European countries to undertake their own colonial ventures.

European expansion also had major consequences for ecosystems. Numerous species of fruits, vegetables, and animals were introduced to Europe from America and vice versa. European diseases also devastated America's natives. Spain's imprint on the new territories—Roman Catholicism, economic dependence, and a hierarchical society—is still visible today (see Chapter 18).

THE REFORMATION

WHO WERE the early Protestant leaders?

Reformation The sixteenth-century religious movement that sought to reform the Roman Catholic Church and led to the establishment of Protestantism.

The **Reformation** was a religious reform movement that began in Germany in the sixteenth century and led to the establishment of Protestant Christianity.

RELIGION AND SOCIETY

The Reformation originated in the free imperial cities of Germany and Switzerland. There were about sixty-five such cities, each a little kingdom unto itself. Most had Protestant movements of mixed success and duration.

Cities struggled with higher princely or royal authority, and they also suffered deep internal social and political divisions. Generally, groups that felt bullied allied with the Protestant movement, at least initially. Social and political experience thus coalesced with larger religious issues. When Martin Luther and his comrades wrote, preached, and sang about a priesthood of all believers, scorned the authority of ecclesiastical landlords, and ridiculed papal laws as arbitrary human inventions, they touched political as well as religious nerves in German and Swiss cities. This was also true in the villages, for the peasants on the land also heard in Protestantism a promise of political liberation and even a degree of social betterment.

POPULAR MOVEMENTS AND CRITICISM OF THE CHURCH

The Protestant Reformation could not have occurred without the monumental crises of the late medieval church and the Renaissance papacy. Many people, laity and clerics alike, sought a more heartfelt, idealistic, and often—in the eyes of the pope—heretical religious piety. They experimented with new religious forms, seeking simplicity in imitation of Christ.

A variety of factors contributed to increasing lay criticism of the church. The laity in the cities were becoming increasingly knowledgeable about the world and those who held power. They traveled widely, as soldiers, pilgrims, explorers, and traders. New postal systems and the printing press increased the information at their disposal. The new age of books and libraries raised literacy and heightened curiosity. Laypersons increasingly shaped the cultural life of their communities.

QUICK REVIEW

Criticism of the Church

◆ Many people did not see church as a foundation for religious piety

◆ Laity and clerics interested in alternatives and reform

◆ Laypersons increasingly willing to take initiative

SECULAR CONTROL OVER RELIGIOUS LIFE

On the eve of the Reformation, Rome's international network of church offices began to be pulled apart by a growing sense of regional identity (incipient nationalism) and the increasing competence of local secular administrations. The late medieval church had permitted important ecclesiastical posts ("benefices") to be sold to the highest bidders and had not enforced residency requirements in parishes. Rare was the late medieval German town that did not have complaints about the maladministration, concubinage, or fiscal misconduct of its clergy.

City governments also sought to restrict clerical privileges and to improve local religious life by bringing the clergy under the local tax code and by endowing new clerical positions for well-trained and conscientious preachers.

THE NORTHERN RENAISSANCE

The scholarly works of northern humanists created a climate favorable to religious and educational reforms. The northern humanists tended to come from more diverse social backgrounds and to be more devoted to religious reforms than were their Italian counterparts. They were also more willing to write for lay audiences.

The growth of schools and lay education combined with the invention of cheap paper to create a mass audience for printed books. Johann Gutenberg (d. 1468) invented printing with movable type in the German city of Mainz around 1450. By 1500, printing presses operated in at least sixty German cities and in more than two hundred throughout Europe, providing a new medium for politicians, humanists, and reformers alike.

The most famous northern humanist was Desiderius Erasmus (1466–1536). Idealistic and pacifistic, Erasmus aspired to unite the classical ideals of humanity and civic virtue with the Christian ideals of love and piety. He summarized his own beliefs with the phrase *philosophia Christi*, a simple, ethical piety in imitation of Christ, as opposed to what he saw as the dogmatic, ceremonial, and factious religious practice of the late Middle Ages. Erasmus edited the works of the Church Fathers and made a Greek edition of the New Testament (1516), which became the basis for a new, more accurate Latin translation (1519). Martin Luther later used both these works as the basis for his famous German translation.

The best known early English humanist was Sir Thomas More (1478–1535), a close friend of Erasmus. More's *Utopia* (1516), a criticism of contemporary society, depicts an imaginary society based on reason and tolerance that requires everyone to work and has rid itself of all social and political injustice. Although More himself remained staunchly Catholic, humanism paved the way for the English Reformation.

In Spain, humanism served the Catholic Church. Francisco Jiménez de Cisneros (1437–1517) was a confessor to Queen Isabella and, after 1508 Grand Inquisitor, a position from which he was able to enforce the strictest religious orthodoxy. Jiménez was a conduit for humanist scholarship and learning. He founded the University of Alcalá near Madrid in 1509, printed a Greek edition of the New Testament, and translated many religious tracts that aided clerical reform and control of lay religious life. His greatest achievement, taking fifteen years to complete, was the Complutensian Polyglot Bible, a six-volume work that placed the Hebrew, Greek, and Latin versions of the Bible in parallel columns. Such scholarly projects and internal church reforms joined with the repressive measures of Ferdinand and Isabella to keep Spain strictly Catholic.

INDULGENCES

An **indulgence** was a remission of the temporal penalty imposed by priests on penitents as a "work of satisfaction" for their mortal sins. According to medieval theology, when a priest absolved a penitent of guilt for sins, the penitent remained under an eternal penalty imposed by God. After absolution, however, this eternal penalty was

The Gutenberg Bible. Print and Protestantism would drive the history of the sixteenth century. Well established by the mid–fifteenth century, the printing press made possible the diffusion of both secular and religious learning. In addition to humanistic scholarship, print also served the educational and propaganda campaigns of princes and religious reformers, increasing literacy in both Latin and vernacular languages. In the mid-1520s Martin Luther made separate German translations of the New and the Old Testaments, which became essential works in the Protestant Reformation.

Why were Bibles printed in the vernacular particularly important to Protestants?

QUICK REVIEW

Desiderius Erasmus (1466–1536)

◆ Most famous northern humanist

◆ Saw study of Bible and classics as best path to reform

◆ Edited the works of the Church Fathers and made a Greek edition of the New Testament

indulgence Remission of the temporal penalty of punishment in purgatory that remained after sins had been forgiven.

The Electoral Princes of Saxony, by Lucas Cranach the Elder (ca. 1532). The three princes Luther served: Frederick the Wise, John the Constant, and John Frederick the Magnanimous.

Why did some German princes support Luther?

transformed into a temporal penalty, a manageable "work of satisfaction" that the penitent might perform in earthly time (for example, through prayers, fasting, almsgiving, and pilgrimages). Penitents who failed to complete their works of satisfaction would suffer in purgatory. The laity was genuinely anxious at the prospect of suffering in purgatory for neglected penances or unrepented sins.

Indulgences had earlier been given to Crusaders who did not complete their penances because they had fallen in battle. In 1343, Pope Clement VI (r. 1342–1352) had proclaimed the existence of a "treasury of merit," an infinite reservoir of good works in the church's possession that could be dispensed at the pope's discretion. The church sold "letters of indulgence," which covered the works of satisfaction owed by penitents. By Luther's time, they were regularly dispensed for small cash payments and presented as remitting not only the donor's punishments but also those of their dead relatives presumed to be suffering in purgatory.

In 1517, an indulgence was preached on the borders of Saxony in the territories of Archbishop Albrecht of Mainz, who had large debts. The selling of the indulgence was a joint venture by Albrecht, the Augsburg banking house of Fugger, and Pope Leo X (r. 1513–1521), half the proceeds going to the pope and half to Albrecht and his creditors. The famous indulgence preacher John Tetzel (d. 1519) exhorted the crowds:

> Don't you hear the voices of your dead parents and other relatives crying out, "Have mercy on us, for we suffer great punishment and pain. From this you could release us with a few alms. . . ."[1]

MARTIN LUTHER AND GERMAN REFORMATION TO 1525

Late medieval Germany lacked the political unity to enforce "national" religious reforms during the late Middle Ages. As popular resentment of clerical immunities and ecclesiastical abuses—especially over the selling of indulgences—spread among German cities and towns, opposition to Rome formed. German humanists had long voiced such criticism, and by 1517 it provided a solid foundation for Luther's reform.

Martin Luther (1483–1546) was educated by teachers who had been influenced by the Northern Renaissance. His family hoped he would study law, but instead he entered a monastery and was ordained in 1507. In 1510 he traveled to Rome and witnessed the abuses for which the papacy was being criticized. In 1511, he was transferred to the Augustinian monastery in Wittenberg, where he earned his doctorate in theology and became a leader within the monastery, the new university, and the spiritual life of the city.

Luther was plagued by the disproportion between his own sense of sinfulness and the perfect righteousness that God required for salvation according to medieval theology. Traditional church teaching and the sacraments were no consolation. Between 1513 and 1518 Luther gradually concluded that the righteousness God demands does not come from religious works but is present in full measure in those who believe and trust in the redemptive life and death of Christ, who alone exhibits the righteousness satisfying to God. Luther's belief is known as "justification by faith alone."

When Luther, according to tradition, posted his **ninety-five theses** against indulgences on the door of Castle Church in Wittenberg, on October 31, 1517, he

ninety-five theses   Document posted on the door of Castle Church in Wittenberg, Germany, on October 31, 1517, by Martin Luther protesting, among other things, the selling of indulgences.

---

[1]*Die Reformation in Augenzeugen Berichten*, ed. by Helmar Judghans (Dusseldroft: Karl Rauch Verlag, 1967), p. 44.

protested especially against the impression that indulgences actually remitted sins and released the dead from punishment in purgatory. Luther believed these claims made salvation seem to be something that could be bought and sold.

Luther's theses were quickly endorsed by humanists, but the church began official proceedings to discipline him. Emperor Maximilian I's death (January 12, 1519) diverted official attention to the contest for a new emperor. Charles I of Spain, then nineteen years old, succeeded his grandfather and became Emperor Charles V (r. 1519–1556). Charles was assisted by a long tradition of Habsburg imperial rule and massive Fugger loans, which helped secure votes. The electors also won political concessions from Charles that prevented him from taking unilateral action against Germans, something for which Luther eventually had cause to be grateful (see Map 17–3).

In a June 1519 debate with professor John Eck (1486–1543), Luther challenged the infallibility of the pope and the inerrancy of church councils, arguing for the first time for Scripture as the sole and sovereign authority over faith. He burned all his bridges to the old church when he defended John Huss, a condemned heretic. In 1520, Luther issued three pamphlets elaborating on his beliefs. In April 1521, Luther defended his religious teaching before the imperial **Diet of Worms**, over which newly elected Emperor Charles V presided. Ordered to recant, Luther declared that he could not act against Scripture, reason, and his own conscience. On May 26, 1521, he was placed under the imperial ban and became an "outlaw." Friends hid him in a secluded castle, where he spent almost a year translating the New Testament into German and attempting by correspondence to oversee the first stages of the Reformation in Wittenberg.

The Reformation was greatly helped in these early years by the emperor's wars with France (the Habsburg-Valois wars) and the advance of the Ottoman Turks into eastern Europe. Against both adversaries Charles V needed German troops, so he promoted friendly relations with the German princes. In 1526, each German territory was given freedom to enforce the Edict of Worms against Luther "so as to be able to answer in good conscience to God and the emperor." German princes effectively

Diet of Worms   The meeting of the representative (diet) of the Holy Roman Empire presided over by the Emperor Charles V at the German city of Worms in 1521 at which Martin Luther was ordered to recant his ninety-five theses.

MAP 17–3   **The Empire of Charles V.** Dynastic marriages and good fortune concentrated into Charles's hands rule over the lands shown here plus Spain's overseas possessions. Crowns and titles rained down on him; his election as emperor in 1519 gave him new burdens and responsibilities.

What were the geographical advantages and disadvantages of the empire of Charles V?

A Catholic Portrayal of Martin Luther Tempting Jesus (1547). Reformation propaganda often portrayed the pope as the Antichrist or the devil. Here Catholic propaganda turns the tables on the Protestant reformers by portraying a figure of Martin Luther as the devil (note the monstrous feet and tail under his academic robes).

Versuchung Christi, 1547, Gemälde, Bonn, Landschaftsverband Rheinland/Rheinisches Landesmuseum, Bonn. Inv. Nr. 58.3.

How does this painting illustrate the intense divisions within Christiandom at this time?

Execution of a Peasant Leader. The punishment of a peasant leader in a village near Heilbronn. After the defeat of rebellious peasants in and around the city of Heilbronn, Jacob Rorbach, a well-to-do peasant leader from a nearby village, was tied to a stake and slowly roasted to death.

Why did many German peasants oppose Luther?

gained religious sovereignty. In 1555, the Peace of Augsburg enshrined local control over religion in imperial law.

In the late 1520s and the 1530s, Protestant preachers built sizable congregations in many cities that pressured urban governments to adopt religious reforms. Many magistrates had long pushed for reform and welcomed the preachers as allies. Religious reform became a territorial political movement as well, led by the elector of Saxony and the prince of Hesse. Like the urban magistrates, the princes recognized political and economic opportunities for themselves in the demise of the Roman Catholic Church, and they urged the reform on their neighbors. By the 1530s, there was a powerful Protestant alliance prepared for war with the Catholic emperor.

There were early divisions within the Protestant movement. German peasants, for example, had at first believed Luther to be an ally. They solicited his support of their political and economic rights, including their revolutionary request for release from serfdom. But Lutherans were not social revolutionaries. Luther believed that Christian freedom was an inner release from guilt and anxiety, not the right to an egalitarian society. When the peasants revolted in 1524–1525, Luther condemned them as "unchristian" and urged the princes to crush their revolt without mercy. Tens of thousands of peasants died. (See Document, "German Peasants Protest Rising Feudal Exactions," p. 416.)

Luther also had a disturbing perspective on Jews. In 1523 he published the pamphlet, "Jesus Christ Was Born a Jew," in which he urged Christians to be kind to Germany's Jews in the hope that they might convert to reformed Christianity. But he later decided that Jews threatened German Christians, and he urged German princes to forcibly expel those who refused to convert. Fortunately, the Jews found a protector in Emperor Charles V.

ZWINGLI AND THE SWISS REFORMATION

Switzerland was a loose confederacy of thirteen autonomous cantons or states and allied areas. Some became Protestant, some remained Catholic, and a few managed to compromise. The two preconditions of the Swiss Reformation were the growth of national sentiment and a desire for church reform.

Ulrich Zwingli (1484–1531), based in Zurich, was widely known for opposing superstition and the sale of indulgences. Zwingli's reform guideline was simple and effective: Whatever lacked literal support in Scripture was to be neither believed nor practiced. After a public disputation in January 1523, Zurich became effectively a Protestant city and the center of the Swiss Reformation. Its harsh discipline in pursuit of religious ideals made it one of the first examples of a "puritanical" Protestant city.

Landgrave Philip of Hesse (1504–1567) sought to unite Swiss and German Protestants in a mutual defense pact. His efforts were spoiled by theological disagreements between Luther and Zwingli over the nature of Christ's presence in the Eucharist. Zwingli maintained a symbolic interpretation of Christ's words, "This is my body." Christ was only spiritually present in the bread and wine of the Eucharist. Luther insisted that Christ's human nature shared the properties of his divine nature; where Christ was spiritually present, he could also be bodily present. For Luther, the Eucharistic miracle was not **transubstantiation**, as Rome taught, but "consubstantiation": Christ's body and blood being one with, but not of, the bread and wine of the Eucharist. Philip of Hesse brought Luther and Zwingli together in October 1529, but they were unable to work out their differences. The disagreement splintered the Protestant movement theologically and politically.

ANABAPTISTS AND RADICAL PROTESTANTS

Many people wanted a more rapid and thorough implementation of primitive Christianity. The most important of these radical groups were the Anabaptists, the sixteenth-century ancestors of the modern Mennonites and Amish. The Anabaptists rejected infant baptism, insisting that only the baptism of a consenting adult conforms to Scripture. (*Anabaptism* derives from the Greek word meaning "to rebaptize.") Anabaptists withdrew from society to form communities modeled on the example of the first Christians. Political authorities saw their separatism as a threat, and in 1529 rebaptism became a capital offense throughout the Holy Roman Empire.

JOHN CALVIN AND THE GENEVAN REFORMATION

Calvinism was the religious ideology that inspired or accompanied massive political resistance in France, the Netherlands, and Scotland. Believing in both divine predestination and the individual's responsibility to create a godly society, Calvinists were zealous reformers. In a famous and controversial study, *The Protestant Ethic and the Spirit of Capitalism* (1904), the German sociologist Max Weber argued that this peculiar combination of religious confidence and self-disciplined activism produced an ethic congenial to emergent capitalism.

On May 21, 1536, Geneva voted to adopt the Reformation: "to live according to the Gospel and the Word of God... without... any more masses, statues, idols, or other papal abuses." John Calvin (1509–1564), a reform-minded humanist and lawyer, arrived in Geneva soon thereafter. He wrote articles for the governance of the new church, as well as a catechism to guide and discipline the people. Calvin's measures were too strong for Genevans' tastes, however, and in February 1538 the reformers were exiled from the city.

Calvin then spent two years in Strasbourg, a model Protestant city. He married and wrote a second edition of his masterful *Institutes of the Christian Religion*, which many consider the definitive theological statement of the Protestant faith. Calvin was invited to return to Geneva in 1540.

Calvin and his followers thought the "elect" should live a manifestly God-pleasing life. The consistory, a judicial body composed of clergy and laity, enforced strict moral discipline and was unpopular with many Genevans. But after 1555 the city's magistrates were all devout Calvinists, and more than one third of Geneva's population was Protestants who had been driven out of France, England, and Scotland, so Calvin had strong support.

POLITICAL CONSOLIDATION OF THE LUTHERAN REFORMATION

By 1530 the Reformation was irreversible, but it would take several decades and major attempts to eradicate it before this was accepted. German Lutherans formed regional consistories, which oversaw and

Christ Blessing the Children, by Lucas Cranach the Elder (1538). This novel painting was a Lutheran protest against the Anabaptists, who refused to recognize the efficacy of infant baptism. Appealing to the example of Jesus, who had been baptized as an adult, Anabaptists (the name means "rebaptism") disavowed their infant baptism and sought another when they were old enough to grasp what it meant. Here, Jesus joins a throng of new mothers to caress, kiss, and commend their babies to God. After 1529, Anabaptism became a capital offense in the Holy Roman Empire.

Why were there early divisions within the Protestant movement?

transubstantiation   The doctrine that the entire substances of the bread and wine are changed in the Eucharist into the body and blood of Christ.

A Portrait of the Young John Calvin.

Bibliothèque Publique et Universitaire, Geneva.

Why was Calvin exiled from Geneva, and why did he return?

DOCUMENT

German Peasants Protest Rising Feudal Exactions

In the late fifteenth and early sixteenth centuries, German feudal lords, both secular and ecclesiastical, tried to increase the earnings from their lands by raising demands on their peasant tenants. As the lords restricted the traditional freedoms and property rights of peasants, massive revolts occurred in southern Germany in 1525. The following representative statement of peasant grievances, summarized in twelve articles, came from the town of Memmingen.

- **Are** the peasants more interested in material freedom than in spiritual freedom? Which of their demands are the most revolutionary and which are the least problematic for their lords to grant? Why do some centuries exhibit greater social and political equality than others?

1. It is our humble petition and desire that in the future each community should choose and appoint a pastor, and that we should have the right to depose him should he conduct himself improperly... .

2. We are ready and willing to pay the fair tithe of grain... The small tithes [of cattle], whether [to] ecclesiastical or lay lords, we will not pay at all, for the Lord God created cattle for the free use of man... .

3. We... take it for granted that you will release us from serfdom as true Christians, unless it should be shown us from the Gospel that we are serfs.

4. It has been the custom heretofore that no poor man should be allowed to catch venison or wildfowl or fish in flowing water, which seems to us quite unseemly and unbrotherly as well as selfish and not agreeable to the Word of God... .

5. We are aggrieved in the matter of woodcutting, for the noblemen have appropriated all the woods to themselves... .

CHRONOLOGY

PROGRESS OF PROTESTANT REFORMATION ON THE CONTINENT

1517	Luther posts ninety-five theses against indulgences
1519	Charles I of Spain elected Holy Roman emperor (as Charles V)
1519	Luther challenges infallibility of pope and inerrancy of church councils at Leipzig Debate
1521	Papal bull excommunicates Luther for heresy
1521	Diet of Worms condemns Luther
1521–1522	Luther translates the New Testament into German
1524–1525	Peasants' Revolt in Germany
1529	Marburg Colloquy between Luther and Zwingli
1530	Diet of Augsburg fails to settle religious differences
1531	Formation of Protestant Schmalkaldic League
1536	Calvin arrives in Geneva
1540	Jesuits, founded by Ignatius of Loyola, recognized as order by pope
1545–1563	Council of Trent institutes reforms and responds to the Reformation
1546	Luther dies
1547	Armies of Charles V crush Schmalkaldic League
1555	Peace of Augsburg recognizes rights of Lutherans to worship as they please

administered the new Protestant churches. Educational reforms included compulsory primary education, schools for girls, a humanist revision of the traditional curriculum, and catechetical instruction of the laity in the new religion. The political success of Lutheranism in the empire, by the 1550s, gave Protestant movements elsewhere a new lease on life.

In Denmark, Lutheranism became the state religion under Christian III (r. 1536–1559). In Sweden, Gustavus Vasa (r. 1523–1560), supported by a nobility greedy for church lands, confiscated church property and subjected the clergy to royal authority. The absence of a central political authority made Poland a model of religious pluralism and toleration in the second half of the sixteenth century.

Charles V attempted to enforce a compromise agreement between Protestants and Catholics in 1540 to 1541. Then he turned to a military solution: In 1547 imperial armies crushed the Protestant Schmalkaldic League. The

6. In regard to the excessive services demanded of us which are increased from day to day, we ask that this matter be properly looked into so that we shall not continue to be oppressed in this way... .

7. We will not hereafter allow ourselves to be further oppressed by our lords, but will let them demand only what is just and proper according to the word of the agreement between the lord and the peasant. The lord should no longer try to force more services or other dues from the peasant without payment... .

8. We are greatly burdened because our holdings cannot support the rent exacted from them... We ask that the lords may appoint persons of honor to inspect these holdings and fix a rent in accordance with justice... .

9. We are burdened with a great evil in the constant making of new laws... In our opinion we should be judged according to the old written law... .

10. We are aggrieved by the appropriation... of meadows and fields which at one time belonged to a community as a whole. These we will take again into our own hands... .

11. We will entirely abolish the due called Todfall [that is, *heriot* or *death tax*, by which the lord received the best horse, cow, or garment of a family upon the death of a serf] and will no longer endure it, nor allow widows and orphans to be thus shamefully robbed against God's will, and in violation of justice and right... .

12. It is our conclusion and final resolution, that if any one or more of the articles here set forth should not be in agreement with the Word of God, as we think they are, such article we will willingly retract.

Source: *Translations and Reprints from the Original Sources of European History*, Vol. 2 (Philadelphia: Department of History, University of Pennsylvania, 1897).

emperor issued the Augsburg Interim, an order that Protestants everywhere must readopt Catholic beliefs and practices. But Protestants resisted fiercely, and the emperor relented. The Peace of Augsburg in September 1555 made the division of Christendom permanent by recognizing what had already been established in practice: *cuius regio, eius religio*, meaning that the ruler of a land would determine the religion of the land. Lutherans were permitted to retain all church lands forcibly seized before 1552. Those discontented with the religion of their region were permitted to migrate to another. Calvinism, however, was not recognized by the Peace of Augsburg. Calvinists organized to lead national revolutions throughout northern Europe.

THE ENGLISH REFORMATION TO 1553

Late medieval England had a well-earned reputation for defending the rights of the crown against the pope. The marriage of King Henry VIII (r. 1509–1547) finally precipitated England's break with the papacy.

Henry married Catherine of Aragon (d. 1536), a daughter of Ferdinand and Isabella of Spain and the aunt of Emperor Charles V, in 1509. By 1527 the union had produced only a single surviving child, Mary Tudor (d. 1558). He came to believe that his marriage had been cursed by God because Catherine had briefly been the wife of his late brother, Arthur.

Henry wanted to marry Anne Boleyn (ca. 1504–1536), one of Catherine's young ladies in waiting. This required papal annulment of the marriage to Catherine, which Henry could not get. Henry's ministers proposed a simple solution: Why not have the king declare his supremacy over English spiritual affairs, as he did over English temporal affairs? Then the king could decide the status of his own marriage.

In 1529 Parliament convened for what would be a seven-year session. In 1533 the "Reformation Parliament" put the clergy under royal jurisdiction, and Henry wed the pregnant Anne Boleyn. Parliament's later Act of Supremacy declared Henry "the only supreme head on earth of the church of England."

Despite his political break with Rome, Henry continued to endorse Catholic doctrine in a country seething with Protestant sentiment. When Edward VI (r. 1547–1553), Henry's son by his third wife, Jane Seymour, became king at age ten, his regents enacted much of the Protestant Reformation. In 1553, when Mary Tudor succeeded to the throne, she restored Catholic doctrine and practice with a single-mindedness that rivaled that of her father. It was not until the reign of Anne Boleyn's daughter Elizabeth I (r. 1558–1603) that a lasting religious settlement was worked out in England.

CATHOLIC REFORM AND COUNTER-REFORMATION

Counter-Reformation The sixteenth-century reform movement in the Roman Catholic Church in reaction to the Protestant Reformation.

The medieval church had already faced internal criticisms and efforts at reform before the **Counter-Reformation** was launched in reaction to Protestant successes.

Sixteenth-century popes had resisted efforts to change the laws and institutions of the church. Many new religious orders, however, led a broad revival of piety within the church. The Society of Jesus, the new order of Jesuits, was instrumental in the success of the Counter-Reformation. Organized by Ignatius of Loyola in the 1530s, within a century the society had more than fifteen thousand members scattered throughout the world, including thriving missions in India, Japan, and the Americas.

Ignatius of Loyola (1491–1556) began his spiritual pilgrimage in 1521 while recuperating from battle wounds. Reading Christian classics, he was so impressed with the heroic self-sacrifice of the church's saints that he underwent a profound religious conversion. Ignatius devised a program of religious and moral self-discipline called the *Spiritual Exercises*, which outlined a path to absolute spiritual self-mastery. Ignatius believed that a person could shape his or her own behavior, even create a new religious self, through disciplined study and regular practice. Ignatius's exercises were intended to teach Catholics to submit to higher church authority and spiritual direction. The potent combination of discipline, self-control, and passion for traditional spirituality and mystical experience helped counter the Reformation and won many Protestants back to Catholicism, especially in Austria and Germany.

Pope Paul III (r. 1534–1549) called a general council to reassert church doctrine. Three sessions, spread over eighteen years, met in the imperial city of Trent in northern Italy under firm papal control. The Council of Trent's most important reforms concerned internal church discipline. The selling of church offices was forbidden. The authority of local bishops was strengthened. Parish priests were required to be neatly dressed, better educated, strictly celibate, and active among their parishioners. The council did not make a single doctrinal concession to the Protestants, instead reaffirming traditional beliefs and practices. Parish life revived under the guidance of a devout and better-trained clergy.

The Miracle of St. Ignatius of Loyola, by Peter Paul Rubens. Here the founder of the Society of Jesus, surrounded by angels and members of the new Jesuit Order, preaches to an aroused assembly.

What elements of this painting capture the spirit of the Counter-Reformation?

THE REFORMATION AND DAILY LIFE

Although politically conservative, the Reformation brought about far-reaching changes in traditional religious practices and institutions.

HOW DID family life change during the Reformation era?

RELIGION IN FIFTEENTH-CENTURY LIFE

In the fifteenth century, the church calendar regulated daily life. About one third of the year was given over to some kind of religious observance or celebration. Clerics made up 6 to 8 percent of the total population of the great cities of central Europe, exercising considerable political as well as spiritual power.

Monasteries and nunneries were influential institutions. Local aristocrats were closely identified with particular churches and chapels. The Mass and liturgy were read entirely in Latin. Images of saints were regularly displayed, and on certain holidays their relics were paraded about and venerated. Pilgrims gathered by the hundreds and thousands at religious shrines, searching for cures or seeking diversion. Several times during the year, special preachers appeared with letters of indulgence to sell. Many clergy lived openly with concubines and had children in relationships tolerated by the church if penitential fines were paid.

People complained about the clergy's exemption from taxation and, in many instances, also from the civil criminal code. People grumbled about having to support church offices whose occupants actually worked elsewhere, and many felt that the church had too much influence over education and culture.

RELIGION IN SIXTEENTH-CENTURY LIFE

In these same cities after the Reformation had firmly established itself, the same aristocratic families governed; the rich generally got richer and the poor poorer. But overall numbers of clergy fell by two thirds and religious holidays shrank by one third. Monasteries and nunneries were nearly absent, many having been transformed into hospices for the sick and poor or into educational

G.1431; Rö.MGVK fl   *Taming of the Lion* [334 x 477] 1524 *Berlin*

Taming the Lion

A   No man is ever so high or good
That he cannot be managed by a woman
Who does his will
In friendly love and service.

B   Although he is tyrannical wild,
He is soon calmed by a woman.
She boldly strokes his open mouth,
His anger fades, he does not bite.

C   The lion, most lordly of beasts,
Famous for his strength and nobility,
Favors us women with heartfelt gifts
And good humor accompanies his
  kindness.

D   How wonderfully you reflect
Your taming at woman's hand,
Bearing patiently what another
Does to you against your will.

E   O powerful king and greatest lord
Your equal is neither near nor far.
Excelling all, both large and small,
Upon your head should lie a crown.

F   Lord lion, although you are feared
  by all,
A woman knows how to saddle you,
Bending you to her will by love.
True love finds a home with a
  good man.

G   How well you have been groomed!
Now how lively and cheerful!
One so spirited
May have the company of women.

H   Lord lion, you may have your every wish.
Cover your trail with your tail
And you will not be tracked down.
Those who love in secret know this well.

Lion I let the women amuse themselves
  by serving me.
What harm can they possibly do me?
If I want, I can suddenly turn fierce
  again.
He is a fool who lets himself be taught
  by women.

Taming the Lion. The words of the attendants (wives) serving the lion (husband) raise the question: Who really controls the relationship between the sexes?

How did family relationships in Europe change during this period?

institutions. In the churches, which had also been reduced in number by at least a third, worship was conducted almost completely in the vernacular. Local shrines were closed down, and anyone found openly venerating saints, relics, and images was subject to fine and punishment. Copies of Luther's translation of the New Testament, or excerpts from it, were in private homes. The clergy could marry, and most did. They paid taxes and were punished for their crimes in civil courts. Domestic moral life was regulated by committees composed of roughly equal numbers of laity and clergy, over whose decisions secular magistrates had the last word.

Not all Protestant clergy were enthusiastic about this new lay authority in religion, and the laity themselves were ambivalent about some aspects of the Reformation. Over half of the original converts returned to the Catholic fold before the end of the sixteenth century. Half of Europe's population was Protestant in the mid-sixteenth century, but by the mid-seventeenth century only a fifth remained Protestant.[2]

FAMILY LIFE IN EARLY MODERN EUROPE

Changes in the timing and duration of marriage, family size, and infant and child care suggest that social and economic pressures were influencing family life. The Reformation was only one factor in these changes.

Between 1500 and 1800, men and women in western Europe and England married at later ages than they had previously: men in their mid- to late twenties and women in their early to mid-twenties. After the Reformation, both Protestants and Catholics required parental consent and public vows in church before a marriage could be deemed fully licit. Late marriage in the West reflected the difficulty couples had supporting themselves independently. In the sixteenth century, one in five women never married, and an estimated 15 percent were widows. Women who bore children for the first time at advanced ages had higher mortality rates. Delayed marriage increased premarital sex and the number of illegitimate children.

Marriage tended to be "arranged" in the sense that the parents met and discussed the terms of the marriage. But the wealth and social standing of the bride and the bridegroom were not the only things considered. By the fifteenth century, it was usual for the future bride and bridegroom to have known each other, and their feelings were respected by parents.

The western European family was conjugal, or nuclear, consisting of two parents and two to four children who survived into adulthood. Infant mortality and child death were common. The family lived within a larger household, including in-laws, servants, laborers, and boarders.

Artificial birth control has existed since antiquity, but early birth control measures were not very effective, and for both historical and moral reasons the church opposed them. The church and physicians both encouraged women to suckle their own newborns rather than hand them off to wet nurses (lactating women who sold their services). Because nursing has a contraceptive effect, some women nursed to space out their pregnancies, while those who wanted many children used wet nurses.

Between the ages of eight and thirteen, children were usually sent away from home to school or to begin apprenticeships and take up employment. The widowed often remarried within a few months of their bereavement. Marriages between spouses of vastly different ages were common. In context, these practices made sense. Parents showed love and affection for their children by ensuring that they acquired the skills needed to be self-supporting. The labor involved in maintaining a household pushed people to remarry rapidly, but extreme disparity in ages invited criticism.

Portrait of His Wife and Two Elder Children, by Hans Holbein the Younger (1528). German-English painter Hans Holbein's painting of his wife and two of his children.

What was it like to be a child in early modern Europe?

---

[2]Geoffrey Parker, *Europe in Crisis, 1598–1648* (Ithaca, NY: Cornell University Press, 1979), p. 50.

THE WARS OF RELIGION

After the Council of Trent adjourned in 1563, Catholics began a Jesuit-led counter-offensive against Protestants. At the time of John Calvin's death in 1564, Geneva had become both a refuge for Europe's persecuted Protestants and an international school for Protestant resistance, producing leaders fully equal to the new Catholic challenge. Genevan Calvinism and the reformed Catholicism of the Council of Trent were two equally dogmatic, aggressive, and irreconcilable church systems.

Calvinism adopted a presbyterian form of church government, in which elders representing individual congregations determined church policy. By contrast, the Counter-Reformation affirmed Catholicism's dedication to a centralized episcopal system, governed by a clerical hierarchy and owing absolute obedience to the pope. Calvinism attracted proponents of political decentralization who opposed totalitarian rulers, whereas Catholicism was congenial to proponents of absolute monarchy who believed that order required "one king, one church, one law."

Wars of religion were both national conflicts and international wars. Catholics and Protestants struggled for control of France, the Netherlands, and England. The Catholic governments of France and Spain fought the Protestant regimes in England and the Netherlands. The Thirty Years' War, which began in 1618, illustrated the international nature of religious conflict. Before it ended, it drew in every major European nation.

Huguenots French Calvinists.

FRENCH WARS OF RELIGION (1562–1598)

When Henry II (r. 1547–1559) died accidentally in 1559, his sickly fifteen-year-old son, Francis II (d. 1560), came to the throne under the regency of the queen mother, Catherine de Médicis (1519–1589). With the monarchy weakened, three powerful families competed for control. The Guises were by far the strongest, and they were militant Catholics. The Bourbon and Montmorency-Châtillon families, in contrast, developed strong Huguenot sympathies, largely for political reasons. (French Protestants were called **Huguenots**.)

Ambitious aristocrats and discontented townspeople joined Calvinist churches in opposition to the Guise-dominated French monarchy. Many apparently hoped to establish within France a principle of territorial sovereignty akin to that secured within the Holy Roman Empire by the Peace of Augsburg.

Catherine de Médicis continued as regent for her second son, Charles IX (r. 1560–1574) after Francis II died. Wanting a Catholic France but not a Guise-dominated monarchy, Catherine sought allies among the Protestants. Early in 1562 she granted Protestants limited freedoms—though even limited royal toleration ended when the Duke of Guise surprised a Protestant congregation worshiping illegally at Vassy in Champagne and proceeded to massacre several score of them, marking the beginning of the French wars of religion.

In 1572, apparently to cover up her role in an attempt to assassinate a Huguenot leader, Catherine convinced Charles that a Huguenot coup was afoot. On the eve of Saint Bartholomew's Day, August 24, 1572, three thousand Huguenots were butchered in Paris. Within three days an estimated twenty thousand Huguenots were executed throughout France. This event changed the nature of Protestant-Catholic conflict both within and beyond the borders of France. In Protestant eyes, it became an international struggle for survival against an adversary whose cruelty justified any means of resistance.

Henry III (r. 1574–1589) sought to steer a middle course, and in this effort he received support from a growing body of neutral Catholics and Huguenots who put

The St. Bartholemew's Day Massacre. In this notorious event, here depicted by the contemporary Protestant painter François Dubois, three thousand Protestants were slaughtered in Paris and an estimated twenty thousand others died throughout France. The massacre transformed the religious struggle in France from a contest for political power into an all-out war between Protestants and Catholics.

Le Massacre de la St-Barthélémy, entre 1572 et 1584. Oil on wood, 94 × 154 cm. Musée Cantonal des Beaux-Arts, Lausanne. Photo: J.-C. Ducret Musée Cantonal des Beaux-Arts, Lausanne.

Do you think these events would be portrayed differently by a Catholic artist?

the political survival of France above its religious unity. Such *politiques*, as they were called, were prepared to compromise religious creeds to save the nation. Henry III allied with his Protestant cousin and heir, Henry of Navarre, against the Catholic League, supported by the Spanish, which dominated Paris in the mid-1580s. When a fanatical Dominican friar murdered Henry III, the Bourbon Henry of Navarre became Henry IV of France (r. 1589–1610).

Henry IV believed that a royal policy of tolerant Catholicism would be the best way to achieve peace. On July 25, 1593, he publicly abjured the Protestant faith and embraced the traditional and majority religion of his country. "Paris is worth a Mass," he is reported to have said. Henry IV's famous Edict of Nantes (1598) recognized and sanctioned minority religious rights within what was to remain an officially Catholic country. This religious truce granted the Huguenots, who by this time numbered well over a million, freedom of public worship, the right of assembly, admission to public offices and universities, and permission to maintain fortified towns.

Henry IV was assassinated in 1610. Although he is best remembered for the Edict of Nantes, the political and economic policies he put in place laid the foundations for the transformation of France into the absolutist state it would become in the seventeenth century.

IMPERIAL SPAIN AND THE REIGN OF PHILIP II (1556–1598)

Until the English defeated his mighty Armada in 1588, Philip II of Spain was the greatest ruler in the second half of the sixteenth century. He focused first on Turkish expansion. On October 7, 1571, a Holy League of Spain, Venice, and the pope defeated the Turks at Lepanto. Before the engagement ended, thirty thousand Turks had died and over one third of the Turkish fleet was sunk or captured. But Philip failed when he attempted to impose his will within the Netherlands and on England and France.

The Milch Cow. This sixteenth-century satirical painting depicts the Netherlands as a land all the great powers of Europe wish to exploit. Elizabeth of England is feeding her (England had long-standing commerical ties with Flanders); Philip II of Spain is attempting to ride her (Spain was trying to reassert its control over the entire region); William of Orange is trying to milk her (he was the leader of the anti-Spanish rebellion); and the king of France holds her by the tail (France hoped to profit from the rebellion at Spain's expense).

The "Milch Cow." Rijksmuseum, Amsterdam.

Which character shown here could be considered most successful in the way history actually played out?

The Netherlands was the richest area in Europe. The merchant towns of the Netherlands were Europe's most independent, and many were Calvinist strongholds. A stubborn opposition to the Spanish overlords formed when Philip II insisted on enforcing the decrees of the Council of Trent in the Netherlands. William of Nassau, the Prince of Orange (r. 1533–1584), emerged as the leader of a broad movement for the Netherlands' independence from Spain. Like other successful rulers in this period, William of Orange was a *politique* who placed the Netherlands' political autonomy and well-being above religious creeds.

The ten largely Catholic southern provinces (roughly modern Belgium) came together in 1576 with the seven largely Protestant northern provinces (roughly the modern Netherlands) in unified opposition to Spain. This union, known as the Pacification of Ghent, declared internal regional sovereignty in matters of religion. In January 1579 the southern provinces made peace with Spain. The northern provinces continued the struggle. Spain was preoccupied with France and England, and the northern provinces drove out all Spanish soldiers by 1593.

ENGLAND AND SPAIN (1558–1603)

Elizabeth I (r. 1558–1603), the daughter of Henry VIII and Anne Boleyn, may have been the most astute politician of the sixteenth century. She repealed the anti-Protestant legislation of her predecessor Mary Tudor and guided a religious settlement through Parliament that prevented England from being torn asunder by religious differences in the sixteenth century.

Catholic extremists hoped to replace Elizabeth with the Catholic Mary Stuart, Queen of Scots (1542–1587), but Elizabeth acted swiftly against assassination plots and rarely let emotion override her political instincts.

Elizabeth dealt cautiously with the Puritans, Protestants who sought to "purify" the national church. The Puritans had two special grievances: (1) the retention of Catholic ceremony and vestments within the Church of England, and (2) the continuation of the episcopal system of church governance. Sixteenth-century Puritans were not separatists, however. They worked through Parliament to create an alternative national church of semiautonomous congregations governed by representative presbyteries (hence, Presbyterians). More extreme Puritans wanted every congregation to be autonomous. Elizabeth refused to tolerate these Congregationalists, whose views she considered subversive.

Despite the sincere desires of both Philip II and Elizabeth, a series of events—culminating in Elizabeth's execution of Mary, Queen of Scots, on February 18, 1587—led inexorably to war between England and Spain. On May 30, 1588, a mighty fleet of 130 Spanish ships bearing 25,000 sailors and soldiers set sail for England. But the day belonged completely to the English. English and Dutch ships, assisted by an "English wind," dispersed the waiting Spanish fleet, over a third of which never returned to Spain.

The Armada's defeat gave heart to Protestant resistance everywhere. Spain never fully recovered from it. By the time of Philip's death on September 13, 1598, his forces had been rebuffed by the French and the Dutch. His seventeenth-century successors were all inferior leaders. The French soon dominated the Continent, while the Dutch and the English whittled away Spain's overseas empire. Elizabeth died on March 23, 1603, leaving behind her a strong nation poised to expand into a global empire.

Elizabeth I (1558–1603) Standing on a Map of England in 1592. An astute politician in foreign and domestic policy, Elizabeth was one of the most successful rulers of the sixteenth century.

What qualities of kingship are conveyed in this portrait of Elizabeth 1?

THE THIRTY YEARS' WAR (1618–1648)

The Thirty Years' War in the Holy Roman Empire was the last and most destructive of the wars of religion. Religious and political hatreds had become entrenched, and various groups were determined to sacrifice all for their territorial sovereignty and religious beliefs. As the conflicts multiplied, virtually every major European land became involved either directly or indirectly. When the hostilities ended in 1648, the peace terms shaped much of the map of northern Europe as we know it today.

During the second half of the sixteenth century, Germany was an almost ungovernable land of 360 autonomous political entities. The Peace of Augsburg (1555) had given each a significant degree of sovereignty within its own borders. Political decentralization and fragmentation characterized Germany as the seventeenth century opened; it was not a unified nation like Spain, England, or even strife-torn France. (See Map 17–4.)

The Holy Roman Empire was about equally divided between Catholics and Protestants, the latter having perhaps a slight numerical edge by 1600. After the Peace of Augsburg, Lutherans had gained political control in many Catholic areas, as had the Catholics in a few previously Lutheran areas. There was also religious strife between liberal and conservative Lutherans and between Lutherans and the growing numbers of Calvinists. Calvinism had not been recognized as a legal religion by the Peace of Augsburg, but it established a strong foothold within the empire when the devoutly Calvinist Elector Frederick III (r. 1559–1576) made it the official religion within the Palatinate in 1559. By 1609 Palatine Calvinists headed a Protestant defensive alliance supported by Spain's sixteenth-century enemies: England, France, and the Netherlands.

Jesuits were also active within the Holy Roman Empire. From staunchly Catholic Bavaria, supported by Spain, Jesuits launched successful missions throughout the empire. In 1609 Maximilian, Duke of Bavaria (1573–1651), organized a Catholic League to counter the Palatine-based Protestant alliance. When the Catholic League fielded a great army, it launched the Thirty Years' War, the worst European catastrophe since the Black Death of the fourteenth century.

MAP 17–4   **Religious Division ca. 1600.**   By 1600 few could expect Christians to return to a uniform religious allegiance. In Spain and southern Italy Catholicism remained relatively unchallenged, but note the existence elsewhere of large religious minorities, both Catholic and Protestant.

Why did the wars of religion fail to reestablish religious uniformity in the Holy Roman Empire?

MAP EXPLORATION

To explore this map further, go to http://www.prenhall.com/craig_maps

Lutheran
Calvinist
Anglican
Roman Catholic
Minorities
L   Lutheran
C   Calvinist
A   Anabaptist
R   Roman Catholic

In 1648 all hostilities within the Holy Roman Empire were brought to an end by the Treaty of Westphalia. It firmly reasserted the major feature of the Peace of Augsburg (1555): Rulers were again permitted to determine the religion of their lands. The treaty also gave the Calvinists their long-sought legal recognition, while denying it to sectarians. The independence of the Swiss Confederacy and the United Provinces of Holland, long recognized in fact, now became law.

The Treaty of Westphalia perpetuated German division and political weakness into the modern period, although Austria and Brandenburg-Prussia attained international significance during the seventeenth century. In Europe at large, distinctive nation-states, each with its own political, cultural, and religious identity, reached maturity in the seventeenth century and firmly established the competitive nationalism of the modern world.

SUPERSTITION AND ENLIGHTENMENT: THE BATTLE WITHIN

WHO WERE some of the most significant writers and thinkers between 1500 and 1700?

Religious reform and warfare moved intellectuals to rethink human nature and society. One side of that reconsideration was dark and cynical, perhaps because the peak years of religious warfare had also been those of the great European witch hunts. Another side was brilliantly skeptical and constructive, reflecting the growing scientific movement of the years between 1500 and 1700.

WITCH HUNTS AND PANIC

The witch hunts and panics that erupted in almost every Western land reveal the dark side of early modern thought and culture. Between 1400 and 1700, courts sentenced an estimated 70,000 to 100,000 people to death for harmful magic (*maleficium*) and diabolical witchcraft. In addition to harming their neighbors, witches were said to fly to mass meetings known as *sabbats*. They were accused of indulging in sexual orgies with the devil. They were said to practice cannibalism (especially the devouring of small Christian children) and a variety of ritual acts and practices that denied or perverted Christian beliefs.

Many factors contributed to the great witch panics of the second half of the sixteenth and the early seventeenth centuries. Religious division and warfare were major influences. The church had traditionally provided defenses against the devil and demons; the Reformation forced people to find alternative ways to handle their anxieties. The growing strength of governments intent on weeding out nonconformists also played a part.

In village societies, feared and respected "cunning folk" had long helped people cope with natural disasters and disabilities by magical means. For local people, these were important services, and possession of magical powers made one an important person in the village. Vulnerable people, such as old, single women, often claimed power. Witch beliefs may also have been a way for villagers to defy urban Christian society's attempts to impose its beliefs, laws, and institutions on the countryside.

The Christian clergy also practiced magic, transforming bread and wine into the body and blood of Christ, and eternal punishments for sins into temporal ones. Clergy exorcised demons, too. In the late thirteenth century the church declared its magic the only legitimate magic. Since such power was not human, the theologians reasoned, anyone who practiced magic outside the church did so on behalf of the devil. Attacking accused witches became a way for the church to extend its spiritual hegemony. To accuse, try, and execute witches was a declaration of moral and political authority.

Roughly 80 percent of the victims of witch hunts were women, most single and between forty-five and sixty years of age. Older single women were particularly vulnerable for many reasons. More women than men laid claim to supernatural powers, so they were at disproportionate risk. Many of these women were midwives, so they were associated with deaths during childbirth. Both the church and their neighbors were prepared to think and say the worst about them.

Many factors helped end the witch hunts. A more scientific worldview made it difficult to believe in the powers of witches. Witch hunts also tended to get out of hand. Tortured witches sometimes alleged having seen leading townspeople at sabbats, at which point the trials threatened anarchy.

WRITERS AND PHILOSOPHERS

By the end of the sixteenth century, many could no longer embrace either the old Catholic or new Protestant absolutes. Intellectually as well as politically, the seventeenth century would be a period of transition. Some writers and philosophers of the late sixteenth and seventeenth centuries embraced the emerging new science wholeheartedly (Hobbes and Locke), some tried to straddle the two ages (Cervantes and Shakespeare), and still others ignored or opposed the new developments that seemed mortally to threaten traditional values (Pascal).

In Spain, the intertwining of Catholic piety and Spanish political power fostered a literature preoccupied with medieval chivalric virtues, especially honor and loyalty. Generally acknowledged to be the greatest Spanish writer of all time, Miguel de Cervantes Saavedra (1547–1616) educated himself by insatiable reading in vernacular literature and immersion in the school of life. In 1570 he became a soldier and was decorated for gallantry at Lepanto (1571). He began his most famous work, *Don Quixote*, in prison in 1603, after conviction for theft.

Many believe the intent of *Don Quixote* was to satirize the chivalric romances so popular in Spain, but Cervantes shows deep affection for his characters. Don Quixote, a none-too-stable middle-aged man, is driven mad by reading too many chivalric

QUICK REVIEW

Witch Hunts

- "Cunning folk" traditionally helped villagers
- Christian clergy monopolized "magic"
- Older, single women most vulnerable to accusations of witchcraft
- Witch trials could be destabilizing

romances. He comes to believe that he is an aspirant to knighthood and must prove his worthiness. He acquires a rusty suit of armor, mounts an aged horse, and chooses for his inspiration a peasant girl whom he fancies to be a noble lady. Sancho Panza, a wise peasant who serves as Don Quixote's squire, watches with skepticism and sympathy as his lord repeatedly makes a fool of himself. The story ends tragically with Don Quixote's humiliating defeat by a well-meaning friend who forces him to renounce his quest for knighthood. Throughout *Don Quixote*, Cervantes juxtaposed the down-to-earth realism of Sancho Panza with the old-fashioned religious idealism of Don Quixote. Cervantes admired the one as much as the other and demonstrated that to be truly happy, men and women need dreams—even impossible ones—just as much as a sense of reality.

Surprisingly little is known about William Shakespeare (1564–1616), the greatest playwright in the English language. He apparently worked as a schoolteacher, acquiring broad knowledge of Renaissance learning and literature. He took the new commercialism and the bawdy pleasures of the Elizabethan Age in stride and with amusement. References to contemporary political events fill his plays. By modern standards he was a political conservative, accepting the social rankings and the power structure of his day and demonstrating unquestioned patriotism.

Shakespeare was a playwright, actor, and part owner of a theater. His work brought together the best past and current achievements in the dramatic arts. He particularly mastered the psychology of human motivation and passion. Shakespeare wrote histories, comedies, and tragedies. Four of his best tragedies were written within a three-year period: *Hamlet* (1603), *Othello* (1604), *King Lear* (1605), and *Macbeth* (1606). In his lifetime and ever since, Shakespeare has been immensely popular with both audiences and readers. As Ben Jonson (1572–1637), a contemporary classical dramatist who created his own school of poets, put it in 1623: "He was not of an age, but for all time."

Blaise Pascal (1623–1662) was a French mathematician and a physical scientist widely acclaimed by his contemporaries. He was torn between the continuing dogmatism and the new skepticism of the seventeenth century. Pascal believed that reason and science, although attesting to human dignity, remained of no avail in religion. Here only the reasons of the heart and a "leap of faith" could prevail. Pascal saw two essential truths in the Christian religion: A loving God, worthy of human attainment, exists, and human beings, because they are corrupted in nature, are utterly unworthy of God.

Pascal made a famous wager with the skeptics. It is a better bet, he argued, to believe that God exists and to stake everything on his promised mercy than not to do so; if God does exist, everything will be gained by the believer, whereas the loss incurred by having believed in a nonexistent God is minimal. Pascal urged his contemporaries to seek self-understanding by "learned ignorance" and to discover humankind's greatness by recognizing its misery, thereby countering what he saw as the false optimism of the new rationalism and science.

The most controversial thinker of the seventeenth century was Baruch Spinoza (1632–1677), the son of a Jewish merchant of Amsterdam. He criticized the dogmatism of Dutch Calvinists and championed freedom of thought. Spinoza's most influential writing, *Ethics*, appeared after his death in 1677. Religious leaders universally condemned it for its apparent espousal of pantheism. According to Spinoza there is only one substance, which is self-caused, free, and infinite, and God is that substance. Everything that exists is in God and cannot even be conceived of apart from him. Such a doctrine is not literally pantheistic, but in Spinoza's view, statements about the natural world are also statements about divine nature. Mind and matter are seen to be extensions of the infinite substance of God; what transpires in the world of humankind and nature is a necessary outpouring of the Divine.

This teaching risked portraying the world as eternal and human actions as unfree and inevitable, the expression of a divine fatalism. Such points of view had been considered heresies by Jews and Christians because these views deny the creation of the world by God and destroy any voluntary basis for personal reward and punishment.

Thomas Hobbes (1588–1679) was the most original political philosopher of the seventeenth century. Although he never broke with the Church of England, he came to share basic Calvinist beliefs, especially the low view of human nature and the ideal of a commonwealth based on a covenant, both of which find eloquent expression in his political philosophy. Hobbes was an enthusiastic supporter of the new scientific movement. During the 1630s he visited Paris, where he came to know Descartes; after the outbreak of the Puritan Revolution (see Chapter 20) in 1640, he lived as an exile in Paris until 1651. Hobbes also spent time with Galileo (see Chapter 22) in Italy and took a special interest in the works of William Harvey, the physiologist famed for the discovery of how blood circulates through the body.

Hobbes was driven to political philosophy by the English Civil War (see Chapter 20). In 1651 his *Leviathan* appeared. Its subject was the political consequences of human passions, and its originality lay in (1) its making natural law, rather than common law (i.e., custom or precedent), the basis of all positive law, and (2) its defense of a representative theory of absolute authority against the theory of the divine right of kings. Hobbes maintained that statute law found its justification only as an expression of the law of nature and that rulers derived their authority from the consent of the people.

The key to Hobbes's political philosophy is a brilliant myth of the original state of humankind. According to this myth, human beings in the natural state are generally inclined to a "perpetual and restless desire of power after power that ceases only in death."[3] Whereas earlier and later philosophers saw the original human state as a paradise from which humankind had fallen, Hobbes saw it as a corruption from which only society had delivered people. According to Hobbes, people escape the impossible state of nature only by entering a social contract that creates a commonwealth tightly ruled by law and order. The social contract obliges every person, for the sake of peace and self-defense, to agree to set aside personal rights. The social contract also establishes the coercive force necessary to compel compliance. Hobbes conceived of the ruler's power as absolute and unlimited. There is no room in Hobbes's political philosophy for political protest in the name of individual conscience or for resistance to legitimate authority by private individuals—features of *Leviathan* criticized by Catholics and Puritans alike.

John Locke (1632–1704) has proved to be the most influential political thinker of the seventeenth century.[4] His political philosophy was embodied in the so-called Glorious Revolution of 1688 to 1689 (Chapter 20). Although he was not as original as Hobbes, his political writings were a major source of the later Enlightenment criticism of absolutism, and they gave inspiration to both the American and French Revolutions.

Locke's two most famous works are the *Essay Concerning Human Understanding* (1690) (discussed in Chapter 22) and *Two Treatises of Government* (1690), in which he argued that rulers are not absolute in their power. Rulers remain bound to the law of nature, which is the voice of reason, teaching that "all mankind [are] equal and independent, [and] no one ought to harm another in his life, health, liberty, or possessions,"[5] since all human beings are the images and property of God. People enter social contracts, empowering legislatures and monarchs to arbitrate their disputes, precisely to preserve their natural rights, not to give rulers an absolute power over them. From Locke's point of view, absolute monarchy was "inconsistent" with civil society and could be "no form of civil government at all."[6]

Leviathan. Thomas Hobbes's political treatise, *Leviathan*, portrayed rulers as absolute lords over their lands, incorporating in their persons the individual wills of all their people.

Look closely at this picture: What does it show?

[3] *Leviathan*, Parts I and II, ed. by H. W. Schneider (Indianapolis, IN: Bobbs-Merrill, 1958), p. 86.

[4] Locke's scientific writings are discussed in Chapter 24.

[5] *The Second Treatise of Government*, ed. by T. P. Peardon (Indianapolis, IN: Bobbs-Merrill, 1952), chap. 2, sects. 4–6, pp. 4–6.

[6] Ibid.

SUMMARY

WHY DID western Europeans start exploring, trading, and settling around the world in the fifteenth century?

The Discovery of a New World. In the late fifteenth century, Europe began to expand around the globe. Driven by both commercial and religious motives, the Portuguese pioneered a sea route around Africa to India and the Far East, and the Spanish discovered the Americas. The social, political, and biological consequences were immense. *page 406*

WHO WERE the early Protestant leaders?

The Reformation. The Reformation began in Germany with Martin Luther's attack on indulgences in 1517. The Reformation shattered the religious unity of Europe. In Switzerland, Zwingli and Calvin launched their own versions of Protestantism. In England, Henry VIII repudiated papal authority when the pope refused to grant him a divorce. The different Protestant sects were often as hostile to each other as they were to Catholicism. The Roman Catholic Church also acted to reform itself. The Council of Trent tightened church discipline and reaffirmed traditional doctrine. The Jesuits converted many Protestants back to Catholicism. *page 410*

HOW DID family life change during the Reformation era?

The Reformation and Daily Life. The Reformation led to far-reaching changes in religious beliefs, practices, and institutions. Family life changed in this period, as couples married later in life. *page 419*

WHY DID religious divisions lead to war?

The Wars of Religion. The religious divisions of Europe led to more than a century of warfare from the 1520s to 1648. The chief battlegrounds were in France, the Netherlands, and Germany. When the Thirty Years' War ended in 1648, Europe was permanently divided into Catholic and Protestant areas. *page 421*

WHO WERE some of the most significant writers and thinkers between 1500 and 1700?

Superstition and Enlightenment: The Battle Within. The Reformation led to both dark and constructive views of human nature. Witch crazes erupted across Europe. Thousands of innocent people, mostly women, were persecuted and executed as witches between 1400 and 1700. In literature and philosophy, these years witnessed an outpouring of creative thinking. Among the greatest thinkers of the age were Cervantes, Shakespeare, Pascal, Spinoza, Hobbes, and Locke. *page 424*

INTERPRETING THE PAST

European Expansion and Conquest

The primary source documents and visual sources below chronicle the beginnings of Europe's exploration, conquest, and exploitation of the non-Western world that began in the fifteenth century. As the text sources indicate, explorers like Columbus and da Gama were the eyes and ears of their sovereigns, intently observing the landscape, resources, and cultures of the Americas, Africa, and India. Without available indigenous written accounts describing their first meetings with Europeans, we must carefully analyze European texts to discern the nature of these momentous encounters. In the following exercise, use the source documents along with the images to address the following thematic questions. Use specific examples from the documents to back up your assertions.

Sources from MyHistoryLab for Chapter 17

1) Columbus, Journal Excerpt and Letter

2) Excerpt from *The Travel Journal of Vasco da Gama*

3) Duarte Barbosa, *Account of His Journeys in Africa and India*

REVIEW QUESTIONS

1. What impact did European expansion have on European economies?

2. What were the main problems of the church that contributed to the Protestant Reformation? Why was the church unable to suppress dissent as it had earlier?

3. How did the theologies of Luther, Zwingli, and Calvin differ? Were their differences only religious, or did they have political consequences for the Reformation as well?

4. Why did the Reformation begin in Germany and not in France, Italy, England, or Spain?

5. What was the Catholic Reformation? Did the Council of Trent alter the character of traditional Catholicism?

6. Why did Henry VIII break with the Catholic Church? Was the "new" religion he established really Protestant?

7. Were the wars of religion really over religion? Explain.

8. Henry of Navarre (later Henry IV of France), Elizabeth I, and William of Orange have been called *politiques*. What does that term mean, and how might it apply to each?

9. Why was England more successful than other lands in resolving its internal political and religious divisions peacefully during the sixteenth and seventeenth centuries?

10. Consider some of the leading intellectuals of this period: Cervantes, Shakespeare, Pascal, Spinoza, Hobbes, and Locke. Whose ideas do you find most challenging, and why? Which one would you most like to meet?

KEY TERMS

Counter-Reformation (p. 418)
Diet of Worms (p. 413)
Huguenots (HYEW-guh-nahts) (p. 421)

indulgence (p. 411)
ninety-five theses (p. 412)
Reformation (p. 410)
transubstantiation (p. 415)

Note: To learn more about the topics in this chapter, please turn to the Suggested Readings at the end of the book.

Visual Sources from MyHistoryLab

1) Indians planting corn
2) American cannibals

The text sources vary widely in the geographic areas they describe, but they were written within several decades of each other, and the authors are all European explorers or colonizers encountering a distant culture for the first time. Christopher Columbus's journal excerpt and letter offers great detail, although much of it is of questionable accuracy. In reading this revealing document, keep in mind these questions: Who was Columbus writing to? What were the possible motives shaping his narrative? In the excerpts from the travel journal of Vasco da Gama, the author discusses encountering the people and culture of the coastal Indian city of Calicut. It too includes a number of inaccuracies along with much valuable information. The third text source, by Duarte Barbosa, written in 1518, recounts Portuguese efforts to trade as well as to dominate East Africa very early in the colonial era. The images listed above also show indigenous cultures, in this case North American (Indians planting corn) and South American (American cannibals) from the perspective of Europeans.

Questions

Discuss the observations of Europeans, their accuracy or inaccuracy (if it can be determined), and their motives. Also assess how their activities and behavior would have been perceived to indigenous peoples living in the Americas, Africa, or India.

Specifically, in reading each of these texts, analyze the goals, explicit or implied, espoused by Columbus, da Gama, and Barbosa. Are they religious, economic, a combination of both, or something else? What actions do they take to achieve their goals? How do the Europeans perceive the indigenous inhabitants—civilized or uncivilized? peaceful or violent? intelligent or ignorant? Are these descriptions consistent? How accurate do you think these descriptions are? (One example of a rather important inaccuracy—da Gama's journal states that the inhabitants of Calicut are Christians and includes a description of a Christian church. The residents of Calicut, however, were Hindus, and the journal describes a Hindu temple.)

What are the consequences of the Europeans' encounters? Analyze the short-term results of these encounters first. Did the Europeans indicate a desire to fundamentally change the environment or culture of the lands they visited?

Christianity is based on the teaching of Jesus of Nazareth, a Jew who lived in Palestine during the Roman occupation. His simple message of faith in God and self-sacrificial love of one's neighbor attracted many people. The Roman authorities, perceiving his large following as a threat, crucified him. After Jesus' crucifixion, his followers proclaimed that he had been resurrected from the dead and that he would return in glory to defeat sin, death, and the devil, and take all true believers with him to heaven—a radical vision of judgment and immortality that has driven Christianity's appeal since its inception. In the teachings of the early church, Jesus became the Christ, the son of God, the long-awaited Messiah of Jewish prophecy. His followers called themselves Christians.

Christianity proclaimed the very incarnation of God in a man, the visible presence of eternity in time. According to early Christian teaching, the power of God's incarnation in Jesus lived on in the preaching and sacraments of the church under the guidance of the Holy Spirit. According to the Christian message, in Jesus, eternity has made itself accessible to every person here and now and forevermore.

The new religion attracted both the poor and powerless and the socially rising and well-to-do. For some, the gospel of Jesus promised a better material life. For others, it imparted a sense of spiritual self-worth regardless of one's place or prospects in society.

In the late second century the Romans began persecuting Christians as "heretics" (because of their rejection of the traditional Roman gods) and as social revolutionaries (for their loyalty to a lord higher than the emperor of Rome). At the same time dissenting Christians, particularly sects claiming direct spiritual knowledge of God apart from Scripture, internally divided the young church. To meet these challenges the church established effective weapons against state terrorism and Christian heresy: an ordained clergy, a hierarchical church organization, orthodox creeds, and a biblical canon (the New Testament). Christianity not only gained legal status within the Roman Empire, but also, by the fourth century, most favored religious status thanks to Emperor Constantine's embrace of it.

After the fall of the Western Roman Empire in the fifth century C.E., Christianity became one of history's great success stories. Aided by the enterprise of its popes and the

Pentecost. This exquisite enamel plaque, from the Mosan school that flourished in France in the eleventh and twelfth centuries, shows the descent of the Holy Spirit upon the apostles, fifty days after the resurrection of Jesus, on the ancient Jewish festival called the "feast of weeks," or Pentecost.

Mosan, The Pentecost, ca. 1150–1175. Champlevé enamel on copper gilt; 4 1/16 x 4 1/16 in. (10.3 x 10.3 cm). The Metropolitan Museum of Art, The cloisters Collection, 1965 (65.105). Photograph ©1989 The Metropolitan Museum of Art.

How did the church gain power in Europe?

example of its monks, the church cultivated an appealing lay piety centered on the Lord's Prayer, the Apostles' Creed, veneration of the Virgin, and the sacrament of the Eucharist. Clergy became both royal teachers and bureaucrats within the kingdom of the Franks. Despite a growing schism between the Eastern (Byzantine) and Western churches, and a final split in 1054, by 1000 the church held real economic and political power. In the eleventh century reform-minded prelates put an end to presumptuous secular interference in its most intimate spiritual affairs by ending the lay investiture of clergy in their spiritual offices. For several centuries thereafter the church remained a formidable international force, able to challenge kings and emperors and inspire crusades to the Holy Land.

By the fifteenth century the new states of Europe had stripped the church of much of its political power. It was thereafter progressively confined to spiritual and moral authority. Christianity's greatest struggles ever since have been not with kings and emperors over political power but with materialistic philosophies and worldly ideologies, matters of spiritual and moral hegemony within an increasingly pluralistic and secular world. Since the sixteenth century a succession of humanists, skeptics, Deists, Rationalists, Marxists, Freudians, Darwinians, and atheists have attempted to explain away some of traditional Christianity's most basic teachings. In addition, the church has endured major internal upheavals. After the Protestant Reformation (1517–1555) made the Bible widely available to the laity, the possibilities for internal criticism of Christianity multiplied geometrically. Beginning with the split between Lutherans and Zwinglians in the 1520s, Protestant Christianity has fragmented into hundreds of sects, each claiming to have the true interpretation of Scripture. The Roman Catholic Church, by contrast, has maintained its unity and ministry throughout perilous times, although present-day discontent with papal authority threatens the modern Catholic Church almost as seriously as the Protestant Reformation once did.

Christianity has remained remarkably resilient. It possesses a simple, almost magically appealing gospel of faith and love in and through Jesus. In a present-day world whose religious needs and passions still run deep, evangelical Christianity has experienced a remarkable revival. The Roman Catholic Church, still troubled by challenges to papal authority, has become more pluralistic than in earlier periods. The pope has become a world figure, traveling to all continents to represent the church and advance its position on issues of public and private morality. A major ecumenical movement emerging in the 1960s has promoted unprecedented cooperation among evangelical Christian denominations. Everywhere Christians of all stripes are politically active, spreading their divine, moral, and social messages. Meanwhile, old hot-button issues, such as the ordination of women, are being overtaken by new ones, particularly the marriage of gay men and women and the removal of clergy who do not maintain the moral discipline of their holy orders.

◆ Over the centuries what have been some of the chief factors attracting people to Christianity?

◆ What forces have led to disunity among Christians in the past and what factors cause tensions among modern Christians?

Gay Bishop. V. Gene Robinson is applauded after his investiture as the Episcopal Church's bishop of New Hampshire in March 2004. Robinson is the Episcopal Church's first openly gay bishop. The issue of homosexuality has divided Christian churches across the world.
What other controversies have divided Christians?

431

18

Conquest and Exploitation: The Development of the Transatlantic Economy

Negroes for Sale.

A Cargo of very fine stout Men and Women, in good order and fit for immediate service, just imported from the Windward Coast of Africa, in the Ship Two Brothers.—— Conditions are one half Cash or Produce, the other half payable the first of January next, giving Bond and Security if required.

The Sale to be opened at 10 o'Clock each Day, in Mr. Bourdeaux's Yard, at No. 48, on the Bay. May 19, 1784. JOHN MITCHELL.

Thirty Seasoned Negroes

To be Sold for Credit, at Private Sale.

AMONGST which is a Carpenter, none of whom are known to be dishonest.

Also, to be sold for Cash, a regular bred young Negroe Man-Cook, born in this Country, who served several Years under an exceeding good French Cook abroad, and his Wife a middle aged Washer-Woman, (both very honest) and their two Children. Likewise, a young Man a Carpenter. For Terms apply to the Printer.

Slave Auction Notice. Africans who survived the voyage across the Atlantic were immediately sold into slavery in the Americas. This eighteenth-century advertisement from Charleston, South Carolina describes a group of slaves "imported" from the Windward Coast of West Africa (the modern countries of Liberia and the Ivory Coast). Note how the advertisement alerts prospective buyers to the skills of the slaves.

Why were Africans treated as commodities during the era of the Transatlantic slave trade?

PERIODS OF EUROPEAN OVERSEAS EXPANSION *page 434*

WHAT WERE the four periods
of European contact with the world?

MERCANTILIST THEORY OF ECONOMIC EXPLOITATION *page 435*

WHAT WAS mercantilism?

ESTABLISHMENT OF THE SPANISH EMPIRE IN AMERICA *page 436*

WHAT ROLES did the Roman Catholic Church play
in Spanish America?

ECONOMIES OF EXPLOITATION IN THE SPANISH EMPIRE *page 438*

HOW DID Spaniards attempt to control labor
in the Americas?

COLONIAL BRAZIL *page 439*

HOW WERE sugar and slavery
entwined in colonial Brazil?

FRENCH AND BRITISH COLONIES IN NORTH AMERICA *page 441*

HOW WERE the economies of the French and British North
American colonies integrated into the transatlantic economy?

THE COLUMBIAN EXCHANGE: DISEASE, ANIMALS,
AND AGRICULTURE *page 442*

WHAT WAS the "Columbian Exchange"?

SLAVERY IN THE AMERICAS *page 444*

WHY WAS the transatlantic slave trade so
economically important?

AFRICA AND THE TRANSATLANTIC SLAVE TRADE *page 448*

HOW DID the slave trade impact Africa?

434

GLOBAL PERSPECTIVE

THE ATLANTIC WORLD

The exchanges of people, goods, ideas, and plants, animals, and microcosms among the American, European, and African continents in the fifteenth and sixteenth centuries transformed world history. In the Americas, the native peoples—whose ancestors had migrated from Asia millennia before—had established a wide variety of civilizations. Some of their most remarkable architectural monuments and cities were constructed during the very centuries when European civilizations were reeling from the collapse of Roman power. While trade and culture had long linked parts of Africa and regions in Eurasia (see Chapter 15) the civilizations of the Americas and the civilizations of Eurasia and Africa had had no significant contact with each other prior to the era of European exploration.

Within half a century of the landing of Columbus, millions of America's native peoples in Florida, the Caribbean islands, Mesoamerica, and South America had encountered Europeans intent on conquest, exploitation, and religious conversion. The Europeans' rapid conquest was the result of several factors—their advanced weapons and navies, the new diseases they brought with them, and internal divisions among the Native Americans. Thereafter, Spain and

Portugal dominated Central and South America (what we now, as a result of this history, call Latin America), and England, France, and Holland set out to settle North America. The Europeans imported their own food crops, such as wheat and apples, while also taking advantage of American plants, such as potatoes, corn, and tobacco.

Throughout the Americas and the Caribbean basin, Europeans established economies of exploitation. In Latin America, they developed various institutions to extract native labor. Plantation owners from the Mid-Atlantic English colonies through the Caribbean and into Brazil preferred slaves forcibly imported from Africa. African slaves were hardier than indigenous laborers, who lacked immunity to European diseases, and they could be better controlled than indentured servants from Europe. With the exception of tobacco, plantation crops derived largely from the Old World; some Africans were already familiar with the cultivation of, for example, rice. The emergent Atlantic World drew the economies and peoples of Europe, Africa, and the Americas into a vast worldwide web of production based on slave labor.

The European encounter with the Americas in the late fifteenth century made the Americas a region where European languages, legal and political institutions, trade patterns, and religion prevailed. African populations, economies, and political structures were altered by the slave trade. These developments gave Europe more influence over other world cultures and civilizations than it would otherwise have achieved.

Within decades of the European voyages of discovery, Native Americans, Europeans, and Africans began to interact in a manner unprecedented in human history. The Native Americans of North and South America encountered bands of European conquerors and missionaries. Technological and military superiority as well as political divisions among the Native Americans allowed the Europeans to realize their material and religious ambitions. By the middle of the sixteenth century Europeans had begun to import Africans into the American continents as chattel slaves, converting them to Christianity in the process. By the close of the sixteenth century Europe, the Americas, and Africa had become linked in a vast transatlantic economy that extracted material and agricultural wealth from the American continents largely on the basis of the nonfree labor of impressed Native Americans and imported African slaves. ■

PERIODS OF EUROPEAN OVERSEAS EXPANSION

WHAT WERE the four periods of European contact with the world?

Since the late fifteenth century, European contacts with the rest of the world have gone through four distinct stages. The first was that of the European discovery, exploration, initial conquest, and settlement of the Americas and commercial expansion elsewhere. The second was an era of trade rivalry among Spain, France, and Great Britain. During

Slavery had its most striking impact on the lives of the millions of humans who were torn from their birthplaces, their families, and their cultures. African slaves suffered from high mortality and sharply reduced birthrates; they were subjected to harsh working conditions and brutally dehumanizing treatment.

Beyond the egregious harms done to individual slaves and their descendants, slavery influenced political, economic, and social history throughout the Atlantic world. The slave trade corroded the political and social structures of African societies. Some historians have suggested that the plantation economy's efficient organization and use of labor created models of efficient productive organization and use of labor that became adapted in the Industrial Revolution in Europe and North America (see Chapter 20). Recent historical scholarship has highlighted ways in which the inherent contradictions between the institution of slavery, Enlightenment ideals of human will and behavior, and new political philosophies of the state in Europe and the Americas contributed some of the underpinnings for the wave of revolutions in the eighteenth and nineteenth centuries (see Chapters 22 and 23).

Focus Questions

- How did the encounter of Europe and Africa with the Americas change the global ecological balance?

- Why was the Spanish Empire based on economies of exploitation? How was the labor of non-European peoples drawn into the economy of this empire?

- How and why did the plantation economy develop? Why did it rely on African slaves for its labor? What were the consequences of the slave trade for individuals and institutions in each of the three continents constituting the Atlantic world?

- Why do we think of the plantation economy as a global, rather than regional, system of production? Why was it the "engine" of Atlantic basin trade?

---

this period (to 1820), the British colonies of North America and the Spanish colonies of Mexico and Central and South America broke free from European control. The third period spanned the nineteenth century and was characterized by the development of European empires in Africa and Asia. Imperial ideology at this time involved theories of trade, national honor, race, religion, and military strength. The last period of European experience with empire occupied the mid-twentieth century and was a time of decolonization—a retreat from empire.

Technological advantages, not innate cultural superiority, enabled Europeans to exercise global dominance disproportionate to Europe's size and population for four and a half centuries. The legacy of European imperialism continues to influence contemporary international relations.

El Morro, Puerto Rico. This fortress was built by the Spanish in the sixteenth century to protect Spain's valuable trading rights against British, Dutch, and pirate ships.

Why did Spain strive to control sea lanes?

MERCANTILIST THEORY OF ECONOMIC EXPLOITATION

The early modern European empires of the sixteenth through the eighteenth centuries were based on commerce. Extensive trade rivalries sprang up around the world and competitors developed navies to protect their interests. Spain, with the largest empire, constructed elaborate naval, commercial, and political structures to exploit and govern it. These empires depended largely on slave labor. The Atlantic slave trade forcibly

WHAT WAS mercantilism?

Mercantilism. As this painting of the Custom House Quay in London suggests, trade from European empires and the tariffs imposed on it were expected to generate revenue for the home country. Behind many of the goods carried in the great sailing ships in the harbor and landed on these docks lay the labor of African slaves working on the plantations of North and South America.

What kinds of trade goods are visible in this painting?

brought together the lives and cultures of peoples in Africa and the New World. It also enriched many European merchants.

To the extent that any formal economic theory lay behind the conduct of these empires, it was **mercantilism**, a system in which governments heavily regulate trade and commerce to increase national wealth. From beginning to end, the economic well-being of the home country was the primary concern. Mercantilists believed that a nation had to gain more gold and silver bullion than its rivals and that one nation's economy could grow only at the expense of others. Governments did this by establishing colonies overseas to provide markets and natural resources for the home country, which furnished military security and political administration for the colonies. The home country and its colonies were to trade exclusively with each other. For decades, both sides assumed that the colonies were the inferior partner in a monopolistic relationship.

Mercantilist ideas were always neater on paper than in practice. By the early eighteenth century, it was clear that mercantilist assumptions did not correspond with reality. Colonial and home markets did not mesh. Spain, for instance, could not produce enough goods for South America, while manufacturing in the British North American colonies challenged production in England and led to British attempts to limit certain colonial industries, such as iron and hat making.

Colonists of different countries wished to trade with each other. English colonists could buy sugar more cheaply from the French West Indies than from English suppliers. The eighteenth century became the "golden age of smugglers."[1] Governments could not control the activities of all their subjects, and they could be dragged into war by clashes among their colonies. Problems associated with the mercantile empires led to conflicts around the world.

ESTABLISHMENT OF THE SPANISH EMPIRE IN AMERICA

WHAT ROLES did the Roman Catholic Church play in Spanish America?

mercantilism Term used to describe close government control of the economy that sought to maximize exports and accumulate as much precious metal as possible to enable the state to defend its economic and political interests.

QUICK REVIEW

Francisco Pizarro (ca. 1478–1541)

◆ Invasion force landed in South America in 1532

◆ Forces included 200 men, horses, guns, and swords

◆ Executed the Inca ruler and captured Cuzco in 1533

CONQUEST OF THE AZTECS AND THE INCAS

Within twenty years of the arrival of Columbus (1451–1506), Spanish explorers in search of gold had claimed the major islands of the Caribbean and brutally suppressed the native peoples. These actions presaged what was to occur on the continent.

In 1519 Hernán Cortés (1485–1547) landed in Mexico with about five hundred men and a few horses. He opened communication with Moctezuma II (1466–1520), the Aztec emperor. Moctezuma may initially have believed Cortés to be the god Quetzalcoatl, who, according to legend, had been driven away centuries earlier but had promised to return. Whatever the reason, Moctezuma hesitated to confront Cortés, attempting at first to appease him with gifts of gold. Cortés forged alliances, most importantly with Tlaxcala, a traditional enemy of the Aztecs. His forces then marched on the Aztec capital of Tenochtitlán (modern Mexico City), where Moctezuma welcomed him. Cortés soon made Moctezuma a prisoner. When Moctezuma died in unexplained circumstances, the Spaniards were driven from Tenochtitlán and nearly wiped out. But they returned, and the Aztecs were defeated in late 1521. Cortés proclaimed the Aztec Empire to be New Spain.

---

[1]Walter Dorn, *Competition for Empire, 1740–1763* (New York: Harper, 1940), p. 266.

In 1532, Francisco Pizarro (ca. 1478–1541) landed on the western coast of South America to take over the Inca Empire. His force included about two hundred men armed with guns, swords, and horses, the military power of which the Incas did not understand. Pizarro lured the Inca ruler, Atahualpa (ca. 1500–1533), into a conference, then seized him and had him garroted in 1533. The Spaniards then captured Cuzco, the Inca capital, ending the Inca Empire. The Spanish faced insurrections, however, and fought among themselves for decades. Effective royal control was not established until the late 1560s.

The conquests of Mexico and Peru are among the most dramatic and brutal events in modern world history. Small military forces armed with advanced weapons and in alliance with indigenous enemies of the rulers subdued, in a remarkably brief time, two advanced, powerful peoples. European diseases, especially smallpox, aided the conquest, since much of the native population succumbed to diseases against which they had no immunity. But beyond the drama and bloodshed, these conquests marked a turning point. Whole civilizations with long histories and a record of enormous social, architectural, and technological achievement were effectively destroyed. Native American cultures endured, but European culture had the upper hand.

Spanish Conquest of Mexico. A sixteenth-century drawing depicts a battle during the Spanish conquest of Mexico. The Aztecs are on the right. Note how the Spaniards bring up the rear, behind their native allies, the Tlaxcalteca.

How does the position of the Tlaxcalteca leading the attack on the Aztecs offer a different perspective on the conquest of the Americas?

THE ROMAN CATHOLIC CHURCH IN SPANISH AMERICA

The Spanish conquest of the West Indies, Mexico, and South America opened a vast region to the Roman Catholic faith. Religion played a central role in the conquest of the New World, as it had in the reconquest of the Iberian Peninsula from the Moors. In both cases, the obligation Christians felt to spread their faith was used to justify military conquest and the extension of political control and dominance. As a consequence, the Roman Catholic Church in the New World was a conservative force working to protect the political power and prestige of the Spanish authorities. Indeed, the papacy turned over much of the control of the church in the New World to the Spanish monarchy. In the sixteenth century, as the papacy and the Habsburg monarchy fought Protestantism, the Roman Catholicism that spread throughout the Spanish domains of America was the zealous faith of the Counter-Reformation.

The Roman Catholic Church, with the aid first of the Franciscans and Dominicans and later the Jesuits, sought to convert the Native Americans and eradicate Indian religious practices. Converts, however, did not enjoy equality with Europeans; even late in the eighteenth century there were few Native American Christian priests. Real tension existed between the early Spanish conquerors and the mendicant friars. Without conquest the church could not convert the Native Americans, but the priests often deplored the harsh conditions imposed on the native peoples. By far the most effective and outspoken critic was Bartolomé de Las Casas (1474–1566), a Dominican. He contended that conquest was not necessary for conversion. One result of his campaign was new royal regulations after 1550.

Las Casas's writings inspired the "**Black Legend**," according to which all Spanish treatment of Native Americans was inhumane. Although substantially true, the Black Legend exaggerated the case against Spain. Certainly the rulers of the native empires—as the Aztec demands for sacrificial victims attest—had often themselves been cruel to their subject peoples.

Black Legend The argument that Spanish treatment of native Americans was uniquely inhumane.

By the end of the sixteenth century the church in Spanish America largely upheld the colonial status quo. Although individual priests defended the communal rights of Native American tribes, the colonial church prospered through its exploitation of the resources of the New World. Those who spoke for the church did not challenge Spanish domination, and the church only modestly moderated the forces exploiting human labor and material wealth. By the late eighteenth century, the Roman Catholic Church had become one of the most conservative forces in Latin American society.

ECONOMIES OF EXPLOITATION IN THE SPANISH EMPIRE

HOW DID Spaniards attempt to control labor in the Americas?

Colonial Spanish America had an economy of exploitation in two senses. First, its organization of labor involved dependent servitude or slavery. Second, America's resources were exploited for the economic advantage of Spain.

VARIETIES OF ECONOMIC ACTIVITY

conquistadores Meaning "conquerors." The Spanish conquerors of the New World.

The early **conquistadores** ("conquerors") had been interested primarily in gold, but by the middle of the sixteenth century silver mining provided the chief source of metallic wealth. The great silver mining centers were Potosí in present-day Bolivia and in northern Mexico. The Spanish crown received one fifth (the *quinto*) of all mining revenues. The mining industry experienced a recession early in the seventeenth century because of lack of new investment and the increasing costs involved in deeper mines, but it boomed in the eighteenth century. Overall, silver was a great source of wealth, and its production for the benefit of Spaniards and the Spanish crown epitomized the extractive economy on which Latin American colonial life was based.

This extractive economy required labor, but there were too few Spanish colonists to provide it, and most of the colonists who came to the Americas did not want to work for wages. So, the Spaniards turned first to the native population for workers and then to African slaves. Indian labor dominated on the continent and African labor in the Caribbean.

encomienda The grant by the Spanish crown to a colonist of the labor of a specific number of Indians for a set period of time.

The Spanish devised a series of institutions to exploit Native American labor. The first was the **encomienda**, a formal grant by the crown of the right to the labor of a specific number of Native Americans for a particular time. The Spanish crown disliked the *encomienda* system. The monarchy was distressed by reports from clergy that the Native Americans were being mistreated and feared that *encomienda* holders were becoming a powerful noble class in the New World. *Encomienda* as an institution declined by the middle of the sixteenth century.

repartimiento A labor tax in Spanish America that required adult male native Americans to devote a set number of days a year to Spanish economic enterprises.

The *encomienda* was followed by another arrangement of labor servitude, the **repartimiento**, which was largely copied from the draft labor practices of the Incas. *Repartimiento*, in an adaptation of the Incan *mita*, required adult male Native Americans to devote a set number of days of labor annually to Spanish economic enterprises. The time limitation on *repartimiento* led some Spanish managers to work teams of men to exhaustion—sometimes to death—before replacing them with the next rotation.

hacienda A large landed estates in Spanish America.

peninsulares Native-born Spaniards who emigrated from Spain to settle in the Spanish colonies.

Outside the mines, the major institution using dependent labor in the Spanish colonies was the **hacienda**. This institution, which dominated rural and agricultural life in Spanish colonies on the continent, developed when the crown made grants of land. These grants led to the establishment of large landed estates owned by **peninsulares** (whites born in Spain) or Creoles (whites born in America). This use of the resources of the New World for royal patronage did not directly burden Native Americans because the grazing that occurred on the haciendas required less labor than did the mines. But laborers on the hacienda were usually in formal servitude to the owner and had to buy goods for everyday living on credit from him. They were rarely able to repay the resulting debts and thus could not leave. This system was known as **debt peonage**. The hacienda economy produced foodstuffs for mining areas and urban centers, and haciendas became one of the most important features of Latin American life.

COMMERCIAL REGULATION AND THE *FLOTA* SYSTEM

Because Queen Isabella of Castile (r. 1474–1504) had commissioned Columbus, the legal link between the New World and Spain was the crown of Castile. Its powers both at home and in America were subject to few limitations. Government of America was assigned to the Council of the Indies, which, in conjunction with the monarch, nominated the viceroys of New Spain and Peru. These viceroys were the chief executives in the New World. Each of the viceroyalties included subordinate judicial councils known as *audiencias*. Local officers included the *corregidores*, who presided over municipal councils. These offices provided the monarchy with a vast array of opportunities for patronage. Political power flowed from the top of this political structure downward; there was little or no local initiative or self-government (see Map 18–1).

Colonial political structures existed largely to support the commercial goals of Spain. Spanish control of its American empire involved a system of monopolistic trade regulation, although Spain's trade monopoly was often breached. The Casa de Contratación (House of Trade) in Seville regulated all trade with the New World. Cádiz was the only Spanish port to be used for the American trade. The Casa de Contratación was the single most influential institution of the Spanish Empire. The entire organization was geared to benefit the Spanish monarchy and privileged merchant groups.

A complicated system of trade and bullion fleets administered from Seville was at the heart of the trade monopoly. Each year a fleet of commercial vessels (the *flota*) controlled by Seville merchants, escorted by warships, carried merchandise from Spain to a few specified ports in America. These included Portobello, Veracruz, and Cartagena. There were no authorized ports on the Pacific coast. Buenos Aires and other areas received goods only after the shipments had been unloaded at one of the authorized ports. After selling their wares, the ships were loaded with silver and gold bullion. They usually wintered in heavily fortified Caribbean ports and then sailed back to Spain. Each year a Spanish ship also crossed the Pacific from Spanish Manila to Acapulco, bringing Chinese silk and porcelain. It returned to Manila laden with Mexican silver. The *flota* system worked imperfectly, but trade outside it was illegal. Spanish colonists within the American empire were prohibited from trading directly with each other, and foreign merchants were forbidden to breach the Spanish monopoly.

The Silver Mines of Potosí.   Worked by conscripted Indian laborers under extremely harsh conditions, these mines provided Spain with a vast treasure in silver.

What does the puny size of the Indians in this painting say about their status in the Spanish-American society?

debt peonage   A system that forces agricultural laborers (peons) to work and live on large estates (*haciendas*) until they have repaid their debts to the estate's owner.

COLONIAL BRAZIL

Spain and Portugal originally had rival claims to the Americas. In 1494, by the Treaty of Tordesillas, the pope divided the seaborne empires of Spain and Portugal by drawing a line west of the Cape Verde Islands. In 1500 a Portuguese explorer landed on the coast of what is present-day Brazil, which extended east of the papal line of division, and thus Portugal gained a major hold on the South American continent. Portugal, however, had fewer resources to devote to its New World empire than did Spain. Its rulers, therefore, left exploitation of the region to private entrepreneurs. Because the native peoples in the lands that Portugal claimed were nomadic, the Portuguese, unlike

HOW WERE sugar and slavery entwined in colonial Brazil?

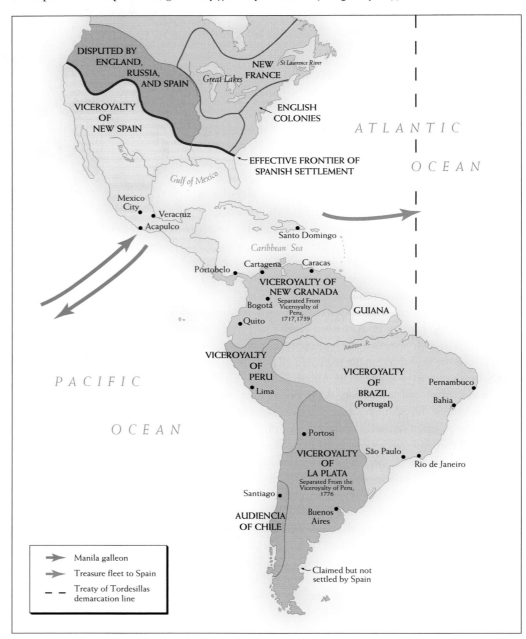

MAP EXPLORATION

To explore this map further, go to **http://www.prenhall.com/craig_maps**

MAP 18–1   The Americas, ca. 1750. Spain organized its vast holdings in the New World into viceroyalties, each of which had its own governor and other administrative officials. The English colonies clung to the North American seaboard. French possessions centered on the St. Lawrence River and the Great Lakes. Portuguese holdings in Brazil were mostly confined to the coast.

Based on this map, what were the strengths and weaknesses of the Spanish Empire in the Americas?

DISPUTED BY ENGLAND, RUSSIA, AND SPAIN

NEW FRANCE

St Lawrence River

Great Lakes

VICEROYALTY OF NEW SPAIN

ENGLISH COLONIES

ATLANTIC

OCEAN

EFFECTIVE FRONTIER OF SPANISH SETTLEMENT

Rio Grande

Gulf of Mexico

Mexico City

Veracruz

Acapulco

Santo Domingo

Caribbean Sea

Portobelo

Cartagena

Caracas

VICEROYALTY OF NEW GRANADA
Separated From Viceroyalty of Peru, 1717,1739

Bogotá

Quito

GUIANA

Amazon R.

VICEROYALTY OF PERU

VICEROYALTY OF BRAZIL (Portugal)

Pernambuco

Bahia

Lima

PACIFIC

OCEAN

Portosi

São Paulo

Rio de Janeiro

VICEROYALTY OF LA PLATA
Separated From the Viceroyalty of Peru, 1776

Santiago

Buenos Aires

AUDIENCIA OF CHILE

Claimed but not settled by Spain

→ Manila galleon

→ Treasure fleet to Spain

– – Treaty of Tordesillas demarcation line

QUICK REVIEW

Brazil's Colonial Economy

- Indigenous peoples were nomads, so Portuguese entrepreneurs imported African slaves for labor
- Sugar production and gold mining were most significant elements of economy
- Portuguese crown less involved in colonial administration than Spanish crown

the Spanish, imported Africans as slaves rather than using the native Indian population as their work force.

By the mid-sixteenth century, sugar production had gained preeminence in the Brazilian economy, although some minerals were discovered and some cattle raised. Because sugar cane was grown on large estates (*fazendas*) with African slave labor, the dominance of sugar meant also the dominance of slavery. Slavery became even more important when, in the early eighteenth century, significant gold deposits were discovered in southern Brazil. The expansion of gold mining increased the importation of African slaves. Nowhere, except perhaps in the West Indies, was slavery as important as it was in Brazil, where it persisted until 1888.

The taxation and administration associated with gold mining brought new, unexpected wealth to the eighteenth-century Portuguese monarchy, allowing it to rule without recourse to the Cortés or traditional parliament for taxation. Through transatlantic trade the new wealth generated from Brazilian gold also filtered into all the major trading nations, which could sell their goods to Portugal as well as profit from the slave trade.

The Portuguese crown attempted to regulate Brazilian trade. Brazil, however, required less direct control by the Portuguese than the Spanish Empire required from Spain, and as a result, Brazil's colonial settlers may have felt less resentment toward their government. In Brazil, the basic unit of production was the plantation, which did not require a vast colonial administration; agricultural products were much easier to keep track of than the precious metals of Spanish-American mines. The Portuguese were willing to allow more local autonomy than was Spain. In Spanish America the use of Native American labor was supervised by the government. Brazil, less dependent on Native American labor, felt no such constraints. Indeed, the Portuguese government condoned policies whereby indigenous tribes were driven into the backcountry or exterminated. Throughout the eighteenth century the Portuguese government also favored the continued importation of slaves.

Sugar plantations of Brazil and the West Indies were a major source of the demand for slave labor. Slaves are here shown grinding sugarcane and refining sugar, which was then exported to the consumer markets in Europe.

How did the labor requirements for sugar production differ from other colonial economic activities?

FRENCH AND BRITISH COLONIES IN NORTH AMERICA

French explorers had pressed down the St. Lawrence River valley in Canada during the seventeenth century. French fur traders and Roman Catholic Jesuit missionaries had followed, with the French government supporting the missionary effort. By the end of the seventeenth century a significant but sparsely populated French presence existed in Canada (see Map 18–1). The largest settlement was Quebec, founded in 1608. Since trade rather than settlement generally characterized the French effort, there was little conflict between the French and the Native Americans; some Frenchmen married Native American women. It was primarily through the fur trade that French Canada participated in the early transatlantic economy.

From the first successful settlement in Jamestown, Virginia, in 1607, through the establishment of Georgia in 1733, English colonies spread along the eastern seaboard of the future United States. The Dutch, Swedes, and others founded settlements too, but all of them were taken over during the seventeenth century by the English. Settlements were founded for a variety of reasons. Virginia and New Amsterdam (after 1664, New York) aimed for enrichment through farming and trade. Others, such as the Carolinas, were developed by royal favorites who were given vast land tracts. James Oglethorpe founded Georgia as a refuge for English debtors. But the pursuit of religious liberty constituted the major driving force of the Pilgrim and Puritan founders of Massachusetts, the Baptist Roger Williams in Rhode Island, the Quaker William Penn in Pennsylvania, and the Roman Catholic Lord Baltimore in Maryland.

With the exception of Maryland, these colonies were Protestant. The Church of England dominated the southern colonies. In New England, varieties of Protestantism associated with or derived from Calvinism were in the ascendancy. In their religious affiliations, the English-speaking colonies manifested two important traits

HOW WERE the economies of the French and British North American colonies integrated into the transatlantic economy?

QUICK REVIEW

British North America

- ◆ Jamestown, Virginia: Became first successful British settlement in 1607
- ◆ Religion shaped the organization of British colonies
- ◆ English colonies had a complex relationship with Native Americans

Roanoke. The first successful English colonies in North America in the seventeenth century were preceded by two failed efforts on Roanoke Island in what is now North Carolina in the late sixteenth century. John White accompanied both attempts, the second as governor. White was a perceptive and sensitive observer whose watercolor paintings provide invaluable information about Native American life in the coastal Carolina region at the time of contact. This painting shows the Algonquin village of Secoton. The houses were bark covered. In the lower left is a mortuary temple. The dancers in the lower right are performing a fertility ceremony. The man sitting in the platform in the upper right is keeping birds away from the corn crop.

What factors influenced the relationships between English settlers and Native Americans?

Columbian Exchange Biological exchange of plants, animals, and diseases between the Americas and the rest of the world.

derived from the English experience. First, much of their religious life was organized around self-governing congregations. Second, their religious outlook derived from those forms of Protestantism that were suspicious of central political authority. In this regard, their cultural and political outlook differed sharply from that of the Roman Catholics of the Spanish Empire. In a sense, the ideologies of the extreme Reformation and Counter-Reformation confronted each other in the Americas.

The English colonists had complex interactions with the Native American populations. They had only modest interest in missionary enterprise. New diseases imported from Europe took a high death toll among the native population. North America had no large Native American cities; indigenous populations were dispersed, and intertribal animosity was intense. The English often encountered well-organized resistance, as from the Powhatan conspiracy in Virginia and the Pequots in New England. The most powerful of the Native American groups was the Iroquois Nation, organized in the early eighteenth century in New York. The Iroquois battled successfully against other tribes and long negotiated successfully with both the Dutch and the English. The English often used one tribe against another, and the Native Americans also tried to use the English or the French in their own conflicts. The outcome of these struggles between the English settlers and the Native Americans was rarely full victory for either side. From the late seventeenth century through the American Revolution, Native Americans were drawn into the Anglo-French wars that were fought in North America as well as Europe. Indeed, Native American alliances became important for the Anglo-French conflict on the Continent, which was intimately related to their rivalry over transatlantic trade (see Chapter 20).

The economies of the English-speaking colonies were primarily agricultural. From New England through the Middle Atlantic, there were mostly small farms tilled by free white labor; from Virginia southward a plantation economy dependent on slavery predominated. The principal ports of Boston, Newport, New York, Philadelphia, Baltimore, and Charleston were the chief centers through which goods moved back and forth between the colonies and England and the West Indies. The commercial economies of these cities were all related to the transatlantic slave trade.

Until the 1760s the political values of the Americans resembled those of their English counterparts. The colonials were thoroughly familiar with events in England and sent many of their children there to be educated. They were monarchists but, like their English counterparts, suspicious of monarchical power. Their politics involved vast amounts of patronage and individual favors. Their society was clearly hierarchical with an elite that functioned like a colonial aristocracy and many ordinary people who were dependent on that aristocracy. Throughout the colonies during the eighteenth century, the Anglican Church grew in influence and membership. The prosperity of the colonies might eventually have led them to separate from England, but in 1750 few people thought that would occur.

Both England and France had important sugar islands in the Caribbean with plantations worked by African slaves. The trade and commerce of the northern British colonies were closely related to meeting the needs of these islands.

THE COLUMBIAN EXCHANGE: DISEASE, ANIMALS, AND AGRICULTURE

WHAT WAS the "Columbian Exchange"?

The European encounter with the Americas produced remarkable ecological transformations that have shaped the world to the present time (see Map 18–2). Alfred Crosby, the leading historian of the process, has named this cross-continental flow the **Columbian Exchange**.

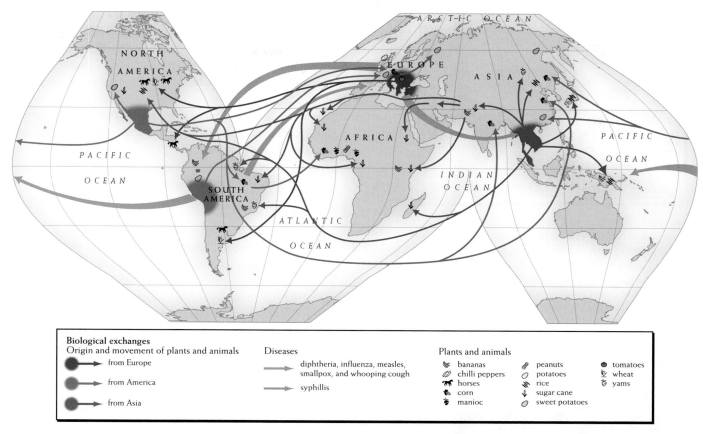

Biological exchanges
Origin and movement of plants and animals

from Europe

from America

from Asia

Diseases

diphtheria, influenza, measles, smallpox, and whooping cough

syphillis

Plants and animals

bananas
chilli peppers
horses
corn
manioc

peanuts
potatoes
rice
sugar cane
sweet potatoes

tomatoes
wheat
yams

MAP 18–2 **Biological Exchanges.**   The worldwide movement of plants, animals, and diseases.

How did the Columbian Exchange alter environments around the world?

DISEASES ENTER THE AMERICAS

The American continents had been biologically separated from Europe, Africa, and Asia for tens of thousands of years. (A few overseas ships such as the Vikings had reached American shores, but the numbers of people involved were miniscule.) The only animal native to the Americas that could serve as a beast of burden was the llama, which could transport only about a hundred pounds. Nor did animals constitute a major source of protein for Native Americans, whose diets consisted largely of maize, beans, peppers, yams, and potatoes. The American continents included vast grassland that lacked grazing animals to transform those plants into animal protein. It appears that native peoples had not experienced major epidemics.

By the second voyage of Columbus (1493), that picture began to change in remarkable ways. Columbus brought a number of animals and plants to Hispaniola and other islands of the Caribbean that were previously unknown to the New World. His sailors and the men on subsequent European voyages also carried diseases new to the Americas.

European diseases ultimately played at least as big a role in defeating indigenous Americans as advanced European weaponry did. Much controversy surrounds the question of the actual size of the populations of Native Americans in the Caribbean islands, Mexico, Peru, and the North Atlantic coast. Those populations were quite significant, with those of Mexico numbering many millions. In the first two centuries after the encounter, wherever Europeans went, extremely large numbers of Native Americans died from diseases they had

Smallpox. Introduced by Europeans to the Americas, smallpox had a devastating effect on Native American populations. It swept through the Aztec capital of Tenochtitlán soon after the Spaniards arrived, contributing to the fall of the city. This illustration of the effect of the plague in the Aztec capital is from a postconquest history known as the Florentine Codex, compiled for Spanish church authorities by Aztec survivors.

What other diseases did Europeans bring to the Americas?

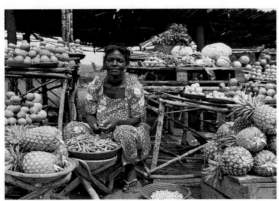

Global Foods. A woman in the African country of Uganda offers beans and pineapples for sale, both of which originated in the Americas.

What other American plants were introduced to Africa?

never before encountered. Smallpox, the most deadly, destroyed millions of people. Bubonic plague, typhoid, typhus, influenza, measles, chicken pox, whooping cough, malaria, and diphtheria produced deadly results in more localized epidemics. An unknown disease, but quite possibly typhus, caused major losses among the Native Americans of New England between approximately 1616 and 1619.

On the reverse side of the equation it appears that syphillis, which became a rampant venereal disease in Europe at the close of the fifteenth century and eventually spread around the globe, originated in the New World. Until the discovery of penicillin in the 1940s, syphillis remained a major public health concern throughout the world.

ANIMALS AND AGRICULTURE

The introduction of European livestock revolutionized American agriculture. The most important new animals were pigs, cattle, horses, goats, and sheep. The horse became first the animal of conquest and then the animal of colonial Latin American culture. Because Native Americans had no prior experience with such large animals that would obey the will of a human rider, they were fearful of the mounted Spanish horsemen. After the conquest, however, the Americas from Mexico southward became the largest horse-breeding region of the world. By the nineteenth century, the possession of horses allowed the Plains Indians of North America to resist European encroachment. Pigs, cattle, and sheep produced enormous quantities of hides and wool. Their large numbers also meant the Americas from the sixteenth century through the present would support a diet more plentiful in animal protein than anywhere else in the world.

Europeans also brought their own plants to the New World, including peaches, oranges, grapes, melons, bananas, rice, onions, radishes, and various green vegetables. Sugarcane cultivation created the major demand for slavery throughout the transatlantic plantation economy. European wheat, over time, allowed the Americas not only to feed themselves but also to export large amounts of grain throughout the world.

The only American animal that came to be raised in Europe was the turkey. The Americas, however, were the source of plants that eventually changed the European diet: maize, potatoes, sweet potatoes, peppers, beans, manioc (tapioca), peanuts, squash, pumpkins, pineapples, cocoa, and tomatoes. Maize and potatoes had the greatest impact on European farming, transforming the European diet. Both crops grow rapidly, supplying food quickly and steadily if not attacked by disease. There is good reason to believe the cultivation of the potato was a major cause of the population increase in eighteenth- and nineteenth-century Europe. Africa received many of these same foodstuffs, as well. Maize became a staple in Africa. Tobacco also originated in the Americas.

SLAVERY IN THE AMERICAS

WHY WAS the transatlantic slave trade so economically important?

Slavery was the final mode of forced or subservient labor in the New World. Enslavement of Africans and their descendants extended throughout the Spanish Empire, Portuguese Brazil, and the English-speaking colonies of North America. The heartland of transatlantic slavery lay in the Caribbean islands.

THE BACKGROUND OF SLAVERY

Virtually every premodern state around the globe depended on slavery to some extent (see Map 18–3). Slave institutions in sub-Saharan Africa were ancient and included traffic with the Mediterranean world. The Islamic states of southwestern Asia and

MAP EXPLORATION

To explore this map further, go to **http://www.prenhall.com/craig_maps**

MAP 18–3   The Slave Trade, 1400–1860.   Slavery is an ancient institution, and complex slave-trading routes were in existence in Africa, the Middle East, and Asia for centuries, but it was the need to supply labor for the plantations of the Americas that led to the greatest movement of peoples across the face of the earth.

How does this map show the global nature of the slave trade?

North Africa continued and even increased this traffic, importing slaves from both the Sudan and Horn of Africa as well as the East African coast, although they took fewer slaves from Africa than from eastern Europe and Central Asia. Both Mediterranean Christian and Islamic peoples were using slaves—mostly Greeks, Bulgarians, Turkish prisoners of war, and Black Sea Tartars, but also Africans—well before the voyages of discovery opened sub-Saharan sources of slaves for the new European colonies overseas.

Not all forms of slavery were as dehumanizing as the chattel slavery that came to predominate—with the sanction of Christian authorities—in the Americas. Islamic law, for example, permitted slavery but also ameliorated it. All slavery, however, involved the forceful exploitation and degradation of some human beings for the profit of others, the denial of basic freedoms, and sometimes the violent sundering of even

Sugar Plantation. African slaves on the Caribbean island of Antigua bring sugarcane to a windmill where it will be crushed into juice. A white overseer closely watches the proceedings.

What kinds of investments did plantation owners have to make before they could profit from sugarcane?

the closest family ties. Although there were some variations in the legal and social structures of slavery in the Atlantic world, slaves brought from Africa and their descendants were invariably chattel slaves: They were outright possessions of their masters, indistinguishable from any material possession; they were not recognized as persons under the law, so they had no legal rights; they could not claim any control over their bodies, their time, their labor, or even their own children.

African societies suffered immense political, economic, and social devastation when they were the chief supplier of slaves to the world. The New World societies that were built to a great extent on the exploitation of African slavery also suffered enduring consequences, including racism.

ESTABLISHMENT OF SLAVERY

As the numbers of Native Americans in South America declined due to disease and exploitation, the Spanish and the Portuguese turned to the labor of imported African slaves. By the late 1500s, in the West Indies and many cities of South America, black slaves surpassed the white population.

On much of the South American continent dominated by Spain, slavery declined during the late seventeenth century, but it continued to thrive in Brazil and in the Caribbean. In British North America, beginning with the importation of slaves to Jamestown in 1619, it quickly became a fundamental institution.

One of the forces that led to the spread of slavery in Brazil and the West Indies was the cultivation of sugar. Sugarcane required a large investment in land and equipment, and only slave labor could provide enough low-cost workers to make the plantations profitable. As the production of sugar expanded, the demand for slaves increased.

By 1700, the world center for sugar production was in the Caribbean Islands. As the European appetite for sugar grew, so did the slave population. By 1725, black slaves may have constituted almost 90 percent of the population of the West Indies. There and in Brazil and the southern British colonies, prosperity and slavery went hand in hand. The wealthiest colonies were those that raised consumer staples, such as sugar, rice, tobacco, or cotton, by slave labor.

OVERVIEW The Columbian Exchange

TO THE AMERICAS

Diseases	smallpox, influenza, bubonic plague, typhoid, typhus, measles, chicken pox, malaria, and diphtheria
Animals	pigs, cattle, horses, goats, sheep, and chickens
Plants	apples, peaches, pears, apricots, plums, oranges, mangos, lemons, olives, melons, almonds, grapes, bananas, cherries, sugarcane, rice, wheat, oats, barley, onions, radishes, okra, dandelions, cabbages, and other green vegetables

FROM THE AMERICAS

Diseases	syphillis
Animals	turkeys
Plants	maize, tomatoes, sweet peppers, chilis, potatoes, sweet potatoes, squash, pumpkins, manioc (tapioca), beans, cocoa, peanuts, pecans, pineapples, guavas, avocados, blueberries, and tobacco

THE PLANTATION ECONOMY AND TRANSATLANTIC TRADE

The **plantation economy** encompassed plantations that stretched from Maryland through the West Indies and into Brazil. They formed a vast corridor of slave societies in which social and economic subordination was based on both involuntary servitude and race. This kind of society, in its total dependence on slave labor and racial differences, had not existed before the European discovery and exploitation of the Americas. The social and economic influence of plantation slavery touched not only the plantation societies themselves but also West Africa, western Europe, and New England. It persisted from the sixteenth century through the second half of the nineteenth century, ending with the British effort to outlaw the slave trade during the first half of the nineteenth century, the Latin American wars of independence, the Emancipation Proclamation of 1862 in the United States, and the Brazilian emancipation of 1888. Every society in which it existed still contends with its effects.

The slave trade was part of the larger system of transatlantic trade that linked Europe, Africa, and the European colonies in South America, the Caribbean, and North America. In this system the Americas supplied labor-intensive raw materials like tobacco, sugar, coffee, precious metals, cotton, and indigo. Europe supplied manufactured goods like textiles, liquor, guns, metal wares, and beads, and cash in various forms. Africa supplied gold, ivory, wood, palm oil, gum, and other products, as well as the slaves who provided the labor to create the American products. By the eighteenth century slaves were the predominant African export.

SLAVERY ON THE PLANTATIONS

The American plantations to which African slaves arrived were always in a fairly isolated rural setting. The plantation might raise food for its owners and their slaves, but the main production was intended for export. Plantation owners imported virtually all the finished or manufactured goods they used.

The conditions of the lives of plantation slaves differed from colony to colony. Most owners possessed relatively few slaves. Black slaves living in Portuguese areas had the fewest legal protections. In the Spanish colonies the church attempted to provide some protection for black slaves but devoted much more effort to protecting Native Americans. Slave codes were developed in the British and the French colonies during the seventeenth century, but they provided only the most limited protection. Virtually all slave owners feared a slave revolt; slave laws favored the master rather than the slave. Masters were permitted to punish slaves by whipping and other harsh corporal punishment, and slaves were often forbidden to gather in large groups lest they plan a revolt. Marriages of slaves were not recognized by law in most places. The child of an enslaved woman was born a slave, the property of the mother's owner. Slave families could be separated at whim by the owner or the owner's heirs.

The daily life of most slaves was one of hard agricultural labor, poor diet and clothing, and inadequate housing. The death rate among slaves was high. Their welfare and their lives were sacrificed to the ongoing expansion of the plantations that made their owners wealthy and that produced goods demanded by consumers in Europe.

The African slaves who were transported to the Americas were, like the Native Americans, converted to Christianity: in the Spanish domains to Roman Catholicism,

African American Culture.   This eighteenth-century painting depicts a celebration in the slave quarters on a South Carolina plantation. One planter's description of a slave dance seems to fit this scene: the men leading the women in "a slow shuffling gait, edging along by some unseen exertion of the feet, from one side to the other—sometimes curtseying down and remaining in that posture while the edging motion from one side to the other continued." The woman, he wrote, "always carried a handkerchief held at arm's length, which was waved in a graceful motion to and fro as she moved."

Abby Aldrich Rockefeller Folk Art Museum, Colonial Williamsburg Foundation, VA.

Why did slave owners suppress traditional African religious practices?

plantation economy   The economic system stretching between the Chesapeake Bay and Brazil that produced crops, especially sugar, cotton, and tobacco, using slave labor on large estates.

King Affonso I   of the Kongo holds an audience with European ambassadors who kneel before him.

What roles did Africans play in the transatlantic slave trade?

and in the English colonies to various forms of Protestantism. They were forbidden to practice their traditional faiths. Slave owners often did not know whether particular activities were religious, but they erred on the side of caution: Activities that were not directly related to economic production, or that suggested links to African culture, were suppressed. Some African practices survived in muted forms, however, and slaves did manage to mix African religion with Christianity.

European settlers and slave traders were prejudiced against black Africans. Many Europeans thought Africans were savage or looked down on them simply because they were slaves. These attitudes had been shared by both Christians and Muslims in the Mediterranean world. Furthermore, many European languages attached negative connotations to blackness. In virtually all plantation societies, race was an important element in keeping black slaves subservient. Although racial thinking in regard to slavery became more important in the nineteenth century, the fact that slaves were differentiated from the rest of the population by race as well as by their status as chattel property was fundamental to the system.

AFRICA AND THE TRANSATLANTIC SLAVE TRADE

HOW DID the slave trade impact Africa?

The establishment of plantations demanding the use of slave labor drew Africa and its peoples into the heart of the transatlantic economy. As Native American peoples were decimated by conquest and European diseases or proved unsatisfactory as plantation laborers, colonial entrepreneurs began to look elsewhere for people to work their plantations. First the Portuguese and then the Spanish, Dutch, French, English, and Americans turned to western, central, and southeastern Africa for an ample supply of slaves.

The Portuguese were the principal carriers in the early history of the trade. Their virtual monopoly was broken by the Dutch in the 1640s. The French and the English came into the trade later, yet during the eighteenth century, which saw the greatest number of slaves shipped, they carried almost half the total traffic. Americans, too, were avid slavers who managed to make considerable profits before and even after Britain and the United States outlawed the transatlantic slave trade in 1807 and 1808, respectively.

Slaving was an important part of the massive new overseas trade that financed much European and American economic development during the nineteenth century. The success and considerable profits of this trade, bought at the price of immense human suffering, helped propel Europe and some of its colonial offshoots in the Americas into world dominance.

SLAVERY AND SLAVING IN AFRICA

The trade that long before the fifteenth century supplied African slaves to the Mediterranean and Asia has conventionally been termed the "Oriental" slave trade. The Sudan and the Horn of Africa were the two prime sources of slaves for this trade. The Afro-European trade, conventionally called the **"Occidental" slave trade,** can be traced at least to the thirteenth century, when Europeans established sugarcane plantations on Cyprus. This industry subsequently spread westward to Crete and Sicily and, in the fifteenth century, to the Portuguese Atlantic islands of Madeira and São Tomé. The Portuguese developed the plantation system of slave labor as they began their expansion into the Atlantic and beyond. Voyages beginning in the fifteenth century by the Portuguese and other Europeans made the western coasts of Africa as far south as Angola the prime slaving areas. A less important source region for both Occidental and Oriental trades was the eastern coast of Africa below the Horn.

"Occidental" slave trade The trade in slaves from Africa to the Islamic Mediterranean and Asia that predated the transatlantic slave trade.

Prior to the full development of the transatlantic slave trade, slavery and slave trading had been no more significant in Africa than anywhere else in the world.[2] Indigenous African slavery resembled that of other premodern societies. Probably about ten thousand slaves per year, most of them female, were taken from sub-Saharan Africa through the Oriental slave trade.

By about 1650 the newer Occidental slave trade of the Europeans had become as large as the Oriental trade and for the ensuing two centuries far surpassed it. It affected all of Africa, disrupting especially western and central African societies. As a result of the demand for young male slaves on the plantations of the Americas, West Africa experienced a sharp drain on its productive male population. With the growing demand for slaves came an increase in internal warfare in western and central Africa. Moreover, as the external trade destroyed the regional male-female population balance, an internal market for female slaves arose.

These developments accelerated during the eighteenth century, at the height of the Occidental trade. During this period, African states and slave traders were most heavily involved as regulators and suppliers of the trade. Slave prices increased accordingly. Owing to population depletion and regional migrations, however, the actual number of slaves sold declined in some areas. The population declined sharply in the coastal and inland areas hardest hit by the ravages of the trade in the later eighteenth century and continued to decline in places even until 1850.

As European and American nations slowly began to outlaw first the slave trade and then slavery itself in the nineteenth century, the Oriental and internal trades increased. Slave exports from East Africa and the Sudan and Horn increased significantly after about 1780, and indigenous African slavery, predominantly of women, also expanded. By about 1850 the internal African trade surpassed the combined Oriental and (now outlawed and decreasing) Occidental trade. This traffic was dominated by the same figures—merchants, warlords, and rulers—who had previously profited from external trade.

Indigenous African slavery began a real decline only at the end of the nineteenth century, in part because of the dominance of European colonial regimes and in part because of internal changes. The formal end of African indigenous slavery occurred only in 1928 in Sierra Leone. Late in the twentieth century, however, in various locations around the world—mostly places with endemic, severe poverty and weak civil authority, including the Sudan—patterns emerged of involuntary servitude and human trafficking that constitute modern-day slavery.

CHRONOLOGY

CONQUEST OF THE AMERICAS AND THE TRANSATLANTIC SLAVE TRADE

1494	Treaty of Tordesillas divides the seaborne empires of Spain and Portugal
1500	The Portuguese arrive in Brazil
1519–1521	Hernán Cortés conquers the Aztec Empire
1531–1533	Francisco Pizarro conquers the Inca Empire
1607	Jamestown, Virginia, first permanent English settlement in North America
1608	The French found Quebec
1619	First African slaves brought to British North America
1700s	Over 6 million slaves imported from Africa to the Americas
1794	Slavery abolished throughout the French empire
1807	Importation of slaves abolished in British domains
1808	Importation of slaves abolished in the United States
1817–1820	Spain abolishes the slave trade
1833	Slavery abolished throughout the British empire
1850	Importation of slaves abolished in Brazil
1874–1928	Indigenous African slavery abolished
1888	Slavery abolished in Brazil

---

[2]The summary follows closely that of P. Manning, *Slavery and African Life: Occidental, Oriental, and African Slave Trades* (Cambridge: Cambridge University Press, 1990), pp. 127–140.

THE AFRICAN SIDE OF THE TRANSATLANTIC TRADE

Africans were actively involved in the transatlantic slave trade. Except for the Portuguese in central Africa, European slave traders generally obtained their human cargoes from private or government-sponsored African middlemen at coastal forts or simply at anchorages along the coast. Africans were motivated to control the inland trade, and Europeans were vulnerable to tropical disease. Thus it was largely African middlemen who undertook the actual capture or procurement of slaves and the difficult, dangerous task of marching them to the coast. These middlemen were generally either wealthy merchants who could mount slaving expeditions inland or the agents of African kingdoms who sought to profit from the trade.

The media of exchange for slaves varied. At first they usually involved mixed barter for goods that ranged from gold dust or firearms to beads and alcohol. As time went on they came increasingly to involve some form of monetary payment. This exchange drained productive resources (human beings) from Africa in return for nonproductive wealth.

The chief western and central African slaving regions provided different numbers of slaves at different times, and the total number of exported slaves varied sharply between periods (see Map 18–4). When one area was unable to produce sufficient numbers to meet demand, the European traders shifted their buying to other points. Thus, between 1526 and 1550 the major sources of the slaves for the transatlantic trade were the Kongo-Angola region (34 percent), the Guinea coast of Cape Verde (25.6 percent), and Senegambia (23.5 percent).[3] By contrast, between 1761 and 1810 the French drew some 52 percent of their slaves from Angola and 24 percent from the Bight of Benin, but only 4.8 percent from Senegambia, whereas the British relied most heavily on the Bight of Biafra and central Africa.[4] Traders naturally went where population density and the presence of active African merchant or state suppliers promised the most slaves and the lowest prices, although prices do not seem to have varied radically in a given period.

Slaves in the Streets of Zanzibar, nineteenth century. Slaving was a part of East African trade for centuries.

Why did the slave trade persist even after it was abolished?

Middle Passage The transatlantic crossing of ships carrying slaves from Africa to the Americas and Caribbean.

THE EXTENT OF THE SLAVE TRADE

Historians now estimate that from the sixteenth through the nineteenth century there were over 35,000 transatlantic slave ship voyages forcibly transporting more than 11 million Africans to America; many other Africans were lost in passage or through brutality associated with the trade. (See Document, "Olaudah Equiano Recalls His Experience at the Slave Market in Barbados.") The slave trade varied sharply in extent from period to period (see Figure 18–1). The period of greatest activity from 1701 to 1810 accounted for over 60 percent of the total. Despite Great Britain's abolishing the slave trade in its colonies in 1807 and the United States in 1808, the Portuguese still transported more than a million slaves to Brazil between 1811 and 1870. Other nations also continued to trade in slaves in the nineteenth century. In fact, more slaves landed in the Americas in the final years of the trade than during the entire seventeenth century.[5] It is

FIGURE 18-1. The Atlantic Slave Trade, 1400–1800. From Canizares-Esguerra, Jorge; Seeman, Eric, *The Atlantic in Global History, 1500–2000,* © 2007. Electronically reproduced by permission of Pearson Education, Inc., Upper Saddle River, New Jersey.

Why did the slave trade increase so dramatically in the eighteenth century?

---

[3]Scholars have spent decades attempting to assemble trustworthy statistics on the slave trade; the database by Eltis et al., *The Trans-Atlantic Slave Trade: A Database on CD-ROM* (Cambridge and New York: Cambridge University Press, revised 2008), has marshaled a great deal of information in one spot, but new data continue to emerge. Philip Curtin, *The Atlantic Slave Trade: A Census* (Madison: University of Wisconsin Press, 1969), p. 101.

[4]Curtin, *The Atlantic Slave Trade*, pp. 101, 129; James A. Rawley, *The Trans-Atlantic Slave Trade: A History* (New York: W. W. Norton, 1981), p. 129. Note that precise statistics are subject to revision in light of more recent scholarship; see, for example, Eltis et al., *The Trans-Atlantic Slave Trade: A Database on CD-ROM.*

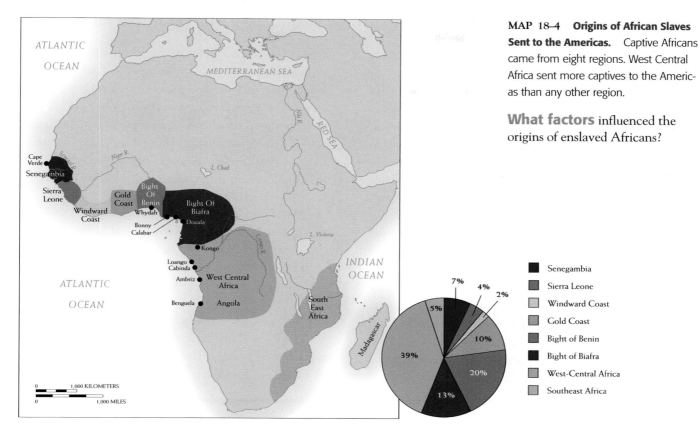

MAP 18–4   Origins of African Slaves Sent to the Americas.   Captive Africans came from eight regions. West Central Africa sent more captives to the Americas than any other region.

What factors influenced the origins of enslaved Africans?

- ■ Senegambia
- ■ Sierra Leone
- ■ Windward Coast
- ■ Gold Coast
- ■ Bight of Benin
- ■ Bight of Biafra
- ■ West-Central Africa
- ■ Southeast Africa

sobering to contemplate how long it took the "modern" Western nations to abolish the trade in African slaves.

The overall number of African slaves exported during the Occidental trade—effectively between 1451 and 1870—is still debated. A major unknown for both the Occidental and the Oriental trades is the number of slaves who died under the brutal conditions to which they were subjected when captured and transported overland and by sea. The **Middle Passage**, the portion of the journey in which Africans were packed onto dangerous and unhealthy boats for the voyage across the Atlantic Ocean, claimed untold numbers. The most reliable estimates pertain only to those slaves who actually landed abroad, and these estimates are more reliable for the Occidental trade than for the older, smaller, and more dispersed Oriental trade. Those who actually reached an American or Old World destination in the Occidental trade totaled more than 10 million.

Another 5 million or more were lost to the Oriental trade. Finally, the Occidental trade spurred an apparently huge increase in internal slavery, and according to the estimate of one expert, an additional 15 million people were enslaved within African societies themselves.[6]

Slave Ship.   Loading plan for the main decks of the 320-ton slave ship *Brookes*. The *Brookes* was only 25 feet wide and 100 feet long, but as many as 609 slaves were crammed on board for the nightmarish passage to the Americas. The average space allowed each person was only about 78 inches by 16 inches. Note how humans were grouped by size and how every adult depicted on the C and D decks has one leg shackled.

How does this drawing convey the inhumanity of the slave trade?

---

[5]Rawley, *The Transatlantic Slave Trade*, p. 429; Curtin, *Atlantic Slave Trade*, p. 268.
[6]Manning, *Slavery and African Life*, pp. 37, 170–171.

DOCUMENT

Olaudah Equiano Recalls His Experience at the Slave Market in Barbados

Olaudah Equiano composed one of the most popular and influential slave narratives of the late eighteenth and early nineteenth centuries. He had led a remarkable life. Born in West Africa in what is today Nigeria, he spent his early life among the Ibo. He was captured, sold into slavery, and made the dreaded Atlantic crossing. In the passage that follows, he recounts his arrival in Barbados and the experience of cultural disorientation, sale into slavery, and seeing Africans separated from their families. Equiano's life did not end in slavery, the most destructive aspects of which he also described in vivid detail. He achieved his freedom and then led an adventuresome life on various commercial and military ships plying the Caribbean, the Atlantic, and the Mediterranean. He also made a trip to the Arctic Ocean. Equiano's account consequently describes not only the life of a person taken from Africa and sold into American slavery but also the life of a person who, once free, explored the entire transatlantic world. His autobiographical narrative, which first appeared in 1789 and displayed Equiano's wide reading, served two purposes for the antislavery campaign that commenced in the second half of the eighteenth century. First, it provided a firsthand report of the slave experience in crossing from Africa to America. Second, his powerful rhetoric and clear arguments demonstrated that, if free, Africans could achieve real personal independence. Many defenders of slavery had denied that Africans possessed the character and intelligence to be free persons.

- **What** were the fears of the Africans on the slave ship as they approached the port? How were older slaves in Barbados used to calm their fears? How did the sale of slaves proceed? What happened to African families in the process of the sale?

At last, we came in sight... of Barbados,... and we soon anchored... off Bridgetown. Many merchants and planters now came on board.... They put us in separate parcels, and examined us attentively. They also made us jump, and

Job ben Solomon. Captured by Mandingo enemies and sold to a Maryland tobacco planter, Job ben Solomon accomplished the nearly impossible feat of returning to Africa as a freeman. By demonstrating his talents as a Muslim scholar, including his ability to write the entire Qur'an from memory, he astonished his owners and eventually convinced them to let him go home.

The New York Public Library. Art Resource, N.Y.

What was a more typical fate for a slave in the Americas?

CONSEQUENCES OF THE SLAVE TRADE FOR AFRICA

These statistics hint at the massive impact slave trading had on African life and history. The question of specific effects remains difficult.

We cannot be certain whether the transatlantic trade brought net population loss or gain to specific areas of West Africa. The wide and rapid spread of maize and cassava cultivation after these plants had been imported from the Americas may have fueled African population increases that offset losses through slaving. We know, however, that slaving took away many of the strongest young men in various areas and, in the Oriental trade zones, most of the young women.

Similarly, we do not know if more slaves were captured as by-products of local wars or from targeted slave raiding, but we do know they were captured and removed from their societies. Nor do we know if slaving always inhibited development of trade or perhaps sometimes stimulated it because commerce in a range of African products—from ivory to wood and hides—often accompanied that in slaves. We do know that the exchange of productive human beings for money or goods that were generally not used to build a productive economy was a great loss for African society as a whole.

Finally, because we do not yet have accurate estimates of the total population of Africa at different times over the four centuries of the transatlantic slave trade, we cannot determine with certainty its demographic impact. We can, however, make some educated guesses. If, for example, tropical Africa had possibly 50 million inhabitants in 1600, it would then have had 30 percent of the combined population of the Americas, the Middle East, Europe, and North Africa. If in 1900, after the depredations of the slave trade, it had 70 million inhabitants, its population would have dropped to only slightly more than 10 percent of the combined population of the same world regions. Accordingly, current best estimates indicate that overall African population growth suffered significantly as a result of the devastating numbers of people lost to enslavement or to the increased warfare and decreased birthrate tied to the slave trade. Figures like these also give some idea pointed to the land, signifying we were to go there. We thought by this we should be eaten by these ugly men, as they appeared to us; and when, soon after we were all put down under the deck again, there was much dread and trembling among us, and nothing but bitter cries to be heard all the night from these apprehensions, insomuch that at last the white people got some old slaves from the land to pacify us. They told us we were not to be eaten, but to work, and were soon to go on land, where we should see many of our country people. This report eased us much.... . We were conducted immediately to the merchant's yard, where we were all pent up together like so many sheep in a fold, without regard to sex or age. As every object was new to me, everything filled me with surprise... and indeed I thought these people were full of nothing but magical arts.... . We were not many days in the merchant's custody before we were sold after their usual manner which was this: On a signal given (as the beat of a drum), the buyers rush at once into the yard where the slaves are confined, and make choice of that par-

cel they like best. The noise and clamour with which this is attended, and the eagerness visible in the countenances of the buyers, serve not a little to increase the apprehension of the terrified Africans, who may well be supposed to consider them as the ministers of that destruction to which they think themselves devoted. In this manner, without scruple, relations and friends separate, most of them never to see each other again. I remember in the vessel in which I was brought over, in the men's apartment, there were several brothers who, in the sale, were sold in different lots; and it was very moving on this occasion to see and hear their cries at parting.... . Surely this is a new refinement in cruelty, which, while it has no advantage to atone for it, thus aggravates distress, and adds fresh horrors even to the wretchedness of slavery.

Source: *The Interesting Narrative of the Life of Olaudah Equiano or Gustavus Vassa, The African, Written by Himself* (first published 1789), as quoted in Henry Louis Gates Jr. and William L. Andrews, eds., *Pioneers of the Black Atlantic: Five Slave Narratives from the Enlightenment, 1772–1815* (Washington, DC: Counterpoint, 1998),

of slavery's probable impact on Africa's ability to engage with developments that, elsewhere in the world, led to the emergence of the modern industrializing world.[7]

It is important to remember that even in West and Central Africa, which bore the brunt of the transatlantic trade, its impact and the response to it were varied. In a few cases, kingdoms such as Dahomey (the present Republic of Benin) seem to have sought and derived immense economic profit by making slaving a state monopoly. Other kingdoms, such as Benin, sought to stay almost completely out of slaving. In instances including the rise of Asante power or the fall of the Yoruba Oyo Empire, it appears that increased slaving was a result as well as a cause of regional instability and change. Increased warfare meant increased prisoners to be enslaved and a surplus to be sold off. Whether slaving was a motive for war is still an unanswered question.

Similarly, the consequences of the major increase in indigenous slavery are unknown, and they varied with the specifics of regional situations. For example, in West Africa relatively more men were taken as slaves than women, whereas in the Sahelian Sudanic regions relatively more women than men were taken. In the west the loss of so many men increased the pressures for polygamy, whereas in the Sahelian Sudanic regions the loss of women may have stimulated polyandry and reduced the birthrate significantly.

Even though slavery existed previously in Africa, the scale of the transatlantic trade was unprecedented and, hence, had an unprecedented impact on indigenous social, political, and economic realities. The slave trade measurably changed patterns of life and balances of power, whether by stimulating trade or warfare, by disrupting previous market and political structures, by substantially increasing slavery inside Africa, or by disturbing the male-female ratio and, consequently, the workforce balance and birthrate patterns. The overseas slave trade siphoned indigenous energy into ultimately counterproductive or destructive directions. True economic development was inhibited, especially in central and coastal West Africa. The transatlantic slave trade must by any standard be described as one of the most tragic aspects of European involvement in Africa.

QUICK REVIEW

Difficulties in Determining Consequences of the Slave Trade

- Do not know how the slave trade affected specific West African regions
- Cannot determine number of slaves captured during wars and captured during slave raiding
- Do not know how slave trading affected commerce in African products

---

[7]On all of the preceding points regarding probable impact of the trade, see Manning, *Slavery and African Life*, pp. 126–148, 168–176. Also consult Eltis et al., *The Trans-Atlantic Slave Trade: A Database on CD-ROM*.

SUMMARY

WHAT WERE the four periods of European contact with the world?

Periods of European Overseas Expansion. Europe's disproportionate influence on world history has gone through four phases: conquest and commercial exploitation (roughly 1500–1700); trade rivalry, especially among Spain, France, and Great Britain (roughly 1700–1820); European colonization in Africa and Asia (nineteenth century and first half of twentieth century); and decolonization (mid-twentieth century). *page 434*

WHAT WAS mercantilism?

Mercantilist Theory of Economic Exploitation. Early European empires were based on mercantilism, the idea that the nation could be enriched by controlling trade with colonial markets. *page 435*

WHAT ROLES did the Roman Catholic Church play in Spanish America?

Establishment of the Spanish Empire in America. Within half a century of the landing of Columbus, millions of America's native peoples had encountered Europeans intent on conquest, exploitation, and religious conversion. Because of their advanced weapons, navies, and the new diseases they brought with them, as well as internal divisions among the Native Americans, the Europeans achieved a rapid conquest. The Roman Catholic Church was generally aligned with the conquerers, but some priests became advocates for Native Americans. *page 436*

HOW DID Spaniards attempt to control labor in the Americas?

Economies of Exploitation in the Spanish Empire. In Spanish America, various institutions were developed to extract native labor. The *flota*, controlled by administrators in Seville, sought to monopolize trade. *page 438*

HOW WERE sugar and slavery entwined in colonial Brazil?

Colonial Brazil. Brazil was Portugal's largest American holding. The Brazilian economy was dominated by sugarcane, which depended on African slave labor. *page 439*

HOW WERE the economies of the French and British North American colonies integrated into the transatlantic economy?

French and British Colonies in North America. Early French colonists were few in number. They were more interested in commerce (especially transatlantic fur-trading) and Christianity than settlement, so their relationships with Native Americans were relatively nonconfrontational. English colonists were mostly agriculturalists who had varied and complicated interactions with Native American populations. The economies of North America's port cities were intertwined with the transatlantic slave trade. *page 441*

WHAT WAS the "Columbian Exchange"?

The Columbian Exchange: Disease, Animals, and Agriculture. Until the European explorations, the civilizations of the Americas, Eurasia, and Africa had had no significant contact with each other. Native Americans had no immunity to several significant European diseases, so many died. Exchanges of plants and animals transformed agriculture in the Americas, Europe, and Africa. *page 442*

WHY WAS the transatlantic slave trade so economically important?

Slavery in the Americas. From the Mid-Atlantic English colonies through the Caribbean and into Brazil, slave-labor plantation systems were established. The economies and peoples of Europe, Africa, and the Americas were thus drawn into a vast worldwide web of production based on slave labor. The United States received slightly more than a quarter as many slaves as did Brazil alone or the British and French Caribbean regions together, yet the forced migration of Africans as slaves into the United States had profound consequences. *page 444*

HOW DID the slave trade impact Africa?

Africa and the Transatlantic Slave Trade. On the African continent, the impact of the slave trade was immense, though difficult to document specifically. The social, economic, and personal effects were enormous, given the extent and duration of the trade. The loss of population and productive resources helped set the stage for European colonization. The Atlantic slave trade's impact continues to be felt at both ends of the original "trade." *page 448*

REVIEW QUESTIONS

1. How were small groups of Spaniards able to conquer the Aztec and Inca Empires?

2. What was the basis of the mercantilist theory of economics? What was the relationship between the colonial economies and those of the homelands?

3. What was the relationship between conquistadores and missionaries in Spain's American colonies?

4. Describe the economies of Spanish America and Brazil. What were the similarities and differences between them and the British and French colonies in the Caribbean and North America? What role did the various colonies play in the transatlantic economy?

5. Why do we think of the plantation economy as a global, rather than regional, system of production? Why was it the "engine" of Atlantic basin trade?

6. Explain the chief factors involved in the Columbian Exchange. Which animals from Europe flourished in the Americas? Why? Which American plants had broad impact in Europe and elsewhere in the world?

7. Why did forced labor and slavery develop in the Americas? How was slavery in the Americas different from slavery in earlier societies?

8. What historical patterns emerged in the slave trade(s) within and out of Africa? Consider the gender and age distribution of slaves, their places of origin, and their destinations.

9. Compare and contrast the Oriental and Occidental slave trades. What was the effect of the transatlantic slave trade on West African societies? On East Africa? What role did Africans themselves play in the slave trade?

KEY TERMS

Black Legend (p. 437)
Columbian Exchange (p. 442)
conquistadores (kon-KEES-tuh-DOR-ays) (p. 438)
debt peonage (p. 439)
encomienda (EN-koh-MYEN-dah) (p. 438)
hacienda (HAH-see-EN-dah) (p. 438)

mercantilism (MUR-kuhn-tihl-izm) (p. 436)
Middle Passage (p. 450)
"Occidental" slave trade (p. 448)
peninsulares (p. 438)
plantation economy (p. 447)
repartimiento (ray-PAHR-tih-MYEN-toh) (p. 438)

Note: To learn more about the topics in this chapter, please turn to the Suggested Readings at the end of the book.

INTERPRETING THE PAST

Seeing Both Sides of Slavery: African Americans in the New World

Sources from MyHistoryLab for Chapter 18

myhistorylab

1) Bryan Edwards, excerpts from *Observations on the Maroon Negroes on Jamaica*

2) Olaudah Equiano, excerpt from *The Interesting Narrative*

3) Phillis Wheatley, *To the Right Honorable William, Earl of Dartmouth*

4) Five African Spirituals

5) Willem Bosman describes the slave trade

Visual Sources from MyHistoryLab

1) Advertisement for a slave auction

2) The slave ship *Brookes*

These primary source documents and images offer different perspectives on slavery during the height of the transatlantic slave trade. Three of the documents are authored by Africans or African Americans, and two are written by Europeans who participated in the slave trade. Together, these accounts tell a complex tale of resistance, accommodation, and exploitation.

Common to the works of Equiano and Wheatley is the theme of self-improvement, a virtue that came to define America's self-image. The five spirituals, like the chronicle of Bryan Edwards's experience in Jamaica, detail both overt and covert resistance to slavery. Finally, Captain Willem Bosman's description of the slave trade contrasts with Equiano's account.

Using these source documents and images, consider how Africans resisted a seemingly inexorable system and evaluate the perspectives of European participants in the transatlantic slave trade.

Questions

How did African culture survive in the Americas? How did African customs and traditions help Africans in the New World?

Both Equiano and Wheatley were pioneering and popular black writers. Equiano was a committed abolitionist: Wheatley expressed herself mostly in elegant poetry. In her poem addressed to the Earl of Dartmouth, Wheatley pleads with the Secretary to the North American colonies to support increased liberty. How does she invoke her African heritage and the experience of slavery?

What are the attitudes of the two white writers toward the Africans they encounter? Are there signs of accommodation with Africans who have gained a measure of power in the Americas?

19

East Asia in the Late Traditional Era

Seventeenth-Century Screen Painting of a Shintō River Festival in Tsushima (a town near Nagoya city) held annually in July to ward off epidemics in the heat of the summer. Among the throng of spectators at the river's edge are shopkeepers, other townspeople, Buddhist priests, and palanquin bearers (at the left). Of the five boats on the river (which are not shown), each with 550 lanterns, only one mast with five red lanterns can be seen at the center of the panel.

Tosa (attributed to): people along the river. Detail from screen representing the River Festival. 17th century. Painting on paper. Photo: Arnaudet. Musee des Arts Asiatiques-Guimet, Paris, France. Reunion des Musees Nationaux/Art Resource, NY.

What overall impression of Japanese society is conveyed by this painting?

LATE IMPERIAL CHINA

MING (1368–1644) AND QING (1644–1911) DYNASTIES *page 459*

WHERE DID China expand under the Qing?

JAPAN

WARRING STATES ERA (1467–1600) *page 466*

WHAT IMPACT did military technology have on Japanese society in this period?

TOKUGAWA ERA (1600–1868) *page 468*

HOW WAS Japanese culture transformed during the Tokugawa era?

KOREA AND VIETNAM

KOREA *page 476*

WHAT WAS Korea's relationship to China?

VIETNAM *page 478*

HOW DID Vietnam expand southward during this time?

GLOBAL PERSPECTIVE

East Asia in the Late Traditional Era

Why did the West, and not East Asia or anywhere else, open the door to modernity? Why did an industrial revolution not develop within the sophisticated commercial economies of Japan and China? The answer, obviously, must be found within Western history. Still, a few comparisons with the West may illuminate aspects of premodern East Asia.

1. The sociologist Max Weber saw Western capitalism as inspired by the Protestant ethic—which he found lacking in India, China, and Catholic Europe. But is the East Asian family-centered ethic of frugality, savings, and hard work not a "Protestant ethic" of sorts? And if a deeper Calvinist anxiety about salvation is required, as Weber stated, then why has East Asia achieved such explosive growth since World War II?

2. Was the scientific revolution of the seventeenth century critical to the industrial revolution? Some historians say that revolution was well under way before science made a substantial contribution.

3. The self-educated technicians of England who invented the water loom and steam engine reaped enormous honors and rewards. In China and Japan no patents protected inventors and no economists wrote of inventors as the benefactors of society. Wealth and honors were reserved for officials and gentry, who were literary and political in orientation and despised those who worked with their hands. (Of course, in earlier dynasties, Chinese had been brilliantly inventive without patent protection.)

4. Bureaucracy is sometimes viewed as a key component of modernity. Bureaucracy does for administration what the assembly line does for production: It breaks complex tasks into simple ones to achieve huge gains in efficiency. In the West bureaucracies appeared only in recent centuries. They strengthened monarchies and nation-states against landed aristocrats; they represented the triumph of ability over hereditary privilege. Chinese bureaucrats shared many of the same virtues. They were an elite of talent educated in the Confucian classics, as British officials were educated in those of Greece and Rome. But they were somehow different. They had wielded power for at least a millennium and were a segment of the landed

---

This chapter underlines the dynamism of China and Japan during the centuries between the "medieval" and the "modern" eras. China, Japan, Korea, and Vietnam—or at least their elites—shared a range of social values largely based on Confucianism. The similarity may have been greatest in the mid-nineteenth century, when Japan, Korea, and Vietnam had become more Confucian than ever before.

But when we compare their histories and institutions, the similarities diminish. China and Japan were furthest apart. Korea and Vietnam, even while forging an identity in reaction to China, were more directly influenced by China. Tang-dynasty Chinese (618–907) had forged a pattern of government so efficient and closely geared to the deeper familial and educational constitution of the society that it was rebuilt after each dynastic breakdown. The histories of the Ming (1368–1644) and the Qing (1644–1911) dynasties have a recognizable cyclical cast, though they also demonstrate historical trends that cut across dynastic lines. Japanese political history, in contrast, is not cyclical. Like Europe, Japan never found a pattern of rule that worked so well and was so deeply embedded in the institutions of the society that it was recreated over and over again.

In both China and Japan, society became more integrated and the apparatus of government more sophisticated. These advances shaped responses to the West during the nineteenth century. ■

gentry class in a country from which hereditary aristocrats had long since disappeared. Despite their talent, in the nineteenth century they would constitute a major obstacle to modernity.

Putting aside comparisons with Europe, we also note the difference between Chinese and Japanese attitudes toward outside civilizations. When the Jesuits tried to introduce science, the Chinese response was occasional curiosity and general indifference. A few Jesuits were appointed as interpreters or court astronomers or were used to cast cannons for China's armies. The Chinese lack of interest in foreign cultures can be explained by the coherence of China's core institutions: the emperor, bureaucracy, examination system, Confucian schools, and gentry. These were so deeply rooted and highly appreciated as to constitute a closed system. In contrast, despite a national policy of seclusion, the Japanese reached out for Dutch medicine and science—as they had earlier reached out for Chinese Neo-Confucianism. In the middle of the nineteenth century, this greater openness helps explain their rapid advance.

That Vietnam and Korea did not achieve industrial revolutions requires less explanation. They were smaller and less commercially developed than China or Japan. Vietnam was preoccupied with wars and its expansion to the south. In Korea, sometimes called the "hermit kingdom," the elites were open only to Chinese culture and engaged in endless factional struggles.

Focus Questions

◆ What features of Japan or China, other than those mentioned above, bear on their lack of progress from commerce to industry? Are there still other factors treated in the chapters on Europe that are also relevant?

◆ Why was Tokugawa Japan more open to Western learning that Qing China? Was population a plus, a minus, or a factor that did not matter?

LATE IMPERIAL CHINA

MING (1368–1644) AND QING (1644–1911) DYNASTIES

The Ming and the Qing were China's last dynasties. The former was Chinese, whereas the latter was a foreign dynasty (Manchus) established by conquest. The two were nevertheless remarkably similar in their institutions and pattern of rule.

WHERE DID China expand under the Qing?

LAND AND PEOPLE

China's population reached about 410 million people in the mid-nineteenth century, from a level of 60 to 90 million at the start of the Ming dynasty (1368). This population density stimulated commerce and gave new prominence to the scholar-gentry. Population growth was paralleled by an increase in the food supply.

There are many unanswered questions regarding the population growth during these centuries. Was there a decline in the death rate? Or did the development of new lands and technology enable more mouths to be fed? Certainly, the Ming–Qing era was the longest continuous period of good government in Chinese history. But by the early nineteenth century, the Chinese standard of living may have begun to decline. An ever-increasing population was no blessing.

Fisherman on an Autumn River, a Ming dynasty scroll painting by Dai Qin (1390–1460).

Tai Chin, "Fisherman on an Autumn River," (1390–1460). Painting Ink and color on paper 18 1/8 x 291 1/4 in. (46 x 740 cm). Courtesy of Freer Gallery of Art, Smithsonian Institution, Washington, D.C.

What activities do you see in this image?

CHINA'S THIRD COMMERCIAL REVOLUTION

Commerce in China expanded and contracted cyclically. Early Ming emperors were isolationists with an agrarian orientation. They established government monopolies that stifled enterprise and depressed the southeastern coastal region by restricting maritime trade and shipping. In the mid-sixteenth century, commerce started to grow again, buoyed by the surge of population and agriculture and a relaxation of government controls. If the growth during the Han and Song dynasties may be called China's first and second commercial revolutions, then the expansion between 1500 and 1800 was its third. By the early nineteenth century, China was the most highly commercialized nonindustrial society in the world.

One stimulus to commerce was imported silver. The Chinese balance of trade was favorable. Beginning in the mid-sixteenth century, silver from Japan entered China, and from the 1570s, Spanish galleons brought in Mexican and Peruvian silver. In the eighteenth century, private **Shanxi banks** opened branches throughout China to facilitate the transfer of funds and extend credit for trade. As in Europe, the influx of silver and the overall increase in liquidity led to inflation and commercial growth in China.

Shanxi banks Private financial institutions specializing in long-distance funds transfers for business and trade; they appeared first in Shanxi province.

Urban growth between 1500 and 1800 was mainly at the level of market towns, which provided the link between the local markets and the larger provincial capitals and cities. Interregional trade also gained, but China did not develop a national economy. Seven or eight regional economies, each the size of a large European nation, were the focus for most economic activity. But a new level of trade developed among them, especially where water transport made such trade economical.

The Confucian family ideal changed little. A woman was expected to obey her parents, then her husband, and finally her son. Physically, women were more restricted as footbinding spread through the upper classes and to some commoners (see Figure 19–1). One exception to the rule was the Manchus. One Manchu (Qing) emperor issued an edict banning footbinding, but it was ignored.

As population grew and the size of the average landholding shrank, more women worked at home, making products for commercial markets. And as their contribution to the household income grew, their voice in household decisions often became larger than Confucian doctrines would suggest.

QUICK REVIEW

Women Under Qing and Ming

- Confucian family ideals changed little during the Ming and Qing eras
- Footbinding spread among the upper classes and some commoners
- As population grew, more women worked at home

POLITICAL SYSTEM

Despite these massive demographic and economic changes, political structures in China changed little. Government during the Ming and Qing was much like that of the Song or Yuan, only stronger. Sources of strength included the spread of education, the use of

Confucianism as an ideology, stronger emperors, better government finances, more competent officials, and a larger gentry class with an expanded role in local society.

Confucian teachings were more widespread than ever before. There were more schools in villages and towns. Academies preparing candidates for the civil service examinations multiplied. Publishing flourished, and literacy outpaced population growth. The Confucian view of society was patriarchal. The family, headed by the father, was the basic unit. The emperor, the son of heaven and the ruler-father of the empire, stood at its apex. In between were the district magistrates, the "father-mother officials." The idea of the state as the family writ large was not just a matter of metaphor but also carried with it duties and obligations at every level.

In comparison to Europe, where religious philosophies were less involved with the state and where a revolution in science was reshaping religious and political doctrines, Neo-Confucian metaphysics gave China greater unity and a more integrated worldview.

Ming–Qing emperors made all important decisions. They wielded despotic powers at their courts. They had secret police and prisons where those who committed even minor offenses might be tortured. The dedication and loyalty even of officials who were cruelly mistreated attest to the depth of their Confucian ethical training. During the Qing the life-and-death authority of emperors did not diminish, but officials were generally better treated. As foreign rulers, the Manchu emperors took care not to alienate Chinese officials.

The Forbidden Palace in Beijing was an icon of the emperor's majesty. The entire palace complex focused on the ruler. Its massive walls and vast courtyards progressed to the audience hall where the emperor sat on an elevated dais above the officials, who knelt before him. Behind the audience hall were the emperor's private chambers and his harem. By the seventeenth century, there were nine thousand palace ladies and perhaps as many as seventy thousand eunuchs.

Government was better financed than during earlier dynasties. As late as the 1580s, huge surpluses were accumulated at both the central and the provincial levels. Only during the last fifty years of the Ming did soaring military expenses bankrupt the government. When, in the second half of the seventeenth century, the Manchus reestablished a strong central government, they restored the flow of taxes to levels close to those of the Ming.

The good government of the Ming–Qing system in China was largely a product of the ethical commitment and ability of its officials. No officials in the world today approach in power or prestige those of the Ming and the Qing. When the Portuguese arrived early in the sixteenth century, they called these officials "mandarins." The rewards of an official career were so great that the competition to enter it became ever fiercer. After being screened at the district office, a candidate took the county examination. If he passed, he became a member of the gentry and was exempted from state labor service. This examination required years of study. About half a million passed each year. The second hurdle was the provincial examination held every third year. Only one in a hundred was successful. The final hurdle was the metropolitan examination, passed by fewer than ninety each year.

The **gentry** class was an intermediate layer between the elite bureaucracy above and the village below. The Chinese gentry was largely urban, living in market towns or district seats. Socially and educationally, its members were of the same class as the bureaucracy's district magistrates—a world apart from clerks, runners, or village headmen. As absentee landlords whose lands were worked by sharecroppers,

FIGURE 19–1. A Bound Foot. This diagram shows the twisted and cramped bone structure of a bound ("lily") foot, as compared with that of a normal foot. Bound tightly with cloth from the age of five, a little girl's foot grew painfully into this deformed but erotically admired shape.

From *East Asia, The Great Tradition*, E.O. Reischauer, J.K. Fairbank, Houghton Mifflin, 1960.

What were the roles of women in late imperial China?

gentry In China, a largely urban, landowning class that represented local interests and functioned as quasi-bureaucrats under the magistrates.

Examination Stalls. The dilapidated remains of the examination stalls at Nanjing. Doors to individual cubicles can be seen to the right and left of the three-story gate. Thousands of such cubicles made up the old examination stalls. Those who passed the exams governed China.

Corbis-Bettmann.

Why was the examination system so central to Chinese government?

they were often exploitative, but they were also local leaders, representing community interests to the bureaucracy. They performed quasi-official functions on behalf of their communities: maintaining schools and Confucian temples; repairing roads, bridges, canals, and dikes; and writing local histories. The gentry class was the local upholder of Confucian values.

The collapse of the Ming dynasty in 1644 and the establishment of Manchu rule was less of a break than might be imagined. First, the transition was short. Second, the Manchus, unlike the Mongols, were already partially Sinicized. Even before entering China, they had ruled over the Chinese settled in Manchuria.

In the late sixteenth century an able leader unified the Manchurian tribes and proclaimed a new dynasty, establishing a Confucian government with Chinese institutions. When the Ming collapsed and rebel forces took over China, the Manchus presented themselves as the conservative upholders of the Confucian order. The Chinese gentry preferred the Manchus to Chinese rebel leaders. Most Chinese scholars and officials served the new dynasty. The Qing as a Chinese dynasty dates from 1644, when the capital was moved to Beijing.

As a tiny minority, the Manchus adopted institutions to maintain themselves as an elite group. One was their military organization. Manchu garrison forces were segregated and not put under the jurisdiction of Chinese officials. They were given stipends and lands to cultivate. They were forbidden to marry Chinese, their children had to study Manchu, and they were not permitted to bind the feet of their daughters. In 1668, northern and central Manchuria was cordoned off by a willow palisade to keep Chinese immigrants out.

The second institutional feature was the appointment of one Chinese and one Manchu to each key post in the central government. At the provincial level, Chinese governors were overseen by Manchu governor-generals. Most officials and all district magistrates beneath the governors were Chinese.

CHRONOLOGY

LATE IMPERIAL CHINA

Ming Dynasty 1368–1644

1368–1398	Reign of first Ming emperor; Chinese armies invade Manchuria, Mongolia, and eastern Central Asia
1402–1424	Reign of third Ming emperor; Chinese armies invade Vietnam and Mongolia
1405–1433	Voyages of Zheng He to India and Africa
1592–1598	Chinese army battles Japanese army in Korea

Qing (Manchu) Dynasty 1644–1911

1661–1722	Reign of Kangxi
1668	Manchuria closed to Chinese immigrants (by willow palisade)
1681	Suppression of revolts by Chinese generals
1683	Taiwan captured
1689	China and Russia sign Treaty of Nerchinsk
1736–1795	Reign of Qianlong
1793	Macartney mission

An important strength of the Manchu dynasty was the long reigns of two extremely able emperors, Kangxi (1661–1722) and Qianlong (1736–1795). Kangxi was a model emperor. A man of great vigor, he rose at dawn to read official documents before meeting with officials. He presided over palace examinations. Well versed in the Confucian classics, he won the support of scholars. Kangxi studied European science with Jesuit court astronomers; he opened four ports to foreign trade; he carried out public works; and he made six tours of China's southern provinces.

Qianlong, Kangxi's grandson, began his reign in 1736. Under his rule the Qing dynasty attained its highest level of prosperity and power. But in his last years Qianlong permitted a court favorite to practice corruption on an almost unprecedented scale. In 1796, the White Lotus Rebellion broke out. Qianlong's successor put down the rebellion, but the ample financial reserves that had existed throughout the eighteenth century were never reestablished. China nevertheless entered the nineteenth century with its government intact and with a peaceful and stable society.

MING–QING FOREIGN RELATIONS

By the time the first Ming emperor (r. 1368–1398) died, China controlled the northern steppe and had recovered jurisdiction over the southern tier of Chinese provinces (see Map 19–1). During the reign of the third Ming emperor (1402–1424), northern Vietnam became a Chinese province and remained so for two decades.

The Ming emperors "managed" China's frontiers using a tribute system. Ambassadors of vassal kings acted out their subordination to the universal ruler of

Emperor Qianlong. The great Manchu emperor Qianlong (r. 1736–1795).

Unidentified Artist. © Metropolitan Museum of Art, Rogers Fund, 1942.

What image of the Emperor is conveyed by this portrait?

MAP 19–1 The Ming Empire and the Voyages of Zheng He. The inset map shows the voyages of Zheng He to Southeast Asia and India. Some ships of his fleet even reached East Africa. (Zheng himself did not.)

What was the purpose of Zheng He's voyages?

Giraffe with Attendant. Some emperors had private zoos and gladly received exotic animals as gifts from tribute states. A painting by Shen Du (1357–1438).

1977-42-1. Tu, Shen. "The Tribute Giraffe with Attendant." *Philadelphia Museum of Art*: Gift of John T. Dorrance, 1977.

Besides keeping exotic animals, what were some other ways Chinese emperors made their power visible?

the celestial kingdom by approaching the emperor, performing the kowtow (kneeling three times and each time bowing his head to the floor three times), and presenting gifts. In return, the vassal kings were sent seals confirming their status, given permission to use the Chinese calendar and year-period names, and appointed to the Ming nobility.

The most far-ranging ventures of the third Ming emperor were the maritime expeditions that sailed to Southeast Asia, India, the Arabian Gulf, and East Africa between 1405 and 1433. They were commanded by the eunuch Zheng He, a Muslim from Yunnan (see Map 19–1). The first of these armadas had sixty-two major ships and carried twenty-eight thousand sailors, soldiers, and merchants. The expeditions were intended to make China's glory known to distant kingdoms and to enroll them in the tribute system. They ended abruptly: They were costly and offered little return at a time when the dynasty was fighting in Mongolia and building Beijing. What was remarkable about these expeditions was not that they came half a century earlier than the Portuguese voyages of discovery, but that China had the necessary maritime technology and yet decided not to use it. China lacked the combination of restlessness, greed, religious faith, and curiosity that would motivate the Portuguese.

The chief threat to the Ming dynasty was the Mongols. In the 1430s, they captured the emperor, and in 1550 they overran Beijing. They were defeated by a Chinese army in the 1560s and signed a peace treaty in 1571.

A second threat came from Japan, whose pirates raided the Chinese coast in the fifteenth and sixteenth centuries. After Hideyoshi unified Japan, he twice invaded and occupied Korea in 1592 and between 1597 and 1598. China sent troops, and the Japanese withdrew after the death of Hideyoshi. But the strain on Ming finances weakened the dynasty.

The final foreign threat to the Ming was the Manchus. After coming to power in 1644, the Manchu court spent decades consolidating its rule within China. The emperor Kangxi took Taiwan in 1683, making it part of China for the first time.

As always, the principal foreign threats to Qing China came from the north and northwest. By the 1660s, Russian traders, trappers, and adventurers had reached northern Manchuria, where they built forts and traded with the eastern Mongols. During the 1680s, Kangxi drove the Russians from the lower Amur River. This victory during the early years of the reign of Peter the Great (1682–1725) led to the 1689 Treaty of Nerchinsk, which excluded Russia from northern Manchuria while permitting its caravans to visit Beijing.

In the west there was a complex, three-corner relationship among Russia, the western Mongols, and Tibet. Kangxi, and then Qianlong, campaigned against the Mongols, invaded Tibet, and in 1727 signed a new treaty with Russia. During the campaigns, the Chinese temporarily came to control millions of square miles of new territories. Ever since, even after China's borders contracted, the Chinese have insisted that the Manchu conquests define their legitimate borders. The roots of the present-day border contentions, and the Chinese claim to Tibet, go back to these events during the eighteenth century.

Europeans had reached China during the Tang and the Yuan dynasties. But only with Europe's oceanic expansion in the sixteenth century did they arrive in large numbers. Some came as missionaries, of whom the most successful were the Jesuits. They studied Chinese and the Confucian classics and conversed with scholars. They used their knowledge of astronomy, geography, engraving, and firearms to win entry to the court at Beijing and appointments in the bureau of astronomy. When the Manchus came to power, the Jesuits kept their position. They tried to propagate Christianity, attacking Daoism and Buddhism, but arguing that Confucianism as a rational philosophy complemented Christianity. They interpreted the Confucian rites of ancestor worship as secular and compatible with Christianity. A few high court officials were converted. But the Jesuits' rivals, Franciscans and Dominicans, reported to Rome that the Jesuits condoned Confucian rites. Papal bulls in 1715 and 1742 forbade Chinese Christians to participate in ancestor worship, and the emperor banned Christianity in China.

Other Europeans came to China to trade. The Portuguese came first in the early sixteenth century but behaved badly and were expelled. They returned in midcentury and were permitted to trade on a tiny peninsula at Macao that was walled off from China. They were followed by Dutch from the East Indies (Indonesia), by the British East India Company in 1699, and by Americans in 1784. By the early eighteenth century, Westerners could trade only at Canton. They could not bring their wives to China. They were subject to Chinese law and were controlled by official merchant guilds. Nevertheless, the trade was profitable to both sides.

The British East India Company developed a triangular commerce among China, India, and Britain. For China, this trade produced an influx of specie, and the Chinese officials in charge grew immensely wealthy. Chafing under the restrictions, in 1793 the British government sent negotiators. The emperor Qianlong permitted Lord Macartney (1736–1806) to present his gifts, which the Chinese described as tribute, but he turned down Macartney's requests. Western trade remained encapsulated at Canton.

Le Pere Adam Schaal.

Jesuit Missionary. A late seventeenth-century color engraving of the Jesuit missionary Johann Adam Schall depicts him in traditional Confucian dress holding a sextant and a compass. A globe is behind him on the left.

Why were the Manchus interested in Western science?

MING–QING CULTURE

Chinese culture had begun to turn inward during the Song dynasty in reaction to Buddhism. This tendency continued into the Ming and Qing, when Chinese culture became virtually impervious to outside influences. This reflected a tradition and a social order that had stood the test of time, but it also indicated a closed system of ideas.

Ming and Qing Chinese highly esteemed the traditional categories of high culture: painting, calligraphy, poetry, and philosophy. Porcelains of great beauty were also produced. The pottery industry of Europe began during the sixteenth century to imitate these wares, and Chinese and Japanese influences have dominated Western ceramics ever since.

Chinese today see the novel as the characteristic cultural achievement of the Ming and Qing. The novel in China grew out of plot-books used by earlier storytellers. Most novels were written in colloquial Chinese.

QUICK REVIEW

Chinese Contacts with the West

- Europeans arrived in China in large numbers after the sixteenth century
- The most successful missionaries were the Jesuits
- By the eighteenth century, Europeans could trade only at Canton

JAPAN

The two segments of "late traditional" Japan could not be more different. The Warring States era (1467–1600), the last phase of Japan's medieval history, saw internal wars and anarchy. Within a century all vestiges of the old estate system had been scrapped and virtually all the Ashikaga lords had been overthrown. The Tokugawa era (1600–1868) that followed saw Japan reunited under a highly competent government. Japanese culture was brilliantly transformed.

WHAT IMPACT did
military technology
have on Japanese
society in this period?

WARRING STATES ERA (1467–1600)

In 1467 a dispute arose over who would be the next Ashikaga shōgun. The dispute led to wars throughout Japan for eleven years. Most of Kyoto was destroyed in the fighting, and the authority of the Ashikaga bakufu came to an end. This first war ended in 1477, but the fighting resumed and continued for more than a century.

WAR OF ALL AGAINST ALL

daimyo   Meaning "great name," these men were the most powerful feudal leaders in Japan from the tenth to the nineteenth century.

Even before 1467, the Ashikaga equilibrium had been precarious. The regional **daimyo** lords had relied on their relationship to the bakufu to hold their stronger vassals in check, while relying on these vassals to preserve their independence against strong neighbors. The collapse of bakufu authority after 1467 left the regional lords standing alone, removing the last barrier to internecine wars. The regional lords became prey to the stronger among their vassals as well as to powerful neighboring states.

By the end of the sixteenth century, hundreds of little "Warring States daimyo" had emerged. The constant wars among these men were not unlike those of the early feudal era in Europe. The most efficient in revamping their domains for military ends survived. The less ruthless, who clung to old ways, were defeated and absorbed.

As fighting continued, local states gave way to regional states until the late sixteenth century, when all of Japan was brought under the hegemony of a single lord, Toyotomi Hideyoshi (1536–1598). But it was only with the victory of Tokugawa Ieyasu (1542–1616) at the Battle of Sekigahara in 1600 that true unification was finally achieved. Ieyasu radically transformed Japanese society.

FOOT SOLDIER REVOLUTION

During the Warring States period, the foot soldier replaced the aristocratic mounted warrior as the backbone of the military. Soldiers were still called samurai and were still vassals of a lord, but their numbers, social status, and techniques of warfare changed dramatically. All public lands and estates, including the emperor's, were seized and converted into fiefs, which were privately governed by the fief holder. A fief was not divided among heirs but passed intact to the ablest son.

Daimyo Castle.   Construction of the "White Heron" castle in Himeji was begun during the Warring States Era and was completed shortly after 1600. During the Tokugawa peace, it remained as a monument to the glory of the daimyo. Today it can be seen from the "bullet train."

How was central authority reasserted over the daimyo?

With larger revenues, Warring States daimyo built bigger armies. They recruited mainly from the peasantry. By the late sixteenth century hundreds of thousands of troops were deployed in major campaigns. In the mid-fourteenth century a new weapon was developed: a thrusting spear with a thick shaft and a heavy chisel-like blade. Held in both hands, it could penetrate medieval armor as a sword could not. It could also be swung about like a quarterstaff. It was used by soldiers positioned at intervals of three feet in a pincushion tactic to impale charging cavalry. The weapon spelled the end of the aristocratic warrior in Japan. Its use coincided with the recruitment of peasant soldiers, for it required only short training. A second change in military technology was the introduction of the musket by the Portuguese in the mid-sixteenth century. Warring States generals quickly adopted it. As individual combat gave way to mass armies, warfare became pitiless, cruel, and bloody.

The society that emerged from the Warring States period might, in some sense, be described as feudal. By the late sixteenth century, all warriors in Japan were part of a pyramid of vassals and lords headed by a single overlord, and warriors of rank held fiefs and vassals of their own. But in other respects, Japan was more like postfeudal Europe. First, most of the military class were soldiers, not aristocrats. Even though they were called samurai and were vassals, they were not given fiefs but were paid with stipends of rice. Second, in mid-sixteenth-century Japan the military may have reached 7 or 8 percent of the population, making it comparable in size to European mercenary armies of the fourteenth or sixteenth centuries. Third, the recruitment of village warriors caused problems. Taxes became harder to collect. Local samurai were often involved in uprisings that sometimes spread through whole provinces. Again, the parallels with postfeudal Europe seem closer. Fourth, even in a feudal society, not everything is feudal. Commercial growth continued in the Warring States Era.

FOREIGN RELATIONS AND TRADE

Japanese pirate-traders plied the seas of East Asia during the fifteenth and sixteenth centuries. To halt their depredations, the Ming emperor invited the third Ashikaga shōgun to trade with China. An agreement was reached in 1404. However, piracy stopped only after Japan was reunified at the close of the sixteenth century.

Early Japanese exports to China were raw materials, but by the sixteenth century, manufactured goods were rising in importance. In exchange, Japan received copper cash, porcelains, paintings, books, and medicines. After establishing his hegemony over Japan, Hideyoshi permitted only ships with his vermilion seal to trade with China, a policy the Tokugawa continued. Between 1604 and 1635 over 350 ships went to China in this "vermilion-seal trade." Then, in 1635, the policy of national seclusion ended Japan's foreign trade. No Japanese were permitted to leave Japan, and the construction of large ships was prohibited.

CHRONOLOGY	
WARRING STATES JAPAN AND THE ERA OF UNIFICATION (1467–1600)	
1467–1568	Battles throughout Japan
1543	Portuguese arrive in Japan
1588	Hideyoshi starts sword hunt
1590	Hideyoshi completes unification
1592, 1597–1598	Hideyoshi sends armies to Korea
1597	Hideyoshi bans Christianity
1598	Hideyoshi dies; his generals battle for succession
1600	Battle of Sekigahara; Tokugawa Ieyasu reunifies Japan

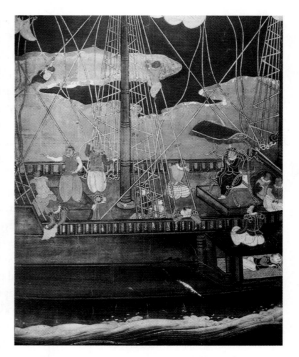

Arrival of the Portuguese in Japan.   Portuguese merchants arrived in Japan in 1543 from India and the East Indies. Their crews were multiethnic, and they brought Jesuit priests as well.

"Arrival of the Portuguese in Japan." Detail—central section of the boat, 1594–1618. Screen. Paint, gold, paper. Museo, Soares Dos Reis, Porto, Portugal. Bridgeman-Giraudon/Art Resource, N.Y.

How are the Portuguese depicted in this painting?

Overlapping Japan's maritime expansion in the seas of East Asia was the arrival of European ships. Portuguese pirate-traders arrived in Japan in 1543. Spanish galleons came in 1587, followed by the Dutch and the English after the turn of the century. The Portuguese became important as shippers, carrying Southeast Asian goods and Japanese silver to China and Chinese silk to Japan and using their profits to buy spices for the European market.

Traders brought with them Jesuit missionaries, who concentrated their efforts on the samurai. Christian converts numbered about three hundred thousand in 1600—a higher percentage of Japanese than are Christian today. It is difficult to explain why Christianity met with greater success in Japan than in other Asian lands. When introduced, it was seen as a new Buddhist sect. There seemed little difference to the Japanese between the cosmic Buddha of Shingon and the Christian God. The Japanese also noted the theological similarity between the pietism of the Pure Land sect and that of Christianity. The personal example of the Jesuits was also important.

The fortunes of Christianity began to decline in 1597, when six Spanish Franciscans and twenty Japanese converts were crucified in Nagasaki, apparently because a Spanish pilot had boasted that merchants and priests were preparing Japan for conquest. Sporadic persecutions continued until 1614, when Tokugawa Ieyasu formally banned the foreign religion. The last resistance was an uprising in 1637 to 1638 in which thirty-seven thousand Christians died. After that, Christianity survived in Japan only as a hidden religion.

TOKUGAWA ERA (1600–1868)

HOW WAS Japanese culture transformed during the Tokugawa era?

POLITICAL ENGINEERING AND ECONOMIC GROWTH DURING THE SEVENTEENTH CENTURY

After the unifications of 1590 and 1600, Japan's leaders sought to create a peaceful, stable, orderly society. By the middle or late seventeenth century, Japan's society and political system had been radically reengineered. Economic and demographic growth was vigorous. This combination of political and economic change made the seventeenth century a period of great dynamism.

In the summer of 1588, Hideyoshi ordered a "sword hunt" to disarm the peasants. Once the hunt was completed, the 5 percent of the population who were still equipped as samurai used their monopoly on weapons to control the other 95 percent.

Hideyoshi next froze the social classes. Samurai were prohibited from quitting the service of their lord. Peasants were barred from abandoning their fields to become townspeople. Samurai, farmers, and townspeople tended to marry within their respective classes, and each class developed a unique cultural character.

Hideyoshi ordered surveys to define each parcel of land by location, size, soil quality, product, and cultivator's name, laying the foundation for a systematic land tax. Domains and fiefs were henceforth ranked in terms of their assessed yield.

Hideyoshi assumed that his vassals would honor their oaths of loyalty to his heir, and he was especially trustful of his great ally Tokugawa Ieyasu. This trust, however, was misplaced. After his death in 1598, Hideyoshi's former vassals broke into two opposing camps. In 1600, they fought a great battle from which Ieyasu emerged victorious. Ieyasu established his headquarters in Edo (modern Tokyo), in the center of his military holdings in eastern Japan (see Map 19–2). He took the title of shōgun in 1603 and called his government the bakufu. Ieyasu then used his military power to reorganize Japan.

"Picture-Treading" Plaque. *Fumi-e,* or "picture-treading" plaques are bronze images representing Christ or the Virgin, used by the Tokugawa with increasing intensity from 1614 onward to extirpate the foreign religion. In the *fumi-e* ceremony suspected converts were obliged to tread on the plaques to show that they rejected Christianity.

Why was Christianity banned in Japan?

Edo Castle.   Edo first became a castle town in the mid-fifteenth century. Tokugawa Ieyasu made the castle his residence and headquarters in 1590 and, after his great victory in 1600, rebuilt and extended it. This early Edo period screen painting shows (upper right) the keep or inner citadel, which was not rebuilt after a fire in 1657. Korean envoys (bottom center) enter the castle grounds. They have brought tiger skins and other gifts. Onlookers gawk at their unfamiliar garb. Warriors (top, far right) practice archery. The inner castle compounds shown in the painting were only the central part of an elaborate system of moats, stone-block ramparts, and gates. In 1868, after the Meiji Restoration, Edo was renamed Tokyo (Eastern Capital) and became the residence of the emperor.

How does Edo castle symbolize the power of Tokugawa Ieyasu?

MAP 19–2   **Tokugawa Japan and the Korean Peninsula.**   The area between Edo and Osaka in central Honshu was both the political base of the Tokugawa bakufu and its rice basket. The domains that would overthrow the Tokugawa bakufu in the late nineteenth century were mostly in outlying areas of southwestern Japan.

What controls did the Tokugawa impose to restrain the daimyo?

Daimyo.   A daimyo seated in a palanquin carried by commoner porters. The screen at the side is rolled up so that he can observe the sights of Edo. Surrounding the palanquin are several dozen of his samurai retainers. In the right foreground are Edo townsmen.

What seems to be the relationship between the daimyo and other people depicted here?

Ieyasu's first move was to confiscate the lands of his defeated enemies and use them to reward his vassals and allies. During the first quarter of the seventeenth century, the bakufu confiscated the domains of 150 daimyo and transferred 229 daimyo from one domain to another. The transfers severed long-standing ties between daimyo and their disarmed former village retainers. When a daimyo was transferred to a new fief, he took his samurai retainers with him. The rearrangement created a defensive system, with the staunchest Tokugawa supporters nearest to the center of power.

The Tokugawa established other controls. Legal codes regulated the imperial court, the temples and shrines, and the daimyo. Military houses were enjoined to use men of ability and to practice frugality. Only with bakufu consent could daimyo marry or repair their castles. The Tokugawa also established a hostage system that required the wives and children of daimyo to reside permanently in Edo and the daimyo themselves to spend every second year in Edo. This transformed feudal lords into courtiers.

Another key control was the national policy of seclusion. Seclusion was no barrier to cultural imports from China and Korea. But except for small Chinese and Dutch trading contingents at Nagasaki, no foreigners were permitted to enter Japan, and on pain of death no Japanese were allowed to go abroad. Nor could oceangoing ships be built. This policy was strictly enforced until 1854. Seclusion enclosed the system of Tokugawa rule, cutting off outside political contacts.

The political dynamism of the period from Hideyoshi through the first century of Tokugawa rule was matched by economic growth. Resources no longer needed for war were allocated to land reclamation and agriculture. This doubled food production, which led to a doubling of population from about 12 million in 1600 to 24 million in 1700. The production of agricultural by-products, including cotton, silk, indigo, lumber, dyes, and *sake*, also grew.

Medieval guilds were abolished and Japan's central markets were freed from monopolistic restrictions. The result was a burgeoning of trade and the formation of a national market network. As this network expanded, economic functions became more differentiated and efficient.

The sharp decline in foreign trade caused by seclusion did not dampen Japan's domestic economy because of the tax system and consumption patterns. Tokugawa tax policy was based on land, not commerce. Taxes took about one third of the peasant's production. It was a heavier tax rate than that in neighboring China and bespeaks the effective grasp that the military class had on Japanese society. The 87 percent of the population who lived in the countryside paid almost one third of the country's agricultural wealth to the 5 percent in the military class. The remaining 8 percent of townspeople also lived off the tax flow by providing goods and services for samurai. This distribution of benefits was mirrored in the three-area city planning common to all castle towns: a large parklike area with castle, trees, stone

The Commercial District of Osaka, the "kitchen" of Tokugawa Japan. Warehouses bear the crests of their merchant houses. Ships (upper right) loaded with rice, cotton goods, *sake*, and other goods are about to depart for Edo (Tokyo). Their captains vied with one another to arrive first and get the best price.

How did commerce develop in the Tokugawa period?

walls, and moats for the daimyo and his government; an extensive samurai quarter; and a meaner townspeople's quarter. Just as the castle towns were the consumption centers of the regional tax economies, so was Edo the national consumption center and a super-castle town. It had the same three-area layout on a grander scale. By 1700 Edo had a population of about 1 million.

Economic growth and the national integration of the economy led to a richness and diversity in urban life. Townsmen governed their districts. Samurai city managers watched over the city as a whole. Official services were provided by schools, police, and firefighters. But there were also servants, restaurant owners, priests, sword sharpeners, instructors in the martial arts, prostitutes, and bathhouse attendants. In the popular arts, there were woodblock printers and artists, book publishers, puppeteers, acrobatic troupes, and **Kabuki** and **Nō** actors. Merchant establishments included money changers, pawnbrokers, peddlers, small shops, single-price retail establishments like the House of Mitsui, and great wholesale merchants.

EIGHTEENTH AND EARLY NINETEENTH CENTURIES

By the late seventeenth century, the political engineering of the Tokugawa state was complete. In the economy, too, dynamic growth gave way to slower growth within a high-level equilibrium. Yet changes of a different kind were under way.

The eighteenth century began with high drama. In 1701, a daimyo at Edo Castle drew his sword and wounded an official who had insulted him. It was a capital crime to unsheath a sword within the castle, and the daimyo was ordered to commit *harakiri* (that is, to disembowel himself), which he promptly did. This made his retainers *rōnin*, masterless samurai. Almost two years later, they avenged their master by beheading the official whose insult had cost them their daimyo. All forty-seven of them then obeyed an order to kill themselves. They were widely acclaimed for the purity of their sense of duty and their loyalty to their lord, but Tokugawa society held law to be the only basis of social order. The law forbade personal vendettas, and the law could not be trumped by ethical considerations.

Viewed historically, three points may be noted about the incident. First, in a similar situation the more practical samurai of the Warring States period would have forgotten their former lord and rushed to find a new one. But in the Tokugawa era, with the authority of the daimyo backed by that of the shōgun, there was no room for disloyalty. So loyalty became deeply internalized and was viewed almost as a religious obligation. Second, the incident tells something of the state in Tokugawa Japan. The 1615

Kabuki A realistic form of Japanese theater similar to English Elizabethan drama.

Nō A highly stylized form of Japanese theater performed on a simple stage.

QUICK REVIEW

The Japanese Economy

◆ Agricultural production doubled from 1600 to 1700

◆ Peace sustained economic growth

◆ Economic growth and national integration led to a rich and diverse urban society

Bridal Procession. The bridal procession of Yohime, the twenty-first daughter of the eleventh Tokugawa shōgun, approaches the Edo mansion of the Kaga daimyo. The red gate (upper right), built in 1827 for this occasion, is today an entrance to the main campus of Tokyo University. The eleventh shōgun had twenty-eight sons and twenty-seven daughters by his more than forty concubines. Of his children, thirteen sons and twelve daughters survived to maturity. This woodblock print by Kunisada is a "national treasure."

What does this image suggest about the relationship between society and government during the Tokugawa?

"Laws for the Military Houses" contains the passage: "Law is the basis of the social order. Reason may be violated in the name of law, but law may not be violated in the name of reason."[1] One Tokugawa law forbade private vendettas. So, despite the moral purity of their act, the forty-seven "virtuous warriors" had to die. Third, loyalty and idealism were not the monopoly of males. In the drama, at least, samurai wives and daughters displayed the same heroic spirit of self-sacrifice.

Most political history of late Tokugawa Japan is written in terms of alternating cycles of laxity and reform. Even during the mid-seventeenth century, the expenses of the bakufu and daimyo states were often greater than their income. Taxes were based on agriculture in an economy that was becoming commercial. It was simple mathematics: After the samurai were paid their stipends, not enough was left for the expenses of domain government and the costs of the Edo establishments. In part, it was the toll of extraordinary costs, such as a bakufu levy, the wedding of a daimyo's daughter, or the rebuilding of a castle after a fire. And, finally, it was a taste for luxury among daimyo and retainers of rank.

Over the years a familiar pattern emerged. To make ends meet, domains would borrow from merchants. Then, as finances became even more difficult, a reformist clique of officials would return the domain to a more frugal and austere way of life. But since no one likes to practice frugality forever, a new round of spending would begin. The bakufu carried out three great reforms on Tokugawa lands:

1716–1733	Tokugawa Yoshimune	17 years
1787–1793	Matsudaira Sadanobu	6 years
1841–1843	Mizuno Tadakuni	2 years

The first two reforms were long and successful; the third was not. Its failure set the stage for the ineffective response of the bakufu to the West in the mid-nineteenth century.

The balance between centralization and decentralization lasted until the end of the Tokugawa era. Not a single domain ever tried to overthrow the bakufu hegemony. Nor did the bakufu ever try to extend its control over the domains. But bureaucracy grew steadily. Public authority extended into areas that had been private. In 1600 most samurai fiefs were run by their samurai fief holders. By 1850, however, district officials administered all but the largest of samurai fiefs. They collected the standard domain taxes and forwarded their income to the samurai. In periods of retrenchment, samurai were often paid only half the amount due. Paperwork proliferated: records of births, adoptions, name changes, samurai ranks, fief registers, court proceedings, and so on.

Of course, there were limits to bureaucratization. Only samurai could aspire to official posts, and decision-making posts were limited to upper-ranking samurai. But in periods of financial crises a demand arose for men of ability, and middle- or lower-middle-ranking samurai became staff assistants to bureaucrats of rank.

---

[1]R. Tsunoda, W. T. de Bary, and D. Keene, eds., *Sources of the Japanese Tradition* (New York: Columbia University Press, 1958), p. 336.

By 1700, the economy approached the limit of expansion within the available technology. The population reached 26 million early in the eighteenth century and remained at that level into the mid-nineteenth century, a period during which the population of China more than doubled. After 1700, taxes were stabilized and land surveys were few. Evidence suggests little increase in grain production and only slow growth in agricultural by-products. Some families made conscious efforts to limit their size to raise their standard of living. Contraception and abortion were commonplace, and infanticide was practiced in hard times. But periodic disease, shortages of food, and late marriages among the poor were more important factors in limiting population growth.

Some farmers remained independent cultivators, but by the mid-nineteenth century, about a quarter of all cultivated lands were worked by tenants. Most landlords had small holdings. The misery of the lower stratum of rural society contributed to an increase in peasant uprisings during the late eighteenth and early nineteenth centuries. Authorities had no difficulty quelling them, and no uprising in Japan approached those that erupted in late Manchu China.

Commerce grew slowly during the late Tokugawa. In the early eighteenth century, it was again subjected to regulation by guilds. Merchants paid set fees in return for monopoly privileges in central marketplaces. Guilds were also reestablished in the domains, and some domains created domain-run monopolies on products such as wax, paper, indigo, or sugar. The problem facing domain leaders was how to share in the profits without injuring the competitive standing of domain exports. Most late Tokugawa commercial growth was in rural industries—*sake*, soy sauce, dyes, silks, or cotton. Some were organized and financed by city merchants. Others competed with city merchants, shipping directly to the end markets to circumvent monopoly controls. The expansion of labor in rural industries may explain why the population of late Tokugawa cities declined.

The largest question about the Tokugawa economy concerns its relation to Japan's rapid industrialization in the late nineteenth century. Some scholars have suggested that Japan had a "running start." Others have stressed Japan's backwardness in comparison with European developers. The question is unresolved.

TOKUGAWA CULTURE

Two hundred fifty years of peace and prosperity provided a base for an increasingly complex culture and a broader popular participation in cultural life. In the villages, Buddhism became more deeply rooted, and new folk religions proliferated. By the early nineteenth century, most well-to-do farmers could read and write. The aristocratic culture of the ranking samurai houses also remained vigorous. Nō plays continued to be staged. The medieval tradition of black ink painting was continued by the Kanō school and other artists. The Ashikaga tradition of restraint, simplicity, and naturalness in architecture was extended. The gilded and colored screen paintings that had surged in popularity during Hideyoshi's rule developed further, culminating in the powerful works of Ogata Kōrin (1658–1716). Zen Buddhism, having declined during the Warring States period, was revitalized by the monk Hakuin (1686–1769), who was also a writer, a painter, a calligrapher, and a sculptor.

Some scholars have described Tokugawa urban culture as having two divisions. One was the work of serious, high-minded samurai, who produced a vast body of Chinese-style paintings, poetry, and philosophical treatises. The other was the product of the townspeople: low-brow, irreverent, secular, satirical, and often scatological. The samurai esteemed Song-style paintings of mountains and waterfalls, often adorned with

Mother Bathing Her Son. Woodblock print by Kitagawa Utamaro (1753–1806). Utamaro was so popular a master of his genre that publishers hired unknown artists to produce fakes in his name. This led him to sign some works "the genuine Utamaro." He boasted of his high fees, comparing himself to a great courtesan and his imitators to streetwalkers. Note the tub's skillful design, the mother's wooden clog and her simple yet elegant kimono. A second kimono hangs to dry at the upper-right corner.

Kitagawa Utamaro (1753-1806), "Mother Bathing Her Son". Print. Color woodblock print, oban, tate-e, nishiki-e, mica 14 7/8" x 10 1/8" (37.8 x 25.7 cm.). The Nelson-Atkins Museum of Art, Kansas City, Missouri (Purchase: Nelson Trust). © The Nelson Gallery Foundation. All Reproduction Rights Reserved.

What commentary on women's roles does this woodblock print provide?

The Virtuous Wife

The three-generation stem family, composed of the older parents, their eldest son and his "bride," and their children, was the ideal during the Edo period. The principal family bond was between the parents and their elder son. The son's "bride," at least until she produced children of her own, was less than a full family member, as the adage "the womb is borrowed" suggests. Kaibara Ekken (1630–1714), an early Confucian moralist, propounded an ethic appropriate to such a family in his Greater Learning for Women. It reflects the accepted wisdom of his age.

- **Can** people accept and practice any ethic that serves their society? Or are some ethics more "natural" than others? How did a girl raised in Tokugawa society feel? Could she embrace Ekken's teachings? Or does the following passage suggest, at least obliquely, that some human feelings are universal and difficult to deny?

GIRL'S INSTRUCTION

Seeing that it is a girl's destiny, on reaching womanhood, to go to a new home, and live in submission to her father-in-law, it is even more incumbent upon her than it is on a boy to receive with all reverence her parents' instructions. Should her parents, through their tenderness, allow her to grow up self-willed, she will infallibly show herself capricious in her husband's house, and thus alienate his affection; while, if her father-in-law be a man of correct principles, the girl will find the yoke of these principles intolerable. She will hate and decry her father-in-law, and the end of these domestic dissensions will be her dismissal from her husband's house and the covering of herself with ignominy. Her parents, forgetting the faulty education they gave her, may, indeed, lay all the blame on the father-in-law. But they will be in error; for the whole disaster should rightly be attributed to the faulty education the girl received from her parents.

quotations from the Confucian classics or Tang poetry. The townspeople collected prints of people and scenes from everyday life. Samurai moralists saw money as the root of evil; merchants saw it as their goal in life.

The greatest works of literature and philosophy of Tokugawa Japan were produced between 1650 and 1725, just as the initial political transformation was being completed but the economy was still growing and the society was not yet set in its ways. One of the major literary figures and certainly the most entertaining was Ihara Saikaku (1642–1693), who is generally credited with having recreated the Japanese novel with works including *The Life of an Amorous Man* and its sequel, *The Life of an Amorous Woman*. The ethicist Kaibara Ekken (1630–1714) wrote about family life and other topics (see Document, "The Virtuous Wife").

Another major figure was the dramatist Chikamatsu Monzaemon (1653–1724). Born a samurai, Chikamatsu wrote for both the Kabuki and the puppet theater. Kabuki had begun early in the seventeenth century as suggestive skits and erotic dances performed by actresses. In 1629, the bakufu forbade women to perform on the stage. By the 1660s, Kabuki had evolved into a more serious drama with male actors playing both male and female roles.

The most important change in Tokugawa intellectual life was that the ruling elite abandoned the religious worldview of Buddhism in favor of the more secular values of Confucianism. The great figures of Tokugawa Confucianism adapted Chinese Confucianism to fit Japanese society in the late seventeenth and early eighteenth centuries. For example, in Chinese Confucianism there was no place for a shōgun, whereas in the Japanese tradition of sun-line emperors, there was no room for the Mandate of Heaven. Most Tokugawa thinkers handled this discrepancy by saying that heaven gave the emperor its mandate and that the emperor then entrusted political authority to the shōgun. (This solution was not very realistic, since the emperor was just a figurehead.) Another problem

THE INFIRMITIES OF WOMAN

The five worst infirmities that afflict the female are indocility, discontent, slander, jealousy, and silliness. Without any doubt, these five infirmities are found in seven or eight out of every ten women, and it is from these that arises the inferiority of women to men. A woman should cure them by self-inspection and self-reproach.

THE WIFE'S MISCELLANEOUS DUTIES

A woman has no particular lord. She must look to her husband as her lord, and must serve him with all worship and reverence, not despising or thinking lightly of him. The great lifelong duty of a woman is obedience. In her dealings with her husband, both the expression of her countenance and style of her address should be courteous, humble, and conciliatory, never peevish and intractable, never rude and arrogant—that should be a woman's first and chiefest care. When the husband issues his instructions, the wife must never disobey them. In doubtful cases she should inquire of her husband, and obediently follow his commands. If ever her husband should inquire of her, she should answer to the point—to answer in a careless fashion would be a mark of rudeness. Should her husband be roused at any time to anger, she must obey him with fear and trembling, and not set herself up against him in anger and forwardness. A woman should look on her husband as if he were Heaven itself, and never weary of thinking how she may yield to her husband and thus escape celestial castigation.

Source: Kaibara Ekken, *Greater Learning for Women*, in K. Hoshino, *The Way of Contentment* (London: John Murray, 1913, reprinted 1979), pp. 33–34, 44–45.

was the difference between China's centralized bureaucratic government and Japan's system of lord–vassal relationships. Samurai loyalty was clearly not that of a scholar-official to the Chinese emperor. Some Japanese Confucianists solved this problem by saying that it was China that had deviated from the feudal society of the Zhou sages, whereas in Japan, Tokugawa Ieyasu had recreated that society. A third problem concerned the "central flowery kingdom" and the barbarians around it. No philosopher could bring himself to say that Japan was the real middle kingdom, but some argued that centrality was relative, whereas others suggested that China under barbarian Manchu rule had lost its claim to universality.

Japanese thought retained its intellectual vitality into the mid-nineteenth century. Thinkers were stimulated in part by disputes among different schools of Confucianism and, perhaps, by Japan's lack of an examination system. The best energies of its samurai youth were not channeled into writing sterile essays. Official preferment—within the constraints of Japan's hereditary system—was more likely to be obtained by writing a proposal for domain reforms.

Schools expanded rapidly, beginning in the early eighteenth century. By the mid-nineteenth century, about 40 to 50 percent of the male population and 15 to 20 percent of the female population was literate—a far higher rate than in most of the world and on a par with some late developers in Europe.

Two important schools of scholarship—National Studies and Dutch Studies—were diametrically opposed in most respects but alike in criticizing the Chinese influence on Japanese life and culture. **National Studies** began as a philological examination of ancient Japanese texts. Scholars in the National Studies tradition tried to find in the Japanese classics the original true character of Japan before it had been contaminated by Chinese ideas. They concluded that the early Japanese spirit was spontaneous, lofty, and honest, in contrast to the Chinese spirit, which they characterized as rigid, cramped, and artificial. National Studies also reaffirmed Japan's imperial

National Studies A Japanese intellectual tradition that emphasized native Japanese culture and institutions and rejected the influence of Chinese Confucianism.

CHRONOLOGY

TOKUGAWA ERA (1600–1868)

1600	Tokugawa Ieyasu reunifies Japan
1615	"Laws of Military Houses" issued
1639	Seclusion policy adopted
1642	Edo hostage system in place
1653–1724	Chikamatsu Monzaemon, dramatist
1701	The forty-seven rōnin avenge their lord
1853, 1854	Commodore Matthew Perry visits Japan

Dutch Studies Scholarship based on books imported by Dutch traders, particularly medical and scientific texts.

institution. National Studies became influential during the late Tokugawa era and influenced the Meiji Restoration. Its doctrines continued thereafter as one strain of Japanese ultranationalism.

A second development was **Dutch Studies**. After Christianity had been proscribed and the policy of seclusion adopted, all Western books were banned in Japan. The ban on Western books (except for those propagating Christianity) was ended in 1720 by the shōgun Tokugawa Yoshimune (r. 1716–1745). Japanese pioneers recognized early that Western anatomy texts were superior to Chinese. By the mid-nineteenth century, there were schools of Dutch Studies in the main cities of Japan. Those who studied Dutch focused on medicine, but some knowledge of other Western sciences and arts also entered Japan.

Starting in the late eighteenth century, the Japanese began to think of the West, and especially of Russia, as a threat to Japan. A sudden expansion in Dutch Studies occurred after Commodore Matthew Perry's visits to Japan in 1853 and 1854. During the 1860s, Dutch Studies became Western Studies, as English, French, German, and Russian were added to the languages studied at the bakufu Institute for the Investigation of Barbarian Books. In sum, Dutch Studies laid a foundation on which the Japanese built quickly when the need arose for knowledge of the West.

KOREA AND VIETNAM

A recurring feature of world history is the spread of heartland civilizations into their surrounding areas. In East Asia the heartland civilization was that of China; the surrounding areas that were transformed were Japan, Korea, and Vietnam. Like the Japanese, Koreans and Vietnamese devised writing systems using Chinese ideographs. They partially modeled their governments on those of China. They accepted Chinese Buddhism and Confucianism and with them Chinese conceptions of the universe, state, and human relationships. The Confucian definitions of the relations between ruler and minister, father and son, and husband and wife were emphasized in Korea and Vietnam. But Koreans and Vietnamese, who spoke non-Chinese tongues, saw themselves as separate peoples and gradually came to take pride in their independence. Germany might be a parallel case in Europe: It became civilized by borrowing the heartland Graeco-Christian culture of the Mediterranean area, but it kept its original tongue and elements from its earlier culture.

KOREA

WHAT WAS Korea's relationship to China?

The Korean peninsula is a distinct geographical unit. The weak Koryo state (918–1392) survived as long as it did by serving as a tributary to China's dynasties. The Choson period (1392–1910) was also defined by a tributary relationship with China.

KOREA: THE CHOSON ERA

In 1392, a Koryo general, Yi Songgye, founded a new dynasty, the Choson. It lasted until 1910; its amazing longevity was directly related to the stability of Ming–Qing China.

If the Koryo was Korea's Buddhist age of faith, the Choson was its Neo-Confucian age. By the late fifteenth century, Korean philosophers were making original contributions to Neo-Confucian philosophy. This pattern of changes may be seen as "East Asian" in that it paralleled changes that had occurred in China during the Song dynasty and would occur in Japan during the Tokugawa era.

After seizing power, Yi carried out an extensive land reform and strengthened his government by absorbing members of the great Koryo families into his officialdom. These elite families, known as **yangban**, monopolized education, official posts, and land. Beneath them were the commoners, the "good people," taxpaying free subjects of the king. Beneath the commoners and constituting perhaps one third of the population were government and private slaves. Korean slaves were property, often attached to land, to be used as their owners willed; they could be given as gifts, and their children were slaves. Following Confucian teachings, husbands and wives were not separated.

King Sejong (r. 1418–1450) illustrates the potential of a wise monarch. He reformed land taxes, made loans of grain to farmers during spring planting, and encouraged the spread of better agricultural technology. After reforming the army and navy, he attacked pirate strongholds on Tsushima Island and expanded Korea's borders. In 1420, he established a Hall of Worthies to encourage scholarship. But there were limits that even Sejong could not overcome. Sejong promoted the use of coins and paper money to stimulate commerce, but they never caught on. Sejong had twenty sons and fourteen daughters, but after his death, his uncle usurped the throne.

At mid-dynasty, invasions dealt a severe blow to Choson society. Having brought all of Japan under his control, Hideyoshi decided to conquer China through Korea. His samurai armies devastated Korea in 1592 and 1596. The invasions ended with his death in 1598. On both occasions the Ming court sent troops to aid its tributary, but the Chinese armies devastated the land almost as badly as the Japanese. A third disaster occurred in 1627 and 1637 when Manchu troops invaded pro-Ming Korea. The result of these multiple incursions was a roughly 75 percent drop in taxable land. Behind this statistic lay famine, death, and misery.

Had the late-sixteenth-century Choson government been stronger, it might have recovered. But cliques of officials had begun to fight among themselves over official positions. Many in the losing factions were executed or imprisoned. The effectiveness of government declined. High officials in Seoul used their power to garner private agricultural estates and established local academies to prepare their own kinsmen for the official examinations.

From the mid-seventeenth century on, Korea offers a mixed picture. Literacy rose and a new popular fiction of fables, romances, and novels appeared. Women writers became important for the first time. Among some yangban there was a call for "practical learning" to renew Korean society, and scholars outlined plans for administrative reforms and the encouragement of commerce. Their recommendations were not adopted, and society continued its decline. More Koreans died in the famine of 1671 than during Hideyoshi's invasions. Overtaxation, drought, floods, pestilence, famine, and crime became commonplace. Disgruntled officials led peasants in revolts in 1811 and 1862. Because of the concentration of officials, wealth, and military power at Seoul and because of Manchu support for the ruling house, neither revolt toppled the dynasty, but Korea was weak.

yangban Elite Korean families of the Choson period.

A Badge of Rank. In Choson Korea—as in China—the rank of an official was indicated by the embroidered square affixed to his gown. Some squares showed ducks, pheasants, egrets, leopards, or tigers. Here we see a crane flying among the clouds and rainbows below.

How did badges of rank reflect Confucian values in Korean society?

VIETNAM

HOW DID Vietnam expand southward during this time?

EARLY HISTORY

The history of Vietnam's second millennium is conventionally broken into dynastic blocks named after the ruling family: Ly (1009–1225), Tran (1225–1400), Le (1428–1787), and Nguyen (1802–1880s). Unlike China's, however, Vietnamese dynasties were not strong, centralized, bureaucratic states. Often several independent states coexisted during the time span of a single "dynasty." Every Vietnamese dynasty became a "tributary" of China, though submission was purely formal. Tensions between the center and the periphery as well as Chinese invasions were among the influences on Vietnamese history.

LATE TRADITIONAL VIETNAM

The first four centuries of an independent Vietnam, the Ly and Tran dynasties (1009–1400), were not remarkable. Vietnam was often divided into regional states that frequently fought wars with each other or with Champa to the south. The Tran dynasty weakened at the end; Vietnam was conquered by Chinese armies in 1407 and was ruled by a Chinese governor for twenty years. Chinese rule, however, proved so exploitative that a rebellion rose against it. The rebellion was led by Le Loi, a landowner from Thanh Hoa, who used war-elephants against the Chinese troops. After his victory, he went on to establish the Le dynasty (1428–1787).

Two momentous developments began in Vietnam during the fifteenth century under Le. One was centralization and a more extensive use of Chinese institutions. Le Thanh Tong (1442–1497), an immensely talented early ruler, divided his realm into thirteen provinces and then into prefectures, counties, and departments. He weakened the nobility by holding civil service examinations for the selection of officials and set up nine ranks of civil and military officials. He established schools, introduced Neo-Confucian learning, and promoted public works. He registered the population and reinstituted a Chinese-type land tax. In the decades after his death, many reforms broke down, but in time other reformers appeared and carried the process a step further. Overall, the influence of Chinese culture was greater than that of occupation by Chinese armies.

The second development, which also was begun by Le Thanh Tong, was what Vietnamese historians call "the march to the south." Vietnamese armies conquered the state of Champa in 1471. This opened the way for a centuries-long movement of Vietnamese into the central and southern portions of what is today Vietnam (see Map 19–3). To secure the lands he had conquered, Le established self-supporting colonies of Vietnamese soldier-peasants along the coast of the former kingdom. These became a part of the local population. To rule the Muslim Chams, in 1483 he promulgated a Confucian-tinged legal code that remained in effect through most of the dynasty. It appealed to "uni-

CHRONOLOGY

KOREA AND VIETNAM

Korea

1392	Yi Songgye founds Choson dynasty
1592, 1587	Japanese invasions
1627, 1637	Invasions by Manchu troops
1671	Famine
1811, 1862	Peasant revolts

Vietnam

1471	Vietnam conquers Champa
1483	Confucian legal code promulgated by Le Thanh Tong
1644	Fall of Ming dynasty leads to wave of Chinese immigration
1698	Nguyen court extends rule south to Saigon
1757	Nguyen rule extended over entire Mekong delta
1802	Nguyen unifies Vietnam and establishes a new dynasty

versal" values that could be accepted by both Vietnamese and Chams. Le's successors were unable to maintain control over the central coast, and autonomous Vietnamese states arose in the area.

Politics and demography became entwined. During the complex history of the middle and late Le dynasty, northern Vietnam was governed, in fact, by the Trinh family, and central Vietnam was ruled by the Nguyen from their capital city of Hue. In the seventeenth century, the Mekong delta (today's south Vietnam) was sparsely settled, mostly by Chams and Cambodians. The Nguyen court in Hue extended its rule south to Saigon in 1698 by sending an official to settle a commercial dispute between a Chinese and a Cambodian. By 1757, the Nguyen had further extended their control over the entire Mekong delta westward to the Gulf of Siam. Political control facilitated the continued movement of Vietnamese from the densely settled north to the south, though they remained a minority in southern Vietnam throughout the eighteenth century.

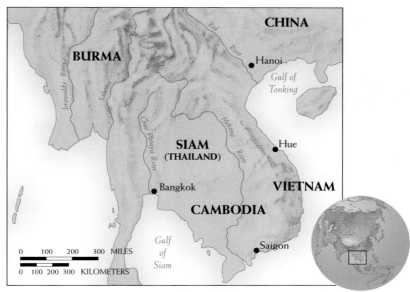

MAP 19–3   **Vietnam and Neighboring Southeast Asia.**

How did China's proximity influence Vietnamese history?

Another phenomenon affecting Vietnam was the Chinese diaspora to Southeast Asia. The fall of the Ming dynasty in 1644 led to the first wave of Chinese emigrants. By the century's end substantial numbers of Chinese had settled and formed communities in the Mekong delta. Some became Saigon merchants, selling rice to Chinese merchants in Singapore. Today, about a million partially assimilated Chinese live in southern Vietnam and play a major role in its economy.

In the late eighteenth century, wars broke out between the north and the Nguyen in Hue. By 1802 the Nguyen had defeated the northern armies, unified the country, and established a new dynasty. It kept its capital at Hue. The new emperor had been aided by French advisers and adventurers, several of whom were rewarded with high official posts. But the second emperor turned against the French and adopted anti-Christian policies. The Nguyen dynasty became more Chinese than any previous dynasty. It adopted the law codes of Manchu China, established Chinese-style institutions, and recruited a hierarchy of civil and military officials by examinations. The reasons for these initiatives were to placate Confucian scholars in the north, to strengthen the court, and to weaken the military figures who had helped the dynasty's rise.

During the first half of the nineteenth century, Vietnam was probably governed better than any other Southeast Asian state, but it had weaknesses. There were tensions between the north, which was overpopulated, well schooled, and furnished most of the official class, and the south, which was ethnically diverse, educationally backward, and poorly represented in government. Trade and artisanal industries were less developed than in China and Japan, only small amounts of specie circulated, and periodic markets were more common than market towns. The government rested on a society composed largely of self-sufficient villages. In sum, Vietnam entered the second half of the nineteenth century even less prepared than China or Japan for the challenges it would soon face.

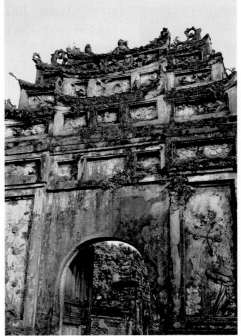

Hue.   A gate from the imperial citadel.

Where is Hue?

SUMMARY

WHERE DID China expand under the Qing?

China: Ming and Qing Dynasties. China's last two imperial dynasties were the Ming (1368–1644) and the Qing or Manchus (1644–1911). Chinese society became more integrated and its government more sophisticated. The population reached 410 million, cities grew, and commerce expanded. Chinese government rested on a bureaucracy educated in Confucian teachings and the gentry class. Under the Qing, China expanded to the west and east, establishing claims to Tibet, Central Asia, and Taiwan. Trade with the West grew under the control of Chinese officials. *page 459*

WHAT IMPACT did military technology have on Japanese society in this period?

Japan: Warring States Era. With the collapse of the Ashikaga bakufu, daimyo lords fought among themselves. The military was transformed by new weapons and tactics, and Europeans arrived as traders and missionaries. *page 466*

HOW WAS Japanese culture transformed during the Tokugawa era?

Japan: Tokugawa Era. The Tokugawa shōgun (1600–1868) restored order. The government, based at Edo, controlled the military houses and encouraged economic growth. Japan became closed to the outside world except for a small Dutch presence at Nagasaki. Japanese drama, literature, and art flourished, as did commercial life. *page 468*

WHAT WAS Korea's relationship to China?

Korea. Korea was a tributary of China but developed according to its own internal dynamics. Korea was notable for its Confucian culture and yangban aristocracy. *page 476*

HOW DID Vietnam expand southward during this time?

Vietnam. Vietnamese history during this period was notable for its conquest and peopling of the Mekong delta. Fifteenth-century ruler Le Thanh Tong took an early lead in introducing administrative reforms based on Chinese government, and in expanding to the south. *page 478*

INTERPRETING THE PAST

Japan, the Shōgunate, and the West

Sources from MyHistoryLab for Chapter 19

myhistorylab

1) Tokugawa Shōgunate, The Laws for the Military House
2) Japan Encounters the West, 1587–1640

Visual Sources from MyHistoryLab

1) The Tokaido Road
2) Jesuit Martyrs in Japan
3) Title Page from a Japanese Anatomy Text, 1775

The primary sources for this chapter illustrate Japan's unique social system and government that existed from the late traditional

REVIEW QUESTIONS

1. What factors led to economic and population growth in late traditional China? Was the pattern the same in Japan during those centuries?

2. How was Manchu rule like Mongol rule during the Yuan dynasty? How was it like the rule by Chinese emperors during the Ming?

3. What were the social and administrative foundations of the absolute power of Ming–Qing emperors?

4. Compare and contrast the bureaucracies of China and Japan in this period. What influences might you expect their differences to have on the later histories of these countries?

5. How did advances in military technology change warfare in sixteenth-century Japan? How was the strategic balance of power reflected in the government created by Tokugawa Ieyasu?

6. Did literacy change the samurai? How did literate samurai "fit" the changed society of the late eighteenth century?

7. What was Dutch Studies? With what ideas did Dutch Studies compete, and why is it important?

8. Who were the yangban, and how did they influence Korean history?

9. How and why did Vietnam expand to the south?

10. Summarize the relationship between Vietnam and China and between Korea and China. Was either relationship stronger or more significant? Explain.

KEY TERMS

daimyo (dye-myoh) (p. 466)
Dutch Studies (p. 476)
gentry (p. 461)
Kabuki (p. 471)

Nō (p. 471)
National Studies (p. 475)
Shanxi banks (p. 460)
yangban (yahng-bahn) (p. 477)

Note: To learn more about the topics in this chapter, please turn to the Suggested Readings at the end of the book.

era to the middle of the nineteenth century. Japanese military leaders (shōguns) created what has been termed "a premodern police state" as well as heavily restricting contact with Westerners by the early seventeenth century. The first document lists some of the rules that shōguns imposed on daimyos (regional nobility and warlords) within their own provinces as well as at the shōgun's court at Edo (Tokyo) where they were required to be in attendance at certain times of the year. The second document details the gradual "closing of Japan" from the 1580s to the 1630s. The visual sources add context to the shōgun's policy of insulating Japan from foreign influence for over two centuries.

Use the sources to address the following thematic questions that deal with Japanese leadership's harsh domestic policies, as well as their efforts to strictly control contacts with Westerners and their culture. Use specific examples from the documents to back up your assertions.

Questions

What methods did the Tokugawa shogunate employ in its efforts to maintain strict control over regional daimyo? Would these methods help or hinder the shōgun's attempts to limit the spread of Christianity?

Examine the Tokaido Road color print. How did Japan's physical environment assist the shōgun's policy of insulating Japan from outside influence?

What policy changes are evident in the *Japan Encounters the West* documents dating from 1587 to 1640? How are Europeans depicted? How are Japanese depicted?

Consider the title page and excerpt from a 1775 Japanese anatomy. How and why did Western knowledge (medicine and science) penetrate Japan's formidable policy of isolation?

20

State Building and Society in Early Modern Europe

Schonbrunn Palace, Vienna. To symbolize his vast royal authority Louis XIV of France constructed a vast new palace at Versailles outside Paris as the center of his government. Subsequently, other European monarchs built similar palaces. Between 1743 and 1763 the Austrian Empress Maria Theresa carried out the construction of the Schonbrunn Palace on the outskirts of Vienna to symbolize Habsburg authority.

Compare this photograph of Schonbrunn Palace with the painting of Versailles on page 488. How are the two buildings similar?

EUROPEAN POLITICAL CONSOLIDATION *page 485*

HOW DID England and France provide models for governance in early modern Europe?

EUROPEAN WARFARE: FROM CONTINENTAL TO WORLD CONFLICT *page 493*

WHY WERE the European wars of the eighteenth century global in scope?

THE OLD REGIME *page 496*

WHAT WERE the political and economic structures of the Old Regime?

FAMILY STRUCTURES AND THE FAMILY ECONOMY *page 499*

WHAT WAS the role of women in family economy?

THE REVOLUTION IN AGRICULTURE *page 502*

WHAT WAS the connection between population increase and agricultural improvements in the eighteenth century?

THE EIGHTEENTH-CENTURY INDUSTRIAL REVOLUTION: AN EVENT IN WORLD HISTORY *page 504*

WHY DID the Industrial Revolution begin in England?

EUROPEAN CITIES *page 507*

HOW DID population growth lead to changes in urban social structures?

THE JEWISH POPULATION: AGE OF THE GHETTO *page 509*

HOW WERE European Jews segregated from European society?

GLOBAL PERSPECTIVE

EARLY MODERN EUROPE

During the seventeenth and eighteenth centuries political and economic developments occurred in Europe that set the continent on a path that by the nineteenth century resulted in a period of European world domination that ultimately proved temporary. The major states of northwestern Europe consolidated themselves politically and militarily in strong, often aggressive political units. The economy of this region of Europe would take the first steps toward industrialization and the capacity to produce vast quantities of both consumer and capital goods. These same states developed sophisticated financial structures that fueled their overseas commercial empires, which in the cases of the Netherlands, France, and Great Britain could be protected by strong navies.

It is important to recognize that all of those world-transforming developments occurred slowly. At the beginning of this era of political and economic consolidation much of Europe resembled other major world civilizations. By the second quarter of the eighteenth century, the major European powers were not yet nation-states in which the citizens felt themselves united by a shared sense of community, culture, language, and history. They were still monarchies in which the personality of the ruler and the personal relationships of the great noble families considerably influenced public affairs. As yet they differed little in political and social structures from many other societies in the world, and they still lagged behind India, China, and some parts of the Islamic world in population density and urbanization. However, industry

and military technology were beginning to reverse the global balance of power between Europe and Asia.

These European states displayed certain problems that also characterized the governments of China and Japan during the same epochs. In particular, as in Japan, the problem of a balance between centralization and decentralization arose in virtually all the European states. In France, Russia, and Prussia, the forces of centralization proved quite strong. In Austria the forces of decentralization were powerful. England achieved a rather delicate balance. Furthermore, as in Tokugawa Japan, European states of the eighteenth century generally saw an increase in legal codification and in the growth of bureaucracy. Only in Prussia did the military influence on society resemble that in Japan.

The role of the personality of the monarch in Europe bore some resemblance to that of certain Manchu emperors in China, such as Kangxi (1662–1722) and Qianlong (r. 1736–1795). Louis XIV and Peter the Great had no less influence on their nations than did these great Manchu emperors. All of them built up military strength and fostered innovation. However, although European rulers developed state bureaucracies, none of them put together so brilliant a group of trained civil servants as those who administered China. The roots of the Chinese civil service went back centuries, and Chinese civil servants, unlike those in Europe, tended to resist modernization of the Chinese government and economy for both practical and ideological reasons. Civil servants in Europe, perhaps because they rose to power simultaneously with Europe's

B etween the early seventeenth and mid-twentieth centuries, Europe dominated the world politically, militarily, and economically, as no region had before. Two broad factors accounted for this situation. First, by the mid-eighteenth century five major states—Great Britain, France, Austria, Prussia, and Russia—had come to dominate European politics and would continue to do so until at least World War I. These states began to fight among themselves, first in Europe and then also in their colonial empires, in the late seventeenth century. These conflicts had major consequences for the non-European world.

The second factor was that the peoples living primarily in northwestern Europe undertook a series of economic advances that laid the foundation for the social and economic transformation of the world. Europeans began for the first time in their history to achieve a more or less stable food supply. The population of Europe commenced a major period of growth. New inventions and institutions, known collectively as the Industrial Revolution, gave Europe a productive capacity previously unknown in human history. Economic advances gave Europeans the tools to dominate much of the world. ∎

industrialization, tended to foster rather than obstruct modernization, which posed no threat to their power or worldview.

The global commercial empires of the Netherlands, France, Spain, and England gave rise to fierce commercial rivalries. The drive for empire and commercial supremacy propelled these states into contact with Africa, Latin America, India, China, and Japan. Spain and Portugal had long exploited Latin America as their own monopoly, an arrangement that England challenged in the eighteenth century. China's lack of interest in dominating the Indian Ocean opened the way for European adventurers and traders in India. France and England fought for commercial supremacy in India, and by the 1760s England had, in effect, conquered the subcontinent. The slave trade between Africa and the New World flourished throughout the seventeenth and the eighteenth centuries. European merchants and navies also sought to penetrate East Asia, although their success was limited until the advent of nineteenth-century "gunboat diplomacy." As this term implies, European success in Africa, Asia, and the Indian Ocean was always closely linked to its sophisticated military technology, and especially the construction of sturdy ships able to carry heavy cannons. As a result of these developments, European commerce dominated the world for the next two centuries. Europe and its colonists extracted labor and other natural resources from virtually all the other continents of the world. These assets in turn only widened the growing gap in wealth and power that separated Europe from the rest of the world in the nineteenth and twentieth centuries.

Consequently, by the mid-eighteenth century, the European states that just two centuries earlier lagged behind China in wealth and technology had made their power and influence felt throughout the world. Beginning in the early eighteenth century with the slow but later steady growth of industrialism, the political power of the European states became linked to a qualitatively different economic base than any seen elsewhere in the world. That political and economic combination allowed Europe to dominate the world from the 1750s to the Second World War.

Focus Questions

◆ How did European states resemble those in other parts of the world in the mid-eighteenth century? How did they differ?

◆ What was the relationship between military technology, especially naval power, and the growth of European colonial empires?

◆ What factors led to the political and economic transformation of western Europe and its emergence as a region that would eventually (for a time) dominate much of the world?

EUROPEAN POLITICAL CONSOLIDATION

TWO MODELS OF EUROPEAN POLITICAL DEVELOPMENT

In the second half of the sixteenth century, changes in European military organization, weapons, and tactics sharply increased the cost of warfare and forced monarchs to seek new revenues. Rulers like the king of France, who established secure financial bases without the support of nobles or assemblies, exercised absolute rule. The English monarch, however, could govern only with Parliament by the end of the seventeenth century. These two governmental systems—**absolutism** in France and **parliamentary monarchy** in England—shaped Europe's political evolution.

TOWARD PARLIAMENTARY GOVERNMENT IN ENGLAND

When Elizabeth I died in 1603, the English crown passed to the son of Mary, Queen of Scots, who became James I of England (r. 1603–1625), founder of the Stuart dynasty. The Stuart kings aspired to absolute power, and their pursuit of an income to

HOW DID England and France provide models for governance in early modern Europe?

absolutism Term applied to strong centralized continental monarchies that attempted to make royal power dominant over aristocracies and other regional authorities.

parliamentary monarchy A state headed by a monarch but whose power is shared with a national representative body.

Charles I ruled for several years without calling Parliament, but once he began a war with Scotland, he needed revenues that only Parliament could supply.

Musée du Louvre, Pans/Superstock.

Compare this image of Charles I with the portraits of Louis XIV on page 487 and the Qianlong emperor on page 463. How are the three portraits similar? How are they different?

QUICK REVIEW

Charles II (r. 1660–1685)

◆ England returned to the 1642 status quo when Charles assumed the throne

◆ Charles favored religious toleration

◆ Issued Declaration of Indulgence in 1672 suspending all laws against non-Anglicans

Puritans English Protestants who sought to "purify" the Church of England of any vestiges of Catholicism.

Glorious Revolution The largely peaceful replacement of James II by William and Mary as English monarchs in 1688. It marked the beginning of constitutional monarchy in Britain.

support it threatened the economic well-being of the nobility and elites represented in Parliament. These groups invoked traditional English liberties and effectively resisted the Stuarts. **Puritans** (Calvinists), who wanted a more radical reformation of the Anglican Church, also opposed the kings. Both James I and his son Charles I (r. 1625–1649), who had Catholic sympathies, confronted a combined political and religious opposition to their absolutist policies.

In 1642, the conflict between Charles I and Parliament erupted into civil war, which the parliamentary and Puritan forces won in 1645. In 1649, a "rump" Parliament (one from which the opposition had been removed) beheaded Charles I and abolished the monarchy, the House of Lords, and the established church. England became a Puritan republic led by the victorious general Oliver Cromwell (1599–1658). After Cromwell died, disillusionment with Puritan strictness and republican mismanagement prompted restoration of the Stuart monarchy under Charles II (r. 1660–1685). His Parliament was dominated by conservative members of the Church of England, and the policies it pursued severely restricted both Protestant Non-Conformists and Roman Catholics. Parliament's Test Act established as a qualification for office an oath that no Roman Catholic could take in good conscience.

James II (r. 1685–1688), the brother who succeeded Charles in 1685, was a Roman Catholic. He decreed toleration for both Roman Catholics and Protestant Non-Conformists and imprisoned seven Anglican bishops who refused to publicize his suspension of laws against Catholics. James's policy of toleration had as its goal the extension of royal authority over all English institutions.

Members of England's Parliament hoped that James would be succeeded by his eldest daughter, Mary (r. 1689–1694), a Protestant married to William of Orange (1650–1702), stadtholder of the Netherlands. But on June 20, 1688, James II's Catholic second wife gave birth to a Catholic male heir to the throne. This prompted Parliament to invite William of Orange to invade England to preserve its "traditional liberties," that is, the Anglican Church and parliamentary government.

THE "GLORIOUS REVOLUTION"

William of Orange's army met no opposition when it landed in England in November 1688. James fled to France, and Parliament proclaimed William III and Mary II the new monarchs. This bloodless coup was celebrated as the **Glorious Revolution**; the government it established limited the powers of the monarchy and guaranteed the civil liberties of the English privileged classes. Henceforth, England's monarchs would rule by the consent of Parliament, which convened every three years. Roman Catholics were declared ineligible to inherit the English throne. The Toleration Act of 1689 permitted all forms of Protestant worship but outlawed Roman Catholicism.

The Act of Settlement in 1701 ended a century of strife by bequeathing the English crown to Germany's Protestant House of Hanover if Anne (r. 1702–1714), the second daughter of James II and the heir to the childless William and Mary, died childless. At Queen Anne's death in 1714, the Elector of Hanover became George I of England (r. 1714–1727), the third foreigner to occupy its throne in just more than a century.

Under the Hanoverians, Britain achieved political stability and economic prosperity during the first quarter of the eighteenth century. Robert Walpole

(1676–1745), George I's chief minister from 1721 to 1742, was adept at handling the House of Commons and exercising influence through patronage. He maintained peace abroad and promoted the status quo at home. Britain's foreign trade spread from New England to India. Agriculture became more productive. Because the dominant economic groups were represented in Parliament, they were willing to pay the taxes to support a powerful military force, particularly a strong navy. As a result, Great Britain became not only a European power of the first order but also eventually a world power.

The power of the British monarchs and their ministers was limited, and Parliament could not ignore popular pressure. Many members of Parliament held independent views. Newspapers and public debate flourished. Free speech could be exercised, as could freedom of association. No standing army intimidated the populace. The English state showed how military power could coexist with political liberty, and Britain became the model for European progressives who opposed the absolutist regimes on the Continent. The political ideas that emerged in the British Isles during the seventeenth century also took root in Britain's North American colonies.

CHRONOLOGY

ENGLAND

1603	James VI of Scotland becomes James I of England
1625	Charles I becomes king of England
1629	Charles I dissolves Parliament and embarks on eleven years of personal rule
1640	April–May, Short Parliament; November, Long Parliament convenes
1642	Outbreak of the Civil War
1649	Charles I executed
1649–1660	Various attempts at a Puritan Commonwealth
1660	Charles II restored to the English throne
1670	Secret Treaty of Dover between France and England
1672	Parliament passes the Test Act
1685	James II becomes king of England
1688	Glorious Revolution
1689	William III and Mary II come to the throne of England
1701	Act of Settlement provides for Hanoverian Succession
1702–1714	Queen Anne, the last of the Stuarts
1714	George I of Hanover becomes king of England
1721–1742	Ascendancy of Sir Robert Walpole

RISE OF ABSOLUTE MONARCHY IN FRANCE: THE WORLD OF LOUIS XIV

The French monarchy trod a very different political path. Louis XIV (r. 1643–1715) came to the throne at the age of five. His regent, Cardinal Mazarin (1602–1661), tried to strengthen royal power. These efforts aroused widespread rebellions between 1649 and 1652 known as the Fronde (after the slingshot used by street boys).

YEARS OF PERSONAL RULE

After Mazarin's death in 1661, Louis XIV assumed personal control of the government. Louis concentrated unprecedented authority in the monarchy but, with the Fronde in mind, respected local social and political institutions. Because he governed directly, rebels could not defend themselves from a charge of treason by claiming that they opposed only bad ministers and not the king.

Louis ruled through powerful councils, whose members he chose from families long in royal service or people just beginning to advance socially. Unlike the ancient noble families, they had no power bases in the provinces and depended solely on the king for their positions.

Louis XIV of France (r. 1643–1715) was the dominant European monarch in the second half of the seventeenth century. The powerful centralized monarchy he created established the prototype for the mode of government later termed *absolutism*.

Bridgeman-Giraudon/Art Resource, N.Y.

What do you notice about Louis XIV's body, his clothes, and his surroundings?

Versailles. Louis XIV constructed his great palace at Versailles, as painted here in 1668 by Pierre Patel the Elder (1605–1676), to demonstrate the new centralized power he sought to embody in the French monarchy. The central building is the hunting lodge his father Louis XIII had built earlier in the century. Its interior and that of the wings added to it were decorated with themes from mythology presenting Louis XIV as the "Sun King" around whom all his king-dom revolved. The gardens and ponds behind the main structure were the sites of elaborate entertainment, concerts, and fireworks.

Pierre Patel (1605-1676), "View of the Chateau Versailles in 1668". Chateaux de Versailles et de Trianon, Versailles. Reunion des Musees Nationaux/Art Resource, N.Y.

How does the layout of Versailles convey royal power?

divine right of kings The theory that monarchs are appointed by and answerable only to God.

boyars The Russian nobility.

streltsy Professional troops who made up the Moscow garrison. They were suppressed by Peter the Great.

Louis XIV was innovative in the use of the physical setting of his court to enhance his political power. The palace at Versailles, which was built between 1676 and 1708, was a temple to royalty. Its splendor proclaimed the majesty of the Sun King, as Louis was known. It housed thousands of the more important nobles, royal officials, and servants, and preoccupation with elaborate court ceremonies kept nobles from the real business of government.

Louis owed his concept of royal authority to his devout tutor, the political theorist Bishop Jacques-Bénigne Bossuet (1627–1704). Bossuet defended what he called the **divine right of kings** by citing examples of Old Testament rulers divinely appointed by and answerable only to God. Medieval popes had insisted that only God could judge a pope, and Bossuet made the same claim for a king. As God's regents on Earth, kings could not be bound by nobles and parliaments, for as Louis XIV allegedly explained: "*L'état, c'est moi*" ("I am the state").

Louis insisted on religious conformity, and in October 1685 he revoked the Edict of Nantes (1598), which had protected France's Huguenots. Protestant churches and schools were closed, Protestant ministers exiled, nonconverting laity condemned as galley slaves, and Protestant children taken to be baptized by Catholic priests. More than a quarter million people fled and joined France's opponents in England, Germany, the Netherlands, and the New World.

As will be seen later in the chapter, Louis used most of the wealth and authority he had amassed to lead France into a long series of wars that weakened the nation. Despite this, he established a model for strong centralized monarchy that other monarchs in central and eastern Europe copied. They saw Louis as more successful than the Stuarts of Great Britain, who could only rule through Parliament.

RUSSIA ENTERS THE EUROPEAN POLITICAL ARENA

The emergence of Russia as an active European power was a new development. Previously, Russia had hardly been considered part of Europe, and prior to 1673 it maintained no permanent ambassadors in western Europe. Hemmed in by Sweden on the Baltic and by the Ottoman Empire on the Black Sea, Russia had no warm-water ports. Its chief outlet for trade to the west was Archangel on the White Sea, which was icebound part of the year.

BIRTH OF THE ROMANOV DYNASTY

The last half of the reign of Ivan IV (r. 1533–1584), or Ivan the Terrible, was a time of enormous political turmoil in Russia. An era called the Time of Troubles followed, and in 1613, an assembly of nobles tried to stabilize the situation by electing as tsar a seventeen-year-old boy, Michael Romanov (r. 1613–1645). He began the dynasty that ruled Russia until 1917, but his country remained weak and impoverished. The *boyars*, the old nobility, controlled its bureaucracy, and the *streltsy*, or guards of the Moscow garrison, constantly threatened mutiny.

CHRONOLOGY

FRANCE

1649–1652	The Fronde, a revolt of nobility and townspeople against the crown
1661	Louis XIV assumes personal rule
1667	Louis XIV invades Flanders
1672	France invades the United Provinces
1678–1679	Peace of Nijmwegen
1682	Louis XIV establishes his court at Versailles
1685	Edict of Nantes revoked
1689–1697	Nine Years' War between France and the League of Augsburg
1697	Peace of Ryswick
1702–1714	War of the Spanish Succession
1713	Treaty of Utrecht between England and France
1714	Treaty of Rastadt between the emperor and France

OVERVIEW   Great Powers and Declining Powers in Europe

In the seventeenth and eighteenth centuries, five European states—Britain, France, Austria, Prussia, and Russia—became great European powers. All except Austria remained powerful, even after the end of World War I in 1918. At the same time, four other states that had been major European powers declined permanently into secondary status. The table below lists the main strengths of the rising powers and the main sources of weakness of the declining states.

FIVE GREAT POWERS

State	Government	Strengths
Britain	Constitutional Monarchy	Commercial and financial resources; navy; colonial empire; overseas trade; intellectual liberty; growing industry; religious toleration
France	Absolute Monarchy	Army; large population; cultural preeminence; colonial empire; intellectual vibrancy
Austria	Absolute Monarchy	Imperial prestige; dynastic loyalty; army
Prussia	Absolute Monarchy	Army; efficient bureaucracy
Russia	Absolute Monarchy	Army; large population; extensive natural resources; imperial control over church and state

FOUR DECLINING POWERS

State	Government	Weaknesses
Spain	Absolute Monarchy	Stagnant economy; inefficient government; weak military; enforced religious and intellectual conformity
Ottoman Empire	Absolute Monarchy	Backward economy; unstable government; resistance to change; outmoded military
Sweden	Constitutional Monarchy	Small population; weak economy
Netherlands	Republic	Divided government; small population; declining economy

Peter the Great (r. 1682–1725), seeking to make Russia a military power, reorganized the country's political and economic structures. His reign saw Russia enter fully into European power politics. Here he is depicted as a latter-day St. George, slaying a dragon.

The Apotheosis of Tsar Peter I the Great 1672-1725 by unknown artist 1710. Historical Museum Moscow Russia. E.T. Archive.

What forces might the dragon symbolize?

PETER THE GREAT

In 1682, a ten-year-old boy named Peter (r. 1682–1725) ascended the throne with the help of the *streltsy*, who expected to exploit him. Like Louis XIV, the turmoil of his youth convinced Peter that the power of the tsar had to be made supreme over the *boyars* and the *streltsy* and that the tsar needed a strong military.

Northwestern Europe, particularly the military resources of the maritime powers, fascinated Peter I, who eventually became known as Peter the Great. In 1697, Peter toured western Europe incognito (allowing him to avoid the ceremony that would have attended an official royal visit). He spent his happiest moments inspecting shipyards, docks, and shops that produced military hardware, and he returned to Moscow determined to copy the technology he had seen abroad. He also understood that his plans for making Russia into a great nation would require him to oppose the long-standing power and traditions of the Russian nobles.

While Peter was abroad, the *streltsy* had rebelled. On his return, Peter suppressed the revolt. Approximately a thousand rebels were put to death, and their corpses remained on public display to discourage future disloyalty. Peter then built a new military that would serve him, not itself. He employed ruthless methods of conscription and over the course of his reign drafted about three hundred thousand men. He adopted policies for the officer corps and general military discipline patterned on those of west European armies.

Peter attacked the *boyars* and their attachment to tradition. He personally shaved the long beards of the court *boyars* and sheared off the customary long hand-covering sleeves of their shirts and coats, which had made them the butt of jokes among other European courts. Peter skillfully balanced one group against another as he rebuilt Russian government and military forces along the lines of the more powerful European states.

Peter built a navy to compete with the Ottoman Empire in the Black Sea, and in 1695 he began a war with the Ottomans. He also constructed a Baltic fleet to fight the Great Northern War with Sweden (1700–1721). In 1721, the Peace of Nystad confirmed Russia's conquest of Estonia, Livonia, and part of Finland. Peter had acquired the ice-free ports that were to give Russia influence in European affairs.

Peter's domestic and foreign policies intersected on the Gulf of Finland where he founded his new capital city, St. Petersburg, in 1703. He built government structures and compelled the *boyars* to construct town houses. St. Petersburg symbolized a new Western orientation for Russia and Peter's determination to hold his position on the Baltic coast.

Peter was jealous of his son Aleksei, who had never demonstrated much intelligence or ambition. Late in 1717, Peter suspected that Aleksei had become the focal point for a seditious plot. He personally interrogated Aleksei, who was eventually condemned to death and died under mysterious circumstances on June 26, 1718.

The interrogations surrounding Aleksei had revealed greater degrees of court opposition than Peter had suspected. Recognizing he could not eliminate his numerous opponents the way he had attacked the *streltsy* in 1698, Peter undertook radical administrative reforms designed to bring the nobility and the Russian Orthodox Church more closely under the authority of persons loyal to the tsar.

In 1717 Peter reorganized his domestic administration, using the model of Swedish institutions called *colleges*—bureaus of several persons operating according to written instructions rather than departments headed by a single minister. He established eight colleges to handle matters such as the collection of taxes, foreign relations, war, and economic affairs. Each college had a foreign advisor, and by making careful appointments Peter balanced influence within these colleges between nobles and people he trusted.

He also curtailed the independence of the Russian Orthodox Church, some of whose clergy sympathized with the tsar's son. In 1721, Peter abolished the post of patriarch and submitted the church to a government department called the Holy Synod, consisting of several bishops headed by a layman, the procurator general. It made sure that the church supported the tsar's secular agenda.

In 1722 Peter published a **Table of Ranks** intended to draw the nobility into state service. That table equated a person's social position and privileges with his rank in the bureaucracy or the military rather than with his lineage among the traditional landed nobility, many of whom continued to resist Peter's agenda. Peter thus made the social standing of individual *boyars* a function of their willingness to serve the state.

Peter took many decisive actions, but he never settled on a successor. When Peter died in 1725, he left no obvious heir to the throne. For about thirty years, soldiers and nobles decided who ruled Russia. Peter had laid the foundations of a modern Russia, but not a stable state.

THE HABSBURG EMPIRE AND THE PRAGMATIC SANCTION

In 1648, the Habsburg family established a permanent hold on the title of Holy Roman Emperor, but their power depended on eliciting cooperation from scores of political entities of various kinds.

Vüe des bords de la Neva en descendant la rivière entre le Palais d'hyver de Sa Majesté Imperiale & les batimens de l'Académie des Sciences

St. Petersburg. Peter the Great built St. Petersburg on the Gulf of Finland to provide Russia with better contact with western Europe. He moved Russia's capital there from Moscow in 1703. This is an eighteenth-century view of the city.

Why would a view of St. Petersburg emphasize its position on the sea?

Table of Ranks   An official hierarchy established by Peter the Great in imperial Russia that equated a person's social position and privileges with his rank in the state bureaucracy or army.

CHRONOLOGY

RISE OF RUSSIAN POWER

1533–1584	Reign of Ivan the Terrible
1584–1613	Time of Troubles
1613	Michael Romanov becomes tsar
1682	Peter the Great becomes tsar as a boy
1689	Peter assumes personal rule
1697	European tour of Peter the Great
1698	Peter suppresses the *streltsy*
1700	The Great Northern War opens between Russia and Sweden; Russia defeated at Narva by Charles XII
1703	Saint Petersburg founded
1709	Russia defeats Sweden at Poltava
1718	Death of Aleksei, son of Peter the Great
1721	Peace of Nystad ends the Great Northern War
1721	Peter establishes control over the Russian Orthodox Church
1722	The Table of Ranks
1725	Peter dies, leaving an uncertain succession

While establishing their authority over the German states, the Habsburgs also consolidated their power within their hereditary possessions outside the Holy Roman Empire: the kingdom of Bohemia (in modern Czechoslovakia), the duchies of Moravia and Silesia, Hungary, Croatia, and Transylvania. In each of their territories, the Habsburgs needed help from local nobles, and they often had to bargain with nobles in one part of Europe to maintain their position in another.

Despite these internal weaknesses, Leopold I (r. 1658–1705) blocked the advances of the Turks into central Europe and thwarted aggression by Louis XIV. The Ottomans recognized his sovereignty over Hungary in 1699 and extended his territorial holdings over much of the Balkan Peninsula and western Romania.

In the early eighteenth century the Habsburg emperor Charles VI (r. 1711–1740) had no male heir, and Charles feared that after he died the Austrian Habsburg lands might fall prey to the surrounding powers. He devoted most of his reign to seeking the approval of his family, the estates of his realms, and the major foreign powers for a document called the **Pragmatic Sanction**. This provided the legal basis for a single line of inheritance within the Habsburg dynasty through Charles VI's daughter Maria Theresa (1740–1780). When Charles VI died, he believed that he had secured legal recognition of the unity of the Habsburg Empire and the succession of his daughter. However, his failure to provide Maria Theresa with a strong army or a full treasury left her lands vulnerable to foreign aggression. Less than two months after his death in December 1740, Frederick II of Prussia invaded the Habsburg province of Silesia, and Maria Theresa had to fight for her inheritance.

Pragmatic Sanction The legal basis negotiated by the Emperor Charles VI (r. 1711–1740) for the Habsburg succession through his daughter Maria Theresa (r. 1740–1780).

THE RISE OF PRUSSIA

Prussia expanded into a German power vacuum created by the Peace of Westphalia. It was built by the Hohenzollern family, rulers of Brandenburg since 1417. By inheritance, the Hohenzollerns acquired a series of territories, most of which were not contiguous with Brandenburg, but which, by the late seventeenth century, consituted a block of territory within the Holy Roman Empire second only to that of the Habsburgs. Beginning in the mid-seventeenth century, Hohenzollern rulers forged their geographically separated holdings into a powerful state and built an army that empowered them to rule without the approval of the local nobility.

There was, however, a political and social trade-off between the Hohenzollerns and their nobles, the **Junkers**. In exchange for obedience to the Hohenzollerns, the Junkers received the right to total authority over the serfs on their estates. Furthermore, the heaviest taxes were imposed on the peasants and the urban classes. Junkers increasingly dominated the army officer corps, and all officials and army officers took an oath of loyalty to the Hohenzollern rulers. The army provided the state with a semblance of unity and made Prussia a desirable ally. As thanks for aiding the Habsburg emperor in 1701, the Hohenzollerns were permitted the title of "King" in Prussia, one of their parcels of territory that lay inside Poland and outside the authority of the Holy Roman Emperor.

Junkers The noble landlords of Prussia.

Frederick William I (r. 1713–1740) of Prussia governed through a bureaucracy structured along military lines and mobilized his small realm to support the third or fourth largest army in Europe. Prussia's population, in contrast, ranked thirteenth. Separate laws applied to soldiers and to civilians. Given that the officer corps was the highest social class, military service attracted the sons of Junkers. The army, the

Junker nobility, and the monarchy fused into a single political entity. The military dominated Prussian government, society, and daily life as in no other state in Europe. Other nations had armies; the Prussian army had a nation.

Although Frederick William I built the best army in Europe, he avoided conflict. His army was a symbol of Prussian power and unity, not an instrument for foreign adventures or aggression. At his death in 1740, the army passed to his son Frederick II (Frederick the Great, r. 1740–1786). Almost immediately Frederick II upset the Pragmatic Sanction and invaded Silesia. Austrian-Prussian competition for control of Germany dominated central European affairs for more than a century.

A Prussian Military Camp. This print shows a Prussian encampment in the Pomerania, on the south coast of the Baltic Sea. By 1800 this entire region had come under Prussian control.

What role did the military play in the Prussian rise to power?

EUROPEAN WARFARE: FROM CONTINENTAL TO WORLD CONFLICT

Whereas religious zeal had fueled the European wars of the Reformation Era, dynastic and commercial rivalry drove wars from the reign of the Louis XIV through the conclusion of the Seven Years' War in 1763. European powers developed their military weapons and naval prowess in conflicts with each other and then turned their new technologies against non-European peoples.

WHY WERE the European wars of the eighteenth century global in scope?

THE WARS OF LOUIS XIV

By the late 1660s France was superior to any other European nation in administrative bureaucracy, armed forces, and national unity. Louis XIV could afford to raise and maintain a large and powerful army and was in a position to dominate Europe.

In 1667, Louis XIV led France into the first of four major wars designed to expand his territory, and he was soon regarded as a menace to the whole of western Europe, Catholic and Protestant alike. In 1681, Louis's forces occupied the free city of Strasbourg, prompting defensive coalitions to form against him. One of these, the League of Augsburg, grew to include England, Spain, Sweden, the United Provinces, and the major German states, including the Habsburg empire. Between 1689 and 1697, the League of Augsburg and France battled each other on European fronts in the Nine Years' War, while England and France also warred in North America. In 1697, the Peace of Ryswick secured Holland's borders and thwarted Louis's expansion into Germany.

On November 1, 1700, Charles II of Spain (r. 1665–1700) died and bequeathed his estate to Louis's grandson, Philip of Anjou, or Philip V of Spain (r. 1700–1746). This tipped the balance of power in Europe in France's favor, and England, Holland, and the Holy Roman Empire formed the Grand Alliance as a countermeasure. The War of the Spanish Succession (1701–1714) soon enveloped western Europe. France finally made peace with England at Utrecht in July 1713 and with Holland and the emperor at Rastadt in March 1714. Philip V retained Spain, but England got Gibraltar, a base for action in the Mediterranean. The long war left France economically and politically exhausted.

THE EIGHTEENTH-CENTURY COLONIAL ARENA

The Treaty of Utrecht in 1713 established boundaries for the colonial empires of the first half of the eighteenth century. Except for Portugal's Brazil, Spain claimed all of mainland South America, Mexico, Cuba, half of Hispaniola, Florida, and California. Britain held the North Atlantic seaboard, Nova Scotia, Newfoundland, Jamaica, and Barbados as well as a few trading stations on the Indian subcontinent. The Dutch controlled Surinam (Dutch Guiana) and various trading stations in Ceylon, Bengal, and Java (modern-day Indonesia). The French claimed the St. Lawrence River valley; the Ohio and Mississippi river valleys; Saint Domingue (Haiti), Guadeloupe, and Martinique in the West Indies; and trading stations in India and West Africa. French and English settlers in North America clashed throughout the eighteenth century.

Each of the powers sought to make its imperial holdings into impenetrable trading areas, but the Spanish government in particular lacked the capacity to maintain a commercial monopoly over its sprawling territory. The Treaty of Utrecht gave the British a thirty-year *asiento*, or contract, to furnish slaves to the Spanish Empire and the right to send one ship each year to the trading fair at Portobello (in present-day Panama). The British cheated, and when the Spanish decided to enforce its restrictions, the stage was set for conflict.

A Dutch Merchant and His Wife in Batavia (Java). Attributed to Jacob Cuyp (1594–1651), this painting from 1650 shows the Dutch merchant Jacob Mathieusen and his wife in front of Batavia's harbor, on the island of Java in the East Indies. The merchant points to his ships while a slave shelters the couple from the tropical sun with a parasol.

How is the relation between the merchant and his wife depicted? Between the Europeans and the non-European?

WAR OF JENKINS'S EAR

In 1731, when a Spanish patrol boarded a British vessel to search for contraband, a fight ensued and an English captain, Robert Jenkins, had his ear cut off. He preserved it in a jar of brandy and in 1738 displayed it to the British Parliament as evidence of alleged Spanish atrocities inflicted on British merchants. Late in 1739, Great Britain went to war with Spain and, in junction with Prussia's aggression on the continent, began a series of worldwide European wars.

THE WAR OF THE AUSTRIAN SUCCESSION (1740–1748)

In December 1740, Frederick II of Prussia seized the Austrian province of Silesia. Maria Theresa of Austria preserved the Habsburg Empire by sacrificing some of the power of its crown. She ensured the loyalty of the Magyars of Hungary, the most important of her domains, by granting them considerable local autonomy. The link between her war with Prussia, the War of the Austrian Succession, and the British–Spanish commercial conflict was made by France. French aristocrats pushed their government to support Prussia against Austria, France's long-standing enemy. French aid to Prussia helped consolidate a new and powerful German state, a threat that brought Great Britain into the continental war against France and Prussia. In 1744, the conflict expanded beyond the continent when France decided to support Spain against Britain in the New World. The war ended in stalemate in 1748. By the Treaty of Aix-la-Chapelle, Prussia retained Silesia. This was a truce, not a permanent peace.

THE SEVEN YEARS' WAR (1756–1763)

In 1756, a dramatic shift of alliances occurred. Prussia and Great Britain signed the Convention of Westminster. The Prussians and the British hoped that their alliance would dissuade Russia and France from invading Germany. When Austria countered the loss of its British ally by turning to France, the European alliances of the previous century were reversed.

In August 1756, Prussia invaded Saxony to head off what Frederick II thought was a conspiracy by Saxony, Austria, and France. This began the Seven Years' War. In the spring of 1757, France and Austria formed a new alliance targeted at Prussia, and Sweden, Russia, and the smaller German states joined them. Two factors in addition to Frederick's strong leadership saved Prussia: British financial aid and the death in 1762 of Empress Elizabeth of Russia (r. 1741–1762). Her successor, Tsar Peter III (d. 1762), fervently admired Frederick and immediately made peace with Prussia. The Treaty of Hubertusburg of 1763 ended the Seven Years' War with no changes in borders.

More impressive than Prussia's survival were Great Britain's victories in every theater of conflict. These were the work of William Pitt the Elder (1708–1778), who was named secretary of state in charge of the war in 1757. North America, however, was Pitt's real concern. He won control of all of North America east of the Mississippi for Great Britain in what American historians call the French and Indian War. Pitt's aspirations were global. He took Quebec from the French in 1759 and

CHRONOLOGY	
EUROPEAN CONFLICTS OF THE MID-EIGHTEENTH CENTURY	
1739	Outbreak of War of Jenkins's Ear between England and Spain
1740	War of the Austrian Succession commences
1748	Treaty of Aix-la-Chapelle
1756	Convention of Westminster between England and Prussia
1756	Seven Years' War opens
1759	British forces capture Quebec
1763	Treaty of Hubertusburg
1763	Treaty of Paris

The Taking of Quebec. The capture of Quebec in September 1759 by British forces, followed by the seizure of Montreal a year later, signaled the demise of French power in Canada.

General James Wolfe's expedition against Quebec in 1759: English engraving, 1760. The Granger Collection, New York.

How did the French lose control in Canada?

View of the Taking of Quebeck by the English Forces Commanded by Gen.ˡ Wolfe Sep: 13.1759.

Old Regime Term applied to the pattern of social, political, and economic relationships and institutions that existed in Europe before the French Revolution.

QUICK REVIEW

The Seven Years' War (1756–1763)

◆ Prussian invasion of Saxony sparked war

◆ War spread into North America

◆ Treaty of Paris ended war in 1763

Montreal a year later. The French West Indies fell to the British fleet. British forces on the Indian subcontinent, under Robert Clive (1725–1774), defeated the French in 1757 and cleared the way for the conquest of all India by the British East India Company. Never had a European power experienced such a complete worldwide military victory.

The Treaty of Paris of 1763 was somewhat less triumphant. George III (r. 1760–1820) had succeeded to the British throne and Pitt was no longer in office. Britain received all of Canada, the Ohio River valley, and the eastern half of the Mississippi River valley. France retained footholds in India at Pondicherry and Chandernagore and regained the West Indies sugar islands of Guadeloupe and Martinique.

The midcentury wars established a new balance of power in European and on the high seas (see Map 20–1). Prussia became a great continental power, and Great Britain gained a world empire. France's retreat from North America opened the way for a continent dominated by the English language and Protestantism. Latin America remained dominated by the Spanish and Portuguese languages and Roman Catholicism. On the subcontinent of Asia the foundation was laid for British rule. The global power of the European states was a function not only of their wars but also of dramatic economic and political developments that allowed Europe to dominate the world from the 1750s to the Second World War.

WHAT WERE the political and economic structures of the Old Regime?

THE OLD REGIME

The period before the French Revolution's outbreak in 1789 is called the *ancien régime* (the **Old Regime**). Politically, the age was characterized by absolute monarchies, growing bureaucracies, and aristocratically led armies. Economically, it featured the predominance of agriculture, food shortages, slow transportation, a low level of iron production, unsophisticated financial institutions, and in some cases, competitive commercial overseas empires. Socially, people saw themselves more as members of groups than as individuals.

MAP 20–1   The Colonial Arena.   The acquisition of overseas colonies by European powers led to intense rivalries on a global scale. Territories frequently changed hands during the eighteenth century.

Why were colonies central to European conflicts in the eighteenth century?

MAINTENANCE OF TRADITION

Few people outside the political, commercial, and intellectual elite wanted change or innovation. This was especially true of social relationships. Both nobles and peasants repeatedly called for the restoration of traditional or customary rights. Nobles defended their ancient rights against intrusion by expanding monarchical bureaucracies. Peasants called for the revival or maintenance of their customary manorial rights. Except for early signs of industrial development in Britain, economies were predominantly traditional. Everything depended on the quality and quantity of the grain harvest.

HIERARCHY AND PRIVILEGE

The medieval sense of hierarchy became more rigid during the century. Some cities tried to enforce sumptuary laws that forbade persons to dress like their social superiors, but it was the corporate nature of social relationships that enforced hierarchy. Each state or society was a community composed of smaller communities. Eighteenth-century Europeans did not claim individual rights. Their rights were those of the communities of which they were a part. A "community" might be a village, nobility, a guild, a university, or a parish. Its privileges might involve exemption from taxation or degrading punishment or the right to practice a trade or craft.

ARISTOCRACY

The eighteenth century was the great age of the aristocracy. Nobles constituted about 1 to 5 percent of the population of any given country. They were the single wealthiest group, and land was the chief source of their income. They possessed the widest range of powers and dominated polite society. Aristocracy everywhere was a matter of birth and legal privilege, but in other respects, aristocrats differed markedly from country to country. Great Britain boasted the smallest, wealthiest, best defined, and most socially responsible aristocracy. Moving eastward across Europe, aristocrats became more numerous, not always wealthy, but possessing increasing degrees of arbitrary, repressive authority.

A European-wide **aristocratic resurgence** marked the eighteenth century as various nobilities sought to defend their privileges against the expanding power of monarchies and the growing wealth of commercial classes. The nobles restricted entry into their ranks and institutions. By monopolizing appointments to the officer corps of the armies, the bureaucracies, the government ministries, and the church, they tried to control the power of the monarchies. They tried to curtail royal authority by using institutions they already controlled: the British Parliament, the French *parlements*, their local estates, and provincial diets. Nobles also pressed the peasantry for higher rents or long-forgotten feudal dues as a way to shore up their position and reassert traditional privileges.

aristocratic resurgence Eighteenth-century aristocratic efforts to resist the expanding power of European monarchies.

parlement French regional court dominated by hereditary nobility. The most important was the Parlement of Paris, which claimed the right to register royal decrees before they could become law.

QUICK REVIEW

Servants under the Old Regime
- Worked in exchange for room, board, and wages
- Usually young and not socially inferior to the employer
- Work as servants allowed young people to save toward independence

THE LAND AND ITS TILLERS

Land was the economic basis of eighteenth-century European life. Well over three fourths of Europe's population lived on the land. Most spent their entire lives within a few miles of their birthplaces; they were poor, and their lives were hard.

PEASANTS AND SERFS

Most people who worked the land were subject to domination by landowners. This was true to different degrees for free peasants, such as English tenants and most French cultivators, and for the serfs of Germany, Austria, and Russia, who were bound to individual plots of land and particular lords. Generally, the power of landlords increased the farther east one traveled. Most French peasants owned some land, but nearly all peasants were subject to feudal dues and to forced labor on a lord's estate for a certain number of days each year.

What seems to be the relationship between husband and wife and between the humans and the land?

In Prussia and Austria, despite attempts by the monarchies to improve the lot of serfs, landlords exercised almost complete control over them. Moreover, throughout continental Europe the burden of state taxation fell on the tillers of the soil. Through various legal privileges and the ability to demand concessions from their monarchs, the landlords escaped the payment of numerous taxes. The serf's condition was worst in Russia. Russian serfs were regarded merely as economic commodities. Their services were attached to an individual lord rather than to a particular plot of land. Their landlords could demand up to six days a week of labor from them, and like Prussian and Austrian landlords, they could punish their serfs. Although serfs had little recourse against their lords, custom, tradition, and law provided a few protections. For example, the marriages of serfs, unlike those of most slaves, were legally recognized. The landlord could not disband the family of a serf (see Document, "Russian Serfs Lament Their Condition").

Peter the Great gave whole villages of serfs to favored nobles, and Catherine the Great (r. 1762–1796) confirmed the authority of the nobles over their serfs in exchange for the nobility's political cooperation. More than fifty peasant revolts between 1762 and 1769 culminated between 1773 and 1774 in Pugachev's Rebellion, the largest peasant uprising of the eighteenth century. When it was finally and brutally suppressed, any discussion of liberalizing the condition of Russia's serfs was postponed for a generation. Smaller peasant revolts or disturbances occurred in Bohemia in 1775, in Transylvania in 1784, in Moravia in 1786, and in Austria in 1789. Peasants and serfs normally directed their wrath against property rather than persons, and they sought to reassert traditional or customary rights against practices they perceived as innovations. In this respect, the peasant revolts were conservative.

family economy   The basic structure of production and consumption in preindustrial Europe.

FAMILY STRUCTURES AND THE FAMILY ECONOMY

In preindustrial Europe, the household was the basic unit of production and consumption. Very few productive establishments employed more than a handful of people not belonging to the owner's family. In rural areas, small towns, and cities, the household mode of organization predominated: farms, artisans' workshops, and small merchants' shops. This created what is called the **family economy**.

WHAT WAS the role of women in family economy?

DOCUMENT

Russian Serfs Lament Their Condition

As with other illiterate groups in European history, it is difficult to recapture the voices of Russian serfs. The following verses from "The Slaves' Lament," a popular ballad from the era of Pugachev's Rebellion (1773–1775), indicate that the serfs were aware of how the legislation of that era, which favored the landowning classes, affected their lives. The verses embody the resentment that Pugachev's Rebellion ignited. Note how the verses suggest that the tsar may be more favorable to serfs than their landowners are. Pugachev claimed to be Tsar Peter III, and many Russian serfs believed him and thus considered him a liberator from landlord tyranny. Throughout this ballad, serfs present themselves as slaves.

- **What** specific complaints about landlords are expressed in these verses? What charges indicate that serfs may believe their situation has worsened? What hope do they seem to place in the tsar? What idealized picture of the world do the serfs believe they would themselves create?

O woe to us slaves living for the masters!
We do not know how to serve their ferocity!
Service is like a sharp scythe;
And kindness is like the morning dew.
Brothers, how annoying it is to us
And how shameful and insulting
That another who is not worthy to be equal with us
Has so many of us in his power.
And if we steal from the lord one half kopeck,
The law commands us to be killed like a louse.
And if the master steals ten thousand,
Nobody will judge who should be hanged.
The injustice of the Russian sheriffs has increased:
Whoever brings a present is right beyond argument.
They have stopped putting their trust in the Creator
  for authority,
And have become accustomed to own us like cattle.
All nations rebuke us and wonder at our stupidity,
That such stupid people are born in Russia.

THE FAMILY ECONOMY

Throughout Europe, family members saw themselves as working together in an interdependent rather than an independent or individualistic manner. The goal of the family household was to produce or secure through wages enough food to support its members. In the countryside, they usually farmed. In cities and towns, artisan production or working for another person was the usual pattern. Almost everyone lived within a household. Except for members of religious orders, people living outside a household were viewed as potentially criminal, disruptive, or a drain on the charity of others.

Every member of a family in the family economy had to work. Few peasant households in western Europe had enough land to support themselves by farming alone. One or more of their family members had to work elsewhere and send wages home. It was not uncommon for a father to become a migrant worker and shift the burden of farm work to his wife and younger children. Within the family economy, all of the goods and income produced benefited the household, not individual family members. The need to survive poor harvests or economic slumps meant no one could be idle.

In the urban version of the family economy, the father was usually a chief craftsman who employed one or more servants. But he also expected his children to work in his shop. His eldest child was usually trained in the trade, and his wife might sell the wares he produced or pursue another trade. The wife of a merchant also often ran her husband's business, especially when he traveled to purchase new goods. When business was poor, family members looked for other employment to help the family unit survive.

And indeed, stupidity was rooted in us long ago,
as each honour here has been given to vagrants.
The master can kill the servant like a gelding;
The denunciation by a slave cannot be believed.
Unjust judges have composed a decree
That we should be tyrannically whipped with a knout
for that.
Better that we should agree to serve the tsar.
Better to live in dark woods
Than to be before the eyes of these tyrants;
They look on us cruelly with their eyes
And eat us as iron eats rye. No one wants to serve
the tsar
But only to grind us down to the end.
And they try to collect unjust bribes,
And they are not frightened that people die cruelly.
Ah brothers, if we got our freedom,
We would not take the lands or the fields for ourselves.
We would go into service as soldiers, brothers,

And would be friendly among ourselves,
Would destroy all injustice
And remove the root of evil lords.
They [the landlords] sell all the good rye to the merchants,
And give us like pigs the bad.
The greedy lords eat meat at fast time,
And even when meat is allowed, the slaves
must cook meatless cabbage soup.
O brothers, it is our misfortune
always to have rye kasha.
The lords drink and make merry,
And do not allow the slaves even to burst out laughing.

Source: Paul Dukes, trans. and ed., *Russia under Catherine the Great: Select Documents on Government and Society* (Newtonville, MA: Oriental Research Partners, 1978), pp. 115–117. Reprinted by permission of Oriental Research Partners.

Farm Family. Painted by the English artist Francis Wheatley (1747–1801) near the close of the eighteenth century, this scene is part of a series illustrating a day in the life of an idealized farm family. Note the artist's assumptions about the division of labor by gender. Men work in the fields, women work in the home or look after the needs of men and children. As other illustrations in this chapter show, many eighteenth-century women in fact worked outside the home, but considerable social pressure was developing at this time to restrict them to domestic roles. This painting and the others in the series are thus more prescriptive than descriptive, intended in part to persuade their viewers that women belonged in their separate family sphere. Many, perhaps most, families living in the countryside could not maintain the closeness that these paintings extol. To survive, many had to send members to work on other farms or even to other regions.

Francis Wheatley (RA) (1747–1801), "Evening," signed and dated 1799, oil on canvas, 17 1/2 × 21 1/2 in. (44.5 × 54.5 cm), Yale Center for British Art, Paul Mellon Collection, Bridgeman Art Library (B1977.14.118).

How have images such as this one influenced the way we view pre-industrial society?

WOMEN AND THE FAMILY ECONOMY

The family economy constrained the lives of women in preindustrial western Europe. A woman's life experience was largely a function of her ability to establish and maintain a household. Marriage was an economic necessity, since a woman outside a household was highly vulnerable. Unless she was an aristocrat or a member of a religious order, she could probably not support herself. Consequently, much of a woman's life was devoted first to serving her parents' household and then to establishing one of her own. In most cases, bearing and rearing children were subordinate to these goals.

By the age of seven, a girl was expected to begin to do household work. On a farm, she might look after chickens or water animals or carry food to adults working the land. In an urban artisan's household, she would do some form of light work, such as cleaning, carrying, sewing, or weaving. She remained in her parents' home until they found more remunerative work for her elsewhere. An artisan's daughter might not leave home until marriage because she was learning valuable skills from her parents. Girls who grew up on farms usually left home by the age of twelve or fourteen. They were likely to migrate to a nearby town or city to become household servants but would rarely travel more than thirty miles from their parents' home.

A young woman's chief goal was to accumulate a dowry, some capital she could contribute to setting up a household with her husband. Marriage within the family economy was a joint economic undertaking. It might take a young woman ten years or more to accumulate a dowry. This meant that marriage was usually postponed until a woman's mid- to late twenties. Within marriage, domestic duties, childbearing, and child rearing were subordinate to economic survival. Consequently, couples would often practice birth control.

A married woman's work was in many ways a function of her husband's occupation. If economic disaster struck the family, more often than not it was the wife who took the lead in sending off family members to find work elsewhere or even to beg in the streets. Women led active, often decisive roles in the family economy.

THE REVOLUTION IN AGRICULTURE

WHAT WAS the connection between population increase and agricultural improvements in the eighteenth century?

The main goal of traditional European peasant society was to ensure the stability of the local food supply. That supply was never certain and became more uncertain the farther east one traveled. A failed harvest could mean death from either outright starvation or protracted debility. Food was often harder to find in the country than in cities because city governments usually stored reserve supplies of grain.

Poor harvests meant higher prices. Even small increases in food costs could squeeze peasant or artisan families. If prices increased sharply, many families sought help from their local government or the church. Peasants felt powerless before the whims of nature and the marketplace, and they resisted change on the assumption that traditional cultivation practices best ensured the food supply.

During the eighteenth century, bread prices rose slowly but steadily, spurred by demand from a growing population. Prices rose faster than urban wages and brought no advantage to the small peasant producer. The beneficiaries were landlords and the wealthier peasants who had surplus grain to sell. The increasing price of grain encouraged innovation in farm production and began an **agricultural revolution**.

agricultural revolution The innovations in farm production that began in the eighteenth century and led to a scientific and mechanized agriculture.

enclosure The consolidation or fencing in of common lands by British landlords to increase production and achieve greater commercial profits. It also involved the reclamation of waste land and the consolidation of strips into block fields.

NEW CROPS AND NEW METHODS

The agricultural revolution began during the sixteenth and seventeenth centuries in the Low Countries, where Dutch landlords and farmers devised better ways to build dykes and to drain land so that they could farm larger areas. They experimented with new crops, such as clover and turnips, that would increase the supply of animal fodder and replenish the soil.

The Dutch innovations spread to England during the early eighteenth century. They ensured adequate food for cities and freed surplus agricultural labor for industrial work, but the landlords' new approach to farming undermined traditional peasant life. The objective of farming ceased to be the provision of a local food supply and became the pursuit of the largest possible profit.

Agricultural innovations were adopted slowly; many were incompatible with the existing organization of land in Britain. In 1700 approximately half the arable land in Britain was farmed by the "open-field method." Small cultivators in village communities usually tilled unconnected strips, and their traditional two- or three-field systems of rotation left much land fallow and unproductive each year. Decisions about planting were made communally. The system discouraged innovation and aimed to produce a steady, but not a growing, supply of food. By the second half of the century, the rising price of wheat encouraged landlords to consolidate or enclose their lands to increase production. **Enclosure** involved fencing common lands, reclaiming previously untilled waste, and transforming cultivated strips into block fields. These procedures disrupted the economic and social life of the countryside and incited riots. The larger landlords resorted to parliamentary acts for help in enclosing lands. Between 1761 and 1792, almost 500,000 acres were enclosed through parliamentary acts. In 1801, a general enclosure act streamlined the process.

The enclosures have remained controversial. They increased food production but disrupted small traditional communities. They forced off the land some independent farmers, who had needed the common pasturage, and very poor cottagers, who had lived on the reclaimed waste land. In some counties where the enclosures took place, however, the population increased. New soil had come into production, and services subsidiary to farming also expanded.

POPULATION EXPANSION

Agricultural improvement was both a cause and a result of an immense growth in the population of Europe. Exact figures are lacking, but the best estimates suggest that in 1700 Europe's population was between 100 million and 120 million people. By 1800, the figure had risen to almost 190 million, and by 1850, to 260 million (see Figure 20–1). Such extraordinary growth put new demands on all resources and considerable pressure on existing social organization. Causes of this growth are unclear. The death rate declined, thanks to fewer wars and epidemics in the eighteenth century. But changes in the food supply itself may have been the chief reason for sustained population growth. One contributing factor was the widespread cultivation of a New World

English Children. Few children in the eighteenth century were as privileged as the ones in this landed English family. Most began working to help support their families as soon as they were physically able. It was during the eighteenth century, however, that Europeans apparently began to view childhood as a distinct period in human development. Even though Arthur Devis has painted these children to look something like little adults, he has included various toys associated with childhood.

Arthur Devis (c. 1711–1787), "Children in an Interior," © 1742–1743, oil on canvas, 39 × 49 3/4 in. (99.0 × 125.5 cm), Yale Center for British Art, Paul Mellon Collection, B1978.43.5.

Do the children seem happy in this painting? Why or why not?

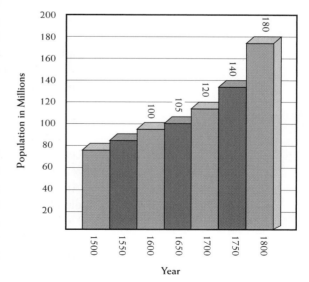

FIGURE 20–1.   Population of Europe, 1500–1800.

What caused population growth to accelerate in the eighteenth century?

tuber, the potato. Enough potatoes could be raised on a single acre to feed one peasant's family for an entire year. With this more certain food supply, more children could be reared, and more could survive.

THE EIGHTEENTH-CENTURY INDUSTRIAL REVOLUTION: AN EVENT IN WORLD HISTORY

WHY DID the Industrial Revolution begin in England?

In the second half of the eighteenth century the European economy began very slowly to industrialize. This development, more than any other, distinguished the West from the rest of the world for the next two centuries. While this economic development was occurring, people did not call it a *revolution*. That term came to technology-based advances in productivity only after the French Revolution, when writers contended that what had taken place in Britain was the economic equivalent of the political events in France. From this comparison arose the concept of an *industrial* revolution.

Economies had always been relatively static. But since the late eighteenth century, Europe's ecomomy has expanded at a relatively steady rate. At considerable social cost and dislocation, industrialism produced more goods and services than ever before in human history. Industrialism in Europe eventually overcame the economy of scarcity. The new means of production demanded new kinds of skills, new discipline in work, and a large labor force. The produced goods met immediate consumer demand and created new demands. In the long run, industrialism raised standards of living and gave human beings more control over the forces of nature than they had ever known. But industrialism also upset the political and social structures of the Old Regime and prompted political and social reform. The economic elite of the emerging industrial society challenged the political dominance of the aristocracy. Traditional communities declined, people were displaced, and cities grew. This occurred wherever industrialization spread during the next two centuries.

The consumer products of industrialization encouraged more international trade in which Western nations supplied finished goods in exchange for raw materials. Other areas of the globe became economically dependent on European and American demand. The wealth achieved through this uneven commerce allowed Europeans to dominate world markets for almost two centuries. Furthermore, by the early nineteenth century iron and steel production and the new technologies of manufacture allowed European states and later the United States to build more powerful military forces, especially navies, than those of Africa, Latin America, or Asia. Both the economic and the military dominance of the West arose directly from the industrialization.

Much of the history of the non-Western world from the middle of the eighteenth century to the present can be understood in terms of how the nonindustrialized nations reacted to Westerners made wealthy and powerful through industrialized economies. Africa and Latin America became generally dependent economies. Japan, by the middle of the nineteenth century, decided it must imitate the European pattern. China became indirectly ruled by Europeans; revolutions of the twentieth century largely represented Chinese efforts to achieve self-direction. Southeast Asia and the Middle East supplied resources to the West; they could move toward economic independence only through imitation or—like Arab nations in the early 1970s—by refusing to supply oil to the West. The process of industrialization that commenced in small factories in eighteenth-century Europe has changed the world more than any other single development in the last two centuries.

INDUSTRIAL LEADERSHIP OF GREAT BRITAIN

Great Britain was the home of the **Industrial Revolution** for several reasons. Britain was the single largest free-trade area in Europe, with good roads and waterways and no internal trade barriers. There were rich deposits of coal and iron ore. The political structure was stable, and property rights were secure. Banking and public credit systems created a good investment climate. Taxation was heavy, but fair. There was both domestic consumer demand and demand from the North American colonies. Finally, British society was relatively open and allowed people who earned money to rise socially. (See Map 20–2.)

Textile production inaugurated the Industrial Revolution. The peasant family living in a one- or two-room cottage, not the factory, was the basic unit of production. The family economy, rather than the industrial factory economy, characterized the eighteenth century. Small-scale household manufacturing permeated the European countryside. The same peasants who tilled the land in spring and summer often spun

Industrial Revolution Mechanization of the European economy that began in Britain in the second half of the eighteenth century.

MAP 20–2   The Industrial Revolution in Britain.   Richly endowed with coal and iron ore and possessing many natural ports and a network of navigable waterways, Britain exploited these advantages to become the world's first industrial nation.

How does this map show the connections between industry and urbanization?

OVERVIEW   Why the Industrial Revolution Began in Britain

Great Britain was the home of the Industrial Revolution, and until the middle of the nineteenth century, it maintained the industrial leadership of Europe. Several factors contributed to the early industrialization of Britain.

Natural Resources	• Britain had extensive deposits of coal and iron ore.
Infrastructure	• Britain had an extensive network of roads and canals that facilitated the shipment of raw materials and goods.
Society	• The predominance of London: London was the largest city in Europe and the social, commercial, financial, and political center of Britain. It was thus both an enormous market for consumer goods itself and created a demand for these goods in the rest of Britain, which sought to emulate London fashions.
	• The prevalence of newspapers: Newspapers thrived in Britain, and advertisements in them increased consumer demand for goods.
	• Wealth in Britain brought status: British society was relatively mobile. Wealthy merchants and entrepreneurs could rise socially, enter the aristocracy, and enjoy political influence.
Government, Financial Institutions, and Empire	• The rule of law: Britain had a stable government that guaranteed property rights.
	• Britain was a free-trade area. No internal tolls inhibited the shipment of goods and raw materials within Britain.
	• Britain had a sound system of banking and public credit that created a stable climate for investing in commerce and industry.
	• Taxes were collected efficiently and fairly. No class was exempt from paying taxes.
	• The colonial empire: British colonies were both a market for British goods and sources of raw materials for British manufacturers.

domestic or putting-out system Method of production in which agents furnished raw materials to households, whose members created finished products, which the agents then sold.

spinning jenny A machine invented in England by James Hargreaves around 1765 to mass-produce thread.

water frame A water-powered device invented by Richard Arkwright to produce a more durable cotton fabric. It led to the shift in the production of cotton textiles from households to factories.

thread or wove textiles in winter. Under the **domestic** or **putting-out system**, agents of urban textile merchants distributed wool or other fibers to the homes of peasants, who spun it into thread. The agent then transported the thread to other peasants, who wove it into cloth, and the merchant sold the final product. Sometimes spinners or weavers owned their own equipment, but more often the merchant capitalist provided the machinery as well as the raw material.

By midcentury, production bottlenecks had developed within the domestic system. Thanks to population growth, especially in Great Britain, demand for cotton textiles was growing more rapidly than production. The most famous inventions of the Industrial Revolution were devised in response to this consumer demand for cotton textiles. John Kay's invention of the flying shuttle in the 1730s gave weavers the technical capacity to produce enough fabric to satisfy demand, but spinners could not make enough thread for the weavers. Manufacturers offered prizes for the invention of a machine to correct this imbalance, and about 1765 James Hargreaves (d. 1778) invented the **spinning jenny**.

The spinning jenny was a piece of machinery for cottage use. The invention that moved cotton textile manufacture into the factory was Richard Arkwright's (1732–1792) **water frame**, patented in 1769. When Arkwright lost his patent rights, other manufacturers used his invention, and numerous factories sprang up in the countryside near streams that provided water power. By 1815, cotton composed 40 percent of the value of British domestic exports, and by 1830 just over 50 percent.

The critical invention that enabled industrialization to spread from one industry to another was the steam engine. For the first time in history, human beings were able to tap an unlimited source of inanimate power. Unlike engines powered by water or wind, the steam engine, fueled by coal, provided a portable, steady source of power that could be applied to many industrial and transportation uses.

The first practical engine using steam power was invented by Thomas Newcomen (1663–1729) in the early eighteenth century. It was large, inefficient, and practically immovable, but English mine operators used it to pump water out of coal and tin mines. In 1769, James Watt (1736–1819) patented an improved design, but it required precise metalwork. Watt's partner Matthew Boulton (1728–1809), a toy manufacturer, worked with John Wilkinson (1728–1808), a cannon manufacturer, to find ways to drill the precise metal cylinders required by Watt's engines. In 1776, the Watt steam engine found its first commercial application pumping water from mines. Boulton persuaded Watt to adapt the engine for use in running cotton mills, and by the early nineteenth century the steam engine had become the prime mover in every industry. Applied to ships and then to wagons on iron rails, it also revolutionized transportation.

Blacksmith Shop. During the eighteenth century, most goods were produced in small workshops, such as this English blacksmith shop shown in a painting by Joseph Wright of Derby (1734–1797), or in the homes of artisans. Not until very late in the century, with the early stages of industrialization, did a few factories appear.

Joseph Wright of Derby, The Blacksmith's Shop, 1771, oil on canvas, 50 1/2 x 41 in. (128.3 x 104.1 cm). Yale Center for British Art, Paul Mellon Collection.

How does this painting reveal the artist's attitude toward what is going on here?

The manufacture of high-quality iron was essential for industrial development. In the course of the eighteenth century, British ironmakers began to use coke (derived from coal) instead of charcoal to smelt ores, and the steam engine provided power for high-temperature blast furnaces. Britain had large coal deposits, and the steam engine improved iron production while increasing demand for iron. In 1784, Henry Cort (1740–1800) introduced a new method for melting and stirring molten ore that yielded a purer iron. He also developed a rolling mill that shaped molten metal into bars, rails, or other forms. Previously, metal had to be pounded into shape. All of these innovations achieved a better, more versatile, and cheaper product, and by the early nineteenth century, annual British iron production amounted to more than a million tons. The lower cost of iron in turn lowered the cost of steam engines and allowed them to be used more widely.

CHRONOLOGY

MAJOR INVENTIONS IN THE TEXTILE-MANUFACTURING REVOLUTION

1733	John Kay's flying shuttle
1765	James Hargreaves's spinning jenny (patent 1770)
1769	James Watt's steam engine patent
1769	Richard Arkwright's water frame patent
1787	Edmund Cartwright's power loom

EUROPEAN CITIES

PATTERNS OF PREINDUSTRIAL URBANIZATION

Remarkable changes occurred in the pattern of city growth between 1500 and 1800. In 1500 there were approximately 156 cities within Europe (excluding Hungary and Russia) with a population greater than 10,000. Only four cities—Paris, Milan, Venice, and Naples—had more than 100,000 inhabitants. By 1800 approximately 363 cities had

HOW DID population growth lead to changes in urban social structures?

10,000 or more inhabitants, and 17 had populations larger than 100,000. The percentage of the European population living in urban areas had risen from just over 5 percent to just over 9 percent. The urban concentration had also shifted from southern Mediterranean Europe to the north.

URBAN CLASSES

At the top of the urban social structure stood a generally small group of nobles, major merchants, bankers, financiers, clergy, and government officials. They usually constituted a self-appointed and self-electing oligarchy who governed the city through its corporation or city council. In a few cities, artisan guilds featured in urban governments, but most city councils were dominated by the local nobility and the commercial elite.

The middle class, or *bourgeoisie*—prosperous but not immensely wealthy merchants, tradesmen, bankers, and professional people—were the most dynamic element of the urban population. The middle class had less wealth than most nobles but more than urban artisans. They lived in the cities and towns, and their sources of income had little or nothing to do with the land. They normally supported reform, change, and economic growth. Resenting aristocratic privilege and social exclusiveness, they wanted rational regulations for trade and commerce.

As the century passed, the bourgeoisie increasingly begrudged the aristocracy, and as the middle class grew in size and wealth and aristocratic control of political and ecclesiastical power tightened, tension increased. The middle class tended to fear the lower urban classes as much as they resented the nobility. The lower orders constituted a potentially violent element in society; a potential threat to property; and, in their poverty, a drain on national resources. The lower orders, however, were much more varied than either the city aristocracy or the middle class cared to admit.

Shopkeepers, artisans, and wage earners constituted the single largest group in any city, and they suffered from the grasping of both the middle class and the local nobility. They had their own culture, values, and institutions and, like the rural peasants,

Dress Shop. Consumption of all forms of consumer goods increased greatly in the eighteenth century. This engraving illustrates a shop, probably in Paris. Here women, working apparently for a woman manager, are making dresses and hats to meet the demands of the fashion trade.

What spurred the growing demand for consumer goods?

were conservative. Their economic position was highly vulnerable, and their lives centered on their work. They usually lived near or at their place of employment and worked in shops with fewer than a half dozen other people. They formed guilds to protect their interests, but by the eighteenth century these had declining influence and reinforced conservative values. The guilds constituted the chief protection for artisans against the operation of the commercial market and were particularly strong in central Europe.

THE JEWISH POPULATION: AGE OF THE GHETTO

HOW WERE European Jews segregated from European society?

There were small Jewish communities in Amsterdam and other western European cities, but most European Jews lived in eastern Europe. In 1762, Catherine the Great of Russia specifically excluded Jews from a manifesto that welcomed foreigners to settle in Russia, although she eased this a few years later. The first partition of Poland in 1772 (see Chapter 23) gave Russia a large Jewish population and created larger Jewish communities in Prussia and Austria.

Jews did not have the same rights as Christians, unless such rights were specifically granted to them by a sympathetic monarch. They were resident aliens whose status could change at the whim of a government. Under the Old Regime, they lived apart from non-Jews—in cities usually in districts called **ghettos**—and in the countryside in separate villages. They were treated as a distinct people religiously and legally and often bore the burden of discriminatory legislation.

ghettos Separate communities in which Jews were required by law to live.

During the seventeenth century, a few Jews helped finance wars for major rulers. The most famous of these "court Jews" was Samuel Oppenheimer (1630–1703), who helped the Habsburgs fund the struggle against the Turks that defended Vienna. The court Jews were exceptional, for most European Jews lived in poverty and worked at the lowest occupations. Their religious beliefs, rituals, and community set them apart, and numerous issues kept them in positions of social inferiority. But under the Old Regime, the discrimination they suffered was based on religious separateness, not racial prejudices. Jews who converted to Christianity were admitted to the political and social institutions of European society.

Ghetto in Cracow. During the Old Regime, European Jews were separated from non-Jews, typically in districts known as ghettos. Relegated to the least desirable section of a city or to rural villages, most lived in poverty. This watercolor painting depicts a street in Kazimlesz, the Jewish quarter of Cracow, Poland.

Judaica Collection. Max Berger, Vienna Austria/©Erich Lessing/Art Resource, N.Y.

Even though this painting shows an outwardly peaceful scene, how does it also show segregation?

SUMMARY

HOW DID England and France provide models for governance in early modern Europe?

Models of European Political Development. In the seventeenth and eighteenth centuries, Britain, France, Russia, Austria, and Prussia emerged as great powers in Europe. Through their military strength, economic development, and in some cases colonial empires, they would affect virtually every other world civilization. In the seventeenth century, conflict between the Stuart kings and Parliament led to civil war, the execution of Charles I, a short-lived English republic under Oliver Cromwell, and the Glorious Revolution (1688–1689) that finally established the supremacy of Parliament. Under Louis XIV (r. 1643–1715), France became the model of an absolute monarchy. Russia became a great power under Peter the Great (r. 1682–1725), who opened Russia to Western influence. The Habsburgs remained Holy Roman Emperors, but the rise of Prussia under the Hohenzollerns challenged Habsburg dominance in central Europe. The Hohenzollern rulers built Prussia into a great power by developing an efficient bureaucracy and a powerful army. *page 485*

WHY WERE the European wars of the eighteenth century global in scope?

European Warfare: From Continental to World Conflict. In a series of worldwide colonial struggles with France, Britain used its commercial resources and navy to profit from France's entanglements in Europe and emerge supreme in North America and India. Louis pursued an aggressive foreign policy that expanded France's borders but cost France dearly in wealth and resources and provoked strong opposition from the other European powers. In the War of the Spanish Succession, he succeeded in placing his grandson on the throne of Spain, but the war left France exhausted. Prussia emerged from a series of wars with Austria, France, and Russia as one of the strongest European states and the rival to Habsburg power in central Europe. *page 493*

WHAT WERE the political and economic structures of the Old Regime?

The Old Regime. Eighteenth-century European society was traditional, hierarchical, corporate, and privileged—features that had characterized Europe and the world for centuries. All societies also confronted the scarce food supplies. For the eighteenth century, however, an improved food supply helped support a larger population. New agricultural techniques and the expanding population created pressures on social structures. *page 496*

WHAT WAS the role of women in family economy?

Family Structures and the Family Economy. Production and consumption in pre-industrial Europe were organized around the household. The family, not the individual, was the basic economic unit. Women's dowries helped establish households, and marriages were economic partnerships. *page 499*

WHAT WAS the connection between population increase and agricultural improvements in the eighteenth century?

The Revolution in Agriculture. Traditional economic and social organization had presupposed a stable or declining population. Traditional agriculture focused on avoiding famine; it discouraged innovation. Growing population and new techniques transformed food production. Agriculture became more commercialized. *page 502*

WHY DID the Industrial Revolution begin in England?

The Eighteenth-Century Industrial Revolution: An Event in World History. The eighteenth century witnessed the beginning of industrial production. New inventions greatly increasing productive capacity first appeared in the English textile industry. The steam engine provided a portable source of energy. Industrialization affected Europe's relations with the rest of the world. *page 504*

HOW DID population growth lead to changes in urban social structures?

European Cities. Cities expanded and commerce grew during the eighteenth century. The expansion of the European population stimulated change and challenge to tradition and hierarchy. The social hierarchy had to accommodate more people. Corporate groups, such as the guilds, had to confront an expanded labor force. New wealth meant that birth would cease to determine social relationships. *page 507*

HOW WERE European Jews segregated from European Society?

The Jewish Population: Age of the Ghetto. Europe's Jews were segregated from non-Jews in separate villages or, within cities, in ghettoes. They did not have the same rights and privileges as their compatriots, unless those rights had been specifically granted by their monarch. *page 509*

REVIEW QUESTIONS

1. By the end of the seventeenth century, England and France had different systems of government with different religious policies. What were the main similarities and differences? Why did each nation develop as it did?

2. How and why did Russia emerge as a great power? Discuss the character of Peter the Great. How were his domestic reforms related to his military ambitions?

3. What were the main points of conflict between Britain and France in North America, the West Indies, and India? What were the results of these conflicts by 1763? Which countries emerged stronger from the Seven Years' War and why?

4. Why were Europe's wars during this period so significant for the rest of the world?

5. In what ways could aristocrats and peasants be described as conservative? Was conservatism a wise choice for nobles? For peasants? Why or why not?

6. How would you define the term *family economy*? In what ways were the lives of women constrained by the family economy in preindustrial Europe?

7. What caused the agricultural revolution? How did technological innovations help change European agriculture? What were some of the reasons for peasant revolts in Europe in the eighteenth century?

8. What factors led to the Industrial Revolution of the eighteenth century? What were some of the technological innovations and why were they important? Why did Great Britain take the lead in the Industrial Revolution?

9. Describe city life during the eighteenth century. What changes took place in the distribution of population in cities and towns?

10. What was the status of European Jews in the Old Regime? How were they made to live as a people apart from the rest of the European population?

KEY TERMS

absolutism (p. 485)
agricultural revolution (p. 502)
aristocratic resurgence (p. 498)
boyars (boh-YAHRZ) (p. 488)
divine right of kings (p. 488)
domestic or putting-out system (p. 506)
enclosures (p. 502)
family economy (p. 499)
ghettos (p. 509)
Glorious Revolution (p. 486)
Industrial Revolution (p. 505)

Junkers (YOONG-kurs) (p. 492)
Old Regime (p. 496)
parlement (p. 498)
parliamentary monarchy (p. 485)
Pragmatic Sanction (p. 492)
Puritans (p. 486)
spinning jenny (p. 506)
streltsy (p. 488)
Table of Ranks (p. 491)
water frame (p. 506)

Note: To learn more about the topics in this chapter, please turn to the Suggested Readings at the end of the book.

INTERPRETING THE PAST

State Building, Modern Society, and Aristocracy in Europe

Sources from MyHistoryLab for Chapter 20
myhistorylab

1) Jean Domat, *On Social Order and Absolutist Monarchy*

2) The Marquis de Mirabeau, *The Friend of Men; or, Treatise on Population* (1756)

3) Louis Sebastien Mercier, *Portrait of Paris: The Saint-Marcel Neighborhood*

4) Voltaire on Social Conditions in Eighteenth-Century France

Europe experienced a resurgence of aristocratic power in the eighteenth century, yet within a century most traditional aristocratic privileges had been revoked. Why?

These primary source documents illustrate Europe's sharp class divisions. Jean Domat explains how absolutism conforms with natural law and religious principles. The Marquis de Mirabeau offers prescient warnings about those who replaced the traditional nobility in the French countryside.

Louis Sebastien Mercier describes problems encountered by those who moved from the country to the city. Finally, Francois-Marie Arouet (Voltaire) discusses the realities of day-to-day living.

Use the source documents to address the following questions that focus on the benefits and drawbacks of traditional (aristocratic and royal) rule.

Questions

How does Jean Domat justify absolute monarchy?

Why is the Marquis de Mirabeau, himself an aristocrat, so concerned about the tensions between landowners and peasants?

How does Mercier's depiction of urban Paris life among common workers and newly arrived peasants conform with the writings of Domat, Mirabeau, and Voltaire?

What position does Voltaire ultimately take on inequality?

21

The Last Great Islamic Empires, 1500–1800

Akbar Inspecting the Construction of Fatehpur-Sikri, ca. 1590. Sometime around 1570, work began on the construction of a new Mughal capital, Fatehpur-Sikri ("City of Victory"), a few miles southwest of Agra. Akbar (r. 1556–1605), the great emperor who ordered the building of Fatehpur-Sikri, had a keen interest in architecture, and here he stands at the construction site, gesturing to one of the masons as the imperial entourage looks on. In every sense, he lived up to his epithet as the "architect of the spiritual and material world."

Why was cultural patronage important to a ruler like Akbar?

THE LAST GREAT ISLAMIC EMPIRES

The Islamic region's vitality between 1450 and 1800 was exemplified by the three prosperous and great empires and societies of the Ottomans, the Safavids, and the Mughals. All built extensive civilian and military bureaucracies using inspired military and civilian leaders, revived Islamic social and cultural ties, and improved tactics and strategies learned from their predecessors.

While Islamic ideology, society, and culture accounted for some of the Ottoman, Safavid, and Mughal successes, each of their own imperial military, social, and commercial innovations marked their respective rise to global importance. They also built arguably the greatest cities in the world of their time, such as Istanbul, Isfahan, and Dehli, and patronized the arts, stimulating important new traditions of Islamic literature, calligraphy, painting, and architecture. Yet they were essentially conservative societies. Economically they remained closely tied to agricultural production, long-distance trade, and taxation based on land. Perhaps because they were such powerful, wealthy, and successful societies, they did not undergo the kind of social or religio-political revolutions that rocked Europe after 1500. Thus, much like the societies of China and Japan in the same period, they did not experience the sort of generative changes in material and intellectual life that the still comparatively underdeveloped western Europe experienced in the sixteenth, seventeenth, and eighteenth centuries (although European intellectual culture was vibrant and diverse in regions such as Italy, Germany, and France). There was no compelling challenge to traditional Islamic ideals of societal organization and human responsibility, even though many Islamic movements of the eighteenth century did call for communal and personal reform.

As one historian has put it, the striking growth of Islamic societies and cultures in this age was "not one of *origination*, but rather one of *culmination* in a culture long already mature." Even in their heydays, these empires produced much scientific work, but no scientific revolution; much art, architecture, and literature of high quality, but none that departed radically in concept or inspiration from previous traditions; political consolidation and also expansion, but no conquest of significant new markets or territories; commercial prosperity in long-distance trade, but no beginnings of a real commercial or industrial revolution. By the mid-nineteenth century, all were at various stages of economic, political, social, and military disarray in comparison to Europe. By contrast, western Europe, having lagged behind the Islamic world in economic, social, and cultural development as well as political

---

etween 1450 and 1650 Islamic culture, society, and statecraft blossomed. By 1600, the simultaneous growth of the Ottoman, Safavid, and Mughal Empires, sometimes called the "gunpowder empires," marked the global apogee of Islamic society, culture, and economic power. Around these empires were arrayed Muslim khanates of Central Asia and Russia, sultanates of Southeast Asia, Islamic savanna-land empires of West Africa, the city-ports of East Africa, the Sharifian state of Morocco, and regional empires of the Sudan in which Islam played a significant role. The ideal of a universal Islamic caliphate yielded to the reality of multiple secular, albeit distinctively "Islamic," polities (see Map 21–1).

In 1600, Islamic civilization seemed as strong and vital as that of western Europe, China, or Japan. Yet by the late seventeenth century, Islamic power was in retreat before the rising tide of western European military and economic imperialism, even though Islamic cultural life and Muslim religion flourished.

Hindus were the chief religious group the Muslims displaced in some regions of Southeast Asia. Islam also succeeded in most of Malaysia, Sumatra, Java, and the Moluccas (the Spice Islands). ■

THE OTTOMAN EMPIRE AND THE EAST MEDITERRANEAN WORLD

WHY DID the Ottoman Empire find it increasingly difficult to compete with European powers?

ORIGINS AND DEVELOPMENT OF THE OTTOMAN STATE BEFORE 1600

The Ottomans were a Turkish dynasty that originated in the groups of western Oghuz Turks from the steppes of Central Asia who came to Anatolia as settlers and Muslim and military might during the Middle Ages and much of the early modern period, was by the nineteenth century in the midst of industrial, financial, social, and military revolutions and finally poised to challenge successfully the Islamic empires from the Mediterranean to the Indian Ocean.

Thus it is not entirely surprising that European global expansionism gradually dominated Africa, India, Indonesia, and the heartland culture of the Islamic world, rather than the reverse. Neither the great imperial Islamic states, the smaller Islamic sultanates and emirates, the diverse Hindu kingdoms, nor the varied African states (let alone the smaller societies of Africa, the Americas, and the South Pacific) fared well in their eventual clashes with Europeans during this age. The growing European domination of the seas, of the flow of gold and silver, and of global consumable products allowed Europeans to contain as well as to bypass the major Islamic lands in their quest for commercial empires.

Industrial development and military technology joined economic wealth, social prosperity, and political stability by the early 1800s to give western Europe global military supremacy for the first time. Before 1800 the Europeans were able to bring only minor Islamic states under colonial administrations. However, the footholds they gained in Africa, India, and Southeast Asia laid the groundwork for rapid colonial expansion by the 1850s. The age of the last great Islamic empires was the beginning of the rise of the first great modern European empires. The colonialism of the nineteenth century accompanied the aggressive advance of western European industrial, commercial, and military power that held sway into the mid-twentieth century.

Focus Questions

◆ How did the trajectory of development between the Islamic empires and Europe differ in the period from 1500 to 1800?

◆ Why, after centuries as the "underdog," was Europe by the early nineteenth century finally able to challenge the power of the Islamic empires?

◆ Why was the Islamic world, more than China and Japan, increasingly subject to European intrusion during the early modern period?

frontier warriors.[1] The Ottomans reached Anatolia (Asia Minor) in the time of the Seljuks of Rum (1098–1308), who were the first western Turks to have founded a lasting state there (see Chapter 13). By about 1300, the newcomers had built one of several small military states along the Byzantine-Seljuk frontier in western Anatolia. In the fourteenth century several vigorous leaders expanded their territories east into central Anatolia and west across the Dardanelles (in 1356) onto European soil in the Byzantine lands of Macedonia and modern Bulgaria. Exchanging grants of revenue-producing conquered land (*timars*) for military service, the Ottomans built both a formidable fighting force and a loyal military aristocracy.

By 1402 the center of Ottoman rule had shifted northwest to Edirne on the Balkan Peninsula itself. Ottoman control then extended northwest as far as the Danube and east across central Anatolia. Constantinople formed an alien pocket within these dominions, and it finally fell in 1453 to Sultan Mehmed II, "the Conqueror" (r. 1451–1481). Constantinople, now renamed Istanbul, became the Ottoman capital. Proud Byzantium, for hundreds of years the center of Eastern Christendom, was no more, although the Ottomans allowed the Christian patriarch to preside in Istanbul over the Eastern church. The fall of Constantinople, or the "liberation of Istanbul," was both the culmination of previous war efforts and also a springboard for Ottoman European ambitions. As their expansionist and extraordinary conquests continued, often justified in the name of Islam, they became in Christian European eyes the scourge of God.

---

[1]The Ottomans, sometimes called *Osmanlis*, are named after Osman (1259–1326), also rendered *Othman* or *Uthman*, a *ghazi* said to have founded the dynasty when he set up a border state about 1288 on the Byzantine frontier in northwestern Anatolia.

MAP EXPLORATION

To explore this map further, go to http://www.prenhall.com/craig_maps

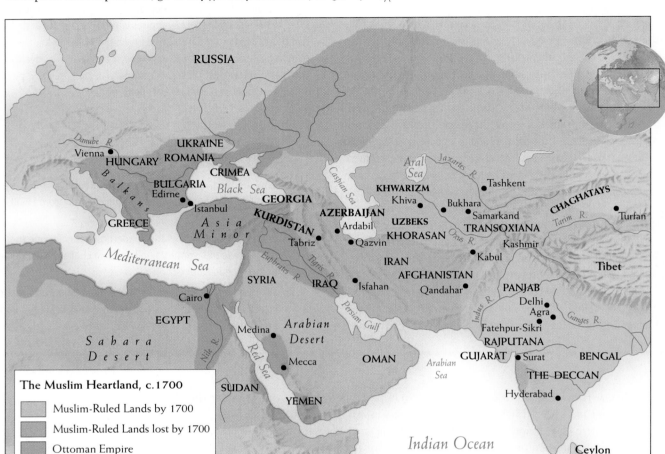

MAP 21–1 **The Islamic Heartlands, ca. 1700.** The three rival "gunpowder" empires—the Safavid, Mughal, and Ottoman empires— dominated the Islamic heartlands. Despite variations, the three empires demonstrated similar organizational structures.

Does this map suggest that the Islamic World was in decline by 1700?

By 1512 Ottoman rule was secure in virtually all of southeastern Europe and north of the Black Sea in most of the Ukraine. Under Selim I (r. 1512–1520) and Süleyman, "the Lawgiver" (known in the West as "Süleyman the Magnificent," r. 1520–1566), this sovereignty was greatly expanded. Selim subjugated the Egyptian Mamluks (1517) and annexed Syria-Palestine, most of North Africa, the Yemen, and western Arabia, including Mecca and Medina. Selim also nullified the Shi'ite threat from Iran in the east (discussed later). Süleyman extended Ottoman control over Kurdistan and Georgia (in the Caucasus), as well as Mesopotamia and Iraq. He also advanced Ottoman borders in eastern Europe. Having won much of Hungary and nearly taken Vienna by siege in 1526 to 1529, he was able by battle and treaty to bring virtually all of Hungary under direct Ottoman rule in the 1540s.

The Ottoman ruler could now claim to be the Abbasid heir and caliph for all Muslims. This claim was symbolized by the addition (begun by Selim I, after the Mamluk conquest in 1517) of the title "Protector of the Sacred Places [Mecca and Medina]" to that of emperor (**padishah**). At this point, Ottoman military might was unmatched by any state in the world, except possibly China. It controlled a large geographical area—home to numerous linguistic and ethnic groups—making the Ottoman an empire in every sense of the word (see Map 21–1).

THE "CLASSICAL" OTTOMAN ORDER

Mehmed II was the true founder of the Ottoman order. He replaced the tribal chieftains with loyal servants of the ruler, he initiated a tradition of formal governmental legislation with his **Qanun-name** (*Lawbook*), and he organized the *ulama* into a hierarchy under a single "Sheikh of Islam." In the next century Süleyman earned his title "Lawgiver" by his legislation touching all aspects of life and all social ranks, his reconciliation of customary law and **Shari'a** (religious law), and his efforts to regularize both law and bureaucracy.

The entire Ottoman state was organized as one vast military institution. All members, whatever their function, held military ranks as the standing "army" of the state under the hereditary leadership of the sultan. This centralized state was supported by the productivity of its Muslim and non-Muslim subjects, such as Jewish and Armenian merchants. The ruling class was Muslims, shared the common Ottoman culture, and had to give utter allegiance to the sultan. The state organization included the palace and three other functional divisions: the administrative or ruling institution, the military institution, and the religious or learned institution. The palace included the sultan, his **harem**, his ministers, and the servants. The privy council, headed by the grand vizier, together with the chancery, the imperial treasury, and the remaining civil bureaucracy, formed the backbone of the ruling or administrative institution. Although men held the keys to power, women also had certain important roles, most often concealed from the public eye. Traditional Turkish customs assumed that power was vested collectively in the family. Women had some ceremonial functions; they also played vital roles in court politics, especially in the selection of officers and in negotiating economic policy.

Several measures helped ensure the ongoing strength of the sultan. Young Ottoman princes were given administrative and leadership training in the provinces, which kept them from being sheltered in the palace and gave them experience of life outside the capital. Stability of succession was traditionally guaranteed by the practice of fratricide in the ruling family, which, legalized formally in Mehmed II's *Qanun-name*, continued until the late sixteenth century. Thus the succession was theoretically left to God, the strongest aspirant to the sultanate having to assert himself and seize power, after which he was expected to execute his brothers to eliminate future competing claims to the throne.

The Ottomans co-opted the legal-religious and educational-intellectual roles of the religious scholars, or *ulama*, for the service of the state, making them an arm of the government under a single religious authority, the **Grand Mufti** or "Sheikh of Islam." This highly organized branch of the state was open only to Muslim men and included the entire system of courts and judges. It was based on a comprehensive network ranging from local mosque schools to the four elite madrasas built around the Süleymaniye Mosque in Istanbul during Süleyman's reign. Scholars' ranks within the graded hierarchy of the *ulama* reflected the level of schooling and teaching they had attained.

padishah   Persian for "master-king"; the title is comparable to emperor.

Qanun-name   A book of laws promulgated by Ottoman sultans.

Shari'a   Islamic religious law.

harem   The wives, concubines, female relatives, and servants in a Muslim household—usually confined to a section of a house or palace.

Grand Mufti   The chief religious authority of the Ottoman Empire. Also called "the Shaykh of Islam."

Istanbul, from a 1537 Turkish map. Its strategic location on the Bosphorus straits gave it a commanding position to dominate trade in the eastern Mediterranean.

What features of Istanbul does this map draw attention to?

518 **PART 4** THE WORLD IN TRANSITION, 1500 TO 1850 C.E.

While the *ulama* were thus under state control, the state itself was formally committed to maintaining the divinely ordained *Shari'a*, and the *ulama* enjoyed great esteem. This structure may account for the fact that whereas the *ulama* in both Safavid Iran and Mughal India often differed with their rulers, the Ottoman *ulama* usually functioned tamely as part of the state apparatus. (See Map 21–2.)

Although the religious establishment upheld the supremacy of the *Shari'a* and the sultan recognized its authority, the functional law of the land was the highly organized state administrative law—the practical code, or **Qanun**, established by the ruler. The *Shari'a* as interpreted by the *ulama* theoretically governed the *Qanun*, and often the sultan formally applied traditional religious norms in his regulations. The conformity of these regulations to the *Shari'a* sometimes came from the genuine piety of a particular administrator or ruler and was sometimes only a pious fiction, something also true for Safavid Iran and Mughal India.

The key ingredient to Ottoman power, however, was the military. The Ottoman rulers kept the military's loyalty by two means: checks on the power of the old landed

Qanun Ottoman administrative law.

MAP 21–2 The Ottoman Empire at Its Zenith. This large and multiethnic empire spanned three continents and lasted for more than four hundred years.

What were the strengths and weaknesses of the Ottoman Empire's geographical position?

aristocracy by careful registry and control of *timar* lands, and the use of slave soldiers with allegiance only to the sultan. The army was based originally on the provincial cavalry whose officers were supported with *timar* land revenues in lieu of cash wages. The state held all conquered agricultural land as its direct property, granting peasants hereditary land use but not ownership. Careful records were kept of the revenue due on all lands, and as long as the state was strong, so too was its control over productive land and the cavalry-gentry whom *timar* revenues supported. But even as early as 1400 the Ottoman rulers tried to reduce the cavalry-gentry's preeminence by employing specialized infantry troops of well-trained and well-paid slave soldiers (equipped, unlike the cavalry, with firearms) whose loyalty was to the sultan alone.

To sustain the quality of these slave troops, the Ottomans developed a unique institution: the provincial slave levy, or **devshirme**. This institution selected young Christian boys from the provincial peasantry to be raised as Muslims; most came from the Balkan peasantry. They were trained to serve in both army and bureaucracy at all levels, from provincial officer to grand vizier. The most famous slave corps was the *yeni cheri* (young troops), or **Janissaries**, the elite infantry troops of the empire. Muslim boys were not allowed into the slave corps, although some parents tried to buy them a place in what offered the most promising careers in the empire. Until 1572 marriage was forbidden to the slave soldiers, which further ensured loyalty and prevented hereditary claims on office.

devshirme The system under the Ottoman Empire that required each province to furnish a levy of Christian boys who were raised as Muslims and became soldiers in the Ottoman army.

Janissaries Elite Ottoman troops who were recruited through the devshirme.

AFTER SÜLEYMAN: CHALLENGES AND CHANGE

The reign of Süleyman marked the peak of Ottoman prestige and power. Further territorial gains were made in the seventeenth century, and the Ottoman state long remained a major force in European and Asian politics, but beginning with the reign of Süleyman's weak son, Selim II (1566–1574), the empire was plagued by military corruption, governmental decentralization, and maritime setbacks. Economically there were agricultural failures, commercial imbalances, and inflation. Yet culturally and intellectually, the seventeenth and eighteenth centuries were periods of impressive accomplishments and lively activity. Overall, these ensuing two centuries witnessed a seesaw pattern between decline and vitality.

The post-Süleyman era began badly, with the loss of territory in the Caucasus and Mesopotamia to the Safavids of Iran (1603). By this time the Ottoman military apparatus was already weakened, partly from fighting two-front wars with the Safavids and the Habsburgs and partly because of European advances in military and naval technology. The Janissaries became increasingly disruptive. By 1600 they had largely replaced the provincial cavalry as new warfare styles made cavalry obsolete. By 1600 Muslims were allowed into the Janissary corps, marriage was possible, and the *devshirme* was declining in use (it ended just over a century later). During the seventeenth century, the Janissaries became increasingly corrupt as they tampered with politics, trying to influence decision making and even dynastic succession. Finally, the increasing employment of mercenaries resulted in the peacetime release of masses of unemployed armed men into the countryside, leading to the sacking of provincial towns, banditry, and revolts.

Murad IV (r. 1623–1640) introduced reforms and ruled with an iron hand, but his death left a weak central authority again. The Köprülüs, father and son, two capable viziers (r. 1656–1676), briefly renewed strong administrative control and military success, but thereafter the central institutions decayed.

Süleyman the Lawgiver. Süleyman giving advice to the Crown Prince, Mehmed Khan. From a contemporaneous Ottoman miniature.

Suleyman I (Kanuni); Shehzade by Talikizade Suphi. Folio 79a of the Talik-izade Shehnamesi, Library at the Topkapi Palace Museum, A3592, Photograph courtesy of Talat Halman.

What regions did Süleyman bring under Ottoman control?

Topkapi Palace, Istanbul. Inside the imperial harem, this elegant room was used to entertain the sultan who watched the proceedings from his large throne.

What organizational features of the Ottoman Empire helped sultans hold onto their power?

QUICK REVIEW

Ottoman Culture

- Katib Chelebi (d. 1657): most illustrious figure in Ottoman literature
- Distinctly Ottoman artistic forms emerged in the late sixteenth century
- Sinan (d. 1578) was the leading Ottoman architect of his day

ayan   Ottoman notables.

millets   Within the Ottoman Empire, ethnic communities that administered their own educational, charitable, and judicial affairs.

Financing the Ottoman state grew ever more difficult. The increase in the Janissary corps from 12,000 to 36,000 men between the early 1500s and 1600 drained state coffers. Inflation grew as the coinage was debased. In contrast to the mercantilist and protectionist policies of European powers, the Ottomans discouraged exports and encouraged imports since too many exports would have raised domestic prices. This damaged the economy in the long run. The population doubled in the sixteenth century, and unemployment grew after 1600. Increased decentralization paved the way for the rise of provincial notables (***ayan***), who became virtually independent in the eighteenth century. Tax farming also went hand-in-glove with the rise of large private estates. New taxes were imposed and old emergency levies regularized, and taxes were required in cash rather than in kind. Increasingly, taxes were levied on a communal rather than an individual basis.

The seventeenth and eighteenth centuries were an era of genuine vitality in poetry, prose, music, painting, cartography, historiography, astronomy, and other fields. The Ottoman patronage of the arts and sciences was one way to assert the Ottoman claim to Islamic and universal authority. The seventeenth century saw especially lively intellectual exchange, both religious and secular. But it was also a time when the *ulama* became an aristocratic and increasingly corrupt elite. Major religious posts became hereditary sinecures for sons and other relatives of a handful of families who had produced prominent *ulama*, and the posts were often sold or leased.

Of the many individuals who were learned in many fields, Katib Chelebi (d. 1657) was the most illustrious; he wrote histories, social commentary, geographies, and encyclopedic works. Other important writers were the great historian of the Ottomans, Na'ima (d. 1716), the tireless traveler and travel writer Evliya Chelebi (d. ca. 1685), and probably the greatest Ottoman poet, Nedim (d. 1730). Ottoman art had been highly eclectic in the first century after Mehmed II. Thanks to the imperial master architect Sinan (d. 1578) and others, the Ottomans developed distinctive artistic and architectural forms in the late sixteenth century. The first half of the eighteenth century was the golden age of Ottoman poetry and art; it also saw the first Ottoman printing press and the beginning of strong European influence in the arts, architecture, and manners. In the popular sphere, the now classical form of Turkish theater (in which two men play male and female parts) began as early as the sixteenth century, perhaps under Jewish immigrant influence.

Socially, the period saw the consolidation of Ottoman society as a multiethnic and multireligious state. The empire encompassed a dizzying array of languages, religions, and ethnic identities. All subjects, both Muslim and non-Muslim, were organized into small communities called **millets** that were responsible for their community members from the cradle to the grave. The millets administered their educational, charitable, and judicial affairs and assisted the central government in tax collection. Typically the millets were headed by a religious leader and enjoyed some degree of internal autonomy. Thus early on the Ottoman Empire proved to be a haven for a number of minority groups, especially Jews. Considerable immigration of Jews into Ottoman societies following their expulsion from Spain during the Spanish Inquisition (1492) had brought new craftsmen, physicians, bankers, scholars, and even entertainers.

The large Christian population of the empire was generally well treated, but in the eighteenth and nineteenth centuries they began to suffer from increasing taxes and other forms of discrimination. As a result the Christians looked to Christian Europe and Russia for liberation.

State policy encouraged just treatment of all subjects. In the eighteenth century, however, relations between Muslims and non-Muslims deteriorated, in part because of the remarkable rise in the economic and social status of non-Muslims—in particular the mercantile middle class. Non-Muslims virtually monopolized foreign trade, and in the eighteenth century European countries gave many of them citizenship. This qualified them for the trade privileges that the sultan granted to foreign governments.

One of the major social institutions of later Ottoman society, the coffeehouse, flourished from the mid-sixteenth century on. It probably originated as a Sufi institution that came with coffee to the Mediterranean from the Yemen. The Ottoman coffeehouse rapidly became a major common space for socializing. People gathered to drink coffee, play games, watch puppet shows, read books, discuss public affairs, and even engage in political agitation. The sheikh of Islam banned coffee because of its stimulant qualities, but it could not be suppressed. The coffeehouse fostered a common Ottoman urban culture among lower and middle classes.

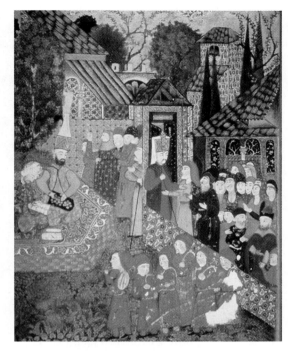

Devshirme. An Ottoman portrayal of the *devshirme*. This miniature painting from about 1558 depicts the recruiting of young Christian children for the sultan's elite Janissary corps. The children, dressed in red, are at the bottom, while their parents, who look pleased, congregate on the right.

Arifi, "Suleymanname," Topkapi Palace Museum, II 1517, fol. 31b, photograph courtesy of Talat Halman.

Why would parents be pleased at their children's recruitment as Janissaries?

THE DECLINE OF OTTOMAN MILITARY AND POLITICAL POWER

After their failure in 1683 to take Vienna, the Ottomans were driven out of Hungary and Belgrade; they never seriously threatened Europe again. In 1774 Russia took the Crimea and became the formal protector of the Orthodox Christians in the Islamic empire. Whereas in the seventeenth century the Ottoman Empire was a relatively self-contained and self-sufficient empire, by the late eighteenth century the empire was increasingly dependent on the international market systems, particularly those of western Europe. Its economic growth had been based on conquest and the control of land as a source of wealth. When its expansion was stopped, the Ottoman sultans were not prepared to adjust to changes in an increasingly western European world economy, geared toward capitalist accumulation and industrialization. The Ottomans never regained their earlier power and influence before their empire collapsed in 1918.

CHRONOLOGY

THE OTTOMAN EMPIRE

1301	Foundation of early Ottoman principality in Bursa by Osman
1356	Ottomans cross Dardanelles into Europe
1451–1481	Rule of Sultan Mehmed II, "the Conqueror"
1453	Fall of Constantinople to Mehmed the Conqueror
1512–1520	Rule of Selim I
1517	Ottoman conquest of Egypt, assumption of claim to Abbasid caliphal succession from Mamluks
1520–1566	Rule of Süleyman, "the Lawgiver"
1526–1529	First Ottoman siege of Vienna
1578	Death of Ottoman master architect, Sinan
1656–1676	Governance of Koprülüs as viziers
1683	Second Ottoman siege of Vienna
1699	Treaty of Karlowitz, loss of Hungarian and other European territory
1774	Loss of Crimea to Russia; tsar becomes formal protector of Ottoman Orthodox Christians
1918	End of empire

A Turkish Coffeehouse. This early nineteenth-century view of a coffeehouse in Istanbul captures the exoticism that made the Ottoman Empire so intriguing to Western visitors.

What role did coffeehouses play in Ottoman society?

Outflanked by Russia to the north and by European sea power to the south and west, the Ottomans were blocked in the east by their implacable Safavid foes in Iran. They could not sustain the level of external trade needed to support their expensive wars, especially after Italian, French, British, and Dutch traders obtained special concessions for trade in the Fertile Crescent, Persian Gulf, and Red Sea regions that Ottoman merchants did not have. Ultimately, their dependence on a decentralized agrarian-age, local market economy proved insufficient to face the rising global commercial and industrial powers of Europe.

THE SAFAVID EMPIRE AND THE WEST ASIAN WORLD

WHAT ROLE did Shi'ite ideology play in the Safavid Empire?

Sufi Sufism is a mystic tradition within Islam that encompasses a diverse range of beliefs and practices dedicated to Divine love and the cultivation of the elements of the Divine within the individual human being. The chief aim of all Sufis is to let go of all notions of duality, including a conception of an individual self, and to realize the Divine unity.

pirs Shi'ite holy men.

ORIGINS

As noted in Chapter 13, Iranian history changed under the Safavid dynasty after 1500. The Safavids had begun in the fourteenth century as hereditary Turkish spiritual leaders of a Sunni **Sufi** order in the northwestern Iranian province of Azerbaijan. In the fifteenth century the Safavid order evolved a new and militant Shi'ite Sufi ideology. By claiming descent from the imams of Twelver Shi'ism (see Chapter 13), the Safavid spiritual masters (*sheikhs* and **pirs**) became the focus of Shi'ite religious allegiance. Many adherents were won to the *tariqa*, or Sufi brotherhood, and eventually to Shi'ism from among the Turkoman tribesmen of eastern Anatolia, northern Syria, and northwestern Iran. These mounted warriors were called *Qizilbash* ("Red Heads") because of their distinctive red uniform hats, which signaled their allegiance to the twelve Shi'ite imams and their Safavid Sufi master.

The growing strength of the Safavid brotherhood brought about conflicts with the dominant Sunni Turkoman groups in the region around Tabriz. The Safavids emerged victorious in 1501 under the leadership of the young Safavid Sufi master-designate Isma'il. Recognized as a divinely appointed representative of the "hidden" imam (see Chapter 11), Isma'il extended his sovereignty over the southern Caucasus, Azerbaijan, the Tigris-Euphrates valley, and all of western Iran by 1506. Unified by religious identity and in league with Babur, the Timurid ruler of Kabul, the Safavids by

1512 had taken from the Uzbek Turks all of eastern Iran from the Oxus River in the north to the Arabian Sea in the south. Thereafter, the Uzbeks became implacable foes of the Safavids because of the loss of lands to the Safavids and the Uzbek (and later nineteenth-century Turcoman) pastoral migratory life and border raids. Throughout the ensuing century the Safavids were often forced to fight a debilitating two-front war, against Uzbeks in the east and Ottomans in the west.

A strong central rule now united traditional Iranian lands for the first time since the heyday of the Abbasid caliphate. It was a regime based on the existing Persian bureaucratic institutions, which in turn were based on Seljuk institutions. Shah Isma'il ruthlessly enforced Shi'ite conformity, which slowly took root across the realm—perhaps bolstered by a rising Iranian Sufi self-consciousness and identity in the face of the Sunni Ottomans, Arabs, Uzbeks, and Mughals who surrounded Iran. In the latter part of his reign, Shah Isma'il began to develop a more centralized bureaucracy at the expense of his Sufi enthusiasts. The shah was determined to govern, both culturally and politically, through a reconstruction of the historic Iranian monarchy. Although the shah had loyal tribal and religious support within his domain, Isma'il had tenuous ties with his neighbors, especially the leaders of the Ottoman Empire, who vigorously ensured that this Sufi-inspired monarchy would not spread farther into Ottoman eastern Anatolian lands widely populated by other Sufi orders.

In 1514 the better-armed Ottoman army of Selim I soundly defeated the Safavid forces at Chaldiran in Iranian Azerbaijan, marking the beginning of an extended series of Ottoman-Safavid border wars over the next two centuries. Chaldiran also marked the beginning of Qizilbash disaffection with Shah Isma'il and consequent efforts to take power from the Safavids. Furthermore, this defeat gave the Ottomans control of the Fertile Crescent and forced the Safavids to move their capital and their focus eastward, first to Qazwin, and then to Isfahan.

SHAH ABBAS I

Isma'il's successor, Tahmasp I (r. 1524–1576), survived repeated attacks by both Ottomans and Uzbeks, in part through the strength of Shi'ite religious feeling and the allegiance of the Iranian bureaucracy. A few years later, however, the most able of the Safavid rulers, Shah Abbas I (r. 1588–1629), brought able leadership to the Safavid domains. He regained provincial land for the state and used the revenue to pay for new troops from his Caucasian territories, thereby providing a counterweight to the sometimes unruly Qizilbash, who were supported by land revenue assignments. Shah Abbas not only pushed the Ottomans out of Azerbaijan and Iraq but also turned back new Uzbek invasions in Khorasan. He sought alliances with the Ottomans' European enemies. This latter tactic, used by a number of the Safavid rulers, reflected one of the several military and economic divisions in the assumed unity within the Islamic world. Empires, whether Islamic or not, were essentially divided from each other over their own self-interests: that is, absolute control of the empire's land and all its resources. Abbas also broke the century-long Portuguese monopoly on trade along Persian shores and opened trade relations with the English and Dutch East India commercial companies. His reign brought considerable prosperity to Iran, symbolized by

Dancing Sufis, their arms raised in ecstasy, congregate at the tomb of the great Persian medieval poet Sa'adi.

What were some highlights of Persian culture under the Safavids?

the magnificent capital he built at Isfahan, which epitomized Safavid grandeur and vision, shown most vividly in its regal central piazza-like square, the Maydan-i-Shah.

The most enduring aspect of Safavid consolidation of power in Iran was the replacement of Sunni Islam with Shi'ite Islam as the official religion. Because Twelver Shi'ism was not widely grounded in Iranian religious tradition, the Safavid shahs imported religious scholars (*ulama*) primarily from today's Lebanon and Syria, placing them squarely in the service of the state to give legitimacy to the government. The Safavids discouraged pilgrimage to Mecca but instead emphasized visits to Karbala, or to the shrine of Husayn, the grandson of the Prophet Muhammad. Eventually, however, the relations between the government and the *ulama* became strained. By the seventeenth century, the *ulama* withdrew from political participation and refused to bestow direct legitimacy on the shah.

Safavid Decline

After Shah Abbas, the empire rarely enjoyed able leadership. This contributed to its decline and collapse, the chief causes of which were (1) continued two-front pressure from Ottoman and Uzbek armies, (2) economic decline, (3) social unrest among the provincial elites, and (4) the increasing landholding power of the Shi'ite *ulama*. The conservative *ulama* not only introduced a form of Islamic legalism but also emphasized their own authority as interpreters of the law over that of the monarch. They persecuted religious minorities and encouraged hatred of Sunni Muslims. Some of the

Maydan-i-Shah. The enormous rectangular-shaped plaza at the top of this aerial photo connects with the equally impressive Masjd-i-Shah Mosque, constructed between 1611 and 1638.

How does this photo show the close connection between spiritual and temporal power in Safavid society?

Iranian *ulama* and *tujjar* or merchants sought closer ties with the European commercial communities. Local administrators were content to maintain the traditional decentralized Safavid system in their own respective interests, which only accelerated the country's dependency on the introspective and corrupt Safavid family.

In the end, an Afghan leader captured Isfahan and forced the abdication of Husayn I (1694–1722). A few of the Safavid princes managed to retake control of western Iran, but the empire's greatness was gone. A revived, but officially Safavid, monarchy under the talented Qizilbash tribal leader Nadir Shah (r. 1736–1747) and several successors restored much of Iran's lost territories. However, Nadir Shah's military ventures, which included an invasion of northwestern India and the conquest of Delhi, sapped the empire's finances. After Nadir's autocratic and brutal reign ended in 1747, Iran's provincial elites, *ulama*, and merchants struggled to regain some of the previous political and economic stability over the next sixty years. By early in the nineteenth century, some success was achieved under the Qajar kings (see Chapter 27).

CHRONOLOGY	
THE SAFAVID EMPIRE	
1334	Death of Safi al-Din, founder of Safavid Sufi order
1501	Rise of the Sufi Safavid shahs under Shah Isma'il I
1501–1510	Safavid conquest of greater Iran; Shi'ite state founded
1588–1629	Rule of Shah Abbas I
1722	The Afghan invasion and forced abdication of Sultan Husayn
1722–1737	The rise of pretenders to the Safavid throne under the Safavid banner of Tahmasp II and his son, Abbas III
1736–1747	Rule of the Sunni Afshar leader, Nadir Shah; revival of Sunni monarchy in Iran
1739	Nadir Shah invades northern India, sacks Delhi

CULTURE AND LEARNING

The most impressive aspects of Safavid times were the conversion of Iran to Shi'ite Islam and the cultural and intellectual renaissance of the sixteenth and seventeenth centuries. The traditions of painting, with their origins in the powerful miniatures of the preceding century—notably those from Herat after 1450, exemplified by the work of the painter Bihzad (1440–1514) in late Timurid times—were cultivated and modified in Safavid times. Portraiture and scenes from everyday life became popular. Among the most developed crafts were ceramic tile, porcelain, shawls, and carpets. The magnificent architecture of Isfahan, especially evident in the exquisite gardens and grand arches and domes constructed in Shah Abbas's time, gives breathtaking evidence of the developed sense of proportion, color, and design in addition to the superb architectural technology and urban planning of Safavid taste. So impressive and ambitious was the scope of Isfahan that it became known as being "half the world," a lofty epithet suggesting that it was the quintessence of the religious and imperial Iranian world. It marks a point in the sophisticated use of space and lavish use of ceramic tiles to decorate the facades and especially the great domes of major buildings.

The lasting visible legacies of Safavid rule were Iranian cultural artifacts, buildings, roads, town squares, homes, gardens, and bridges. These were handsomely decorated and financed by the Safavid fortunes from trade in silk, silver, and other long-distance commercial products, as well as the Safavid patronage in literature, theology, philosophy, painting, crafts, and architecture. The Safavid age also saw a distinctively Shi'ite and Sufi piety develop and gave a firmly Shi'ite Islamic character to Iranian culture and traditions. It focused on commemorating the suffering of the imams, life as a struggle for social justice, and loyalty to the Shi'a *ulama*, who alone provided guidance in the absence of the "hidden" imam (see Chapter 11).

In intellectual life, the *Ishraqi* or "illuminationist" school of theological-philosophical thought brought together the mystical and Sufi bent of Iranian Islamic

Safavid Art. *Woman with a Veil,* by Riza Abbasi, ca. 1595. During Safavid times, Persian artists began to depict everyday life and people, such as this graceful and sinuous young woman.

What were the roots of the Safavid artistic tradition?

thought and the long Islamic traditions of Aristotelianism and Platonism in the form of Shi'a religious speculation into the nature of divine truth and its accessibility to human reason and imagination. The illuminationists' two key ideas were the concept of transcendence and the notion of a "realm of images." They conceived of transcendence in terms of a divine light identified with the Light of Truth, which was expressed most fully in Muhammad and the Shi'a imams. The realm of images was a sphere of being in which the attuned spirit could experience true visions. These ideas reconceived human experience of the Divine in a way that transcended logic and had to be experienced individually. At stake were basic notions of the human psyche and the larger cosmos. The most prominent exponent of the *Ishraqi* school was Mulla Sadra (d. 1640).

WHAT ROLE did religious intolerance play in the decline of the Mughal Empire?

Mughals Descendants of the Mongols who established an Islamic empire in India in the sixteenth century with its capital at Delhi.

THE MUGHALS

ORIGINS

In a recurring pattern of Indian history, invaders from beyond the Oxus River to the northwest began a new era in the subcontinent in the early sixteenth century. These invaders were Chaghatay Turks descended from Timur (Tamerlane) and known to history as the **Mughals** (a Persianate form of *Mongol*). They ended the political fragmentation that by 1500 had reduced the Delhi sultanate to only one among many Indian states. In 1525 to 1527 the founder of the Mughal dynasty, Babur, marched on India, replaced the last sultan of Delhi, and then defeated a Rajput confederacy. Before his death in 1530, he ruled an empire stretching from the Oxus to Bihar and the Himalayas to the Deccan. But the real founder of the Mughal Empire and the greatest Indian ruler since Ashoka (ca. 264–223 B.C.E.) was Akbar "the Great" (r. 1556–1605). He was at least as great a ruler as his famous contemporaries, Elizabeth I of England (r. 1558–1603), the Holy Roman Emperor Charles V (r. 1519–1556), and Shah Abbas I (r. 1587–1629).

AKBAR'S REIGN

Akbar began his reign, like so many other illustrious rulers, with an impressive record of military success. He added North India and the northern Deccan to the Mughal dominions. Even more significant, however, were his governmental reforms, cultural patronage, and religious toleration. He completely reorganized the central and provincial governments and rationalized the tax system. His marriages with Rajput princesses and his appointment of Hindus to positions of power eased Muslim–Hindu tensions. So did his cancellation of the poll tax on non-Muslims (1564) and his efforts to reduce the power of the more literalist, "hard-line" *ulama*. Under his leadership the Mughal Empire became a truly Indian empire.

Akbar was a religious eclectic who showed not only tolerance of all faiths but also unusual interest in different religious traditions. He frequently brought together representatives of all faiths—Jain and Buddhist monks, Brahmans, *ulama*, Parsis (Zoroastrians), and Jesuits—to discuss religion. These debates took place in a special hall in Akbar's magnificent palace complex at Fatehpur-Sikri outside the Mughal capital, Agra.

THE LAST GREAT MUGHALS

Akbar's three immediate successors were Jahangir (r. 1605–1627), Shah Jahan (r. 1628–1658), and Awrangzeb (r. 1658–1707). They left behind significant achievements, but the problems of sustaining an Indian empire took their toll on Mughal power. The reigns of Jahangir and Shah Jahan were arguably the golden age of Mughal

QUICK REVIEW

Akbar (r. 1556–1605)

- Added North India and the northern Deccan to Mughal Empire
- Carried out extensive governmental reforms
- Interested in a variety of religious faiths

culture, notably in architecture and painting, which developed its own Mughal style based on traditional Hindi and Persian elements. But the burdens imposed by new building, by military campaigns, and by the erosion of Akbar's administrative and tax reforms led to economic decline. Jahangir set a fateful precedent in permitting English merchants to establish a trading post, or "factory," at Surat on the western coast in Gujarat. Shah Jahan brought the Deccan wholly under Mughal control but lost Kandahar to Safavid forces in 1648. His wars further strained the Mughal economy. No less a burden on the treasury were his elaborate building projects, the most magnificent of which was the white-stoned Taj Mahal (built 1632–1653), the unparalleled tomb with its Persian-styled dome that he built for his beloved consort, Mumtaz.

With Shah Jahan, religious toleration retreated; under his son, Awrangzeb, a narrow religious fanaticism all but reversed Akbar's earlier policies. The resulting internal disorder and instability hastened the decline of Mughal power. Awrangzeb persecuted non-Muslims, destroying Hindu temples, reimposing the poll tax (1679), and alienating the Rajput leaders, whose forebears Akbar had so carefully cultivated. His intransigent policies coincided with and perhaps contributed to the spread of the militant reformism of the Sikh movement throughout the Punjab and the rise of Hindu Maratha nationalism in western India.

SIKHS AND MARATHAS

In the late sixteenth and early seventeenth centuries the Sikhs, who trace their origins to the teachings of Guru Nanak (d. 1538), developed into a distinctive religious movement. Neither Muslim nor Hindu, they had their own scripture, ritual, and moralistic and reformist ideals. Awrangzeb earned their lasting enmity by persecution that culminated in the martyrdom of their ninth leader, or guru, Teg Bahadur, in 1675. Thereafter, the tenth and last Sikh guru, Gobind Singh (d. 1708), developed the Sikhs into a formidable military force. Awrangzeb and his successors had to contend with repeated Sikh uprisings.

The Hindu Marathas, led by the charismatic Shivaji (d. 1680), rose in religious and nationalistic fervor to found their own regional empire in about 1646. On Shivaji's death, the Maratha state controlled the mountainous western coast, and its army was the most disciplined force in India. Despite Awrangzeb's subsequent defeat of the Marathas and his conquest of the entire south of India, the Marathas continued to fight him. After his death they brought about a confederation of almost all the Deccan states under their leadership. While formally acknowledging Mughal sovereignty, the Marathas actually controlled far more of India after about 1740 than did the Mughals.

POLITICAL DECLINE

In addition to the Rajput, Sikh, and Maratha wars, other factors sealed the fate of the once great Mughal Empire after Awrangzeb's death in 1707: the rise in the Deccan of the powerful Islamic state of Hyderabad in 1724; the Persian invasion of North India by Nadir Shah in 1739; the invasions (1748–1761) by the Afghan tribal leader Ahmad Shah Durrani (r. 1747–1773), "founder of modern Afghanistan"; and the British victories over Bengali forces at Plassey in Bengal (1757) and over the French on the southeastern coast (1740–1763). By 1819 the dominance

Fatehpur-Sikri. The Diwan-i-Khas, one of the many pavilions found in the enormous imperial palace complex.

How does this building reflect the grandeur of Mughal imperial architecture?

DOCUMENT

Guru Arjun's Faith

These lines are from the pen of the fifth guru of the Sikh community, Arjun (d. 1606). In them he repeated the teaching of Kabir, a fifteenth-century Indian saint whose teachings are included with those of Guru Nanak and other religious poets in the Sikh holy scripture, the Adi Granth. This teaching focuses on the error of clinging to a doctrinaire communalist faith, be it that of the Hindus or of the Muslims.

- **Why** might syncretic teachings, such as those of the Sikhs, have been appealing in seventeenth-century India?

I practice not fasting, nor observe the [month of] Ramadan:
I serve Him who will preserve me at the last hour.
The one Lord of the earth is my God,
Who judgeth both Hindus and Muslims.

---

of the British East India Company had eclipsed Mughal as it did Maratha and almost all regional Indian power, even though the Mughal line did not officially end until 1858.

RELIGIOUS DEVELOPMENTS

The period from about 1500 to 1650 was of major importance for Indian religious life. Akbar's eclecticism mirrored the atmosphere of the sixteenth century in India. A number of religious figures preached a spiritually or mystically oriented piety that transcended the legalism of both the *ulama* and the Brahmans and rejected caste distinctions. In these ideas, we can see both Muslim Sufi and Hindu *bhakti* influences at work. Guru Nanak, the spiritual father of the Sikh movement, took up Kabir's ideas and preached faith and devotion to one loving and merciful God. (See Document, "Guru Arjun's Faith.") He opposed narrow allegiance to particular creeds or rites and excessive pride in external religious observance. Nanak's hymns of praise contain both Hindu and Muslim ideas and imagery. Dadu (d. 1603) preached a similar message. He was born a Muslim but, like Kabir and Nanak, strove to get people to go beyond either Muslim or Hindu allegiance to a more spiritual love and service of God.

There was also an upsurge of *bhakti* devotionalism that amounted to a Hindu revival. It was epitomized by the Bengali Krishna devotee Chaitanya (d. ca. 1533), who stressed total devotion to Lord Krishna. The forebears of present-day Hare Krishna devotees, his followers spread widely his ecstatic public praise of God and his message that all are equal in God's sight. The other major figure in Hindu devotionalism in this era was Tulasidas (d. 1623), whose Hindi retelling of the story of the Sanskrit *Ramayana* remains among the most popular works of Indian literature. Tulasidas used the story of Rama's adventures to present *bhakti* ideas that remain as alive in current everyday Hindu life as do his verses.

Muslim eclectic tendencies came primarily from the Sufis. By 1500 many Sufi retreat centers had been established in India. Sufis' enthusiastic forms of worship and their inclination to play down the externals of religion proved particularly congenial to Indian sensibilities. Such Sufis were, however, often opposed by the more puritanical *ulama*, many of whom held

Jahangir and Shaykh Husain. Jahangir showing preference to the Chishti Sufi *shaykh* and saint Husain over three temporal rulers: the Ottoman emperor, the king of England, and a Hindu prince. The Timurid emperor presents a book to Shaykh Husain, the descendant of the great Chishti saint Mu'inuddin, while ignoring the temporal rulers in the lower-left corner. The artist copied the likeness of King James I from an English portrait given to Jahangir by Sir Thomas Roe, the British ambassador from 1615 to 1619. The magnificent floral borders to the miniature (ca. 1615–1618) were added in 1727 by Muhammad Sadiq.

Bichitr, Jahangir Preferring a Sufi Shakikh to Kings, ca. 1660–70, Album Page; Opaque watercolor, gold and ink on paper, 25.3 × 18.1 cm. Courtesy of the Freer Gallery of Art, Smithsonian Institution, Washington, D.C.

How did Hindu and Persian styles influence Mughal culture?

> I go not on a pilgrimage to Mecca, nor worship at Hindu
>   places of Pilgrimage.
> I serve the one God and no other.
> I neither worship as the Hindus, nor pray as the Muslims.
> I take the Formless God into my heart, and there make
>   obeisance unto Him.
> I am neither a Hindu nor a Muslim.
>
> The soul and the body belong to God whether He be
>   called Allah or Ram.
> Kabir hath delivered this lecture.
> When I meet a true guru or pir, I recognize my own Master.
>
> Source: From Max Arthur Macauliffe, *The Sikh Religion*, 6 vols.
> (Oxford: Clarendon Press, 1909), p. 422.

powerful positions as royal advisers and judges. To check puritan bigotry among the *ulama*, Akbar named himself the supreme spiritual authority in the empire and then ordered that toleration be the law of the land.

After Akbar's death the inevitable reaction set in. It was summed up in the work of the Indian leader of the central Asian Sufi order of the Naqshbandiya, Ahmad Sirhindi (d. 1624). He sought to purge Sufism of its extreme tendencies and of all popular practices not sanctioned by the schools of law. He crusaded against any practices that smacked of Hindu influence and also against tolerant treatment of the Hindus themselves. Among Akbar's royal successors, Awrangzeb, as noted earlier, was known for his strictures against non-Muslims. His intolerance has often been unfairly exaggerated, but in the end its spirit won the day. The possibilities for Hindu–Muslim rapprochement that had emerged in Akbar's time waned, presaging the communal strife that has marred southern Asian history in recent times.

CHRONOLOGY

INDIA: THE MUGHALS AND CONTEMPORARY INDIAN POWERS

1525–1527	Rule of Babur, founder of Indian Timurid state
1538	Death of Guru Nanak, founder of Sikh religious tradition
1556–1605	Rule of Akbar "the Great"
1605–1627	Rule of Jahangir
1628–1658	Rule of Shah Jahan, builder of the Taj Mahal
1646	Founding of Maratha Empire
1658–1707	Rule of Awrangzeb
1680	Death of Maratha leader, Shivaji
1708	Death of tenth and last Sikh guru, Gobind Singh
1724	Rise of Hyderabad state
1739	Iranian invasion of North India under Nadir Shah
1757	British East India Company victory over Bengali forces at Plassey
1857–1858	Indian uprising and the death of the last Mughal ruler, Bahadur Shah II

CENTRAL ASIA: ISLAMIZATION IN THE POST-TIMUR ERA

Islam established a solid footing in Central Asia in the post-Timur era of the fifteenth century. In the preceding century, as the peoples of western Central Asia had begun to shift from nomadic to settled existence, the familiar pattern of Islamic diffusion from trading and urban centers to the countryside had set in. Islamization by Sunni and Shi'a Sufis, traders, and tribal rulers continued thereafter, even as far as western China and Mongolia. It was slowed only in the late sixteenth century by the conversion of the tribes of Mongolia proper to the Buddhism of the Tibetan lamas. Thus, after 1500 the Safavid Shi'ite empire was bounded by Islamic Sunni states in India, Afghanistan, Anatolia, Mesopotamia, Transoxiana, and western Turkestan (Khwarizm, the region between the Aral and Caspian Seas). In these last two areas, the most important states were those founded by Uzbek and Chaghatay Turks, both of whom were ruled by Muslim descendants of Genghis Khan.

WHAT WERE the most important Islamic states in central and southern Asia?

UZBEKS AND CHAGHATAYS

During the fifteenth century Timur's heirs had ruled Transoxiana and most of Iran (see Chapter 13). To the north, above the Jaxartes River (Syr Darya) and the Aral Sea, a new steppe khanate had been formed by the unification in 1428 of assorted clans of Turks and Mongols known as the Uzbeks. Muhammad Shaybani (d. 1510), an Uzbek leader who was descended from Genghis Khan, invaded Transoxiana (1495–1500). There he founded a new Uzbek Islamic empire that replaced Timurid rule, which shifted south to Kabul and eventually India, as described earlier. Muhammad's line continued Uzbek rule in Transoxiana at Bukhara into the eighteenth century, while another Uzbek line ruled the independent khanate of Khiva in western Turkestan from 1512 to 1872.

Of the other Central Asian Islamic states after 1500, the most significant was that of the Chaghatay Turks. The Chaghatays had been the successors of Genghis Khan in the whole region from the Aral Sea and the Oxus River to China (see Map 21–1). After 1350, Timur's invasion broke up their khanate. From about 1514 a revived Chaghatay state flourished in eastern Turkestan. Although the Chaghatay rulers lasted until 1678 in one part of the Tarim basin, their real power was lost after about 1555 to various Khoja princes, Sunni zealots who claimed to be *Sharifs* (descendants of the Prophet).

CONSEQUENCES OF THE SHI'ITE RIFT

On the face of it, the Ottoman, Mughal, Safavid, and Central Asian Islamic states had much in common: Muslim faith and culture, similar systems of taxation and law, the Persian language, and Turkish rulers. Yet the deep religious division between the Shi'ite Safavids and all their Sunni neighbors proved stronger than their bonds. The result was a serious geographic division that isolated Central Asian Muslims in particular.

Shi'ite–Sunni political competition was sharpened by Safavid militancy, to which the Sunni states responded in kind. Attempts to form alliances with non-Muslim states, previously unheard of in the Islamic world, became commonplace in Shi'ite political strategy. The Sunnis also resorted to such tactics: The Ottomans, for example, made common cause with Protestants against their Catholic Habsburg enemies. Although trade continued, the presence of a militant Shi'ite state astride the major overland trade routes of the larger Islamic world hurt the international flow of Islamic commerce.

The Safavid Shi'ite schism also changed the shared cultural traditions of the "Abode of Islam." This change was especially reflected in the fate of Persian literary culture. As a result of its ever stronger association with Shi'ite religious ideas after the rise of the Safavids, Persian made little further progress as a potential common language alongside Arabic in Sunni lands. Outside Iran it was destined to remain a language of high culture, the court, and bureaucracy, where it was the mark of the educated and cultural person: Persian language and mastery of the Persian classics largely defined what it meant to be an Ottoman or Mughal "gentleman." In India, Urdu became the common Muslim idiom (see Chapter 13), and in Ottoman and Central Asian lands, one or another Turkic tongue was spoken in everyday life. The Persian classics inspired Persian learning among educated Sunnis, but Safavid Persian literature was largely ignored.

Central Asia was ultimately the Islamic region most decisively affected by the Shi'ite presence in Iran. Combined with the growing pressure of Christian Russian power from the West, the militant Shi'ism of Iran isolated

The Great Central Square of the Registan, in Samarkand, with the seventeenth-century Shir Dar Madrasa on the right and the fifteenth-century Ulugh Beg Madrasa on the left. Samarkand and other major Central Asian cities were centers of Islamic culture and learning as well as political power.

What are the similarities between this square and the photographs on pages 524 and 527? What does this suggest?

OVERVIEW   Major Islamic States, ca. 1600

The age of the last great Islamic empires lasted from the fifteenth century to the eighteenth century. These states dominated the Islamic world, which stretched from Morocco on the Atlantic coast of North Africa across the Near East and along the eastern coast of Africa to the southeast Asian islands that today make up the Republic of Indonesia. Despite these political divisions and the religious divide between Sunni and Shi'ite Muslims, in many respects the Islamic world formed a single cultural unit.

STATE	LOCATION	ISLAMIC TRADITION
Ottoman Empire	Balkans, Anatolia, North Africa, Syria, Iraq, Arabia	Sunni
Safavid Empire	Iran, Afghanistan Caucasus	Shi'ite
Mughal Empire	India	Sunni
Uzbeks	Central Asia: Kiva, Bokhara	Sunni
Chaghatays	Central Asia: Turkistan	Sunni
Acheh	Sumatra	Sunni

Central Asia from the rest of the Muslim world. Political and economic relations with other Islamic lands became increasingly difficult after 1500, as did religious and cultural interchange. However healthy Islam remained in this region, its contact with the original Islamic heartlands (and even with India) shrank. Contact came primarily through a few pilgrims, members of Sufi orders, *ulama*, and students. Central Asian Islam mostly developed in isolation, a large but peripheral area to the Islamic mainstream communities.

POWER SHIFTS IN THE SOUTHERN OCEANS

SOUTHERN OCEANS TRADE

HOW DID the arrival of Europeans affect maritime trade in Southeast Asia?

The period from 1000 to 1500 witnessed the gradual spread of Islamic religion and culture along the southern rim of Asia, from the Red Sea and East Africa to Indonesia and the South China Sea. In ports in Java, Sumatra, the Malay Peninsula, South India, Gujarat, East Africa, Madagascar, and Zanzibar, Islamic traders established thriving communities. Their enclaves often became the dominant presence in these cities. Initially the Muslims' economic stature attracted the socially and religiously mobile peoples of these cosmopolitan centers; many of them also found the ideas and practices of Islam compelling. Typically this first stage of conversion was followed by Islam's transmission to surrounding areas and finally to inland centers. In this transmission, Sufi orders and their preachers and holy men played the main role. However, conquest by Muslim coastal states quickened the process in Indonesia and East Africa.

The international trade network that the Muslims inherited in the Indian Ocean to South China sea areas was ancient. Before 1200 much of the trade in these waters had been dominated by Hindu or Buddhist kingdoms on the Malay Peninsula or Sumatra (see Chapter 13). Arab traders had also been active at least in the Indian Ocean. Hindu culture had been carried, along with an Indonesian language, as far as Madagascar in the first millennium C.E. Hindus were the chief religious group the Muslims displaced. In the East, Islam never ousted the Indian Buddhist cultures of Burma, Thailand, and Indochina, although Muslim traders lived in their ports. Islam did, however, gradually win most of Malaysia, Sumatra, Java, and the "Spice Islands" (the Moluccas)—always the coastal areas first, then the inland regions.

CONTROL OF THE SOUTHERN SEAS

The Portuguese reached the East African coast in 1498. For three centuries, the history of the lands along the trade routes of the southern Asian seas was bound closely with Islamic religious, cultural, and commercial networks and also with the rising power of Christian western Europe. The key attractions of these diverse lands were their commercial and strategic possibilities (see Map 21–3).

In the sixteenth century the Europeans began to displace by force the Muslims who dominated the maritime southern rim of Asia. They owed their success to support from their homelands and their superior warships. Using superior naval power, and exploiting indigenous rivalries and terrorizing all who opposed them, the Portuguese carved out a major power base along the west coast of India at the expense of Muslim traders.

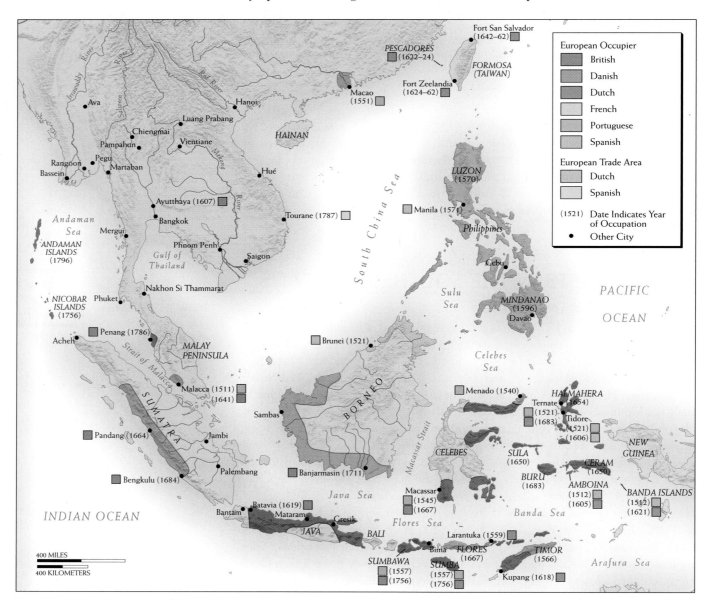

MAP 21–3   European Commercial Penetration of Southeast Asia.   Beginning with the Portuguese and Spanish in the sixteenth century, and then the Dutch and British in the seventeenth, western European powers established commercial bases throughout Southeast Asia, often cooperating with local Islamic, Hindi, or Buddhist rulers.

What were the motives for European maritime imperialism in Southeast Asia?

OVERVIEW The Religions of Southeast Asia

Predominately Buddhist	Burma
	Thailand, but with a significant Muslim minority
	Cambodia
	Laos
	Vietnam, but with a large Roman Catholic minority
	Singapore, but with Muslim, Christian, and Hindu minorities
Predominately Muslim	Indonesia, but the island of Bali is Hindu, and there is a large Christian minority
	Malaysia, but with Hindu, Buddhist, Chinese, and Christian minorities
	Brunei
Predominately Christian	Philippines, but with a sizable Muslim minority
	East Timor

Islamization continued, however, even in the face of Christian proselytizing and growing European political and commercial presence. The Muslims, unlike most of the European Christians, never kept aloof from the native populations and were largely assimilated everywhere. They rarely abandoned their faith, which proved generally attractive to new peoples they encountered. The result was usually an Islamized and racially mixed population.

As a result, while European gunboat imperialism had considerable military and economic success, often at the expense of Islamic states, European culture and Christianity made little headway against Islam. From East Africa to the Pacific, only in the northern Philippines did a substantial population become largely Christian.

THE EAST INDIES: ACHEH

The history of the Indonesian archipelago has always revolved around the international demand for its spices, peppers, and other produce. By the fifteenth century the coastal Islamic states were centered on the trading ports of the Malay Peninsula, the north shores of Sumatra and Java, and the Moluccas, or "Spice Islands." The last great Hindu kingdom of inland Java was defeated by an Islamic coalition of states in the early 1500s. Several substantial Islamic sultanates arose in the sixteenth and seventeenth centuries, even as Europeans were carving out their own economic empires in the region. The most powerful of these Islamic states was Acheh, in northwestern Sumatra (ca. 1524–1910).

In its early years Acheh provided the only counterweight to the Portuguese presence across the straits in Malacca (Malaysia). Although the Acheh sultans were unable to drive out the better-armed invaders, neither could the Portuguese subdue them. Despite Portuguese control of Indies commerce, Acheh managed to dominate the pepper trade of Sumatra and to thrive until the end of the sixteenth century. In the first half of the seventeenth century the sultanate controlled both coasts of Sumatra and parts of the Malay Peninsula. Meanwhile, the Dutch had replaced the Portuguese in the business of milking the Indies of their wealth, and by the eighteenth century they were doing it just as ruthlessly and more efficiently. In the early twentieth century the Dutch finally won full control in the region, but only after nearly forty years of intermittent war with Acheh (1873–1910).

CHRONOLOGY

THE SOUTHERN SEAS: ARRIVAL OF THE EUROPEANS

1498	The Portuguese come to the East African coast and to the west coast of India
1500–1512	The Portuguese establish bases on west Indian coast, replacing Muslims as Indian Ocean power
early 1500s	Muslim sultanates replace Hindu states in Java and Sumatra
1524–1910	State of Acheh in northwestern Sumatra
1600s	Major increase in Islamization and connected spread of Malay language in the archipelago
1641	Dutch conquest of Malacca
ca. 1800	Dutch replace Muslim states as main archipelago power
1873–1910	War between Holland and Acheh

SUMMARY

WHY DID the Ottoman Empire find it increasingly difficult to compete with European powers?

The Ottoman Empire and the East Mediterranean World. The period from 1500 to 1800 marks the cultural and political blossoming of the last Islamic empires and their gradual decline. The Ottoman Empire built up from a small principality in the fourteenth century, to a great empire under rulers including Mehmet II and Süleyman in the fifteenth and sixteenth centuries. The empire was well organized and had one of the strongest militaries in the world. In the seventeenth century, it still posed a threat to Europe, but in the eighteenth century it declined particularly in relation to the industrializing west. *page 514*

WHAT ROLE did Shi'ite ideology play in the Safavid Empire?

The Safavid Empire and the West Asian World. Shi'ite Sufi Safavids unified the traditional Iranian heartland under Shah Isma'il early in the sixteenth century. Shah Abbas I, whose rule straddled the turn of the seventeenth century, was a masterful ruler who consolidated Shi'te power in Iran. Safavid artists and intellectuals left a rich legacy, and the capital city of Isfahan was renowned as "half the world." *page 522*

WHAT ROLE did religious intolerance play in the decline of the Mughal Empire?

The Mughals. India was reunified under the Mughals in the sixteenth century. The great ruler Akbar (1558–1603) expanded Mughal territory and modeled religious tolerance. But Hindu–Muslim tensions increased after Akbar's reign, and both Sikhs and Hindu Marathas resisted Mughal authority. In the nineteenth century, the British East India Company gained power. *page 526*

WHAT WERE the most important Islamic States in central and southern Asia?

Central Asia: Islamization in the Post-Timur Era. The Uzbeks and Chaghatays of Central Asia were Sunni Muslims, geographically isolated from the mainstream Islamic community by the militant Shi'ism of the Safavids. *page 529*

HOW DID the arrival of Europeans affect maritime trade Southeast Asia?

Power Shifts in the Southern Oceans. Islamic traders attracted converts and established vibrant, multiethnic seaport communities around the rim of east Africa and southern Asia. Europe's growing economic and naval dominance allowed it to control many southern sea trade centers, but Islamization continued. *page 531*

INTERPRETING THE PAST

Islamic Empires: The Importance of Leadership

Sources from MyHistoryLab for Chapter 21

myhistorylab

1) Excerpt from *Biography of Emperor Akbar of India*
2) Sunni vs. Shi'ite: *Letter from Selim I to Ismail I*
3) Ogier Ghiselin de Busbecq: *Süleyman the Lawgiver*
4) Fathers Simon and Vincent: *Report on Shah Abbas I, the Safavid Ruler of Persia*

Visual Sources from MyHistoryLab

1) Safavid Battle Tunic
2) Ottoman Law Book, 1517

Islamic societies prospered throughout Southwest Asia in the years between 1450 and 1800, while three imperial states vied for dominance: the Ottomans (Turkey/Mesopotamia), the Safavids (Iran/Mesopotamia/Afghanistan), and the Mughals (India/Pakistan). Each state favored a different sect of Islam, depending on the religious orientation of its rulers and population. Yet each also faced the challenge of ruling a heterogeneous population with peoples of different religions, ethnicities, and

REVIEW QUESTIONS

1. Why did the Ottoman Empire expand so rapidly? Why did the empire fail to hold certain areas in Europe?

2. Why did the Safavid Empire succeed in Iran? What role did Islamic religion, a favorable geographic position, and access to the Indian Ocean have in this development? Who were the major foes of this empire?

3. What were the most important elements that united all Islamic states? Why was there a lack of unity between these states from 1500 to 1850? How and why were the European powers able to promote division among these various states?

4. What were Akbar's main policies toward the Hindu population? Why did he succeed and his followers fail in this area? What were his main governmental reforms?

5. How and why did the Sikhs develop into a formidable military power? Why did they become separatists in their orientation to the larger Indian world?

6. Akbar, Abbas, and Süleyman are considered some of the most successful world leaders in history. Compare and contrast their strengths, weaknesses, and long-term influence.

7. Compare the Sunni-Shi'ite differences and similarities within the Islamic world (1500–1800) with that of the Protestant–Catholic split within the Christian world during that same period. For example, can we compare relations between England and Spain in the sixteenth century to those between the Ottomans and the Safavids? Explain.

8. Why were outside powers attracted to the lands of the southern seas? Why did the European powers triumph in the struggle to control this area?

9. Which of the cultures described in this chapter seems most appealing to you? Which would you most like to live in, and why?

KEY TERMS

ayan (p. 520)
devshirme (dev-sheer-MEH) (p. 519)
Grand Mufti (grand MOOF-tee) (p. 517)
harem (p. 517)
Janissaries (JAN-nihss-AYR-ees) (p. 519)

millets (p. 520)
Mughals (MOO-gahlz) (p. 526)
padishah (p. 517)
pirs (p. 522)
Qanun (p. 518)
Qanun-name (p. 517)
Shari'a (sha-REE-ah) (p. 517)
Sufi (SOO-fee) (p. 522)

Note: To learn more about the topics in this chapter, please turn to the Suggested Readings at the end of the book.

economic interests. A second and equally difficult task was the necessity of maintaining secure borders.

This exercise involves reading four primary sources, from 1550 to about 1605, that document Ottoman, Safavid, and Mughal rulers and their methods. Because several of the writers lavishly praise the imperial rulers they were describing, you must read carefully "between the lines" in order to better analyze the historical events and circumstances being discussed.

The first document, part of a biography written by Abdu'l Fazl 'Allami, Emperor Akbar's key aide (also a historian and theorist), records the life of the imperial household and the ruler's methods in a highly flattering but also revealing manner. The second text is a letter from the Ottoman leader Selim I to the Safavid ruler Ismail I, offering a succinct and rather pointed summary of the reasons why Ismail should cease attacking Ottoman borders. The third text, *Süleyman the Lawgiver*, offers an outsider's assessment of the Ottoman emperor, his court, and society. It is highly complimentary, contrasting the Ottomans with European society and its aristocratic leadership. Finally, two Catholic friars (members of the Carmelite religious order) who visited Safavid Persia in 1605 present their views of their host, Shah Abbas, who freely allowed them to seek converts, as well as to gather information.

Use the text sources and the images to gain understanding about how these rulers governed their societies and attempted to secure the borders of their realms from encroachments from aggressive neighbors, including fellow Muslims. Use specific examples from the documents to back up your assertions.

Questions

What were the challenges of running a large empire, and what kinds of skills were necessary to achieve a stable, prosperous state? Compare each of the documents.

What roles do women perform in Mughal society, according to the biography of Akbar?

How did rulers deal with disputes with other leaders and states (see the Letter from Selim I to Ismail I, especially)? How was religion used in the effort to dissuade further attacks?

Compare the traits of each of the leaders discussed in these texts. Were there any common features? Akbar, Abbas, and Süleyman are considered some of the most successful world leaders in history. Are any of their potential weaknesses in evidence?

22

The Age of European Enlightenment

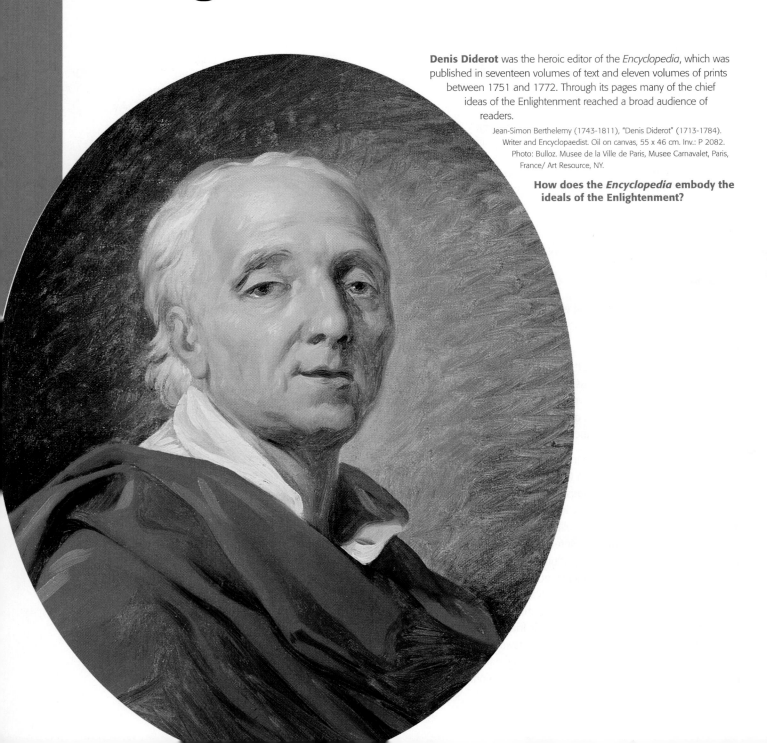

Denis Diderot was the heroic editor of the *Encyclopedia*, which was published in seventeen volumes of text and eleven volumes of prints between 1751 and 1772. Through its pages many of the chief ideas of the Enlightenment reached a broad audience of readers.

Jean-Simon Berthelemy (1743-1811), "Denis Diderot" (1713-1784). Writer and Encyclopaedist. Oil on canvas, 55 x 46 cm. Inv.: P 2082. Photo: Bulloz. Musee de la Ville de Paris, Musee Carnavalet, Paris, France/ Art Resource, NY.

How does the *Encyclopedia* embody the ideals of the Enlightenment?

THE SCIENTIFIC REVOLUTION *page 538*

WHY IS the Scientific Revolution important to world history?

THE ENLIGHTENMENT *page 545*

HOW DID Enlightenment thinkers argue for the reform of society?

THE ENLIGHTENMENT AND RELIGION *page 546*

WHY DID the *philosophes* regard the church as the chief enemy of reform and human happiness?

THE ENLIGHTENMENT AND SOCIETY *page 549*

HOW DID the *philosophes* hope that reason would change society?

ENLIGHTENED ABSOLUTISM *page 554*

WHAT WERE the goals of enlightened absolute rulers?

GLOBAL PERSPECTIVE

THE EUROPEAN ENLIGHTENMENT

Of all the movements of modern European thought, the most influential are the Scientific Revolution and the Enlightenment. A direct line of intellectual descent exists from those movements to the science and social criticism of the present day. Wherever modern science and technology are pursued and their effects felt, the spirit of the Enlightenment persists. From the eighteenth century to the present, the writers of the Enlightenment provided a pattern for intellectuals who wished to make their societies more rational, scientific, and secular, and thus "modern." Moreover, the Enlightenment model of society has become so influential in the West (and via the West in the rest of the world) that it has become synonymous with "modern." As a result, societies worldwide are judged to be modernized to the extent that their economies are industrialized and market oriented and their societies scientific and secular.

The Enlightenment writers valued emotions and passions as well as reason, but they used reason as a weapon for reform and the basis for a more productive economic life. In the centuries since the Enlightenment, such a use of critical reason has become a mark of reforming and progressive social and intellectual movements. The Enlightenment writers first used reason against Christianity and the strong influence of churches in European society and politics. However, reason came to be used against other world religions as well, leading to the tendency in the modern world to view science and religion in potential conflict and to consider less scientifically advanced societies as inherently culturally backward. This particular view of modernization tended to make the European and later North American experience regarded as the necessary pattern for all advanced society. This outlook originated with the majority of Enlightenment writers themselves. A minority of those writers of the eighteenth century, as with many present-day commentators, questioned whether even a rational, critical, and economically productive Europe should be the pattern for all human societies. Virtually all Enlightenment writers believed in some form of religious toleration or recognition of religious pluralism in their societies.

In terms of political thought the heritage of the Enlightenment was complex with different strands of political thought often in tension or outright conflict with each other. One strand of Enlightenment political thought that often drew upon the English political experience contributed to constitutionalism and modes of government in which the power and authority of the central government stand sharply circumscribed. Montesquieu, for example, influenced the Constitution of the United States and the

Enlightenment The eighteenth-century movement led by the *philosophes* that held that change and reform were both possible and desirable through the application of reason and science.

Western science and technology have transformed every region of the world during the past three centuries. Science, with the technology and medicine that flow from its understanding of nature, is a dominant force in modern life. Scientific knowledge with its attendant medical and economic progress, as well as its military advantages, is a goal of modern states.

The impact of science could make itself felt first in Europe and then elsewhere only when the conviction spread that change and reform were possible and desirable. This attitude came into its own in Europe only after 1700. The movement that fostered it is called the **Enlightenment**. It was an expression of confidence in the power of rational criticism to challenge the intellectual authority of tradition and revealed religion. Enlightenment thinkers believed human beings could comprehend the operation of physical nature and mold it to the ends of material and moral improvement. The rationality of the material world became a standard against which the customs and traditions of society could be measured and criticized. The spirit of innovation and improvement came to characterize modern Western society. This outlook has perhaps been Europe's most important cultural export to the rest of the world. ■

WHY IS the Scientific Revolution important to world history?

THE SCIENTIFIC REVOLUTION

The sixteenth and seventeenth centuries witnessed a sweeping change in the scientific view of the universe. Instead of being considered the center of the universe, the Earth was now seen as only another planet orbiting around the sun. The sun itself became one of millions of stars. This transformation led to a vast rethinking of moral and religious matters as well as of scientific theory. Science and the scientific method became numerous constitutions that document later influenced. Another strand of Enlightenment political thought, found in Voltaire, contributed to the growth of strong monarchial governments, which was the case with enlightened absolutism. Advocates of this mode of government believed that a monarch and a strong central bureaucracy could formulate and impose rational solutions to political and social problems and hence overcome competing interests. Still another strand of political thought, arising from Rousseau, led to the socialist concern with inequality of wealth and a desire for radical democratic government. Because of the complexity of Enlightenment political thought, modern governments displaying liberalism, socialism, and bureaucratic centralism may find roots in eighteenth-century thinkers. Modern political movements finding themselves essentially at odds with the Enlightenment heritage are those attached to radical Islamic groups who define themselves in opposition to most Western values. Those Western values tend to be values derived from the Enlightenment.

Much of what has been best about the Western cultural legacy to global culture derives from the Enlightenment. It is also important to remember that, as we observed in Chapter 18, the seventeenth and eighteenth centuries, whose ideas fostered the Enlightenment, also saw the rise of European colonial empires and the establishment of plantation economies based on slavery. Europeans' treatment of non-Europeans, as well as their warfare against each other in this era, often belied the principles of the Enlightenment. By the same token, some of the most admirable principles of Western culture, including advocacy of democracy and human rights, can be traced to Enlightenment roots.

Focus Questions

- How did Enlightenment values as well as Enlightenment admiration of science become one of the chief defining qualities of societies regarded as advanced, progressive, and modern?

- How has the political thought of the Enlightenment influenced the development of modern political philosophies and modern governments?

- How could modes of thought developed to criticize various aspects of eighteenth-century European society be transferred to other traditions of world civilizations?

so impressive and so influential that they set a new standard for evaluating knowledge in the Western world.

The process that established the new view of the universe is usually termed the **Scientific Revolution**. The revolution-in-science metaphor must be used carefully, however. Not everything associated with the "new" science was necessarily new. Sixteenth- and seventeenth-century natural philosophers were often reexamining and rethinking theories and data from the ancient world and the late Middle Ages. Moreover, the word *revolution* normally denotes rapid, collective political change involving large numbers of people. The Scientific Revolution was *not* rapid. It was a complex movement with many false starts and brilliant people suggesting wrong as well as useful ideas. Nor did it involve more than a few hundred people who labored in widely separated studies and crude laboratories located in Poland, Italy, Bohemia, France, and Great Britain. Furthermore, the achievements of the new science were not simply the function of isolated brilliant scientific minds. The leading figures of the Scientific Revolution often drew on the aid of artisans and craftspeople to help them construct new instruments for experimentation and to carry out their experiments. Thus, the Scientific Revolution involved a reappropriation of older knowledge as well as new discoveries. Additionally, because the practice of science involves social activity as well as knowledge, the revolution also saw the establishment of new social institutions to support the emerging scientific enterprise.

From the early seventeenth century through the end of the twentieth century science achieved greater cultural authority in the Western world than did any other form of intellectual activity, and the authority and application of scientific knowledge became one of the defining characteristics of modern Western civilization. Although

Scientific Revolution The sweeping change in the scientific view of the universe that occurred in the West in the sixteenth and seventeenth centuries.

new knowledge emerged in many areas during the sixteenth and seventeenth centuries, including medicine, chemistry, and natural history, the scientific achievements that most captured the learned imagination and persuaded people of the cultural power of natural knowledge were those that occurred in astronomy.

NICOLAUS COPERNICUS REJECTS AN EARTH-CENTERED UNIVERSE

Nicolaus Copernicus (1473–1543) was a Polish astronomer who enjoyed a high reputation during his life. In 1543, the year of his death, Copernicus published *On the Revolutions of the Heavenly Spheres*, which provided an intellectual springboard for a complete criticism of the then-dominant view of the position of the Earth in the universe.

Ptolemaic system The pre-Copernican explanation of the universe, which placed the Earth at the center of the universe.

At the time, the standard explanation of the place of the Earth in the heavens was the **Ptolemaic system**. It combined the mathematical astronomy of Ptolemy, contained in the *Almagest* (150 C.E.), with the physical cosmology of Aristotle. Over the centuries, most writers commenting on Ptolemy's system had assumed that the Earth was the center of the universe, an outlook known as *geocentricism*. Drawing on Aristotle, these commentators assumed that above the Earth lay a series of concentric spheres, one of which contained the moon, another the sun, and still others the planets and the stars. At the outer regions of these spheres lay the realm of God and the angels. The Earth had to be the center because of its heaviness. The stars and the other heavenly bodies had to be enclosed in the spheres so that they could move, since nothing could move unless something was actually moving it. The state of rest was presumed natural; motion required explanation. This was the astronomy found in such works as Dante's *Divine Comedy*.

Numerous problems were associated with the Ptolemaic model, and these had long been recognized. The most important was the observed motions of the planets, which at times appeared to go backwards. The Ptolemaic system explained these strange motions by proposing the *epicycle*: a second revolution by a planet in an orbit tangent to its primary orbit around the Earth. The Ptolemaic explanations were effective as long as one accepted Aristotelian physics and the Christian belief that the Earth rested at the center of the created universe.

Copernicus challenged this picture in the most conservative way possible. He suggested that if the Earth were assumed to move about the sun in a circle, there were fewer difficulties with the Ptolemaic system. With the sun at the center of the universe, mathematical astronomy would make more sense. The epicycles became smaller, and the retrograde motion of the planets could be explained as an optical illusion arising from an observer viewing the planets from a moving Earth. Except for the modification in the position of the Earth, most of Copernicus's book was Ptolemaic. It prompted others who were discontented with the Ptolemaic system to think in new ways, however. Copernicus's combination of mathematics, empirical data, and observation established the model for scientific thinking.

The Ptolemaic System. The "Emperor's Astronomy" (dedicated to the Holy Roman Emperor Charles V) elegantly depicts the cosmos and heavens according to the 1,400-year-old Ptolemaic system, which maintained that the sun revolved around the Earth. By means of hand-colored maps, Petrus Apianus (1495–1552) laid out the mechanics of a universe that was earth- and human-centered. Within three years of Apianus's book, this view was challenged by Copernicus's assertion that the Earth revolved around the sun.

Why was the question of the Earth's position in the universe of such importance?

TYCHO BRAHE AND JOHANNES KEPLER

The next major step toward the conception of a sun-centered system was taken by the Danish astronomer Tycho Brahe (1546–1601). He spent most of his life opposing Copernicus and advocating a different kind of Earth-centered system. He suggested that the moon and the sun revolved around the Earth and that the other planets revolved around the sun. His major weapon against Copernican astronomy was a series of new astronomical observations made with the naked eye. Brahe constructed the most accurate tables of observations that had been drawn up for centuries.

When Brahe died, these tables came into the possession of Johannes Kepler (1571–1630), a German astronomer. Kepler was a convinced Copernican but for philosophical, not scientific, reasons. Kepler was deeply influenced by Renaissance Neo-Platonists who, following upon Plato's (ca. 428–ca. 328 B.C.E.) association of knowledge with light, honored the sun. These Neo-Platonists were also determined to discover mathematical harmonies that would support a sun-centered universe. After much work, Kepler discovered that to keep the sun at the center of things, he must abandon the Copernican concept of circular orbits. The mathematical relationships that emerged from Brahe's observations suggested that the orbits of the planets were elliptical. Kepler published his findings in 1609 in a book entitled *On the Motion of Mars*. He had solved the problems of planetary orbits by using Copernicus's sun-centered universe and Brahe's empirical data.

None of the available theories could explain why the planetary orbits were elliptical. That solution awaited the work of Sir Isaac Newton.

GALILEO GALILEI

From Copernicus to Brahe to Kepler, there had been little new information about the heavens that might not have been known to Ptolemy. However, in 1609 an Italian scientist named Galileo Galilei (1564–1642) first turned a telescope on the heavens. He saw stars where none had been known to exist, mountains on the moon, spots moving across the sun, and moons orbiting Jupiter. The heavens were far more complex than anyone had formerly suspected. None of these discoveries proved that the Earth orbited the sun, but they did reveal the inadequacy of the Ptolemaic system, which could not accommodate these new phenomena. Some of Galileo's colleagues at the University of Padua were so unnerved that they refused to look through the telescope because it revealed the heavens to be different from the teachings of the church and from Ptolemaic theories.

Galileo publicized his findings and arguments for the Copernican system in his *Dialogues on the Two Chief Systems of the World* (1632). It was condemned by the Roman Catholic Church, which compelled him to recant his opinions. He did so, but reputedly muttered, "It [the Earth] still moves."

Galileo's most important achievement was to articulate the concept of a universe totally subject to mathematical laws. Copernicus had thought that the heavens conformed to mathematical regularity; Galileo saw this regularity throughout all physical nature. He believed that the smallest atom behaved with the same mathematical precision as the largest heavenly sphere.

Earlier in the century the English philosopher Francis Bacon had advocated a method based solely on empiricism. As the century passed, both empirical induction and mathematical analysis proved fundamental to scientific investigation.

FRANCIS BACON: THE EMPIRICAL METHOD

Francis Bacon (1561–1626) was a multitasking Englishman: He was a lawyer, a high royal official, and the author of histories, moral essays, and philosophical discourses. Traditionally, he has been regarded as the father of **empiricism** and of experimentation in science. Much of this reputation was unearned, but he did help set an intellectual tone and create a climate conducive to scientific work.

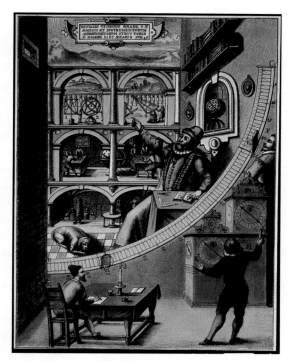

Tycho Brahe in the Uranienburg observatory on the Danish island of Hven (1587). Brahe made the most important observations of the stars since antiquity. Kepler used his data to solve the problem of planetary motion in a way that supported Copernicus's sun-centered view of the universe. Ironically, Brahe himself had opposed Copernicus's view.

How was empiricism at the center of the Scientific Revolution?

empiricism The use of experiment and observation derived from sensory evidence to construct scientific theory or philosophy of knowledge.

Portrait of Galileo Galilei (1636) by the Flemish Baroque painter Justus Sustermans.

How does the artist's use of light and shadow contribute to this portrayal of Galileo?

In books such as *The Advancement of Learning* (1605), the *Novum Organum* (1620), and the *New Atlantis* (1627), Bacon attacked the scholastic belief that most truth had already been discovered. He urged contemporaries to strike out on their own in search of a new understanding of nature. Bacon was one of the first major European writers to champion the desirability of innovation and change. Bacon believed that human knowledge should produce useful results. In particular, knowledge of nature should be brought to the aid of the human condition. By directing natural philosophy toward an examination of empirical evidence, Bacon hoped that it would achieve new knowledge and thus new capabilities for humankind.

Bacon's own theory of induction from empirical evidence was unsystematic, but his insistence on appealing to experience influenced others whose methods were more productive. He and others of his outlook received almost daily support from the reports of European explorers and also of ordinary seamen who now sailed all over the world and could describe wondrous cultures, as well as plants and animals, unknown to the European ancients.

Bacon's linkage of science and material progress, although not fully accurate, has continued to influence Western civilization to the present day. It has made science and those who can appeal to the authority of science major forces for change and innovation. Thus, though not making any major scientific contribution himself, Bacon directed investigators of nature to a new method and a new purpose. As a person actively associated with politics, Bacon also believed that the pursuit of new knowledge would increase the power of governments and monarchies. Here too, his thought opened the way for the eventual strong linkage between governments and the scientific enterprise.

ISAAC NEWTON DISCOVERS THE LAWS OF GRAVITATION

The question that continued to perplex seventeenth-century scientists who accepted the theories of Copernicus, Kepler, and Galileo was how the planets and other heavenly bodies moved in an orderly fashion. This was the issue that the Englishman Isaac Newton (1642–1727) addressed and, in so doing, established a basis for physics that endured for more than two centuries.

In 1687 Newton published *The Mathematical Principles of Natural Philosophy*, better known by its Latin title of *Principia Mathematica*. Galileo's mathematical bias permeated Newton's thought, as did his view that inertia applied to bodies both at rest and in motion. Newton reasoned that the planets and all other physical objects in the universe moved through mutual attraction, or gravity. Every object in the universe affected every other object through gravity. Newton proved the gravitational relationship between the planets mathematically; he made no attempt to explain the nature of gravity itself.

Newton was a mathematical genius, but he also upheld the importance of empirical data and observation. Like Francis Bacon, he believed that one must observe phenomena before attempting to explain them. The final test of any theory or hypothesis for him was whether it described what was actually observed. Newton was a great opponent of the rationalism of the French philosopher René Descartes (1596–1650), which he believed included insufficient guards against error. Consequently, as Newton's own theory of universal gravitation became increasingly accepted, so, too, was Baconian empiricism.

WOMEN IN THE WORLD OF THE SCIENTIFIC REVOLUTION

Historians speculate about the relationship of women to the new science. Factors that had long excluded women from intellectual life continued during the Enlightenment to block their participation in the Scientific Revolution. The institutions of European intellectual life all but excluded women. With a few exceptions in Italy, women were

QUICK REVIEW

Francis Bacon (1561–1626)

◆ Attacked belief that most truth had already been discovered

◆ One of the first Europeans to champion innovation and change

◆ Persuaded others that scientific thought must proceed by means of empirical observation

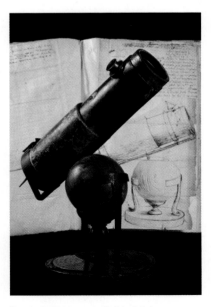

Newton's Telescope. Behind it is a copy of *Principia Mathematica*, his most famous work.

What was the significance of Newton's work on gravity?

not admitted to European universities until the end of the nineteenth century. Women could and did exercise influence over princely courts where natural philosophers, such as Galileo, sought patronage, but they usually did not determine those patronage decisions or benefit from them. Queen Christina of Sweden was an exception; she engaged René Descartes to provide the regulations for a new science academy. When various scientific societies were founded, women were not admitted to membership. There were virtually no social spaces that permitted women to pursue science.

A few isolated women—from both the nobility and the artisan class—did engage in scientific research, but only with the aid of men in their families. Margaret Cavendish (1623–1673) had access to a circle of natural philosophers who gathered around her husband, the Duke of Newcastle. She understood the new science, spoke against the ideas of Descartes and Hobbes, and criticized the Royal Society for being more interested in novel scientific instruments than in solving practical problems. Her most important works were *Observations upon Experimental Philosophy* (1666) and *Grounds of Natural Philosophy* (1668). She was the only woman in the seventeenth century to be allowed to visit a meeting of the Royal Society of London.

Women associated with artisan crafts achieved greater freedom in pursuing the new sciences than did noblewomen. Traditionally, women had worked in artisan workshops, often with their husbands, and sometimes took over the business when their spouse died. Much German astronomy, for example, occurred with women assisting their fathers or husbands. German astronomer Maria Cunitz published a book on astronomy that many people thought her husband had written until he added a preface supporting her sole authorship. Elisabetha and Johannes Hevelius constituted a wife-and-husband astronomical team, as did Maria Winkelmann and her husband Gottfried Kirch. Although Winkelmann discovered a comet in 1702, not until 1930 was the discovery ascribed to her rather than to her husband. Kirch was the official astronomer of the Berlin Academy of Sciences and was responsible for establishing an official calendar published by the Academy. When her husband died in 1710, Winkelmann applied for permission to continue the work, basing her application for the post on the guild's tradition of allowing women to continue their husband's work. After much debate, the Academy formally rejected her application on the grounds of her gender, although its members knew of her ability and previous accomplishments.

Some women were able to use books or personal friendships as a narrow path around such policies of exclusion. Margaret Cavendish had composed a *Description of a New World, Called the Blazing World* (1666) to introduce women to the new science. Other scientific writings for a female audience were Bernard de Fontenelle's *Conversations on the Plurality of Worlds* and Francesco Algarotti's *Newtonianism for Ladies* (1737). During the 1730s, Emilie du Châtelet aided Voltaire in his composition of an important French popularization of Newton's science. Her knowledge of mathematics was more extensive than his.

Still, with only a few exceptions, women were barred from science and medicine until the late nineteenth century, and only in the twentieth century did they enter these fields in any significant numbers. Not only did the institutions of science exclude them but also the ideas associated with medical practice, philosophy, and biology suggested that women and their minds were essentially different from, and inferior to, men and theirs. By the early eighteenth century, despite isolated

Women and Learning. René Descartes, the French philosopher, is on the right, tutoring Queen Christina (1626–1689) of Sweden, seated on the left.
Pierre-Louis the Younger Dumesnil (1698-1781), "Christina of Sweden (1626-89) and her Court: detail of the Queen and René Descartes (1596-1650) at the Table." Oil on canvas. Chateau de Versailles, France/Bridgeman Art Library.

What roles did women play in the Scientific Revolution?

John Locke (1632–1704), defender of the rights of the people against rulers who think their power is absolute.

"John Locke (1632-1704)." By courtesy of the National Portrait Gallery, London.

What are the similarities between Locke's and Newton's views of the universe?

precedents of women pursuing natural knowledge, reading scientific literature, and engaging socially with natural philosophers, it had become a fundamental assumption of European intellectual life that the pursuit of natural knowledge was a male vocation.

JOHN LOCKE

John Locke (1632–1704) attempted to discover laws governing the human mind similar to those that Newton had discovered as explanations for natural phenomena. No other philosopher had so profound an impact on European and American thought during the eighteenth century.

Locke's *Essay Concerning Human Understanding* (1690) postulated that the human mind is blank at the time of birth. People have no innate ideas. All their knowledge derives from information that comes through their physical senses. Given that people's intellects are shaped by the interaction between their minds and the world, Locke argued that human nature can be molded by modifying the environment. Locke in effect rejected the Christian view that human beings were flawed by original sin. Human beings do not need to wait for divine aid; they can take charge of their own destinies.

In his *Two Treatises of Government*, written during the reign of Charles II (r. 1660–1685), Locke made a case against absolute monarchy. Nature's rational law, he argued, dictates that all people voluntarily relinquish some of their freedom and contract with their rulers for the protection and preservation of their natural rights. Rulers are, therefore, not absolute but bound by nature's laws. A monarch who does not comply can legitimately be overthrown. In his *Letter Concerning Toleration*, Locke argued that governments existed to protect property and civil order. They should not legislate on religion, for the pursuit of salvation is the responsibility of the individual. Locke himself drew the line in England against toleration of Roman Catholics and Unitarians. During the eighteenth century, however, the logic of his argument was extended to advocate toleration for those faiths as well.

OVERVIEW Major Figures in the Scientific Revolution

Nicolaus Copernicus (1473–1543)	On the basis of mathematical analysis argued that the Earth moved around the sun.
Tycho Brahe (1546–1601)	Compiled accurate tables of astronomical observations.
Johannes Kepler (1571–1630)	Used Brahe's data to argue that the orbits of the planets were elliptical.
Galileo Galilei (1564–1642)	First astronomer to use a telescope. Argued that mathematical laws governed the universe.
Francis Bacon (1561–1630)	Argued that scientific thought must conform to empirical evidence. Championed innovation and change.
René Descartes (1596–1650)	Invented analytical geometry. Argued that the world was governed by mathematical laws that could be deduced by reason.
Isaac Newton (1642–1727)	Described the effect of gravity mathematically and established a theoretical basis for physics that endured until the late nineteenth century.
John Locke (1632–1704)	Argued that the human mind is a blank slate that may be molded by modifying the environment. Human beings could thus take charge of their own destiny without divine aid.

THE ENLIGHTENMENT

The movement known as the Enlightenment included writers living at different times in various countries. Its early exponents, the ***philosophes***, popularized the rationalism and scientific ideas of the seventeenth century. They exposed contemporary social and political abuses and argued that reform was necessary and possible. They confronted oppression and religious condemnation and by midcentury had brought enlightened ideas to the European public in a variety of formats.

HOW DID Enlightenment thinkers argue for the reform of society?

philosophes The eighteenth-century writers and critics who forged the new attitudes favorable to change. They sought to apply reason and common sense to the institutions and societies of their day.

VOLTAIRE

The most influential of the *philosophes* was François Marie Arouet, called Voltaire (1694–1778). During the 1720s, Voltaire offended the French authorities and was briefly imprisoned. In 1733, after visiting England, he published *Letters on the English*, which praised the intellectual and political freedom found in England and indirectly criticized French society. In 1738, he published *Elements of the Philosophy of Newton*, which popularized the thought of the great scientist.

Thereafter, Voltaire lived part of the time in France and part near Geneva, just across the French border, where the royal authorities could not bother him. His essays, history, plays, stories, and letters made him the literary dictator of Europe. He turned the bitter venom of his satire and sarcasm against one evil after another in French and European life. His most famous satire is *Candide* (1759), in which he attacked war, religious persecution, and what he regarded as unwarranted optimism about the human condition. Like most *philosophes*, Voltaire believed that human society could and should be improved. But he was never certain that reform, if achieved, would be permanent. The optimism of the Enlightenment constituted a tempered hopefulness rather than a glib certainty. Pessimism was an undercurrent in most of the works of the period.

FRANÇOIS · DE · VOLTAIRE · COPIÉ · D'APRÈS · LE TABLEAU · FAIT · PAR · LARGILIÈRE · EN · 1718 · ÉLU · EN · 1746

Voltaire. Philosopher, dramatist, poet, historian, and popularizer of scientific ideas, Voltaire (1694–1778) was the most famous and influential of the eighteenth-century philosophers. His sharp satire and criticism of religious institutions opened the way for a more general critique of the European political and social status quo.

What were some of Voltaire's most important ideas?

THE *ENCYCLOPEDIA*

One of the greatest monuments of the Enlightenment was the *Encyclopedia*. Under the heroic leadership of Denis Diderot (1713–1784) and Jean le Rond d'Alembert (1717–1783), the first volume appeared in 1751. When completed in 1772, it numbered seventeen volumes of text and eleven of plates. The *Encyclopedia* was the product of the collective effort of more than one hundred authors, and its editors had solicited articles from all the major French *philosophes*. Attempts were made to censor it and halt its publication, but it was ultimately completed. The *Encyclopedia* made a plea for freedom of expression and set forth the most advanced critical ideas in religion, government, and philosophy. It also provided practical information in areas such as manufacturing, canal building, and agriculture.

Between 14,000 and 16,000 copies of various editions of the *Encyclopedia* were sold before 1789. The project had been designed to secularize learning and the articles concentrated on humanity and its well-being. The encyclopedists looked to antiquity rather than to the Christian centuries for their inspiration, and they believed that the welfare of humankind lay not in the pursuit of revelation but in the application of reason to human relationships. The *Encyclopedia* diffused enlightened thought throughout the continent and drew German and Russian thinkers into the movement (see Map 22–1).

THE ENLIGHTENMENT AND RELIGION

WHY DID the *philosophes* regard the church as the chief enemy of reform and human happiness?

In the eyes of the *philosophes*, the chief enemy of the improvement and happiness of humankind was the church. They were especially critical of Roman Catholicism. But all the Christian churches advocated a religious rather than a scientific view of humankind and taught the idea that human beings were sinful and in need of divine grace. Religion turned attention away from this world and the solution to its problems to the world to come. The *philosophes* also indicted the churches for fostering intolerance and bigotry.

DEISM

The *philosophes* believed that religion should be reasonable and lead to moral behavior. Newton argued that nature was a rational system; many believed that the God who had created it must also be rational. Locke argued that all human knowledge derived from empirical experience, casting doubt on the possibility of divine revelation. The rational religion of the Enlightenment is called **deism**. The deists regarded God as resembling a divine watchmaker who had set the mechanism of nature to work and then let it operate without intervention.

There were two major points in the deists' creed. The first was a belief in the existence of God, which they thought could be empirically deduced from the contemplation of nature. Because nature provided evidence of a rational God, that Deity must also favor rational morality. Consequently, the second point in the deists' creed was a belief in life after death, when rewards and punishments would be meted out according to the virtue of the life a person led on this earth.

Deism was empirical, tolerant, reasonable, and capable of encouraging virtuous living. It was the major positive religious component of the Enlightenment.

Illustration from the *Encyclopedia*. Denis Diderot in the *Encyclopedia* included illustrations of machinery and working people from across the globe. Diderot was also deeply hostile to slavery. This engraving illustrated a sugar mill and sugar boiling house run with slave labor in the New World. The sugar produced in such mills was used in the European coffeehouses where the ideas of the *philosophes* were often discussed.

How does this illustration show the *Encyclopedia's* emphasis on practical learning?

TOLERATION

The centuries immediately preceding the Enlightenment had been characterized by bloody religious wars, and *philosophes* hoped that the triumph of reason and science would end denominational hatred and establish religious toleration.

Voltaire championed this cause. In 1762, the French authorities ordered the execution of a Huguenot named Jean Calas (1698–1762) for having allegedly murdered his son to prevent him from converting to Roman Catholicism. Calas was tortured but died without confessing his guilt. In 1763, Voltaire published the *Treatise on Toleration*, and he continued to hound the authorities until the decision against Calas was reversed in 1765. For Voltaire, the case illustrated the dangers of religious fanaticism and the need for rational judicial reform. In 1779, Gotthold Lessing's (1729–1781) play about a Jew, *Nathan the Wise*, broadened the plea for toleration beyond Christian sects to include all religious faiths. These calls for toleration argued that secular values were more important than religious ones.

deism A belief in a rational God who had created the universe, but then allowed it to function without his interference according to the mechanisms of nature and a belief in rewards and punishments after death for human action.

ISLAM IN ENLIGHTENMENT THOUGHT

Beyond the Balkans, there were few Muslims in eighteenth-century Europe. European merchants traded in Islamic regions, but most Europeans came to know what little they did know about the Islamic world and Islam as a religion through books—the religious

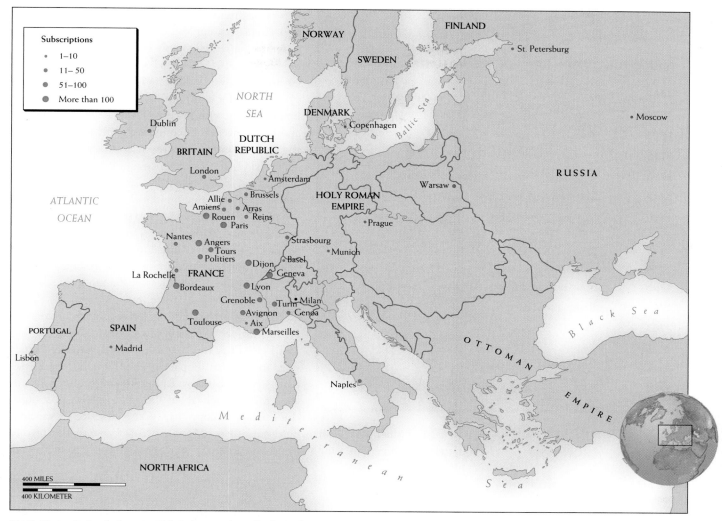

Subscriptions
- 1–10
- 11–50
- 51–100
- More than 100

NORWAY

FINLAND

SWEDEN

• St. Petersburg

NORTH
SEA

DENMARK

• Moscow

Dublin

Copenhagen

Baltic Sea

DUTCH
REPUBLIC

BRITAIN

RUSSIA

London

Amsterdam

ATLANTIC
OCEAN

Brussels

Warsaw •

Allie

HOLY ROMAN
EMPIRE

Amiens   Arras

Rouen   Reins

Prague

Paris

Nantes

Strasbourg

Angers   Munich

Tours

Politiers

Dijon   Basel

La Rochelle   FRANCE   Geneva

Bordeaux   Lyon

Grenoble   Turin   Milan

Toulouse   Avignon   Genoa

Aix

PORTUGAL   SPAIN   Marseilles

Black Sea

Lisbon   Madrid

O T T O M A N

Naples

E M P I R E

Mediterranean

NORTH AFRICA

S e a

400 MILES

400 KILOMETER

MAP 22–1   Subscriptions to Diderot's *Encyclopedia* throughout Europe.

Why are the greatest number of subscriptions to the *Encyclopedia* concentrated in Western Europe?

commentaries of Christian missionaries, histories, and the reports of travelers—that generally were hostile to Islam and deeply misleading.

Islam continued to be seen as a rival to Christianity. European writers portrayed Islam as a false religion and Muhammad as an impostor because he had not performed miracles. They also attacked Islam as an exceptionally carnal or sexually promiscuous religion because of its teaching that heaven was a place of sensuous delights, its permission for a man to have more than one wife, Muhammad's own polygamy, and the presence of harems in the Islamic world. Christian authors ignored the Islamic understanding of the life and mission of Muhammad. They referred to Islam as Muhammadanism, implying that Muhammad was divine rather than a human being with whom God had chosen to communicate. (For Muslims, the suggestion that Muhammad was divine is blasphemous.)

Several European universities established chairs of Arabic studies in the seventeenth century, but the professors who held them tended to agree with the Christian theologians and to equate Islam with religious fanaticism. Even scholarly books based on considerable knowledge of Arabic and Islamic sources were largely hostile to their subject.

CHRONOLOGY

MAJOR PUBLICATION DATES OF THE ENLIGHTENMENT

1687	Newton's *Principia Mathematica*
1690	Locke's *Essay Concerning Human Understanding*
1696	Toland's *Christianity Not Mysterious*
1733	Voltaire's *Letters on the English*
1738	Voltaire's *Elements of the Philosophy of Newton*
1748	Montesquieu's *Spirit of the Laws*
1750	Rousseau's *Discourse on the Moral Effects of the Arts and Sciences*
1751	First volume of the *Encyclopedia* edited by Diderot and d'Alembert
1755	Rousseau's *Discourse on the Origin of Inequality*
1762	Rousseau's *Social Contract*
1763	Voltaire's *Treatise on Tolerance*
1776	Smith's *Wealth of Nations*
1779	Lessing's *Nathan the Wise*
1792	Wollstonecraft's *A Vindication of the Rights of Woman*

Enlightenment *philosophes* spoke with two voices regarding Islam. For Voltaire, Muhammad and Islam in general represented simply one more example of the religious fanaticism he had so often criticized among Christians. Edward Gibbon (1737–1794), who blamed Christianity for contributing to the fall of the Roman Empire, wrote with respect of Muhammad's leadership and Islam's success in conquering so vast a territory in the first century of its existence. Other commentators approved of Islam's tolerance and the charitable work of Muslims. Some *philosophes* criticized Islam on cultural and political grounds. Baron de Montesquieu (1689–1755), discussed later in this chapter, associated Islamic society with the passivity that he ascribed to people subject to political despotism. Montesquieu believed the excessive influence of Islamic religious leaders prevented the Ottoman Empire from adapting itself to new advances in technology.

One of the most positive commentators on eighteenth-century Islam was a woman. Between 1716 and 1718, Lady Mary Wortley Montagu (1689–1762) lived in Constantinople with her husband, the British ambassador to Turkey. In her *Turkish Embassy Letters*, she praised much about Ottoman society and urged the English to copy the Turkish practice of vaccination against smallpox. Unlike European males, Montagu had access to the private quarters of women in Istanbul, and she thought upper-class Turkish women were

Map of Turkey and View of Constantinople (Istanbul). Few Europeans visited the Ottoman Empire. What little they knew about it came from reports of travelers and from illustrations such as this view of Istanbul, the empire's capital.

Why did the Ottoman Empire arouse so much interest among Enlightenment thinkers?

remarkably free and well treated by their husbands. Montagu repeatedly criticized the misinformation that prevailed in Europe about the Ottoman Empire and declared that many of the hostile comments about Islam and Islamic morality were simply wrong.

Yet the European voices demanding fairness for Islam were rare. Nor were Muslims very curious about the Christian West. Only a handful of people from the Ottoman or Safavid empires visited western Europe in the eighteenth century, and no Islamic writers showed much interest in contemporary European authors. The *ulama*, the Islamic religious establishment, taught that God's revelations to Muhammad meant that Islam had superceded Christianity as a religion and, therefore, there was little to be learned from the Christian culture of Europe.

QUICK REVIEW

Enlightenment and Islam: Cross-Cultural Views

- ◆ European popular view of Islam biased
- ◆ European scholarship on Islam hostile
- ◆ Lady Montagu provided sympathetic view of Islam
- ◆ Islam dismissive of Christianity, disinterested in European writers

THE ENLIGHTENMENT AND SOCIETY

The *philosophes* believed that the application of human reason to society would reveal laws in human relationships similar to those found in physical nature. Although the term did not appear until later, the idea of social science originated with the Enlightenment. The purpose of discovering social laws was to remove the inhumanity that was a by-product of ignorance.

HOW DID the *philosophes* hope that reason would change society?

MONTESQUIEU AND *THE SPIRIT OF THE LAWS*

Charles Louis de Secondat, Baron de Montesquieu's (1689–1755) *The Spirit of the Laws* (1748) was perhaps the most influential book of the century. Montesquieu took an empirical approach to the study of law, passing his conclusions on legal texts from ancient as well as modern nations. He concluded that no single set of laws could apply to all peoples at all times and in all places. Only a careful examination and evaluation of many variables could reveal what mode of government would prove most beneficial for a given people. A century later such speculations would have been classified as sociology.

The French, Montesquieu believed, would be best served by a monarchy whose power was limited by intermediary institutions: the aristocracy, the towns, the *parlements*, and other corporate bodies whose liberties the monarch had to respect. Their role was to preserve the liberty of subjects by restraining the power of their ruler. Montesquieu was a political conservative, but he believed that France's oppressive and inefficient monarchy was degrading life in France and it needed reform.

One of Montesquieu's most influential ideas was the division of power. He thought that Great Britain provided an excellent example of this principle in action. It vested executive power in its monarch, legislative power in its Parliament, and judicial power in its courts, and any two of these branches of government could check the power of the other. His perception of the eighteenth-century British constitution was incorrect, but his analysis made a strong case for limiting the power of rulers by constitutional means and relying on legislatures, not monarchs, to make laws. Although Montesquieu set out to defend the political privileges of the French aristocracy, his ideas had a profound and enduring effect on the liberal democracies of the next two centuries.

ADAM SMITH ON ECONOMIC GROWTH AND SOCIAL PROGRESS

The most important Enlightenment exposition of economics was Adam Smith's (1723–1790) *An Inquiry into the Nature and Causes of the Wealth of Nations* (1776). Smith urged abolition of England's mercantile system. Mercantilists claimed that economic regulation by the state was needed to preserve the wealth of a nation as well as

Printing Shops. Shops such as this were the productive centers for the book trade and newspaper publishing, which spread the ideas of the Enlightenment.

How did printing spread Enlightenment ideas?

laissez-faire French phrase meaning "allow to do." In economics, the doctrine of minimal government interference in the working of the economy.

QUICK REVIEW

Adam Smith (1723–1790)

◆ Advocated abolition of mercantile system

◆ Saw nature as a set of physical resources to be exploited by human beings

◆ Was in favor of limited government activity in the economy

to increase wealth by taking it away from other nations. But Smith believed that such regulation constricted wealth and production. He believed that if individuals were unleashed to pursue their self-interest, the result would be economic expansion, for the rational demands of the marketplace would guide their productive activities.

It was a basic assumption of mercantilism that the earth's resources are limited and scarce, so that one nation can acquire wealth only at the expense of others. Smith's book challenged this assumption. He saw the resources of nature—water, air, soil, and minerals—as boundless. To him, they demanded exploitation for the enrichment and comfort of humankind. In effect, Smith was saying that the nations and peoples of Europe need not be poor.

Smith is usually regarded as the founder of *laissez-faire* economic thought and policy, which favors a limited role for the government in economic life. *The Wealth of Nations* was, however, a complex book. Smith was no simple dogmatist. For example, he did not oppose all government activity touching the economy. The state, he argued, should provide schools, armies, navies, and roads. It should also undertake certain commercial ventures, such as the opening of dangerous new trade routes that were economically desirable but too expensive or risky for private enterprise. Smith, like most of the *philosophes*, was less doctrinaire than any brief summary of their thought suggests.

Smith's theories helped to justify Western imperialism. Smith endorsed a model popular with other social theorists of his day: the *four-stage theory*. It divided human societies into four categories according to their economic basis: hunting and gathering, pastoral or herding, agricultural, and commercial. Movement through these stages was assumed to be progress. This meant that economic development was the indicator of where a group fell on the continuum between barbarism and civilization. Smith's theory allowed Europeans to view their society as the pinnacle of human achievement and to justify their pursuit of imperial domination of the world as a civilizing mission.

ROUSSEAU

Jean-Jacques Rousseau (1712–1778) held a different view of political power. Rousseau was a strange, isolated genius who never felt comfortable with the other *philosophes*. Yet perhaps more than any other writer of the mid-eighteenth century, he transcended the thought and values of his own time. His *Discourse on the Moral Effects of the Arts and Sciences* (1750) contended that civilization and enlightenment had corrupted, not elevated, human nature. In a *Discourse on the Origin of Inequality* (1755), he agreed that economic problems were at the root of evil in the world, but the problem was maldistribution of property, not production. Rousseau felt that the purpose of society should be to nurture better, not wealthier, people. His vision of reform was much more radical than that of other philosophers.

Rousseau carried these same concerns into his political thought. *The Social Contract* (1762) outlines the kind of political structure that Rousseau believed would overcome the evils of contemporary society. Most eighteenth-century political thinkers regarded society as a collection of independent individuals pursuing selfish goals, and they advocated liberating these individuals from the undue bonds of government. Rousseau, however, claimed that society was more important than the individual, because individuals are what they are only because of their relationship to the larger community. Lone, independent human beings can achieve little, but in a community they become moral creatures capable of significant action. Rousseau, drawing on Plato and Calvin, claimed that true freedom was obedience to law—that is, rules determined by the general will. The general will, Rousseau believed, was the opinion of the majority of voting citizens who acted with adequate information and under the influence of virtuous customs and morals. This majority was always right and to obey it was to be free. If a minority disagreed, it had (paradoxically) to be forced to be free. Radical direct democracy entailed collective action against individual citizens. Rousseau assaulted the eighteenth-century cult of the individual and selfishness and was at odds with the commercial spirit that was transforming his world.

ENLIGHTENED CRITICS OF EUROPEAN EMPIRE

Most European thinkers associated with the Enlightenment favored the extension of European empires across the world, believing that this amounted to the spread of progress and civilization. There were, however, a few Enlightenment voices who criticized the European empires. They were troubled by the European conquest of the Americas, the treatment of Native Americans, and the enslavement of Africans on the two American continents. The most important of these critics were Denis Diderot and two German philosophers, Immanuel Kant (1724–1804) and Johann Gottfried Herder (1744–1803).

Rousseau. The writings of Jean-Jacques Rousseau (1712–1778) raised some of the most profound social and ethical questions of the Enlightenment. This portrait by Maurice Quentin was made about 1740.

What did Rousseau believe should be the goal of Enlightened reform?

These critics shared important ideas. They argued for the existence of a form of shared humanity that the sixteenth-century European conquerors and their successors in the Americas and in other areas of imperial conquest had ignored. Kant wrote, "When America, the Negro countries, the Spice Islands, the Cape, and so forth were discovered, they were to them [the Europeans], countries belonging to no one, since they counted the inhabitants as *nothing*."[1] Kant, Diderot, and Herder rejected this dismissive outlook and the harsh policies that had flowed from it. They believed no single definition of human nature could be made the standard throughout the world and then used to dehumanize people whose appearance or culture differed from that standard.

Diderot, Kant, and Herder also shared the conviction that the people whom Europeans had encountered in the Americas possessed cultures that should have been respected and understood rather than being destroyed. As Herder wrote in the late eighteenth century, " 'European culture' is a mere abstraction, an empty concept. Where does or did it actually exist in its entirety? In which nation? In which period? . . . The culture of man is not the culture of the European; it manifests itself according to time and place in every people."[2] For Herder, human beings living in different societies possessed the capacity as human beings to develop in culturally different fashions. This outlook later became known as cultural relativism.

A third, closely related idea was that human beings may develop distinct cultures possessing intrinsic values that cannot be directly compared. Each culture possesses

---

[1]Quoted in Sinkar Muthu, *Enlightenment Against Empire* (Princeton: Princeton University Press, 2003), p. 267. This section draws primarily from this excellent book.

[2]F. M. Barnard, *Self-direction and Political Legitimacy: Rousseau and Herder* (Oxford: Clarendon Press, 1988), p. 227.

DOCUMENT

Rousseau Argues for Separate Spheres for Men and Women

Rousseau published Émile, a novel about education, in 1762. In it he made one of the strongest and most influential arguments of the eighteenth century for distinct social roles for men and women. Furthermore, he portrayed women as fundamentally subordinate to men.

- **How** does Rousseau move from the physical differences between men and women to an argument for distinct social roles and social spheres? What would be the proper kinds of social activities for women in Rousseau's vision? What kind of education would he think appropriate for women?

There is no parity between the two sexes in regard to the consequences of sex. The male is male only at certain moments. The female is female her whole life or at least during her whole youth. Everything constantly recalls her sex to her; and, to fulfill its functions well, she needs a constitution which corresponds to it. She needs care during her pregnancy; she needs rest at the time of childbirth; she needs a soft and sedentary life to suckle her children; she needs patience and gentleness, a zeal and an affection that nothing can rebuff in order to raise her children. She serves as the link between them and their father; she alone makes him love them and gives him the confidence to call them his own. How much tenderness and care is required to maintain the union of the whole family! And, finally, all this must come not from virtues but from tastes, or else the human species would soon be extinguished.

The strictness of the relative duties of the two sexes is not and cannot be the same. When woman complains on this score about unjust man-made inequality, she is wrong. This inequality is not a human institution—or, at least, it is the work not of prejudice but of reason. It is up to the sex that nature has charged with the bearing of

deep inner social and linguistic complexities that make any simple comparison impossible. Indeed, Diderot, Kant, and Herder argued that one fundamental aspect of humanity is the ability to develop a variety of distinctly different cultures.

These arguments critical of empire often involved criticism of New World slavery and were part of the antislavery movement to be discussed in a later chapter. Whereas the antislavery arguments took strong hold in both Europe and America from the late eighteenth century onward, the arguments critical of empire did not. They stand generally isolated from the rest of Enlightenment political thought and would not be strongly revived until new anticolonial voices were raised in Europe and the non-European world at the close of the nineteenth century.

WOMEN IN THE THOUGHT AND PRACTICE OF THE ENLIGHTENMENT

Women, especially in France, helped promote the careers of the *philosophes*. In Paris the salons of women such as Marie-Thérèse Geoffrin (1699–1777), Julie de Lespinasse (1733–1776), and Claudine de Tencin (1689–1749) gave the *philosophes* access to useful social and political contacts and a receptive environment for their ideas. These women were well connected to major political figures who could help protect the *philosophes* and secure them pensions. The marquise de Pompadour (1721–1764), the mistress of Louis XV, for example, played a key role in overcoming efforts to censor the *Encyclopedia*. She also helped block the circulation of works attacking the *philosophes*.

Despite their reliance on female patrons, their general enthusiasm for reform, and their tendency to reject ascetic views of sexual relations, the *philosophes* advocated no radical changes in the social condition of women. Montesquieu, for example, believed that women were not naturally inferior to men and that they should play a greater role in society, but he also believed that men should dominate marriage and family. Furthermore, although he supported the right of women to divorce and opposed laws that oppressed them, he exalted chastity as the primary female virtue.

children to be responsible for them to the other sex. Doubtless it is not permitted to any one to violate his faith, and every unfaithful husband who deprives his wife of the only reward of the austere duties of her sex is an unjust and barbarous man. But the unfaithful woman does more; she dissolves the family and breaks all the bonds of nature. ...

Once it is demonstrated that man and woman are not and ought not be constituted in the same way in either character or temperament, it follows that they ought not to have the same education. In following nature's directions, man and woman ought to act in concert, but they ought not to do the same things. The goal of their labors is common, but their labors themselves are different, and consequently so are the tastes directing them. ...

The good constitution of children initially depends on that of their mothers. The first education of men depends on the care of women. Men's morals, their passions, their tastes, their pleasures, their very happiness also depend on women. Thus the whole education of women ought to relate to men. To please men, to be useful to them, to make herself loved and honored by them, to raise them when young, to care for them when grown, to counsel them, to console them, to make their lives agreeable and sweet—these are the duties of women at all times, and they ought to be taught from childhood. So long as one does not return to this principle, one will deviate from the goal, and all the precepts taught to women will be of no use for their happiness or for ours.

Source: From *Émile; or, On Education, by Jean-Jacques Rousseau*, Allan Bloom, trans. Copyright © 1979 by Basic Books, a member of Perseus Books L.L.C.

The views about women expressed in the *Encyclopedia* were less generous. Diderot and d'Alembert saw no need to include many articles by women. Most of the articles that dealt with women emphasized their physical weakness and inferiority, usually attributed to menstruation or childbearing. Contributors disagreed on the social equality of women. The articles conveyed a general sense that women were reared to be frivolous. The encyclopedists discussed women primarily in a family context and considered motherhood their most important occupation. On sexual behavior, the encyclopedists upheld a double standard. In contrast to the articles, however, illustrations in the *Encyclopedia* showed women deeply involved in the economic activities of the day. The illustrations also showed the activities of lower- and working-class women, about whom the articles have little to say.

Rousseau urged women to embrace their traditional roles. In his novel *Émile* (1762), he declared that women should be educated to be subordinate to men and to center their lives on bearing and rearing children. He portrayed women as weaker and inferior to men, except perhaps for their capacity for feeling and giving love. He excluded them from public affairs and confined them to the domestic sphere. Many of these attitudes were not new—some have roots in Roman law—but Rousseau's powerful presentation and the influence of his other writings gave them new life, including in the legislation of the French Revolution. (See Document, "Rousseau Argue for Separate Spheres for Men and Women.")

Paradoxically, despite these views (and his own ill treatment of the many women he impregnated), Rousseau achieved a vast following among women. They may have responded to the stress he put on women's emotions and subjective feelings. By portraying domestic life and the roles of wife and mother as noble vocations, he gave middle- and upper-class women confidence that their lives had purpose.

Enlightenment Salon. The salon of Madame Marie-Thérèse Geoffrin (1699–1777) was one of the most important gathering spots for Enlightenment writers during the middle of the eighteenth century. Well-connected women such as Madame Geoffrin were instrumental in helping the *philosophes* they patronized to bring their ideas to the attention of influential people in French society and politics.

What kinds of people are depicted here?

In 1792 in *A Vindication of the Rights of Woman*, Mary Wollstonecraft (1759–1797) brought Rousseau before the judgment of the rational Enlightenment ideal of progressive knowledge. Wollstonecraft (who, like many women of her day, died shortly after childbirth of puerperal fever) argued that to confine women to the separate domestic sphere was to make them the sensual slaves of men. As victims of male tyranny, women could never achieve their own moral or intellectual identity. Denying good education to women would impede the progress of all humanity. Wollstonecraft was demanding for women the kind of intellectual liberty that male writers of the Enlightenment had been championing for men for more than a century.

ENLIGHTENED ABSOLUTISM

WHAT WERE the goals of enlightened absolute rulers?

During the last third of the century it seemed that several European rulers had embraced many of the reforms set forth by the *philosophes*. *Enlightened absolutism* indicates monarchical government dedicated to the rational strengthening of the central absolutist administration at the cost of lesser centers of political power. The monarchs most closely associated with it—Frederick II of Prussia, Joseph II of Austria, and Catherine II of Russia—often found that the political and social realities of their realms caused them to moderate both their enlightenment and their absolutism. Frederick II corresponded with the *philosophes*, invited Voltaire to his court, and even wrote history and political tracts. Catherine II consciously created the image of being enlightened. She read the works of the *philosophes*, became a friend of Diderot and Voltaire, and made frequent references to their ideas, all in the hope that her nation might seem more modern and Western. Joseph II continued numerous initiatives begun by his mother, Maria Theresa, and imposed a series of religious, legal, and social reforms that contemporaries believed he had derived from suggestions of the *philosophes*.

The relationship between these monarchs and the writers of the Enlightenment was complicated. The rulers did wish to see their subjects enjoy better health, more accessible education, a more rational political administration, and economic prosperity. But they also sought the rational economic and social integration of their realms so they could achieve military strength. After the Seven Years' War all the states of Europe understood that they would require stronger armed forces, which meant they needed new revenues. The search for more political support for their rule led these monarchs to make "enlightened" reforms. Consequently, they and their advisers used rationality to pursue many goals admired by the *philosophes* but also to further what the *philosophes* considered irrational militarism.

JOSEPH II OF AUSTRIA

No eighteenth-century ruler embodied rational, impersonal authority more than Emperor Joseph II of Austria, the son of Maria Theresa (r. 1740–1780). He prided himself on his narrow, passionless rationality, but he genuinely wanted to improve the lot of his people. Paradoxically, his well-intentioned efforts prompted rebellions by both aristocrats and peasants from Hungary to the Austrian Netherlands.

The Habsburgs' empire was Europe's most diverse political entity. Its rulers never succeeded in creating a unified government or enlisting the loyalties of its various groups of aristocrats. Maria Theresa preserved the monarchy during the War of the Austrian Succession (1740–1748) by guaranteeing independence for aristocrats, especially the Hungarians. But she also improved her position in Austria and Bohemia by imposing a more efficient system of tax collection. Even clergy and nobles were compelled to pay.

She established central councils to deal with political problems. She expanded primary schooling, and she tried to redirect educational institutions to training officials for royal service. Concern for peasants and serfs (from whom she recruited her military manpower) led her to limit the services that landowners could demand from them.

Joseph II's reforms were more wide ranging than his mother's. He was ambitious to expand at the expense of Poland, Bavaria, and the Ottoman Empire. But his greatest ambition was to overcome the pluralism of the Habsburg holdings by increasing the power of the central monarchy in areas of political and social life that Maria Theresa had wisely not disturbed. In particular, Joseph sought to lessen Hungarian autonomy. He refused to have himself crowned king of Hungary and even had the Crown of Saint Stephen sent to Vienna. He thus avoided having to guarantee existing or new Hungarian privileges in a coronation oath. He reorganized local government in Hungary to increase the authority of his own officials, and he required the use of the German language in all governmental matters. But the Magyar nobility resisted, and in 1790 Joseph had to rescind most of his centralizing measures.

Another target of Joseph's assertion of royal absolutism was religion. In October 1781 Joseph extended freedom of worship to Lutherans, Calvinists, and the Greek Orthodox. They were permitted to have their own churches, sponsor schools, enter skilled trades, and hold academic appointments and public service positions. From 1781 through 1789 Joseph relieved the Jews of certain taxes and signs of personal degradation and gave them the right of private worship. Despite these benefits, the Jews still did not enjoy general legal rights equal to those of other Habsburg subjects.

Above all, Joseph sought to bring the various institutions of the Roman Catholic Church directly under his control. He forbade direct communication between the bishops of his realms and the pope. He dissolved over six hundred monasteries and confiscated their lands. He also dissolved the traditional Roman Catholic seminaries, replacing them with eight general seminaries that emphasized parish duties. In effect, Joseph's policies made Roman Catholic priests the employees of the state and ended the influence of the church as an independent institution in Habsburg lands. In many respects his policies, known as *Josephinism*, prefigured those of the French Revolution.

Regarding serfdom and the land, Joseph II expanded policies initiated by Maria Theresa. During his reign he introduced reforms that touched the heart of rural society. He abolished the legal status of serfdom defined in terms of servitude to another person. He gave peasants much more personal freedom. They could marry, engage in skilled work, or have their children trained without permission of the landlord. The procedures of the manorial courts were reformed, and avenues of appeal to royal officials were opened. Joseph also encouraged landlords to change land leases, so that it would be easier for peasants to inherit them or to transfer them to another peasant without bringing into doubt the landlord's title of ownership. Joseph believed that reducing traditional burdens would make the peasant tillers of the land more productive and industrious.

In 1789 Joseph proposed a new and daring system of land taxation. All proprietors were to be taxed, regardless of social status. No longer were the peasants alone to bear the burden of taxation. He commuted compulsory service into a monetary tax, split between the landlord and the state. The decree was drawn up, but resistance from the nobles delayed its implementation. Joseph died in 1790, and the decree never went into effect. However, his measures had stirred up turmoil throughout the Habsburg realms. Peasants revolted over disagreements about the interpretation of their newly granted rights. The nobles of the various realms protested the taxation scheme.

On Joseph's death, the crown went to his brother Leopold II (r. 1790–1792). Although sympathetic to Joseph's goals, Leopold had to repeal many of the most controversial decrees, such as that changing taxation.

QUICK REVIEW

**Joseph II of Austria
(r. 1765–1790)**

- Attempted widespread reforms based on Enlightenment principles
- Resistance forced Joseph to rescind most of his centralizing efforts
- Abolished serfdom and gave peasants more personal freedom

Catherine the Great ascended to the Russian throne after the murder of her husband. She tried initially to enact major reforms, but she never intended to abandon absolutism. She assured the nobility of their rights and by the end of her reign had imposed press censorship.

What were Catherine the Great's goals?

CHRONOLOGY

RUSSIA FROM PETER THE GREAT THROUGH CATHERINE THE GREAT

1725	Death of Peter the Great
1741–1762	Elizabeth
1762	Peter III
1762	Catherine II (the Great) becomes empress
1767	Legislative Commission summoned
1768	War with Turkey
1771–1774	Pugachev's Rebellion
1772	First Partition of Poland
1774	Treaty of Kuchuk-Kainardji ends war with Turkey
1775	Reorganization of local government
1783	Russia annexes the Crimea
1785	Catherine issues the Charter of the Nobility
1793	Second Partition of Poland
1795	Third Partition of Poland
1796	Death of Catherine the Great

CATHERINE THE GREAT OF RUSSIA

Joseph II never grasped the practical necessity of cultivating political support for his policies. Catherine II (r. 1762–1796), who had been born a German princess, understood only too well the fragility of the Romanov dynasty's power base.

After the death of Peter the Great in 1725, the court nobles and the army had determined the Russian succession. As a result, the crown fell into the hands of people with little talent until 1741, when Peter's daughter Elizabeth came to the throne. At her death in 1762 Elizabeth was succeeded by Peter III, one of her nephews. He was a weak and possibly insane ruler who had been married in 1745 to a young German princess, the future Catherine the Great. Catherine had neither love nor loyalty for her demented husband. After a few months of rule, Peter III was deposed and murdered with Catherine's approval, and she was immediately proclaimed empress.

Catherine's familiarity with the Enlightenment and the general culture of western Europe convinced her that Russia must make major reforms to remain a great power. Having come to the throne through a palace coup, she also understood that any major reform must enjoy wide political and social support.

In 1767 Catherine summoned a Legislative Commission to advise her on revising the law and government of Russia. There were over five hundred delegates drawn from all sectors of Russian life. Before the commission convened, Catherine wrote a set of *Instructions*, containing ideas drawn from the political writings of the *philosophes*. The revision of Russian law, however, did not occur for more than half a century. In 1768 Catherine dismissed the commission before several of its key committees had reported. Yet the commission had gathered a vast amount of information about the conditions of local administration and economic life throughout Russia. The inconclusive debates and the absence of programs from the delegates themselves suggested that most Russians saw no alternative to an autocratic monarchy. Catherine herself had no intention of departing from absolutism.

Catherine proceeded to carry out limited reforms on her own authority. She supported the rights and local power of the nobility. In 1775 she reorganized local government to solve problems brought to light by the Legislative Commission. She put most local offices into the hands of nobles rather than creating a royal bureaucracy. In 1785 Catherine issued the Charter of the Nobility, which guaranteed many noble rights and privileges. She issued a similar charter to the towns of her realms. In part, the empress had to favor the nobles. There were too few educated subjects in her realm to establish an independent bureaucracy, and the treasury could not afford an army strictly loyal to the crown. So Catherine wisely made a virtue of necessity. She strengthened the stability of her crown by a convenient alliance with her nobles and urban leaders.

Catherine continued the Russian drive for warm-water ports (see Map 22–2). This led to warfare with the Turks between 1768 and 1774, when the Treaty of Kuchuk-Kainardji gave Russia a direct outlet on the Black Sea, free navigation rights in its waters, and free access through the Bosphorus. Moreover, the Crimea became an independent state, which Catherine painlessly annexed in 1783.

THE PARTITION OF POLAND

These Russian military successes made the other states of eastern Europe uneasy. Their anxieties were allayed by the First Partition of Poland. The Russian victories along the Danube River in what is today Romania were most unwelcome to Austria, which had its own ambitions there. At the same time, the Ottoman Empire was pressing Prussia for aid against Russia. Frederick the Great made a proposal to Russia and Austria that would give each something it wanted, prevent conflict among them, and save appearances. After long, complicated, secret negotiations, the three powers agreed that Russia would abandon the Danubian provinces in return for a large chunk of Polish territory with almost 2 million inhabitants. As a reward for remaining neutral, Prussia annexed most of the Polish territory between East Prussia and Prussia proper, which allowed Frederick to unite two previously separate sections of his realm. Finally, Austria took Galicia, with its important salt mines, and other Polish territory with over 2.5 million inhabitants. The Polish state had lost approximately one third of its territory.

There were two additional partitions of Poland by Russia and Prussia, and one more by Austria. They occurred in 1793 and 1795 and removed Poland from the map of Europe until 1919. The great powers contended that they were saving themselves, and by implication the rest of Europe, from Polish anarchy. The argument was plausible to some contemporaries because of the fears spurred by the French Revolution. However, the truth was that the political weakness of Poland made the country and its resources a rich field for plunderous aggression.

MAP 22–2 Expansion of Russia, 1689–1796.   The overriding territorial aim of the two most powerful Russian monarchs of the eighteenth century, Peter the Great (in the first quarter of the century) and Catherine the Great (in the last half of the century) was to secure navigable outlets to the sea in both the north and the south for Russia's vast empire; hence, Peter's push to the Baltic Sea and Catherine's to the Black Sea. Russia also expanded into Central Asia and Siberia during this time period.

Which empire came into direct conflict with Russian expansion?

Charter of Nobility. Granted by Empress Catherine II in 1785, this charter concluded the legal consolidation of Russian nobility as a class and provided for its political and corporate rights, privileges, and principles of self-organization. In this printing, the imperial title is handwritten in gold and is surrounded by engraved coats of arms of the provinces of the Russian Empire.

How does this charter illustrate the principles of enlightened absolutism?

SUMMARY

WHY IS the Scientific Revolution important to world history?

The Scientific Revolution. The scientific ideas of the sixteenth and seventeenth centuries changed the way Western intellectuals thought about the world and humankind. Western thinkers came to rely on mathematical laws, empirical data, and experimentation. Copernicus, Kepler, and Galileo overturned the ancient idea that the Earth was the center of the universe. Galileo and Descartes maintained that the world was governed by mathematical laws. Francis Bacon encouraged observation and experimentation. Newton hypothesized gravity and established an enduring basis for physics. Locke argued that human beings are shaped by their sense experiences and are hence creatures of their environment subject to reform and possible progress. Women were largely excluded from scientific practice. *page 538*

HOW DID Enlightenment thinkers argue for the reform of society?

The Enlightenment. The Enlightenment *philosophes* used reason as a basis for reform and to advocate progressive social, economic, and political movements. Voltaire's prodigious literary output outlined major issues in Enlightenment thought, and Diderot's *Encyclopedia* helped Enlightenment ideas diffuse throughout Europe. *page 545*

WHY DID the *philosophes* regard the church as the chief enemy of reform and human happiness?

The Enlightenment and Religion. The *philosophes* believed that the Christian church distracted people from finding rational solutions to their problems. They particularly attacked religious intolerance. Many were followers of deism, a belief in a rational, "divine watchmaker" God. Like most Europeans of their age, many *philosophes* had a distorted view of Islam, but some admired aspects of Islamic culture. *page 546*

HOW DID the *philosophes* hope that reason would change society?

The Enlightenment and Society. Montesquieu and other *philosophes* argued for limited, constitutional government. Adam Smith linked economics and social progress. Rousseau wished to reform society in the name of virtue rather than material happiness. He maintained that in the pursuit of virtue the needs of society were more important than those of the individual. Enlightenment thinkers criticized imperial conquest as dehumanizing, but they generally failed to support improvements in women's social standing. The competing strands of the Enlightenment continue to pervade Western society. *page 549*

WHAT WERE the goals of enlightened absolute rulers?

Enlightened Absolutism. Enlightened absolutism was a form of monarchical government dedicated to the rational strengthening of the central government. Many of the reforms enlightened monarchs imposed were influenced by the ideas of the *philosophes*, but the chief goal of these rulers was to increase their own authority and military strength, as witnessed by the partitions of Poland among Russia, Prussia, and Austria at the end of the eighteenth century. The most important enlightened monarchs were Frederick II of Prussia, Joseph II of Austria, and Catherine the Great of Russia. *page 554*

INTERPRETING THE PAST

The Enlightenment and the Quest for Practical Knowledge

Sources from MyHistoryLab for Chapter 22

1) Lady Mary Wortley Montagu, *Letters*

2) James Lind, *A Treatise on Scurvy*

3) Immanuel Kant, *Defining the Enlightenment*

Visual Sources from MyHistoryLab

1) *Drawing of Queen Anne of England Visiting Anton Van Leeuwenhoek* (1698)

2) *Jewish Medical Book: Illustration of the Human Body Compared to a House*

3) Illustration from Newton's *Opticks*

The European Enlightenment was a multifaceted phenomenon, with competing strands of political thought, new social and philosophical theories, and innovative scientific developments that contributed to a public debate about the nature of society. Using reason and empiricism, the *philosophes* attempted to publicize injustice and abuse, particularly by traditional authority—hereditary monarchs, the aristocracy, and

REVIEW QUESTIONS

1. What was the Scientific Revolution? What were the major contributions of Copernicus, Brahe, Kepler, Galileo, Bacon, and Newton? Do you think they regarded themselves as revolutionaries?

2. How and to what extent did women participate in the Scientific Revolution?

3. Define the Enlightenment. Is it best seen as a single movement or a series of related movements? What was the relationship of the Enlightenment to the new science? How did the Enlightenment further the idea of progress and the superiority of European civilization?

4. Why did the *philosophes* believe they must comment so extensively on religion? Why did they criticize Christianity? Why did some of them champion deism?

5. What were the differing views of the *philosophes* toward Islam?

6. Was there a single Enlightenment view of politics? Why could writers so dedicated to reform have so many different political paths to achieve reform?

7. How has the political thought of the Enlightenment influenced the development of modern political philosophies and modern governments?

8. Summarize the Enlightenment critique of European empires. Do you see any flaws in this line of reasoning? Why do you think it was not more influential?

9. What were the prevailing attitudes of the *philosophes* toward women and women's roles? Do these attitudes present any contradiction to other Enlightenment positions? Explain.

10. Define *enlightened absolutism*. What were the similarities in the policies of Frederick the Great, Joseph II, and Catherine the Great? To what extent do their policies actually seem to stem from the ideas of the Enlightenment *philosophes*?

KEY TERMS

deism (DEE-izm) (p. 546)
empiricism (p. 541)
Enlightenment (p. 538)
laissez-faire (leh-say-FAYR) (p. 550)
philosophes (FILL-uh-SOHFS) (p. 545)
Ptolemaic system (TAHL-uh-MAY-ik) (p. 540)
Scientific Revolution (p. 539)

Note: To learn more about the topics in this chapter, please turn to the Suggested Readings at the end of the book.

the church. In so doing, they hoped to reform society by using reason and humor in order to advance the cause of science and rationalism. Their primary tool was the printed word, disseminated in books, journals, and newspapers read by growing numbers of literate people throughout Europe.

This exercise will involve reading three eighteenth-century primary sources that document the attempt to develop practical solutions to improve society through the use of rational thought and scientific methods. Although today we take the application of science and technology to solve problems as routine, during this era these were pioneering and often controversial methods, since they intruded on the customary authority of the church and monarchy.

The first document is written by Lady Mary Wortley Montagu, the wife of the ambassador to Constantinople (capital of the Ottoman Empire) who discusses her observations of Muslim society and particularly the practice of smallpox vaccination. The second document, from James Lind, a Scottish naval surgeon, describes his search for a cure for scurvy, a disease that he discovered was caused by insufficient intake of vitamin C and was fatal if untreated. The third document is from the German *philosophe* Immanuel Kant, who seeks to define the Enlightenment as an empowerment of individuals to think rationally by

actively challenging traditional authority. The accompanying images illustrate how information about technological and medical advances were circulated in printed images.

Use the source documents and the images to enter the world of the *philosophes* and those allied with them in the effort to use reason to improve society. Use specific examples from the documents to back up your assertions.

Questions

How did the experience of living in Constantinople (Istanbul) change Lady Mary's outlook? How would she have come to be aware of Ottoman medical practices such as vaccination? How does she compare the life of the elites in Ottoman society with the life of peasants?

How did James Lind discover a cure for scurvy? Was the "scientific method" involved? If so, how?

How do the visual sources for this exercise illustrate the use of reason, science, and technology to improve human society?

Do the authors of the first two documents illustrate Kant's plea for individuals to empower themselves in the quest for knowledge? Why or Why not?

23

Revolutions in the Transatlantic World

Guerilla Warfare. Haitian slaves ambush French forces during their successful revolt led by Toussaint L'Ouverture and Jean-Jacques Dessalines in 1794. The Haitian revolution was the largest emancipation of slaves to occur in the eighteenth century.

Why was the Haitian revolution the great exception in the American Wars of Independence in the late eighteenth and early nineteenth centuries?

REVOLUTION IN THE BRITISH COLONIES IN
NORTH AMERICA *page 562*

WHAT WAS radical about the American Revolution?

REVOLUTION IN FRANCE *page 565*

HOW DID the French Revolution and Napoleon transform
France's government and society?

WARS OF INDEPENDENCE IN LATIN AMERICA *page 575*

WHY DID Latin American nations reject Spanish
and Portuguese rule?

TOWARD THE ABOLITION OF SLAVERY IN
THE TRANSATLANTIC ECONOMY *page 580*

WHY DID slavery become unacceptable in Western society?

GLOBAL PERSPECTIVE

THE TRANSATLANTIC REVOLUTIONS

The revolutions and the crusade against slavery that occurred throughout the transatlantic world between 1776 and the 1830s transformed the political, social, and economic life of three continents. First in North America, then in France and other parts of Europe, and finally in South America, bold political experiments challenged colonial government, monarchies, and aristocratic governments and laid the foundations for modern liberal democracy. These revolutions and the effort to abolish slavery owed much to the philosophical inspiration of the Enlightenment and bear witness to the immense influence of the Enlightenment in world history.

As a result of the events of this age of transatlantic revolution the largest republic since ancient times was established in North America. In Europe the absolutist governments were overthrown across the continent by the impact of the French Revolution and the armies of Napoleon. Slaves on Haiti overthrew the French colonial regime and established the first black republic. By the close of the first quarter of the nineteenth century, wars of independence across Latin America had closed the era of European empire with the establishment of republics everywhere except Brazil.

No less important, this era witnessed the beginning of an international effort to bring about the abolition of the slave economies that had long dominated the transatlantic economy.

The expanding forms of political liberty found their counterparts in an economic life freed from the constraints of the old colonial empires and eventually from the economies based on plantation slave labor. The new American republic constituted a vast free trade zone, with its commerce and ports open to the entire world.

For the first time since the encounter with Europe, all of Latin America could trade freely with its own peoples and those of the rest of the world.

In Europe the reforms of the French Revolution and the new Napoleonic Code of law removed many regional economic barriers and led to more standard weights and measures.

National law formed the framework for economic activity. The movement to abolish slavery fostered a wage economy of free laborers. That kind of economy generated its own set of problems and social dislocation, including a sort of sharecropping serfdom for many former slaves, but it was nonetheless an economy of free human beings who were the chattel of no other human being.

B etween 1776 and 1824 a world-transforming series of revolutions occurred in France and the Americas. Within half a century the peoples of the two American continents established their independence. The French monarchy collapsed from the forces of aristocratic resistance and popular revolution. All the revolutionary leaders sought to establish new governments based largely, though never entirely, on Enlightenment principles.

From start to finish these revolutions were connected. The financial pressures from the Seven Years' War (1756–1763) had led Britain, Spain, and France to seek revenues in ways that destabilized the Americas and France itself. Once the American Revolution began, France aided the colonists, thus exacerbating its own financial problem. The French Revolution and the ensuing Napoleonic wars created situations in Spain and Portugal to which the colonial elites in Latin America responded by seeking independence. The era also witnessed the commencement of a vast international crusade, first to abolish the slave trade and then to abolish slavery in the transatlantic world. Opponents of slavery were inspired by the same Enlightenment ideas that inspired many of the revolutionaries, as well as by religious convictions. The political and economic dislocations of the revolutionary era helped the antislavery forces achieve their goals. The political, social, and economic life of the transatlantic world was altered forever. ■

REVOLUTION IN THE BRITISH COLONIES IN NORTH AMERICA

WHAT WAS radical about the American Revolution?

RESISTANCE TO THE IMPERIAL SEARCH FOR REVENUE

After the Treaty of Paris in 1763 ended the Seven Years' War, the British government faced two problems. The first was the cost of defending the empire it had acquired. The second was the need to organize a vast new territory: all of North America east of the Mississippi (see Map 23–1).

Finally, the age of transatlantic revolutions saw the emergence of nationalism as a political force. All of the revolutions, because of their popular political base, had given power to the idea of nations defined by their own character and historical past rather than by dynastic rulers. Americans saw themselves as forming a new kind of nation. The French had demonstrated the power of a nation fully mobilized for military purposes. In turn the aggression of France had aroused national sentiment, especially in Great Britain, Spain, and Germany. The new nations of Latin America also sought to define themselves by their heritage and historical experience rather than by their past in the Spanish and Portuguese empires.

These various revolutions, their political doctrines, and their social and economic departures provided examples to peoples elsewhere in the world. But even more important, the transformations of the transatlantic revolutions and eventual abolition of slavery meant that new political classes and newly organized independent nations would become actors on the world scene. Europeans would have to deal with a score of new nations in the Americas. The rest of the world confronted new nations freed from the direction and authority of European powers. In turn, the political changes in Europe meant that those nations and their relationships with the rest of the world would be directed by a broader range of political groups and forces than in the past. Ironically, however, by the close of the nineteenth century several of the European nations as well as the United States that had become liberal democratic states would commence a new wave of colonialism throughout Africa and Asia and would impose new economic dominance on the republics of Latin America.

Focus Questions

◆ What is the relationship between the Enlightenment and the transatlantic revolutions? between the Enlightenment and the crusade against slavery?

◆ How did the transatlantic revolutions fundamentally alter the relationship between Europe and the Americas?

◆ What is the relationship between the transatlantic revolutions and nationalism? Why did such a relationship exist?

The British drive for revenue began in 1764 with the Sugar Act. Britain hoped to enhance revenue from imports of sugar into the colonies by the rigorous collection of what was actually a reduced tax. Smugglers were to be tried in admiralty courts without juries. A year later, Parliament passed the Stamp Act, a tax on legal documents and other items. The British considered these taxes just because they had been approved by Parliament and because the revenue was to be spent in the colonies that paid them. The Americans, however, objected that they were not represented in Parliament and insisted that they alone had the right to tax themselves. Furthermore, the Americans feared that if colonial government were financed from Britain, they would cease to control it. Following disorder in its American lands (particularly in Massachusetts), Parliament repealed the Stamp Act in 1766 but asserted its right to legislate for the colonies.

AMERICAN POLITICAL IDEAS

The American colonists believed that the English Revolution of 1688 had established liberties that belonged to them as well as to the British. They claimed that George III (r. 1760–1820) and the British Parliament were dissolving the bonds of allegiance that united the two peoples by attacking those liberties. The colonists thus appealed to an argument that English aristocrats of an earlier generation had used to justify limiting the power of their king in order to support a popular revolution.

These Whig political ideas, largely derived from John Locke (1632–1704), were only a part of the English ideological heritage that affected the Americans. Colonists had become familiar with a series of British political writers called the *Commonwealthmen*. These authors held republican political ideas that stemmed from the radical branches of the Puritan revolution. They dismissed much parliamentary taxation as nothing more

Boston Massacre. This view of the Boston Massacre of March 5, 1770, by Paul Revere owes more to propaganda than to fact. There was no order to fire, and the innocent citizens portrayed here were really an angry, violent mob.

What were the purposes of propaganda such as this engraving?

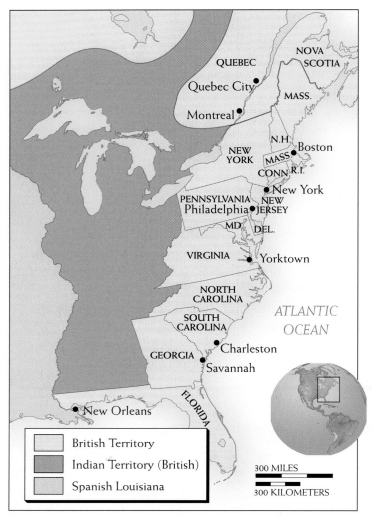

MAP 23–1   North America in 1763. In the year of the victory over France, the English colonies lay along the Atlantic seaboard. The difficulties of organizing authority over the previous French territory in Canada and west of the Appalachian Mountains would contribute to the tensions that precipitated the American Revolution.

How did westward expansion of the colonies lead to tensions with both the British and the Indians?

than a means for financing political corruption, and they feared standing armies as instruments of tyranny. The policy of Great Britain toward America after the Treaty of Paris made many colonists believe that the suspicions of the Commonwealthmen were correct.

CRISIS AND INDEPENDENCE

In May 1773, Parliament allowed the East India Company to import tea directly into the American colonies. Although the law lowered the price of tea, it levied a tea tax that was imposed without the colonists' consent. Protestors in Boston reacted by throwing a shipload of tea into the harbor, an event that became known as the Boston Tea Party.

The British ministry of Lord North (1732–1792) was determined to assert the authority of Parliament over the colonies. In 1774, Parliament closed the port of Boston, reorganized the government of Massachusetts, quartered troops in private homes, and transferred the trials of royal customs officials to England. Parliament also extended the boundaries of Quebec to include the Ohio River valley, an act that the Americans regarded as an attempt to prevent them from spreading, with their political ideas, westward beyond the Appalachian Mountains.

Committees of correspondence, composed of citizens critical of Britain, had been established throughout the colonies, and in September 1774, these committees organized the First Continental Congress in Philadelphia. This body failed to persuade Parliament to abandon its attempt at direct supervision of colonial affairs. In 1775, the battles of Lexington, Concord, and Bunker Hill were fought, and the Second Continental Congress undertook to govern the colonies. In August 1775, George III declared the colonies in rebellion. During the winter, Thomas Paine's (1737–1809) pamphlet *Common Sense* galvanized public opinion in favor of separation from Great Britain. A colonial army and navy were organized, and on July 4, 1776, the Continental Congress adopted the Declaration of Independence. The War of the American Revolution continued until 1781, when the forces of George Washington (1732–1799) defeated those of Lord Cornwallis (1738–1805) at Yorktown. In 1778, however, the war had widened into a European conflict, for the French government supported the rebellion in the hope of weakening its traditional enemy, Great Britain. In 1779, Spain also came to the aid of the colonies. The 1783 Treaty of Paris concluded the conflict and recognized the independence of the thirteen American colonies.

As the crisis with Britain unfolded, the American colonists saw themselves as first preserving traditional English liberties, but as the war went on, they developed a different understanding of what liberty meant. By the mid-1770s, they had rejected monarchy and embraced republicanism. After the Constitution was adopted in 1788, a bill of rights was added to protect civil liberties. They rejected the aristocratic social hierarchy that had existed in the colonies in favor of democratic ideals. Although they limited the right to vote, they asserted the equality of white male citizens before the law and in social relations. They rejected social ranking based on birth and inheritance and asserted that all citizens must have the opportunity to improve their social standing and economic lot by engaging in free commercial activity. Although the American Revolution did not free slaves or address the rights of women and Native Americans, it produced a society freer than any the world had yet seen—one in which political and social liberties would continue to increase. The American Revolution was a genuinely radical movement, the influence of which increased as Americans moved across the continent and as other peoples began to question traditional European government. The political and social values of the American Revolution would inspire the wars of independence in Latin America and, to a lesser extent, both liberal and radical political movements in Europe.

Third Estate The branch of the French Estates General representing all of the kingdom outside the nobility and the clergy.

REVOLUTION IN FRANCE

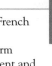

The French monarchy emerged from the Seven Years' War both defeated and deeply in debt. Then French support for the American Revolution exacerbated the financial difficulties. Given the economic vitality of France, the government debt was not overly large, but the government was unable to collect sufficient taxes to service and repay the debt.

HOW DID the French Revolution and Napoleon transform France's government and society?

Between 1786 and 1788, Louis XVI (r. 1774– 1792) appointed several different ministers to deal with the financial crisis. All failed to persuade the aristocracy and the church to pay more taxes. As these negotiations dragged on, the *parlement* of Paris declared that only the Estates General could institute new taxes. The Estates General had not met since 1614, but in 1788, Louis XVI agreed to convene it the following year.

REVOLUTIONS OF 1789

The Estates General had three divisions: the First Estate of the clergy, the Second Estate of the nobility, and the **Third Estate**, representing everyone else. Before the Estates General met at Versailles in May 1789, there had been much public debate over its organization and how voting should be organized. The nobility wanted all votes to be taken by estate, which would have allowed the nobles and clergy to outvote the Third Estate. The Third Estate wanted each member to vote individually so that, with its larger membership, it would dominate.

The Third Estate invited the clergy and the nobles to join it in organizing a new legislative body. A few of the lower clergy did so. On June 17 that body declared itself the National Assembly.

Three days later, finding themselves accidentally locked out of their usual meeting place, the National Assembly moved to a nearby tennis

CHRONOLOGY		
THE AMERICAN REVOLUTION		
1760	George III becomes king	
1763	Treaty of Paris concludes the Seven Years' War	
1764	Sugar Act	
1765	Stamp Act	
1766	Sugar Act repealed and Declaratory Act passed	
1767	Townshend Acts	
1770	Lord North becomes George III's chief minister	
1770	Boston Massacre	
1773	Boston Tea Party	
1774	Intolerable Acts	
1774	First Continental Congress	
1775	Second Continental Congress	
1776	Declaration of Independence	
1778	France enters the war on the side of America	
1781	British forces surrender at Yorktown	
1783	Treaty of Paris concludes the American Revolutionary War	

Storming of the Bastille.   On July 14, 1789, crowds stormed the Bastille, a prison in Paris. This event, whose only practical effect was to free a few prisoners, marked the first time the populace of Paris redirected the course of the revolution.

Anonymous, France, eighteenth century, "Siege of the Bastille, 14 July, 1789." Musée de la Ville de Paris, Musée Carnavalet, Paris, France. Bridgeman-Giraudon/Art Resource, N.Y.

Compare this painting with the illustration on page 563. How do they serve similar ends?

QUICK REVIEW

National Assembly

- ◆ June 17, 1789: Third Estate declares itself National Assembly
- ◆ Tennis Court Oath: Pledge to sit until France had a constitution
- ◆ June 27, 1789: King capitulates to National Assembly

Women's March.   The women of Paris marched to Versailles on October 7, 1789. The following day the royal family was forced to return to Paris with them. Henceforth, the French government would function under the constant threat of mob violence.

Anonymous, eighteenth century, "To Versailles, to Versailles." The Women of Paris going to Versailles, October 7, 1789. French, Musée de la Ville de Paris, Musée Carnavalet, Paris, France. Photograph copyright Bridgeman-Giraudon/Art Resource, N.Y.

Looking at individual faces and dresses, what kinds of women seem to be participating in this demonstration?

court, where its members took the famous Tennis Court Oath to continue to sit until they had given France a constitution. Louis XVI ordered the National Assembly to desist, but shortly afterward most of the clergy and many nobles joined the assembly. On June 27 the king capitulated and the National Assembly reorganized as the National Constituent Assembly, where voting would occur by head rather than by order.

Two new factors soon intruded. First, Louis XVI tried to regain the initiative by mustering troops near Versailles and Paris. The National Constituent Assembly was beginning to demand a constitutional monarchy. Louis refused to consider their proposal and hoped that a show of military force would head off revolution.

The second new factor was the populace of Paris. The mustering of royal troops created anxiety in the city, where already there had been several bread riots. Parisians began organizing a citizen militia. On July 14 a crowd marched to the Bastille, a great fortress that had once held political prisoners, in search of weapons for the militia. Troops in the Bastille fired into the crowd, killing ninety-eight. The crowd then stormed the fortress, released its seven prisoners (none of whom was there for political reasons), and killed several soldiers and the governor. They found no weapons, but the fall of the Bastille signaled that the political future of the nation would not be decided solely by the National Constituent Assembly. Similar disturbances took place in the provincial cities. Soon Louis XVI came to Paris and recognized both the newly elected government of the city and its National Guard.

As disturbances erupted in various cities, the *Great Fear* swept across the French countryside. Peasants rose up to vent their anger at injustices and reclaim rights and property that they had lost during the aristocratic resurgence of the previous quarter century. Châteaux were burned, documents were destroyed, and peasants refused to pay feudal dues. On August 4, 1789, liberal nobles and churchmen in the assembly surrendered their special rights and exemptions, formally giving up what they had already lost. (Many were later compensated.) Now France's laws applied equally to all citizens.

On August 27, 1789, the assembly issued the *Declaration of the Rights of Man and Citizen*, drawing on the political language of the Enlightenment. It proclaimed that all men were born free and equal with natural rights to liberty, property, and personal safety. Governments existed to protect those rights. All political sovereignty resided in the nation and its representatives. All citizens were equal before the law and equally eligible for public offices. There was to be due process of law, and innocence was to be presumed until proof of guilt. Freedom of religion was affirmed. Taxation was to be apportioned equitably according to capacity to pay. Property rights were declared sacred.

When Louis XVI stalled before ratifying both the declaration and the aristocratic renunciation of feudalism, his hesitations fanned suspicions that he might resort to force. Moreover, bread shortages continued. On October 5 several thousand Parisian women marched to Versailles, demanding more bread. This was one of several occasions when women played a major role in the actions of the Parisian crowd. The king agreed to sanction the decrees of the assembly. Then the crowd insisted that Louis and his family return to Paris. On October 6, 1789, the king and his family followed the women back to Paris and settled in the palace of the Tuileries. The assembly joined them. Things then remained relatively quiet until the summer of 1792.

RECONSTRUCTION OF FRANCE

The National Constituent Assembly set about reorganizing France. The assembly was determined to protect property but limit the political influence of small property owners and those who did not own property. While championing equality before the law, the assembly spurned social equality and extensive democracy. In this it charted a course that nineteenth-century liberals across Europe and in other areas of the world were to follow.

The Constitution of 1791 established a constitutional monarchy. There was a unicameral Legislative Assembly. The monarch could delay, but not halt, legislation. Only about 50,000 male citizens of the French nation of 26 million could actually elect or serve in the Legislative Assembly.

Olympe de Gouges (d. 1793), a butcher's daughter who became a leading radical in Paris, quickly composed a *Declaration of the Rights of Woman* (1793), which she ironically addressed to Queen Marie Antoinette (1755–1793). The document was fundamentally the *Declaration of the Rights of Man and Citizen* with the word *woman* strategically inserted. She declared, "Women, wake up; the tocsin of reason is being heard throughout the whole universe; discover your rights."[1] Her demands illustrated how the public listing of rights in the *Declaration of the Rights of Man and Citizen* created universal civic expectations.

The National Constituent Assembly reorganized provincial administration, instituted uniform courts, simplified legal procedures, and abolished the most degrading punishments. It also suppressed the guilds, removed regulations on the grain trade, and established the metric system of uniform weights and measures. In 1790, it placed the burden of proof and the obligation to pay compensation on peasants who tried to rid themselves of residual feudal dues. In 1791, it forbade worker associations, crushing efforts by urban workers to protect their wages. Peasants and laborers were left to the mercy of the free market.

The National Constituent Assembly decided to pay the troublesome royal debt by confiscating and selling the lands of the Roman Catholic Church in France. The Assembly issued ***assignats***, or government bonds, guaranteed by the revenue to be generated from the sale of church property. When the *assignats* began to circulate as currency, the Assembly issued even larger quantities of them, causing their value to fall. Inflation put new stress on the lives of the urban poor.

In July 1790 the Assembly issued the Civil Constitution of the Clergy, transforming the Roman Catholic Church in France into a branch of the secular state. Among many sweeping changes, priests and bishops would be elected and serve as salaried employees of the state. The measure roused immense opposition within the French church. The Assembly unwisely demanded that all clergy take an oath to support the Civil Constitution; few did. In reprisal, the Assembly designated the clergy who had not taken the oath as "refractory" and removed them from their clerical functions.

In February 1791 the pope condemned not only the Civil Constitution of the Clergy but also the *Declaration of the Rights of Man and Citizen*. This marked the

QUICK REVIEW

Constitution of 1791

◆ Established constitutional monarchy

◆ Monarch could delay, but not halt, acts of unicameral Legislative Assembly

◆ Voting limited to 50,000 elite men

assignats Government bonds based on the value of confiscated church lands issued during the early French Revolution.

[1]Quoted in Sara E. Melzer and Leslie W. Rabine, eds., *Rebel Daughters: Women and the French Revolution* (New York: Oxford University Press, 1992), p. 88.

opening of a Roman Catholic offensive against liberalism in Europe and revolution throughout the world that continued for over a century. Within France itself, many were torn between religious devotion and revolutionary loyalty. French citizens quickly divided between those who supported the constitutional priests and those who resorted to the refractory clergy. Louis XVI and his family favored the latter.

In the summer of 1791, the queen and some nobles persuaded Louis XVI to flee, but the royal family was caught and returned to Paris. Assembly leaders now saw the king as a counterrevolutionary. On August 27, 1791, Leopold II of Austria (r. 1790–1792), brother of Marie Antoinette, and Frederick William II (r. 1786–1797) of Prussia promised to intervene in France to protect the royal family if the other major European powers agreed that they could do so. The latter provision rendered the declaration meaningless, since Great Britain would not consent. It had the effect, however, of convincing France's revolutionaries that they were surrounded by aristocratic and monarchical foes.

A SECOND REVOLUTION

In September 1791, a new Legislative Assembly was elected, and it convened on October 1 in an atmosphere that was becoming increasingly radical. Since the earliest days of the revolution, clubs of politically like-minded persons had sprung up in Paris. The best organized were the **Jacobins**, who had links with similar groups in the provinces. On April 20, 1792, the Legislative Assembly, led by a group of Jacobins known as the Girondists (because many came from the department of the Gironde), voted to declare war on Austria, which was allied to Prussia. The war with Austria led to what is usually called the second revolution, which overthrew the constitutional monarchy and established a republic.

Jacobins The radical republican party during the French Revolution that displaced the Girondins.

The war went badly, and the looming threat radicalized French politics. Late in July, under radical working-class pressure, the government of Paris passed from the elected council to a committee, or commune, of representatives from the municipal wards. On August 10, 1792, a large crowd invaded the Tuileries, forcing Louis XVI and Marie Antoinette to take refuge in the Legislative Assembly. Several hundred of the royal guards and many Parisians were killed, the royal family was imprisoned, and the king's political functions were suspended.

Convention French radical legislative body from 1792 to 1794.

sans-culottes Meaning "without breeches." The lower-middle classes and artisans of Paris during the French Revolution.

Early in September, the Paris Commune summarily killed about 1,200 people in the city jails, on the mistaken assumption that they were counterrevolutionaries. The Paris Commune then compelled the Legislative Assembly to call for the election, by universal manhood suffrage, of a new assembly to write a democratic constitution. That body, called the **Convention** after its American counterpart of 1787, met on September 21, 1792. The Convention declared France a republic.

The second revolution had been the work of Jacobins more radical than the Girondists and of the people of Paris known as the **sans-culottes**, meaning "without breeches." (Working men wore long trousers instead of the knee breeches favored by aristocratic courtiers.) The *sans-culottes* were shopkeepers, artisans, wage earners, and a few factory workers. The politics of the Old Regime had ignored them, and the policies of the National Constituent Assembly had not protected them from an unregulated free-market economy.

Execution of Louis XVI. On January 21, 1793, the Convention executed Louis XVI.

Execution of Louis XVI. Aquatint. French, eighteenth century. Musée de la Ville de Paris, Musée Carnavalet, Paris, France. Giraudon/Art Resource, N.Y.

Why would the execution of Louis XVI be held in public?

The *sans-culottes*, whose labor and military service were needed for the war effort, generally knew what they wanted, beginning with price controls for food. They resented most forms of social inequality and were hostile to the aristocracy and the original leaders of the revolution. They advocated a community of small property owners. They were antimonarchical, republican, and suspicious of government. The Jacobins, by contrast, were republicans who favored representative government and an unregulated economy. However, once the Convention began its deliberations, the more extreme Jacobins, known as the Mountain because of their seats high in the assembly hall, worked with the *sans-culottes* to pass revolutionary reforms and win the war.

In December 1792, Louis XVI was put on trial and convicted of conspiring against the state. He was beheaded on January 21, 1793. The killing of a king shocked Europe, and France found itself isolated and at war with virtually everyone. Civil war broke out as well. In March 1793, aristocratic officers and priests raised a royalist revolt in western France and won local popular support.

THE REIGN OF TERROR AND ITS AFTERMATH

The **Reign of Terror** is the name given to the period from autumn 1793 through midsummer 1794 marked by thousands of quasi-judicial executions and murders. Two factors created the environment for the outbreak of the Terror: (1) the fear created by internal and external wars, and (2) the revolutionary aspirations of the Convention and the *sans-culottes*.

In April 1793, the Convention established a Committee of Public Safety charged with saving the revolution from enemies at home and abroad. It eventually assumed quasi-dictatorial power and generally enjoyed a working political relationship with the *sans-culottes* of Paris.

In June 1793, the Parisian *sans-culottes* invaded the Convention, drove out the Girondists, and gave the Mountain complete control. On August 23 the Convention decreed a **levée en masse**, or general military requisition of population. It conscripted males into the army and mobilized economic production for military purposes. On September 29, price controls were imposed in accordance with *sans-culottes*' demands. During these same months, the armies of the revolution crushed many of the counterrevolutionary disturbances in the provinces.

Revolutionary women established their own institutions. In May 1793 Pauline Léon and Claire Lacombe founded the Society of Revolutionary Republican Women. Its members sought stricter price controls and worked to ferret out food hoarders. The women demanded the right to wear the revolutionary cap that male citizens had adopted. By October 1793, the Jacobins in the Convention had begun to fear the turmoil the increasingly radical society was causing, and it banned all women's clubs and societies. Other women's political activities were repressed, too. When Olympe de Gouges spoke out against the Terror, she was tried and guillotined in November 1793. Women were excluded from the French army and from entering the galleries to watch the debates of the Convention.

Reign of Terror   The period between the summer of 1793 and the end of July 1794 when the French revolutionary state used extensive executions and violence to defend the Revolution and suppress its alleged internal enemies.

levée en masse   The French revolutionary conscription (1792) of all males into the army and the harnessing of the economy for war production.

Revolutionary Calendar.   To symbolize the beginning of a new era in human history, French revolutionary legislators established a new calendar. This calendar for Year Two (1794) proclaims the indivisible unity of the revolution and the goals of liberty, equality, and fraternity.

Why would the creation of a new calendar further the aims of a revolutionary regime?

CHRONOLOGY

THE FRENCH REVOLUTION

1789	May 5	Estates General opens at Versailles
	June 17	Third Estate declares itself the National Assembly
	June 20	National Assembly takes the Tennis Court Oath
	July 14	Fall of the Bastille
	August 4	Nobles surrender their feudal rights in a meeting of the National Constituent Assembly
	August 27	*Declaration of the Rights of Man and Citizen*
	October 5–6	Parisian women march to Versailles and force Louis XVI and his family to return to Paris
1790	July 12–14	Civil Constitution of the Clergy adopted and accepted by the king
1791	June 20–24	Louis XVI and his family attempt to flee France and are stopped at Varennes
1792	April 20	France declares war on Austria
	August 10	Tuileries palace stormed, and Louis XVI takes refuge in the Legislative Assembly
	September	September Massacres; monarchy abolished
1793	January 21	Louis XVI executed
	February 1	France declares war on Great Britain
	March	Counterrevolution breaks out in the Vendée
	April 6	Committee of Public Safety formed
	July	Robespierre enters Committee of Public Safety
	August 23	*Levée en masse* proclaimed
	October 16	Queen Marie Antoinette executed
	November 10	Cult of Reason proclaimed; revolutionary calendar beginning in September
1794	May 7	Cult of the Supreme Being proclaimed
	June 8	Robespierre leads the celebration of Festival of the Supreme Being
	July 28	Robespierre executed
1795	August 22	Constitution of the Year III adopted, establishing the Directory

The pressures of war made it relatively easy to dispense with legal due process. But the Convention and the Committee of Public Safety felt morally justified in doing so, for they saw themselves as creating something new in history: a republic devoted to eradicating aristocratic and monarchical corruption and promoting civic virtue.

Most dramatically, the "republic of virtue" attempted to dechristianize France. In the autumn of 1793 the Convention proclaimed a new calendar dating from the first day of the French Republic. There were twelve months of thirty days with names associated with the seasons and climate. The Cathedral of Notre Dame was renamed the Temple of Reason. The legislature enforced dechristianization in the provinces by closing churches and persecuting clergy and believers. Dechristianization roused much opposition and alienated the provinces from the revolutionary government in Paris.

During late 1793 and early 1794, Maximilien Robespierre (1758–1794) emerged as the chief figure on the Committee of Public Safety. The Jacobin Club provided his base of power, and he had the support of the *sans-culottes* of Paris. He considered dechristianization a political blunder.

The Reign of Terror was the work of a series of revolutionary tribunals established by the Convention during the summer of 1793. The tribunals were instituted to try the enemies of the republic, but the definition of enemy broadened as the months passed. Marie Antoinette, other members of the royal family, and many aristocrats were executed in October 1793. They were followed by Girondist politicians. Robespierre gradually turned the Terror against leaders who might have threatened his own position. Robespierre secured a law that permitted the revolutionary tribunal to convict suspects without evidence. By early 1794, the Terror had moved to the provinces, where thousands were executed.

In May 1794, at the height of his power, Robespierre concluded that the worship of reason was too abstract for most citizens. He replaced it with the Cult of the

Supreme Being, but he did not long preside over this new religion. On July 27 his opponents staged a coup, and he was executed the next day.

The Reign of Terror soon ended, having claimed as many as forty thousand victims. Most were peasants and *sans-culottes*. By the late summer of 1794, provincial uprisings had been crushed, and the war against foreign enemies was also going well. Those factors, combined with the feeling in Paris that the revolution had consumed enough of its own children, brought the Terror to an end.

The tempering of the revolution, a phase called the **Thermidorian Reaction**, began in July 1794, with the establishment of a new constitutional regime. The influence of wealthy middle-class and professional people replaced that of the *sans-culottes*. Many of the people responsible for the Terror were removed from public life, and the Jacobin Club of Paris was closed.

The Thermidorian Constitution of the Year III was a conservative document that provided for bicameral legislative government dedicated to protecting the rights of property owners. Its executive branch was a five-person Directory elected by the upper legislative house.

By the Treaty of Basel of March 1795, the Convention concluded peace with Prussia and Spain. With the war effort succeeding, the Convention severed its ties with the *sans-culottes*. True to their belief in an unregulated economy, the Thermidorians repealed the ceiling on prices. Rising prices led to food riots during the winter of 1794–1795, but the Convention suppressed them. On October 5, 1795, when a Paris mob rioted, a general named Napoleon Bonaparte (1769–1821) commanded the cannon and with what he termed a "whiff of grapeshot" dispersed the crowd.

THE NAPOLEONIC ERA

Napoleon Bonaparte was born in 1769 to a poor noble family in Corsica. Because France had annexed Corsica in 1768, he was able to obtain a commission as a French artillery officer. At the start of his career, he was a fiery Jacobin. In 1793, he played a leading role in recovering the port of Toulon from the British. This won him promotion to the rank of brigadier general, and his defense of the Directory in 1794 won him a command in Italy. By October 1797, he had crushed the Austrians and concluded the Treaty of Campo Formio, which took Austria out of the war and left France dominant over Italy and Switzerland.

In November 1797, the triumphant Bonaparte returned to Paris to confront France's only remaining enemy, Britain. Judging it impossible to invade England, he decided to try to capture Egypt from the Ottoman Empire and cut off Britain's communication with India. However, Admiral Horatio Nelson (1758–1805) destroyed the French fleet and stranded the French army in Egypt. The Russians, Austrians, and Ottomans then joined Britain to form the Second Coalition, and in 1799, the Russian and Austrian armies defeated the French in Italy and Switzerland and threatened to invade France.

Bonaparte abandoned his men in Egypt and returned to France. On November 10, 1799, he overthrew the Directory, and in December 1799, he issued the Constitution of the Year VII. It established him in power with the title First Consul. The constitution received approval from the electorate in a rigged plebiscite, and a government called the **Consulate** brought the revolution to an end.

Bonaparte quickly won a peace for France. Russia had already left the Second Coalition, and in 1800, a French victory at Marengo in Italy took Austria out of the war. In 1802, Britain concluded the Treaty of Amiens, and all of Europe was at peace—at least temporarily.

Thermidorian Reaction   The reaction against the radicalism of the French Revolution that began in July 1794. Associated with the end of terror and establishment of the Directory.

Consulate   French government dominated by Napoleon from 1799 to 1804.

Napoleon.   In December 1799 Napoleon seized power and established himself as First Consul. The title of "Consul" came from the ancient Roman Republic; by 1804 Napoleon would assume the title of "Emperor" as the French Republic gave way to the Napoleonic Empire. The simplicity of this modest military dress as First Consul also gave way to flowing imperial robes.

What was the significance of a title derived from ancient Rome?

Bonaparte also restored peace and order at home. Although he used generosity, flattery, and bribery to win over some of his enemies, issued a general amnesty, and employed persons from all political factions, Bonaparte was ruthless and efficient in suppressing political opposition. He established a highly centralized administration in which all departments were managed by prefects directly responsible to the central government in Paris. He employed secret police. He stamped out, once and for all, the royalist rebellion in the west and moved against other royalist plots.

Napoleon placated French Catholics who had been angered by revolutionary attacks on religion. In 1801, he concluded a concordat with Pope Pius VII (r. 1800–1823). Both refractory and constitutional clergy were forced to resign. Their replacements received spiritual investiture from the pope, but the state named the bishops and paid their salaries and the salary of one priest in each parish. In return, the church gave up claims to its confiscated property, the clergy swore oaths of loyalty to the state, and the Organic Articles of 1802 established the supremacy of the state over the church. Similar laws applied to Protestant and Jewish religious organizations, reducing still further the privileged position of the Catholic Church.

In 1802, another plebiscite ratified Bonaparte's appointment as consul for life, and he set about transforming the basic laws and institutions of France on the basis of both liberal principles derived from the Enlightenment and the revolution, and conservative principles going back to the Old Regime and the spirit that had triumphed at Thermidor. This was especially true of the Civil Code of 1804, usually called the Napoleonic Code. It stopped far short of the full equality advocated by liberal rationalists. Fathers were granted extensive control over their children and men over their wives. Labor unions were forbidden, and the rights of workers were subordinated to those of employers.

In 1804, Bonaparte used the fear created by a failed assassination attempt to strengthen his hold on power. A plebiscite ratified another new constitution, which designated Napoleon Emperor of the French. Napoleon summoned the pope to Notre Dame to take part in the coronation. At the last minute the pope agreed that Napoleon should actually crown himself; the emperor did not want anyone to think that his power and authority depended on the approval of the church. Henceforth he was called Napoleon I.

Between his coronation as emperor and his final defeat at Waterloo (1815), Napoleon conquered most of Europe in military campaigns that astonished the world. France's victories changed the map of Europe, ended the Old Regime and its feudal trappings in western Europe, and forced the eastern European states to reorganize. Everywhere, Napoleon's advance unleashed the passions of nationalism.

Napoleon's military interventions led Britain to issue him an ultimatum and finally, in May 1803, to declare war. William Pitt the Younger (1759–1806) was returned to office as prime minister in 1804, and he persuaded Russia and Austria once again to try to block France's expansion. On October 21, 1805, Britain scored a major victory. Lord Nelson destroyed the French and Spanish fleets at the Battle of Trafalgar just off the Spanish coast. He was killed, but his victory guaranteed Britain control of the sea.

William Pitt and Napoleon. In this early nineteenth-century cartoon, England, personified by a caricature of William Pitt, and France, personified by a caricature of Napoleon, are carving out their areas of interest around the globe.

How did Napoleon achieve such great military successes in Europe?

On land, between October 1805 and July 1807, Napoleon defeated the armies of Austria, Prussia, and Russia. He forced Austria to withdraw from northern Italy. He replaced the Holy Roman Empire with the Confederation of the Rhine, and Prussia and Russia were compelled to become his allies.

Napoleon could not be secure, however, until he had defeated Britain. He tried to cut off British trade with Europe, hoping to cripple British commercial and financial power and drive the British from the war. This strategy, called the Continental System, harmed the European economies and roused opposition to Napoleon. The British economy survived because of its access to the Americas and the eastern Mediterranean.

In 1807, a French army invaded the Iberian Peninsula to force Portugal to abandon its alliance with Britain. When a revolt broke out in Madrid in 1808, Napoleon deposed the Spanish Bourbons and placed his brother Joseph (1768–1844) on the Spanish throne. Attacks on the privileges of the church increased public outrage. Napoleon's Spanish opponents launched a guerrilla war, and the British supported them by sending an army under Sir Arthur Wellesley (1769–1852), later the Duke of Wellington. This began a long campaign that played a critical role in Napoleon's ultimate defeat.

Encouraged by the French troubles in Spain, the Austrians renewed the war in 1809. They were swiftly defeated, and Austria lost much territory and 3.5 million subjects. Napoleon married the Archduchess Marie Louise (1791–1847), Francis I's eighteen-year-old daughter, after divorcing his wife Josephine de Beauharnais (1763–1814), with whom he had not produced children.

The Franco-Russian alliance began to falter. The Continental System had harmed the Russian economy, and Napoleon's establishment of a Polish state, the Grand Duchy of Warsaw, on Russia's doorstep angered Tsar Alexander I (r. 1800–1825). Napoleon's annexation of Holland and his marriage to an Austrian princess further disturbed the tsar. In 1810 Russia withdrew from the Continental System and began to prepare for war.

To stifle the Russian military threat, Napoleon amassed a so-called Grand Army of more than 600,000 men and invaded the country. Russia's generals decided to oppose him by retreating before his advance and stripping the countryside of supplies. Russia was too vast for Napoleon to maintain lines to supply, and his men could not live off the devastated land. Terrible rains, fierce heat, shortages of food and water, and the courage of the Russian rear guard eroded the morale of Napoleon's army.

In September 1812 at Borodino, not far west of Moscow, the bloodiest battle of the Napoleonic era cost the French 30,000 casualties and the Russians almost twice as many. Yet the Russian army was not destroyed, and Napoleon had won nothing substantial. By October, after occupying Moscow, the Grand Army was forced to retreat. By December Napoleon realized that the Russian fiasco would encourage plots against him at home, so he returned to Paris, leaving the remnants of his army to struggle westward. Perhaps only 100,000 lived to tell the tale. Even as the news of the disaster reached the West, the total defeat of Napoleon was far from certain. He was able to suppress his opponents in Paris and raise another 350,000 men.

Francisco de Goya, *The Third of May, 1808,* 1814–1815.   Napoleon sent troops into Spain in 1807 after the king of Spain had agreed to aid France against Portugal, which was assisting Britain. By early 1808 Spain had essentially become an occupied nation. On May 2 riots took place in Madrid between French troops and Spanish civilians. In response to the riots, the French marshall Joachim Murat ordered numerous executions, especially of artisans and clergy, during the night of May 2 and 3.

What is the mood of this painting, and with whom does Goya seem to sympathize?

In 1813, patriotic pressure and national ambition brought together the last and most powerful coalition against Napoleon. With British financing, the Russians drove westward to be joined by Prussia and Austria. From the west, Wellington marched his peninsular army into France. Napoleon waged a skillful campaign but met decisive defeat in October at Leipzig. At the end of March 1814, the allied army marched into Paris. Napoleon abdicated and went into exile on the island of Elba off the coast of Italy.

THE CONGRESS OF VIENNA AND THE EUROPEAN SETTLEMENT

Once Napoleon was gone, the allies began to pursue their separate ambitions. The key leader was Viscount Castlereagh (1769–1822), the British foreign secretary. Even before the victorious allied armies entered Paris, he had negotiated the Treaty of Chaumont (March 9, 1814). It restored the Bourbons to the French throne and returned France to its 1792 frontiers. Remaining problems were left for a conference at Vienna.

The Congress of Vienna met from September 1814 until November 1815. The victors agreed that no single state should be allowed to dominate Europe. They constructed a series of states to prevent French expansion (see Map 23–2). They established the kingdom of the Netherlands in the north and added Genoa to Piedmont in the south. Prussia was given new territories in the west to deter French aggression along the Rhine River. Austria obtained control of northern Italy to prevent a repetition of Napoleon's conquests there. Most of Napoleon's arrangements in the rest of Germany were left untouched, and the Holy Roman Empire was not revived. The Congress established the rule of legitimate monarchs and rejected any compromise with the republican and democratic politics that had flowed from the French Revolution.

However, the settlement of eastern Europe sharply divided the victors. Alexander I wanted Russia to govern all of Poland. Prussia wanted all of Saxony. Austria, however, refused to allow Prussia's power to grow and Russia to expand. The Polish-Saxon question gave France a chance to regain influence in international affairs. French Foreign Minister Talleyrand (1754–1838) negotiated a secret treaty with Britain and Austria. When the news leaked out, the tsar agreed to accept jurisdiction over a smaller Poland, and Frederick William III of Prussia (r. 1797–1840) agreed to settle for part of Saxony. Thereafter, France was included as a fifth great power in the deliberations.

Napoleon's escape from Elba on March 1, 1815, unified the victors. Although Napoleon promised a liberal constitution and a peaceful foreign policy, the allies declared him an outlaw (a new device under international law). Wellington and the Prussians defeated

LE CONGRÈS.

Political Cartoon of the Congress of Vienna.   In this cartoon depiction, Talleyrand simply watches which way the wind is blowing; Castlereagh hesitates, while the monarchs of Russia, Prussia, and Austria form the dance of the Holy Alliance. The king of Saxony holds onto his crown and the republic of Geneva pays homage to the kingdom of Sardinia.

What did the Congress of Vienna actually achieve?

Napoleon at Waterloo in Belgium on June 18, 1815. Napoleon was exiled to Saint Helena, a tiny island off the coast of Africa, where he died in 1821.

The Hundred Days, as the period of Napoleon's return is called, made the peace settlement somewhat harsher for France, but the main outlines of the Vienna Settlement remained in place. The Quadruple Alliance between England, Austria, Prussia, and Russia was renewed on November 20, 1815. It was to be a coalition for the maintenance of peace, and its existence and later operation represented an important departure in European affairs. The statesmen at Vienna, unlike their eighteenth-century counterparts, had seen the armies of the French Revolution change borders and overturn the political and social order of the continent. They were determined to prevent a recurrence of those upheavals. Their purpose was not to punish France but to establish a framework for future stability. The great powers, through the Vienna settlement, agreed to work together to defend the status quo.

The Congress of Vienna produced a long-lasting peace. Its work has been criticized for failing to recognize and provide for the great movements that would stir the nineteenth century—nationalism and democracy—but such criticism is unrealistic. The settlement, like all such agreements, was aimed at solving past ills, and in that it succeeded. It spared Europe a general war until 1914.

CHRONOLOGY

NAPOLEONIC EUROPE

1797	Napoleon concludes Treaty of Campo Formio
1798	Nelson defeats French navy at Aboukir
1799	Consulate established
1801	Concordat between France and papacy
1802	Treaty of Amiens
1803	War renewed between France and Britain
1804	Execution of Duke of Enghien; Napoleonic Civil Code issued; Napoleon crowned emperor
1805	Nelson defeats French fleet at Trafalgar (October 21); Austerlitz (December 2)
1806	Continental System established by Berlin Decrees
1807	Treaty of Tilsit
1808	Beginning of Spanish resistance to Napoleonic domination
1809	Wagram; Napoleon marries Archduchess Marie Louise of Austria
1812	Invasion of Russia
1813	Leipzig (Battle of the Nations)
1814	Treaty of Chaumont (March) establishes Quadruple Alliance; Congress of Vienna convenes (September)
1815	Napoleon returns from Elba (March 1); Waterloo (June 18); Holy Alliance formed (September 26); Quadruple Alliance renewed (November 20)
1821	Napoleon dies on Saint Helena

WARS OF INDEPENDENCE IN LATIN AMERICA

The French Revolution and the Napoleonic wars inspired movements for independence throughout Latin America. France was driven from Haiti, Portugal from Brazil, and Spain from all its American empire except Cuba and Puerto Rico.

WHY DID Latin American nations reject Spanish and Portuguese rule?

EIGHTEENTH-CENTURY DEVELOPMENTS

After Spain's defeat in the Seven Years' War in 1763, its king, Charles III (r. 1759–1788), decided that the American colonial system had to be changed. He abolished the monopolies of Seville and Cádiz, opened more South American and Caribbean ports to trade, and authorized direct trade between American ports. In 1776, he organized a fourth viceroyalty that encompassed much of present-day

MAP EXPLORATION

To explore this map further, go to **http://www.prenhall.com/craig_maps**

MAP 23–2   Europe 1815, after the Congress of Vienna.   The Congress of Vienna achieved the post-Napoleonic territorial adjustments shown on the map. The most notable arrangements dealt with areas along France's borders (the Netherlands, Prussia, Switzerland, and Piedmont) and in Poland and northern Italy.

Why did the Congress of Vienna seek to place strong states on the borders of France?

---

peninsulares Native-born Spaniards who emigrated from Spain to settle in the Spanish colonies.

Creoles Persons of European descent who were born in the Spanish colonies.

Argentina, Uruguay, Paraguay, and Bolivia. Charles III also tried to make tax collection more efficient and to eliminate bureaucratic corruption by appointing *intendents*, bureaucrats loyal only to the crown.

These reforms returned the empire to direct Spanish control. Many **peninsulares** (whites born in Spain) went to the New World to fill these new posts, depriving **Creoles** (whites born in America) of opportunity. Expanding trade brought more Spanish merchants to Latin America, where economic activity continued to be organized for the benefit of Spain.

FIRST MOVEMENTS TOWARD INDEPENDENCE

Haiti achieved independence from France in 1804, following a slave revolt that commenced in 1794 led by Toussaint L'Ouverture (1744–1803) and Jean-Jacques Dessalines (ca. 1756–1806). Haiti's revolution involved the popular uprising of a repressed social group, which proved to be the great exception in the Latin American wars for liberty. On the South American continent, it was the Creole elite who led the campaigns against Spain and Portugal. Few Indians, blacks, mestizos, mulattos, or slaves were involved or benefited from the end of Iberian rule. Indeed, the Haitian slave revolt haunted the Creoles, as did an Indian revolt in the Andes in 1780 and 1781. The Creoles were determined that political independence from Spain and Portugal should not cause social disruption or the loss of their social and economic privileges. In this respect the Creole revolutionaries were like American revolutionaries in the southern colonies who wanted to reject British rule but keep their slaves, or French revolutionaries who wanted to depose the king but not extend liberty to the French working class.

Creole complaints resembled those of the American colonists against Great Britain. Latin American merchants wanted to trade more freely, and they wanted commercial regulations that would benefit them rather than Spain. They deeply resented Spanish policies favoring *peninsulares* for political patronage, including appointments in the colonial government, church, and army. They believed the royal patronage system was another device with which Spain extracted wealth and income from America for its own people rather than its colonial subjects.

From the 1790s onward Spain suffered military reverses in the wars associated with the French Revolution and Napoleon, and the commercial situation turned sharply against the inhabitants of the Spanish Empire. The military pressures led the Spanish monarchy into a desperate search for new revenues, including increased taxation and the confiscation of property in the American Empire. The policies harmed the economic life of the Creole elite.

Creole leaders had read the Enlightenment *philosophes* and believed that the political reforms the *philosophes* championed would benefit their region. They were also well aware of the political arguments that had justified the American Revolution. The event that crystallized Creole discontent into revolt against Spain was Napoleon's overthow of the Portuguese monarchy in 1807 and the Spanish government in 1808. The Portuguese royal family fled to Brazil, but the Bourbon monarchy of Spain seemed vanquished. The Creole elite feared that a monarchy headed by Napoleon's brother in Spain would harm their economic and social interests and would drain the region of resources for Napoleon's wars. Creole juntas, or political committees, formed between 1808 and 1810 and claimed the right to govern regions of Latin America. Ten years of warfare ensued before Spain conceded Latin American independence.

Toussaint L'Ouverture. L'Ouverture (1744–1803) began the revolt that led to Haitian independence in 1804.

Why did the Haitian revolution have such repercussions throughout the transatlantic world?

SAN MARTÍN IN RÍO DE LA PLATA

The first region to assert its independence was the Río de la Plata (modern Argentina). In 1810, the junta in Buenos Aires thrust off Spanish authority and sent soldiers to liberate Paraguay and Uruguay. They were defeated, but Paraguay asserted its own independence, and Brazil absorbed Uruguay.

MAP 23–3 **The Independence Campaigns of San Martín and Bolívar.** José de San Martín and Simón Bolívar fought for independence in different parts of South America in the early 1800s. In 1822 they collaborated to liberate Quito, but they disagreed over post-independence political structures: San Martín was a monarchist, while Bolívar was a republican.

How do the wars for independence in Latin America compare with the colonists' revolt against British rule in North America?

The Buenos Aires government then attempted to liberate Peru, the greatest remaining stronghold of royalist power on the continent (see Map 23–3). In 1814, José de San Martín (1778–1850) led an army over the Andes Mountains. By early 1817, he had occupied Santiago in Chile and established Bernardo O'Higgins (1778–1842) as supreme dictator. In 1821, he drove royalist forces from Lima and assumed the title of Protector of Peru.

SIMÓN BOLÍVAR'S LIBERATION OF VENEZUELA

While San Martín had been liberating the southern portion of the continent, Simón Bolívar (1783–1830) had been pursuing a similar task in the north. A firm advocate of independence and republicanism, Bolívar had helped organize a liberating junta in Caracas, Venezuela, in 1810. Between 1811 and 1814, civil war broke out as royalists, slaves, and cowboys challenged his republican government and drove him into exile. (See Document, "Bolívar Denounces Spanish Rule in Latin America.") In 1819, with help from Haiti, he captured Bogotá, capital of New Granada (modern Colombia, Bolivia, and Ecuador) and established a base for attacking Venezuela. In 1821, his forces captured Caracas, and he was named president.

In July 1822, the armies of Bolívar and San Martín liberated the city of Quito, but the two leaders disagreed about the future political structure of Latin America.

San Martín believed in monarchies; Bolívar favored republics. Shortly thereafter, San Martín retired from public life and moved to Europe. In 1823, Bolívar sent troops into Peru and on December 9, 1824, at the battle of Ayacucho, defeated the Spanish royalist forces. The battle marked the end of Spain's effort to retain its American empire.

INDEPENDENCE IN NEW SPAIN

The drive for independence in New Spain (modern Mexico, Texas, California, and the rest of the southwestern United States) illustrates how socially conservative the Latin American colonial revolutions were. As elsewhere, a local governing junta was organized. But before it had time to act, a Creole priest, Miguel Hidalgo y Costilla (1753–1811), incited the Indians of his parish to rebel. They and other repressed groups responded to Father Hidalgo's call for social reform, and he soon had 80,000 followers. But in July 1811, he was captured and executed. Leadership of his movement then passed to José María Morelos y Pavón (1765–1815), a more radical mestizo priest. In 1815, he too was captured and executed.

In 1820, a revolution in Spain forced Ferdinand VII (r. 1813–1833) to accept a liberal constitution, and conservative Mexicans feared that a liberal Spanish monarchy would try to impose liberal reforms on Mexico. Therefore, for the most conservative of reasons, they declared Mexico independent under a government determined to resist social reform.

Great Britain was highly sympathetic to the Latin American independence movements, since they opened the markets of the continent to British trade and investment. In 1823 Great Britain supported the American Monroe Doctrine that prohibited further colonization and intervention by European powers in America, and Britain quickly recognized the Spanish colonies as independent states. Through the rest of the century, British commercial interests dominated Latin America.

Simón Bolívar. Bolívar was the liberator of much of Latin America. He inclined toward a policy of political liberalism.

What were the policy differences between Bolívar and José de San Martín?

BRAZILIAN INDEPENDENCE

Brazilian independence came relatively peacefully. The arrival of the Portuguese royal family and several thousand officials in 1807 (as noted previously) transformed Rio de Janeiro into a court city. The prince regent Joao (r. 1816–1826) in 1815 declared Brazil a kingdom and no longer merely a colony of Portugal. In 1820, a revolution took place in Portugal, and its leaders offered the throne to Joao and demanded the return of Brazil to colonial status. Joao, who had become Joao VI in 1816, returned to Portugal and left his son Pedro (r. 1822–1831) as regent in Brazil. In 1822, Pedro asserted Brazil's independence and became emperor of Brazil. The country remained a monarchy until 1889.

The determination of Brazil's political and social elite to preserve slavery aided the peaceful transition. The wars of independence elsewhere had led to the abolition of slavery or moved the independent states closer to abolition. Any attempt to gain independence from Portugal through warfare might have caused social as well as political turmoil that would open the slavery question.

DOCUMENT

Bolívar Denounces Spanish Rule in Latin America

In September 1815 Simón Bolívar published a long statement, often called The Jamaica Letter, *in which he explained the political and economic difficulties under which the Creole elite of the Spanish Empire had lived. He defined Americans as referring to those persons in Latin America who were neither Indian nor European by birth. He also implicitly excluded black slaves. Consequently, his attack on Spain was voiced on behalf of the white population of the South American continent who had been born there and who demanded rights of political participation and economic freedom.*

- **Why** does Bolívar describe the Creole elite as having lived in a permanent political infancy? What are the economic disadvantages that he describes, and why had those become more burdensome in the half century before he wrote this letter? How had Spanish economic regulation prevented the Creole elite from achieving positions of responsibility in

Latin America? How does this document compare with others concerned with movements of independence and nationalism?

The role of the inhabitants of the American hemisphere has for centuries been purely passive. Politically they were non-existent. We are still in a position lower than slavery, and therefore it is more difficult for us to rise to the enjoyment of freedom. ... We have been harassed by a conduct which has not only deprived us of our rights but has kept us in a sort of permanent infancy with regard to public affairs. If we could at least have managed our domestic affairs and our internal administration, we could have acquainted ourselves with the processes and mechanics of public affairs... .

Americans today, and perhaps to a greater extent than ever before, who live within the Spanish system occupy a position in society no better than that of serfs

TOWARD THE ABOLITION OF SLAVERY IN THE TRANSATLANTIC ECONOMY

WHY DID slavery become unacceptable in Western society?

In 1750, few questioned the institution of slavery, but by 1888, slavery no longer existed in the transatlantic economy. This vast transformation of economic and social life occurred as the result of an international effort, first to abolish the slave trade and then to abolish slavery itself. No previous society in world history had attempted to abolish slavery. Its elimination in the transatlantic world is one of the most permanent achievements of the eighteenth-century Enlightenment and revolutions.

The eighteenth-century crusade against slavery originated among writers of the Enlightenment and religious critics. Although some *philosophes*, including John Locke, were reluctant to question slavery and even defended it, the general Enlightenment rhetoric of equality stood in sharp contrast to the radical inequality of slavery. Montesquieu satirized slavery in *The Spirit of the Laws*. Adam Smith's emphasis in *The Wealth of Nations* on free labor and the efficiency of free markets undermined economic defenses of slavery. Much eighteenth-century literature idealized primitive peoples as embodying a lost human virtue. Slavery, once considered the natural and deserved result of some deficiency in slaves themselves, grew to be regarded as an unmitigated evil. Other Enlightenment ethical thinking led reformers to believe that by working against slavery, they would realize their own highest moral character.

Religious protest against slavery originated among English Quakers, a radical Protestant group founded by George Fox in the seventeenth century. Some early Quakdestined for labor, or at best they have no more status than that of mere consumers. Yet even this status is surrounded with galling restrictions, such as being forbidden to grow European crops, or to store products which are royal monopolies, or to establish factories of a type the [Spanish] Peninsula itself does not possess. To this add the exclusive trading privileges, even in articles of prime necessity, and the barriers between American provinces, designed to prevent all exchange of trade, traffic, and understanding. In short, do you wish to know what our future held?—simply the cultivation of the fields of indigo, grain, coffee, sugar cane, cacao, and cotton; cattle raising on the broad plains; hunting wild game in the jungles; digging in the earth to mine its gold—but even these limitations could never satisfy the greed of Spain.

So negative was our existence that I can find nothing comparable in any other civilized society, examine as I may the entire history of time and the politics of all nations. Is it not an outrage and a violation of human rights to expect a land so splendidly endowed, so vast, rich, and populous, to remain merely passive?

As I have just explained, we were cut off and, as it were, removed from the world in relation to the science of government and administration of the state. We were never viceroys or governors, save in the rarest of instances; seldom archbishops and bishops; diplomats never; as military men, only subordinates; as nobles, without royal privileges. In brief, we were neither magistrates nor financiers and seldom merchants.

Source: From Harold A. Bierck Jr., ed., *Selected Writings of Bolívar*, Vol. 1. Copyright © 1951 The Colonial Press, pp. 110–112.

ers owned slaves in the West Indies and participated in the transatlantic slave trade. During the Seven Years' War (1756–1763), however, many Quakers experienced economic hardship and other difficulties. Certain Quakers decided that the presence of the evil of slavery in the world explained these troubles. They took action against the whole system of slavery that characterized the transatlantic economy.

Just as the slave system was a transatlantic affair, so was the crusade against it. During the American Revolution small groups of reformers, usually spearheaded by Quakers in Philadelphia and elsewhere, had established an antislavery network. Emancipation gradually spread among the northern states. In 1787 the Continental Congress forbade slavery in the newly organized Northwest Territory north of the Ohio River.

Despite these American developments, Great Britain was the center for the antislavery movement. During the early 1780s, reformers there decided to work toward ending the slave trade rather than the institution of slavery itself. The horrors of the slave trade caught the public's attention in 1783 when the captain of the slave ship *Zong* threw more than 130 slaves overboard in order to collect insurance. Soon after, groups from the Church of England and the English Quakers formed the Society for the Abolition of the Slave Trade. The most famous of the new leaders was William Wilberforce, who, each year for the rest of his life, introduced a bill to end the slave trade. For many, the slave trade seemed worse than the holding of slaves, and attacking slavery raised complicating issues of property rights. If the trade were ended, it seemed likely that planters would treat their remaining slaves more humanely.

While the British reformers worked for the abolition of the slave trade, some slaves took matters into their own hands. The slave revolt in Haiti was a warning to

CHRONOLOGY

THE WARS OF LATIN AMERICAN INDEPENDENCE

1759–1788		Charles III of Spain carries out imperial reforms
1776		Organization of Viceroyalty of Río de la Plata
1780–1781		Revolt of Indians in the Andes
1794		Toussaint L'Ouverture leads slave revolt in Haiti
1804		Independence of Haiti
1807		Portuguese royal family flees to Brazil
1808		Spanish monarchy falls to Napoleon
1808–1810		Creole Committees organized to govern much of Latin America
1810		Buenos Aires junta sends forces to liberate Paraguay and Uruguay
1811		Miguel Hidalgo y Costilla leads rebellion in New Spain and is executed
1811–1815		José María Morelos y Pavón leads rebellion in New Spain and is executed
1814		San Martín organizes army
1815		Brazil declared a kingdom
1816		Bolívar invades Venezuela
1817		San Martín occupies Santiago, Chile
1820		Revolution in Spain
1821	February 24	New Spain declares independence
	June 29	Bolívar captures Caracas, Venezuela
	July 28	San Martín liberates Peru
1822	July 26–27	San Martín and Bolívar quarrel at Guayaquil; San Martín goes into exile in Europe
	September 7	Dom Pedro declares Brazilian independence
1824		Battle of Ayacucho—final Spanish defeat

QUICK REVIEW

Impact on Africa of Opposition to Slavery

- British navy blockades West Africa
- Sierra Leone, Libreville, and Liberia established in West Africa
- Reformers spread Christianity and free trade in Africa
- Antislavery campaign within Africa facilitates colonization

slave owners throughout the West Indies. Other slave revolts occurred, such as those in Virginia led by Gabriel Prosser in 1800 and by Nat Turner in 1831; in South Carolina led by Denmark Vesey in 1822; in British-controlled Demarra in 1823 and 1824; and in Jamaica in 1831. Each of these was brutally suppressed.

For economic reasons, some British West Indies planters decided that abolition of the slave trade might be in their best interest. They were experiencing soil exhaustion and increased competition from French planters. There was a glut of sugar on the market, and the price was falling. Without new slaves, the French would lack the labor they needed to exploit their islands. During the Napoleonic wars, the British captured a number of the French islands. To protect the planters of the older British West Indies islands, the British Cabinet in 1805 forbade the importation of slaves into the newly acquired islands, and in 1807 Parliament finally passed Wilberforce's prohibition on slave trading from any British port. Thereafter, suppression of the slave trade became a major goal of nineteenth-century British foreign policy. The British navy maintained a squadron off West Africa to halt slave traders.

Leaders of the Latin American wars of independence were disposed by Enlightenment ideas to disapprove of slavery, and they sought the support of slaves by promises of emancipation. The newly independent nations slowly freed their slaves to maintain good relations with Britain, from which they needed economic support. Slavery had disappeared from Latin America by the middle of the century, with the important exception of Brazil.

British reformers founded the gradualist Abolition Society in 1823. The savagery with which West Indian planters put down slave revolts in 1823 and 1824 and again in 1831 strengthened the abolitionists' resolve. In 1833, following the passage of the Reform Bill in Great Britain, Parliament abolished the right of British subjects to hold slaves. In the British West Indies, 750,000 slaves were freed within a few years.

The other old colonial powers in the New World were slower to abolish slavery. Portugal ended slavery elsewhere in its American possessions in 1836, but Brazil's independent government continued slavery. The Swedes abolished slavery in their

Spanish Slave Ship.   After 1807 the British Royal Navy patrolled the West African coast attempting to intercept slave-trading ships. In 1846 the British ship HMS *Albatross* captured a Spanish slave ship, the *Albanoz*, and freed the slaves. A British officer depicted the appalling conditions in the slavehold in this watercolor.

Why did British reformers focus first on abolishing the slave trade, not slavery itself?

possessions in 1847; the Danes in 1848; but the Dutch not until 1863. France, despite a significant antislavery movement, did not abolish slavery in the West Indies until the revolutions of 1848.

Despite opposition, during the first thirty years of the nineteenth century, slavery expanded in parts of the transatlantic world: the lower south of the United States (for the cultivation of cotton), Brazil (for the cultivation of coffee), and Cuba (for the cultivation of sugar). World demand for the products of these regions made the slave system economically viable. Slavery ended in the United States only after the Civil War. In Cuba it persisted until 1886, and full emancipation did not occur in Brazil until 1888 (see Chapters 25, 26, and 27).

The emancipation crusade, like slave trading, drew Europeans into African affairs, including efforts to move former slaves back to Africa, Christian missionary endeavors, and commercial ventures. When the American Civil War finally halted large-scale demand for transatlantic slaves, reformers concentrated on ending the slave trade in East Africa and the Indian Ocean, contributing to the establishment of the late-nineteenth-century European colonial empires (see Chapters 18 and 27).

SUMMARY

WHAT WAS radical about the American Revolution?

Revolution in the British Colonies in North America. North Americans rejected British attempts to raise revenue through colonial taxes. The ideas of John Locke, the Commonwealthmen, and others pushed the colonists to the American Revolution. As the crisis continued, Americans became increasingly radicalized, rejecting monarchy and aristocratic social structures in favor of democracy and republicanism. The colonies gained independence in 1783 and adopted a constitution in 1788. Though women, slaves, Native Americans and others still lacked rights, American society was the freest yet in the world and helped inspire political movements throughout the Americas and in Europe. *page 562*

HOW DID the French Revolution and Napoleon transform France's government and society?

Revolution in France. The French monarchy, too, was troubled by finances. The need to appease taxpayers led to the 1789 calling of the Estates General. In conjunction with mass action by Parisian women, *sans-culottes*, and others, politics and protest turned, within four years, to two revolutions followed by the Reign of Terror. Some stability returned with Napoleon, whose rule began in 1799, and whose wars remade the map of Europe. In the post-Napoleonic settlement at the Congress of Vienna (1814–1815), European leaders tried to institutionalize peaceful relations throughout the continent. French society had experienced multiple disruptions, perhaps most notably the changes in the role of the church. *page 565*

WHY DID Latin American nations reject Spanish and Portuguese rule?

Wars of Independence in Latin America. The American, French, and Haitian (1794–1804) revolutions, as well as the resentment Creole elites felt toward Iberian exploitation, helped spur independence movements in Latin America. These revolutions were socially conservative, particularly in Mexico. Brazil achieved independence peacefully, in part because slaveholders there wanted to minimize the risk of social disruption that might lead to calls for abolition. *page 575*

WHY DID slavery become an acceptable in Western Society?

Toward the Abolition of Slavery in the Transatlantic Economy. English Quakers were in the forefront of the fight against first slave trading and then slavery itself. Enlightenment ideas and slave revolts throughout the Americas were also significant factors. Abolition proceeded slowly, however, and early in the nineteenth century it coexisted with an expansion of slaveholding in regions where plantation-grown cash crops were highly profitable (cotton in the southern United States, sugar in the Caribbean, and coffee in Brazil). *page 580*

INTERPRETING THE PAST

Women Activists and the French Revolution

Sources from MyHistoryLab for Chapter 23

myhist**o**ry**lab**

1) *Declaration of the Rights of Man and Citizen*

2) Olympe de Gouges: *Declaration of the Rights of Woman and Female Citizen*

The French revolutionary era aroused widespread expectations among the country's citizens that the feudal system would be eliminated and that democracy would replace the hereditary aristocracy that ruled France. Women were at the forefront of the marches, strikes, and riots that prodded the representatives of the Third Estate to push for radical changes in 1789. The resulting reorganization of the French government by the National Assembly and the Constitution of 1791 offered a number of

REVIEW QUESTIONS

1. Discuss the American Revolution in the context of transatlantic history. To what extent were the colonists influenced by their position in the transatlantic economy? To what extent were they influenced by European ideas and political developments? How did their demands for liberty compare and contrast with the ideas of liberty championed during the French Revolution?

2. How was the Estates General transformed into the National Assembly? How does the *Declaration of the Rights of Man and Citizen* reflect the social and political values of the eighteenth-century Enlightenment? What were the chief ways in which France and its government were reorganized in the early years of the revolution?

3. What was the revolution of 1792, and why did it occur? What were the causes of the Reign of Terror, and what political coalitions made it possible?

4. How did Napoleon rise to power? What were his major domestic achievements? Did his rule more nearly fulfill or betray the ideals of the French Revolution?

5. What were the results of the Napoleonic wars? Why did Napoleon decide to invade Russia? Why did he fail? What were the major outlines of the peace settlement achieved by the Congress of Vienna?

6. What political changes took place in Latin America in the twenty years between 1804 and 1824? What were the main reasons for Creole discontent with Spanish rule?

7. How were the Latin American independence movements influenced by the American and French Revolutions? What were the factors that made the Latin American wars of independence different from those two revolutions?

8. A motto of the French Revolution was "liberty, equality, and fraternity." How might one compare the American Revolution, the French Revolution, and the Latin American wars of independence in regard to the achievement of these goals?

9. What intellectual and religious factors contributed to the rise of the antislavery movement? What was the impact of slave revolts? To what extent did nonhumanitarian forces contribute to it? What opposition did it meet? Why did slavery receive a new lease on life during the same years that the antislavery movement emerged?

10. What, if any, advances did women make as a result of these revolutions in the transatlantic world? Which groups tended to benefit most, and which least, from the events discussed in this chapter?

KEY TERMS

assignats (ASS-ihn-YAHTS) (p. 567)

Consulate (p. 571)

Convention (p. 568)

Creoles (p. 576)

Jacobins (p. 568)

levée en masse (le-VAY ahn MAHS) (p. 569)

peninsulares (pen-IN-soo-LAHR-ayes) (p. 576)

Reign of Terror (p. 569)

sans-culottes (SANZ-koo-LAHTZ) (p. 568)

Thermidorean Reaction (p. 571)

Third Estate (p. 565)

Note: To learn more about the topics in this chapter, please turn to the Suggested Readings at the end of the book.

reforms but did not provide for universal suffrage for men or women or other truly democratic measures. The stage was thus set for the second and more radical phase of the revolution to commence.

In this exercise you will read primary sources that focus on the gap between the rights proposed for men and those assumed for women. The exclusion of women from participation in the political system, even after the events of 1789, led to an increase in demands for equal rights, unhindered by women's traditionally subservient roles.

The first document here is the *Declaration of Rights of Man and Citizen,* issued by the National Assembly in late 1789 to declare men born free and forever equal in rights before the law. It was a formal acknowledgment that the individual freedoms that were the hallmark of the American Revolution should apply to France. The second document, from Olympe de Gouges, a writer and

playwright, responded to the *Declaration of Rights of Man* by calling for equal rights for women.

Use the source documents to explore the reasoning and evidence offered by the men and women of the revolutionary era in their demands for expanded rights. Use specific examples from the documents to back up your assertions.

Questions

How does the *Declaration of the Rights of Woman* challenge the idea of citizenship embodied in the *Declaration of the Rights of Man*?

What elements are common to the *Declaration of the Rights of Woman* and *The Declaration of the Rights of Man*? What are the differences?

24

Political Consolidation in Nineteenth-Century Europe and North America

One of the Extraordinary Figures of the Nineteenth Century, Giuseppe Garibaldi (1807–1882), here seen toward the end of his life serenely dressed in his trademark poncho (a mode of dress he adopted in the 1830s and 1840s as a freedom fighter in South America), was the forceful and spiritual leader of the movement for Italian unification, which was achieved after many conflicts, in 1861.

How does Garibaldi's dress contribute to his idealized, romantic image as a "freedom fighter"?

THE EMERGENCE OF NATIONALISM IN EUROPE *Page 589*

WHAT IS nationalism?

EARLY-NINETEENTH-CENTURY POLITICAL LIBERALISM *Page 592*

WHAT WERE the basic goals of European liberals?

EFFORTS TO LIBERALIZE EARLY-NINETEENTH-CENTURY EUROPEAN POLITICAL STRUCTURES *Page 594*

WHY WERE efforts to achieve political liberalism more successful in France and Britain than in Russia?

TESTING THE NEW AMERICAN REPUBLIC *Page 599*

WHAT WERE the causes of the American Civil War?

THE CANADIAN EXPERIENCE *Page 603*

HOW DID Canada achieve united self-government?

MIDCENTURY POLITICAL CONSOLIDATION IN EUROPE *Page 604*

WHAT WERE the steps that led to Italian and German unification?

UNREST OF NATIONALITIES IN EASTERN EUROPE *Page 607*

HOW DID nationalism affect the Habsburg Empire?

RACIAL THEORY AND ANTI-SEMITISM *Page 608*

HOW DID racial theory influence anti-Semitism?

EUROPEAN AND NORTH AMERICAN POLITICAL CONSOLIDATION

During the first three quarters of the nineteenth century the nations of Europe and North America underwent major political consolidation. Great Britain emerged from the Napoleonic wars as the strongest power on the globe and maintained that position for more than a century. France experienced decades of changing political regimes but remained a major political and military force. However, the third quarter of the century saw Germany and Italy transformed from relatively weak regions of small principalities into major unified nation-states. Similarly the Austrian Empire reorganized itself. As will be seen in Chapter 25, Russia also undertook major political and social reforms to consolidate the strength of the tsarist government. On the other side of the Atlantic, the United States became a major nation aspiring to stretch across the North American continent, as did Canada. These developments laid the foundation for the major transatlantic state-system of the late nineteenth and early twentieth centuries.

The movement toward strong, centralized national states in Europe and North America during the nineteenth century had counterparts elsewhere in the world. In Asia during this same period, Japan sought to imitate the military and economic power of the European states. Late-nineteenth-century Latin America enjoyed one of its most successful and stable periods. The governments of that region established centralized regimes on the basis of relatively prosperous economies. In the United States the Civil War established the power of the central federal government over that of the individual states. The role of the war in the forging of a single American nation was similar to the role that military force played in the unifications of Italy and Germany and the suppression of the Paris Commune.

In Italy and Germany many people regarded the triumph of nationalism as a positive achievement. However, the last half of the century also saw various national and ethnic groups use the power of the national state to repress or dominate other groups. Examples include the Hungarian treatment of smaller subject nationalities and the British treatment of the Irish. To some extent, this phenomenon can be explained by the geographical borders of the new nations that were carved out of former European monarchies and empires, such as the Austro-Hungarian Empire. In many cases, the boundaries ignored the reality that many, perhaps most, regions were home to more than one ethnic group, with religions, languages, and ethnicities different from those of their rulers and the governing class. In the premodern world, loyalty to a ruling dynasty, rather than shared history, language, or ethnicity, was the primary determinant of group identity or membership in a polity above the local level. People saw themselves first as members of a tribe, clan, village, or town, and second as the subjects of a ruler who might not even speak their language and whose authority often impinged very little on their daily lives. Thus ethnic or linguis-

D uring the nineteenth century two fundamental long-term developments occurred in the northern transatlantic world that would have a profound impact all around the world. First, in both Europe and North America a process of political consolidation took place that made the nation-states of that region the strongest of the period. Second, and directly contributing to that political strength, powerful industrial economies with a new kind of society no longer based primarily on the land emerged in Europe and North America. As a direct result of this political consolidation and industrialization, the nations of the northern transatlantic became the world's major military powers. By the close of the nineteenth century and well into the twentieth this political and military power allowed the nations of Europe and the United States to exert unprecedented political, military, and economic influence around the globe. On the basis of this power many people in Europe and North America came to claim superiority over people in other cultures and other regions. Moreover, the manner in which Europeans and to a lesser extent Americans developed sets of ideas to explain what was happening politically and economically in their region would later be used by peoples elsewhere in the world as they responded to the worldwide power that the northern transatlantic nations exerted.

This chapter will examine the process of political consolidation in the northern transatlantic world, whereas Chapter 25 will explore the social changes that occurred in the nineteenth century. Although we will consider the two processes separately, each contributed to the other. ◼

tic minorities posed less of an obstacle to monarchical rulers than to governments of nation-states, where national identity is often based on shared language and ethnicity. This problem has continued to bedevil national states in Europe and elsewhere in the world into the modern era and is an important cause for many recent conflicts in regions as diverse as Eastern Europe, Asia, and Africa.

Elsewhere around the globe during the nineteenth century strong central governments often simply repressed minority populations, especially indigenous peoples, or allowed them fewer rights of civic participation and protection. In almost all cases the repression of minority groups generated social and political problems that haunted the twentieth century. Native Americans failed to gain rights in Latin America. In the United States the westward movement brought warfare against Native Americans, and legislation facilitated the segregation of American black citizens. In Canada, English speakers fared better than French speakers. In Australia, Aborigines were killed or forcibly relocated in many regions before and after that country's government gained sovereignty from England.

Finally, the emergence of strong European nation-states set the stage for the transfer of their rivalries from Europe to other areas of the globe. The militarily and economically strong states of Europe soon turned to foreign adventures that subjugated vast areas of Africa and Asia. This imperialism led many colonized peoples to become aware that only strong nationalistic movements of

their own could eventually end subjugation by the militarily stronger Europeans. Consequently, during the first quarter of the twentieth century, the nationalistic principle that less than fifty years earlier had dominated European politics began to influence the politics of the peoples on whom Europeans had imposed their government and administration. As these former colonies achieved independence and established their own nation-states, however, their governments experienced problems similar to those of the European nations in balancing the demands for unity of the majority with the rights of the diverse ethnic and religious minorities inhabiting their territory.

Focus Questions

◆ What role has military and economic power played in strengthening nation-states?

◆ Why do most nation-states have ethnic minorities? Why have these minorities tended to be oppressed?

◆ How did the rivalry among the European nation-states affect other regions of the world? What relationship did it have on the development of nationalism outside of Europe?

THE EMERGENCE OF NATIONALISM IN EUROPE

Nationalism proved to be the single most powerful European political ideology of the nineteenth and early twentieth centuries. Politically, **nationalism** is based on the relatively modern concept that a nation is composed of people who are joined together by the bonds of common language, customs, culture, and history, and who, because of those bonds, should share the same government. The idea that political and ethnic boundaries should coincide came into its own in Europe during the late eighteenth and early nineteenth centuries. Nationalists opposed the principle upheld at the Congress of Vienna that legitimate monarchies or dynasties should provide the basis for political unity. Nationalists rejected the concept of multinational states such as the Austrian or Russian Empires. They also objected to peoples of the same ethnic group, such as Germans and Italians, dwelling in political units smaller than that of the ethnic nation. Consequently, nationalists challenged both the domestic and the international order of the Vienna settlement.

WHAT IS nationalism?

nationalism The belief that one is part of a nation, defined as a community with its own language, traditions, customs, and history that distinguish it from other nations and make it the primary focus of a person's loyalty and sense of identity.

CREATING NATIONS

Nationalists created nations in the nineteenth century. During the first half of the century, writers spread nationalistic concepts. Many were historians who chronicled

DOCUMENT

Mazzini Defines Nationality

No political force in the nineteenth century was stronger than nationalism. It replaced dynastic political loyalty with loyalty based on ethnicity. In 1835 the Italian nationalist and patriot Giuseppe Mazzini (1805–1872) explained his understanding of the concept. Note how he combined a generally democratic view of politics with a religious concept of the divine destiny of nations.

- **What** specific qualities of a people does Mazzini associate with nationalism? How and why does Mazzini relate nationalism to divine purposes? How does this view of nationality relate to the goals of liberalism?

The essential characteristics of a nationality are common ideas, common principles and a common purpose. A nation is an association of those who are brought together by language, by given geographical conditions or by the role assigned them by history, who acknowledge the same principles and who march together to the conquest of a single definite goal under the rule of a uniform body of law.

The life of a nation consists in harmonious activity (that is, the employment of all individual abilities and energies comprised within the association) towards this single goal. ...

But nationality means even more than this. Nationality also consists in the share of mankind's labors which God assigns to a people. This mission is the task which a people must perform to the end that the Divine Idea shall be realized in this world; it is the work which gives a

a people's past or literary scholars who established a national literature by collecting and publishing earlier writings in the people's language. In effect, they gave a people a sense of their past and a literature of their own, which schoolteachers then spread.

The language to be used in schools and government was a point of contention for nationalists. In France and Italy, official versions of the national language were imposed in the schools. In eastern Europe, nationalists attempted to resurrect the national language. Often these resurrected languages were virtually invented by scholars. This process led to far more linguistic uniformity within European nations than had existed before the nineteenth century. Proficiency in the official language became a path to advancement. A uniform language helped to persuade people who had not thought of themselves as constituting a nation to believe that they were a nation. Yet even in 1850, less than half of the inhabitants of France, for example, spoke official French (see Map 24–1).

MEANING OF NATIONHOOD

Nationalists used a variety of arguments to express what they meant by nationhood. Some claimed that gathering Italians, for example, into a unified Italy would promote economic and administrative efficiency. Others insisted that nations, like biological species, were distinct creations of God. Throughout the nineteenth century, for example, Polish nationalists portrayed Poland as the suffering Christ among nations, thus implicitly suggesting that Poland, like Christ, would experience resurrection and a new life. (See Document, "Mazzini Defines Nationality.")

A significant difficulty for nationalism has been determining which ethnic groups could be considered nations, with claims to territory and political autonomy. In theory, any of them could, but in reality nationhood came to be associated with groups that were large enough to support a viable economy, that had a history of significant cultural association, that possessed a cultural elite that could nourish and spread the national language, and that could conquer other peoples to establish and people its rights as a member of Mankind; it is the baptismal rite which endows a people with its own character and its rank in the brotherhood of nations. ...

Nationality depends for its very existence upon its sacredness within and beyond its borders.

If nationality is to be inviolable for all, friends and foes alike, it must be regarded inside a country as holy, like a religion, and outside a country as a grave mission. It is necessary too that the ideas arising within a country grow steadily, as part of the general law of Humanity which is the source of all nationality. It is necessary that these ideas be shown to other lands in their beauty and purity, free from any alien mixture, from any slavish fears, from any skeptical hesitancy, strong and active; embracing in their evolution every aspect and manifestation of the life of the nation. These ideas, a necessary component in the order of universal destiny, must retain their originality even as they enter harmoniously into mankind's general progress.

The people must be the basis of nationality; its logically derived and vigorously applied principles its means; the strength of all its strength; the improvement of the life of all and the happiness of the greatest possible number its results; and the accomplishment of the task assigned to it by God its goal. This is what we mean by nationality.

Source: From *Absolutism to Revolution, 1648–1848,* 2nd ed., Herbert H. Rowen, ed. Copyright © 1969. Reprinted by permission of Prentice Hall, Upper Saddle River, NJ.

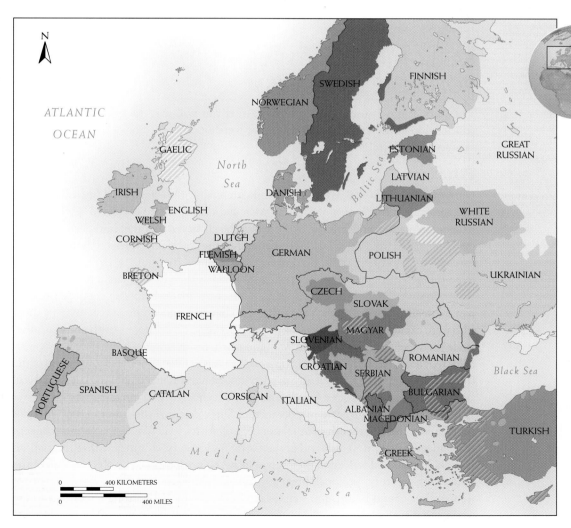

MAP 24–1 Languages of Europe. Although this map provides a good overview of the main languages of nineteenth-century Europe, it does not show the vast number of dialects that were the primary tongue of most speakers. A speaker of the Piedmont dialect from northwestern Italy, for example, would not understand a speaker from Italy's southern Island of Sicily.

Why was language significant for nationalists?

protect their own independence. Many smaller ethnic groups claimed to fulfill these criteria but could not effectively achieve independence or recognition. They could and did, however, create domestic unrest within the political units they inhabited. Such was the situation in Europe, and the American Civil War can be seen as having similar origins.

REGIONS OF NATIONALISTIC PRESSURE IN EUROPE

During the nineteenth century nationalists challenged the political status quo in six major areas of Europe. Irish nationalists wanted independence from Britain, or at least self-government. German nationalists sought political unity for all German-speaking peoples, challenging the multinational Austrian Empire and pitting Prussia and Austria against each other. Italian nationalists sought to unify the peninsula and drive out the Austrians. Polish nationalists struggled to restore Poland as an independent nation. In eastern Europe Hungarians, Czechs, Slovenes, and others sought either autonomy or formal recognition within the Austrian Empire. Finally, in the Balkans national groups sought independence from Ottoman and Russian control. In each area, nationalist activity ebbed and flowed. During the century, however, nationalists changed the political map and political culture of Europe in a way that the Confederate States of America failed to do in the mid-nineteenth-century United States.

EARLY-NINETEENTH-CENTURY POLITICAL LIBERALISM

WHAT WERE the basic goals of European liberals?

The term *liberal* as used in present-day American political rhetoric has virtually no relationship to the kinds of ideologies that were described as liberal in the nineteenth century.

POLITICS

liberalism In the nineteenth century, support for representative government dominated by the propertied classes and minimal government interference in the economy.

European **liberalism** derived from the Enlightenment, the example of English liberties, and the French *Declaration of Rights of Man and Citizen*. Liberals favored legal equality, religious toleration, and freedom of the press. They believed that the legitimacy of government emanated from the freely given consent of the governed expressed through elected parliaments. Most important, free government required that state or crown ministers be responsible to the representatives of the nation rather than to the monarch.

However limited these goals seem, none of the major European countries in 1815 met them all. The people who espoused these changes in government tended to be those who were excluded from the existing political processes, but whose wealth and education made them believe such exclusion was unjustified. Liberals were often products of career fields that admitted and rewarded people on the basis of talent (academics, members of the learned professions, and people involved in commerce and manufacturing). Monarchical and aristocratic regimes often failed to recognize their status and interests.

European liberals were not democrats. They despised the lower classes. Liberals transformed the eighteenth-century concept of aristocratic liberty into a new concept of privilege based on wealth and property. By midcentury, this meant that throughout Europe, liberals had separated themselves from the working class. In the first half of the nineteenth century, political liberals generally did not support political rights for women, but liberal political principles provided women with strong arguments to use when agitating for rights.

ECONOMICS

The economic goals of the liberals furthered their separation from the working class. Liberal elements in the landed and commercial middle class, influenced by the Enlightenment and Adam Smith, wanted to be able to manufacture and sell goods freely. They favored the removal of barriers to trade and, from the 1830s onward, sought construction of rail networks.

Economic liberals opposed the old paternalistic traditions in which governments or guilds passed legislation to fix wages and labor practices. They regarded labor simply as a commodity to be bought and sold freely. Liberals favored an open economy in which people were free to use their talents and property to enrich themselves. They contended that this would lead to more goods and services for everyone at lower prices.

These economic goals found many followers outside Europe among groups that favored the expansion of free trade, new transport systems, and a free market in labor. In the United States, people with this outlook often attacked slavery as inefficient and paternalistic. In Latin America, political liberals sought to repeal legislation that had protected Native Americans under Spanish rule.

RELATIONSHIP OF NATIONALISM AND LIBERALISM

Nationalism was not necessarily or logically linked to liberalism, but they were often complementary. Behind the concept of a people joined naturally together by the bonds of common language, customs, culture, and history lurked the idea of popular sovereignty. The idea of the career open to talent could be applied to suppressed national groups that were not permitted to realize their cultural or political potential. The efficient government and administration required by commerce and industry would mean joining small German and Italian states into larger political units. Nationalist groups in one country could gain the sympathy of liberals in other nations by espousing representative government and political liberty.

LIBERALISM AND NATIONALISM IN MODERN WORLD HISTORY

The French Revolution had demonstrated that the ideals of political liberalism could easily cross dynastic borders. In time those liberal ideals as well as those of nationalism would spread around the globe. Thus, what began as a European development is also important for global history. The concept of the "rights of man and citizen" was used during the wars of independence in Latin America to challenge Spanish government. By the close of the nineteenth century, those same ideals had been turned against European colonial governments in Africa and Asia (see Chapter 27). The belief that people should have the right to govern themselves inspired the settlers who spread across both the United States and Canada as well as those who settled in Australia and New Zealand. Similarly, the belief that individual ethnic groups should constitute independent nations became a major political conviction that led peoples living under European colonial government during the late nineteenth and twentieth centuries to challenge the right of Europeans and

A CONVENTION OF HEMMERS AND STITCHERS HELD AT LYNN, FEB. 28, FOR ADOPTING A LIST OF PRICES; MRS. E. HALL, PRESIDING.—See page 294.)

Female Liberal Political Activism. The ideas of political liberalism spoke deeply to the situation of women throughout the transatlantic world. Women demanded entrance into the political forum, as demonstrated by the first women's rights convention in Seneca Falls, New York, in 1848, and this meeting of women strikers in Lynn, Massachusetts, in 1860.

How successful were women in gaining rights during this period?

later Americans to govern them or dominate their lives through economic power. Thus, political developments in Europe during the early nineteenth century profoundly affected global politics during the twentieth century.

EFFORTS TO LIBERALIZE EARLY-NINETEENTH-CENTURY EUROPEAN POLITICAL STRUCTURES

WHY WERE efforts to achieve political liberalism more successful in France and Britain than in Russia?

European nations moved toward liberal political structures haltingly and in the face of conflict. Most conservatives hoped the Congress of Vienna had established walls against liberal advances. Three examples will indicate the different experiences that European liberals confronted early in the nineteenth century.

RUSSIA: THE DECEMBRIST REVOLT OF 1825 AND THE AUTOCRACY OF NICHOLAS I

In the process of driving Napoleon's army across Europe and then occupying defeated France, many officers in the Russian army were introduced to the ideas of the French Revolution and the Enlightenment. They realized how economically backward and politically stifled Russia was, and groups within the officer corps began to form secret societies. These societies were small and divided in their goals, agreeing only that the Russian government must change. In 1825, they decided to stage a coup d'état the following year.

Events intervened. In November 1825, Tsar Alexander I died unexpectedly, creating two crises. The first was a dynastic one: Alexander had no direct heir. His brother Constantine, who commanded Russian forces in Poland, was next in line to be tsar, but he had renounced any claim to the throne. Secret instructions left by Alexander and made public only after his death named the tsar's younger brother, Nicholas (r. 1825–1855), his successor, but the legality of Alexander's orders was uncertain. Constantine acknowledged Nicholas as tsar, and Nicholas acknowledged Constantine. For about three weeks, Russia actually had no ruler. Then, in early December, the army command reported to Nicholas the existence of a conspiracy among certain officers. Nicholas concluded that he could not delay and had himself declared tsar.

The second crisis now unfolded—a plot by junior officers to rally their troops to compel reform. On December 26, 1825, the army was to take the oath of allegiance to Nicholas, who was less popular than Constantine and regarded as more conservative. Nearly all of the regiments did so, but the Moscow regiment refused. Its chief officers, surprisingly, were not secret society members, but they marched into the Senate Square in Saint Petersburg calling for Constantine and a constitution. Attempts at peaceful settlement failed, and Nicholas ordered cavalry and artillery to attack the insurgents. Five of the plotters were executed, and more than one hundred other officers were exiled to Siberia.

Liberalism was crushed as even a moderate political influence in Russia. Nicholas I manifested extreme conservatism in foreign affairs, too, ever ready to provide troops to suppress liberal and nationalist movements anywhere in Europe. Except for a modest experiment early in the twentieth century, tsarist Russia never experienced liberal political structures.

REVOLUTION IN FRANCE (1830)

In 1824 Louis XVIII (r. 1814–1824), the Bourbon king restored to the French throne by the Congress of Vienna, died and was succeeded by his brother, Charles X (r. 1824–1830). The new king considered himself a monarch by divine right. He wanted to restore lands that the French aristocrats had lost during the revolution and pressed other conservative measures through the Chamber of Deputies. Opposition soon developed. After elections in 1827, Charles moderated his conservatism, but French liberals pressed for a constitutional regime. In 1829, Charles abandoned efforts to accommodate liberals and appointed an ultraroyalist ministry. This move backfired.

In 1830 Charles X called for new elections, and the liberals scored a stunning victory. The king and his ministers decided to undertake a royalist seizure of power. In June and July 1830 the ministry had sent a naval expedition against Algeria. On July 9 reports of its victory, and the consequent foundation of a French empire in North Africa, reached Paris. On July 25, 1830, under the euphoria of this foreign diversion, Charles X issued the Four Ordinances, which restricted freedom of the press, dissolved the recently elected Chamber of Deputies, and called for new elections under a franchise restricted to the wealthiest people in the country.

Liberal newspapers immediately called on the nation to reject the monarch's actions. Parisian laborers, burdened since 1827 by an economic downturn, took to the streets and erected barricades. The king called out troops, and more than 1,800 people died during the ensuing battles. On August 2 Charles X abdicated and left for exile in England. The liberals in the Chamber of Deputies named a new ministry composed of constitutional monarchists. They proclaimed Louis Philippe (r. 1830–1848), the Duke of Orléans and head of the liberal branch of the royal family, the new monarch. Under the **July Monarchy**, Louis Philippe was called the king of the French rather than of France. The king had to cooperate with the Chamber of Deputies; he could not dispense with laws on his own authority. The revolutionary tricolor replaced the white flag of the Bourbons. The Charter, or constitution, was regarded as embodying the rights of the people rather than as a concession granted by the monarch. Catholicism was recognized only as the religion of the majority of the people, not as the official religion. Censorship was abolished. The franchise, though still restricted, was extended.

Socially, however, the Revolution of 1830 proved quite conservative. The landed oligarchy retained its economic, political, and social influence. Money became the path to power and influence in the government. There was much corruption. Most important, the liberal monarchy displayed scant sympathy for the lower and working classes.

July Monarchy   The French regime set up after the overthrow of the Bourbons in July 1830.

Great Reform Bill (1832)   A limited reform of the British House of Commons and an expansion of the electorate to include a wider variety of the propertied classes. It laid the groundwork for further orderly reforms within the British constitutional system.

THE GREAT REFORM BILL IN BRITAIN (1832)

The passage of Britain's **Great Reform Bill**, which became law in 1832, was the result of events different from those that occurred on the Continent. In Britain the forces of conservatism and reform compromised with each other. Great Britain came to be regarded as the exemplary liberal state not only of Europe but also of the world.

English determination to maintain union with Ireland began the reform process. The Act of Union in 1800 between England and Ireland had suppressed the separate Irish parliament

Decembrist Revolt.   When members of the Moscow regiment refused to swear allegiance to Nicholas, he ordered the cavalry and artillery to attack them. Although a total failure, the Decembrist Revolt came to symbolize the yearnings of all Russian liberals in the nineteenth century for a constitutional government.

Why did liberalism fail in Russia?

Liberty Leading the People by Eugene Delacroix is a famous evocation of the Revolution of 1830.

Eugene Delacroix (1798-1863), "Liberty Leading the People". July 28, 1830. Painted 1830. Oil on canvas, 260 x 325 cm. Photo: Hervé Lewandowski. Musee du Louvre/RMN Reunion des Musees Nationaux, France. SCALA/Art Resource, N.Y.

How does Delacroix mythologize the events of 1830?

Catholic emancipation The grant of full political rights to Roman Catholics in Britain in 1829.

Daniel O'Connell, known as the "Liberator," was the preeminent leader of Catholic emancipation in the first half of the nineteenth century.

How did the "Irish Question" influence British politics?

and seated Irish representatives in the British parliament at Westminster. Only Protestant Irishmen, however, could be elected to represent what was an overwhelmingly Catholic country.

During the 1820s, under the leadership of Daniel O'Connell (1775–1847), Irish nationalists organized the Catholic Association to agitate for **Catholic emancipation**, as the movement for legal rights for Roman Catholics was known. In 1828 O'Connell was elected to Parliament but could not legally take his seat. The British ministry of the Duke of Wellington (1769–1852) saw a risk of civil war, so in 1829 Wellington and Robert Peel (1788–1850) steered the Catholic Emancipation Act through Parliament. Roman Catholics could now become members of Parliament. This, together with the repeal in 1828 of restrictions against Protestant nonconformists, ended the monopoly held by members of the Church of England on British political life.

Catholic emancipation alienated many of Wellington's Tory supporters. Many believed that Catholic emancipation only passed because of corruption in the House of Commons, so they elected reform candidates in 1830. The Tories were badly divided. When the Wellington ministry fell, King William IV (r. 1830–1837) turned to the Whigs to form a government.

The Whig ministry soon presented the House of Commons with a major reform bill that had two broad goals. The first was to replace "rotten" boroughs, which had few voters, with representatives for the previously unrepresented manufacturing districts and cities. The second was to increase the number of voters in England and Wales. In 1831 the House of Commons narrowly defeated the bill. After a new election, the House of Commons passed the reform bill, but the House of Lords rejected it. Mass meetings were held throughout the country, and riots broke out in several cities. Finally, William IV agreed to create enough new peers to give a third reform bill a majority in the House of Lords. Under this pressure, the measure became law in 1832.

The Great Reform Act expanded the size of the English electorate, but it was not a democratic measure. The electorate was increased by more than 200,000 persons, or by almost 50 percent. The basis of voting, however, remained a property qualification. New urban boroughs gave the growing cities a voice in the House of Commons. But for every new urban electoral district, a new rural district was also drawn, where the aristocracy was expected to dominate in elections. Nonetheless, the Great Reform Act established the foundations for long-term political stability in Britain. Political structures permitted the absorption of new groups and interests into the existing political processes. A large body of ideas emphasizing competition and individualism was accepted by the members of all classes. Even the leaders of trade unions asked only to receive some of the fruits of prosperity and to prove their own social respectability. During the 1840s a major working-class political movement known as **Chartism** brought the demands of industrial workers into the political process. Great Britain continued to symbolize the confident liberal state.

Benjamin Disraeli (1804–1881), leader of the Conservatives in the House of Commons, thought significant portions of the working class would eventually support Conservative candidates who were responsive to social issues and that the growing suburban middle class would become more conservative. Disraeli supported the Second Reform Act (1867), which increased the number of voters from approximately

1,430,000 to 2,470,000. The election of 1868 dashed Disraeli's hopes: William Gladstone (1809–1898) became the new prime minister. His ministry from 1868 to 1874 witnessed the culmination of classical British liberalism. Gladstone introduced competitive examinations into the civil service, abolished the purchase of army officers' commissions, and introduced the secret ballot. He opened Oxford and Cambridge universities to students of all religious denominations and, by the Education Act of 1870, made the British government responsible for establishing and running elementary schools, which previously had been supported by the various churches.

The liberal policy of creating popular support for the nation by extending political liberty and reforming abuses had its conservative counterpart in concern about social reform. Disraeli succeeded Gladstone as prime minister in 1874. Whereas Gladstone looked to individualism, free trade, and competition to solve social problems, Disraeli believed the state should protect weaker citizens. In his view, paternalistic legislation would alleviate class antagonism. His most important measures were the Public Health Act of 1875 and the Artisans Dwelling Act of 1875, through which the government became involved in providing housing for the working class.

A House of Commons Debate.   William Ewart Gladstone, standing on the right, is attacking Benjamin Disraeli, who sits with legs crossed and arms folded. Gladstone served in the British Parliament from the 1830s through the 1890s. Four times the Liberal Party prime minister, he was responsible for guiding major reforms through Parliament. Disraeli, regarded as the founder of modern British conservatism, served as prime minister from 1874 to 1880.

What were the significant differences between the policies of Gladstone and Disraeli?

Ireland remained a major issue for the British government. From the late 1860s onward, Irish nationalists had sought **home rule**, by which they meant more Irish control of local government. The Irish, like the Hungarians and Czechs in the Habsburg Empire, proved a profoundly disruptive force in British politics. By 1885 Charles Stewart Parnell (1846–1891) had organized eighty-five Irish members of the House of Commons into a tightly disciplined party. In the election of 1885 the Irish Party emerged holding the balance of power between the English Liberals and Conservatives. Gladstone announced support for home rule for Ireland, and Parnell gave his votes to the formation of a Liberal ministry. The issue split the Liberal Party, however. In 1886 a group known as the Liberal Unionists joined with the Conservatives to defeat Gladstone's Home Rule Bill. Gladstone called for a new election, which the Liberals lost. The new Conservative ministry of Lord Salisbury (1830–1903) attempted to reconcile the Irish to the English government through public works and administrative reform. The policy had only marginal success.

In 1892 Gladstone returned to power and sponsored a second Home Rule Bill that passed the House of Commons but was defeated in the House of Lords. With the failure of this bill, further action on the Irish question was suspended until a Liberal ministry passed the third Home Rule Bill in the summer of 1914. However, the implementation of home rule was suspended for the duration of World War I.

Normal British domestic issues could not be adequately addressed because of the political divisions created by Ireland. The split of the Liberal Party hurt the cause of further social and political reform. Because the two traditional parties failed to deal with social questions, by the turn of the century a newly organized Labour Party began to fill the vacuum.

QUICK REVIEW

William Gladstone (1809–1898)

◆ Became prime minister in election of 1868

◆ Witnessed the culmination of classical British liberalism

◆ Carried out reforms of governmental abuses and extended political liberty

Chartism   The first large-scale European working-class political movement. It sought political reforms that would favor the interests of skilled British workers in the 1830s and 1840s.

home rule   The advocacy of a large measure of administrative autonomy for Ireland within the British Empire between the 1880s and 1914.

1848: YEAR OF REVOLUTIONS IN EUROPE

In 1848 a series of liberal and nationalistic revolutions and revolts spread across Europe (see Map 24–2). No single factor caused this revolutionary groundswell, but similar conditions existed in several countries. Severe food shortages had prevailed since 1846 due to poor harvests. The commercial and industrial economy was in recession, causing widespread unemployment. However, the dynamic for change in 1848 originated not with the working classes but with middle-class political liberals, who pushed for more representative governments, civil liberty, and unregulated economic life.

To put additional pressure on their governments, the liberals began to appeal for the support of the urban working classes, even though their goals were different. The working

MAP 24–2   Centers of Revolution, 1848–1849.   The revolution that toppled the July Monarchy in Paris in 1848 soon spread to Austria and many of the German and Italian states. Yet by the end of 1849, most of these uprisings had been suppressed.

Which regions were most affected by the uprisings of 1848 and 1849?

classes sought improved employment and better working conditions. The liberals refused to follow political revolution with social reform and thus isolated themselves from their temporary working-class allies. Once separated from potential mass support, the liberal revolutions were easily suppressed by the armies of reactionary governments. As a result, the revolutions of 1848 failed to establish genuinely liberal or national states.

The results of the continental revolutions of 1848 were important for the individual nation-states. In France the monarchy of Louis Philippe was overthrown and briefly replaced by a republic. In 1851 the republic was in turn overthrown in a military coup led by Louis Napoleon, a nephew of the first Napoleon. Thereafter Louis Napoleon created the Second Empire and took the title of Napoleon III. In Prussia and the Austrian Empire short-lived revolutions brought political liberals and nationalists to the fore, but in each case those revolutions were put down by the military. The same was true of efforts by Italian nationalists to thrust off Austrian rule of Italy.

From the standpoint of world history, the chief importance of the failed revolutions of 1848 was the emergence on the European continent of strongly conservative governments that would dominate the next quarter century. The turmoil of 1848 through 1850 ended the era of liberal revolution that had begun in 1789; political initiative passed for a time to the conservatives. Liberals and nationalists had discovered that rational argument and local insurrections would not help them to achieve their goals. The working class also adopted new tactics and organization. The era of the riot and urban insurrection was ending. In the future, workers would turn to trade unions and political parties to achieve their political and social goals.

The defeat of liberal political forces in 1848 also influenced the modernization of Japan. Within a few years Japan would emerge from its long self-imposed isolation. After the Meiji Restoration, the new leaders of Japan looked to European examples of successful modern nations. The nation they would most clearly copy was the conservative, militaristic Germany that emerged after the defeat of the liberals of 1848.

TESTING THE NEW AMERICAN REPUBLIC

TOWARD SECTIONAL CONFLICT

WHAT WERE the causes of the American Civil War?

While the nations of western Europe hesitantly embraced political liberalism, the United States was continuing its bold republican political experiment. By the first quarter of the century, however, serious sectional tensions had arisen, the most important of which related to the presence of black slavery in the southern states.

The Constitutional Convention of 1788 had debated several aspects of slavery. A compromise allowed the slaveholding states to count three fifths of their slaves when calculating their population for representation in Congress. The Constitution also forbade any federal attempt to prevent the importation of slaves before 1808.

Westward expansion raised new questions about slavery. The Ordinance of 1787, passed by Congress under the Articles of Confederation, had prohibited slavery in the Northwest Territory. Territory south of the Ohio River and beyond the Mississippi River was, however, open to slavery, and there it spread. By 1820, when Missouri was admitted as a slave state and Maine as a free one, the number of slave and free states was evenly divided; this meant an equal number of senators from slave and free states. It was decided that in the future no slave states would be carved out of land north of the southern border of Missouri. For the time being, this Missouri Compromise ended congressional debate over slavery (see Map 24–3).

Meanwhile, the economies of the North and the South were rapidly diverging. In the North, family farms, free labor, commerce, and early industrialization in textiles

MAP EXPLORATION

To explore this map further, go to http://www.prenhall.com/craig_maps

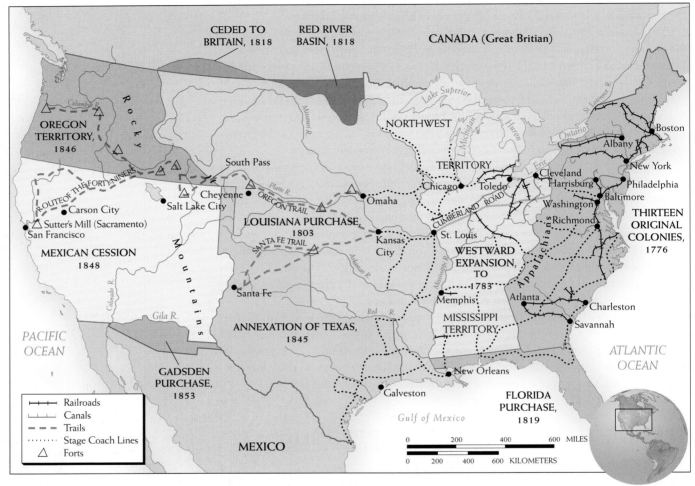

MAP 24–3   The United States, 1776–1850.   During the nineteenth century, the United States expanded across the entire North American continent. The revolutionary settlement had provided most of the land east of the Mississippi. The single largest addition thereafter was the Louisiana Purchase of 1803. The annexation of Texas, and later the Mexican Cession following the Mexican War, added the major southwestern territories. The borders of the Oregon Territory were settled through long, difficult negotiations with Great Britain.

What is the connection between the westward expansion of the United States and the Civil War?

characterized the economy. Northern farms were relatively small and worked by families, producing mostly foodstuffs for the local community. Farm laborers were free, as were workers in the towns, on the ships, and in the factories of the North. The political spokesmen for the North tended to favor tariffs to protect their young industries from cheaper foreign competition. (In this, many American liberals differed from their European counterparts.) Northern textile factories used cotton that was produced in the South, though most southern cotton was sold overseas.

Nineteenth-century innovations in transportation led to the fuller integration of different parts of the northern economy. Canals were built to link the major rivers with manufacturing and agricultural markets. The Ohio, Mississippi, and Missouri Rivers were made navigable for steamboats. By the late 1840s, in America as in Europe, the major transportation innovation was the railroad. Most railways linked the Northeast and the

West and fostered the commercial agriculture of the Midwest, making much of the northern economy just as rural and agricultural as the southern. Railway construction aided the development of the northern coal and iron industries. The midcentury expansion of railways caused new sectional tensions, as it became clear the railways could open vast territories for settlement and could thus also open a national debate over slavery.

What most distinguished North from South was free versus slave labor. The southern economy depended on slavery. Cotton was king in the South. The invention of the cotton gin by Eli Whitney (1765–1825) in 1793 made cotton cultivation much more profitable because the seed no longer had to be laboriously picked by hand out of the new cotton. The industrial revolution in textiles kept cotton prices high, and the expansion in world population kept the demand for cotton cloth steady. The South profited from growing the cotton, New England from shipping it, and other parts of the North from supplying the manufactured goods the South needed. The South had virtually no incentive to diversify its agriculture. In some respects, the southern economy resembled the economies of many Latin American countries, which were based on exporting a single crop or natural resource and on slave labor.

In keeping with the egalitarian values of the American Revolution, slavery was abolished in the North by the early nineteenth century. But in the South, the expansion of the cotton empire in the Mississippi Delta in the early nineteenth century gave slavery a new lease on life. Although most southern families never owned slaves, and most slave owners possessed only a few slaves, the institution of slavery survived for many reasons. For one, it was economically viable, and no one could devise a way to abolish it that was politically or socially acceptable to white Southerners. Throughout American society, North and South, there was a strong commitment to the protection of private property, which included slaves. Perhaps most basic, however, was the racist thinking—in the North and in the South—that saw blacks as fundamentally inferior to whites.

All American slaves were nonwhite, the descendants of Africans who had been forcibly captured and shipped in wretched conditions to the United States (see Chapter 17). Despite racial mixing among Africans and their white slave owners and Native Americans, slave codes defined as black virtually anyone who had African ancestors. Slaves were regarded as chattel property; that is, they could be sold, given away, or even gambled away like any other piece of property. They had no recourse to law or constitutional protections and could be whipped or beaten. Although owners wanted to see their slave investments reproduce themselves, slaves suffered from overwork and from diseases associated with poor nutrition, substandard sanitation, and inferior housing.

Slaves worked primarily in the fields, where they plowed, hoed, and harvested cotton, rice, sugar, tobacco, or corn. They were usually organized into work gangs supervised by white overseers. This work, like all farming, was seasonal, but during planting or harvest seasons, labor would persist from sunrise to sunset. Children would help in the fields. Older or more privileged slaves might work in the house.

Slave communities helped preserve the family life and inner personalities of slaves. Some elements of African culture persisted: African legends were passed on orally. Religion proved extraordinarily important. Slaves adopted for their own cultural needs the Old Testament stories of the Jews' liberation from Egypt. They also often combined elements of African religion with evangelical Protestantism. Yet the marriages and family lives of slaves had no legal recognition, and the integrity of the slave family could be violated at any time. White masters and their sons often sexually exploited black slave women. Families could be separated by sale or after an owner's death. Many young children were

The Excelsior Iron Works, located in New York City. This print from the 1840s shows the works as a beehive of activity. Iron mills produced the material for railroads, ships, and machinery.

How did the economy of the North differ from that of the South?

Scars of Slavery. This Louisiana slave named Gordon was photographed in 1863 after he had escaped to Union lines during the Civil War. He bears the permanent scars of the violence that lay at the heart of the slave system. Few slaves were so brutally marked, but all lived with the threat of beatings if they failed to obey.

Do you believe evidence of the cruelty of slavery, such as this photograph, influenced Lincoln's declaration to issue the Emancipation Proclamation?

reared by other slaves to whom they were not related. In a world of white dominance, the institutions, customs, and religions of the slave community were the only means black slaves had to protect the autonomy of their own personalities.

THE ABOLITIONIST MOVEMENT

During the 1830s a militant antislavery movement emerged in the North. Its leaders and followers regarded it as a moral compromise to live in a nation that tolerated slavery. (See Chapter 23 for a discussion of abolitionism in Britain and elsewhere.) Abolitionists such as William Lloyd Garrison condemned the Union and the Constitution as structures that perpetuated slavery. Former slaves, such as Frederick Douglass and Sojourner Truth, and freeborn black Americans, such as Daniel A. Payne, also joined the cause. The antislavery movement, which was initially only one of many American reform movements, gained new adherents during the 1840s as the question of extending slavery into the new territories came to the fore toward the end of the Mexican War (1846–1848). Victory added significant new territory in the Southwest and California, in addition to Texas, which had been annexed in 1845. Through negotiations with Britain the United States also acquired the vast Oregon Territory in the Northwest in 1846 (see Map 24–3).

Southerners feared that changing attitudes and the opening of territories where slavery might be prohibited would give the South a minority status. Northerners believed that a slave-power conspiracy controlled the federal government. The Compromise of 1850, a group of laws that balanced slave and free interests, briefly restored political calm. The Kansas-Nebraska Bill was introduced by Stephen A. Douglas (1813–1861) in 1845. Based on the principle of popular sovereignty, the bill proposed that the people of each new territory decide whether to permit slavery. The Republican Party was organized in 1854 largely in opposition to the Kansas-Nebraska Bill. During 1854, "Bleeding Kansas" was in a state of civil war over slavery.

In the 1857 *Dred Scott* decision, the Supreme Court effectively repealed the Missouri Compromise by declaring that Congress could not prohibit slavery in the territories, that slaves did not become free by living in free states, and that slaves did not have basic rights. Thereafter, slavery dominated national political debate.

In 1859 John Brown seized the federal arsenal at Harpers Ferry, Virginia, as part of an effort to foment a slave rebellion. He was captured, tried, and hanged, further increasing sectional polarization.

The Republican Party opposed slavery, although most Republicans did not favor outright abolition. In 1860 Abraham Lincoln (1809–1865), the Republican candidate, was elected president. Neither he nor the Republican Party had campaigned for the abolition of slavery. Nonetheless, Southerners perceived his election as a threat. In December 1860 southern states began to secede, forming the Confederate States of America. When Confederate forces fired on Fort Sumter in Charleston harbor in April 1861, the most destructive war in U.S. history began.

The Civil War lasted almost exactly four years, and a different nation emerged from the violence. In 1863 Lincoln emancipated the slaves in the rebelling states. The Emancipation Proclamation transformed the northern cause from that of suppressing a southern rebellion into that of extending liberty. By the time the Confederacy was defeated in 1865, the South was occupied by northern armies, its farms were often fallow, its transportation network disrupted, and many of its cities in ruins. Southern political leaders had virtually no impact on the immediate postwar decisions. The Thirteenth, Fourteenth, and Fifteenth Amendments to the Constitution largely recast the character of the Union. The Thirteenth abolished slavery, the Fourteenth granted citizenship to the former slaves, and the Fifteenth allowed them to vote. The Fourteenth Amendment also prohibited much political activity by people who had taken up arms against the Union. These amendments resolved the issues of slavery and the relative roles of the state and federal governments.

The Civil War and the Reconstruction era that followed it overturned the social and political order of the South. For a time, freed slaves participated broadly and actively in the politics of the southern states. For more than ten years federal troops occupied parts of the South. Many of the antebellum southern leaders left political life. Economically, the South remained generally rural and still dependent on cotton. For the first time since the earliest colonial days, it became an area of free labor. Many of the freed slaves and poor whites who tilled the land remained hopelessly in debt to wealthier landowners. Attempts to bring manufacturing into the South met with limited success. Rampant racism blocked free economic development. For the rest of the century the South remained in a semicolonial relationship to the North. Throughout the rural South, poverty was the norm.

Within the context of world history, the American Civil War is important for several reasons. With the exception of the Taiping Rebellion in China from 1851 to 1864, it was the greatest war that occurred anywhere in the world between the defeat of Napoleon in 1815 and the onset of World War I in 1914. It resulted in the establishment of a continent-wide free labor market, even though freed blacks lived in great poverty, and the rural South was economically dependent. The free labor market helped open the entire North American continent to economic development. Debates over the role of industrial labor in the United States resembled those in Europe to be discussed in Chapter 25. American political and economic interests could henceforth develop without the distraction of debates over states' rights and the morality of slavery.

Harvest of Death.   Corpses of dead soldiers are strewn across the battlefield in Gettysburg, Pennsylvania. The battle, which lasted from July 1 to 3, 1863, resulted in 51,000 casualties.

How is the Civil War an example of modern warfare?

THE CANADIAN EXPERIENCE

HOW DID Canada achieve united self-government?

Under the Treaty of Paris of 1763, all of Canada came under the control of Great Britain. Canada then, as now, included both an English-speaking and a French-speaking population, the latter concentrated in Quebec. The Quebec Act of 1774 made the Roman Catholic Church the established church in Quebec. During the American Revolution approximately thirty thousand English loyalists fled the colonies and settled in Canada. They strengthened English influences and were staunchly loyal to the British Crown.

Tension between the French and English populations contributed to the Constitutional Act of 1791, which divided the colony into Upper Canada (primarily English in ethnic composition) and Lower Canada (primarily French). Each section had its own legislature, and a governor-general presided over the two provinces on behalf of the British Crown. Newfoundland, Nova Scotia, New Brunswick, Cape Breton Island, and Prince Edward Island remained separate colonies.

In the early nineteenth century relations with the United States were often tense. There were local disputes over the fur trade and fear that the United States would dominate Canada. That apprehension, and the Anglo-French ethnic divisions, became two of the major themes of Canadian history.

By the late 1830s, tension arose between long-established families with powerful economic interests in both Upper and Lower Canada and new settlers who hoped to achieve prosperity for themselves. There were quarrels over the influence of the British Crown in local affairs. In 1837 rebellions occurred in both Upper and Lower Canada. There were relatively few casualties, but the British took action.

ROAD TO SELF-GOVERNMENT

The British government, operating in the more liberal political climate following the first Reform Act (1832), was determined to avoid another North American revolution. Consequently, it sent the Earl of Durham (1792–1840) to Canada with extensive powers to make

Canadian Railroads. Passengers board a train of the Great Western Railway at Clifton Depot in southern Ontario, sometime in the late 1850s. As in the United States, the growth of railroads transformed Canada in the nineteenth century.

Were there significant regional differences within Canada?

reforms. His 1839 *Report on the Affairs of British North America* advocated uniting both Canadian provinces into one political unit. He believed that most Canadian affairs should be in the hands of a Canadian legislature and that only foreign policy and defense should remain under British control. In effect, Durham wanted Canadians generally to govern themselves, so that English culture would dominate. His policy was carried out in the Canada Act of 1840, which gave the nation a single legislature composed of two houses.

The Durham *Report* established the political pattern that the British government followed, to a greater or lesser extent, with its other English-speaking colonies during the nineteenth century. Britain sought to foster responsible self-government in Australia, New Zealand, and South Africa. But, until well into the twentieth century, the British government and other Western imperial powers generally believed that nonwhite peoples, such as those of India, required direct colonial administration.

KEEPING A DISTINCTIVE CULTURE

Canadians exercised self-government, but distinct English and French cultures continued to exist. Within the legislature there were frequent trade-offs between the eastern and western sections of the nation. During the American Civil War, fears that the American republic might seek to invade or dominate Canada led to an attempt to unite the Maritime Provinces in 1862 and to consideration of a stronger federation among all the parts of Canada.

The British North America Act of 1867 created a Canadian federation. Canadians hoped to avoid what they regarded as flaws in the constitution of the United States. The Canadian system of government was federal but with much less emphasis on states' rights than in the United States. Canadians established a parliamentary mode of government but also chose to retain the presence of the British monarchy in the person of the governor-general as head of state. John A. MacDonald (1815–1891) was the person most responsible for establishing this new government, and he led it for most of the period between 1867 and 1891.

MIDCENTURY POLITICAL CONSOLIDATION IN EUROPE

WHAT WERE the steps that led to Italian and German unification?

While the United States and Canada were establishing themselves as strong, unified political entities in North America, major political consolidation occurred in Europe that would have an enormous impact on the rest of the world. As has often been true in modern European history, war made change possible. In this case, a conflict disrupted the international balance that had prevailed since 1815 and unleashed forces that upset the internal political situation in several states. The war itself was in some respects less important than the political consequences that flowed from it.

THE CRIMEAN WAR

The Crimean War (1854–1856), named after the Black Sea peninsula on which it was largely fought, originated from a long-standing rivalry between Russia and the Ottoman Empire over the Ottoman provinces of Moldavia and Walachia (now in Romania). In 1853 Russia went to war against the Ottomans on a pretext. The next year France and Great Britain supported the Ottoman Empire to protect their interests in the eastern Mediterranean, while Austria and Prussia remained neutral. The war bogged down after the French and the British invaded the Crimea. In March 1856 a peace conference in Paris concluded a treaty highly unfavorable to Russia.

The Crimean War shattered the image of Russian invincibility that had prevailed since the close of the Napoleonic wars. It also shattered the power of the Concert of Europe to settle international disputes on the Continent. The major European powers were no longer willing to cooperate to maintain the existing borders between themselves and their neighbors. For the next twenty-five years instability prevailed in European affairs, allowing a largely unchecked adventurism in foreign policy.

ITALIAN UNIFICATION

Italian nationalists had long wanted to unite the small absolutist principalities of the peninsula into a single state but could not agree on how to do it. Romantic republicans such as Giuseppe Mazzini (1805–1872) and Giuseppe Garibaldi (1807–1882) sought to drive out the Austrians by popular military force and then to establish a republic. They not only failed but also frightened more moderate Italians. The person who eventually achieved unification was Count Camillo Cavour (1810–1861), the prime minister of Piedmont.

Piedmont (officially the "Kingdom of Sardinia"), in northwestern Italy, was the most independent state on the peninsula. It had unsuccessfully fought against Austria in 1848 and 1849. Following the second defeat, King Charles Albert (r. 1831–1849) abdicated in favor of his son, Victor Emmanuel II (r. 1849–1878). In 1852 the new monarch chose Cavour—a moderate liberal in economics and a strong monarchist who rejected republicanism—as his prime minister.

Cavour believed that if Italians proved themselves to be efficient and economically progressive, the great powers might decide that Italy could govern itself. He worked for free trade, railway construction, credit expansion, and agricultural improvement. He also fostered the Nationalist Society, which established chapters in other Italian states to press for unification under the leadership of Piedmont. Cavour joined the French and British side in the Crimean War because he wanted French help with unification. France's Napoleon III (r. 1852–1870) was sympathetic, and in 1858 Cavour and the French emperor plotted to start a war with Austria.

In April 1859 war erupted between Piedmont and Austria, and France came to Piedmont's aid. But Napoleon III did not want too extensive a Piedmontese victory, so after the Austrians had lost a few battles he concluded a separate peace with Austria. Piedmont received Lombardy, but the Veneto

CHRONOLOGY

GERMAN AND ITALIAN UNIFICATION

Year	Date	Event
1854		Crimean War begins
1855		Cavour leads Piedmont into war on side of France and England
1856		Treaty of Paris concludes Crimean War
1858		Secret conference between Louis Napoleon and Cavour
1859		War of Piedmont and France against Austria
1860		Garibaldi lands his forces in Sicily and conquers southern Italy
1861	March 17	Proclamation of the Kingdom of Italy
	June 6	Death of Cavour
1862		Bismarck becomes prime minister of Prussia
1864		Danish War
1866		Austro-Prussian War; Veneto ceded to Italy
1867		North German Confederation formed
1870	June 6–July 12	Crisis over Hohenzollern candidacy for the Spanish throne
	July 13	Bismarck publishes misleading press dispatch
	July 19	France declares war on Prussia
	September 1	France defeated at Sedan and Napoleon III captured
	September 4	French Republic proclaimed
	October 2	Italian state annexes Rome
1871	January 18	Proclamation of the German Empire at Versailles
	March 18–May 28	Paris Commune
	May 10	Treaty of Frankfurt between France and Germany

remained under Austrian control. Cavour felt betrayed by France, but nonetheless the war had driven Austria from most of northern Italy. Later that summer Parma, Modena, Tuscany, and the Romagna voted to unite with Piedmont.

Soon the forces of romantic republican nationalism compelled Cavour to pursue the complete unification of Italy. In May 1860 Garibaldi began a successful unification campaign in the south. To forestall a republican victory Cavour rushed troops south to confront Garibaldi. On the way Cavour's troops conquered the Papal States except for the area around Rome, which remained under the direct control of the pope.

Garibaldi's nationalism won out over his republicanism, and he unhappily accepted the Piedmontese domination. In late 1860 Naples and Sicily voted to join the northern union forged by Piedmont. In March 1861 Victor Emmanuel II was proclaimed king of Italy. Three months later Cavour died. The new state was governed by the conservative constitution promulgated in 1848 by Charles Albert. Italy gained the Veneto in 1866 as a result of the war between Austria and Prussia, and Rome in 1870 as a result of the Franco-Prussian War.

GERMAN UNIFICATION

kleindeutsch Meaning "small German." The argument that the German-speaking portions of the Habsburg Empire should be excluded from a united Germany.

The unification of Germany was the single most important political development in Europe between 1848 and 1914. It was spearheaded by Prussia's conservative army, monarch, and prime minister, who outflanked the kingdom's liberals.

William I's (r. 1861–1888) primary concern was the Prussian army. In 1860, his war minister and chief of staff proposed enlarging the army and increasing the service of conscripts from two to three years, but the liberal-dominated parliament refused to approve the necessary taxes. A two-year deadlock ensued.

In September 1862 William I turned for help to Otto von Bismarck (1815–1898), the person who did more than anyone else to shape the next thirty years of European history. Bismarck came from Junker stock, and he held traditional Prussian values: admiration for the monarchy, the nobility, and the army. After being appointed prime minister and foreign minister in 1862, Bismarck contended that further parliamentary votes on taxes were not required, since the Prussian constitution permitted the government to function on the basis of taxes that had already been approved. The army and most of the bureaucracy backed his interpretation of the constitution, but new elections in 1863 sustained the liberal majority in the parliament. Bismarck sought a cause that would draw popular support away from the liberals and toward the monarchy and the army. He used foreign affairs to divert public attention from domestic matters by having Prussia assume leadership of the effort to unify Germany.

Creating Nations. The proclamation of the German Empire in the Hall of Mirrors at Versailles, January 18, 1871, after the defeat of France in the Franco-Prussian War. Kaiser Wilhelm I is standing at the top of the steps under the flags; Otto von Bismarck is in the center in a white uniform. The new nation possessed enormous economic resources and nationalistic ambitions.

What was the significance of German unification?

Bismarck favored what was known as the **kleindeutsch** ("small German") solution to unification. It excluded Austria. To promote his plan, he fought two brief wars. In 1864, he went to war with Denmark over the status of the duchies of Schleswig and Holstein, German-speaking areas that had long been administered by the Danish monarchy. The Austrians helped defeat Denmark and joined Prussia in jointly administering the two duchies. Bismarck then made alliances with France and Italy against Austria, and in the summer of 1866, decisively defeated Austria in the Seven Weeks' War. The consequent Treaty of Prague excluded the Habsburgs from German affairs and left Prussia the only major power among the German states.

In 1867 Hanover, Hesse, Nassau, and the city of Frankfurt, all of which had supported Austria during the war, were annexed by Prussia and their rulers deposed. Prussia and these newly incorporated territories, plus Schleswig and Holstein and the rest of the German states north of the Main River, constituted the North German Confederation. Prussia was its undisputed leader.

THE FRANCO-PRUSSIAN WAR AND THE GERMAN EMPIRE

Bismarck looked for an opportunity to bring the states of southern Germany into the confederation. It appeared as a result of complex diplomacy surrounding the possibility of a cousin of William I of Prussia becoming king of Spain. France was, of course, opposed to the idea of a second state on its borders ruled by a Hohenzollern. Bismarck goaded the French into war by tricking them into believing that William I had insulted the French ambassador. Napoleon III hoped that victory would give his regime a new and stronger popular base. Once the war began, the states of southern Germany supported Prussia. On September 1, 1870, the Germans defeated the French army and captured Napoleon III. Paris was besieged, and it capitulated on January 28, 1871. Ten days earlier, in the Hall of Mirrors at the Palace of Versailles, the German Empire had been proclaimed. The rulers of the states of southern Germany had requested that William I accept the imperial title—allowing them to retain their kingly titles and thrones.

The unification of Germany established a strong, coherent state in the middle of Europe. It had been forged by the Prussian army and monarchy and would be dominated by Prussian institutions. It possessed enormous economic resources and nationalistic ambitions. For some, the unification of Italy and Germany showed that nationalistic aspirations could only be fulfilled by armed force. France, in the wake of its defeat by Prussia, again became a republic—the Third Republic—governed by a chamber of deputies, a senate, and a president.

UNREST OF NATIONALITIES IN EASTERN EUROPE

In an age increasingly characterized by national states, liberal institutions, and industrialism, the Habsburg domains remained dynastic, absolutist, and agrarian. Following the revolutions of 1848, Emperor Francis Joseph (r. 1848–1916) and his ministers attempted to impose a centralized administration on the multinational empire. The system amounted to a military and bureaucratic government dominated by German-speaking Austrians. This particularly annoyed the Hungarians. Austria's shrinking power compelled Francis Joseph to come to terms with the Hungarian nobility. The **Ausgleich** (Compromise) of 1867 transformed the Habsburg Empire into a dual monarchy. Francis Joseph was crowned king of Hungary in Budapest. Except for the common monarch, foreign policy, and army, Austria and Hungary functioned largely as separate states (see Map 24–4).

Czechs, Romanians, Serbo-Croatians, and other national groups within the empire opposed the compromise because it permitted the German-speaking Austrians and the Hungarian Magyars to dominate all other nationalities. The Czechs of Bohemia were the most vocal group. For more than twenty years, they were conciliated by generous Austrian patronage and posts in the bureaucracy, but by the turn of the century they were becoming restive. They and German-speaking groups in the Austrian Reichsrat disrupted the Parliament rather than permit a compromise on language issues. This ended constitutional government, for the emperor ruled thereafter by imperial decree with the support of the bureaucracy. Constitutionalism survived in Hungary only because the Magyars used it to dominate competing national groups.

Nationalist unrest within the Habsburg Empire constituted one of the major sources of political instability for all of central and eastern Europe. Virtually all the nationality problems had a foreign policy as well as a domestic political dimension. Both the Serbo-Croatians and the Poles believed they deserved a wholly independent state in union with their fellow nationals who lived outside the empire. Ukrainians, Romanians, and Bosnians saw themselves as potentially linked to Russia, Romania,

HOW DID nationalism affect the Habsburg Empire?

Ausgleich Meaning "compromise." The agreement between the Habsburg Emperor and the Hungarians to give Hungary considerable administrative autonomy in 1867. It created the Dual Monarchy, or Austria-Hungary.

MAP 24–4　Nationalities Within the Habsburg Empire. The patchwork appearance reflects the unusual problem of the numerous ethnic groups that the Habsburgs could not, of course, meld into a modern national state. Only the Magyars were recognized in 1867, leaving nationalist Czechs, Slovaks, and the others chronically dissatisfied.

How did the Compromise of 1867 affect the Habsburg Empire?

racism The pseudoscientific theory that biological features of race determine human character and worth.

QUICK REVIEW

Nationalist Unrest

◆ Significant impact on German, Russian, and Austrian Empires

◆ Hungarian Magyars won significant rights

◆ Many Slavic groups oriented toward Russia

◆ Destabilizing influence; led to World War I

Serbia, or a larger, yet-to-be-established Slavic state. Many nationalities looked to Russia for protection, contributing to the tensions that would spark World War I. The dominant German population of Austria proper was generally loyal to the emperor. However, a significant segment was strongly nationalistic and yearned to be part of the united German state being established by Bismarck. These nationalistic Germans in the Austrian Empire often hated the non-German national groups, particularly the Jews. These attitudes influenced Adolf Hitler (1889–1945) in his youth, shaping his political opinions.

　　Each of the three great central and eastern European empires—German, Russian, and Austrian—was touched by nationality problems from the 1860s through the outbreak of World War I. All had Polish populations. Each shared at least two other major national groups. Each nationality regarded its own aspirations and discontents as more important than the larger good. The government of each empire would be overturned during the war, and the Austrian Empire would disappear. The same unresolved problems of central and eastern European nationalism would then lead directly to World War II. During more recent years, they have led to civil war in what was formerly Yugoslavia and to the breakup of what used to be called Czechoslovakia.

HOW DID racial theory influence anti-Semitism?

RACIAL THEORY AND ANTI-SEMITISM

Racial thinking, or **racism**, had long existed in Europe, but articulated racial theory constituted a new component of late-century nationalistic unrest. Late eighteenth-century linguistic scholars, who had observed similarities between many of the European languages and Sanskrit, had postulated the existence of an ancient race called the Aryans, speakers of the original language from which the rest derived. During the Romantic period, writers had called the different cultures of Europe *races*. The debates over slavery in the European colonies and the United States had spurred the development of racial theory. In the late nineteenth century the concept of race emerged as a single dominant explanation of the history and the character of large groups of people.

Arthur de Gobineau (1816–1882), a reactionary French diplomat, theorized that race was the major determinant of human history. In his four-volume *Essay on the Inequality of the Human Races* (1853–1854) Gobineau portrayed the troubles of Western civilization as being the result of the long degeneration of the original white Aryan race, caused by unwise intermarriage with inferior races. Gobineau saw no way to reverse this degeneration.

Houston Stewart Chamberlain (1855–1927), an Englishman who settled in Germany, put racial theory on an alleged scientific basis in his widely read two-volume work entitled *Foundations of the Nineteenth Century* (1899). He championed the concept of biological determinism through race. Using contemporary genetic theory, Chamberlain argued in opposition to Gobineau that the human race could be improved and that a superior race could be developed. He pointed to the Jews as the major obstacle to European racial regeneration. Chamberlain's book and others claiming that Jews threatened traditional German national life aided the spread of **anti-Semitism**.

ANTI-SEMITISM AND THE BIRTH OF ZIONISM

Political and racial anti-Semitism, which cast such dark shadows across the twentieth century, emerged in part from this atmosphere of racial thought. Religious anti-Semitism dated from at least the Middle Ages, but following the French Revolution, western European Jews had gradually gained entry into civil society in Austria, Britain, France, and Germany. Popular anti-Semitism, which identified the Jewish community with money and banking interests, persisted. Racial thought contributed to anti-Semitism the belief that no matter how well Jews assimilated, the problem of race was not in their behavior but in their blood. In Austria, France, and Germany various political leaders and parties used their anti-Semitism to considerable political advantage.

An important Jewish response to this new, rabid anti-Semitism was the launching in 1896 of the Zionist movement to found a separate Jewish state. Its founder was the Austro-Hungarian Theodor Herzl (1860–1904). The advance of political anti-Semitism, especially in Austria and France, as well as Herzl's personal experiences of discrimination, convinced him that the institutions of the liberal state could not protect the Jews in Europe. In 1896 Herzl published *The Jewish State*, calling for a separate state in which the Jews of the world might be assured of those rights and liberties that they should be enjoying in the liberal states of Europe. Herzl followed the tactics of late-century mass democratic politics by directing his appeal in particular to the economically poor Jews who lived in the ghettos of eastern Europe and the slums of western Europe. The original call to **Zionism** thus combined a rejection of the anti-Semitism of Europe with a desire to establish some of the ideals of both liberalism and socialism in a state outside Europe.

Racial thinking and revived anti-Semitism were part of a wider late-century aggressive nationalism. Previously, nationalism had been a literary and liberal movement. From the 1870s onward, however, nationalism became a movement with mass support, well-financed organizations, and political parties. Nationality was redefined in terms of race and blood. The new nationalism opposed the internationalism of both liberalism and socialism; it was used to overcome the pluralism of class, religion, and geography. The nation and its duties could become a secular religion, for example, in the hands of state schoolteachers, who were replacing the clergy as the instructors of youth. This aggressive, racist nationalism would prove to be the most powerful ideology of the early twentieth century.

Revolutionary. In 1848, Ana Ipatescu helped to lead Transylvanian revolutionaries against Russian rule. (Transylvania is part of present-day Romania.) The revolutions of 1848 in eastern Europe were primarily the rising of nationalist or liberal groups. Although generally repressed in the revolutions of that year, subject nationalities would prove a source of political upheaval and unrest in the region throughout the rest of the century, ultimately providing the spark for the outbreak of World War I.

Where was nationalist unrest most prevalent?

anti-Semitism Prejudice, hostility, or legal discrimination against Jews.

Zionism The movement to create a Jewish state in Palestine (the Biblical Zion).

Theodor Herzl. Herzl's visions of a Jewish state would eventually lead to the creation of Israel in 1948.

Why did anti-Semitism become more virulent in the nineteenth century?

SUMMARY

WHAT IS nationalism?

The Emergence of Nationalism in Europe. Nationalism is the modern concept that people who share the same customs, culture, language, and history should also share the same government. It became the most powerful European political ideology of the nineteenth and early twentieth centuries. Nationalists challenged both the domestic and the international order of the Vienna settlement in the decades after 1815. *page 589*

WHAT WERE the basic goals of European liberals?

Early-Nineteenth-Century Political Liberalism. Politically, nineteenth-century liberals sought to establish constitutional governments that recognized civil liberties and made the executive responsible to a legislature elected by men of wealth and property. Economically, liberals wanted a laissez-faire economy with minimal government involvement. Liberals often supported nationalists' efforts to create a single national state that could function as a more efficient economic unit. *page 592*

WHY WERE efforts to achieve political liberalism more successful in France and Britain than in Russia?

Efforts to Liberalize Early-Nineteenth-Century European Political Structures. Efforts to liberalize tsarist Russia failed, particularly after the ultra-conservative Tsar Nicholas fired on his own officers during the 1825 Decembrist Revolt. Liberalism largely triumphed in France after the Revolution of 1830 and in Britain after the passage of the Great Reform Bill. The British were, however, unable to resolve the problem of Irish nationalism in the nineteenth century. *page 594*

WHAT WERE the causes of the American Civil War?

Testing the New American Republic. In the United States, westward expansion and war against Mexico brought vast new territories under the republic from the Mississippi River to the Pacific, but sectional conflict between North and South over economic issues and slavery led to the outbreak of the Civil War in 1861. Northern victory led to the abolition of slavery, the creation of a continent-wide free labor market, and enormous economic development. *page 599*

HOW DID Canada achieve united self-government?

The Canadian Experience. Canada achieved self-government with the Canada Act of 1840, and created a united Canadian federation in 1867. However, Canada remained part of the British Empire and retained its connection with the British monarchy. Anglo-French tension is a recurring theme in Canadian history, but legislative tradeoffs and the federation's de-emphasis on states' rights have maintained Canadian unity. *page 603*

WHAT WERE the steps that led to Italian and German unification?

Midcentury Political Consolidation in Europe. With French assistance, Piedmont under Count Camillo Cavour managed to unite most of the peninsula in the Kingdom of Italy by 1860. German unification was achieved by Prussia under the leadership of Otto von Bismarck between 1864 and 1871. In three victorious wars against Denmark, Austria, and France, Bismarck forged the German states into a German Empire dominated by Prussia. *page 604*

HOW DID nationalism affect the Habsburg Empire?

Unrest of Nationalities in Eastern Europe. Nationalism created problems for the three eastern European empires: Germany, Russia, and Austria, but Habsburg Austria faced the greatest challenge from nationalism because it was a dynastic, not a national, state. In 1867 Hungary became an autonomous kingdom under the Habsburg emperor. Czechs, Croats, and other Slavs in the empire became increasingly dissatisfied. *page 607*

HOW DID racial theory influence anti-Semitism?

Racial Theory and Anti-Semitism. In the late nineteenth century, biological determinism, the concept that some peoples or races were inherently superior to others, took root in Western thought. In Germany, Austria, and France, some nationalists used the concept of race to blame the Jews for their countries' economic and political problems. Part of the Jewish response was the launching of the Zionist movement to found a separate Jewish state. *page 608*

REVIEW QUESTIONS

1. Define *nationalism*. What were the goals of nationalists? What were the difficulties they confronted in realizing those goals? Why was nationalism a special threat to the Austrian Empire? What areas saw significant nationalist movements between 1815 and 1830? Which were successful and which were unsuccessful?

2. What were the tenets of liberalism? Who were the liberals and how did liberalism affect the political developments of the early nineteenth century? What relationship does liberalism have to nationalism?

3. Compare and contrast the movement toward political liberalism between 1815 and 1830 in Russia, France, and Great Britain.

4. What economic differences between the American North and South gave rise to sectional conflict? Why was slavery the core issue in that conflict? How did westward expansion contribute to making slavery such an important issue?

5. How did Canada unify and become self-governing?

6. What is the significance of the Crimean War? How did it impact Russia? Why did the Crimean War have a destabilizing effect on Europe?

7. Why was it so difficult to unify Italy? What were the contributions of Mazzini, Cavour, and Garibaldi to Italian unification?

8. Who was Otto von Bismarck, and why did he try to unify Germany? What was Bismarck's method of unification, and why did he succeed? What effect did the unification of Germany have on the rest of Europe?

9. How did British politicians handle the Irish Question? What were the parallels between England's relationship with Ireland and the nationality problem of the Austrian Empire?

10. What were the origins of the modern idea of racial theory? Who were its major proponents? How did the rise of such a theory change European anti-Semitism?

KEY TERMS

anti-Semitism (p. 609)
Ausgleich (OWS-gleyek) (p. 607)
Catholic emancipation (p. 596)
Chartism (p. 597)
Great Reform Bill (p. 595)
home rule (p. 597)

July Monarchy (p. 595)
kleindeutsch (KLEYEN-doytch) (p. 606)
liberalism (p. 592)
nationalism (p. 589)
racism (p. 608)
Zionism (ZEYE-ahn-izm) (p. 608)

Note: To learn more about the topics in this chapter, please turn to the Suggested Readings at the end of the book.

INTERPRETING THE PAST

The Meaning and Purpose of the Nation

Source from MyHistoryLab for Chapter 24

myhistorylab

1) Samuel Smiles, Excerpt from *Self Help*

Source from for Chapter 24

1) *Mazzini Defines Nationality* (p. 590)

As the most potent and influential political ideology in Europe during the nineteenth and much of the twentieth centuries, nationalism helped unify previously disparate peoples and offered new possibilities for the development of democratic governments. The concept that people with shared language, customs, and culture should share the same government lay at the core of nationalism. It directly contradicted the traditional role of monarchies and family dynasties.

In this exercise, you will read documents that spotlight views on the meaning and purpose of the nation, both for the individual within the nation and for the larger world of which the nation is a part. The perspectives vary from the "liberal nationalist" Giuseppe Mazzini, to the motivational directives of Scottish writer Samuel Smiles.

The first document is a definition of nationalism by Mazzini, a philosopher and politician who was one of the founders of the modern Italian state. The second source is an excerpt from Smiles's most famous book, *Self Help, with Illustrations of Character and Conduct*. Smiles emphasized the potential power of the individual, but here he also asserted that the virtues of a nation are the virtues of its individual citizens, magnified.

Use the source documents to analyze and compare perspectives regarding the meaning and purpose of the nation and to answer the following questions. Use specific examples from the documents to back up your assertions.

Questions

What qualities does Giuseppe Mazzini attribute to nationalism? What kind of justification does he offer for his positive endorsement of this ideology?

What does Smiles see as the proper relationship between the individual and the nation? Does he assume that the reader already shares his point of view? What do you think are the strengths and weaknesses of Smiles's argument?

Based on the information in these documents, on what points do Mazzini and Smiles agree? About what do they differ?

25

Northern Transatlantic Economy and Society, 1815–1914

Russian Society. A detail from *the Parade on Tsarina's Meadow* by G. G. Chernetson, 1831. Tsarina's Meadow was a vast space outside St. Petersburg that often held military parades and reviews in nineteenth-century Russia. The different classes and ethnic groups of the Russian empire can be seen mingling about.

How do the different clothing styles worn by the people in this painting comment on Russian society during this time?

EUROPEAN FACTORY WORKERS AND URBAN ARTISANS *Page 615*

WHAT IS *proletarianization?*

NINETEENTH-CENTURY EUROPEAN WOMEN *Page 617*

WHAT SOCIAL and legal disabilities did European women confront in the nineteenth century?

JEWISH EMANCIPATION *Page 622*

HOW DID emancipation affect Jewish life in Europe outside of Russia?

EUROPEAN LABOR, SOCIALISM, AND POLITICS TO WORLD WAR I *Page 623*

WHY DID Marxism become so influential among European socialists?

NORTH AMERICA AND THE NEW INDUSTRIAL ECONOMY *Page 628*

HOW DID industrialization in the United States differ from industrialization in Europe?

THE EMERGENCE OF MODERN EUROPEAN THOUGHT *Page 633*

WHO WERE some of the intellectuals at the forefront of modern European thought?

ISLAM AND LATE-NINETEENTH-CENTURY EUROPEAN THOUGHT *Page 637*

WHAT WERE some influential views on the relationship between Islam and the West?

GLOBAL PERSPECTIVE

THE BUILDING OF NORTHERN TRANSATLANTIC SUPREMACY

Between 1850 and 1914 Europe had more influence throughout the world than it had before or has had since. Although Europe and North America together were the most industrially advanced regions of the world, the preponderance of economic power lay with Europe. Its industrial base was more advanced than that of any other region, including the still-developing United States. European banks exercised vast influence across the globe. Europeans financed the building of railways in Africa, Asia, and the Americas. Financial power brought political influence. The armaments industry gave European armies and navies predominant power over the peoples of Africa and Asia, whereas the United States began to exercise such power only as a result of the Spanish-American War. These economic developments established a pattern that still persists. First European, and later American, banks, companies, and corporations penetrated the economies and societies of Asia, Africa, and Latin America. These nonpolitical groups often expected their own governments to protect their interests. Thus, what started as commercial contact often evolved into the exercise of direct political influence even over nations that had never been European colonies.

During these years European culture was probably also enjoying its greatest influence. Capital cities in Latin America, especially Buenos Aires and Montevideo, adopted European-style architecture. Paris became synonymous with high fashion. Paris, London, and Vienna were world intellectual centers. The rest of the world regarded the advanced industrial and urban civilization of Europe as a model, in part because more non-Europeans were visiting and studying in Europe than ever before. During this period many American artists and writers flocked to Europe to absorb its culture. Another cultural feature of western Europe and the United States that affected the rest of the world during the era was the emerging role of women. In particular, the demand for the entrance of women into the political process and the professions became a hallmark of the twentieth century. On both sides of the Atlantic, women assumed leadership roles in social reform movements.

The nation that most clearly understood the nature of European power and sought to imitate it was Japan. After the Meiji Restoration (1868), Japanese administrators came to Europe to study the new technology, political structures, and military organizations. The Japanese political and military reorganization that resulted proved sufficiently successful to allow them to defeat Russia in 1905, providing the first example of a non-European nation using Western weapons, organizations,

 During the nineteenth century, northwestern Europe and the United States developed major industrial economies, which produced unprecedented levels of goods and services. This economic achievement undergirded the enormous international political power exerted by the industrial nations of the West from that time to the present.

In the first half of the nineteenth century, a new kind of industrial labor force emerged, especially in Europe. These laborers worked in factories and generally lived in cities. The presence and growth of this new labor force were the most important social developments of the century. It was out of the experiences of this workforce that the political movement known as socialism arose.

In the second half of the nineteenth century European and American political, economic, and social life assumed many characteristics of our present-day world. In Europe nation-states with large electorates, political parties, centralized bureaucracies, and universal military service emerged. In the United States the politics associated with the Progressive movement brought the presidency to the center of American political life. On both sides of the North Atlantic, business adopted large-scale corporate structures, and the labor force organized itself into trade unions. The number of white-collar laborers grew and urban life became predominant throughout western Europe. But even as new vast cities arose in the United States, farming continued to spread across the central Midwest and upper Southwest. During this period, too, women began to assert new political awareness and to become politically active in both Europe and America.

Europe grew dependent on the resources and markets of the rest of the world. Farms in the United States, Canada, Latin America, Australia, and New Zealand supplied food to much of and economic power to defeat a European nation. In the twentieth century other non-European nations found ways to import or manufacture technology that permitted them to challenge European and later American hegemony. Indeed, today the proliferation of weaponry usually developed in the United States or Europe has allowed regional powers to challenge Western dominance. This destabilizing arms trade began in the second half of the nineteenth century.

In contrast to Japan, China, India, the countries of the Middle East, and Africa were overwhelmed by the economic and military power of Europe. In time, however, the peoples of those lands under European domination embraced the ideologies of revolutionary protest, most particularly those of nationalism and socialism. As people from the colonial world came to work or study in Europe, they encountered ideas and criticisms that were most effective against European and Western culture. They adapted those ideas to their own cultural contexts and then turned them against their colonial governors.

Europeans eventually turned their military power against each other in 1914. World War I destroyed the late-nineteenth-century European self-confidence. At home, the Bolsheviks brought revolution to Russia. Abroad after the war, anticolonial movements began to grow, especially in India, in a manner that most Europeans in 1900 could not have imagined. In turn, those movements found many sympathetic supporters in Europe as a result of the spread of ideas regarding social justice and public policy. Furthermore, because the political and economic systems of the world had become so interconnected during the second half of the nineteenth century, the influence and impact of the European conflict could not be limited to Europe. The United States was drawn into World War I and was never again able to avoid worldwide responsibilities.

Focus Questions

◆ What was the relationship between nineteenth-century Europe's economic power and its political hegemony around the globe?

◆ How did European colonies use ideologies fostered in Europe against their colonial rulers?

the world. Before World War I this dependence was concealed by Europe's industrial, military, and financial supremacy. Europeans assumed their supremacy to be natural, but the twentieth century would reveal it to have been temporary. While it prevailed, Europeans dominated most of the other peoples of the earth and displayed extreme self-confidence. The United States, having achieved the status of a major industrial power as well as an agricultural supplier, entered the world stage as a military power, defeating Spain in the Spanish-American War in 1898. With that victory, the United States also acquired its first colonial territories.

At the same time, major new sets of ideas arose. Theories of evolution in biology, relativity in physics, the irrational in philosophy, and psychoanalysis in psychology shaped much of the intellectual outlook for the next century. ■

EUROPEAN FACTORY WORKERS AND URBAN ARTISANS

Industrial production had begun in the eighteenth century, and in the nineteenth century much of Europe headed toward a more fully industrial society. By 1830 only Great Britain had attained that status, but new factories and railways were being constructed elsewhere. What characterized the second quarter of the century, though, was less the triumph of industrialism than the final gasps of those economic groups that opposed it and were displaced by it. Intellectually, the period saw the formulation of the major creeds supporting and criticizing the new society.

WHAT IS *proletarianization?*

proletarianization   The process whereby independent artisans and factory workers lose control of the means of production and of the conduct of their own trades to the owners of capital.

QUICK REVIEW

Factory Work

◆ Proletarianization: loss of ownership of the means of production

◆ Factory work demanded submission to a new kind of work discipline

◆ Factory workers were better off than the hand-loom workers who competed with them

Il Quarto Stato (The Fourth Estate), 1901.   Giuseppe Pellizza da Volpedo (1868–1907) was a powerfully committed Italian socialist artist. The title of his painting is taken from the French socialist Jean Jaurès, who believed that workers would soon displace the traditional three estates of the clergy, aristocracy, and commoners. Pellizza and other artists embracing social realism moved painting away from nostalgic, sentimental depictions of peasants to images of industrial or farm laborers experiencing hunger, poverty, and awakening political consciousness.

Oil on canvas, 283 cm × 550 cm. Civica Galleria d'Arte Moderna-Milano. Photo by Marcello Saporetti.

What is the significance of the woman carrying the baby?

QUICK REVIEW

Improved Conditions in Cities

◆ Cholera epidemics spurred action

◆ New awareness of the value of modern water and sewer systems

◆ Expanded involvement of government in public health

The specter of poor harvests still haunted Europe. The worst was the failure of potato crops that produced the Irish famine from 1845 to 1847. Half a million Irish peasants starved to death; hundreds of thousands emigrated. All over Europe there was a vast uprooting of people from the countryside as the revolution in landholding led to greater agricultural production.

In northern Europe both artisans and factory workers underwent a process of **proletarianization**, meaning they entered into a wage economy and lost significant ownership of the means of production, such as tools and equipment, and control over the conduct of their own trades. The process occurred rapidly wherever the factory system arose. The factory owner provided the financial capital to construct the factory, purchase the machinery, and secure the raw materials. The factory workers contributed their labor for a wage. Those workers submitted to factory discipline, which meant that work conditions became largely determined by the demands for smooth operation of the machines. Factory workers had no direct say over the quality of the product or its price. (It should be noted that factory conditions were often better than those of textile workers who resisted the factory mode of production.)

Urban artisans in the nineteenth century experienced proletarianization more slowly than factory workers, and machinery had little to do with the process. The emergence of factories in itself did not harm urban artisans. Many even prospered. Metal workers and craftsmen in the building trades, for example, saw increased demand for their work. The lower prices for machine-made textiles aided artisans involved in the making of clothing by reducing the costs of their raw materials. Where the urban artisans encountered difficulty and found their skills and livelihood threatened was in the organization of production.

In the eighteenth century a European town or city workplace had usually consisted of a few artisans laboring for a master, first as apprentices and then as journeymen, according to established guild practices. The master owned the workshop and the larger equipment, and the others owned their tools. The journeyman could expect to become a master. This guild system had allowed considerable worker control over labor recruitment and training, production pace, product quality, and price. In the nineteenth century, political and economic liberals disapproved of labor and guild organizations and attempted to make them illegal.

There were other changes in the organization of artisan production. Masters often found themselves under increased competitive pressure from larger establishments. Many masters began to follow a practice, known in France as *confection*, whereby goods such as shoes, clothing, and furniture were produced in standard sizes and styles rather than by individual order. This practice increased the division of labor in the workshop, so less skill was required of each artisan and the particular skills possessed by a worker became less valuable. Migrants from the countryside sometimes created a surplus of relatively unskilled workers. The dilution of skills and lower wages made it more difficult for urban journeymen to become masters with their own workshops. Increasingly, artisans became lifetime wage laborers.

In the United States defenders of slavery frequently compared what they claimed to be the protected situation of slaves with the plight of factory workers. They argued that a free market in wage labor left workers worse off than slaves.

OVERVIEW Major European Cities, 1850–1914

	1850	1880	1914
Berlin	419,000	1,122,000	2,071,000
Birmingham	233,000	437,000	840,000
Frankfurt	65,000	137,000	415,000
London	2,685,000	4,470,000	7,256,000
Madrid	281,000	398,000	600,000
Paris	1,053,000	2,269,000	2,888,000
Vienna	444,000	1,104,000	2,031,000

NINETEENTH-CENTURY EUROPEAN WOMEN

WOMEN IN THE EARLY INDUSTRIAL REVOLUTION

WHAT SOCIAL and legal disabilities did European women confront in the nineteenth century?

The industrial economy had an immense impact on the home and the family life of women. First, it took virtually all productive work out of the home and allowed many families to live on the wages of the male spouse alone. This allowed a new concept of gender-determined roles. Women came to be associated with domestic duties and men almost exclusively with breadwinning. Children were reared to match these gender patterns. Previously, this domestic division of labor had prevailed only among the relatively small middle and gentry classes. Second, industrialization created new modes of employment that allowed many young women to earn enough money to marry or, if necessary, to support themselves independently. Third, industrialism, although fostering more employment for women, lowered the skills required of them.

The early Industrial Revolution began in textile production, so women and their labor were deeply involved from the start. When spinning and weaving had been domestic industries, women worked in all stages of production. When these activities moved into factories and involved large machines, however, men displaced women. With the next generation of machines in the 1820s, unmarried women rapidly became employed in the factories. However, their jobs tended to require few skills. There was thus a certain paradox in the impact of the factory on women: New jobs opened to them, but those jobs were less skilled than those that had been available to them before. Women in the factories were almost always young and single or widows. Factory owners disliked employing married women because of the likelihood of pregnancy, the influence of husbands, and the duties of child rearing.

At midcentury, industrial factory work accounted for less than half of all employment for women. The largest group of employed women in France continued to work on the land. In England they were domestic servants. Domestic industries, such as garment making, employed many women. The charwoman was a common sight across the Continent. Women's conditions of labor were almost always harsh, wherever they worked, and they were vulnerable to exploitation. Women's employment was insecure, and much of it was seasonal. Many working-class women feared they might be compelled to turn to prostitution.

Cities and the more complex economy did allow a greater variety of jobs. Movement to cities and entrance into the wage economy gave women wider opportunities for

QUICK REVIEW

Women's Work

◆ Women involved in preindustrial textile production

◆ In the 1820s, unmarried women found employment in textile factories

◆ In mid-nineteenth-century England the largest group of employed women was domestic servants

Women in Textile Factories.   As textile production became increasingly automated in the nineteenth century, textile factories required fewer skilled workers and more unskilled attendants. To fill these unskilled positions, factory owners turned increasingly to unmarried women and widows, who worked for lower wages than men and were less likely to form labor organizations. The two women shown here, holding "shuttles" used in textile factories, worked in the Lowell Mills in Massachusetts around 1860.

What do you notice about these women's clothes, hair, shoes, and bodies?

marriage. Cohabitation before marriage seems to have been common. Parents did not arrange marriages as frequently as in the past. Marriage generally meant that a woman would leave the workforce to live on her husband's earnings. If all went well, that arrangement might improve her situation, but if the husband became ill or died, or deserted her, she would have to reenter the market for unskilled labor at an advanced age.

Many traditional practices associated with the family economy survived into the industrial era. As a young woman came of age, family needs and her desire to marry still directed her activities. The most likely early occupation for a young woman was domestic service. A girl born in the country normally migrated to a nearby town or city for such employment, often living initially with a relative. As in the past, she would attempt to earn enough in wages to give herself a dowry. If she became a factory worker, she would probably live in a supervised dormitory. The life of young women in the cities seems to have been more precarious than it had been earlier, with fewer family and community ties, and perhaps more available young men. These men, too, were more mobile, so relationships between men and women were often fleeting. Illegitimate births increased.

The wage industrial economy altered marriage, making it less of an economic partnership: The husband might be able to support the entire family, and it was difficult for women to combine domestic duties with work. When married women worked, it was usually in the nonindustrial sector of the economy. Children rather than women were sent to work, which may help explain the increase of fertility within marriages. Married women worked outside the home only when family needs or illness or the death of a spouse required them to do so.

Within the home, the domestic duties of working-class women were an essential factor in the family wage economy. Wives were primarily concerned with food and cooking, but they often also were in charge of the family's finances. The role of the mother expanded when the children still living at home became wage earners. The longer period of home life of working children may also have strengthened the affection between those children and their mothers.

SOCIAL DISABILITIES CONFRONTED BY ALL WOMEN

During the early nineteenth century, virtually all European women faced social and legal disabilities in property rights, family law, and education. By the close of the century each area had shown improvement. All Europeans led lives that reflected their social rank, yet within each rank, women remained economically dependent and legally inferior to men.

Until late in the nineteenth century in most European countries no married women could own property in their own names. Women's legal identities were subsumed into their husbands', and they had no independent standing before the law. Reform of women's property rights came slowly. By 1882 Great Britain allowed married women to own property in their own right. In France, however, a married woman could not even open a savings account in her own name until 1895, and not until 1907 were married women granted possession of their own wages. In 1900 Germany allowed women to take jobs without their husbands' permission, but a German husband retained control of most of his wife's property except for her wages. Similar laws prevailed elsewhere in Europe.

European family law also worked to the disadvantage of women. Legal codes required wives to obey their husbands. The Napoleonic Code and the remnants of Roman law made women legal minors throughout Europe. Divorce was difficult. Extramarital sexual relations of husbands were more tolerated than those of wives. The authority of husbands also extended to children. A husband could take children away from their mother and give them to someone else to rear. Contraception and abortion were illegal. The law on rape normally worked against women. Wherever they turned—whether to physicians or lawyers—women confronted an official world populated and controlled by men.

Throughout the nineteenth century women had less access to education than did men, and what was available to them was inferior. Most women were educated only enough for the domestic careers they were expected to follow. The percentage of illiterate women exceeded that of men.

University and professional education remained reserved for men until at least the third quarter of the century. Italian universities were more open to both women students and women instructors than similar institutions elsewhere in Europe. Educated, professional men feared the competition of women. Restricting women's access to secondary and university education helped bar women from social and economic advancement. Women would benefit only marginally from the expansion of professional employment that occurred during the late nineteenth and early twentieth centuries. Although a few women did enter the professions, especially medicine, most nations prevented women from becoming lawyers until after World War I.

Schoolteaching at the elementary level became a professional haven for women. The few women who pioneered in the professions were seen as challenging the clear separation of male and female spheres that had emerged during the nineteenth century. Women themselves often hesitated to support feminist causes because they had been so thoroughly acculturated into the recently stereotyped roles.

NEW EMPLOYMENT PATTERNS FOR WOMEN

During the late nineteenth century, two major developments affected the economic lives of women. The first was an expansion in the variety of jobs available outside the better-paying learned professions. The second was a withdrawal of married women from the workforce. These two seemingly contradictory developments require explanation.

The expansion of governmental bureaucracies, the emergence of large-scale businesses, and the expansion of retail stores opened many new employment opportunities for women. The need for elementary schoolteachers grew with compulsory education laws. Innovations such as the typewriter and eventually the telephone exchange fostered female employment. Women by the thousands became secretaries and clerks for governments and private businesses, while others became shop assistants.

Although these jobs did open new and often better employment opportunities for women, they nonetheless required low-level skills and involved

Middle-Class Family. Family was central to the middle-class conception of a stable and respectable social life. This portrait of the Bellelli family is by Edgar Degas. Notice that the husband and father sits at his desk, suggesting his association with business and the world outside the home, whereas the wife and mother stands with their children, suggesting her domestic role.

Edgar Degas (1834–1917), The Bellelli Family, c. 1858–60. Musée d'Orsay, Paris, France. Photo by Erich Lessing. Reunion des Musees Nationaux/Art Resource, N.Y.

How were gender roles established in the nineteenth century?

CHRONOLOGY

MAJOR DATES IN LATE-NINETEENTH-CENTURY AND EARLY-TWENTIETH-CENTURY EUROPEAN WOMEN'S HISTORY

1857	Revised English divorce law
1865	University of Zurich admits women for degrees
1869	John Stuart Mill's *The Subjection of Women*
1878	University of London admits women as candidates for degrees
1882	English Married Woman's Property Act
1894	Union of German Women's Organizations founded
1901	National Council of French Women founded
1903	British Women's Social and Political Union founded
1907	Norway permits women to vote on national issues
1910	British suffragettes adopt radical tactics
1918	Vote extended to some British women
1918	Weimar constitution allows German women to vote
1920–1921	Oxford and Cambridge Universities award degrees to women
1922	French Senate defeats bill extending vote to women
1928	Britain extends vote to women on same basis as men

Women Working at a Telephone Exchange. The invention of the telephone opened new employment opportunities for women.

What made telephone exchanges suitable workplaces for women?

minimal training. They were occupied primarily by unmarried women or widows. Employers continued to pay women low wages because they assumed that a woman did not need to support herself independently.

The industrial occupations that women had filled in the mid-nineteenth century, especially textile and garment making, were shrinking. The decline in the number of births also meant that fewer married women were needed to look after other women's children. The real wages paid to male workers increased during this period, reducing families' need for a second income. Thanks to improving health, men lived longer, so wives were less likely to be thrust into the workforce by an emergency. Smaller families also lowered the need for supplementary wages. Working children stayed at home longer and continued to contribute to the family's wage pool.

Finally, the cultural dominance of the middle class established a pattern of social expectations. The more prosperous a working-class family became, the less involved in employment its women were supposed to be.

LATE-NINETEENTH-CENTURY WORKING-CLASS WOMEN

Women Laundry Workers. Although new opportunities opened to them in the late nineteenth century, many working-class women, like these women ironing in a laundry, remained in traditional occupations. As the wine bottle suggests, alcoholism was a problem for women as well as men engaged in tedious work. The painting is by Edgar Degas (1834–1917).

Réunion des Musées Nationaux/Art Resource, N.Y.

Compare this painting with the photograph on page 618. What is similar? What is different?

Although less dominant than earlier in the century, the textile industry and garment making continued to employ many women. The German clothing-making trades illustrate women's vulnerable economic situations. The manufacture of mass-made clothes in Germany was designed to require minimal capital investment. A major manufacturer would arrange to produce clothing through a putting-out system: He would purchase the material and then put it out for tailoring. The clothing was made in independently owned, small sweatshops or by workers in their homes.

In Berlin in 1896 there were more than eighty thousand garment workers, mostly women. When business was good, employment for these women was high. If business became poor, however, women were idled. In effect, the workers who actually sewed the clothing carried much of the risk of the enterprise. Even women in factories were subject to layoffs. Women were nearly always treated as casual workers.

THE RISE OF POLITICAL FEMINISM

Liberal society and its values neither automatically nor inevitably improved the lot of women. In particular, it did not give them the vote or access to political activity. Male liberals feared that granting the vote to women would benefit political conservatives because women were thought to be unduly controlled by the clergy. Consequently, anticlerical liberals often had difficulty working with feminists.

Women were often reluctant to support feminist causes. Some women considered their class and economic interests higher political priorities. Others subordinated feminist political issues to national unity and nationalistic patriotism. Still others would not support particular feminist organizations because of differences over tactics. Except in England, it was often difficult for working-class and middle-class women to cooperate. Roman Catholic feminists were uncomfortable with radical secularist feminists.

Liberal society and law presented women with many obstacles but also provided feminists with many intellectual and political tools. As early as 1792 in Britain, Mary Wollstonecraft (1759–1797) had applied the revolutionary doctrines of the rights of man to the predicament of women in *The Vindication of the Rights of Women*. John Stuart Mill (1806–1873) and his wife Harriet Taylor (1804–1858) had applied the logic of liberal freedom to the position of women in *The Subjection of Women* (1869). The arguments for utility and efficiency so dear to middle-class liberals could be used to expose the human and social waste implicit in the inferior role assigned to women.

Furthermore, the socialist criticism of capitalist society often included a harsh indictment of the social and economic position to which women had been relegated. The earliest statements of feminism arose from critics of the existing order and were often associated with people who had unorthodox opinions about sexuality, family life, and property. This hardened resistance to the feminist message, especially on the Continent.

These difficulties prevented Continental feminists from raising the kind of massive public support or mounting the large demonstrations that feminists in Great Britain and the United States could. Everywhere in Europe the feminist cause was badly divided over both goals and tactics.

Europe's most advanced women's movement was in Great Britain. Millicent Fawcett (1847–1929) led the moderate National Union of Women's Suffrage Societies. She believed Parliament would grant women the vote only when convinced that women would be responsible in their political activity. In 1908 this organization could rally almost half a million women in London. Her tactics were those of English liberals.

Emmeline Pankhurst (1858–1928) led a much more radical branch of British feminists. She was familiar with the disruptive political tactics used in both labor and Irish nationalist politics. In 1903 Pankhurst and her daughters founded the Women's Social and Political Union. For several years they and their followers, known derisively as **suffragettes**, lobbied for women's suffrage. By 1910 they turned to the violent tactics of arson, window breaking, and sabotage of postal boxes. They marched en masse on Parliament. The Liberal government of Herbert Asquith (1852–1928) imprisoned many of the demonstrators and force-fed those who went on hunger strikes in jail. The government refused to extend the franchise. Only in 1918, and then as a result of their contribution to the war effort, did some British women receive the vote.

The cases of France and Germany show how advanced the British women's movement was. In France, when Hubertine Auclert (1848–1914) began campaigning for the vote in the 1880s, she stood virtually alone. French Roman Catholic feminists, such as Marie Mauguet (1844–1928), supported the franchise. Almost all French feminists rejected violence: They were also never able to organize mass rallies. The leaders of French feminism believed that the vote could be achieved through careful legalism. French women did not receive the right to vote until 1944 at the end of World War II.

Women's Suffrage.   The creator of this poster cleverly reveals the hypocrisy and foolishness of denying the vote to women.

Private collection/Bridgeman Art Library.

How does this poster show the obstacles that stood in the path of women's suffrage?

suffragettes   British women who lobbied and agitated for the right to vote in the early twentieth century.

German law actually forbade German women from political activity. By 1902 the Union of German Women's Organizations (BDFK) was calling for the right to vote, but it was largely concerned with improving women's social conditions, their access to education, and their right to other protections. The German Social Democratic Party also supported women's suffrage, but the party was so disdained by the German authorities and German Roman Catholics that this support only made suffrage more suspect in their eyes. Women received the vote in Germany only in 1918 under the constitution of the Weimar Republic. Before World War I, only in Norway (1907) could women vote on national issues.

JEWISH EMANCIPATION

HOW DID emancipation affect Jewish life in Europe outside of Russia?

One of the most important social impacts of political liberalism on European life during the nineteenth century was the emancipation of European Jews from the narrow life of the ghetto into a world of equal or nearly equal citizenship and social status.

EARLY STEPS TO EQUAL CITIZENSHIP

Emancipation began in the late eighteenth century and continued throughout the nineteenth. It moved at different paces in different countries. In 1782 Joseph II (r. 1765–1790), the Habsburg emperor, issued a decree that placed the Jews of his empire under more or less the same laws as Christians. In France the National Assembly recognized Jews as French citizens in 1789. During the Napoleonic wars, Jewish communities in Italy and Germany were allowed to mix on a generally equal footing with the Christian population.

These various steps toward political emancipation were vulnerable to changes in rulers or governments. Even in countries that granted them political rights, Jews could not own land and could be subject to discriminatory taxes. Nonetheless, by the first half of the nineteenth century Jews in western Europe and to a much lesser extent in central and eastern Europe had begun to acquire equal or nearly equal citizenship.

In Russia, however, the traditional modes of prejudice and discrimination continued unabated until World War I. Jews were treated as aliens under Russian rule. The government undermined Jewish community life, limited publication of Jewish books, restricted areas where Jews might live, required internal passports from Jews, and banned them from many forms of state service and from many institutions of higher education. The police and others were allowed to conduct **pogroms**—organized riots—against Jewish neighborhoods and villages.

pogroms Organized riots against Jews in the Russian Empire.

BROADENED OPPORTUNITIES

After the revolutions of 1848, especially in western Europe, the situation of European Jews improved for several decades. Throughout Germany, Italy, the Low Countries, and Scandinavia, Jews were allowed full rights of citizenship. After 1858 Jews in Great Britain could sit in Parliament. In Austria-Hungary full legal rights were extended to Jews in 1867. From approximately 1850 to 1880 there was relatively little organized or overt prejudice toward Jews. Legal prohibitions against marriages between Jews and non-Jews were repealed during the last quarter of the century.

Outside of Russia, Jewish political figures served in the highest offices of the state. Politically they tended to be aligned with liberal parties because such groups had championed equal rights. Especially in eastern Europe, many Jews became associated with the Socialist parties.

Jews still encountered personal prejudice throughout Europe, but in western Europe the Jewish populations seem to have felt relatively secure from the old dangers of legalized persecution and discrimination. Religious prejudice persisted in rural Russia and eastern Europe, and hundreds of thousands of European Jews immigrated to the United States from these regions.

Attitudes changed again during the last two decades of the nineteenth century. In the 1870s, some attributed the economic stagnation of that decade to Jewish bankers and financial interests. In the 1880s organized anti-Semitism erupted in Germany, as it did in France in the 1890s. As we saw in the previous chapter, those developments gave birth to Zionism, the movement to establish a Jewish state in Palestine. Most Jewish leaders, however, believed that attacks on Jewish life were temporary recurrences of older prejudice; they felt that their communities would remain safe under the nineteenth century's legal protections, an analysis that would be proved disastrously wrong during the 1930s and 1940s.

Dedication of a New Synagogue.   The social life of Europe was transformed in numerous ways during the nineteenth century. Beyond the expansion of cities and the rise of industrial society, numerous changes also occurred in religious life. One of the most important of these changes was the gradual emancipation of European Jews from sharply restricted lives in urban ghettos to fuller political participation and social assimilation. This painting by G. E. Opitz portrays the dedication of a new synagogue in Alsace in 1820.

How does this painting show the assimilation of Jews into nineteenth-century European society?

EUROPEAN LABOR, SOCIALISM, AND POLITICS TO WORLD WAR I

THE WORKING CLASSES IN THE LATE NINETEENTH CENTURY

WHY DID Marxism become so influential among European socialists?

After 1848 European workers ceased taking to the streets to riot over their grievances. They also stopped trying to revive the old paternalistic guilds. After midcentury the labor force accepted the fact of modern industrial production and attempted to receive more benefits from that system. Workers turned to new institutions and ideologies to defend their interests: trade unions, democratic political parties, and socialism.

Legal protections were extended to unions throughout the second half of the century. Unions became fully legal in Great Britain in 1871 and were allowed to picket in 1875. In France the Third Republic fully legalized unions in 1884. After 1890 they could function in Germany with little disturbance. Most trade unions were slow to enter the political process directly, as long as the traditional governing classes looked after labor interests.

Midcentury union efforts aimed to improve the wages and working conditions of skilled workers. By the close of the century large industrial unions for unskilled workers were also being organized. They confronted extensive opposition from employers. In the decade before 1914 strikes were common throughout Europe as the unions attempted to raise wages to keep up with inflation. Unions represented a new collective way for workers to confront the economic difficulties of their lives. Union membership grew in 1910 to approximately 3 million in Britain, 2 million in Germany, and 977,000 in France, but they never included a majority of the industrial labor force.

The democratic franchise gave workers direct political influence. Except for Russia, all the major European states adopted broad-based, if not perfectly democratic, electoral systems, leading to the formation of organized mass political parties. Previously,

Trade Union Membership Certificate. Trade unions continued to grow in late nineteenth-century Great Britain. The effort to curb the unions eventually led to the formation of the Labour Party. The British unions often had quite elaborate membership certificates, such as this one for the National Union of Gas Workers and General Labourers of Great Britain and Ireland.

How are labor and work depicted here?

most voters had been men of property who understood what they had at stake in politics. The expansion of the electorate brought into the political processes many people who had to be organized and taught the nature of power and influence in the liberal democratic state. The organized political party—with its workers, newspapers, offices, social life, and discipline—was the vehicle that mobilized the new voters. The largest single group in these mass electorates was the working class. The democratization of politics presented the Socialists with opportunities and required the traditional ruling class to vie with them for the support of the new voters.

MARXIST CRITIQUE OF THE INDUSTRIAL ORDER

During the 1840s, Karl Marx (1818–1883) produced the most influential critique of the industrial order. Later in the century his analysis was adopted by the leading Socialist political party in Germany, which in turn influenced most other European Socialist parties including a small group of exiled Russians. Marx's Jewish middle-class parents sent him to the University of Berlin, where he became deeply involved in radical politics. German authorities drove him into exile—first in Paris; then in Brussels, and finally in London.

In 1844 Marx met Friedrich Engels (1820–1895), another young middle-class German, and they became fast friends. Late in 1847 they were asked to write a pamphlet for a short-lived secret Communist league. *The Communist Manifesto*, published in German, appeared early in 1848. Marx, Engels, and the league had adopted the name *Communist* because it implied the outright abolition of private property, making it more radical than *Socialist*. The *Manifesto* was a work of fewer than fifty pages. It would become the most influential political document of modern European history, though its initial impact was minimal, and it did not have any effect on the revolutionary events of 1848.

In *The Communist Manifesto* Marx and Engels contended that human history must be understood rationally. History is the record of humankind's coming to grips with physical nature to produce the goods necessary for survival. That basic productive process determines the structures, values, and ideas of a society. The organization of the means of production has always involved conflict between the classes who owned and controlled the means of production and the classes who worked for them. That necessary conflict has provided the engine for historical development; it is not an accidental by-product of mismanagement or bad intentions. Consequently, only a radical social transformation, not piecemeal reforms, can eliminate the social and economic evils inherent in the very structures of production. Such a revolution will occur as the inevitable outcome of the development of capitalism.

In Marx's and Engels's eyes, during the nineteenth century the class conflict that had characterized previous Western history had become a struggle between the bourgeoisie and the proletariat or between the middle class and the workers. The character of capitalism ensured the sharpening of the struggle. Capitalist production and compe-

tition would steadily increase the size of the unpropertied proletariat. As business structures grew larger, smaller middle-class units would be squeezed out. Competition would
intensify the suffering of the proletariat, and as workers' suffering increased, they would
foment revolution and finally overthrow the few remaining owners of the means of
production. For a time the workers would organize the means of production through a
dictatorship of the proletariat, which would eventually give way to a propertyless and
classless communist society.

This proletarian revolution was inevitable, according to Marx and Engels. Although
the class conflict involved in the contemporary process resembled that of the past, it
differed in that the struggle between the capitalistic bourgeoisie and the industrial
proletariat would culminate in a wholly new society, free of class conflict. The victorious
proletariat, by its very nature, could not be a new oppressor class. The victory of the proletariat over the bourgeoisie represented the culmination of human history and would result
in "an association, in which the free development of each is the condition for the free
development of all."[1] Marx's analysis was conditioned by the unemployment and depriva-
tion of the 1840s. Capitalism, however, did not collapse as he predicted, nor did the
middle class become proletarianized.

In reality, more people came to benefit from the industrial system. Nonetheless, within a generation Marxism had captured the imagination of many Socialists
and large segments of the working class. Its doctrines were allegedly based on the
empirical evidence of hard economic fact. The purported scientific basis of **Marxism**
helped popularize the ideology, as science became more influential during the second
half of the century. As Marxist thought permeated the international Socialist movement during the next seventy-five years, it would provide the ideological basis for
some of the most momentous and ultimately repressive political movements in the
modern world.

GERMANY: SOCIAL DEMOCRATS AND REVISIONISM

Marxism was adopted by the German Social Democratic Party (SPD). Founded in 1875,
the SPD was vehemently opposed by Otto von Bismarck (1815–1898). Following an
1878 attempt to assassinate Emperor William I (r. 1861–1888), Bismarck unfairly blamed
the Socialists and steered antisocialist laws through the Reichstag, the German Parliament. These measures suppressed the SPD, but the party steadily polled more votes in
Reichstag elections.

When repression failed, Bismarck enacted social welfare legislation to wean
German workers from socialist loyalties. These measures provided health insurance, accident insurance, and old age and disability pensions. The German state itself thus organized
a system of social security that did not change the system of property holding or politics.

In 1891, after forcing Bismarck's resignation, Emperor William II (r. 1888–1918)
legalized the SPD. In the Erfurt Program of 1891, party leaders declared the imminent
doom of capitalism and the necessity of socialist ownership of the means of production.
However, these goals were to be achieved by legal political participation rather than by
revolutionary activity. Since the revolution was inevitable, they argued, the immediate
task of Socialists was to improve workers' lives. In theory, the SPD was vehemently hostile to the German Empire, but in practice the party functioned within its institutions.

In response, Eduard Bernstein (1850–1932) wrote the first important internal
socialist challenge to Marxism. Bernstein, who was familiar with the British
Fabians, questioned whether Marx and his followers were correct in their

Karl Marx.   Marx's Socialist philosophy
eventually triumphed over most alternative versions of socialism in Europe, but
his monumental work has been subject to
varying interpretations, criticisms, and
revisions that continue to this day.

**Why was the Marxist analysis of history so
powerful?**

Marxism   The theory of Karl Marx
(1818–1883) and Friedrich Engels
(1820–1895) that history is the result of
class conflict, which will end in the
inevitable triumph of the industrial
proletariat over the bourgeoisie and the
abolition of private property and social
class.

Fabians   British socialists in the late
nineteenth and early twentieth century
who sought to achieve socialism
through gradual, peaceful, and democratic means.

---

[1]Robert C. Tucker, ed., *The Marx-Engels Reader* (New York: W. W. Norton, 1972), p. 353.

Beatrice and Sidney Webb. These most influential British Fabian Socialists, shown in a photograph from the late 1920s, wrote many books on governmental and economic matters, served on special parliamentary commissions, and agitated for the enactment of socialist policies.

What were the beliefs of the Fabians?

revisionism The advocacy among nineteenth-century German socialists of achieving a humane socialist society through the evolution of democratic institutions, not revolution.

pessimistic appraisal of capitalism and the necessity of revolution. In *Evolutionary Socialism* (1899), Bernstein pointed to the rising standard of living in Europe, the ongoing power of the middle class, and the opening of the franchise to the working class. He argued that a humane socialist society required not revolution but more democracy and social reform. Bernstein's doctrines, known as **revisionism**, were widely debated among German Socialists. Bernstein's critics argued that evolution toward social democracy might be possible in liberal, parliamentary Britain but not in authoritarian, militaristic Germany. The German SPD continued to advocate revolution.

GREAT BRITAIN: THE LABOUR PARTY AND FABIANISM

No form of socialism made significant progress in Great Britain, the most advanced industrial society of the day. The members of the growing trade unions normally supported Liberal Party candidates. The "new unionism" of the late 1880s and the 1890s organized the dock workers, the gas workers, and similar unskilled groups. Employer resistance to unions heightened class antagonism. In 1892 Keir Hardie (1856–1915) became the first independent worker elected to Parliament. In 1893 the Socialist Independent Labour Party was founded, but it remained ineffective.

In 1901, however, a court decision removed the legal protection previously accorded union funds. The Trades Union Congress responded by launching the Labour Party, which sent twenty-nine members to Parliament in the election of 1906. Their goals did not yet encompass socialism. The British labor movement also became more militant, staging scores of strikes for wages to meet the rising cost of living. The government intervened to mediate.

British socialism itself remained primarily the preserve of intellectuals. The Socialists who exerted the most influence were from the Fabian Society, founded in 1884. The society took its name from a Roman general who defeated Hannibal by waiting before attacking, indicating the society's gradualist approach to social reform. Its leading members were Sydney Webb (1859–1947) and Beatrice Webb (1858–1943), H. G. Wells (1866–1946), and George Bernard Shaw (1856–1950). Many Fabians were civil servants who believed that the problems of industry, the expansion of ownership, and the state direction of production could be handled gradually, peacefully, and democratically. They sought to educate the country to the rational wisdom of socialism. They were particularly interested in collective ownership on the municipal level, or so-called gas-and-water socialism.

RUSSIA: INDUSTRIAL DEVELOPMENT AND THE BIRTH OF BOLSHEVISM

Following its defeat in the Crimean War, Russia's tsarist government had undertaken major reforms. The most important reform was the emancipation of the serfs in 1861, through a complicated process that in effect required serfs to pay for their land. The poverty of the emancipated serfs became a political cause for groups of urban revolutionaries. One such group, The People's Will, assassinated Tsar Alexander II (r. 1855–1881) in 1881. Thereafter, the government pursued a policy of political repression.

The late-nineteenth-century tsarist government was determined to make Russia an industrial power. It favored the growth of heavy industries, such as railways, iron, and steel. A small but significant industrial proletariat arose. By 1900 Russia had approximately 3 million factory workers, whose working and living conditions were bad by any standard.

New political organizations emerged. The Social Revolutionary Party, founded in 1901, opposed industrialism and looked to the communal life of rural Russia as a model for the economic future. In 1903 the Constitutional Democratic Party, or Cadets, was formed. The Cadets were drawn from people who participated in the *zemstvos* (local governments), and they modeled themselves on the Liberal parties of western Europe. They wanted a parliamentary regime with responsible ministries, civil liberties, and economic progress.

The situation for Russian Socialists differed radically from that in other major European countries. Russia had no representative political institutions and only a small working class. The Russian Social Democratic Party had been established in 1898. It was Marxist, and its members greatly admired the German SPD, but tsarist repression meant that it had to function in exile. The leading late-nineteenth-century Russian Marxist was Georgii Plekhanov (1857–1918), based in Switzerland. His chief disciple was Vladimir Illich Ulyanov (1870–1924), who took the name of Lenin. After briefly practicing law in St. Petersburg, Lenin was exiled to Siberia from 1895 to 1900 and spent most of the following seventeen years in Switzerland.

Russian Social Democrats quarreled about the proper nature of a Marxist revolution in primarily rural Russia. They were modernizers who favored further industrial development. Most believed that Russia must develop a large proletariat before the revolution could come, and they hoped to mold a mass political party like the German SPD.

Lenin dissented from both positions. In *What Is to Be Done?* (1902), he condemned accommodations and criticized trade unionism that settled for short-term gains rather than true revolutionary change for the working class. Lenin further rejected the concept of a mass party composed of workers. He believed that an elite party of professional revolutionaries had to bring revolutionary consciousness to the working class.

In 1903, at the London Congress of the Russian Social Democratic Party, Lenin's faction assumed the name **Bolsheviks**, meaning "majority" (despite having lost most votes at the Congress), and the more moderate, democratic revolutionary faction became known as the **Mensheviks**, or "minority." In 1905 Lenin published a program for revolution in Russia, urging that the socialist revolution unite the proletariat and the peasants. He grasped the profound discontent in the Russian countryside and knew that an alliance of workers and peasants in rebellion could not be suppressed. Lenin's two principles—an elite party and a dual social revolution—allowed the Bolsheviks to capture the leadership of the Russian Revolution in late 1917.

The Russian Socialists had no immediate influence within Russia. In 1904 Russia went to war with Japan and lost. On January 22, 1905, a priest led thousands of workers to petition the tsar for improvements in industrial conditions. As the petitioners approached the Winter Palace in St. Petersburg, troops opened fire, killing about a hundred people.

Revolutionary disturbances spread throughout Russia. In early October 1905 strikes broke out in St. Petersburg, and worker groups, called *soviets*, virtually controlled the city. Tsar Nicholas II (r. 1894–1917) promised constitutional government. Early in 1906 the tsar announced the election of a bicameral parliament, the **Duma**.

CHRONOLOGY

MAJOR DATES IN THE DEVELOPMENT OF SOCIALISM

1864	International Working Men's Association (the First International) founded
1875	German Social Democratic Party founded
1876	First International dissolved
1878	German antisocialist laws passed
1884	British Fabian Society founded
1889	Second International founded
1891	German antisocialist laws permitted to expire
1895	French *Confédération Générale du Travail* founded
1899	Eduard Bernstein's *Evolutionary Socialism*
1902	Formation of the British Labour party
1902	Lenin's *What Is to Be Done?*
1903	Bolshevik-Menshevik split

Bolsheviks   Meaning the "majority." Term Lenin applied to his faction of the Russian Social Democratic Party. It became the Communist Party of the Soviet Union after the Russian Revolution.

Mensheviks   Meaning the "minority." Term Lenin applied to the majority moderate faction of the Russian Social Democratic Party opposed to him and the Bolsheviks.

soviets   Workers' and soldiers' councils formed in Russia during the Revolution.

Duma   The Russian parliament, after the revolution of 1905.

Bloody Sunday. On Bloody Sunday, January 22, 1905, troops of Tsar Nicholas II fired on a peaceful procession of workers who sought to present a petition at the Winter Palace in St. Petersburg. After this event, there was little chance of reconciliation between the tsarist government and the Russian working class.

Why did soldiers fire on the workers?

He reserved important appointments for himself and named as his chief minister P. A. Stolypin (1862–1911). Neither the tsar nor his minister was sympathetic to the Duma. The government's sole conciliatory gesture was to forgive any payments still owed by peasants from the emancipation of the serfs in 1861. Thereafter Stolypin repressed rural discontent.

Stolypin was assassinated in 1911. The imperial family was surrounded by scandal over the influence of Grigori Rasputin (1871?–1916), who seemed able to heal the tsar's hemophilic son. The undue influence of this strange and uncouth man, the continued social discontent, and the conservative resistance to liberal reforms rendered the position of the tsar uncertain after 1911.

EUROPEAN SOCIALISM IN WORLD HISTORY

The German SPD was the most successful prewar Socialist party, and its rejection of reform influenced Lenin and other leaders of the Russian Revolution. In later history, wherever Soviet Marxism was influential, its goal was revolution, not reform. The debates among late-nineteenth- and early-twentieth-century European Socialists were significant to world history for two additional reasons. First, Europeans who immigrated to North and South America carried many of these socialist ideas and quarrels with them. Second, by the end of the nineteenth century numerous students from the European empires in Africa and Asia traveled to Europe for education, where they, too, were immersed in these debates. Many of those students later became leaders of their own political movements.

NORTH AMERICA AND THE NEW INDUSTRIAL ECONOMY

HOW DID industrialization in the United States differ from industrialization in Europe?

Industrialization in the United States largely followed the European pattern: The first industry to become thoroughly mechanized was textile manufacture, followed by growth in the iron and steel industries. There were significant differences, however. The United States industrialized considerably later than Great Britain. Its

Immigrant Labor. Chinese laborers, known as "coolies," performed most of the backbreaking work on the construction of the railroads in the American West. The workers depicted here are laying down track near Promontory, Utah.

What role did railroads play in the industrialization of the United States?

major expansion in iron and steel took place after the Civil War, approximately contemporary to the economic rise of the newly united Germany. American manufacturers and commercial developers encountered little of the prejudice against trade and commerce that existed among the European aristocracy. Wealthy American businessmen had considerable political influence. The United States possessed an immense internal market free of trade restraints. British bankers saw the United States as an area of secure investment, so they provided much of the necessary capital. Finally, the United States had a relative shortage of labor and consequently relatively high wages, factors that attracted many immigrants to the industrial sector during the second half of the nineteenth century.

In America as in Europe, railways spurred the most intense industrial growth. The number of railway miles increased from approximately 50,000 in the mid-1860s to almost 200,000 by 1900. Much of the construction was made possible by vast European investments in the United States. The railways created enormous demand for iron, steel, coal, and lumber. They also stimulated settlement, vastly expanded markets, and helped to knit the country together.

EUROPEAN IMMIGRATION TO THE UNITED STATES

The same conditions that made life difficult for black people and Native Americans (see Chapter 23) turned the United States into a land of vast opportunity for white European immigrants. These immigrants faced religious and ethnic discrimination as well as frequent poverty in the United States, but the social and economic structures of the United States allowed for assimilation and remarkable upward social mobility. This was especially true of those immigrants who arrived between approximately 1840 and 1890—the great period of German, English, Welsh, Scottish, and Irish immigration (see Map 25–1).

Toward the end of the nineteenth century and well into the twentieth—in what is sometimes known as the New Immigration—millions of people arrived from economically depressed areas of the Mediterranean, eastern Europe, and the Balkans. These new immigrants, who generally came to work in the growing industrial cities, were perceived

MAP EXPLORATION

To explore this map further, go to **http://www.prenhall.com/craig_maps**

Legend:
- Emigration from Europe
- Emigration from Japan
- Emigration from China
- Emigration from India
- Migration from European Russia

Number of Immigrants	
From Asia	700,000
Main groups	
Chinese	370,000
Japanese	275,000
From Canada	2,200,000
From Europe	30,000,000
Main groups	
Germans	5,000,000
Irish	4,500,000
Italians	4,500,000
Poles	2,600,000
English	2,600,000
Jews	2,000,000
From Latin America	900,000

MAP 25–1 Patterns of Global Migration, 1840–1900. Emigration was a global process by the late nineteenth century. More immigrants went to the United States than to every other nation combined.

How did global migration alter societies of the late nineteenth century?

as fundamentally different from those who had come before them. Predominately Roman Catholic, Orthodox, and Jewish, they encountered much intolerance. The same kind of racial theory that spread through Europe during these years was present in the United States, so these new immigrants were regarded as being from less desirable racial stocks. They often settled into communities of people from their own ethnic background, held together by various private organizations including churches and synagogues.

Although none of these immigrants faced the same legal discrimination as did American blacks, Jews encountered restricted covenants on real estate and other obstacles. Asian immigrants to the West Coast of the United States faced harsher prejudice.

Ellis Island. In 1892 the federal government opened the immigration station on Ellis Island, located in New York City's harbor, where about 80 percent of the immigrants to the United States landed. As many as 5,000 passengers per day reported to federal immigration officers for questions about their background and for physical examinations, such as this eye exam. About 1 percent were quarantined or turned away for health problems.

How did immigration patterns change over time?

UNIONS: ORGANIZATION OF LABOR

As in Europe, American workers attempting to organize labor unions faced resistance from employers and those who feared that unions would lead to socialism. Other difficulties were peculiar to the United States: White laborers would not organize alongside black workers, and different ethnic minorities would not cooperate. The ongoing flood of immigration ensured a supply of workers willing to work for low wages. The owners of businesses could divide and conquer the sprawling, ethnically mixed labor force.

The National Labor Union attempted to organize railroad unions in the 1780s. In 1881 the American Federation of Labor (AFL) was founded, focusing on higher wages and better working conditions for skilled workers. Among its most effective leaders was Samuel Gompers (1850–1924). Other unions, such as the United Mine Workers and the Railway Brotherhoods, organized workers by industry.

Serious depressions occurred in both the 1870s and the 1890s. What little relief there was came from local authorities and private charities, a pattern that would continue until the Great Depression of the 1930s. Economic turmoil of the 1880s and 1890s spawned violent strikes and the notorious breaking of the Pullman strike in Chicago in 1894 by federal troops. The major goal of labor thereafter was to achieve the full legal right to organize, achieved only through the legislation of Franklin Roosevelt's (1882–1945) New Deal in the 1930s.

Socialism was a path closed to American labor. The leaders of conservative unions worked against the Socialists, and businesses blocked Socialist influence. The federal and state governments repressed Socialist activities. Virtually all American Socialists were persecuted as Bolshevists during the 1920s and beyond. Thus, in the United States, many social issues were addressed by trade unions rather than by Socialist parties. Although many conservative American political and business leaders disliked them, unions were not legally attacked in the United States.

In many European countries, Socialist parties (or leaders attempting to outflank the Socialists) passed legislation providing social security and other social services. No significant legislation of this kind was passed in the United States, at either the federal or state level, until the New Deal.

THE PROGRESSIVES

Political bosses held much of the power in American politics in the decades after the Civil War. This system depended on patronage: In return for jobs, contracts, licenses, favors, and sometimes actual services, the boss received political support. Government was a vehicle for distributing spoils. Boss politics was a crude way of organizing the disorderly social and economic forces of the great and growing cities with diverse populations.

Deeply disturbed by the corruption, reform-minded political figures ushered in what has been called the Progressive era, which lasted from approximately 1890 through 1914. Usually upper-middle-class whites who feared a loss of political and social influence, these reformers found the urban environment with its slums an unacceptable picture of disorder. They wanted to see more efficient government acting as a direct agent of change and reform.

The Progressives began in the cities and then launched into national politics. They believed boss politics robbed cities of the money needed to make them livable. In place of patronage, they demanded social and municipal services. Progressive mayors called for lower utility rates and streetcar fares.

SOCIAL REFORM

Churches joined the Progressive crusade. The "Social Gospel" preached that Christianity involved civic action. Young men and women began to work in settlement houses in the slums. The most famous was Chicago's Hull House, led by Jane Addams (1860–1935). Other middle-class young people became active in housing and health reform, education, and charities. They believed that the urban environment could be cleaned up and social order, as envisioned by the white middle class, made to prevail.

On the state government level, Progressives attempted to protect groups of people perceived as unable to protect themselves against exploitation. Virtually all of these reformers partook of the cult of science that was so influential in the late nineteenth century. They believed that the problems of society were susceptible to scientific, rational management. The general public interest should replace special interests.

THE PROGRESSIVE PRESIDENCY

Theodore Roosevelt became president in 1901 after the assassination of William McKinley (1843–1901). By force of personality and intelligence, Roosevelt created the modern American presidency, making it the most important and powerful branch of government. He set the agenda for national affairs, surrounded himself with strong advisers, and used his own knowledge of party patronage to beat the bosses at their game.

In domestic policy, Roosevelt believed no economic power should be stronger than the federal government. He successfully moved against some of the most powerful business trusts and financiers in the country, such as J. P. Morgan and John D. Rockefeller. Through "Square Deal" legislation, Roosevelt attempted to assert the public interest. He was not opposed to big business in itself, but he wanted it to operate according to rules established by the government for the public good.

In 1902 Roosevelt brought the moral power of the presidency to the aid of mine workers who were on strike, appointing a commission to arbitrate the dispute. Roosevelt sought to make the presidency and the federal government the guarantor of fairness in economic relations. Thus he fostered the passage of the Pure Food and Drug Act and the Meat Packing Act in 1906, which protected the public against adulterated foodstuffs. His conservation policies ensured that millions of acres of national forests came under the care of the federal government.

Roosevelt's foreign policy was vigorous and imperialistic. In 1898 McKinley had led the nation into the Spanish-American War, and the United States had emerged as an imperial power with control of Cuba, Puerto Rico, Guam, and the Philippines. Roosevelt believed that the United States should be a major world power, and he sent a war fleet around the world. In Latin America naval intervention assured a new government in Panama, and a treaty allowed the United States to construct and control a canal across the Isthmus of Panama. The imperialist policies of the United States were built on a conviction of racial superiority.

Roosevelt was succeeded in 1909 by William Howard Taft (1857–1930), and the 1912 election was a three-way contest among Taft, Roosevelt (running as a third-party candidate), and Woodrow Wilson. The Democrat Wilson won and brought a different concept of progressivism to the White House.

Woodrow Wilson (1856–1924) was a former president of Princeton University and a reforming governor of New Jersey. Like Roosevelt, Wilson accepted a modern industrialized nation. Wilson intrinsically disliked big business, however, and believed the government should protect the weak. Wilson termed his policy the New Freedom, although in office he followed a policy of moderate regulation of business. Wilson saw the presidency as responsible for leading Congress to legislative decisions. He presented Congress with a vast agenda of legislation and then worked carefully with the Democratic leadership to see that it was passed.

Wilson retained many beliefs that have disappointed later admirers. For example, he reinstated racial segregation in the federal civil service and opposed female suffrage.

War broke out in Europe in August 1914. Although Wilson was reelected in 1916 on the slogan "He Kept Us Out of War!" in April 1917 he led the nation into the European conflict. The expertise Progressives had brought to efficient domestic government was turned to making the nation an effective military force. These two impulses—the first toward domestic reform, the second toward a strong international role—had long marked the progressive movement and would shape American history in the years after the war.

The American Progressives resembled political leaders of their generation in Great Britain, France, and Germany, who had supported various social reforms to forestall the advance of socialism and to address the problems of industrialization and urbanization. All had favored unprecedented use of central government authority.

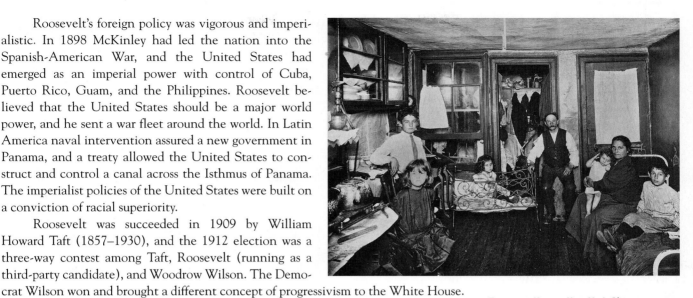

Tenement House, New York City, ca. 1890. Social reformers, such as the journalist Jacob Riis, drew the attention of millions to urban poverty and the plight of industrial workers. In his path-breaking book *How the Other Half Lives*, Riis shocked Americans with a portrait of New York City's poor. The seven members of an immigrant family shown here, who live in a one-room tenement apartment in New York's Lower East Side, are probably wearing their best clothes.

Room in a Tenement flat, 1910, detail, gelatin silver print 8 x 10 inches (20.3 x 25.4 cm.). Museum of the City of New York: Jacob A. Riis Collection.

What possessions can you identify in this family's apartment?

THE EMERGENCE OF MODERN EUROPEAN THOUGHT

Parallel with the striking changes in European economic and social life there emerged major new departures in thought.

WHO WERE some of the intellectuals at the forefront of modern European thought?

Around 1850, Voltaire would have felt at home in a general discussion of scientific concepts. The basic Newtonian picture of physical nature still prevailed. Learned persons regarded the physical world as rational, mechanical, and dependable. Its laws could be ascertained objectively through experiment and observation. By 1850, science had a strong institutional life in French and German universities; the word *scientist* had been coined in the early 1830s.

DOCUMENT

Darwin Defends a Mechanistic View of Nature

In the closing paragraphs of On the Origin of Species (1859), Charles Darwin contrasted the view of nature he championed with that of his opponents. He argued that an interpretation of organic nature based on mechanistic laws was actually nobler than an interpretation based on divine creation. In the second edition, however, Darwin added the term Creator to these paragraphs.

- **Why** does Darwin believe a mechanistic creation suggests no less dignity than creation by God? How does the insertion of the term *Creator* change this passage? What is the grandeur that Darwin finds in his view of life?

Authors of the highest eminence seem to be fully satisfied with the view that each species has been independently created. To my mind it accords better with what we know of the laws impressed on matter by the Creator, that the production and extinction of the past and present inhabitants of the world should have been due to secondary causes, like those determining the birth and death of the individual. When I view all beings not as special creations, but as the lineal descendants of some few beings which lived long before the first bed of the Cambrian [geological] system was deposited, they seem to me to become ennobled. ...

It is interesting to contemplate a tangled bank, clothed with many plants of many kinds, with birds

The last quarter of the nineteenth century and the first decade of the twentieth century were the crucible of modern Western thought. Western intellectuals began to portray physical reality, human nature, and society in ways different from those of the past. The vast change in thinking commenced in the realm of biology.

DARWIN'S THEORY OF NATURAL SELECTION

Charles Darwin's (1809–1882) *On the Origin of Species*, published in 1859, carried the mechanical interpretation of physical nature into the world of living things. (See Document, "Darwin Defends a Mechanistic View of Nature.") The concept of evolution had already been widely discussed, but Darwin and, working independently, Alfred Russel Wallace (1823–1913) formulated the principle of natural selection, which explains *how* species evolve over time.

The two scientists contended that more living organisms come into existence than can survive in their environment. Organisms with any advantage in the struggle for existence produce more surviving offspring and repopulate their species. This principle of survival of the fittest Darwin called **natural selection**. What could not be explained in the nineteenth century was the origin of the variations that gave some living things new traits. Only after 1900, when Gregor Mendel's (1822–1884) work on heredity received public attention, did the mystery of those variations begin to be unraveled.

Darwin's and Wallace's mechanistic theory removed the idea of preconceived divine purpose from organic nature. Thus it not only contradicted the biblical narrative of the Creation but also undermined both the deistic argument for the existence of God from the design of the universe and the belief that the universe was a fixed, stable system. If the world of nature was in flux, it implied that society, values, customs, and beliefs might also be changeable.

In 1871, in *The Descent of Man*, Darwin applied the principle of evolution by natural selection to human beings. Darwin contended that humankind's moral nature and religious sentiments, as well as its physical frame, had evolved in response to the requirements of survival. Neither the origin nor the character of humankind required postulating a deity to explain their existence. The blow to human pride was comparable to Copernicus removing the Earth from the center of the universe.

The theory of evolution by natural selection was criticized by both the religious and the scientific communities. The broad scientific community accepted Darwin's

natural selection According to Darwin, the process in nature by which only the organisms best adapted to their environment tend to survive and transmit their genes, while those less adapted tend to be eliminated.

relativity Theory of physics, first expounded by Albert Einstein in 1905, in which time and space exist not separately, but rather as a combined continuum.

singing on the bushes, with various insects flitting about, and with worms crawling through the damp earth, and to reflect that these elaborately constructed forms, so different from each other, and dependent upon each other in so complex a manner, have all been produced by laws acting around us. These laws, taken in the largest sense, being Growth with Reproduction; Inheritance which is almost implied by reproduction; Variability from the indirect and direct action of the conditions of life, and from use and disuse: a Ratio of Increase so high as to lead to a Struggle for Life, and as a consequence to Natural Selection, entailing Divergence of Character and the Extinction of less-improved forms.

Thus, from the war of nature, from famine and death, the most exalted object which we are capable of conceiving, namely the production of the higher animals, directly follows. There is grandeur in this view of life, with its several powers, having been originally breathed by the Creator into a few forms or into one; and that, whilst this planet has gone cycling on according to the fixed law of gravity, from so simple a beginning endless forms most beautiful and most wonderful have been, and are being evolved.

Source: Charles Darwin, *On the Origin of Species and the Descent of Man* (New York: Modern Library, n.d.), pp. 373–374.

mechanism of natural selection only after it was combined with modern genetics in the 1920s and 1930s.

THE REVOLUTION IN PHYSICS

By the late 1870s, many physical scientists were questioning whether mechanistic models, solid atoms, and absolute time and space truly described the universe. In 1883, Ernst Mach (1838–1916) published *The Science of Mechanics,* in which he urged that scientists consider their concepts descriptive not of the physical world but of the sensations of the scientific observer. Similarly, the French scientist Henri Poincaré (1854–1912) urged that the theories of scientists be regarded as hypothetical constructs of the human mind rather than as true descriptions of nature. By World War I, few scientists believed they could portray the "truth" about physical reality.

Discoveries in the laboratory supported the view that nature was more complex than Newton had imagined. In December 1895, Wilhelm Roentgen (1845–1923) published a paper on his discovery of X rays, a form of energy that penetrated opaque materials. Major steps in the exploration of radioactivity followed within months. In 1896, Henri Becquerel (1852–1908) discovered that uranium emitted a similar form of energy. The next year, J. J. Thomson (1856–1940), at Cambridge University, formulated the theory of the electron, and the interior world of the atom became a realm for human exploration. In 1902, Ernest Rutherford (1871–1937) explained radiation as the disintegration of atoms of radioactive materials. He also speculated on the immense store of energy in the atom.

The discovery of radioactivity contributed to revolutionary theories in physics. In 1900, Max Planck (1858–1947) pioneered the quantum theory of energy, according to which energy is a series of discrete quantities, or packets, rather than a continuous stream. In 1905, Albert Einstein (1879–1955) published his first papers on **relativity** in which he contended that time and space form a continuum, and that measurement of time and space depends on the observer as well as on the entities being observed. In 1927, Werner Heisenberg's (1901–1976) uncertainty principle stated that the behavior of subatomic particles can only be inferred by statistical probability. The physical universe had become ambiguous.

The mathematical complexity of twentieth-century physics meant that science would rarely again be intelligible to the masses, although it started to affect daily life

Darwin's Theories about the evolution of humankind from the higher primates aroused enormous controversy. This caricature shows him with a monkey's body holding a mirror to an apelike creature.

Why are Darwin's theories still controversial?

more than ever. Scientists from the late nineteenth century onward won the financial support of governments and private institutions for their work, and they have altered modern life more significantly than any other intellectuals.

FRIEDRICH NIETZSCHE AND THE REVOLT AGAINST REASON

During the second half of the century, philosophers such as the German Friedrich Nietzsche (1844–1900) began to question the adequacy of rational thinking. Nietzsche attacked Christianity, democracy, nationalism, rationality, science, and progress. He sought less to change values than to probe their sources in the human character. He wanted to tear away the masks of respectable life and explore how human beings made such masks.

His first important work was *The Birth of Tragedy* (1872) in which he urged that the nonrational aspects of human nature are as important and noble as reason itself. He insisted that instinct and ecstasy had important functions and that the strength to live heroically derived from sources beyond rationality.

In later works including *Thus Spake Zarathustra* (1883) Nietzsche criticized democracy and Christianity, claiming that they promoted mediocrity and sheepish behavior. He announced the death of God and proclaimed the coming of the *Overman* (*Übermensch*). The term was frequently interpreted as referring to a superman or superrace, but Nietzsche had in mind the kind of heroism that had motivated the ancient Greeks. He thought humans were hobbled by the values of Christianity and bourgeois morality.

In two of Nietzsche's most profound (and difficult) works, *Beyond Good and Evil* (1886) and *The Genealogy of Morals* (1887), he sought to uncover the social and psychological sources of judgments of good and evil. He claimed that morality was only a human convention and that people could create new life-affirming values, glorifying pride, assertiveness, and strength.

THE BIRTH OF PSYCHOANALYSIS

The major figures of late-nineteenth-century science, art, and philosophy shared a determination to probe beneath surface appearances. They sought to discern the undercurrents, tensions, and complexities within atoms, families, rationality, and social relationships. This was particularly true of Sigmund Freud (1856–1939).

In 1886, Freud, an Austrian Jew, opened a medical practice in Vienna, where he lived until driven out by the Nazis in 1938. His earliest medical interests were psychic disorders; he had studied the use of hypnosis to treat cases of hysteria.

In the mid-1890s, Freud abandoned hypnosis and began urging patients to talk spontaneously about themselves. He found that they associated their particular neurotic symptoms with a chain of experiences going back to childhood and that sex was significant in his patients' problems. By 1897, he had developed a theory of infantile sexuality, suggesting that human beings are sexual creatures from birth. He thus questioned the concept of childhood innocence and made sexuality one of the bases of mental order and disorder.

Freud also examined dreams, believing there must be a reasonable, scientific explanation for their seemingly irrational content. He concluded that dreams give free play to unconscious wishes and drives that have been excluded from everyday conscious life. During waking hours, the mind represses or censors certain wishes, which are as important to the individual's psychological makeup as conscious thought is. In fact, Freud argued, unconscious drives and desires contribute to conscious behavior. Freud developed these ideas in his most important book, *The Interpretation of Dreams* (1900).

In later books and essays, Freud developed a new model of the mind as an arena in which three entities struggle: the id, the superego, and the ego. The **id** consists of

id According to Freudian psychoanalysis, the part of the mind that consists of amoral, irrational, driving instincts for sexual gratification, aggression, and physical and sensual pleasure.

QUICK REVIEW

Sigmund Freud

- ◆ Founder of psychoanalysis
- ◆ Worked in Vienna until he was driven out by the Nazis in 1938
- ◆ Focused attention on infantile sexuality
- ◆ Emphasized the importance of what happens in the mind below the level of consciousness

amoral, irrational instincts for sexual gratification, aggression, and general physical and sensual pleasure. The **superego** embodies the external moral imperatives and expectations imposed on the personality by society and culture. The **ego**, by mediating between the impulses of the id and the standards of the superego, helps the personality cope with the inner and outer demands of its existence.

Freud was a realist who wanted human beings to live free of fear and illusion by rationally understanding themselves and their world. He understood the immense sacrifice of instinctual drives required for rational civilized behavior. He believed that excessive repression could lead to mental disorder, but he also believed that civilization and the survival of humankind required some repression of sexuality and aggression. Freud thought the sacrifice and struggle were worthwhile, but he was pessimistic about the future of civilization in the West.

superego According to Freud, the part of the mind that embodies the external moral imperatives and expectations imposed on the personality by society and culture.

ego According to Freudian theory, the part of the mind that mediates between the impulses of the id and the asceticism of the superego and allows the personality to cope with the inner and outer demands of its existence.

ISLAM AND LATE-NINETEENTH-CENTURY EUROPEAN THOUGHT

WHAT WERE some influential views on the relationship between Islam and the West?

The few late-nineteenth-century European thinkers who wrote about Islam interpreted it, consistent with the contemporary scientific outlook, as a historical phenomenon that, like the other great world religions, was merely a product of a particular culture. The influential French writer Ernest Renan (1823–1892) and sociologists such as the German Max Weber saw Muslim religion and cultures as incapable of developing science and closed to new ideas. Their views were opposed by one of the rare Islamic writers who directly contested a European thinker, Jamal al-din Al-Afghani (1839–1897), an Egyptian intellectual who argued that given time (since Islam was six hundred years younger than Christianity), Islam would produce cultures as modern as those in Europe.

European racial and cultural outlooks framed concepts of the Arab world. Christian missionaries reinforced this by blaming Islam for Arab economic backwardness, for mistreating women, and for condoning slavery. Because the penalty for abjuring Islam is death, missionaries made few converts among Muslims. So they turned their efforts to establishing schools and hospitals, hoping these Christian foundations would eventually lead some Muslims to Christianity. Few Muslims converted, but these institutions taught young Arabs Western science and medicine, and many of their students became leaders in the Middle East. As missionary families lived for long periods among Arabs, they became more sympathetic to Arab political aspirations.

Within the Islamic world, political leaders who championed Western scientific education and technology confronted a variety of responses from religious thinkers. Some of these thinkers (the Salafi or the salafiyya movement, for example) believed there was no inherent contradiction between science and Islam. They believed that Muhammad had addressed the issues of his day and that similarly a reformed Islamic faith could modernize itself without imitating the West. The Arab world should cease direct imitation of the West and modernize itself on the basis of a pure, restored Islamic faith. The Salafi emphasized a rational reading of the Qur'an and saw Ottoman decline as the result of Muslim religious error. This outlook, which had originally sought to reconcile Islam with the modern world, in the twentieth century led many Muslims to oppose Western influence.

Other Islamic religious leaders simply rejected the West and modern thought. They included the Mahdist movement in Sudan, the Sanussiya in Libya, and the Wahhabi movement in the Arabian peninsula (see Chapter 27). Such religious-based opposition was strongest in portions of the Middle East where the European presence was least direct. It had little influence in Morocco, Algeria, Egypt, and Tunisia, which were effectively under the control of Western powers by 1900, and Turkey, where Ottoman leaders had long been deeply involved with the West.

Al-Afghani. One of the most influential thinkers in the Muslim world in the nineteenth century, Al-Afghani tried to reconcile modern science with Islam.

What kind of future did al-Afghani foresee for Islam?

QUICK REVIEW

Islam and the West

- European thinkers applied the same scientific critique to Islam as they did to Christianity
- European racism shaped attitudes toward Arabs
- Response to Western ideas and technology varied in the Islamic world

SUMMARY

WHAT IS *proletarianization?*

European Factory Workers and Urban Artisans. During the course of the nineteenth century, European workers underwent a process of proletarianization as the process of industrialization spread across the Continent. Workers labored for wages; they lost ownership of their tools and equipment, and they lost control over the conduct of their trades. *page 615*

WHAT SOCIAL and legal disabilities did European women confront in the nineteenth century?

Nineteenth-Century European Women. Nineteenth-century women were divided along class lines. Unlike working-class women, most women of the upper and middle classes adopted a cult of domesticity and did not work outside the home. Most jobs available to women were low paying and insecure. Women of all classes faced social, political, and legal disabilities that were only gradually improved in the late nineteenth and early twentieth centuries. Before World War I, only Norway allowed women to vote, and few women could earn university degrees or enter the professions. *page 617*

HOW DID emancipation affect Jewish life in Europe outside of Russia?

Jewish Emancipation. With the exception of Russia, European countries had abolished their legal restrictions on Jews by the mid-nineteenth century. Jews became more fully integrated into European political and economic life. After 1880, however, anti-Semitism increased as Jews were blamed for economic and social problems. *page 622*

WHY DID Marxism become so influential among European socialists?

European Labor, Socialism, and Politics to World War I. To protect their interests, European workers joined trade unions and socialist parties, such as the Labour Party in Britain. The Marxist critique of modern capitalism strongly influenced European socialism when the German Social Democratic Party adopted the thought of Karl Marx. Lenin founded the Bolsheviks as an elite Marxist party that advocated the overthrow of Russia's tsarist regime through a revolution of workers and peasants. *page 623*

HOW DID industrialization in the United States differ from industrialization in Europe?

North America and the New Industrial Economy. Despite the creation of a mass industrial workforce, socialism did not take root in the United States. Under presidents Theodore Roosevelt and Woodrow Wilson, the Progressive movement enacted social and political reforms. The United States also embarked on a more aggressive foreign policy with the acquisition of a colonial empire and, under Wilson, participation in World War I. *page 628*

WHO WERE some of the intellectuals at the forefront of modern European thought?

Modern European Thought. In 1850, learned Europeans regarded the physical world as rational, mechanical, and dependable. By the early twentieth century intellectuals began to portray physical reality, human nature, and society in ways that seem familiar to us today. Leaders in this intellectual transformation included the biologist Charles Darwin, Albert Einstein and other physicists, philosopher Friedrich Nietzsche, and pioneering psychoanalyst Sigmund Freud. *page 633*

WHAT WERE some influential views on the relationship between Islam and the West?

Islam and Late-Nineteenth-Century European Thought. Within the Islamic world, modern European thought produced a variety of often conflicting responses. Egyptian intellectual Jamal al-din Al-Afghani wrote that Islamic culture was simply younger than Christian Europe's, but would in time become modern. Leaders of the Salafi movement held that Islam could modernize without imitating the West. The Sudanese Mahdist movement and others rejected Western modernism. *page 637*

REVIEW QUESTIONS

1. What were the chief factors accounting for the proletarianization of the European labor force? How much of the change in the situation of workers was a result of technology, and how much was the result of changes in how they were organized?

2. How did the class position of a European woman determine much of her experience? How did industrialization change women's experiences? What factors limited all women's opportunities? How had women's positions improved by 1914?

3. What were the major characteristics of Jewish emancipation in the nineteenth century? How did late-century economic developments contribute to increasing prejudice against Jews?

4. What were the essential ideas of Karl Marx? How did his ideas come to dominate late-nineteenth-century European socialism?

5. What was the status of the working-class groups in the United States and Europe in 1860? What improvements if any had been achieved by 1914?

6. What caused the emergence of trade unions and organized mass political parties in Europe?

7. How did the American Progressives, as reformers, differ from the various European Socialists?

8. How did Lenin's view of socialism differ from that of Socialists in western Europe? Why did socialism not emerge as a major political force in the United States?

9. What were the major changes in science in the late nineteenth century? How did both Darwin and Einstein challenge assumptions of earlier science? How did Nietzsche and Freud undermine confidence in human rationality?

10. What were the chief characteristics of Western attitudes toward Islam in the nineteenth century? How did Islamic thinkers respond to modern Western thought?

KEY TERMS

Bolsheviks (BOHL-shuh-vihks) (p. 627)
Duma (DOO-muh) (p. 627)
ego (p. 637)
Fabians (FAY-bee-uhns) (p. 625)
id (p. 636)
Marxism (p. 625)
Mensheviks (MEN-shuh-vihks) (p. 627)

natural selection (p. 634)
pogroms (poh-GRAHMZ) (p. 622)
proletarianization (p. 616)
relativity (p. 634)
revisionism (p. 626)
soviets (p. 627)
suffragettes (p. 621)
superego (p. 637)

Note: To learn more about the topics in this chapter, please turn to the Suggested Readings at the end of the book.

INTERPRETING THE PAST

Workers and Factory Owners

Sources from MyHistoryLab for Chapter 25
myhistorylab

1) *The Sadler Report—Child Labor in the United Kingdom, 1832*

2) Edwin Chadwick, *Summary from Poor Law Commissioners*

3) Andrew Ure, *Philosophy of Manufactures*

The development of industrial economies in western Europe and the United States during the nineteenth century produced a labor force that differed from any in world history. Working in factories instead of their homes, small workshops, or marketplaces, these workers posed unique challenges to industry owners as well as European and American political leaders. The social and political responses to worker concerns shaped later-nineteenth-century and twentieth-century life.

In this exercise you will read documents that spotlight some of the most intractable problems posed by the industrial labor force and the rapidly growing urban centers where they lived and worked. The first source is an excerpt of the result of a British Parliamentary investigation of working conditions in textile factories in

England—the Sadler Report. The second document is a report by Edwin Chadwick, a British lawyer responsible for writing a report on sanitary conditions and public health for a royal commission. The final document is an excerpt from an essay that forcefully argues the case for factory owners against potential reformers.

Use the source documents to analyze and compare viewpoints relating to the living and working conditions of nineteenth-century industrial labor. Answer the following questions in an essay. Use specific examples from the documents to back up your assertions.

Questions

What is most problematic about the scenes described by the Sadler Report? What would be the effect of this description on readers?

What would be the benefits of improving public health, according to Chadwick? What key innovation is central to improving sanitary conditions for the working classes?

What is Andrew Ure's argument in defense of the factory system and its owners? How does he view unions and workers organizing to improve conditions? How does he view factory and mill owners?

26

Latin America from Independence to the 1940s

Mexico City. Juan O'Gorman (1905–1982) was best known as an architect whose most famous work is the library at the Universidad Nacional Autónima de Mexico. In 1932, he took the helm of Mexico City's department of building and construction. His interests in architecture, art (he became a renowned muralist), and the development of Mexico City are all on display in his 1949 painting *El Ciudad de Mexico*. The painting, complete with angels heralding "Viva Mexico," shows the city and the country as a work in progress.

What elements make this painting of Mexico City distinctly Latin American?

LATIN AMERICAN HISTORY

Since the early nineteenth century, Spanish- and Portuguese-speaking America, stretching from the Rio Grande to Cape Horn, has posed a paradox. Languages, religion, economic ties, and many political institutions render the area part of the Western world. Yet the economics, politics, and social life of Latin America have developed differently from other parts of the West. Despite being exceedingly rich in natural resources and possessing gold, silver, nitrates, and oil, the region has been plagued with extreme poverty. As other Western nations have moved toward liberal democracy and social equality, the states of Latin America have had millions of citizens living in situations of marked inequality and social dependence. For over a century and a half, the political life of Latin America has been characterized by uncertain democracy, authoritarian regimes, and a general tendency toward instability. Three major explanations have been set forth to account for these difficulties that have led to so much tragedy and human suffering.

The first and most widely accepted view contends that after the wars of independence the new states of Latin America remained economically and culturally dependent on Europe and, later, the United States. In effect, proponents of this view—called **dependency theory**—argue that the colonial framework was never abolished. Under Spanish and Portuguese rule, Latin America's wealth was extracted and exported for the benefit of those powers. After independence, the Creole elite turned toward foreign investors, first British and then American, to finance economic development and to provide the technology for mining, transport, and industry. As a result, Latin America became dependent on wealthy foreign powers for investment and for markets. These foreign powers, more interested in strong governments that would protect their interests than in developing the economies and political structures of the Latin American states, threw their support behind dictators whose policies impoverished their people and suppressed democratic dissent.

A second explanation emphasizes the Iberian heritage. Its advocates contend that Latin America should be viewed as a region on the periphery of the Western world in the same manner that Spain, Portugal, and Italy lie on the Mediterranean periphery of Europe. All of these Latin nations, dominated by Roman Catholicism, have had similar unstable and often authoritarian governments. They have frequently tended toward some version of dictatorship, uneven development, anticlericalism, and social cleavage between urban and rural areas and between wealthy middle-class or landed elites and poor peasant populations. Viewed in this Iberian-Mediterranean context, Latin America seems less puzzling than when it is viewed in the context of northern Europe.

dependency theory Theory that contends that after the states of Latin America achieved independence in the early-mid nineteenth century, they remained economically and culturally dependent on Europe and later the United States.

By the mid-1820s, Latin Americans had driven out their colonial rulers and broken the colonial trade monopolies. Although rich in natural resources, the region did not achieve widespread prosperity and long-lasting political stability for more than a century after independence.

There are several reasons the economic and political development of Latin America has been different from that of much of Europe or the United States despite many shared cultural features. One is that the Latin American wars of independence had not been popular grassroots movements, but rather they were attempts to break the colonial trade monopolies and preserve the existing social structure. The wars destroyed much of the region's economic infrastructure, leaving Latin America dependent on Great Britain and, later, the United States.

Perhaps most important is the role Latin America played in the integrated global economic system that began to develop in the nineteenth century. Most Latin American nations developed export economies devoted to raw materials or semifinished goods. Unfortunately, these kinds of export products are vulnerable to worldwide fluctuations in demand. Latin American nations became susceptible to undue influence from foreign business and banking interests and to political interference by the governments of the United States and Europe.

Latin America had much in common with Africa and Asia during the nineteenth and early twentieth centuries. In all three regions, nations or areas would specialize in a particular niche, providing, for example, sugar or coffee to the world economy. Huge mining industries, meanwhile, extracted resources such as copper, phosphates, gold, and diamonds. Virtually all such enterprises were dominated by Europeans or North Americans. Supplying raw products

A third explanation emphasizes conscious political, economic, and cultural decisions the Latin American Creole elite took after independence. This explanation contends that the elite, including the army officers who won the wars, sought to enrich themselves and to maintain their positions at the cost of all other segments of the population, who in many of these countries differed ethnically and racially from the elites. These officers, landowners, and urban middle-class leaders aligned their national economies with the industrializing regions of Europe and North America, with which they aligned themselves culturally as well, thus differentiating themselves from the lower classes and indigenous peoples and cultures. They also adopted European liberal political and economic ideologies to justify unlimited exploitation of economic resources on the basis of individualist enterprise. They then used the wealth generated by this exploitation to maintain their power. They embraced European concepts of progress to dismiss the legitimacy of the culture and communal values of the Indians or the peasants.

To understand the region and its past, all three viewpoints are relevant. In addition, it helps to view Latin America within a global perspective. Beginning in the nineteenth century much of the region, like much of Asia and Africa, was drawn into an integrated worldwide economic system dominated by Europe and North America. Many nations in Latin America and elsewhere developed narrow economies based on the export of one or a few raw materials or semifinished products. They were vulnerable to fluctuations in worldwide demand for these products and to political and economic interference from Europe and North America. The results were often economic turbulence and political instability.

Focus Questions

◆ What is dependency theory? How can it help to explain the history of Latin America since independence?

◆ Is Latin America's Iberian heritage a likely explanation of why Latin America has developed along such different lines from those of North America?

◆ What role did the Creole elite play in the economic and political instability that has characterized Latin America in the modern era?

might bring initial prosperity, but it provided too narrow an economic base for sustained economic well-being. In contrast, the economic advance of the United States and Europe was largely due to their ability to exploit niche economies around the globe. ■

INDEPENDENCE WITHOUT REVOLUTION

IMMEDIATE CONSEQUENCES OF LATIN AMERICAN INDEPENDENCE

HOW DID the absence of a social revolution affect Latin America after independence?

The wars of independence liberated Latin America from direct European control but left it economically exhausted and politically unstable (see Map 26–1). Only Brazil prospered. The new republics of the former Spanish Empire felt themselves vulnerable. Since the wars of independence had been civil wars, much of the population did not support the new governments. Economic life contracted: In 1830, overall production was lower than in 1800. Rugged terrain over vast distances made interregional trade difficult, and few institutions fostered it. The old patterns of overseas trade had been disrupted. There was an absence of funds for investment. Many wealthy *peninsulares* departed. Consequently, Latin American governments and businesses looked to Britain for protection, markets, and investment.

Independence also created new sources of discontent. There was much disagreement about the character of the future government. Institutions, such as the Roman Catholic Church, sought to maintain their privileges. Indian communities found

MAP 26–1 **Latin America in 1830.** By 1830 most of Latin America had been liberated from Europe. This map shows the initial borders of the states of the region with the dates of their independence. The United Provinces of La Plata formed the nucleus of what later become Argentina.

Which countries' borders differ significantly from what they are today?

themselves subject to new exploitation. Quarrels arose between the Creole elites of different regions of the new nations. The agricultural hinterlands resented the predominance of the port cities. Investors or merchants from one Latin American nation found themselves in conflict with those of others over tariffs or mining regulations. Civilians became rivals of the military for political authority.

ABSENCE OF SOCIAL CHANGE

All the elites opposed substantial social reform. The Creole victors in the wars of independence granted equal rights to all persons and, except in Brazil, had abolished slavery by 1855. However, the right to vote depended on a property qualification, and peasants remained subservient to their landlords. Colonial racial codes disappeared, but not racial prejudice. **Mestizos, mulattos**, and even Indians who achieved economic success were assimilated into the higher ranks of the social structure. Whites or light-complexioned people tended to constitute the elite of Latin America. Most important, there were no major changes in landholding; the ruling classes protected the interests of landholders.

Except for Mexico in 1910, no Latin American nation until the 1950s experienced a revolution that overthrew the social and economic structures dating from the colonial period. The absence of such social revolution is perhaps the most important factor in Latin American history during the first century of independence. The rise and fall of political regimes represented quarrels among the elite. Everyday life for most of the population did not change. Throughout the social structure, there was no mutual trust or allegiance to the political system.

CONTROL OF THE LAND

Most Latin Americans during the nineteenth century lived in the countryside. Agriculture was dominated by large *haciendas*, or plantations. The landowners ruled these estates as small domains. The *latifundia* (the large rural estates) grew larger during the nineteenth century from confiscated church lands and conquered Indian territories. Work was labor intensive because little machinery was available. For some products—salted meats, for example—there was a limited manufacturing stage in Latin America. Most crops, including grains, tobacco, sugar, coffee, and cacao, were exported.

Landowners constituted a society of their own. They sometimes formed family alliances with the wealthy urban classes who were involved in export commerce or the law. Younger sons might enter the army or the church. Landowners served in the national parliaments. Their wealth, literacy, and social connections made them the rulers of the countryside, and the army would protect them from any social uprising. The landowners lived well and comfortably, although often on isolated estates.

The rural workforce was socially and economically dependent on the landowners. In Brazil, slavery persisted until 1888. In other rural areas, many people lived as virtual slaves. **Debt peonage** was widespread and often tied a peasant to the land like a serf. Later in the nineteenth century, the new lands that were opened were generally organized as large holdings with tenants rather than as small landholdings with independent farmers. This was different from both the United States and Canada. Poor transportation made internal travel difficult and kept many people on the land. Little effort was made to provide education, leaving Latin American peasants ignorant, lacking technological skills, and incapable of improving their condition.

The second half of the nineteenth century witnessed a remarkable growth in Latin American urban life (see Figure 26–1). There was some movement from the countryside

mestizos Persons of mixed Native American and European descent.

mulattos Persons of mixed African and European descent.

debt peonage A system that forces agricultural laborers (peons) to work and live on large estates (*haciendas*) until they have repaid their debts to the estate's owner.

QUICK REVIEW

Landowners
- *Haciendas*: large plantations that dominated Latin American agriculture
- Landowners controlled the institutions of the government
- Rural workforce was dependent on the landowners

	1870	1914
Rio de Janiero	275,000	1,000,000
São Paulo	31,000	450,000
Buenos Aires	178,000	1,200,000
Lima	90,000	200,000
Guayaquil, Ecuador	12,000	75,000
Mexico City	200,000	700,000

FIGURE 26–1 Population of Latin American Cities, 1870–1914

Source: United Nations.

to the city and an influx of European immigrants as well as some from Asia. The Creole elite favored European immigration, which increased the size of the white population; Asian immigration was a source of inexpensive labor. Throughout this period there arose a political and social trade-off between the urban and rural elites. Each permitted the other to pursue its economic self-interest and repress discontent. Nonetheless, the growth of the urban centers shifted political influence to the cities and gave rise to an urban working class. Urban growth in Latin America created difficulties not unlike those that arose in Europe and the United States at about the same time.

SUBMISSIVE POLITICAL PHILOSOPHIES

The political philosophies embraced by the educated and propertied Creole elites discouraged any real challenge to the social order. The political ideas associated with European liberalism, which flourished in Latin America immediately after independence, supported republican government but also limited the franchise to property holders. Thus in Latin America, as in Europe, liberalism protected property and tended to ignore the social problems of the poor and propertyless. The Creole elite also frequently exhibited racial prejudice toward the mulatto, mestizo, and Indian populations.

Economic liberalism and the need for British investment led to free trade. After independence, Latin America exported less than it had under colonial rule and achieved a trade balance only by exporting precious metals. Because these metals often came from stocks mined years earlier, this amounted to a flight of capital. The general economic view was that Latin America would produce raw materials for export in exchange for manufactured goods imported from Europe, especially from Britain.

positivism The philosophy of Auguste Comte that science is the final, or positive, stage of human intellectual development because it involves exact descriptions of phenomena, without recourse to unobservable operative principles, such as gods or spirits.

For most of the nineteenth century, the landed sector of the economy dominated because cheap imports and a shortage of local capital discouraged indigenous industrialism. Latin American liberals championed the extension of great landed estates and the social dependence associated with them. The produce of the new land could contribute export goods to pay for the import of finished goods. Liberals favored confiscating land owned by the church and the Indians because they did not exploit their lands in what liberals considered a progressive manner.

During the second half of the century, **positivism**—the political ideas stemming from the French positivist philosopher Auguste Comte (1798–1857)—swept across Latin America. Comte and his followers had advocated the cult of science and technological progress. This highly undemocratic outlook suggested that either technocrats or dictatorial governments could best achieve modernization. It was especially popular among military officers and influenced the ongoing Latin American struggle between civilian and military elites. The great slogan of Latin American positivism, emblazoned on the flag of the Brazilian republic, was "Order and Progress." Social or political groups that created disorder or challenged the existing social order were by definition unprogressive.

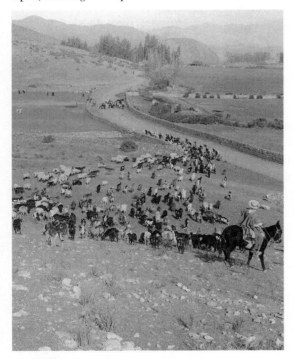

A Chilean Cattle Estate. The great landowners of Latin America ruled their huge estates as small domains.

What impact did landowners have on Latin American society?

Toward the close of the century the military forces in various countries—following Germany's model—became more professionalized. Their training often made the officer corps the most important educated elite in a country. Their education and loyalty gave them considerable influence, generally of a conservative character.

Finally, the late-nineteenth-century European theories of "scientific" racism were used to preserve the social status quo. Racial theory could attribute the economic backwardness of the region to its vast nonwhite or mixed-blood population. This explanation shifted responsibility for the economic difficulties of Latin America away from the mostly white governing elites toward Indians, blacks, mestizos, and mulattos, who had long been exploited or repressed.

This conservative intellectual heritage affected twentieth-century political thought. It can be seen in the ongoing tendency of military groups in Latin America to view themselves as the guarantors of order, ready to protect the status quo or thwart social change. It is also reflected in the way the political elites of Latin America opposed communism after the Russian Revolution. Although many Latin American nations had small organized communist parties, governments used the fear of communism to resist virtually all political movements that advocated social reform or questioned property arrangements. From the 1920s onward, the fear of communism brought support to conservative governments, whether civilian or military. Communism would become an even more powerful regional issue after the successful Cuban Revolution of 1957 installed a communist state in Latin America.

ECONOMY OF DEPENDENCE

The wars of independence destroyed the Spanish and Portuguese colonial trade monopolies. Latin America had many new trading partners, but it remained heavily dependent on external economies. Trade was free and the nations were politically independent, but other nations continued to shape Latin American economic life.

WHAT WAS the economy of dependence?

One of the chief reasons for this dependence was the absence of large internal markets. Trade after independence flowed in the same direction that it had flowed before independence because Europe remained the source of imports of finished goods. Geographical barriers hindered internal trade. The jungles of the Amazon and the Andes Mountains prevented any easy east–west trade. A lack of road systems prevented goods from moving between countries or even easily within, and there was little domestic investment in transport. European and American investments in railways generally facilitated exports rather than internal trade.

NEW EXPLOITATION OF RESOURCES

The wars of independence disrupted the Latin American economy. Mines were flooded; machinery was in disrepair; labor was dispersed. Agricultural production was also disrupted. To restore old industries such as mining and gain access to steamships and railroads, Latin Americans had to turn to Europe and North America. For decades, Britain economically dominated Latin America. The desire to pour manufactured goods into Latin America led Britain and other nations to discourage the development of manufacturing industries there. Foreign investment did help revive the mining industry in Mexico, Peru, and Chile, but mining produces raw materials, not manufactured goods.

To pay for imports and foreign services, Latin American nations turned to the production of agricultural commodities for which there was great European demand. Rural areas and the commercial centers serving agriculture became politically and economically more important than many of the old colonial urban centers. The production of wheat, beef, hides, hemp, coffee, cocoa, and other foodstuffs for the export market also raised the value of land and led governments to expand into previously unsettled territory and to confiscate the lands of the church. Because so much land was

Brazilian Coffee being loaded onto a British ship. Most Latin American countries developed an export economy based on the exchange of agricultural products, raw materials, and semifinished goods for finished goods and services from abroad. Until recently, the coffee industry dominated both the political and economic life of Brazil.

Compare this photograph with the one on page 649. Both photos are from the same time period. How are they similar?

available, agricultural production was increased by putting more land under cultivation rather than by finding more efficient ways to farm. So much wealth could be accumulated through land speculation and land development that little incentive existed for alternative investments in manufacturing. It would also have been difficult, if not impossible, for new Latin American industries to compete with the cheap goods imported from more established industrial economies abroad.

After 1850, the Latin American republics became relatively more prosperous. Chile exported copper and nitrates as well as wheat. Peru exported guano for fertilizer. Coffee was becoming king in Venezuela, Brazil, Colombia, and Central America. Sugar continued to be produced in the West Indies and Cuba, which remained under Spanish control. Argentina supplied hides and tallow. But this limited prosperity was based on the export of agricultural commodities or raw materials and the importation of finished goods.

The period from approximately 1870 through 1930 came to be seen as a kind of golden age. The economies of the Latin American nations grew because industrial production in Europe and the United States created a demand for more exports. The Latin American export economy allowed large quantities of new products to be imported from Europe and the United States. Both the exports and the imports drew Latin America more deeply than ever into the world economy.

There were three broad varieties of late-nineteenth-century Latin American exports. First were foodstuffs that were more or less like those that could be raised in Europe, chiefly wheat and beef products, for which Argentina became the great exporter. Second were distinctly tropical products, such as bananas, sugar, and coffee. Third were natural resources, including metals, of which copper was the most important; minerals, such as nitrates; and later oil.

Both the trading patterns for these goods and internal improvements in Latin American production linked the economy of the region to Europe and, after 1900, to the United States. Europeans and North Americans provided capital and the technological skills to build bridges, roads, railroads, steam lines, and mines. But whenever the economy of Europe or the United States floundered, Latin America was hurt. The region could not control its own economic destiny.

INCREASED FOREIGN OWNERSHIP AND INFLUENCE

During the late nineteenth century, the relative prosperity of the export sector increased the degree of dependence. The growing European demand gave Latin Americans a false sense of security. The vast profits to be made through mining and agricultural exports discouraged investment in local industry. Foreigners saw no reason to capitalize local industry that might replace imported goods. By late in the century, the wealthy in Latin America had, in effect, lost control of valuable sectors of their economy. For example, in 1901 British and other foreign investors owned approximately 80 percent of the Chilean nitrate industry. Foreigners also owned and operated most of the steamship lines and railroads.

The European and American economic penetration of Latin America was more subtle than that experienced by India or China, but it was no less real. Foreign powers also used their political and military influence to protect their economic interests. Britain, as the dominant power until the turn of the century, was frequently involved in the political affairs of the Latin American nations. From the Spanish-American War of 1898 onward, the United States began to exercise more direct influence in the region. In 1903, to facilitate its plans to build a canal across Panama, the United States participated in the rebellion that allowed Panama to separate from Colombia. The U.S. military intervened in the Caribbean and Central America. By the 1920s, the United States had replaced Britain as the dominant trading partner of Latin America.

U.S. interventions were one cost of Latin America's dependent economy. More significant costs, however, arose from fundamental shifts in world trade that were brought on by World War I and continued through the 1920s. First, the amount of trade carried on by European countries decreased. Second, during the 1920s, world prices of agricultural commodities dropped. Latin American nations had to produce more goods to pay for their imports. Third, synthetic products manufactured in Europe or North America replaced the natural products supplied by Latin America. Finally, petroleum began to replace other natural products as an absolute percentage of world trade. This shift meant that petroleum-exporting countries, such as Mexico, gained a greater share of export income.

Banana Republic.   For most of the twentieth century the United Fruit Company, a U.S. conglomerate, exerted tremendous economic influence throughout Central America. The company also wielded significant political power, especially in Guatemala, where workers in this photograph hang banana bunches from a pole.

Why were foreign entities able to exert so much power in Latin America?

ECONOMIC CRISES AND NEW DIRECTIONS

The Great Depression produced a crisis in this **neocolonial economy**. Commodity prices collapsed. The republics of Latin America could not repay their debts to foreign banks. The Depression led to the beginning of a new economic era in Latin America after the conclusion of World War II. It was marked by economic nationalism and a determination to create national economies that were not wholly dependent on foreign events and wealth.

With the Depression, it became necessary to substitute domestic manufactured goods for those imported from abroad. Various nations pursued policies called **import substitution**, and by the mid-1940s there were three varieties of manufacturing in Latin America. First, there were industries that, as in the past, transformed raw materials for export, such as food processing, mining, and petroleum refining. Second, there were industries addressing local demands, such as power plants and machine shops. Third, there were industries, basically assembly plants, that transformed imported materials to take advantage of cheap labor. None of this manufacturing was particularly sophisticated, and none of it involved heavy industry. Not until the 1950s would significant steel production, for example, occur in the region.

neocolonial economy   An economic relationship between a former colonial state and countries with more developed economies in which the former colony exports raw materials to and imports manufactured goods from the more developed nations.

import substitution   The replacement of imported goods with those manufactured domestically.

SEARCH FOR POLITICAL STABILITY

The new states of independent Latin America had little or no experience in self-government. The Spanish Empire had been ruled directly by the monarchy and by Spanish-born royal bureaucrats. This monarchical or paternalistic heritage survived in two forms. First, many traditionalists and conservatives favored the establishment of monarchies in Latin America, including José de San Martín (1778–1850). Monarchy was briefly established in Mexico. In Brazil, an emperor from the Portuguese royal family governed until 1889.

The second heritage of the colonial monarchy was the proclivity of the Latin American political elites to tolerate or support strong executives. The early republic

WHO WERE the *caudillos?*

caudillo Latin American strongman, or dictator, usually with strong ties to the military.

constitutions were frequently suspended or rewritten, so that a strong leader could consolidate his power. Such figures were called **caudillos**. They usually came from the officer corps or enjoyed strong ties to the army. The real basis of their rule was force. *Caudillos* might support conservative causes, such as protection of the church or strong central government, or they might pursue liberal policies, such as the confiscation of church land, the extension of landed estates, and the development of education.

Initially, such dictatorial government was accepted simply to ensure political stability. In many countries the early years of independence saw internal conflicts. A national *caudillo* might reach a compromise with various regional *caudillos* that allowed them to retain substantial local control. Strongmen also encountered little opposition because of their repressive policies. Later in the century the relative prosperity of expanding economies quieted potential discontent. The dictators became more skilled at both repression and patronage. The political and social elites rallied to their support when, around the turn of the century, the young labor movement called strikes. Even when *caudillos* were forced from office and parliamentary government was more or less restored, the regimes that replaced them were neither genuinely liberal nor democratic. Parliamentary governments usually ruled by courtesy of the military and in the economic interest of the existing elites. No matter who ruled, the life of the overwhelming mass of the population changed little. Except for the Mexican Revolution of 1910, Latin American politics was run by and for the elite.

THREE NATIONAL HISTORIES

WHY ARE the histories of Argentina, Mexico, and Brazil so different in spite of these nations' commonalities?

Argentina, Mexico, and Brazil possess more than 50 percent of the land, people, and wealth of the region. Their histories illustrate the general themes of Latin American history.

ARGENTINA

Argentine history from independence to World War II can be divided into three eras. From the rebellion against Spain in 1810 until midcentury, the question of which region of the nation would be dominant was foremost. From 1853 until 1916, Argentina experienced economic expansion and large-scale immigration from Europe, which transformed its society and its world position. From 1916 to 1943, Argentines failed to establish a democratic state and struggled with an economy they did not control.

In 1810, the junta in Buenos Aires overturned Spanish government. However, the other regions of the viceroyalty of Río de la Plata refused to accept its leadership. Paraguay, Uruguay, and Bolivia went their separate ways. Conflicts between Buenos Aires and the remaining provinces dominated the first seventy years of Argentine history. Eventually, Buenos Aires established its primacy because it dominated trade on the Río de la Plata and controlled the international customhouse, which assured revenue.

Between 1821 and 1827 Bernardino Rivadavia (1780–1845) worked to create a liberal political state, but he could not overcome the forces of regionalism. His major accomplishment was a commercial treaty in 1823 that established Great Britain as a dominant trading partner. Thus began a deep intermeshing of trade and finance between the two nations that would continue for over a century. After Rivadavia's resignation in 1827 came the classical period of *caudillo* rule in Argentina. The strongman of the province of Buenos Aires was Juan Manuel de Rosas (1793–1877). In 1831 he negotiated the Pact of the Littoral, whereby Buenos Aires was put in charge of foreign relations, trade, and the customhouse, while the other provinces were left to run their own internal affairs. Within Buenos Aires, Rosas set up what amounted to dictatorial rule. One of his devices was the secret *Mazorca* (ear of corn) association, which terrorized his opponents. His major policies were expansion of trade and agriculture, suppression of the Indians, and nationalism.

Rosas's success in strengthening Buenos Aires bred resentment in other provinces, and in 1852 he was overthrown. The next year a federal constitution was promulgated for the Argentine republic. Buenos Aires remained aloof until the republic conquered the province in 1859. Disputes continued. In 1880 the city of Buenos Aires was made a distinct federal province, separate from its rich hinterland. Provincials had hoped that this arrangement would lessen the influence of the city, but the economic prosperity of the end of the century simply gave the capital new prominence.

The Argentine economy was overwhelmingly agricultural, the chief exports at midcentury being animal products. Internal transportation was poor and the country was sparsely populated. Technological advances changed this situation during the last quarter of the century. In 1876 the first refrigerator ship, *La Frigiorique*, steamed into Buenos Aires. Henceforth, it would be possible to transport large quantities of Argentine beef to Europe. Furthermore, at about the same time it became clear that wheat farming could be extended throughout the pampas. In 1879 and 1880 a government army under General (and later President) Julio Roca (president 1880–1886, 1898–1904) carried out a major campaign against the Indian population known as the Conquest of the Desert. The British soon began to construct and manage railways to carry wheat from the interior to the coast, where it would be loaded on British and other foreign steamships. Government policy made the purchase of land by wealthy Argentines simple and cheap. The owners, in turn, rented the land to tenants. The predominance of both large landowners and foreign business interests thus continued throughout the most significant economic transformation in Argentine history.

The development of the **pampas** and the vastly increased production of beef and wheat made Argentina one of the wealthiest nations of Latin America and a major agricultural rival of the United States. The opening of land, even if only for tenant farming and not ownership, encouraged hundreds of thousands of Europeans, particularly from Spain and Italy, to immigrate to Argentina. The immigrants also provided workers for the food-processing, service, and transportation industries in Buenos Aires. By 1900 Argentina had changed drastically. It was much more urbanized and industrialized. More people had reason to be politically discontent. Moreover, the children of the nineteenth-century immigrants often became the strongest Argentine nationalists during the twentieth century.

Prosperity quieted political opposition for a time. The conservative landed oligarchy governed under presidents who perpetuated a strong export economy. Like similar groups elsewhere, they ignored the social questions raised by urbanization and industrialization.

They also ignored the political aspirations of the urban middle and professional classes, whose members wanted a greater share in political life and an end to political corruption. In 1890 these groups founded the Radical Party, which achieved little until, in 1912, the conservative government expanded the franchise and provided for the secret ballot. Four years later, Radical Party leader Hipólito Irigoyen (1850–1933), was elected president (first term 1916–1922). Without significant support in the legislature, his presidency

Juan Manuel de Rosas (1793–1877), a *Caudillo* of Buenos Aires from 1827 to 1852. Rosas was the archetypal *caudillo*, waging relentless war on the natives of Patagonia.

How do the *caudillos* compare with modern dictators?

pampas The fertile South American lowlands that include the Argentine provinces of Buenos Aires, La Pampa, Santa Fe, and Córdoba, most of Uruguay, and the southernmost end of Brazil, Rio Grande do Sul, covering more than 750,000 km^2 (289,577 sq mi).

Immigrant Hotel, Buenos Aires, ca. 1900. More than 8 million people from Europe and Asia immigrated to South America and the Caribbean between 1860 and 1920. In this photograph, European immigrants to Buenos Aires dine in a communal hall at a hotel set aside specifically for them.

Look closely at this photo. Why are there no women present?

CHRONOLOGY

ARGENTINA

1810	Junta in Buenos Aires overthrows Spanish government
1827–1852	Era of Juan Manuel de Rosas's dictatorial government
1876	Ship refrigeration makes possible export of beef around the world
1879–1880	General Julio Roca carries out Conquest of the Desert against the Indian population
1914–1918	Argentina remains neutral in World War I
1930s	Period of strong influence of nationalist military
1943–1956	Era of Juan and Eva Perón

nacionalismo A right-wing Argentine nationalist movement that arose in the 1930s and resembled European fascism.

Perónism An authoritarian, nationalist movement founded in Argentina in the 1940s by the dictator Juan Perón.

brought few changes. He remained neutral in World War I, so Argentina could trade with both sides. Nonetheless, the war put great pressure on the economy, and much labor agitation resulted. Although previously sympathetic toward labor, Irigoyen as president used troops against strikers. The most violent labor clash occurred in January 1919, when troops quelled a general strike in Buenos Aires during what became known as the *Semana Trágica*, or Tragic Week. Thereafter, the Radical Party attempted to consolidate support among conservatives and pursued policies that benefited landowners and urban business interests. This was possible because of the close relationship between agricultural producers and processors and because both the landed and the middle classes wanted to resist concessions to the working classes.

By the end of the 1920s, the Radical Party had become corrupt and directionless. The worldwide commodity depression hurt exports. In 1930, the military staged a coup. The officers returned power to conservative civilians, and Argentina remained dependent on the British export market. U.S. interests also began to establish plants in Argentina, removing still more economic activity from Argentine control.

In the 1930s, a right-wing nationalistic movement, **nacionalismo**, arose among writers, journalists, and a few politicians. It resembled the fascist political movements then active in Europe. Its supporters equated British and American domination of the economy with imperialism. They rejected liberalism, detested communism, were anti-Semitic, and supported the Roman Catholic Church. Nacionalismo advocated social reforms that recognized the needs of workers and the poor while seeking social harmony rather than communist revolution or socialist reconstruction of the economy. In effect, these groups were anti-imperialistic, socially concerned, authoritarian, and sympathetic to the rule of a modern *caudillo*. World War II gave these attitudes and their supporters new influence.

The war closed almost all of Europe to Argentine exports, creating an economic crisis. The country's leadership seemed incapable of responding to the crisis, and in 1943 the military again seized control. Its leaders had lost patience with politicians more interested in patronage than in patriotism. Many of the officers were fiercely nationalistic children of immigrants. They distrusted liberal politics. Some officers had become deeply impressed by the Fascist and Nazi movements and their rejection of European liberal politics. The officers also shared the Fascist and Nazi hostility to Britain. They contended that the government must address social questions, industrialize the country, and liberate it from foreign economic control. In all these respects, they echoed the *nacionalistas*.

Between 1943 and 1946 Juan Perón (1895–1974), one of the colonels involved in the 1943 coup, forged this social discontent and these authoritarian political attitudes into a remarkable political movement known as **Perónism**. It was authoritarian, initially militaristic, anticommunist, and socially progressive. Perón understood better than his fellow officers that political power could be exerted by appeals to the Argentine working class, particularly in Buenos Aires. He gained the support of the trade unions that were opposed to communism. In 1945 he had been arrested by other military leaders, but he was freed when it became clear that he alone could silence working-class discontent. In 1946 he made himself the voice of working-class democracy, even though after his election to the presidency he created an authoritarian regime that only marginally addressed industrial problems. He was greatly aided by his wife, the former actress Eva Duarte (1919–1952). She enjoyed charismatic support among trade-union members and the working class. (See Document, "Eva Perón Explains the Sources of Her Popularity.")

Perón became the most famous of the postwar Latin American dictators, but his power and appeal were rooted in the antiliberal attitudes that had been fostered by the corruption and aimlessness of Argentine politics during the Depression. He was the supreme twentieth-century embodiment of the *caudillo*. He was ousted in 1956, but stability would continue to elude Argentine politics.

MEXICO

The heritage of Mexican independence was a combination of the thwarted social revolution led by Father Hidalgo and José María Morelos between 1811 and 1815, and the conservative political coup carried out in 1820 by the Creole elite against a potentially liberal Spanish crown. For the first century of independence conservative forces held sway, but in 1910 the Mexican people launched the most far-reaching revolution in Latin American history.

The years from 1820 to 1876 were a time of turmoil, economic floundering, and humiliation. Independent Mexico attempted no liberal political experiments. Its first ruler was Agustín de Iturbide (1783–1824), who ruled until 1823 as an emperor. Thereafter, Mexico was governed by a succession of *caudillo* presidents, who depended on the army for support. The strongest of these figures was Antonio López de Santa Anna (1795–1863), a general and a political opportunist who usually supported conservative political and social interests. He ruled in a thoroughly dictatorial manner. More than once he was driven from office, but he inevitably returned until finally exiled in 1855.

The midcentury movement against Santa Anna's autocracy was called *La Reforma*. In theory, its supporters were liberal, but Mexican liberalism was associated primarily with anticlericalism, confiscation of church lands, and opposition to military influence on politics. *La Reforma* aimed to produce political stability, civilian rule, and an economic policy that would attract foreign capital and immigrants. Having deposed Santa Anna, the leaders of the reform movement passed legislation to break up large landed estates, particularly those owned by the church, and to promote the establishment of small farms. However, the actual content of the laws permitted existing landowners to purchase additional land cheaply and thus made great estates even larger. The legislative attack on privileges of the church led to further civil war between 1857 and 1860. In January 1861 Benito Juárez (1806–1872) entered Mexico City as the temporary victor.

Political instability was matched by economic stagnation. After 1820 many Spanish officials and merchants fled Mexico, taking with them large quantities of gold and silver. The mines that had produced Mexico's colonial wealth were in poor condition, and the country could not repair them. The hacienda system left farming in a backward condition. Cheap imports of manufactured goods stifled domestic industries. Transportation was primitive. The government's remedy was massive foreign borrowing, and soon interest payments consumed the national budget.

Political weakness and economic disarray invited foreign intervention. The territorial ambitions of the United States impinged on Mexico in two ways. In 1823 the Mexican government allowed Stephen F. Austin (1793–1836) to begin the colonization

Argentine president Juan Domingo Perón and his wife Eva address a throng of supporters from a balcony in Buenos Aires.
What were the bases of Perón's support?

La Reforma The nineteenth-century Mexican liberal reform movement that opposed Santa Anna's dictatorship and sought to foster economic progress, civilian rule, and political stability. It was strongly anti-clerical.

Benito Juárez led *La Reforma,* a mid-nineteenth-century movement opposed to the autocracy of Santa Anna. Juárez is portrayed with the tools of an engineer in front of a background of railway building to suggest his dedication to economic progress and modernization in Mexico.
What do you notice most about Benito Juárez in this image, and why?

DOCUMENT

Eva Perón Explains the Sources of Her Popularity

The Perónist movement in Argentina drew broad support from workers and the poor. The movement involved a cult of personality around both Perón and his wife, Eva. In 1951 Eva Perón published a book entitled My Mission in Life (La Razón de mi Vida)*. Here she explains how she sought to relate to her husband's political supporters.*

- **Why** was Eva Perón's acceptance of the name "Evita" a political act? How did her use of this name separate her from the ruling elites of Argentina? What is the role she projects for herself in her relationship to various social groups in Argentina? Do you believe her discussion of herself to be sincere or politically opportunistic?

When I chose to be "Evita," I chose the path of my people. ...

Only the people call me "Evita." Only the *descamisados* [the "unshirted," as Perón's working-class followers were termed] learned to call me so. ...

I appeared to them thus the day I went to meet the humble of my land, telling them that I preferred being "Evita" to being the wife of the president, if that "Evita" could help to mitigate some grief, or dry a tear.

If a man of the government, a leader, a politician, an ambassador, who normally calls me "Señora," should call me "Evita," it would sound as strange and out of place to me as if a street-urchin, a workingman, or a humble person of the people should call me "Señora." ...

Now, if you ask me which I prefer, my reply would be immediately that I prefer the name by which I am known to the people.

---

of Texas. During the next decade, the policies of Santa Anna stirred resentment among the Texas settlers, and in 1835 they rebelled. The next year Santa Anna destroyed the defenders of the Alamo but was decisively defeated at the battle of San Jacinto. Texas became an independent republic that was annexed by the United States in 1845. Border clashes between Mexican and U.S. forces enabled President James Polk to launch a war against Mexico in 1846 that saw the United States army occupy Mexico City. Through the treaty of Guadalupe Hidalgo (1848), the United States gained a vast portion of Mexican territory, including what is now New Mexico, Arizona, and California.

Further foreign intervention occurred as a result of Juárez's liberal victory in 1861. Mexican conservatives and clerics invited the Austrian Archduke Maximilian (1832–1867) to become the emperor of Mexico. Napoleon III (r. 1852–1870) of France, who portrayed himself as a defender of the Roman Catholic Church, provided support for this venture. In May 1862, French troops invaded Mexico. Maximilian became emperor but was unable to gain support from much of the population. In 1867, Juárez captured the unhappy emperor and executed him. The Mexicans had been victorious, but their vulnerability to foreign powers had again been exposed.

Once restored to office, the liberal leaders continued their measures against the church but failed to rally significant popular support. In 1876 Porfirio Díaz (1830–1915) seized power and retained it until 1911. He maintained one of the most successful dictatorships in Latin American history by giving almost every political sector something it wanted. He allowed landowners to purchase public land cheaply; he cultivated the army; and he made peace with the church. He used repression against opponents and bribery to cement the loyalty of his supporters. Wealthy Mexicans grew even richer, and Mexico became a respectable member of the international financial community. Unprecedented quantities of foreign capital flooded the nation. Foreign companies, especially from the United States, invested heavily in what, by 1900, appeared to be a thoroughly stable country.

When a street-urchin calls me "Evita," I feel as though I were the mother of all urchins, and of all the weak and the humble of my land.

When a workingman calls me "Evita," I feel glad to be the companion of all the workingmen of my country and even of the whole world.

When a woman of my country calls me "Evita," I imagine myself her sister, and that of all the women of humanity.

And so, almost without noticing it, I have classified in these three examples the principal activities of "Evita" relating to the humble, the workers, and women.

The truth is that, without any artificial effort, at no personal cost, as though I had been born for all this, I feel myself responsible for the humble as though I were the mother of all of them; I fight shoulder to shoulder with the workers as though I were another of their companions from the workshop or factory; in front of the women who trust in me, I consider myself something like an elder sister, responsible to a certain degree for the destiny of all of them who have placed their hopes in me.

And certainly I do not deem this an honor but a responsibility. ...

Yes. I confess that I have an ambition, one single, great personal ambition: I would like the name of "Evita" to figure somewhere in the history of my country.

Yet problems remained. The peasants wanted land and resented the power of the landlords. Food production actually declined during the Díaz regime, so many Mexicans were malnourished. Labor unrest and strikes afflicted the textile and mining industries, and Díaz used military force against workers. Inflation caused real wages for the working class to decline in the first decade of the twentieth century. The Panic of 1907 in the United States disrupted the Mexican economy. By 1910 the so-called *Pax Porfiriana* was unraveling.

In 1911, Francisco Madero (d. 1913), a wealthy landowner and moderate liberal, led an insurrection that drove Díaz into exile. Shortly thereafter, Madero was elected president. He recognized the rights of trade unions to organize and to strike, but he was unwilling to undertake significant agrarian reform that might have changed the pattern of landholding. He ended by being distrusted both by conservatives, who wanted little or no change from the days of Díaz, and by reformist leaders, who thought the time had come for extensive social and political restructuring. Radical leaders emerged, calling for social change. Pancho Villa (1874–1923) in the north and Emiliano Zapata (1879–1919) in the south rallied mass followings of peasants who demanded fundamental structural changes in rural landholding. In late 1911 Zapata proclaimed his Plan of Ayala, which in effect set forth a program of large-scale peasant confiscation of land. Much of the struggle during the next ten years would be between supporters and opponents of such agrarian reform.

Madero found himself squeezed between the conservative supporters of the deposed Díaz and the radical peasant revolutionaries. No one trusted him, and in early 1913 he was overthrown by General Victoriano Huerta (1854–1916), who had the help

The Execution of Maximilian of Mexico, June 19, 1867, by the French Impressionist painter Édouard Manet. Between 1867 and 1869 Manet completed a series of compositions depicting the execution of the Mexican emperor. This is the final and largest work.

Édouard Manet (1832-1883), "The Execution of Emperor Maximilian of Mexico, June 19, 1867". Oil on canvas. Location: Staedtische Kunsthalle, Mannheim, Germany. © 2009 ARS Artists Rights Society, NY.

Does this painting glorify or belittle the execution of the emperor?

of the United States and was assassinated not long thereafter. Huerta, who was basically a dictator, failed to quash the peasant rebellion. His attacks against the forces of Zapata involved considerable loss of life. In the meantime, Venustiano Carranza (1859–1920), a wealthy landowner, joined Villa's cause. He soon put himself at the head of a large Constitutionalist Army—so called because it advocated the restoration of constitutional government in opposition to the political dictatorship of Huerta—that initially received the support of both Zapata and Villa. Huerta's government collapsed on August 15, 1914, when Constitutionalist forces entered Mexico City. Thereafter disputes erupted between Carranza and Villa and then between Carranza and Zapata. These conflicts arose both from simple political rivalry and from Carranza's refusal to embrace the kind of radical agrarian reform the two peasant leaders sought. Carranza eventually won out, thanks to his political skills and the effectiveness of his army.

Carranza's political skills also helped him build a broad base and edge out both Villa and Zapata as the chief leader of the revolution. One particularly skillful move followed an attempt by U.S. President Woodrow Wilson (1856–1924) to support Carranza by sending U.S. Marines to Veracruz in April 1914. Carranza shrewdly denounced the United States for this action, thus casting himself in the role of patriot and nationalist, and the Marines departed. In another skillful move, he addressed himself to the concerns of urban industrial workers as well as the land hunger of rural peasants, successfully separating the two groups. This division ultimately doomed the effort to implement an agrarian revolution. Carranza made many promises, especially about agrarian reform, that he had little or no intention of carrying out.

Beginning in early 1915 Carranza's military forces began an ultimately successful campaign against Villa and Zapata. The peasant leaders still commanded regional support but could not win control of the nation. During 1916 Carranza confronted U.S. military intervention along the border that continued until early 1917, when the United States became involved in World War I in Europe. Throughout the turmoil in Mexico, the government of the United States attempted to protect American interests. These activities involved ongoing diplomatic initiatives with the various groups in Mexico as well as the threat of military action.

After years of deadly and destructive civil war, Carranza's forces wrote the Constitution of 1917, setting forth a program for ongoing social revolution—never pursued with any vigor—and political reform. Perhaps its two most famous provisions were Articles 27 and 123. Article 27 provided for the government to become the owner of water and mineral rights and other subsoil property rights. This article abrogated all prerevolutionary contracts with foreign companies in regard to oil and minerals. Together with other provisions, it meant that peasant villages could reclaim land they had lost over the past half century. Article 123 guaranteed certain rights for the organization of labor. Many years would pass before all the provisions of the constitution could be enforced, but from 1917 onward it provided the ongoing goals of the revolution and the ideals toward which Mexican governments were expected to strive.

Carranza and his immediate subordinates were much more conservative than either Villa or Zapata. They recognized the agrarian problem but were cautious about changing existing property arrangements. They admired the economic development they had seen in California and were determined to modernize Mexican political life and attract capital investment; Mexican leaders would share these goals from that time onward. Thus, despite the radical rhetoric and the upheaval among peasants that the revolution involved, the Mexican revolution saw the victory of a middle-class elite who would attempt to govern through enlightened paternalism. Although turmoil would persist for many years, with Carranza's victory the general direction of Mexican political life had been established.

QUICK REVIEW

Venustiano Carranza (1859-1920)

- Wealthy landowner who initially joined Villa and Zapata in opposition to Huerta's dictatorship
- Led Constitutionalist Army
- Broke with Villa and Zapata over agrarian reforms; defeated them in civil war
- Constitution of 1917 promised reform; Carranza instead led middle-class elite in imposing enlightened paternalism

The decade after 1917 witnessed both confusion and consolidation. In 1919 Zapata was lured into an ambush and killed. Carranza was assassinated in 1920. Three years later Villa was also assassinated. In this turmoil, Carranza's generals provided stability, serving as presidents in the 1920s. They moved cautiously and hesitated to press land redistribution too quickly. They were opposed by the Roman Catholic Church, which at one point suspended all services for more than two years. In 1929 Plutarco Elías Calles (1877–1945) organized the **PRI**, the Institutional Revolutionary Party, which quickly became the most important political force in the nation. The Mexican political system became dominated by a single party within which most political debate occurred, rather than a system dominated by a single strong leader. Despite external criticism and internal tensions, the PRI oversaw the longest period of political stability experienced by any Latin American nation in the twentieth century.

The Mexican Revolution.   The forces of Emiliano Zapata march on Xochimilco in 1914. Women fought alongside men and played other prominent roles during the Mexican Revolution. **What impressions of the fighters do you get from this photograph?**

In 1934 Lázaro Cárdenas (1895–1970) was elected president and moved directly to fulfill the promises and programs of 1917. He turned tens of millions of acres of land over to peasant villages. In 1938, when Mexico was the third largest producer of petroleum, he expropriated the oil industry. His nationalization policy established PeMex, the Mexican national oil company. Cárdenas left other mineral industries in private and generally foreign hands. His extensive reforms went through smoothly because he worked through bureaucratic and administrative means.

With the election of Manuel Ávila Camacho (1897–1955) in 1940, the era of revolutionary politics ended. Thereafter, the major issues in Mexico were those generally associated with postwar economic development. But unlike other Latin American nations, Mexico, because of its revolution, could confront those issues with a democratic perspective and a sense of collective social responsibility, no matter how imperfectly those goals might be realized.

PRI   The Institutional Revolutionary Party, which emerged from the Mexican Revolution of 1911 and governed Mexico until the end of the twentieth century.

BRAZIL

Postcolonial Brazil, the largest Latin American country, differed in several important respects from other newly independent nations in the region. Its language and colonial heritage were Portuguese rather than Spanish. For the first sixty-seven years of its independence it had a relatively stable monarchical government. And it retained slavery until 1888.

CHRONOLOGY

MEXICO

1820–1823	Agustín de Iturbide rules unsuccessfully as emperor
1833–1855	Santa Anna dominates Mexican political scene
1846–1848	Mexico defeated by United States and loses considerable territory
1861	Victory of liberal forces under Juárez
1862–1867	French troops led by Archduke Maximilian of Austria unsuccessfully invade Mexico
1876–1911	Era of Porfirio Díaz
1911	Beginning of Mexican Revolution
1911	Zapata proclaims Plan of Ayala
1917	Forces of Carranza proclaim constitution
1929	Institutional Revolutionary Party (PRI) organized

Brazil had moved directly from being part of the Portuguese monarchy to becoming an independent empire in 1822. The first emperor, Pedro I (r. 1822–1831), while serving as regent for his father, the king of Portugal, had put himself at the head of the independence movement. Although he granted Brazil a constitution in 1823, Pedro's high-handed rule and his patronage of Portuguese courtiers rather than Brazilians led to his abdication in 1831. Brazilians then took hold of their own destinies.

After a decade of political uncertainty under a regency, Pedro II (r. 1831–1889), the fifteen-year-old son of Pedro I, assumed direct power in 1840 and governed Brazil until 1889. Pedro II made wise and shrewd use of patronage. He established a reputation as a constitutional monarch by asking leaders of both the conservative and the liberal political parties to form ministries. Consequently, Brazil enjoyed remarkable political stability. However, the government took few initiatives to develop the economy.

The great divisive issue in Brazil was slavery. Sugar production remained the mainstay of the economy until the 1850s. Most sugar plantations were located in the coastal provinces of the northeast. Their owners were conservative and resistant to changes in production. Soil exhaustion and inefficient farming methods made profits impossible without the cheap labor of slaves. From about 1850 coffee cultivation began to spread in the southern provinces, and soon coffee cultivation dominated Brazilian agriculture. Coffee producers also used slave labor, but their profits were much larger than those of the sugar producers. Coffee planters also tended to see themselves as economic progressives, so they were more open to emancipation.

As early as 1826 the Brazilian government had made a treaty with Great Britain, agreeing to suppress the slave trade. By 1850 Brazil had virtually ceased importing slaves, freeing the capital once spent on slaves for investments in coffee. The end of slave imports effectively doomed the institution of slavery because the birthrate among slaves was too low for the slave population to reproduce itself, but abolition was still a difficult step.

The Paraguayan War of 1865–1870 postponed consideration of the slave question. This conflict pitted Brazil, Argentina, and Uruguay against Paraguay. The dictator of Paraguay, Francisco Solano López (1827–1870), fought a war of attrition. His death in battle ended the war but only after more than half of the adult male population of Paraguay had been killed.

Slavery returned to the forefront of Brazilian politics. Brazil and the Spanish colonies of Puerto Rico and Cuba were now the only slaveholding countries in the hemisphere. The emperor favored gradual emancipation. A law in 1871 freed slaves owned by the crown and decreed legal freedom for future children of slaves, but it required them to work on plantations until the age of twenty-one. However, throughout the 1870s and 1880s, the abolition movement grew in Brazil. Public figures from across the political spectrum called for an end to slavery. Abolitionists helped slaves escape. The army resented having to enforce laws protecting slavery. In 1888 Pedro II was in Europe for medical treatment, and his daughter was regent. She favored abolition rather than gradual emancipation. When Parliament passed a law abolishing slavery without any compensation to the slave owners, she signed it, ending slavery in Brazil.

The abolition of slavery brought to a head other issues that in 1889 caused the collapse of the monarchy. Planters who received no financial compensation for their slaves were resentful. Roman Catholic clerics were disaffected by disputes

Antislavery Print. Slavery lasted longer in Brazil than in any other nation in North or South America. Antislavery groups circulated prints such as this one published in France to illustrate the brutality of slave life in Brazil.

Why did slavery last so long in Brazil?

with the emperor over education. Pedro II was unwell; his daughter was unpopular and distrusted. The officer corps of the army wanted more political influence. In November 1889 the army sent Pedro II into exile in France.

The Brazilian republic lasted from 1891 to 1930. Like the monarchy, it was dominated by a small group of the wealthy, mostly coffee planters. A political arrangement among the state governors allowed the republic to function smoothly. The president was chosen alternately from the states of São Paulo and Minas Gerais. In turn, the other eighteen governors had considerable local political latitude. Fixed elections and patronage kept the system in operation. Literacy replaced property as the qualification for voting, leaving few people qualified to vote. There was consequently little organized opposition and, for that matter, little political life at all.

From the 1890s onward the coffee industry dominated the nation. Around 1900 Brazil was producing over three fourths of the world's coffee. The crop's success led almost inevitably to overproduction. To meet this problem, the government subsidized prices with loans from foreign banks and taxes on the rest of the economy, which felt exploited by the coffee interests. High world coffee prices encouraged competition from other Latin American producers, which in turn required more price supports in Brazil. Throughout the life of the republic Brazil remained essentially a country producing a single product for export and few goods for internal consumption.

The end of slavery, the expansion of coffee production, and the beginning of a slow growth of urban industry attracted foreign immigrants to Brazil. They tended to settle in the cities and constituted the core of the early industrial labor force. World War I caused major economic disruption. Urban labor discontent appeared. There was a general strike in São Paulo in 1917, with the inevitable military action against the strikers. The failure to address urban and industrial social problems and the political corruption of the republic led to attempted military coups in 1922 and 1924. Both revolts failed, but they indicated profound discontent and demonstrated that certain segments of the military were determined to change the political system. They wanted an economy that was not dependent on a single export crop and a political system that depended on more than corruption and recognized interests besides those of the coffee planters.

Coffee had been "king" of the Brazilian republic, and its collapse brought the republic down with it. In 1929 coffee prices hit record lows; currency exchange rates fell; and foreign loans were unavailable. Millions of bags of coffee lay in warehouses. Government reserves were depleted in an unsuccessful attempt to hold up the price of coffee and to pay for imports no longer being funded by coffee exports. The economic structure of the republic lay in shambles. In October 1930 a military coup installed Getulio Vargas (1883–1954) in the presidency. Vargas governed Brazil until 1945.

The Vargas years were a major turning point. Vargas was initially supported by the reform elements in the military, by professional middle-class groups, and by urban workers. In office, he moved first to the right and then to the left and then back again. He was an experimentalist and pragmatist who primarily wanted to hold on to power and to make Brazil a modern nation. Vargas recognized the new social and economic groups shaping Brazilian political life. First with constitutionalism and then with dictatorship, he attempted to allow the government to act on behalf of those groups without allowing them to influence or direct the government in a genuinely democratic manner. Despite the personal power that accrued to him, he did not form his own political party or movement as Perón would later do in Argentina or as the Mexican revolutionaries had done. Rather, Vargas attempted to function like a ringmaster directing the various forces in Brazilian life. His failure to establish a genuinely stable institutional

QUICK REVIEW

The Brazilian Republic

♦ 1889: Pedro II sent into exile

♦ Brazilian republic (1891–1930) controlled by small group of wealthy persons

♦ Coffee production dominated the Brazilian economy

QUICK REVIEW

Getulio Vargas (1883–1954)

♦ October 1930: Vargas comes to power in military coup

♦ Vargas sought to represent a wider spectrum of Brazilian society without giving up personal power

♦ Vargas assumed dictatorial power in 1937

OVERVIEW Latin American Products for Export, 1820–1930

Argentina	animal products (meat, leather, wool), grain
Bolivia	tin, silver, wool
Brazil	coffee, sugar, rubber
Chile	copper
Colombia	coffee, cattle
Ecuador	bananas
Mexico	silver, cattle, oil
Peru	nitrates, silver
Uruguay	animal products (meat, leather)
Venezuela	coffee, cattle

Estado Novo The "new state" based on political stability and economic and social progress supposedly established by the dictator Getulio Vargas after 1937.

framework for including political interest groups besides coffee planters has influenced Brazil to the present day.

Vargas and his supporters sought to lessen dependence on coffee by fostering industries to produce goods that had been imported from abroad. The policy succeeded, and by the mid-1930s domestic manufacturing was increasing. In the constitution of 1934 Vargas established a legal framework for labor relations. The structures were paternalistic but included an eight-hour day and a minimum wage. The constitution also asserted government responsibility to protect mineral and water rights.

In the Brazilian context these measures appeared reformist, if not necessarily liberal,

Vargas and the Military. Getulio Vargas became ruler of Brazil in 1930 through a military coup. Here he stands with his military supporters. One of the purposes of such pictures was to remind the public that any serious opposition would be put down by the military.

Who seems to be more in power here-Vargas or the military officers?

and marked a departure from government policy dominated by the coffee oligarchy and politics by patronage. However, in the late 1930s Vargas confronted major political opposition from both the Brazilian Communist Party (founded in 1922) and a new right-wing movement called *Integralism*. In 1937, facing these political opponents, Vargas assumed personal dictatorial power. His regime thereafter was repressive. He claimed to have established an **Estado Novo** ("new state"). He wrapped himself in the flag of nationalism and presented himself as the protector of national stability.

Like the European dictators of the same era, Vargas used censorship, secret police, and torture against his political opponents. He used his newly assumed power to diversify and modernize the economy. In 1940 a five-year plan provided more state direction for the economy. His government favored the production of goods from heavy industry that would be used within in Brazil. To maintain the support of workers and trade unions, the state issued a progressive labor code. Siding with the Allies in World War II, Brazil built up large reserves of foreign currency through the export of foodstuffs. This economic activity and imposed political stability allowed the government to secure foreign loans for still further economic development. By the end of the war Brazil was becoming the major Latin American industrial power.

Participation in World War II on the side of the Allies had led many in Brazil to believe that they should not remain subject to a dictatorship. This attitude was widespread in the military, which had fought in Europe and established close contact with the United States. In 1945 Vargas promised that he would lead the nation toward democracy and hold presidential as well as congressional elections. His actions, however, suggested that he planned to manipulate the elections. In response, the military carried out a coup, and Vargas retired temporarily from political life.

The new regime, which was democratic, continued the general policy of economic development through foreign-financed industrialization. The state, however, assumed a much smaller role. When in 1950 Vargas was elected president, his return to office was anticlimactic. He was by then an elderly man, well past his prime. Yet in 1953 he established Petrobas, a state-owned petroleum exploration company. His presidency remained controversial. There was much criticism of him and of the corruption of his appointments. A member of his staff became involved in the assassination of a prominent civilian journalist. The military demanded that Vargas resign. Instead he took his own life in 1954, leaving a public testament in which he presented himself as the protector of the poor and of the broad national interest.

In the decade after Vargas's death, Brazil remained a democracy, although a highly unstable one. The government itself began to undertake vast projects such as the enormously costly construction of the new capital of Brasília, begun in 1957. Located far inland, Brasília required the creation of a vast road system. With Brasília under way, the government of Juscelino Kubitschek (1902–1976), who had supported the building of the new capital, fostered the establishment of a large automobile industry. The rapid growth of cities and the expansion of a working class radicalized political life. The political system could not readily accommodate itself to the concerns of workers and the urban poor. Widespread poverty and illiteracy continued to plague both the cities and the countryside. In a structural problem created by the constitution of 1946, the presidency was controlled by urban voters, whereas the congress was controlled by rural voters.

By the early 1960s, when President João Goulert (1918–1977) took office, Brazilian political life was in turmoil. Goulert's predecessors had attempted to balance interests or to move among various political forces without firmly favoring a single sector. After months of wavering, however, Goulert committed himself to a policy favored by the left. In 1964 he announced his support for land reform. Peasants had already tried to seize land, and landowners had fought them. Political conservatives and moderates expected some favors to urban radicals, which they might have tolerated, but vigorously resisted any hint of significant political or land reform in the countryside. Goulert also questioned the authority of the military hierarchy. Moreover, Brazil faced economic problems: Both industrial and farm production had fallen from the levels achieved in 1960, fostering discontent. In March 1964 the military, claiming to protect Brazil from communism, seized control of the government, ending its post–World War II experiment with democracy.

CHRONOLOGY

BRAZIL

1822	Brazil becomes an independent empire
1840	Pedro II assumes personal rule
1840s and 1850s	Spread of coffee cultivation
1865–1870	Paraguayan War
1871	First law curbing slavery
1888	Slavery abolished
1889	Fall of the monarchy
1917	General strike in São Paulo
1929	Collapse of coffee prices
1930–1945	Vargas era
1957	Construction of Brasília begins
1964	Military takes control of the government

SUMMARY

HOW DID the absence of a social revolution affect Latin America after independence?

Independence Without Revolution. In the 1820s, Latin America threw off Spanish and Portuguese rule, but the traditional elites—landowners, military officers, and the church—remained in control. The Creole elite discriminated against nonwhites. The predominant philosophies were conservative. *page 643*

WHAT WAS the economy of dependence?

Economy of Dependence. Because Latin American economies remained dependent on producing agricultural commodities for export, foreign nations, particularly Britain, dominated Latin American economic life. When commodity prices collapsed during the Great Depression, Latin American economies were devastated. The crisis led to the beginnings of manufacturing in many Latin American countries in an effort to avoid dependence on imports. *page 647*

WHO WERE the *caudillos*?

Search for Political Stability. A series of strongmen called *caudillos* dominated most Latin American republics. They were generally repressive and conservative. *page 649*

WHY ARE the histories of Argentina, Mexico, and Brazil so different in spite of these nations' commonalities?

Three National Histories. Argentina was dominated by Buenos Aires. Agricultural exports contributed to a strong economy. However, urban social discontent and the growth of nationalism in the 1930s led to military intervention in politics and the corporatist dictatorship of Juan Perón from 1946 to 1956. Mexico was unstable after independence. It lost half its territory to the United States and was invaded by France in the 1860s. The long-lasting dictatorship of Porfirio Díaz brought political stability but increasing discontent. The Mexican Revolution that began in 1911 produced cautious reform under the one-party rule of the PRI, the Institutional Revolutionary Party, which remained in power until the end of the century. Brazil was a

stable constitutional monarchy after independence until 1889. It also retained slavery until 1888. The establishment of a republic did not change Brazil's dependence on coffee exports, and the collapse of coffee prices in 1929 led to dictatorship. Although politically repressive, Getulio Vargas instituted social reforms and promoted industrial development, which continued to expand in the decade after his death in 1954. *page 650*

INTERPRETING THE PAST

Latin America: Dependence, Dictators, and Democracy

Sources from MyHistoryLab for Chapter 26

myhistorylab

1) Francisco Bilbao, *America in Danger* (1862)
2) Friederich Hassaurek, *How to Conduct a Latin American Revolution* (1865)

Source from Chapter 26

1) *Eva Perón Explains the Sources of Her Popularity* (1951)

Since gaining independence from European states in the early nineteenth century, Latin American states have been unstable

REVIEW QUESTIONS

1. What was the condition of the Latin American economies after independence? What was their relation to Britain? Why were most Latin American states slow to develop an industrial base? What role did their economies play in the worldwide economy that developed in the nineteenth century?

2. Did the structure of Latin American societies change after independence? What role did the traditional elites play in the economic and political life of their nations? What was the condition of the mass of the population?

3. How did European and U.S. investment in Latin America affect the region economically? Politically?

4. Why did so many Latin American nations find it difficult to develop stable political regimes? What role did the military play?

5. What was the effect of increased European immigration on Argentina? How did the Argentine elite cope with growing urbanization and industrialization?

6. Why was Juan Perón able to seize and hold power? What was the role of "Evita"?

7. Did Mexico experience a real revolution in the early twentieth century? How does this experience distinguish Mexico from other Latin American countries? What caused the turmoil?

8. During the period covered in the book, what influence did the shared border with the United States have on Mexican history?

9. Why was the Brazilian experience of independence and early nationhood different from that of Spanish-speaking Latin America? What was the role of slavery in Brazil's history? How are abolition and coffee connected?

10. How did the Vargas regime change the Brazilian economy? Why did Brazilian democracy end in a military coup in 1964?

KEY TERMS

caudillo (kauw-DEE-lyoh) (p. 650)

debt peonage (p. 645)

dependency theory (p. 642)

Estado Novo (p. 660)

import substitution (p. 649)

La Reforma (p. 653)

mestizos (mess-TEE-zohs) (p. 645)

mulattos (muh-LAHT-ohs) (p. 645)

nacionalismo (p. 652)

neocolonial economy (p. 649)

pampas (PAHM-puhs) (p. 651)

Perónism (p. 652)

positivism (p. 646)

PRI (p. 657)

Note: To learn more about the topics in this chapter, please turn to the Suggested Readings at the end of the book.

politically, inclined to authoritarian regimes and frequent coups. Economic dependency accompanied this political instability. Natural resources and agricultural products were extracted and exported for the benefit of European and North American investors, primarily large corporations.

In this exercise you will examine three documents that spotlight some of the most intractable problems relating to the economic, social, and political life in Latin America in the period after independence. The first document, written by Francisco Bilbao, a liberal political reformer, recapitulates the justifications for the military dictatorships that were prevalent throughout Latin America. The second document is a step-by-step "guide" to the process of revolution, which occurred frequently, as observed by the American Minister to Ecuador in the 1860s. The third primary source, from Chapter 26, is

written by "Evita" the wife of Argentina's authoritarian president Juan Perón.

Assignment

After reading the documents, relate the authors' point of view to the three major explanations for these problems, which are outlined in the "Global Perspective" section on pages 642–643.

Then write an essay that outlines the parallels between the sources and the ways in which they support or undermine the preceding explanations.

27

India, the Islamic Heartlands, and Africa, 1800–1945

The Emir of Bukhara and His Ministers, ca. 1870.   In 1868, Russia defeated the Emir of Bukhara, who ruled one of several petty states in Central Asia that came under Russian domination in the latter half of the nineteenth century. The emir was permitted to rule a greatly diminished territory under Russian protection.

How did Muslim rulers respond to European imperialism in the nineteenth century?

THE INDIAN EXPERIENCE

BRITISH DOMINANCE AND COLONIAL RULE *page 667*

HOW DID British rule affect India?

FROM BRITISH CROWN RAJ TO INDEPENDENCE *page 670*

WHAT ROLE did Gandhi play in ending British rule in India?

THE ISLAMIC EXPERIENCE

ISLAMIC RESPONSES TO DECLINING POWER AND INDEPENDENCE *page 674*

WHY DID Islamic reform movements arise during the eighteenth century?

WESTERN POLITICAL AND ECONOMIC ENCROACHMENT *page 676*

WHY IS the invasion of Egypt by Napoleon's army in 1798 symbolically important?

ISLAMIC RESPONSES TO FOREIGN ENCROACHMENT *page 677*

WHAT WERE three typical Islamic reactions to Western encroachment?

THE AFRICAN EXPERIENCE

NEW POWER CENTERS AND ISLAMIC REFORM MOVEMENTS *page 681*

WHAT WAS the *mfecane*?

PATTERNS IN EUROPEAN COLONIZATION AND AFRICAN RESISTANCE *page 683*

HOW DID Africans resist European colonialism?

THE RISE OF AFRICAN NATIONALISM *page 689*

HOW DID artificial colonial boundaries become important to postindependence Africa?

THE CHALLENGE OF MODERNITY: INDIA, ISLAM, AND AFRICA

The century and a half that began in 1800 was bleak for the fortunes of the Indian subcontinent, Africa, and the Islamic societies of the Middle East and elsewhere. For centuries there had been a rough but long-term balance in advances and setbacks in material and intellectual culture, commercial development, and political stability among the major cultural regions of the world. Suddenly, over a period of 150 years, Europe, long a relative backwater in world history, came to dominate the rest of the world.

The Middle East, Africa, Iran, Central Asia, India, and Southeast Asia, along with Central and South America—later the so-called "Third World" of "developing nations"—were most drastically affected by European imperialism and colonialism. Notwithstanding indigenous developments in these regions, the overarching and decisive development of this era was new and unprecedented domination of the world's economy, intellectual life, and political and military history by a single segment of the global community. Certainly the histories of the less "developed" nations of the world ("developed" in the sense of evolving toward European-style economic, political, and cultural

systems) in this age have their own internal dynamics; in fact, many smaller African or South American societies were not even directly affected by Western dominance until recently. Still, the impact of Western military, economic, and cultural power and influence was considerable. While not synonymous with "progress" as Westerners and modernization theorists have often liked to believe, it has been, nevertheless, a hallmark of the "modern" age in most of Asia, Africa, and South America. Whether by rejection, adaptation and syncretism, or outright imitation, peoples worldwide had to contend with the immense power of the West.

The vitality of so many of the cultures and traditions that bore the brunt of the Western onslaught has been striking. Arab, Iranian, Indian, African, and other encounters with Western material and intellectual domination produced different and often very creative responses and initiatives. These have borne full fruit in political, economic, and intellectual independence only since 1945, although most began much earlier. For example, modern Islamic reform and resurgence began in the eighteenth century, although

T he encroachment of the European nations on the rest of the world from the late fifteenth century onward brought radical, often devastating changes. Within the West itself, spiritual and material disruption accompanied the Renaissance, the Reformation, the Enlightenment, and the Industrial and Scientific Revolutions. The effects of these watershed European developments on the Indian, Asian, and African worlds came more rapidly, in greater concentration, and with less preparation than they had in the West.

To speak of these complex processes under the rubric of "modernization" does not reflect the acute differences between events in western Europe and the more disruptive changes that European imperialism and colonialism brought to other parts of the world. Nor does it do justice to the degree to which the West appropriated the very concept of "modernity." Modernity is now identified with a novel set of ideas and institutions that evolved in Europe between the Renaissance and the early twentieth century and was then gradually exported to, or imposed upon, other societies around the globe. The expression "the impact of modernity" refers to how "modern" Western civilization affected traditional cultures.

The consequences of the spread of Western culture have been so massive that today non-Western peoples are often seen as merely its passive recipients. A simplistic dualism tends to contrast the "modern" West with the "backward" "Orient," as though all of the world outside Europe, North America, and their most Westernized offshoots were a monolithic, archaic "Other."

As parochial as such chauvinistic generalizations are, the impingement of the West has been a major element in the recent history of African, Asian, and Indian civilizations. Throughout the "Third World," Western modernity encountered cultures that had flourishing social, religious, and political traditions of their own. Through processes of profound transformation, peoples have sought to delicately balance the unforeseen challenges of modernity with the familiarity of tradition. That transformation took place throughout Asia and Africa as it has only recently become a major global factor. Indian national, as opposed to regional, consciousness developed from the late eighteenth century onward in response to British imperial and colonial domination, even though it led to national union and independence only after World War II. Ironically, exposure of the indigenous elite to European political and social philosophies gave future leaders of colonial independence drives vital intellectual ammunition with which to develop ideologies of self-rule. Creative thinkers like Mohandas K. Gandhi (1869–1948) merged these European philosophies with ideas drawn from their own cultures to create distinctive new ideologies that could inspire sympathizers from the West as well as their own indigenous followers to oppose European imperialism and oppression of all kinds. African nationalist leaders such as Julius Nyerere (1922–1999) and Jomo Kenyatta (1889–1978) similarly found creative ways to merge European nationalist models with indigenous cultural ones.

Certainly one result of the imperial-colonial experience almost everywhere has been to sharpen the cultural self-consciousness and self-confidence of those peoples most negatively affected by Western dominance. The imperial-colonial experiences of the Third World nations may well prove to have been not only ones of misery and reversal but also of transition to positive development and resurgence, despite the problems that plague many of these nations.

Focus Questions

◆ How did Western domination affect the Indian subcontinent, the Islamic heartlands, and Africa in the nineteenth century?

◆ How did these societies eventually develop ideologies of resistance that helped them achieve independence?

these continents became sites in a fierce European competion for raw materials and influence. The "great game" and the "scramble for colonies" would permanently alter the cultural, economic, and political landscapes in Asia and Africa as well as in Europe. ■

THE INDIAN EXPERIENCE

BRITISH DOMINANCE AND COLONIAL RULE

HOW DID British rule affect India?

In the eighteenth century Britain became the dominant power in the southern seas. In India by the early nineteenth century the British had built the largest European colonial empire in the Afro-Asian world. India, the greatest traditional civilization to come under direct European colonial rule, was the "jewel in the crown" of that empire.

BUILDING THE EMPIRE: THE FIRST HALF OF THE NINETEENTH CENTURY

It was no simple undertaking for Britain to penetrate multiethnic, multilingual, multiconfessional India. The British used a multipronged approach to convince various strata of Indian society and various ethnic groups that cooperation with Britain's imperial enterprise was in their best interests.

A half century before the British Crown asserted direct rule over India in 1858, the British wielded effective imperial control through the East India Company. As the company's pressure on smaller states to pay "subsidies" for military "protection" brought them to either collapse or rebellion, the British annexed more territory. Areas not annexed were recognized as independent princely states. Ranging in size from less

MAP 27–1   **British India, 1820 and 1856.**

How did the East India Company add to the territory under its control?

than a square mile to more than 80,000 square miles (Hyderabad), these independent states retained their status only as long as they remained faithfully allied to Britain and contributed money to their common "defense." Members of Indian elites often colluded with the British against local rulers. The state of Mysore, the Maratha confederation, and the Sikhs of the Panjab were overpowered between 1797 and 1853. The India that resulted was a mixture of small and large tributary states and provinces that the British administered directly (see Map 27–1).

The economic impact of company rule was extensive. To pay the debts incurred by their military actions, the company's administrators organized and exploited Indian land revenues. Squeezed by these demands, many peasants deserted their land; by the 1830s land revenues were in sharp decline. In addition, demand for Indian indigo, cotton, and opium declined, and famines brought widespread suffering despite economic and social reforms.

Company rule affected the physical face of India. Company policies encouraged settled agriculture and small commodity production at the expense of the nomadic and pastoralist cultures of northern and central India. British "pacification" involved the clearing of land to deny natural cover to military enemies and the often forced settlement of peasants in new regions. Early in the nineteenth century European entrepreneurs undertook massive commercial logging operations, causing extensive deforestation. This ecological destruction was a major by-product of the transformation of India into a more homogeneous peasant farming society that provided a better base for colonial administration.

Indians were by no means passive in the face of this exploitation. The first half of the nineteenth century saw almost constant revolt in one place or another. The revolts included peasant movements of noncooperation, Muslim farm workers' attacks on British and Hindu estate owners, grain riots, tribal revolts, and other actions. They culminated in the watershed Indian Uprising of 1857 (the so-called Sepoy Mutiny or Rebellion).

QUICK REVIEW

Causes of the Indian Revolt of 1857

- Addition of Sikhs, Gurkhas, and lower-caste soldiers to army
- Deteriorating economic conditions
- Excessive tax rates
- British annexation of Awadh

The immediate trigger of the uprising of 1857 was the concern among Bengal troops that animal grease on newly issued rifles exposed them to ritual pollution, a violation of the rules of their religion. Behind this issue lay a variety of grievances, including the recent addition of Sikhs, Gurkhas, and lower-caste soldiers to the army; the deteriorating economic conditions of many of the Hindu troops' higher-caste relatives back home; outrage at excessive tax rates, especially among troops from Meerut; and anger at the 1856 British annexation of the rich princely state of Awadh (home to many of the troops). There was also a desire to recover and rebuild a pre-British political order in North India. The revolt was not an all-India affair. It centered on Delhi, where the last Mughal emperor joined in the rebel cause, and involved other cities, towns, and in some cases the rural peasantry.

The Indian Uprising of 1857.   The mutinous Sepoy cavalry attacking a British infantry division at the battle of Cawnpore. Although the uprising was suppressed, it was not easily forgotten. In its aftermath the British reorganized the government of India.

What impression does this image give you of the Sepoys' chances of success against the British?

The British eventually won the day. With their forces augmented by Sikhs from the Panjab and Gurkhas from Bengal, they overcame the divided Indian opposition. By the end of 1857, the revolt was broken, often with great brutality. In 1858, the East India Company was dissolved, and India came under direct rule of the British Crown.

The "Mutiny" of 1857 was not a nationalist revolution but rather a series of antiforeigner, anti-British spontaneous uprisings. Still, it highlighted resentment of the burdens of foreign domination that were to grow increasingly oppressive for Indians of all regions and religions during the ensuing ninety years of crown rule, known as the **raj**.

raj   The years from 1858 to 1947 during which India was governed directly by the British Crown.

BRITISH–INDIAN RELATIONS

The overall impact of British presence on the Indian masses was brutal but impersonal and largely economic. India was effectively integrated into Britain's economy, becoming a market for British goods and providing Britain with raw materials and other products. Britain's involvement in India's internal affairs included politics, education, the civil service infrastructure, communications, and transportation, but the consequences of its domination and exploitation of India's labor and resources were especially far-reaching.

British cultural imperialism was never a major nor even an official policy of the East India Company. Many Britons expressed interest in and some openness to Indians and their culture. A few mixed and even intermarried with Indians. The company itself required many of its India officers to learn Persian and Sanskrit. It opposed Christian missionary activity in India until the 1830s and 1840s, partly because the caste system facilitated imperial policy. Nonetheless the British–Indian relationship had a paternalistic and patronizing dimension, both before and after the events of 1857. The ethos of the British rulers included the understanding that they had the task of governing an inferior "race" that could not handle the job by itself. Even Indians whose university degrees or army training gave them impeccable British qualifications were never accepted as true equals. From army to civil service ranks, the upper echelon of command was British; the middle and lower echelons of administration were Indian.

Portrait of Ram Mohan Roy, the most influential Indian thinker in the early nineteenth century.

What does Roy's clothing suggest about his views toward the West?

Despite this unequal relationship, British ideas and ways of doing things influenced a small but powerful Indian elite. Christian and secular values associated with the European Enlightenment influenced Hindu and Muslim educated classes. In the nineteenth century, probably the most influential and controversial member of the Indian elite to engage the British on their own ground was Ram Mohan Roy (1772–1833). Roy, a Bengali Hindu, rose to the top of the native ranks of East India Company service and became a strong voice for reform, both of Hindu life and practice and of British colonial policy where it deviated from European and Christian ideals. The spiritual father of the Brahmo Samaj (1828), a Hindu reform movement opposed to "barbarous" practices that ranged from *sati* (immolation of widows on their husbands' funeral pyres) to "idol worship" and Brahmanic "ritualism," Roy was an avowed modernist who wanted to meld the best of European-Christian morality and thought with the best of Hindu piety and thought. He was quick to oppose autocratic and unfair British legal and commercial practices and campaigned in India and in England to reform the East India Company's policies. He was influenced by the Christian Scriptures and the great thinkers of European civilization and drew on them in his Hindu reform efforts. His wide-ranging writings and public campaigns for education, political involvement, and social progress and against the "backward" practices and ideas of many of his Hindu compatriots alienated most of the leading Hindu thinkers and activists of his age, but twentieth-century Indians have often seen him as a visionary.

Increasingly after 1858, Britons at home became aware of India and Indians. The image that came to them, however, was filtered by interpreters who were often neither sympathetic nor objective. Many company officers developed little interest in Indians beyond what they needed to know to extract economic gain, though others studied Indian cultures and languages and got to know some of the Indian elite as friends. After the implementation of direct crown rule in 1858, however, a stricter social segregation of white rulers from Indian subjects set in. Overall the British, much more than their Central Asian Mughal predecessors, treated Indians all too often as backward heathens in need of the "civilizing" influences of their own "enlightened" culture, law, political system, education, and religion.

Most Indians resented their subordinate status. The nationalist movement at the end of the nineteenth century extended to the grassroots level among tribal groups, peasant farmers, and home or small-industry workers. Whatever their status, the distrust and animosity most Indians felt toward their foreign rulers continued to grow.

FROM BRITISH CROWN RAJ TO INDEPENDENCE

WHAT ROLE did Gandhi play in ending British rule in India?

THE BURDEN OF CROWN RULE

The Revolt of 1857 had numerous consequences beyond the transfer of administration to the British Crown. The bloody conflict exacerbated mutual fear and hatred. Before the revolt, the British had maintained a largely native army under British officers. After the revolt, they tried to maintain a ratio of at least one British to three Indian soldiers. The army was financed by Indian, not British, revenues. This imposed a huge economic burden on India, diverting one third of its annual revenues to pay for its own occupation.

British economic policies and accelerating population growth put great strains on India's poor. Cheap British machine-produced goods were exchanged for Indian raw materials and the products of its home industries, harming or destroying Indian craft industries and forcing multitudes into poverty or onto the land. Industrialization, which might have provided work for India's unemployed masses, was avoided. The Civil War in the United States (1861–1865) interrupted Britain's source of cotton from the American South, causing a shift from food to cotton farming in India. This shift, combined with a drought in the 1870s, led to widespread famine. Many peasants were forced to immigrate to Britain's dominions in South Africa, where they worked as indentured servants.

The Revolt of 1857 also created a poisonous distrust of Indians within the British colonial administration. **Cantonments** segregated white masters from natives in Indian towns and cities. Despite the just intentions expressed in royal statements and the opening of the civil service, at least nominally, to Indian candidates, the raj discouraged equality between Indian and Briton. One exception to this trend was the tenure of the Marquess of Ripon (1827–1909) as viceroy of India from 1880 to 1884. Ripon fought to erase legal racial discrimination, earning him the hatred of most of his British compatriots in India. Although his foes managed by agitation to dilute his measures, they unwittingly gave Indians a model for political agitation of their own.

INDIAN RESISTANCE

Indians soon took up political activism. Late in the nineteenth century they founded the institutions that would help overcome traditional regionalism, build national feeling, and ultimately end colonial rule. In 1885 Indian modernists formed the Indian National Congress to reform traditional Hindu and Muslim practices that were out of line with their liberal ideals and to change British Indian policies that were equally out of line with British democratic ideals. Other Indians agitated for the rejection of British rule altogether. The Muslim League developed as a counterbalance to the Hindu-dominated Congress and ultimately gained a separate independent Muslim state, Pakistan. Heavy-handed British policies in legal administration, political representation, and taxation strengthened the growing desire for independence.

Indian internal divisions were a major obstacle to independence. These divisions included the many language groups and subject princely states of the subcontinent. These, however, were not even the most critical divisions. For much of British rule, every Indian politician was first a representative of his own region or state and second an Indian nationalist. Furthermore, the Indian elite had little in common with the masses beyond antagonism to foreign rule, making unified resistance difficult. Conflict among Hindus, Muslims, Sikhs, and Jains also impeded concerted political action.

Nonetheless, a nationalist movement took root. Three principal elements within the independence movement led to the creation of India and Pakistan in 1947.

The first consisted of those in the National Congress organization who sought gradual reform and progress toward Indian self-governance, or *svarāj*. This position did not preclude outright opposition to the British, but it did mean trying to change the system from within. Among the proponents of this approach were G. K. Gokhale (1866–1915), the champion of moderate, deliberate, peaceful work toward self-determination; the spiritual and political genius Mohandas K. Gandhi (1869–1948), and his follower Jawaharlal Nehru (1889–1964), who became the first prime minister of India. Gandhi was the principal Indian leader after World War I and directed the all-India drive that finally forced the British out. An English-trained lawyer, Gandhi drew

British Officer Reclining. This photograph of a British officer reclining while being fanned and served by two Indian attendants provides a glimpse into the colonial lifestyle in British India. It also gives insight into race, class, and labor divisions.

What factors discouraged peer-to-peer interactions between Indians and Britons?

cantonments The segregation of areas in which Europeans lived in British-ruled India from those areas inhabited by native Indians.

QUICK REVIEW

India's Independence Movement

- Gradualist reformers worked within the system for progress toward self-governance

- Militant Hindu nationalists wanted to revive tradition and exclude Muslims

- Muslims had varying agendas, but all feared being subsumed in Hindu culture

Gandhi on Passive Resistance and *Svarāj*

Gandhi's powerful thinking and prose were already evident in his Hind Svarāj, or Indian Home Rule, of 1909. This work was to remain his basic manifesto. The following excerpts reflect important points in his philosophy. Svadeshiî refers to reliance only on what one produces at home (rather than on foreign goods).

- **How** does Gandhi relate the ideas of passive resistance and *svarāj* to his theory of Indian self-rule? What are the advantages and disadvantages of his strategy for effecting political and social change? How does this document compare with others concerned with movements of independence and nationalism? See for example, "Mazzini Defines Nationality" (Chapter 24).

Passive resistance is a method of securing rights by personal suffering; it is the reverse of resistance by arms.

When I refuse to do a thing that is repugnant to my conscience, I use soul-force. For instance, the government of the day has passed a law which is applicable to me. I do not like it. If by using violence I force the government to repeal the law, I am employing what may be termed body-force. If I do not obey the law and accept the penalty for its breach, I use soul-force. It involves sacrifice of self.

Everybody admits that sacrifice of self is infinitely superior to sacrifice of others. Moreover, if this kind of force is used in a cause that is unjust, only the person using it suffers. He does not make others suffer for his mistakes. …

… The real meaning of the statement that we are a law-abiding nation is that we are passive resisters. When we do not like certain laws, we do not break the heads of law-givers but we suffer and do not submit to the laws. …

The "Great Soul," "Mahatma" Mohandas K. Gandhi, father of the modern state of India.

How did Gandhi shape India's independence movement?

on not only his own native Hindu (and Jain and Buddhist) heritage but also on the ideas of Western liberal and Christian thinkers like Henry David Thoreau (1817–1862) and Leo Tolstoy (1828–1910). In the end, Gandhi became a world figure as well as an Indian leader. (See Document, "Gandhi on Passive Resistance and *Svarāj*.")

The second element consisted of the militant Hindu nationalists, whose leader, the extremist B. G. Tilak (1856–1920), stressed the use of Indian languages and a revival of Hindu culture and learning. Tilak also subscribed to an anti-Muslim, Hindu communalist vision of Indian self-governance. The Hindu extremists looked to a return to traditional Indian values and self-sufficiency. Their ideas still influence Indian political life, as witnessed by the resurgence of Hindu extremist groups in recent years and the communal strife, especially of Hindus with Muslims.

Muslims made up the third element but there were many divergent regional and even sectarian Muslim constituencies. Generally their leaders made common cause only because they feared that as a minority in a Hindu-majority state they would lose what power they had. Muslims had been slower than the Hindus to take up British ideas and education and thus lagged behind the Hindu intelligentsia in numbers and influence with the British or other Indians. Because of their prominence in the 1857 revolt, the British were at first much less inclined to foster Muslim advancement than that of Hindus. Nonetheless, the Muslims sought rapprochement with the British at first, rather than risk being submerged in Hindu-

If man will only realize that it is unmanly to obey laws that are unjust, no man's tyranny will enslave him. This is the key to self-rule or home-rule. ...

Let each do his duty. If I do my duty, that is, serve myself, I shall be able to serve others. Before I leave you, I will take the liberty of repeating:

1. Real home-rule is self-rule or self-control.

2. The way to it is passive resistance: that is soul-force or love-force.

3. In order to exert this force, *Svadeshî* in every sense is necessary.

4. What we want to do should be done, not because we object to the English or because we want to retaliate, but because it is our duty to do so. Thus, supposing that the English remove the salt-tax, restore our money, give the highest posts to Indians, withdraw the English troops, we shall certainly not use their machine-made goods, nor use the English language, nor many of their industries. It is worth noting that these things are, in their nature, harmful; hence we do not want them. I bear no enmity towards the English but do towards their civilization. In my opinion, we have used the term *Svadeshî* without understanding its real significance. I have endeavored to explain it as I understand it, and my conscience testifies that my life henceforth is dedicated to its attainment.

Source: From *Sources of Indian Tradition*, ed. by William Theodore de Bary. Copyright © 1958 by Columbia University Press. Reprinted with permission of the publisher.

led movements of opposition. Sayyid Ahmad Khan (1817–1898), a longtime supporter of modernist ideas and of cooperation with the British, could also be sharply critical of British mistakes in India. His opposition to Muslim participation in the National Congress foreshadowed later Hindu–Muslim tensions and conflict. He was the founder of the Muslim educational initiative that led to the creation of the Muhammadan Anglo-Oriental College at Aligarh, which attempts to integrate Muslim faith with modern Western thought and learning and is still a major Muslim intellectual center today.

HINDU-MUSLIM FRICTION ON THE ROAD TO INDEPENDENCE

In the twentieth century the rift between Muslims and Hindus in the subcontinent grew wider. In the end the great Indo-Muslim poet, thinker, and "spiritual father of Pakistan," Muhammad Iqbal (1873–1938), and the "founder of Pakistan," Muhammad Ali Jinnah (1876–1949), helped move Muslims to separatism.

The independence of India and Pakistan from Western domination was achieved only with violence, in the long battle with the British, in communal violence among Indians themselves, in the violence between Hindus and Muslims that accompanied partition in 1947, and in the ongoing dispute over Kashmir between India and Pakistan. Still, the victory of 1947 gave the peoples of the subcontinent a sense of participation in the world of

CHRONOLOGY

INDIA

1772–1833	Ram Mohan Roy, Hindu reformer
1817–1898	Sayyid Ahmad Khan, Muslim reformer
1835	Introduction of English education
1857–1858	Sepoy Revolt, or "Mutiny," followed by direct crown rule as a British colony
1869–1948	Mohandas K. Gandhi
1873–1938	Muhammad Iqbal
1876–1949	Muhammad Ali Jinnah
1885	Indian National Congress formed
1889–1964	Jawaharlal Nehru
1947	Independence and partition

The Founding Father of Pakistan.
Muhammad Ali Jinnah was the president of India's Muslim League who in the 1930s advanced the "two nations" theory and made the first formal demand for a separate Muslim homeland. His ideas led to the establishment of Pakistan.

Why did Muslims want a separate state?

nations on their own terms. The British left a legacy of administrative and political unity and egalitarian and democratic ideals that Indian nationalists turned to their own uses.

THE ISLAMIC EXPERIENCE

ISLAMIC RESPONSES TO DECLINING POWER AND INDEPENDENCE

WHY DID Islamic reform movements arise during the eighteenth century?

The eighteenth century saw the weakening of the great Muslim empires and the increasing ascendancy of the West in international trade, military-political power, imperialist expansion, industrial specialization and productivity, and technological progress. The diverse Islamic peoples and states were thrust from positions of global power into a struggle for survival. As with India, the decline of Islamic preeminence was due both to the rise of the modern West and to internal problems.

By the nineteenth century all of the largest Muslim empires—Mughal, Ottoman, Safavid/Qajar, Moroccan, and Central Asian—had declined politically, militarily, and economically in relation to western European empires (see Map 27–2). They had grown decentralized, were less stable economically and politically, and were increasingly dominated by entrenched hereditary elites. Furthermore, new sea routes meant that it was no longer necessary to cross through the Middle East to get from Europe to Asia and back. The resulting changes in Middle Eastern and Mediterranean economies made them peripheral to the world economy now centered on western Europe. The Middle East, however, became enmeshed in the European imperial competition for its industrial resources, particularly oil, and most of the area came under Western political and

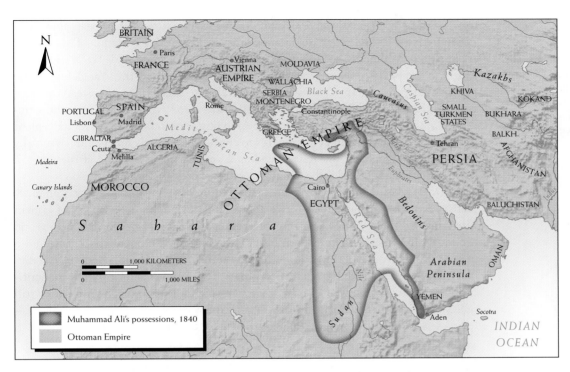

MAP 27–2   West Asia, Central Asia, and the Mediterranean, ca. 1850. Compare this map with Map 21–2 on p. 518. Though the Ottoman Empire still technically ruled a large area, in actuality it had lost much control over regions on the periphery.

Why did the Ottoman Empire lose control of so much territory?

economic domination. The interaction between the people of the Middle East and these new imperial powers was varied. There were some examples of cooperation and accommodation, but the prevailing tone in the nineteenth century was one of conflict.

The fundamental question that engrossed Muslim reformers, politicians, and intellectuals was the basis of European ascendancy. Was the secular learning and technological superiority of Europe something transferable to the Middle East or other non-European regions? Could the once dominant Islamic world regain its vitality by importing European values and education as well as technology? Could Islamic values themselves be adapted or reformed to support and foster the kind of societal progress that Europe seemed to have managed without succumbing to secularization entirely?

During the eighteenth and nineteenth centuries a variety of reform movements sought to revive and purify Islam as a comprehensive guide for living. In major urban areas such as Cairo, Istanbul, and Damascus, influential reformers such as Muhammad Ali (see p. 678) and the sultan Mahmud II proposed adaptionist reform that sought to reengineer the armies, institutions, and societies of the Middle East to conform to the political reality of European domination. Other intellectuals sought to redefine what it meant to be Muslim in a modern age by emphasizing the malleability of the religion in relation to contemporary society. The most famous of such reform efforts was *Tanzimat* (see p. 678) in the Ottoman Empire.

Frontispiece from the Arab Literary-Scientific Journal *al-Muqtataf*, founded by Yaqub Sarruf in the 1860s. A group of such periodicals provided a public arena for political debate despite Ottoman, Egyptian, and British censors. They were a way for the burgeoning educated middle class of the Arab world (especially in Egypt) to construct national identities and debate social, economic, and political issues and policies. The crossed pen and hammer suggest a call to action while the floral border is reminiscent of traditional Islamic manuscripts.

What other institutions or movements helped create national identities in the Middle East?

Wahhabis Followers of Ibn Abd al-Wahhab (1703–1792) who sought to combat the excesses of popular and Sufi piety in Islam and looked to the Qur'an and the traditions of the Prophet as the sole authoritative guidance in religion.

In more rural areas, where neither urban Muslim ideas nor European power had penetrated to the same extent, reformers emphasized a strict construction of what "true" Islam entails. **Wahhabis**, the followers of Ibn Abd al-Wahhab (1703–1792) in Arabia, sought to combat excesses of popular and Sufi piety and to break the stranglehold of the *ulama*'s conformist interpretations of legal and religious issues, favoring instead the exercise of independent judgment. The only authorities were to be the Qur'an and the traditions of the Prophet. Allied with a local Arab prince, Sa'ud, the Wahhabi movement swept much of the Arabian Peninsula. It was crushed in the early nineteenth century by the Ottoman regime but was resuscitated under a descendant of Sa'ud at the onset of the twentieth century and is the guiding ideology of present-day Saudi Arabia.

Other Muslim reform movements reflected similar revivalist and even militantly pietist responses to Islamic decadence and decline. Examples include that of Usman Dan Fodio in Africa in the late eighteenth century (discussed later in this chapter) and the Muslim Brotherhood in modern Egypt (see Chapter 34). Such groups called for a pristine Islam divested of the authoritarianism of the medieval legal schools, *ulama* theological conformity, and degenerate Sufi orders. These movements inspired a noncritical nostalgia for a time when Islamic societies were in ascendance. This memory still rallies movements from Africa to Indonesia and has provided a response to the challenge of Western-style "modernity" and a model for cultural and religious life.

WESTERN POLITICAL AND ECONOMIC ENCROACHMENT

WHY IS the invasion of Egypt by Napoleon's army in 1798 symbolically important?

From the late 1700s until World War II the political fortunes of Islamic states were increasingly dictated from outside by Western powers—including Britain, Russia, Germany, and France—and were at the mercy of the rivalries among them.

Western governments extracted capitulations favorable to their own interests from indigenous governments in exchange for promises of military protection or other considerations. These capitulations took the form of treaty clauses granting commercial concessions, special protection, and "extraterritorial" legal status to European merchant enclaves. Such concessions had originally been reciprocal and had served the commercial purposes of Muslim rulers and some merchants as well as Western traders. However, they eventually provided Western powers with pretexts for direct intervention in Ottoman, Iranian, Indian, and African affairs. The Ottoman Empire suffered from internal disunity; its provincial rulers, or *pashas,* were virtually independent. This disunity, combined with the economic problems facing all the agrarian societies of Asia and Africa, made it easy for the Western powers—with their industrializing economies and militaries—to take control. Repeated Ottoman diplomatic and military defeats made that once great imperial power "the sick man of Europe" after 1800; similar weaknesses allowed Westerners to control Indian and Iranian states.

The onset of European domination of the Islamic heartlands was marked symbolically by Napoleon Bonaparte's (1769–1821) invasion of Egypt in 1798 (see Chapter 23). The invasion highlighted Muslim military weakness and heralded a new era of European imperialism in the Middle East. The British had already wrested control over India and the Persian Gulf from the French; they now became the preeminent Euro-

Linking Asia and Europe. The opening of the Suez Canal in 1869 was a major engineering achievement. It also became a major international waterway, reducing the distance from London to Bombay by half.

How was the Suez Canal as much an imperial achievement as a technological triumph?

pean power in the eastern Mediterranean as well. The French continued to contest British ascendancy in the larger Middle Eastern area, but Russia presented the most serious nineteenth-century challenge to Britain's colonial empire. Russia, having won control of the Black Sea from the Ottomans, sought to gain as much territory and influence in Iran, the Caucasus, and Central Asian regions as possible. Afghanistan, an independent kingdom established by Ahmad Shah Durrani (r. 1737–1773), prevented Russia from penetrating into British India. In the Iranian and Ottoman regions, however, Russia and Britain struggled for supremacy. The Crimean War of 1854 to 1856 (see Chapter 24) was one result.

THE CASE OF IRAN

Beyond the overt political and commercial impact of the West, Western political ideology, culture, and technology proved to be critical factors for change in Islamic societies. Outside of India, this effect was most strongly felt in Egypt, Lebanon, North Africa, and Anatolia (modern Turkey). The Islamic states least and last affected by Western "modernity" were Iran, Afghanistan, and the Central Asian khanates. The Iranian case deserves brief attention.

The rulers of Iran from 1794 to 1925 were the Qajar shahs, whose absolutist reign was not unlike that of the Safavids. However, the Qajars did not claim, as had the Safavids, descent from the Shi'ite *imams*. Under Qajar rule, the *ulama* of the Shi'ite community became less strongly connected with the state apparatus. This period also saw the emergence of a traditionalist doctrine that encouraged all Shi'ites to choose a ***mujtahid***—a qualified scholarly guide—from among the *ulama* and follow his religious and legal interpretations. As a result, the *ulama* were often the chief critics of the government (especially governmental attempts to admit Western influences) and exponents of the people's grievances.

A prime demonstration of *ulama* power occurred when the Qajar shah granted a fifty-year monopoly on tobacco sales to a British corporation in 1890. In 1891 the leading authority in the *ulama* spearheaded a tobacco boycott in protest. This popular action was also supported by modernist-nationalist opponents of the Qajar regime who had strong connections to Iran's commercial, or ***bazaari***, middle classes. The shah had to rescind the concession in a stunning victory for the power of public opinion and a symbolic triumph over Western commercial interests. Yet ironically this action made Iran more dependent on Western capital. The Iranian government was forced to compensate the British corporation, which necessitated a foreign loan from a British bank, making Iran more reliant on Western institutions thereafter.

Iran inevitably felt the impact of Western ideas, especially in the latter half of the century, when younger Iranian intellectuals began to warm to Western liberalism. As in other Islamic countries, the seeds of a new, secular nationalism were sown, coinciding with a growing desire for a voice in government. An uneasy alliance of Iranian radical nationalists, liberal *bazaaris*, and conservative *ulama* proved a sometimes effective counterforce to Qajar absolutism, as in the tobacco boycott and in the early stages of the effort to force the Qajars to accept a constitution in 1906 to 1911. Yet such alliances did not last.

mujtahid A Shi'ite religious-legal scholar.

bazaari The Iranian commercial middle class.

QUICK REVIEW

The Qajar Shahs

◆ Rulers of Iran from 1794 to 1925

◆ Under Qajar rule, the *ulama* of the Shi'ite community was less strongly connected to the state

◆ The *ulama* were often chief critics of Qajar rule

ISLAMIC RESPONSES TO FOREIGN ENCROACHMENT

Western impingement on the Islamic world in the nineteenth and twentieth centuries elicited varied responses. Every people or state had a different experience. There were at least three typical styles of reaction: (1) a tendency to emulate Western ideas and institutions; (2) the attempt to join Western innovations with traditional Islamic

WHAT WERE three typical Islamic reactions to Western encroachment?

Muhammad Ali (1769–1849), the famous viceroy of Egypt.
What were some of Muhammad Ali's attempted reforms?

Tanzimat Reform movement that started in 1839 in an attempt to bring the Ottoman Empire into the modern era and to help integrate non-Muslims and non-Ottomans into the Empire.

institutions; and (3) a traditionalist rejection of things Western in favor of either the status quo or a return to a purified Islamic community, or *Umma*.

EMULATION OF THE WEST

The career of the virtually independent Ottoman viceroy Muhammad Ali (ca. 1769–1849), pasha of Egypt from 1805 to 1849, exemplifies a strategy of emulation. Ali set out to rejuvenate Egypt's failing agriculture, introduce modern mechanized industry, modernize the army, and introduce European education and culture in government schools. Although he ultimately failed to make Egypt as powerful as the European states of his day, Muhammad Ali did set his country on the path to becoming a nation-state. His successors' financial and political successes such as the building of the Suez Canal also led to catastrophes such as the eventual occupation of Egypt by Britain. Although some consider Muhammad Ali to be "the father of modern Egypt," others consider Urabi Pasha, an Egyptian-born military officer, to be the "father of Egyptian nationalist movements." But Muhammad Ali and Urabi Pasha were not alone in the evolution of Egyptian political and militant identities. Sa'd Zaghlul Pasha (1857–1927), an Egyptian statesman and patriot, led a *Wafd* or delegation to Paris in 1919 to protest the 1914 British protectorate imposed on Egypt. Zaghlul Pasha and his companions did not defeat the British occupation, but the *Wafd* party survived well beyond the last occupying British troop.

Efforts to appropriate Western experience and success were made by several Ottoman sultans and viziers after the devastating defeat of the Turks by Russia in 1774. Most notable were the reforms of Selim III (r. 1762–1808), Mahmud II (r. 1808–1839), and the so-called **Tanzimat**, or beneficial "legislation" era, from about 1839 to 1880. Selim made serious efforts at economic, administrative, and military reform. Most important were his destruction of the Janissary corps, tax and bureaucratic reforms, and encouragement of Western military and educational methods among the Ottoman elites. Like Selim and Muhammad Ali, he was less interested in promoting European Enlightenment ideas about citizen rights and equity than in building a stronger, more modern centralized government, which often resulted in the consolidation of poltical power among a select few.

The Tanzimat reforms, introduced by several liberal Ottoman ministers of state, continued the efforts of Selim and Mahmud. They were intended to bring the Ottoman state into line with ideals espoused by the European states, to give European powers less cause to intervene in Ottoman affairs, and to regenerate confidence in the state. They failed to save the empire, but they paved the way for the rise of Turkish nationalism, the "Young Turk" revolution of 1908, and the nationalist revolution of the 1920s that produced modern Turkey. (This development simultaneously frustrated similar nationalist aspirations among old Ottoman minorities like the Greeks, the Armenians, and the Kurds.)

The creation of the Turkish republic out of the ashes of the Ottoman state after World War I is probably the most extreme example of an effort to modernize and nationalize an Islamic state on a Western model. (It could alternatively be the most successful case of integration.) This state was largely the child of Mustafa Kemal (1881–1938), known as "Atatürk" ("father of the Turks"), its founder and first president (1922–1938). Atatürk's major reforms ranged from the introduction of a

European-style code of civil law to the abolition of the caliphate, Sufi orders, Arabic script, and the Arabic call to prayer. These changes constituted a radical attempt to secularize an Islamic state and to separate religious from political and social institutions. Nothing quite like it has ever been repeated. Despite some adjustments and even reversals of Atatürk's measures, Turkey has maintained its independence, reaffirmed its commitment to democratic government, and emerged with a unique but still distinctly Islamic identity.

INTEGRATION OF WESTERN AND ISLAMIC IDEAS

The attempt to join modernization with traditional Islamic institutions and ideas is exemplified in the thought of famous Muslim intellectuals, such as Jamal al-Din al-Afghani (1839–1897), Muhammad Abduh (1845–1905), and Muhammad Iqbal (1873–1938). These thinkers argued for a progressive Islam rather than a materialist Western secularism as the best answer to life in the modern world.

Afghani is best known for his emphasis on the unity of the Islamic world, or **pan-Islamism**, and on a populist, constitutionalist approach to political order. His ideas and his charismatic personality influenced political activist movements in Egypt, Iran, Ottoman Turkey, and elsewhere.

His Egyptian disciple, Muhammad Abduh, sought to modernize Muslim education. He argued that a Qur'anic base could be combined harmoniously with modern science and its open questioning of reality. His modernist reforms affected even the curriculum of the most venerable traditionalist institution of higher learning in the Islamic world, the great al-Azhar in Cairo.

Muhammad Iqbal, the most celebrated Indian Muslim thinker of the twentieth century, argued for a modernist revival of Muslim faith focused on purifying and uplifting the individual self above enslavement either to reason or to traditionalist conformity. Often credited with the original idea of a separate Muslim state in the Indian subcontinent (today's Pakistan), Iqbal still felt that Islam was essentially nonexclusivist and supranationalist. Although Iqbal's poetry and essays excited Muslim fervor and dynamism, it is difficult to say how great his actual impact on Islamic political and social life really was.

WOMEN AND REFORM IN THE MIDDLE EAST

Some Middle Eastern women raised the issue of women's roles in modern society. Most notably, women demanded political rights: Iranian women in December 1911, who confronted the Iranian Parliament to oppose capitulation to Russian-British demands; Egyptian women in 1919, who threw off their veils and declared themselves the new Egyptian women after having accompanied their husbands to Paris where the men had been humiliated by the Versailles powers; Palestinian women in

Tanzimat.   A sitting of the new (1909) Turkish parliament. The sessions were held in a lavish chamber with the delegates from the Balkans, Anatolia, and Fertile Crescent (Syria, Lebanon, Iraq, Jordan, and Palestine) seated facing a high podium at the front of the chamber.

Why did the Ottoman Empire collapse?

pan-Islamism   The movement that advocates that the entire Muslim world should form a unified political and cultural entity.

Kemal Atatürk.   This 1928 photograph shows Atatürk giving instruction in the Latin alphabet, demonstrating his personal engagement in reform.

Why did Atatürk want his countrymen to use the Latin alphabet?

1929, who convened a Women's Congress of Palestine to address the political issues that ensued after the Wailing Wall riots of the same year. It is also noteworthy that a number of journals and magazines devoted to women's concerns emerged in the late nineteenth and early twentieth centuries. Most of them focused on traditional issues such as cooking, parenting, and fashion, but some stressed that women were an essential part of society and should not be excluded from commerce and politics. The Egyptian Feminist Union was founded in 1923 by Huda Sha'rawi (1879–1947) to fight for women's suffrage, reform of marriage laws, and equal access to education. In a well-publicized gesture, Sha'rawi and her colleague Saize Nabrawi removed their veils in the midst of the crowd at Cairo's train station. For them the veil symbolized the inadequate public status of women in Middle Eastern countries. Many Middle Eastern feminists stress, however, that women's inequality is rooted in wide-ranging cultural, political, and economic structures that need to be addressed long before the issue of the veil.

PURIFICATION AND REVIVAL OF ISLAM

A third kind of Muslim reaction to Western domination has emphasized Islamic values and ideals to the exclusion of "outside" forces. This approach has involved either the kind of purist or reformist revivalism seen in Wahhabism or the kind of conservatism often associated with Sunni or Shi'ite "establishment" *ulama*, as Iran since 1979. Both conservative and revivalist Muslim thinkers share the conviction that answers to the questions facing Muslims in the modern world are to be found within the Islamic tradition.

Traditionalist conservatism is much harder to pin down as the ethos of particular movements than is reformist revivalism. Whereas Muslim revivalism (today commonly called "Islamism") usually focuses on Qur'an and Prophetic example as the sole authorities for Islamic life, Muslim conservatism commonly champions those forms of Islamic life and thought embodied in traditional law, theology, and even Sufism. It is seen in the legalistic tendencies that have often resurfaced when Islamic norms have been threatened by the breakdown of traditional society and the rise of secularism. Although such conservatism has been associated with the most reactionary forces in Islamic society, it has also served to preserve basic Muslim values while allowing for gradual change in a way that reformist revivalism could not accept. Where conservatives have formed alliances with governments or simply been co-opted by them, the credibility of the establishment *ulama* has often been destroyed. This is because the masses of Muslims have been increasingly attracted to Islamist agendas for change.

NATIONALISM

Nationalism is a product of modern European history (see Chapter 24). Although not merely a response to Western encroachment, nationalist movements in the Islamic world have been either largely stimulated by Western models or produced in direct reaction to Western imperialist exploitation and colonial occupation. During the late nineteenth century, many intellectuals in Asia or Africa grappled with the question of identity and

CHRONOLOGY

ISLAMIC LANDS, 1700–1938

1703–1792	Ibn Abd al-Wahhab
1737–1773	Rule of Ahmad Shah Durrani, founder of modern Afghanistan
1794–1925	Qajar shahs of Iran
1798	Invasion of Egypt by Napoleon Bonaparte
1805–1849	Rule of Muhammad Ali in Egypt
ca. 1839–1880	Era of the Tanzimat reforms of the Ottoman Empire
1839–1897	Jamal al-Din al-Afghani
1845–1905	Muhammad Abduh
1882–1922	British occupation of Egypt
1908	"Young Turk" revolution
1922–1938	Mustafa Kemal, "Atatürk," in power

whether or not their ethnic or linguistic group constituted a distinct nation or whether they were part of a larger whole. The answer was not always self-evident, given the mosaic of ethnicities, religions, and language groups across Africa and Asia. Yet the often arbitrary division of the colonial world by European administrators eventually demanded an answer. In the European capitals new "nations" were created, such as Nigeria, Lebanon, Congo, or Iraq, that reflected realities and interests of imperialism rather than actual facts on the ground. In due time, these borders have taken on an aura of legitimacy. However, forging nations within artificial parameters has proven to be a difficult and process. As in India, nationalism has been an important aspect of the response to Western domination in the Islamic heartlands. In Turkey in the 1920s it took a secularist form; in Libya, Iran, and elsewhere since the 1970s it has taken an Islamic-revivalist form. As an Afro-Asian phenomenon, it is discussed next and in Chapter 34.

THE AFRICAN EXPERIENCE

The century and a half between 1800 and 1945 saw striking change throughout Africa but especially in sub-Saharan Africa. North Africa and Egypt were more closely bound up in the politics of the Ottoman Empire and Europe throughout this period. Except for South Africa below the Transvaal, tropical and southern Africa did not come under colonial control until after 1880. Before then, internal developments—first, demographic and power shifts and then the rise of Islamic reform movements—overshadowed the increasing European presence in the continent.

Moshoeshwe, king and founder of Lesotho. Not all of the Bantu peoples followed the militaristic example of Shaka. Moshoeshwe, prince of a subtribe of the Sotho Bantus, fought off Zulu attacks and led his people to a mountain stronghold in southern Africa, where, through diplomacy and determination, he founded a small nation that has endured to the present. The kingdom became the British protectorate of Basutoland in 1868. In 1966 it achieved independence as the kingdom of Lesotho under Moshoeshwe's great-grandson, King Moshoeshwe II.

Why were most African states formed during this period short-lived?

NEW POWER CENTERS AND ISLAMIC REFORM MOVEMENTS

SOUTHERN AFRICA

In the south, below the Limpopo River, the first quarter of the nineteenth century saw devastating internal warfare, depopulation, and forced migrations of many Bantu peoples in what is known as the *mfecane*, or "crushing" era. Likely brought on by a population explosion and perhaps fueled by increasing economic competition, the *mfecane* was marked by the rapid rise of sizable military states among the northern Nguni-speaking Bantu. Its result was a period of warfare and chaos; widespread depopulation by death and emigration; and the creation of new, multitribal, multilingual Bantu states in the regions of modern Zimbabwe, Mozambique, Malawi, Zambia, and Tanzania.

The Nguni warrior-king Dingiswayo formed the first of the new military states between about 1800 and 1818. The most important state was formed by his successor, Shaka, leader of the Nguni-speaking Zulu nation and kingdom (ca. 1818–1828). Shaka's brutal military tactics led to the Zulu conquest of a vast dominion in southeastern Africa and the virtual depopulation of some 15,000 square miles. Refugees from

WHAT WAS the *mfecane?*

mfecane   A period of widespread warfare and chaos among Bantu peoples in east-central Africa during the early nineteenth century.

CHRONOLOGY

SOUTHERN AFRICA

ca. 1800–1818	Dingiswayo, Nguni Zulu king, forms new military state
ca. 1800–1825	The *mfecane* among the Bantu of southeastern Africa
1806	British take Cape Colony from the Dutch
ca. 1818–1828	Shaka's reign as head of the Nguni state; major warfare, destruction, and expansion
ca. 1825–1870	Sotho kingdom of King Moshoeshwe in Lesotho
1835–1841	Great Trek of Boers into Natal and north onto the high veld beyond the Orange
1843	British annexation of Natal province
1852–1860	Creation of the Orange Free State and South African Republic

Great Trek The migration between 1835 and 1847 of Boer pioneers (called *voortrekkers*) north from British-ruled Cape Colony to establish their own independent republics.

Shaka's "total war" zone fled north into Sotho-speaking Bantu territory or south to put increasing pressure on the southern Nguni peoples. Virtual chaos ensued, both north and south of Zululand.

The net result, beyond widespread suffering and death, was the creation of many diverse new states. Some people tried to imitate the unique military state of Shaka; others fled to mountainous areas and built up new, largely defensive states; others went west into the Kalahari. The most famous new state was Lesotho, the Sotho kingdom of King Moshoeshwe, which survived as long as he lived (from the 1820s until 1870). Moshoeshwe defended his people from the Zulu and held off the Afrikaners, missionaries, and British until his death.

The new state-building spawned by the *mfecane* was nullified by Boer expansion and British annexation of the Natal province (1843). These developments stemmed from the **Great Trek** of Boer *voortrekers*, which took place between 1835 and 1841. This migration brought about six thousand Afrikaners from the eastern Cape Colony northeastward into the more fertile regions of southern Africa, Natal, and especially the high veld above the Orange River. It resulted in the creation after 1850 of the Afrikaner republics of the Orange Free State between the Orange and Vaal Rivers and the South African Republic north of the Vaal.

EAST AND CENTRAL AFRICA

Farther north in East and Central Africa, increasing external trade was the basis for the formation of several strong regional states. In the Lakes region, peoples such as the Nyamwezi to the east of Lake Tanganyika and the Baganda west of Lake Victoria gained regional power as early as the late eighteenth century through trade with the Arab-Swahili eastern coast and the states of the eastern Congo to the west. The chief traffic in this east–west commerce across central Africa involved slaves, ivory, copper, Indian cloth, firearms, and other manufactured goods.

Elephant Tusks, Congo. Ivory was a prized possession used for decorative purposes and jewelry.

How did the ivory and slave trades interact with European colonization in Africa?

WEST AFRICA

In West Africa the slave trade was only slowly curtailed. European demand for other products, however—notably palm oil and gum arabic—became more important by the 1820s. In the first half of the century *jihad* (holy struggle) movements of the Fulbe (or Fulani) and others shattered the stability of the western savanna and forest regions from modern Senegal and Ghana through southern Nigeria. Protracted wars and dislocation resulted in the rise of regional kingdoms, such as those of Asante and Dahomey (modern Benin), which flourished before succumbing to internal dissension and the colonial activities of Britain and France.

ISLAMIC REFORM MOVEMENTS

The expansive vitality of Islam was one of the significant agents of change in sub-Saharan Africa before the European rush for colonies in the 1880s. It has remained a factor on the wider

African scene ever since. In 1800 Islam was a long-established tradition from West Africa across the Sudan to the Red Sea and along the East African coast, as well as over all of Arabic-speaking North Africa. It had long been widespread in the southern Sahara and northern Sahel and was common among merchant classes in various parts of West Africa. Islam was the law of the land in states such as the sultanate of Zanzibar on the eastern coast and the waning Funj sultanate in the eastern Sudan. Even so, the rural populace was often pagan, and even the ruling and urban elites were frequently only nominally Muslim.

There was a significant series of strong militant Islamic revivalist and reform movements of *jihad* in the nineteenth century. Aimed at a wider allegiance to Muslim values, these movements spread Islam as a lasting part of the African scene. The West African *jihad* movements originated in the seventeenth century with the activities of militant, reformist Sufi brotherhoods from the north. These movements eventually spread to other regions and flourished, especially in the eighteenth century.

The most important *jihad* movement came at the beginning of the nineteenth century and was led by a Fulbe Muslim scholar from Hausa territory in the central Sahel. Usman Dan Fodio (1754–1817) was influenced by the reformist ideas that spread throughout the Muslim world in the eighteenth century from India to Saudi Arabia and Africa. Shortly after 1804 he gathered an immense army of fervent supporters and conquered most of the Hausa lands of modern Nigeria, bringing an explicitly Islamic order to the area. Dan Fodio left behind an impressive sultanate centered on the new capital of Sokoto and governed by one of his sons, Muhammad Bello, until 1837. The Fulbe became the ruling class in the Hausa regions, and Islam spread into the countryside, where it still predominates.

Other reform movements had similar success both in gaining political power and spreading a revivalist, reformist Islamic message. Most notable outside West Africa were the Sanusi movement of Libya and the eastern Sahara (after about 1840) and the famous Mahdist uprising of the eastern Sudan (1880s and 1890s). The Libyan movement provided the focus for resistance to the Italian invasion of 1911. The Sudanese Muhammad Ahmad (1848–1885) condemned the widespread corruption of basic Islamic ideals and declared himself the awaited deliverer, or **Mahdi**, in 1881. He led the northern Sudan in rebellion against Ottoman-Egyptian control, defeating the British forces from Egypt under Charles George Gordon (1833–1885) at Khartoum. His successor governed the Sudan until the British finally destroyed the young Islamic state in 1899 (see Map 27–3).

Mahdi   A redeemer who will appear on earth and establish a just society prior to the final judgement. The Mahdi is central to Shi'ite belief, but controversial in other branches of Islam.

PATTERNS IN EUROPEAN COLONIZATION AND AFRICAN RESISTANCE

EUROPEAN EXPLORERS AND CHRISTIAN MISSIONARIES

HOW DID Africans resist European colonialism?

During the nineteenth century, Europe came to dominate Africa's politics and economy. Before the mid-1800s, Europeans had rarely ventured beyond coastal areas, although the transatlantic slave trade had affected areas farther inland. This changed drastically as, first, trading companies and explorers, then missionaries and, finally, colonial troops and governments moved into Africa. Ironically, the gradual elimination of the slave trade (largely through the efforts of British abolitionists) was accompanied by increased European exploration and increased Western Christian missionary activity in Africa, which ushered in imperial and colonial ventures that had devastating consequences.

CHRONOLOGY	
ISLAMIC REFORM MOVEMENTS	
1810	Dan Fodio founds Islamic sultanate in lands of former Hausa states of northern and central Nigeria
after 1840	Sanusi movement in Libya and eastern Sahara
1881	Muhammad Ahmad declares himself the Mahdi (Sudan)

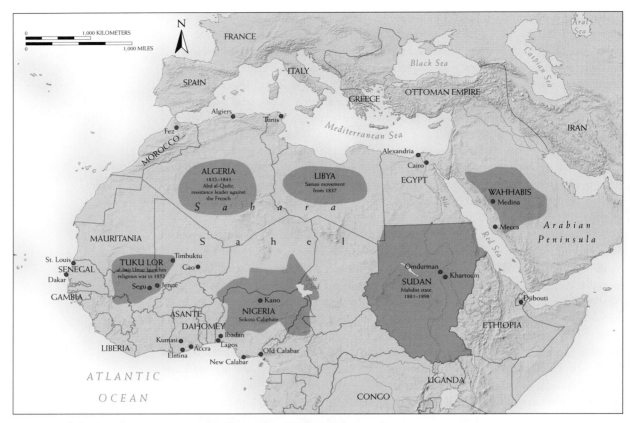

MAP 27–3   Islamic Reform Movements in Africa and Arabia in the Nineteenth Century.

How did reform movements influence African culture and history?

Henry Morton Stanley and His Servant Kalula.   Stanley was a journalist-turned-explorer who "found" abolitionist-turned-explorer David Livingstone near Lake Tanganyika in 1871. Stanley claimed to have greeted him with, "Dr. Livingstone, I presume."

What influence did explorers have on European colonization efforts in Africa?

The nineteenth-century European explorers—mostly English, French, and German—gradually uncovered for Westerners the great "secrets" of Africa: the sources and courses of the Niger, Nile, Zambezi, and Congo Rivers; natural wonders, such as Mount Kilimanjaro and Lake Tanganyika; and fabled places like Timbuktu. The history of European exploration is one of fortune hunting, self-promotion, violence, and mistakes as well as patience, perseverance, bravery, and dedication.

Many of the explorers were also accomplished authors and lecturers; tales of their adventures stimulated European interest in Africa and opened the way for traders, missionaries, and finally soldiers and governors from the Christian West. One of the greatest explorers was Dr. David Livingstone (1813–1873), a Scottish Presbyterian missionary, physician, and abolitionist. Among other things, Livingstone renamed Mosioa-Tunya ("smoke that thunders"), on what is now the Zimbabwe-Zambia border, "Victoria Falls" in honor of Britain's monarch.

The latter nineteenth century saw a mounting influx of Christian missionaries, both Protestant and Catholic (by 1900, some 10,000). Part of their motivation for coming to Africa was to eradicate the remaining slave trade, especially the trade in East Africa run by Arabs from Zanzibar.

The missionaries came to know the African peoples far better than did the explorers. Their accounts of Africa contained chauvinistic and misleading descriptions of the "degraded" state of African culture and religion, but they did bring real knowledge of Africa to Europe. Their translation work and mission schools also brought alphabetic culture and literacy to Africans.

Although their settlements, often in remote areas, provided European governments with convenient pretexts for intervention in the affairs of African tribes and states, the missionaries themselves were more often idealists than opportunists and often worked in opposition to the colonial officers. Half of those who went into the tropical regions succumbed to indigenous diseases, such as malaria, yellow fever, and sleeping sickness. They were often paternalistic, but they also sought to provide Africans with medicine and education. Through the ideals of their faith, they provided Africans—intentionally or not—with a weapon of principle to use against European exploiters. African Christian churches, for example, later played a leading role in the resistance to apartheid in South Africa, despite white Christian oppression and collusion with racism in that country and elsewhere in Africa (see Chapter 34).

THE COLONIAL "SCRAMBLE FOR AFRICA"

Before 1850 the only significant conflict between Europeans and Africans over European attempts to take African territory was in South Africa and Algeria. In South Africa, as we have noted, the Boers came into conflict with Bantu tribes after leaving the British-ruled Cape Colony on their Great Trek to find new lands. The French invaded Algeria in 1830, settled Europeans on choice farmlands, and fought native resistance fighters. Over most of the continent, however, the European presence was felt with real force only from the 1880s. Yet by World War I virtually all of Africa (Ethiopia and Liberia were the exceptions) was divided into a patchwork of large territories ruled by European colonial administrations (see Map 27–4).

European popular and commercial interest in Africa, resulting from the publicity given to African exploration and missionary work, fueled this takeover. The European desire for industrial markets and natural resources, together with intra-European competition for power and prestige, pushed one European state after another to claim whatever segments of Africa they could (see Chapter 29).

The West's superior economic, technological, and military power made the takeover possible. Technical expertise gave Europeans access to the interior of the continent in the late nineteenth century. Except for the Nile and the Niger, the great African rivers have impassable waterfalls only a short way inland from the sea, where the coastal plains rise sharply. European-built steamboats above the falls and railroads around them permitted new levels of commercial and colonial exploitation.

Great Britain and France were the vanguard of the European nations that sought to include African lands in their imperial domains. The British had the largest involvement. They long resisted African colonial involvement and then chose "indirect" as preferable to "direct" colonial administration. British rule was only slightly more enlightened than that of the French, who carved out a colonial empire under their direct control.

Beginning in the mid-1880s the major European powers sought mutual agreement to their claims on particular segments of Africa. Leopold II of Belgium (r. 1865–1909) and Otto von Bismarck (1815–1898) in Germany established their own claims to parts of Africa. France and England set about consolidating their African interests. Italy, too, eventually took African colonial territory in Eritrea, Somaliland, and Libya, but Ethiopia used its newly modernized army to defeat an Italian invasion in 1896. Italy finally conquered Ethiopia in 1935. The **scramble for Africa** was largely over by the outbreak of World War I. After the war Germany lost its African possessions. Europe's colonies in Africa did not gain independence

A Missionary Visit to a Zulu Kraal. The nineteenth-century European and American enthusiasm for working toward "the evangelization of the world in our time" found one of its major outlets in missionary efforts in Africa.

Were missionaries "agents of colonization"?

QUICK REVIEW

Key Factors in "Scramble for Africa"

◆ Popular and commercial interests in Africa spurred by exploration

◆ Intra-European competition for power and prestige

◆ Technological and material superiority of Europe

scramble for Africa The late-nineteenth-century takeover of most of Africa by European powers.

Men Sorting Diamonds, Kimberley, South Africa. Diamond mining in South Africa took off in the late 1860s. By 1880 Kimberley, the biggest mine in the region, had 30,000 people, second only to Cape Town. Whites, such as these diamond sorters, monopolized the well-paid skilled jobs.

What African resources were particularly attractive to Europeans?

MAP EXPLORATION

To explore this map further, go to **http://www.prenhall.com/craig_maps**

MAP 27–4 **Partition of Africa, 1880–1914.** By 1914 the only countries in Africa that remained independent were Liberia and Ethiopia. The occupying powers included most large European states.

Why did Britain and France control so much territory in Africa?

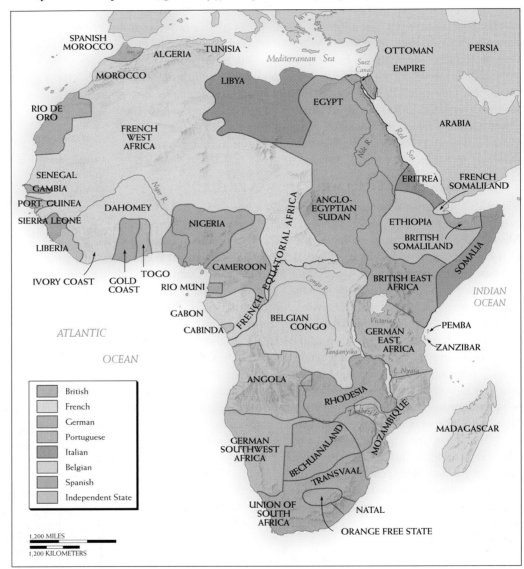

until the changes in the worldwide balance of power and in attitudes toward colonial rule that followed World War II (see Chapter 34).

EUROPEAN COLONIAL RULE

European colonial rule in Africa is one of the uglier chapters of modern history. German, French, Belgian, Portuguese, and Boer rule was notoriously brutal, but Britain too had its share of misrule. The paternalistic attitudes of late-nineteenth-century Europe and America amounted to sheer racism when applied in Africa. The regions with large-scale white settlement produced the worst exploitation. Among the worst legacies of the European presence was the white racist state of modern South Africa, which did not end until 1994. No Western nation can have a clear conscience about its involvement in Africa.

African states were not simply passive objects of European manipulation and conquest. Many astute native rulers sought, by diplomacy, trade, and warfare, to use the European presence to their own advantage. The Baganda king Mutesa in the 1870s (in what is today Uganda) is an example of an African ruler who benefited, at least for a while, from European interest in his territory. Direct armed resistance was always (even for Ethiopia) doomed because of European technological superiority. Nevertheless, such resistance was widespread and continued into the twentieth century. In the end, colonial rule was the product of ongoing conflict and negotiation between European desires, backed up by technological superiority, and the enduring power of African individuals and institutions.

British taxpayers were reluctant to fund colonial ventures. British colonial officials attempted to make a virtue of necessity; since they could afford to pay the salaries of only a very small contingent of British administrators, they put British men at the top of existing African political structures and ruled through indigenous leaders. Often, in the early days of colonial rule, the British would make a show of removing a few high-profile, independent-minded indigenous leaders. In Uganda, for example, the British deposed Mutesa's successor and sent him into exile. The remaining leaders and their British supervisors would then engage in a delicate balancing act: The chiefs and the colonists came to depend on each other for power and legitimacy, but neither could command perfect loyalty from their subjects. Frederick Lugard, who was appointed high commissioner of Northern Nigeria in 1900, formalized this British style of colonial administration and named it, appropriately enough, **indirect rule**.

indirect rule The British practice of administering African colonies through indigenous political structures and leaders.

Other European powers generally ruled their colonies directly: They were willing to bankroll the placement of greater numbers of Europeans in the colonies themselves, and they hired local Africans to work under them within European-style political structures. The French were the most explicit about their intentions, claiming that their goal was for Africans to "evolve"—through education, imitation, assimilation (and, perhaps, over many generations)—into French citizens. In practice, however, French colonial officials were loathe to share the prestige of citizenship.

An important variation in the African colonial experience is between settler and nonsettler colonies. Colonies with relatively high settler populations tended to be places where the environment could support plantation-style, export-oriented agriculture and where the diseases to which Europeans were most susceptible were less prevalent. Settler colonies included Kenya, Mozambique, Rhodesia (Zimbabwe), South Africa, and Algeria.[1]

AFRICAN RESISTANCE

Africans resisted European domination throughout the continent. Often the most efficient way for Africans to resist was to simply disengage, attempting to avoid payment of colonial taxes or participation in forced labor schemes. Riots, marches, and rebellions were more frequent and forceful than colonial administrators wanted to admit, and accounts of such events were sometimes suppressed during the colonial era. Resistance tended to be more overt and sustained in settler

Mutesa of Buganda and His Court.   Noted for his cunning and diplomatic skill and for his autocratic and often cruel conduct, Mutesa was one of the few African rulers who was able to maintain a powerful and successful army and court, which enabled him to deal effectively with Egyptian and British efforts to encroach on his sphere of influence.

Why did direct armed resistance by Africans to European encroachment generally fail?

[1] See E. Gilbert and J. T. Reynolds, *Africa in World History* (Upper Saddle River, NJ: Pearson Prentice Hall, 2004), see chapter 15 for more detailed coverage.

OVERVIEW   Colonialism, 1815–1914

Between the end of the Napoleonic wars and the outbreak of World War I, European powers, the United States, and Japan extended their rule over much of the Near East, Africa, Asia, and the Pacific. The imposition of foreign rule was often the result of conquest, but it also occurred through purchase or the imposition of a protectorate in which a local ruler kept his title but ceded real power, especially over foreign affairs, defense, and finances, to colonial advisers or officials. By 1914, except for the Latin American republics, only Liberia and Abyssinia (Ethiopia) in Africa, the Ottoman Empire in the Near East, and Iran, Afghanistan, Thailand, and China had escaped some form of colonial rule. The following table lists the countries and territories that the Western powers and Japan acquired or dominated as protectorates between 1815 and 1914. In addition, older possessions, such as British India and the Portuguese colonies of Angola and Mozambique, were increased during these hundred years.

NEAR EAST AND NORTH AFRICA

Britain	Aden (in Yemen), Bahrain, Cyprus, Egypt, Kuwait, Oman, Qatar, United Emirates
France	Algeria, Morocco, Tunisia
Italy	Libya, Rhodes

AFRICA

Belgium	Congo (Zaire)
Britain	Botswana, Ghana, Kenya, Lesotho, Malawi, Nigeria, Somaliland, Sudan, Swaziland, Uganda, Zambia, Zanzibar, Zimbabwe, Zululand (in South Africa)
France	Benin, Burkina Faso, Central African Republic, Chad, Congo, Djibouti, Ivory Coast, Madagascar, Mali, Mauretania, Niger
Germany	Burundi, Cameroons, Namibia, Rwanda, Tanganyika (Tanzania), Togo
Italy	Eritrea, Somalia

ASIA

Britain	Brunei, Hong Kong, Malaysia, Myanmar (Burma), Nepal, Papua, Singapore
France	Cambodia, Laos, Vietnam
Germany	New Guiana, Tientsin (in China)
Japan	Korea, Okinawa, Taiwan
Netherlands	Acheh
Russia	Amur Territories (from China), Central Asia, Chechnya
United States	Philippines

PACIFIC

Britain	Fiji, Tonga, Solomons
France	New Caledonia, Tahiti
Germany	Carolines, Marianas
United States	Guam, Hawaii, Midway, Wake

colonies, where Africans and Europeans were most likely to come into direct contact. In places where large swaths of fertile land had been seized by Europeans—the highlands of Kenya, for example—resistance could become violent and chronic, as in the **Mau Mau** uprising that began as a protest against land alienation among Kenya's Kikuyu people. Through the course of the 1950s, tens of thousands of Kenyans were killed, and the British imprisoned many more suspected insurgents and sympathizers in detention camps, while the Mau Mau revolt became a nationalist insurgency.[2]

Mau Mau An uprising that began among the Kikuyu of the Kenya highlands and lasted through the 1950s. The British referred to it as the "Kenya Emergency."

THE RISE OF AFRICAN NATIONALISM

The most important factor in the end of the European colonial period was the rise of nationalism across Africa, especially after World War I. The "national" consciousness of the diverse peoples of a given colonial unit was fueled by common opposition to foreign rule. It was also fed by the use of a common European tongue and through the assimilation of European thought and culture. The ranks of indigenous, educated elites gradually increased in the early twentieth century. From them came the leaders of Africa's nationalist movements between the two world wars and of Africa's new independent nations after World War II.

HOW DID artificial colonial boundaries become important to postindependence Africa?

Mass political parties emerged in the postwar period, including the Convention People's Party in the Gold Coast (Ghana) under Kwame Nkrumah (1909–1972) and the African Democratic Assembly that drew members from a number of French West African colonies under the leadership of Félix Houphouët-Boigny (1905–1993), who became the first president of the Ivory Coast.

It is important to note a countervailing trend, which was the emergence of movements seeking to transcend both colonial boundaries and ethnic or "tribal" divisions and foster an inclusive African identity. One example is **Negritude**, a literary and intellectual movement to celebrate all aspects of African civilization that was exemplified by the writings of Leopold Senghor (1906–2001), who later became the first president of Senegal.

Negritude A movement begun among African students in 1930s Paris to celebrate African culture and thought.

The most severe indigenous critiques of the Western treatment of Africa drew on Western religious and political ideals. The African leaders of the twentieth century learned well from the West and used their learning to help end Western domination. The process culminated in the creation of more than forty self-governing African nations after 1945 (see Chapter 34). African independence movements were based on modern nationalist models from Europe and America rather than ancient ones derived from native tradition. The nationalist and independence movements typically sought to eject the colonial intruders, not to return to an earlier status quo. Their aim was to take over and to run for themselves the Western institutions that colonialism had introduced.

Champion of Negritude, Leopold Senghor, during a visit to France in 1949. He later became president of Senegal.
What is Negritude?

---

[2]The history of Mau Mau is still contested. British administrators deliberately destroyed much of the documentary evidence. For recent attempts to reconstruct events and their meanings, see D. Anderson, *Histories of the Hanged: The Dirty War in Kenya and the End of Empire* (New York: W.W. Norton & Co., 2005), and C. Elkins, *Imperial Reckoning: The Untold Story of Britain's Gulag in Kenya* (New York: Henry Holt & Co., 2004).

SUMMARY

THE INDIAN EXPERIENCE

HOW DID British rule affect India?

British Dominance and Colonial Rule. The East India Company brought increasing areas of India under British control throughout the early nineteenth century. After the Indian Uprising of 1857, Crown rule was instituted. India became part of Britain's economy. Indian labor and resources were exploited. Indian elites were influenced by British culture. Indians of all classes resented their subordination. *page 667*

WHAT ROLE did Gandhi play in ending British rule in India?

From British Crown Raj to Independence. Relations between Indians and Britons were increasingly distrustful. Many strands of Indian nationalism developed, and Gandhi's thought was exceptionally influential. Gandhi's philosophies of passive resistance and self-reliance laid the groundwork for the political movement that brought Indian independence. *page 670*

THE ISLAMIC EXPERIENCE

WHY DID Islamic reform movements arise during the eighteenth century?

Islamic Responses to Declining Power and Independence. Muslim empires were in decline, as Western economic, political, military, and technological power was increasing. Reform movements in the eighteenth and nineteenth centuries proposed various relationships between Islam and the West. *page 674*

WHY IS the invasion of Egypt by Napoleon's army in 1798 symbolically important?

Western Political and Economic Encroachment. European imperialism in the Middle East and Central Asia was encapsulated in Napoleon's invasion of Egypt in 1798. Iran under the Qajar shahs (1794–1925) saw the rise of Shi'ite *ulama* power to oppose Qajar absolutism. *page 676*

WHAT WERE three typical Islamic reactions to Western encroachment?

Islamic Responses to Foreign Encroachment. Emulation of the West, integration of Islamic and Western ideas, Islamic revivalism, and nationalism were among the cultural responses to Western domination in Islamic regions. Women proposed new roles for themselves. *page 677*

THE AFRICAN EXPERIENCE

WHAT WAS the *mfecane*?

New Power Centers and Islamic Reform Movements. In southern Africa, Bantu migrations caused the disruptions of *mfecane*—literally, "crushing," as states and individuals were squeezed by population growth and warfare. This was followed by large-scale displacements of Africans as Boers moved inland in the Great Trek. Elsewhere, trade was generally a precursor to more direct European involvement. A series of Islamic revival and reform movements spread across northern Africa and Arabia in the nineteenth century. Usman Dan Fodio Islamicized Hausa lands, while the Sanssi movement opposed Italians in Libya, and the Mahdist uprising defeated the British at Khartoum. *page 681*

HOW DID Africans resist European colonialism?

Patterns in European Colonization Rule and African Resistance. Different European powers had different strategies and mechanisms for administering African territories, and areas with heavy white settlement generally experienced more exploitation than those with a thinner European presence. A few African rulers were able to use the presence of Europeans to their own advantage, but in general Africans opposed and resisted Europeans. *page 683*

HOW DID artificial colonial boundaries become important to postindependence Africa?

The Rise of African Nationalism. Although colonial boundaries were artificial, they gained cultural meaning as Africans within particular colonies forged nationalist independence movements. There were also pan-African movements, such as Negritude. *page 689*

REVIEW QUESTIONS

1. What does the "impact of modernity" mean to traditional Afro-Asian-Indian cultures? What patterns of reaction can you discern? Why was the West able to impose itself on these cultures?

2. Why was India called the "jewel in the crown" of the British Empire? How did the British gain control of India? What policies did they follow in government and economics?

3. What kinds of political activism against British rule can you cite from Indian history after 1800? What kinds of success or failure did they have?

4. How was the Islamic world internally divided after 1800? How did those divisions influence the coming of European powers?

5. What roles did women play in critiquing Muslim culture during this period?

6. How did nationalism affect European control in South Asia, Africa, and the Middle East? How and when did its various manifestations arise? Were there any successful "national states" from these regions before 1945?

7. Discuss the new African states and power centers of sub-Saharan Africa before 1870. Why did no modern nation-state develop in the area? How did Islam affect the development of new entities? What role did trade play?

8. What were Europeans' main interests in Africa? Why were Africans unable to stop the "scramble for Africa"?

9. What factors influenced Africans' experience of colonial rule in different regions?

10. What was the role of African nationalism in resisting foreign control?

KEY TERMS

bazaari (p. 677)
cantonments (p. 671)
Great Trek (p. 682)
indirect rule (p. 687)
Mau Mau (MOW MOW) (p. 689)
Mahdi (MAH-dee) (p. 683)
mfecane (mm-fuh-KAHN-ay) (p. 681)

mujtahid (p. 677)
Negritude (p. 689)
pan-Islamism (p. 679)
raj (p. 669)
scramble for Africa (p. 685)
Tanzimat (TAHNZ-ee-MAT) (p. 678)
Wahhabis (wah-HAH-bees) (p. 676)

Note: To learn more about the topics in this chapter, please turn to the Suggested Readings at the end of the book.

INTERPRETING THE PAST

The Indian Encounter with Great Britain in the Nineteenth Century

Sources from MyHistoryLab for Chapter 27

myhistorylab

1) Dadabhai Naoroji, *The Benefits of British Rule in India* (1871)
2) Amrita Lal Roy, *English Rule in India* (1886)

Source from Chapter 27

1) Gandhi, from *Indian Home Rule* (1909), page 672

By the mid-nineteenth century Britain dominated India's economy and politics and was actively intervening in its cultural and social life. British policies focused on expanding settled agriculture and commodity production, clearing land, and forced resettlement of peasants. Another British initiative encouraged commercial logging on a large scale, which resulted in deforestation and ecological destruction across large areas of the subcontinent. While reaping economic rewards from India as a result of high taxes levied for "protection," the British also introduced modern technological innovations such as railroads and telegraphs, along with their educational system. These progressive innovations have spurred an active debate about the relative value of Western technology and education compared to the poverty, famine, and other problems caused by British encroachment in almost every facet of India's economy, life, and culture.

The first primary source is written by Dadabhai Naoroji, an Indian scholar, businessman, and political leader who actively sought a measure of political and economic reform of the colonial system in the decades after 1860. Naoroji's essay argues for a continuation of British rule, couched in positive and even-handed terms. The second source is by Amrita Lal Roy, whose "English Rule in India" was published in the *North American Review*, the oldest literary journal in the United States and an influential voice for reform. The final document outlines Gandhi's view of the relationship between passive resistance and Indian independence.

Questions

How does Gandhi make the connection between personal conscience and political power? In this document, does Gandhi present the connection as something specific to India's situation or as a general philosophical principle?

What main points do Naoroji and Roy employ in their arguments for and against British rule? What are the areas of agreement between the two articles? Disagreement?

Research online to find out more about the authors of these three source documents. How might their positions and backgrounds influence their views?

Religions of the World

The Islamic tradition is one of the youngest major world religions. Since its inception during the lifetime of the Prophet Muhammad (632 B.C.E.), it has grown, like the Christian and Buddhist traditions, into a worldwide community not limited by national boundaries or defined in racial or ethnic terms. It began among the Arabs but spread widely. Islam's historical heartlands are those Arabic-, Turkic-, and Persian-speaking lands of the Near East between Egypt and Afghanistan. However, today more than half of its faithful live in Asia east of Karachi, Pakistan; and more Muslims live in sub-Saharan Africa than in all of the Arab lands. There are also growing Muslim minorities in the United States and Europe.

The central vision of Islam is a just and peaceful society where people can freely worship God. It focuses on a human community of worshipers who recognize the absolute sovereignty and oneness of God and strive to do God's will. Muslims believe that divine will is found first in God's revealed word, the Qur'an; then as elaborated and specified in the actions and words of his final prophet, Muhammad; and finally as interpreted and extended in the scriptural exegesis and legal traditions of the Muslim community over the past thirteen and a half centuries.

The Muslim vision thus centers on one God who has guided humankind throughout history by means of prophets or apostles and repeated revelations. God is the Creator of all, and in the end all will return to God. God's majesty would seem to make him a distant, threatening deity of absolute justice; there is such an element in the Muslim understanding of the wide chasm between the human and the Divine. Still, there is an immanent as well as a transcendent side to the Divine in the Muslim view. Indeed, Muslims have given us some of the greatest images of God's closeness to his faithful worshiper, images that have a special place in the thought of the Muslim mystics, who are known as *Sufis* (taken originally from *suf,* "wool," because of the early Muslim ascetics' use of simple wool dress).

Muslims understand God's word in the Qur'an and the elaboration of that word by tradition to be a complete prescription for human life. Thus Islamic law is not law in the Western sense of civil, criminal, or international systems. Rather, it is a comprehensive set of standards for the moral, ritual, social, political, economic, aesthetic, and even hygienic and dietary dimensions of life. By being faithful to God's law the Muslim hopes to gain salvation on the Last Day, when human history shall end and all of God's creatures who have ever lived will be resurrected and called to account for their thoughts and actions during their lives on earth. Some will be saved, but others will be eternally damned.

Thus *Islam,* which means "submission [to God]," has been given as a name to the religiously defined system of life that Muslims have sought to institute wherever they have lived. Muslims have striven to organize their societies and political realities around the ideals represented in the traditional picture of the Prophet's community in Medina and Mecca. This approach necessitated compromise in which power was given to temporal rulers and accepted by Muslim religious leaders as long as those rulers protected God's Law, the *Shari'ah.* The ideal of a single international Muslim community, or *Umma,* has never fully been realized politically, but it remains an ideal.

Many movements of reform over the centuries have called for greater adherence to rigorist interpretations of Islamic law and greater dominance of piety and religious values in sociopolitical as well as individual life. The most famous of these movements, that of the Wahhabis in eighteenth-century Arabia, remains influential in much of the Muslim world, including Saudi Arabia. The Wahhabis' puritanical zeal in fighting what they consider "innovations" in many regional Islamic contexts, such as Shi'ism, Sufi traditions, and more liberal forms of

Muhammad and Ali. This sixteenth-century Persian miniature shows the prophet Muhammad and his kinsman Ali purifying the Ka'ba in Mecca of pagan idols. The Ka'ba is the geographical point toward which all Muslims face when performing ritual prayer.

Art Resource/Bildarchiv Preussischer Kulturbesitz.

What might be the purpose of miniature illustrations such as this?

The Qur'an's First Chapter. This nineteenth-century hand-copied Qur'an in Arabic is open to the *Fatiha*, the opening chapter of Islam's holy book. In seven very short verses, the *Fatiha* sums up man's relation to God in prayer. The first verse, "In the name of God, Most Gracious, Most Merciful," is said out loud by Muslims at the beginning of every major action they undertake each day.

How is God portrayed in these opening lines of the Qur'an?

Muslim School Children in Malaysia, 1997. Though most non-Muslims associate Islam with the Middle East, Islam has deep roots in Southeast Asia. About 212 million Muslims live in Indonesia, making it the most populous Muslim country in the world.

Does this photograph dispel commonly-held perceptions about Islam and the veil?

Islamic practice, continues to the present day. Wahhabism has had considerable success in the past half century and was apparently the spawning ground of the extremist views of Osama bin Laden's al-Qa'ida terrorist movement, which is largely Arab in its ethnic makeup and which has turned from fighting Muslim states it regards as un-Islamic to opposing what it considers the U.S. intrusion into the Arab Islamic world and its unpopular foreign policy in the region. While mainstream Muslims everywhere reject bin Laden's extremism, Wahhabi zealotry has adherents on the fringes of Islamic communities around the world. In this respect, Islam is not unlike Christianity, Judaism, Hinduism, or other major religions, each of which has over its history spawned literalists, zealots, and extremists, who have urged violence in the name of their version of their parent faith.

The major sectarian, or minority, groups among Muslims are those of the Shi'ites, who have held out for an ideal of a temporal ruler who is also the spiritual heir of Muhammad and God's designated deputy on earth. Most Shi'ites, notably those of Iran, hold that after eleven designated blood descendants of the prophets had each failed to be recognized by the majority of Muslims as the rightful leader, or *Imam*, the twelfth disappeared and remains to this day physically absent from the world, although not dead. He will come again at the end of time to vindicate his faithful followers.

Muslim piety takes many forms. The common duties of Muslims are central for Muslims everywhere: faith in God and trust in his Prophet; regular performance of ritual worship (*Salat*); fasting during daylight hours every day in Ramadan (the ninth month of the lunar year); giving one's wealth to the needy (*zakat*); and at least once in a lifetime, if able, making the pilgrimage to Mecca and its environs (*Hajj*). Other regional or popular practices are also important. Celebration of the Prophet's birthday indicates the exalted popular status of Muhammad, even though any divine status for him is strongly rejected theologically. Recitation of the Qur'an permeates all Muslim practice, from daily worship to celebrations of all kinds. Visitation of saints' tombs is a prominent form of popular devotion. Sufi chanting or even ecstatic dancing are also practiced by Muslims around the world.

Muslims vary enormously in their physical environment, language, ethnic background, and cultural allegiances. What binds them now as in the past are not political allegiances but religious affinities and a shared heritage of religious faith and culture. How these allegiances and sensibilities will fare in the face of global challenges will be an important factor in shaping the world of the twenty-first century.

◆ How has the ideal of a single, international Muslim community influenced Islamic history? World history?

◆ What impact have reform movements had on Islam since its inception? What impact do they have today?

28
Modern East Asia

Woodblock, Munakata Shikō, 1945. In modern Japan, woodblock prints are divided between modernists who, initially at least, took their inspiration from the West and those who went through a "Western phase" and then built on the native folk art tradition. Among the latter, the greatest was Munakata Shikō (1903–1975). Munakata was born in Aomori Prefecture, a sparsely populated area in northernmost Honshu known for its long bitter winters, rocky soil, and strong folk religion tradition. At age 24 Munakata went to Tokyo, where for two years he experimented with oils, but then he switched to printmaking. In 1937, at age 34, he took up the Buddhist subjects for which he is best known. His most famous prints are sensuous Buddhist deities and bodhisattvas such as the one depicted here.

What is "modern" about this woodblock print? What elements make it traditional?

MODERN CHINA (1839–1949)

CLOSE OF MANCHU RULE *page 697*

WHAT WERE the most serious threats to Manchu rule in the nineteenth century?

FROM DYNASTY TO WARLORDISM (1895–1926) *page 702*

WHO WERE the key figures in the revolution of 1911?

CULTURAL AND IDEOLOGICAL FERMENT: THE MAY FOURTH MOVEMENT *page 703*

WHY WAS Marxism-Leninism so appealing to Chinese intellectuals?

NATIONALIST CHINA *page 704*

WHO WAS Jiang Jieshi?

MODERN JAPAN (1853–1945)

OVERTHROW OF THE TOKUGAWA *BAKUFU* (1853–1868) *page 708*

WHAT ROLE did the Chōshū and Satsuma play in the overthrow of Tokugawa rule?

BUILDING THE MEIJI STATE (1868–1890) *page 709*

WHAT POWERS did the Meiji Constitution give to the emperor?

GROWTH OF A MODERN ECONOMY *page 711*

WHY DID Japan set out to build a modern economy?

THE POLITICS OF IMPERIAL JAPAN (1890–1945) *page 713*

HOW DID political parties develop in Japan?

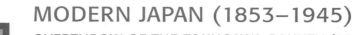

JAPANESE MILITARISM AND GERMAN NAZISM *page 720*

HOW WAS Japan similar to and different from Germany during this period?

GLOBAL PERSPECTIVE

MODERN EAST ASIA

From the late nineteenth century most countries wanted to become modern. They coveted the wealth and power of the West. But what does it mean to be modern?

Three stages may be noted in Japan's development as the world's first and most advanced non-Western modernizer: preconditions, Westernization, and assimilation.

Even before contact with the modern West, Japan had some of the preconditions needed for industrialization: a fairly literate people, an ethic of duty and hard work, a market economy, secular thought, some bureaucracy, and a protonationalism—in sum, an adequate base for an "external modernization."

Building on these preconditions, Japan westernized after 1868, adopting a range of new institutions: post offices, banks, customhouses, hospitals, police forces, joint stock companies, universities with faculties of science and engineering, and so on. Japanese thinkers brought in modern ideas and values: Spencer and Guizot, Turgenev and Tolstoy, Adam Smith and Marx. Japanese writers began experimenting with new forms.

Little by little Japan assimilated what it had borrowed. The *zaibatsu* combines were modern with the most recent technologies, yet their business organizations were unlike those of the West. The spare beauty of traditional architecture was transferred to the glass, steel, concrete, and stone of the modern. A new literature, completely Japanese yet also completely modern, appeared.

Japan may serve as a useful model in that its modernization—as analyzed in terms of the preceding three stages—has gone further than that in any other non-Western country. We note the absence in India or the Islamic world of comparable preconditions. After the end of colonialism, countries in these areas had to create the necessary preconditions even as they borrowed the new technologies. The difficulty explains their limited success. In Africa the dearth of preconditions was even more pronounced.

China, like Japan but unlike countries of South Asia, the Middle East, or Africa, had many of the necessary preconditions—they might be called East Asian preconditions—in place. But when it came to westernization, the government by Confucian literati that had long been China's outstanding asset became its greatest liability. It took decades to topple the dynasty and to advance beyond Confucian ideas.

From the midnineteenth century, the West was expanding, aggressive, and imperialistic, triggering change throughout the world. But the response to the Western impact depended on internal forces in each country. Japan and China were both relatively successful in their responses, for neither became a colony.

The two countries' governing elites were educated in Confucianism, which receded when faced with the powerful secularism of nineteenth-century science and the doctrines associated with it. In both Japan and China, however, core values of the Confucian sociopolitical identity endured, and some of those values transmuted into a strong new nationalism.

In most other respects, modern Japan and China differed. The coming of Commodore Matthew Perry (1794–1858) in 1853 and 1854 precipitated rapid change in Japan. The old Tokugawa regime collapsed, and the Japanese built a modern state. Economic growth followed. By 1900, Japan had defeated China and was about to defeat Russia. After the Great Depression, Japan, like Italy and Germany, became an aggressive and militarized state and was defeated in World War II. But after the war, Japan reemerged more stable and productive with a strong parliamentary government.

The Chinese polity, in contrast, easily weathered the Opium War (1839–1842), an event of considerably greater magnitude than Perry's visit to Japan. The hold of tradition in China was remarkable, as was the effectiveness of traditional remedies in dealing with political ills. In one sense the strength of tradition was China's weakness, for only after the overthrow of the Manchu dynasty in 1911 were the Chinese able to begin the modernization that Japan had started in 1868. Even then they were unsuccessful. Along with typical end-of-dynasty disruptions, new trauma resulted from the rending of the dynastic pattern itself and the unprecedented experience of being confronted by more powerful nations. That China in some sense "failed" during this modern century is the view the Chinese themselves hold. ■

Then, in the maelstrom of the May Fourth Movement, intellectual change occurred at a furious pace, but new doctrines alone could not provide a stable polity. Nationalism emerged as the common denominator of Chinese thought. The nationalists (or Guomindang) drew on it at the Huangpu Academy, during the march north, and in the Nanjing government. But other groups could also appeal to it. The Chinese Communists won out by 1949.

It is beguiling to view the Chinese Communist Party (CCP) cadres as a new class of literati operating the machinery of a monolithic, centralized state with the teachings of Marx and Lenin replacing those of Confucius and local party organization replacing the Confucian gentry. But this interpretation is too simple. Communism stressed science, materialism, and class conflict. It broke with the Chinese past.

Communism itself was also modified in China. Marx had predicted that socialist revolutions would break out in advanced economies where the contradictions of capitalism were sharpest. Lenin had shifted the emphasis from spontaneous revolutions by workers to the small but disciplined revolutionary party, the vanguard of the proletariat. He thereby changed communism into what it has been ever since: a movement capable of seizing power only in backward nations. At the level of doctrine, Mao Zedong modified Lenin's ideas only slightly—by theorizing that "progressive" peasants were a part of the proletariat. But he went beyond this theory in practice, virtually ignoring city workers while relying on China's villages for recruits for his armies, who were then indoctrinated using Leninist techniques.

Yet the organizational techniques that were so effective in creating a party and army would prove less so for economic development. It soon became clear that mass mobilization was no substitute for individual incentives.

Focus Questions

◆ What are the preconditions necessary for modernization along Western lines? Why are they so important?

◆ Compare and contrast the process of modernization in Japan and China in the twentieth century. Which country was more successful? Why?

MODERN CHINA (1839–1949)

China's modern century was not the century in which it became modern but the one in which it encountered the modern West. Its first phase, from the Opium War to the fall of the Qing or Manchu dynasty (1911), was little affected by Western impact. Only during the decade before 1911 did the Confucian tradition begin to be discarded in favor of new ideas from the West. The second phase, from 1911 to the establishment of a communist state in 1949, was a time of turmoil: decades of warlord rule, war with Japan, and then four years of civil war.

CLOSE OF MANCHU RULE

THE OPIUM WAR

The eighteenth-century three-country trade—British goods to India, Indian cotton to China, and Chinese tea to Britain—was in China's favor. The silver flowing into China spurred the monetization of Chinese markets. Then the British replaced cotton with Indian opium, and by the 1820s the balance of trade was reversed.

To check the evil of opium and the outflow of silver, the Chinese government banned opium in 1836. In 1839, the government sent Lin Zexu (1785–1850) to Guangzhou (Canton) to superintend the ban. He destroyed a six-month supply of opium belonging to foreign merchants, leading to a confrontation with the British.

War broke out in November 1839. Chinese troops, with their antiquated weapons, were ineffective. The war ended in August 1842 with the Treaty of Nanjing,

WHAT WERE the most serious threats to Manchu rule in the nineteenth century?

The Opium War, 1840. Armed Chinese junks were no match for British warships. The war ended in 1842 with the Treaty of Nanjing.

How did the Opium War demonstrate Western military superiority?

the first of the "unequal treaties." The treaty gave Britain the island of Hong Kong and a huge indemnity. It also opened five ports: Fuzhou, Guangzhou, Ningpo, Shanghai, and Xiamen (Amoy). British merchants and their families could reside in the ports and engage in trade; Britain could appoint a consul for each city; and British residents within China were subject to British, not Chinese, law. In 1844, similar treaties followed with the United States and France.

After the treaty, Chinese imports of opium increased, but other kinds of trade did not grow rapidly. Western merchants blamed Chinese officials; Chinese authorities were incensed by the export of coolies to work in Cuba and Peru. A second war broke out in 1856, and the British captured Beijing in 1860. New treaties provided for indemnities, the opening of eleven new ports, the stationing of foreign diplomats in Beijing, the propagation of Christianity anywhere in China, and the legalization of the opium trade.

Meanwhile, the Russians were encroaching on China's northern frontier. In 1858, China ceded the north bank of the Amur to Russia, and in 1860, China gave Russia the Maritime Province between the Ussuri River and the Pacific.

REBELLIONS AGAINST THE MANCHU

The Nian, Muslim, and **Taiping Rebellions** convulsed China between 1850 and 1873 (see Map 28–1). The torment and suffering caused by these events were unparalleled in world history. China's population dropped by 60 million.

The Taipings were begun by Hong Xiuquan (1814–1864). Influenced by Protestant tracts, Hong announced that he was the younger brother of Jesus and that God had told him to rid China of Manchus, Confucians, Daoists, and Buddhists. Like earlier rebels, the Taipings combined moral reform, religious fervor, and a vision of egalitarian society. The Taipings were soon joined by peasants, miners, and workers. Fighting spread until the Taipings controlled most of the Yangzi basin and had entered sixteen of the eighteen Chinese provinces. Their army numbered close to a million.

The movement had several weaknesses, most notably poor education among the leadership that prevented them from governing effectively. Many Taiping ideals remained unfulfilled; for example, land was not redistributed.

QUICK REVIEW

Rebellions

- Taiping: Led by Hong Xiuquan (1814–1864), the Taiping assembled an army of close to a million men
- Nian: Located along the Huai River, the Nian came to control a 100,000-square-mile area
- Muslim rebellions: Occurred in the southwest and northwest, areas where China had few officials and little military presence

---

Taiping rebellion A nineteenth-century revolt against China's Manchu dynasty that was inspired by quasi-Christian ideas and that led to enormous suffering and destruction before its collapse in 1868.

MAP 28–1 The Taiping, Nian, and Muslim Rebellions. Between 1850 and 1873 China was wracked by rebellions that almost ended the Manchu dynasty. The dynasty was saved by Chinese "gentry armies."

How did these rebellions influence Chinese history?

Other rebellions were of lesser note but longer duration. The Nian, north of the Taipings along the Huai River, were organized in secret societies and raided the countryside. Eventually they built an army, collected taxes, and ruled 100,000 square miles. Muslims revolted in the southwest and the northwest; one rebel set up an Islamic kingdom with himself as sultan. All these rebellions took advantage of the weakened state of the dynasty and occurred in areas that had few officials and no Qing military units.

Against the rebellions, the imperial forces proved helpless, so in 1852 the court sent Zeng Guofan (1811–1872) to south-central China to organize a local army. Zeng saw the Manchu government, of which he was an elite member, as the upholder of morality and the social order. He recruited members of the gentry as officers. They were Confucian and, as landlords, had the most to lose from rebel rule. They recruited soldiers from their local areas and stopped the Taipings' advance.

In 1860, when the British and French occupied Beijing, a reform government began internal changes, adopted a policy of cooperation with Western powers, and put Zeng in charge of suppressing all the rebellions. The Taipings collapsed when Nanjing was captured in 1864. The Nian were suppressed by 1868 and the Muslim rebellion was put down five years later. Scholar-officials, relying on local gentry, had saved the dynasty.

Between 1850 and 1864, China was wracked by a great civil war between the Taiping rebels and the gentry-led militia of the Qing government. The victory of the latter delayed the collapse of the Qing dynasty until 1912. The scene pictured here shows troops arrayed in battle formation.

How did rebellions help the Manchus to survive?

self-strengthening A movement attempting to restore dynastic power by adopting Western technological innovations while retaining traditional Confucian power structures.

treaty ports Chinese ports ruled by foreign consuls where foreigners enjoyed commercial privileges and immunity from Chinese laws.

The Empress Dowager Cixi. Historians have long criticized the empress dowager as despotic, greedy, and power-hungry, though some believe this criticism is unfair.

Do you think a male leader in an equivalent position would be subject to the same criticisms as Cixi?

SELF-STRENGTHENING AND DECLINE (1874–1895)

Chinese resiliency in the two decades after the suppression of the rebellions was impressive. But if we compare China's progress with that of Japan, then China during the same decades looks almost moribund. China was relatively weaker at the end of the period of "**self-strengthening**" than at the start.

China's inability to act effectively is explained partly by the situation at the court. Prince Gong (1833–1898) and the empress dowager Cixi (1835–1908) were coregents for the young emperor. Prince Gong was eager to exchange ideas with foreigners, but he was outmaneuvered by the empress dowager and was ousted in 1884. The empress dowager had produced the only male child of the former emperor, and her single goal was power. She forged a court just able to survive but too weak to govern effectively.

The most vital figures during these decades were a handful of able governors-general. Each had an army and was in charge of two or three provinces. They were loyal to the dynasty that they had restored and were allowed great autonomy. The governors-general mobilized the gentry again, this time for rebuilding. They set up refugee centers, reduced taxes in the devastated Yangzi valley, reclaimed lands gone to waste, began water-control projects, and built granaries. By the early 1890s, well-being had been restored. Their second task was self-strengthening—the adoption of Western arms and technology. The Chinese built arsenals and shipyards, a telegraph company, railways, and cotton mills. The formula applied in running these enterprises was "official supervision and merchant operation." Major decisions were made by scholar-officials, but day-to-day operations were left to merchants.

The **treaty ports**, of which there were fourteen by the 1860s, were little islands of privilege and security under the rule of foreign consuls, where capital was safe from confiscation, trade was free, and "squeeze" (extortion by officials) was minimal. Foreign companies naturally located in these ports, as well as some Chinese merchants. Well into the twentieth century, the foreign concessions (treaty-port lands leased in perpetuity by foreigners) remained the vital sector of China's modern economy.

Under the low tariffs mandated by the treaties, Chinese industries had little protection from imports. Native cotton spinning was almost destroyed by imports of yarn. Chinese tea lost ground to Indian tea and Chinese silk to Japanese silk. China found few products to export. The level of foreign trade stayed low, and China's interior markets were affected only slightly.

By the 1870s, foreign powers had reached an accommodation with China. They counted on the court to uphold the treaties; in return, they became a prop for the dynasty. By 1900, for example, the court's revenues from customs fees were larger than those from any other source. The fees were collected by the Maritime Customs Service, an efficient and honest treaty-port institution.

THE BORDERLANDS: THE NORTHWEST, VIETNAM, AND KOREA

China's other foreign relations were with fringe lands that China claimed by right of past conquest or as tributaries. During the late nineteenth century, China's self-image as a universal empire was strengthened in the northwest but was dealt a fatal blow in Vietnam and Korea.

In the northwest, China confronted tsarist Russia. Conservatives at the Manchu court ordered Zuo Zongtang, who had suppressed Muslim rebels within China, to suppress a Muslim leader who had founded an independent state in the Tarim basin. By 1878 Zuo's army had regained the area, which was subsequently renamed Xinjiang, or the "New Territories." A treaty signed with Russia in 1881 also restored most of the Ili region in western Mongolia to Chinese control. These victories strengthened court conservatives who wished to take a stronger stance toward the West.

To the south, Vietnam had retained its independence from China since 935 and saw itself as an independent state. China simply saw Vietnam as a tributary. During the 1840s, the Vietnamese emperor moved to reduce French influences and suppress Christianity. The French responded by seizing Saigon and Cochin China in 1859, establishing a protectorate over Cambodia in 1864, and taking Hanoi in 1882. China in 1883 sent troops to aid its tributary, but after a two-year war with France, China was forced to abandon its claims to Vietnam. By 1893, France had brought together Vietnam, Cambodia, and Laos to form the Federation of Indochina, which remained a French colony until 1940.

Unlike Vietnam, Korea saw itself as a tributary of China on Chinese terms. During the last decades of the Choson dynasty (1392–1910), the Korean state was weak. It hung on to power in part by enforcing a policy of seclusion. Its only foreign ties were with China and Japan. In 1876, Japan "opened" Korea to international relations, using much the same tactics that Perry had used against Japan. Japan then contended with China for influence in Korea.

In 1893 a popular religious sect unleashed a rebellion against the Seoul government. China sent troops to help suppress the rebellion, but Japan sent more, and in 1894 war broke out between China and Japan. Japan won handily thanks to the discipline and the superior tactics of the Japanese units. Defeat by Japan convinced many in China that basic changes were inevitable.

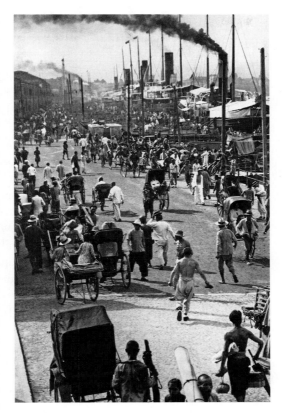

The Bund. After the Opium War, Shanghai became a treaty port in 1842 and foreign settlements arose along the Huangpu River, north of the old walled city. British and other companies built offices along the river's muddy waterfront, which they called the "Bund"—an Anglo-Indian term derived from "band," the Urdu word for embankment. Before World War II, oceangoing ships docked along the Bund in the heart of commercial Shanghai. Today this stretch of the river is fronted by the Zhongshan (Sun Yat-sen) Road. On one side are banks, insurance companies, and hotels; on the other side is a park. Ships no longer dock.

What kinds of people and activities can you identify in this photograph?

The French in Vietnam. Arrival in Saigon of Paul Beau (1857–1927), governor-general of Indochina from 1902 to 1907, from "Le Petit Journal," November 1902.

How are the Vietnamese depicted in this illustration? How do they compare with the way the French are depicted?

QUICK REVIEW

Korea in the Late Nineteenth Century

- Tributary of China
- The Korean state was weak in the last decades of the nineteenth century
- After 1876, Japan contended with China for influence in Korea

FROM DYNASTY TO WARLORDISM (1895–1926)

China was ruled by officials who had mastered the Confucian classics and were intellectually resistant to change. For most officials living in China's interior, the foreign crises of the nineteenth century were "coastal phenomena," soon forgotten. Few officials realized the magnitude of the foreign threat.

China's defeat by Japan in 1895 came as a shock. China responded with a new wave of reforms. Kang Youwei (1858–1927) argued that Confucius himself had been a reformer who had invented the idea of a golden age to persuade the rulers of his own age to adopt his ideas. History was evolutionary—a march forward from absolute monarchy to constitutional monarchy to democracy. Kang's reinterpretation of Confucianism removed a major barrier to the entry of Western ideas into China.

In 1898, the emperor launched "one hundred days of reform." He took as his models Peter the Great (r. 1682–1725) and the Japanese Meiji Emperor (r. 1867–1912). Edicts were issued to reform China's schools, railroads, police, laws, military, bureaucracy, post offices, and examination system. But conservative resistance was nationwide. At court, the empress dowager regained control and ended the reforms. Kang and most of his associates fled to Japan.

The response of the Western powers to China's 1895 defeat was to define spheres of interest, which usually consisted of a leasehold along with railway rights and commercial privileges. Russia gained a leasehold at Port Arthur; Germany acquired one in Shandung. Britain got the New Territories adjoining Jiulong (Kowloon) at Hong Kong. New ports and cities were opened to foreign trade. The United States was in a weaker position, so it enunciated an "open-door" policy: equal commercial opportunities for all powers and the preservation of the territorial integrity of China.

Boxers A nationalistic Chinese religious society that attacked foreigners and their encroachments on China in the late nineteenth century.

Pent-up resentments against foreign encroachments led to the Boxer Rebellion. The **Boxers** (in Chinese, literally the "Righteous and Harmonious Fists") were a religious society with rituals, spells, and amulets that they believed made them impervious to bullets. They rebelled first in Shandung in 1898 and, gaining court support, entered Beijing in 1900. There followed a two-month siege of the foreign legation quarter. Eventually an international force captured Beijing, won a huge indemnity, and obtained the right to maintain permanent military forces in the capital. The Russians occupied Manchuria.

The defeat of the Boxers convinced even conservative Chinese leaders of the futility of clinging to old ways. A more powerful reform movement began with the empress dowager in its vanguard. But the dynasty could not control the movement.

Educational reforms began in 1901. Women were admitted to newly formed schools. In place of Confucianism, instructors taught science, mathematics, geography, and an anti-imperialist version of Chinese history. Western doctrines, such as classical economics, liberalism, socialism, anarchism, and social Darwinism, were introduced. By 1906, there were eight thousand Chinese students in Japan, which became a hotbed of Chinese reformist and revolutionary societies.

Military reforms were begun by Yuan Shikai (1859–1916), whose New Army drew on Japanese and Western models. Young men from gentry families, spurred by patriotism, joined the New Army as officers. Their loyalty was to their commanders and their country, not to the dynasty. In 1905, the examination system was abolished; officials were to be recruited directly from the schools and those who had studied abroad. Provincial assemblies were formed in 1909, and a consultative assembly was established in Beijing in 1910.

OVERVIEW Chinese Intellectuals Respond to the West

In the century after the Opium War, China's leading thinkers responded to the challenge of the West in terms of the following four successive modes of thought:

1. During the 1850s and 1860s, the success of gentry Confucianism in putting down the Taiping and other rebellions and in reestablishing the social order underlined for most Chinese the effectiveness, vitality, and validity of traditional doctrines.

2. From the 1860s to the 1890s, the dominant intellectual modality was "*ti-yong* reformism." The essence (*ti*) was to remain Chinese, but useful contrivances (*yong*) such as arsenals and railroads could be borrowed from the West. This was the ideology of the "self-strengthening" movement.

3. During the last decade of the Manchu dynasty, the *ti* itself was reinterpreted. Kang Youwei argued that Confucius had been a reformer and that Confucianism was a philosophy of change. This line of thought influenced the reforms of 1900 through 1911.

4. A period of experimentation with new doctrines called the May Fourth Movement began in 1914 and extended into the 1920s. Instead of appealing to tradition, leading thinkers judged ideas in terms of their value in solving China's problems. This era of intellectual excitement corresponded with the period of warlord rule that provided a breathing space between the ideological constraints of the old dynasty and those of the Nationalist and Communist eras that would follow.

In sum, during the first decade of the twentieth century the three vital components of the imperial system—Confucian education, the bureaucracy, and the gentry—had been discarded or significantly modified. These changes sparked the 1911 revolution. It began with an uprising in Sichuan province against a government plan to nationalize the main railways. The key figures were the following:

1. Gentry, who stood to lose their investments in the railways.

2. Qing military commanders, who declared their provinces independent.

3. Sun Zhongshan (or Sun Yat-sen) (1866–1925), a republican revolutionary. He organized the Revolutionary Alliance in Tokyo in 1905 and was associated with the Nationalist Party (Guomindang) formed in 1912.

4. Yuan Shikai, who was called on by the court to preserve the dynasty. Instead, he arranged for the last child emperor to abdicate, for Sun to step aside, and for himself to become president of the new Republic of China.

The nationalists won an election called in 1913, but Yuan routed them and proclaimed a new dynasty with himself as emperor. The idea of another dynasty, however, met opposition from all quarters. Yuan died in June 1916. China then fell into the hands of warlord armies. The years until the late 1920s were a time of agony for the Chinese people. Yet they were also a time of intense intellectual ferment.

CULTURAL AND IDEOLOGICAL FERMENT: THE MAY FOURTH MOVEMENT

A period of freedom and vigorous experimentation with new doctrines began in 1914 and extended into the 1920s. It is called the May Fourth Movement because on that date in 1919, thousands of students in Beijing protested the settlement at Versailles that awarded former German possessions in Shandung to Japan. This kind of nationalist

WHY WAS Marxism-Leninism so appealing to Chinese intellectuals?

Jiang Jieshi (or Chiang Kai-shek, 1887–1975), as a young revolutionary officer, stands behind Sun Zhongshan (or Sun Yat-sen, 1866–1925), father of China's 1911–1912 Republican Revolution, taken around 1925.

What were Sun Zhongshan's core beliefs?

fervor also caused leading thinkers to judge ideas in terms of their value in solving China's problems.

Beijing was the center of May Fourth era thought. Cai Yuanpei (1868–1940), the chancellor of Beijing University, and Chen Duxiu (1879–1942), dean of letters, made Beijing University a haven for scholars who had returned from study in Japan or the West. In his magazine *New Youth*, Chen Duxiu called for a generation of progressive, cosmopolitan, and scientific youth who would uphold the values of liberty, equality, and fraternity. China's greatest modern writer, Lu Xun (1881–1936), published *A Madman's Diary* in *New Youth* in 1918. Lu Xun's message was that only the vision of a madman could truly comprehend an abnormal and inhumane society.

May Fourth Movement ideas quickly spread to the rest of China, especially its urban centers. Protest demonstrations against imperialist privilege broke out. Nationalism and anti-imperialist sentiment were stronger than liberalism, although most leaders spoke of democracy. Only members of an older generation of reformers, appalled by the slaughter of World War I and what they saw as Western materialism, advocated a return to traditional philosophies.

At the onset of China's intellectual revolution, Marx's critique of capitalist society did not fit Chinese conditions. More persuasive was the anarchism of Peter Kropotkin (1842–1921), who taught that mutual aid was as much a part of evolution as the struggle for survival. But after the Russian Revolution of 1917, Marxism-Leninism entered China. The Leninist definition of imperialism as the last crisis stage of capitalism put the blame for China's ills on the West and offered "feudal" China the possibility of leapfrogging over capitalism to socialism. Marxist study groups formed in Beijing and other cities. In 1919, a student from Hunan, Mao Zedong, who had worked in the Beijing University library, returned to Changsha to form a study group. The Chinese Communist Party was formed in Shanghai in 1921; Zhou Enlai (1898–1976) formed a similar group in Paris the same year.

NATIONALIST CHINA

WHO WAS Jiang Jieshi?

Guomindang (GMD). China's Nationalist Party, founded by Sun Yat-sen.

GUOMINDANG UNIFICATION OF CHINA AND THE NANJING DECADE (1927–1937)

Sun Zhongshan had fled to Japan during the 1913–1916 rule by Yuan Shikai. He returned to Guangzhou in 1916, but he was a poor organizer, and his **Guomindang (GMD)**—or Nationalist Party—made little headway. Sun began to receive Soviet support in 1923. He reorganized his party on the Leninist model with an executive committee on top of a national party congress, provincial and county organizations, and local party cells.

Sun enunciated "three principles of the people": nationality, livelihood, and rights. Sun's nationalism was directed against Western imperialism. Livelihood was defined in terms of equalizing landholdings and nationalizing major industries. By "people's rights" Sun meant democracy, although he argued that it must be preceded by a preparatory period of single-party dictatorship. Sun sent his loyal lieutenant Jiang Jieshi (Chiang Kai-shek) (1887–1975) to the Soviet Union for study. Jiang returned with a cadre of Russian advisers and established a military academy at Huangpu south of Guangzhou in 1924. Sun died in 1925. By 1926, the Huangpu Academy had graduated several thousand officers, and the GMD army numbered almost a hundred thousand.

The GMD had become the major political force in China; its leadership was divided between a left wing and a right wing.

The growth of the party was spurred by changes within Chinese society. Industries arose in the cities. Labor unions were organized. New ventures were begun outside the treaty ports. A politically conscious middle class developed. Another important sociopolitical element was China's several million students. In May 1925, students demonstrated in Shanghai. Police in the international settlement fired on the demonstrators. The incident inflamed national and anti-imperialist feelings. Strikes and boycotts of foreign goods were called throughout China.

Under these conditions the Chinese Communist Party (CCP) also grew and was influential in student organizations, labor unions, and even within the GMD, which Sun had permitted CCP members to join as individuals.

By 1926, Jiang Jieshi felt ready to march against the warlords. He worried about the growing communist strength, however, and before setting off he ousted the Soviet advisers and CCP members from the GMD offices in Guangzhou. The march north began in July. By the spring of 1927, Jiang's army had reached the Yangzi, defeating warlord armies as it advanced (see Map 28–2). After entering Shanghai in April 1927, Jiang carried out a sweeping purge of the CCP, killing many. Surviving CCP members fled to the mountainous border region of Hunan and Jiangxi to the southwest and established the "Jiangxi Soviet." Jiang's army took Beijing and gained the nominal submission of most northern Chinese warlords during 1928. Most foreign powers recognized the GMD regime in Nanjing as the government of China.

MAP 28–2 The Northern Expeditions of the Guomindang. These expeditions, from 1926 to 1928, unified most of China under the Nationalist (Guomindang) government of Jiang Jieshi, inaugurating the Nanjing decade. Warlord armies continued to hold power on the periphery.

What were the key weaknesses of the Guomindang?

Jiang believed in military force. He was unimaginative, strict, and incorruptible. Jiang venerated Sun Zhongshan and his three "people's principles." But where Sun was a revolutionary, Jiang was conservative and, though a Methodist, often appealed to Confucian values. The New Life Movement begun by Jiang in 1934 was an attempt to revitalize these values. Jiang's power rested on the army, the party, and the bureaucracy. The army was dominated by the Huangpu clique, which was loyal to Jiang, and by officers trained in Japan. After 1927, German advisers reorganized Jiang's army along German lines with a general staff system. The larger part of GMD revenues went to the military, which was expanded into a modernized force of three hundred thousand. Huangpu graduates also controlled the secret military police and used it against communists and any others who opposed the government. The GMD was a dictatorship under a central committee. Jiang became president of the party in 1938.

The densely populated central and lower Yangzi provinces were the area of GMD strength. The party, however, was unable to control outlying areas occupied by warlords, communists, and the Japanese. Warlords ruled some areas until 1949. In 1931, Jiang attacked the Jiangxi Soviet. In 1934, the communists were forced to flee to the southwest and then to Shaanxi province in northwestern China in the epic **Long March**. During this march, Mao Zedong wrested control of the CCP from the Moscow-trained, urban-oriented leaders and established his unorthodox view that a Leninist party could base itself on the peasantry. (See Map 28–3.)

Long March The flight of the Chinese communists from their Nationalist foes to northwest China in 1934.

MAP 28–3   The Long March, 1934–1935.
Arrows trace the Chinese Communists' Long March from Jiangxi Soviet to Yan'an in northwestern China.

How did the Communists gain power?

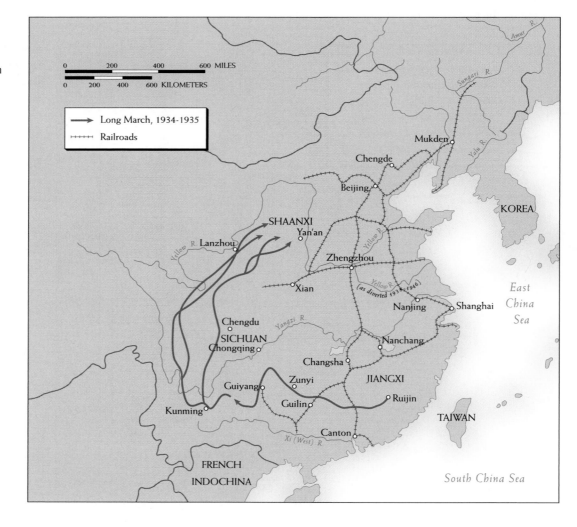

The Japanese had held special rights in Manchuria since the Russo-Japanese War of 1905. When Jiang's march north and the rise of Chinese nationalism threatened the Japanese position, Japan's forces in Manchuria engineered a military coup and established a puppet state in 1932. In the years that followed, Japanese army units moved south as far as the Great Wall. Chinese national sentiment demanded that Jiang resist, but Jiang, well aware of the disparity between his armies and those of Japan, felt that the internal unification of China should take precedence. On a visit to Xian in 1936 Jiang was captured by a northern warlord and held until he agreed to join with the CCP in a united front against Japan. In the following year, however, a full-scale war with Japan broke out, and China's situation again changed.

WAR AND REVOLUTION (1937–1949)

The war with Japan began in July 1937 as an unplanned clash at Beijing and then quickly spread. Beijing and Tianjin fell to Japan within a month, Shanghai was attacked in August, and Nanjing fell in December. During the following year, the Japanese took Guangzhou and set up puppet regimes in Beijing and Nanjing. In 1940, the leader of the left wing of the GMD and many of his associates joined the Japanese puppet government. Japan proclaimed its "New Order in East Asia." It expected Jiang to submit. Instead, in 1938 he relocated his capital to Chongqing, far to the west, and was joined by thousands of Chinese.

Jiang's stubborn resistance won admiration from all sides. But the withdrawal to Chongqing cut the GMD off from most of the Chinese population, programs for modernization ended, and the GMD's former tax revenues were lost. Crippling inflation exacerbated corruption and destroyed morale. The United States sent advisers and military equipment to strengthen Jiang's forces after the start of the Pacific War. Jiang, however, did not want to fight the Japanese but wanted instead to husband his forces for a postwar confrontation with the communists. The surge of anti-Japanese patriotism was not converted to popular support for the GMD.

For the communists headquartered at Yan'an, the Japanese occupation was an opportunity. While compromising with other political and social groups, the party strengthened itself internally. Party membership expanded from 40,000 in 1937 to 1.2 million in 1945. Schools were established in Yan'an to train party cadres. Orthodoxy was maintained by a rectification campaign. Those tainted by impure tendencies were made to repent at public meetings. Mao's thought was supreme. To the Chinese at large, Mao represented himself as the successor to Sun Zhongshan, but within the Communist Party he presented himself as a theoretician in the line of Marx (1818–1883), Engels (1820–1895), Lenin (1870–1924), and Stalin (1879–1953).

Whereas the GMD ruled through officials and often in cooperation with local landlords, the communists learned to operate at the grassroots level. They infiltrated Japanese-controlled areas and also penetrated some GMD organizations and military units. CCP armies were built up from ninety thousand in 1937 to nine hundred thousand in 1945. These armies were supplemented by a rural people's militia and by guerrilla forces. The Yan'an leadership and its party, army, and mass organizations possessed a

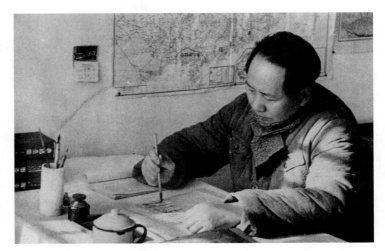

Mao Zedong (1893–1976) at his cave headquarters in Shaanxi province during World War II. He wears a padded winter jacket and writes with a Chinese brush. On his desk are the *Collected Works* of Lu Hsun.

What innovation did Mao introduce to Marxist-Leninist thought?

CHRONOLOGY

MODERN CHINA

Close of Manchu Rule

1839–1842	Opium War
1850–1873	Taiping and other rebellions
1870s–1880s	Self-strengthening movement
1894–1895	Sino-Japanese War
1898	One hundred days of reform
1898–1900	Boxer Rebellion
1912	Republican revolution overthrows Qing dynasty

Warlordism

1912–1916	Yuan Shikai president of Republic of China
1916–1928	Warlord era
1919	May Fourth incident

Nationalist China

1924	Founding of Huangpu Military Academy
1926–1928	Jiang's march north and Guomindang reunification of China
1928–1937	Nanjing decade
1934–1935	Chinese Communists' Long March to Yan'an
1937–1945	War with Japan
1945–1949	Civil war and the establishment of the People's Republic of China

cohesion, determination, and high morale that were lacking in Chongqing. But the strength of the Chinese communists as of 1945 should not be overstated. When the war in the Pacific ended in 1945, China's future was unclear. Even the Soviet Union recognized the GMD as the government of China and expected it to win the postwar struggle. The Allies directed Japanese armies to surrender to the GMD forces in 1945. The United States flew Jiang's troops to key eastern cities. His armies were by then three times the size of the communists' and far better equipped.

A civil war broke out immediately. Efforts by U.S. General George Marshall (1880–1959) to mediate were futile. Until the summer of 1947, GMD armies were victorious, even capturing Yan'an. But the tide turned in July as CCP armies went on the offensive in north China. In January 1949, Beijing and Tianjin fell. A few months later all of China was in communist hands. Many Chinese fled with Jiang to Taiwan or escaped to Hong Kong. In China apprehension was mixed with anticipation. The disciplined, well-behaved soldiers of the Peoples' Liberation Army were certainly a contrast to those of the GMD. As villages were liberated, lands were taken from landlords and given to the landless. In the cities crowds welcomed the CCP troops as liberators. The feeling was widespread that the future of China was once again in the hands of the Chinese.

MODERN JAPAN (1853–1945)

OVERTHROW OF THE TOKUGAWA *BAKUFU* (1853–1868)

WHAT ROLE did the Chōshū and Satsuma play in the overthrow of Tokugawa rule?

From the seventeenth century into the nineteenth century, the natural isolation of the islands of Japan was augmented by the country's policy of seclusion. Then at midcentury, the American ships of Commodore Perry came and forced Japan to sign a treaty opening it to foreign intercourse. Fourteen years later, the entire *bakufu*-domain system collapsed, and a group of talented leaders seized power.

Little changed during the first four years after Perry. The break came in 1858 when the *bakufu*, ignoring the imperial court's disapproval, was persuaded to sign a commercial treaty with the United States. Some daimyo, who wanted a voice in national policy, criticized the treaty as contravening the hallowed policy of seclusion. Younger samurai, frustrated by their exclusion from office, started a movement to "honor the emperor." The *bakufu*, in turn, responded with a purge. But in 1860, the head of the *bakufu* council was assassinated by extremist samurai. His successors lacked the nerve to continue his tough policies.

In 1861, two domains, Chōshū and Satsuma, emerged to heal the breach between the *bakufu* and the court. First, Chōshū officials proposed a policy that favored the *bakufu* but made concessions to the court. Next, Satsuma advocated a policy that made further concessions and ousted Chōshū as "the friend of the court." In response, the moderate reformist government of Chōshū adopted the proemperor policy of its extremist faction and, in turn, ousted Satsuma. Satsuma then seized the court in 1863 in a military coup.

Four points may be noted about the 1861–1863 diplomatic phase of domain action: (1) Even after 250 years of *bakufu* rule, several domains were still able to act autonomously when the opportunity arose; (2) the two domains that acted first and most of those that followed were large domains with many samurai and substantial financial resources; (3) both Satsuma and Chōshū had fought against the Tokugawa in 1600 and remembered an earlier independence; (4) by 1861 to 1863, new politics had opened decision making to middle-ranking samurai officials in a way that would have been impossible before 1853.

The 1863 Satsuma coup at the Kyoto court initiated a military phase of politics. As long as Satsuma and Chōshū remained enemies, politics stalemated and the *bakufu* continued as hegemon. But when the two domains became allies in 1866, the *bakufu* was overthrown in less than two years.

Factors contributing to this process included the movement for a "union of court and camp"; daimyo campaigned for a new conciliar rule in which they would participate together with the emperor and withdrew support from the *bakufu*. A second feature of this period was antiforeignism. A third was the formation of new rifle units, commanded mostly by lower samurai. These units transformed political power in Japan. A fourth development was a cultural shift in Japanese self-perception. During the Tokugawa era, the Japanese had seen themselves as civilized Confucians and much of the rest of the world as barbarians. But in 1868 Fukuzawa Yukichi (1835–1901) proposed that the West, with its technology, science, and humane laws, was "civilized and enlightened"; China, Japan, and countries like Turkey were half civilized; and other areas were dismissed as barbarian. Technology grew out of the Western legal, political, economic, and educational systems. Fukuzawa argued that Western systems required political freedoms and a citizenry with a spirit of independence. Fukuzawa's writings became immensely influential after the Restoration, eventually sparking the "Civilization and Enlightenment Movement" of the 1870s.

West Meets East. Commodore Matthew Perry meeting Japanese officials at Kurigahama in 1853. At the right are two emissaries of the *bakufu*, at the left is Perry's Chinese translator, who speaks English and communicates with the Japanese in written Chinese. Perry's ships are visible in the background along with smaller Japanese craft.

Did Perry's visit result in immediate change in Japan?

Meiji Restoration The overthrow of the Tokugawa *bakufu* in Japan in 1868 and the transfer, or "restoration," of power to the imperial government under the Emperor Meiji.

BUILDING THE MEIJI STATE (1868–1890)

The idea of a "developing nation" did not exist in the mid-nineteenth century. Yet Japan after the 1868 **Meiji Restoration** was just such a nation. (The years from 1868 to 1912 are referred to as the "Meiji period," after the era name that accompanied the accession of the new emperor.) It was committed to wealth and power of the kind Western industrial nations possessed. The government faced tough decisions as it

WHAT POWERS did the Meiji Constitution give to the emperor?

advanced by trial and error. It also demanded that the Japanese people make sacrifices for the sake of the future.

The announcement of the restoration of rule by an emperor was made on January 3, 1868. In the battles that followed, Chōshū and Satsuma troops defeated those of the *bakufu*. Edo surrendered and was renamed Tokyo, the "eastern capital." Edo castle became the imperial palace. At the start the Meiji government was made up of a small group of samurai leaders from Chōshū, Satsuma, and a few other domains. They have been described, only half humorously, as twelve bureaucrats in search of a bureaucracy. But their vision defined the goals of the new government.

CENTRALIZATION OF POWER

Their immediate goal was to centralize political power. By 1871, the young leaders had replaced the domains with prefectures controlled from Tokyo. To ensure a break with the past, each new prefectural governor was chosen from samurai of other regions.

Having centralized political authority, in 1871 about half of the most important Meiji leaders went abroad for a year and a half to study the West. They traveled in the United States and Europe visiting parliaments, schools, and factories.

The second task of the Meiji leaders was to stabilize government revenues. The government converted the grain tax to a money tax. But a third of the revenues still went to pay for samurai stipends, so in 1873 the government raised a conscript army and abolished the samurai class. The samurai were paid off in government bonds, but as the bonds fell during the inflation of the 1870s, most former samurai became impoverished. What had begun as a reform of government finance ended as a social revolution. Some samurai rebelled. The last and greatest uprising was in 1877. When it was suppressed in 1878, the Meiji government became militarily secure.

Diet   The bicameral Japanese parliament.

POLITICAL PARTIES

Other samurai opposed the government by forming political parties and campaigning for popular rights, elections, and a constitution. They drew heavily on liberal Western models and proposed that parties in a national assembly would unite the emperor and the people, curbing the Satsuma-Chōshū clique. Samurai were the mainstay of the early party movement, despite its doctrines proclaiming all classes to be equal. With the government's formation of prefectural assemblies in 1878, more political parties emerged. Many farmers joined, wanting their taxes cut; the poor joined too, hoping to improve their condition. In 1881, the government promised a constitution and a national assembly within ten years. As the date for national elections approached, the parties gained strength, and the ties between party notables and local men of influence grew closer.

THE CONSTITUTION

The government viewed the party movement with distaste but was not sure how to counter it. Under Itō Hirobumi (1841–1909), the conservative Prussian constitution of 1850 was adapted to Japanese uses. As promulgated in 1889, the Meiji Constitution granted extensive powers to the emperor and severely limited the powers of the lower house in the **Diet** (the English term for Japan's bicameral national assembly).

The emperor was sovereign. According to the constitution, he was "sacred and inviolable," and in Itō's commentaries this was

Japan's First Foreign Mission, headed by Prince Iwakura, Ambassador Extraordinary and Plenipotentiary, leaving Yokohama for the United States and Europe on December 23, 1871.

What was Japan's attitude toward the West at this time?

defined in Shinto terms. The emperor was given direct command of the armed forces. The emperor had the right to name the prime minister and to appoint the cabinet. He could dissolve the lower house of the Diet and issue imperial ordinances when the Diet was not in session. The Imperial Household Ministry, which was outside the cabinet, administered the great wealth given to the imperial family during the 1880s. The constitution itself was presented as a gift from the emperor to his subjects. The lower house of the Diet was given the authority only to approve budgets and pass laws, and even these powers were hedged. Itō's intention was not to create a parliamentary system but to devise a constitutional system that included a parliament.

The government also created institutions designed to limit the future influence of the political parties. In 1884, it created a new nobility with which to stock the future House of Peers. Itō, born a lowly foot soldier, ended as a prince. In 1885, he established a cabinet system and became the first prime minister. In 1887, Itō established a Privy Council, with himself as its head, to approve the constitution he had written. Civil service examinations were instituted in 1888. The bureaucracy became highly systematized. In 1890 there were 24,000 officials; by 1908 there were 72,000.

GROWTH OF A MODERN ECONOMY

WHY DID Japan set out to build a modern economy?

The late Tokugawa economy was similar to the economies of other East Asian countries. Almost 80 percent of the population lived in the countryside at close to a subsistence level. Taxes were high, and two thirds of the land tax was paid in kind. Money had only partially penetrated the rural economy. Japan had not developed factory production with machinery, steam power, or large accumulations of capital.

Early Meiji reforms unshackled the economy. Occupations were freed, which meant that farmers could trade and samurai could farm. The abolition of domains threw open regional economies and a groundswell of new commercial ventures and traditional, agriculturally based industries followed. Silk was Japan's wonder crop. The government introduced mechanical reeling, enabling Japan to win markets previously held by China's hand-reeled silk. Silk production rose from 2.3 million pounds in the post-Restoration era to 93 million pounds in 1929.

A parallel unshackling occurred on the land. The land tax reform of the 1870s created a powerful incentive for growth. Progressive landlords bought fertilizer and farm equipment. Rice production rose from 149 million bushels a year during 1880 to 1884 to 316 million during 1935 to 1937. Population grew from about 30 million in 1868 to 45 million in 1900 to 73 million in 1940. Because the farm population remained constant, the extra hands were available for factory and other urban jobs.

The Promulgation of the Meiji Constitution in 1889. The emperor, standing under the canopy, was declared "sacred and inviolable." Seated on the throne, at the left, is the empress.

Shosai Ginko (Japanese, act. 1874–1897), View of the Issuance of the State Constitution in the State Chamber of the New Imperial Palace, March 2, 1889 (Meiji 22), Ink and color on paper, 14 1/8 x 28 3/8 in. "The Metropolitan Museum of Art, Gift of Lincoln Kirstein, 1959 (JP3233-3235) Photograph © The Metropolitan Museum of Art."

What was the basis of the Meiji constitution?

FIRST PHASE: MODEL INDUSTRIES

The modern sector of the economy was the government's greatest concern. It developed in four phases, beginning with the era of model industries, which lasted until 1881. With military strength as a major goal, the Meiji government expanded arsenals and shipyards, built telegraph lines, started railroads, developed mines, and established factories. The quantitative output of these early industries was insignificant; they were pilot-plant operations that doubled as "schools" for technologists and labor.

Just as important to economic development was a variety of other new institutions—banks, post offices, ports, roads, commercial laws, a system of primary and secondary schools, and a government university—patterned after European and American examples.

zaibatsu Large industrial combines that came to dominate Japanese industry in the late nineteenth century.

SECOND PHASE: 1880s–1890s

More substantial growth took place during the 1880s and 1890s. It was marked by the appearance of what would later become the great industrial combines known as **zaibatsu.** One of the first industries to benefit was cotton textiles. By 1896, the production of yarn had reached 17 million pounds, and by 1913 it was more than ten times that amount. Production of cotton cloth rose as well. Another area of growth was railroads, which gave Japan an internal circulatory system, opening up hitherto isolated regions. In 1872, Japan had 18 miles of track; in 1894, 2,100 miles; and by 1934, 14,500 miles.

Cotton textiles and railroads were followed during the 1890s by cement, bricks, matches, glass, beer, chemicals, and other private industries. The government created a favorable climate for growth: The society and the polity were stable, the yen was sound, capital was safe, and taxes on industry were low. The conditions enjoyed by Japan's budding entrepreneurs differed in every respect from those of China.

Silk-Weaving Mill in Japan, late nineteenth century. Note the division of labor: The women do the manual labor, while the man, dressed in formal attire, supervises.

How did the silk industry develop in Japan?

THIRD PHASE: 1905–1929

The economy continued to grow after the 1905 Russo-Japanese War and spurted ahead during World War I. The economy grew slowly during the twenties because of factors including renewed competition from Europe and the great earthquake that destroyed Tokyo in 1923. Agricultural productivity leveled off during the twenties: It became cheaper to import foodstuffs than to invest in new agricultural technology at home.

By the 1920s, Japanese society, especially in the cities, was becoming modern. The Japanese were healthier and lived longer. Personal savings rose with the standard of living. Even factory workers drank beer, went to movies, and read newspapers. By 1925, primary school education was universal. Japan had done what no other non-Western nation had even attempted: It had achieved universal literacy. Nevertheless, an immense cultural and social gap remained between the majority who had only a primary school education and the 3 percent who attended university. This gap emerged as a basic weakness in the 1920s.

It should also be noted that despite overall improvements in the condition of the Japanese, the human costs of growth were high. (See Document, "Natsume Sōseki on the Costs of Rapid Modernization.") Well into the twentieth century more than half of the industrial labor force was women. They went to the textile mills after leaving primary school and returned to their villages before marrying. Their working hours were long, their dormitories crowded, and their movements restricted. Some contracted tuberculosis, the plague of late-nineteenth- and early-twentieth-century Japan, and were sent back to their villages to die.

QUICK REVIEW

Development of the Japanese Economy

◆ First Phase (up to 1881): Development of model industries

◆ Second Phase (1880s–1890s): Emergence of the *zaibatsu* and growth of the railroads

◆ Third Phase (1905–1929): Slow economic growth and modernization of Japanese society

◆ Fourth Phase (1929–1937): Depression and recovery

Planning Began in 1869, one year after the Meiji Restoration, and the first line from the Shiodome station in Tokyo to the port of Yokohama was opened in 1872. In this woodblock print, onlookers (in the foreground) gape outside the fence while passengers in Western dress await the arrival of the train.

What role did railroads play in Japan's economic development?

FOURTH PHASE: DEPRESSION AND RECOVERY

A Japanese bank crisis in 1927, followed by the worldwide Great Depression in 1929, plunged Japan into unemployment and suffering. The political consequences were enormous. Yet most of Japan recovered by 1933, more rapidly than any other industrial nation.

The recovery was fueled by an export boom and military procurements. During the 1930s, the production of pig iron, raw steel, and chemicals doubled. By 1937, Japan had a merchant fleet of 4.5 million tons, the third largest and the newest in the world. The quality of Japan's manufacturers also rose.

THE POLITICS OF IMPERIAL JAPAN (1890–1945)

HOW DID political parties develop in Japan?

Parliaments began in the West. Even a constitution as cautious as that of Meiji had no precedent outside the West. How are we to view the Japanese political experience after 1890? One view is that the Japanese were not ready for constitutional government, so the militarism of the thirties was inevitable. Japanese society certainly had weaknesses, but the Diet was growing in importance, and power was being transferred from the bureaucratic Meiji leaders to political party leaders. The transfer fell short of full parliamentary government, but the advance toward parliamentary government might well have continued if not for the Great Depression and other events.

FROM CONFRONTATION TO THE FOUNDING OF THE SEIYŪKAI (1890–1900)

In 1890 the Meiji leaders—sometimes called *oligarchs*, the few who rule—were concerned with nation building, not politics. They saw the cabinet as "transcendental," serving the emperor and nation, not partisan interests. They saw the lower house of the Diet as a place to let off steam without interfering in the government's serious work of building a new Japan. But the oligarchs had miscalculated, and they were drawn into political struggles.

The first act of the parties in the new 1890 Diet was to slash the government's budget. Prime Minister Yamagata had to make concessions to get some funds restored. This pattern continued for ten years. The government tried to intimidate and bribe the parties but failed. Political parties had the support of the voters,

714

DOCUMENT

Natsume Sōseki on the Costs of Rapid Modernization

Natsume Sōseki (1867–1916) was one of the earliest of a series of great novelists to create a new literature in Japan after the turn of the century. Sōseki could often be humorous. One of his early works, *I Am a Cat*, looks at a Tokyo household from a feline perspective. He advocated ethical individualism as superior to state morality. He also wrote of human isolation in a changing society and of the dark side of human nature.

- **What** were the costs of Japan's rapid modernization? Was the uneasiness experienced by only a few advanced thinkers, or did it cut across the society? Was it different from alienation in the modern West?

THE CIVILIZATION OF MODERN JAPAN

Let us set aside the question of the bragging about the new teachings acquired from the West, which are only superficially mastered. Let us suppose that in forty or fifty years after the Restoration, by the power of education, by really applying ourselves to study, we can move from teaching A to teaching B and even advance to C—without the slightest vulgar fame-seeking, without the slightest sense of vainglory. Let us further suppose that we pass, in a natural orderly fashion, from stage to stage and that we ultimately attain the extreme of differentiation in our internally developed enlightenment that the West attained after more than a hundred years. If, then, by our physical and mental exertions, and by ignoring the difficulties and suffering involved in our precipitous advance, we end by passing through, in merely one-half the time it took the more prosperous Westerners to reach their stage of specialization, to our stage of internally developed enlightenment, the consequences will be serious indeed. At the same time we will be able to boast of this fantastic acquisition of knowledge, the inevitable result will be a nervous collapse from which we will not be able to recover.

PASSERS-BY

This is what your brother said. He suffers because nothing he does appears to him as either an end or a means. He is perpetually uneasy and cannot relax. He cannot sleep and so gets out of bed. But when he is awake, he cannot stay

Russo-Japanese War. Japanese soldiers with flag and bayonets charge across a smoky field to engage Russian troops in the 1904–1905 Russo-Japanese War. Victory over Russia gave Japan a new international standing. The popularity of postcards, such as this one, reflected the new nationalism of Japan.

What were some of the roots of Japanese nationalism?

mostly well-to-do landowners, who opposed the government's heavy land tax.

In 1900, Itō Hirobumi formed a new party, called the Rikken Seiyūkai, or "Friends of Constitutional Government." For most of the next twenty years, it was the most important party in Japan, providing parliamentary support for successive governments through its control of the lower house. This arrangement was satisfactory to both sides: Prime ministers got the support necessary for the government to function smoothly, and party politicians got cabinet posts and pork barrel legislation with which to reward their supporters.

THE GOLDEN YEARS OF MEIJI

The years around turn of the century represented the culmination of what the government had striven for since 1868. Economic development was under way, and the unequal treaties were revised. However, it was events abroad that won Japan recognition as a world power.

The first event was a war with China in 1894 to 1895 over Korea. From its victory, Japan secured Taiwan and other territory, an indemnity, and a treaty giving it still, so he begins to walk. As he walks, he finds that he has to begin running. Once he has begun running, he cannot stop. To have to keep on running is bad enough, but he feels compelled to increase his speed with every step he takes. When he imagines what the end of all this will be, he is so frightened that he breaks out in a cold sweat. And the fear becomes unbearable.

I was surprised when I heard your brother's explanation. I myself have never experienced uneasiness of this kind. And so, though I could comprehend what he was saying, I could feel no sympathy for him. I was like a man who tries to imagine what it is like to have a splitting headache though he has never had one. I tried to think for a while. And my wandering mind hit upon this thing called "man's fate"; it was a rather vague concept in my mind, but I was happy to have found something consoling to say to your brother.

"This uneasiness of yours is no more than the uneasiness that all men experience. All you have to do is to realize that there is no need for you alone to worry so much about it. What I mean to say is that it is our fate to wander blindly through life."

Not only were my words vague in meaning but they lacked sincerity. Your brother gave me one shrewd, contemptuous glance; that was all my remarks deserved. He then said: "You know, our uneasiness comes from this thing called scientific progress. Science does not know where to stop and does not permit us to stop either. From walking to rickshaws, from rickshaws to horsedrawn cabs, from cabs to trains, from trains to automobiles, from automobiles to airships, from airships to airplanes—when will we ever be allowed to stop and rest? Where will it finally take us? It is really frightening."

"Yes, it is frightening," I said.

Your brother smiled. "You say so, but you don't really mean it. You aren't really frightened. This fear that you say you feel, it is only of the theoretical kind. My fear is different from yours. I feel in my heart. It is an alive, pulsating kind of fear."

Source: First selection from M. Kosaka, *Japanese Thought in the Meiji Era.* Copyright © 1958 Pan-Pacific Press, pp. 447–448; second selection from E. McClellan, *Two Japanese Novelists: Sōseki and Tōson* (Chicago: University of Chicago Press, 1974), pp. 49–50.

the same privileges in China as those enjoyed by the Western powers (see Map 28–4). The second event was Japan's participation in the international force that relieved the Boxers' siege in Beijing in 1900. A third development was the Anglo-Japanese Alliance of 1902. For Britain, this alliance ensured Japanese support for its East Asian interests. For Japan, the alliance meant it could fight Russia without fear of intervention by a third party.

The fourth event was the war with Russia that began in 1904. Japanese armies drove the Russians from their railway zones in Manchuria and seized Mukden in March 1905. The Russians sent their Baltic fleet to join the battle, but it was annihilated by Admiral Tōgō (1847–1934). The peace treaty gave Japan the Russian lease in the Liaotung Peninsula, the Russian railway in south Manchuria, the southern half of Sakhalin, and a recognition of Japan's interest in Korea, which was annexed in 1910.

Japan joined the imperialist scramble for colonies because it wanted equality with the great Western powers, and military power and colonies were the best credentials. Enthusiasm for empire was shared by political party leaders, most liberal thinkers, and conservative leaders.

RISE OF THE PARTIES TO POWER

The founding of the Seiyūkai by Itō in 1900 ended a decade of confrontation between the Diet and the government. Hara Takashi (1856–1921) assumed the presidency of the party in 1914. Born a generation after the founding fathers of the Meiji state, he helped Itō to found the Seiyūkai and was the most able politician in

MAP 28–4 **Formation of the Japanese Empire.** The Japanese empire grew in three stages: the Sino-Japanese War of 1894 to 1895, the Russo-Japanese War of 1904 to 1905, and Japanese conquests in Manchuria and northern China after 1931.

Why did Japan want an empire on the Asian mainland?

Japan. His goals, like those of Itō or Yamagata, centered on the expansion of national wealth and power. But he felt that they should be achieved by party government, not oligarchic rule, and he worked to expand the power of his party. The years between 1905 and 1921 were marked by the struggle between these two conceptions of government.

Party strength increased through a buildup of the Seiyūkai party machine and through strengthening of the Diet vis-à-vis other elites within the government in Tokyo. For the former, Hara obtained campaign funds from moneyed interests. Constituencies that supported Seiyūkai candidates got new schools, bridges, dams, roads, or even railroad lines.

In co-opting other governmental elites, the Seiyūkai had mixed success. The party increased its representation in the cabinet and gained some patronage appointments in the bureaucracy, although most bureaucrats remained professionals and resisted the intrusion of political appointees. The House of Peers and the Privy Council, which ratified treaties, remained independent. The Seiyūkai had no success in penetrating the military services.

The weakening of oligarchic control reflected the aging of the "men of Meiji." In 1900, Itō was the last oligarch to become prime minister. From 1901 to 1912, Katsura Tarō (1847–1913), a Chōshū general and Yamagata's protégé, and Saionji, Itō's protégé, took turns in the post. Both had Seiyūkai support. The oligarchs were also weakened by changes within the elites. A younger generation of officers in the military services chafed at the continuing domination by the old cliques. In the civil bureaucracy, younger officials who saw the bureaucracy as an independent service were achieving positions of responsibility. The oligarchs maintained their power to act for the emperor in appointing prime ministers until the deaths of Itō in 1909 and Yamagata in 1922.

A wave of liberalism began during World War I and culminated in the period of party governments from 1924 to 1932. Joining the Allies in World War I, Japan had been influenced by democratic thought. Scholars discussed revising the Meiji Constitution. Labor unions were organized. A social movement was launched to improve conditions in Japan's industrial slums and to pass social and labor legislation. Japan's second political party, the Kenseikai, which had been out of power since 1916, grew more liberal and adopted several of the new social causes as its own, such as universal manhood suffrage. When Hara cut the tax qualification for voting from 10 to 3 yen—a considerable extension of the franchise—the Kenseikai criticized the change as insufficient.

In 1924, the Kenseikai and the Seiyūkai formed a coalition government. For the next eight years, the presidents of one or the other of the two major parties were appointed as prime ministers.

The cabinets (1924–1926) of Katō Kōmei are considered the peak of parliamentarianism in prewar Japan. Katō advocated a British model of government. His ministry passed universal manhood suffrage, cut the military budget, and enacted social and labor legislation. Katō's cabinet brought Japan close to a true parliamentary government.

MILITARISM AND WAR (1927–1945)

The future of Japan's parliamentary government seemed assured during the mid-1920s. The economy was growing, society was stable, and party leaders were experienced. Japan's international position was secure. But by 1945 Japan had been defeated in a devastating war and was occupied by foreign troops for the first time in its history.

A small shift in the balance of power among the governmental elites established by the Meiji constitution had produced a major change in Japan's foreign policy. The parties had forced the other elites to compromise between 1890 and 1926. Beginning in 1932 military men replaced party presidents as prime ministers. In 1937 Japan went to war with China; by the end of 1941 Japan was allied with Germany and Italy, had clashed with the Soviet Union, and had gone to war with the United States.

From their inception, the military services in Japan had been constructed on different principles from Japan's civilian society. The armed services had their own schools, which inculcated discipline, bravery, and loyalty. Soldiers saw themselves as the true heirs of the founders of the modern Japanese state and the guardians of Japanese tradition. They contrasted their loyalty to the emperor and their concern for all Japanese with the special-interest pandering by the political parties.

Yearning for Military Heroes. Japanese patriotic society members dressed as samurai around 1925.

What had happened to the real samurai?

The military resented its diminished national stature during the 1920s, when military budgets were cut and the prestige of a military career declined. But there had been no change in the constitutional position of the services. The general staffs remained directly responsible to the emperor. With the passing of the Meiji oligarchs, this meant they were responsible to no one but themselves.

New multilateral treaties (the 1921–1922 Washington Conference and the 1930 London Conference) recognized the existing colonies of the victors in World War I but opposed new colonial ventures. Japan's position in Manchuria was ambiguous. Because Japan maintained its interests through a tame Chinese warlord, Manchuria was not, strictly speaking, a colony. But Japan saw its claim to Manchuria as similar to that of Western nations and their colonies. The Guomindang unification of China and the blossoming of Chinese nationalism threatened Japan's special position. Japanese army units murdered the Manchurian warlord when he showed signs of independence. In 1931, while the party government in Tokyo equivocated, the army provoked a crisis, took over Manchuria, and proclaimed it an independent state in 1932. When the League of Nations condemned this action, Japan withdrew from the league.

The Great Depression cast doubts on the international economic order and on the *zaibatsu*, which were seen as rich capitalist profiteers in a country full of suffering and want. While Japan's government acted effectively to counter the Great Depression, the recovery came too late to help the political parties. By 1936, political trends that had begun during the worst years of the Depression had become irreversible.

The Depression galvanized the political left and right. The political left was composed mainly of socialist moderates. Supported by unionists and white-collar workers, they would reemerge as a stronger force after World War II. There was also a radical left, consisting of many little Marxist parties and of the Japanese Communist Party, founded in 1922. Although small, the radical parties became influential in intellectual circles during the twenties and thirties.

During the 1930s, an array of right-wing organizations went beyond the emperor-centered nationalism in which all Japanese were steeped to challenge the status quo. Civilian ultranationalists used Shinto myths and Confucian values to attack Western liberalism. Some bureaucrats looked to the example of Nazi Germany and argued for the exclusion of party politicians from government. Military officers envisioned a "defense state"; they urged military expansion and an autarchic colonial empire insulated from the uncertainties of the world economy. Young officers of the revolutionary right advocated "direct action" against the elites of the parliamentary coalition and called for a second restoration of imperial power.

The last group precipitated political change. On May 15, 1932, junior army and navy officers attacked key civilian offices and murdered Prime Minister Inukai. This attack occurred at the peak of right-wing agitation and the pit of the Depression. Saionji decided it would be unwise to appoint another party president as prime minister, choosing instead a moderate admiral. For the next four years cabinets were led by moderate military men but with continuing party participation. These cabinets satisfied neither the parties nor the radical young officers. Japanese politics continued to drift to the right. In 1936, young officers attempted a coup in Tokyo. They killed cabinet ministers and occupied the Diet and other government buildings. They wanted their army superiors to form a new government. Saionji and other men about the emperor stood firm; the navy opposed the rebellion, and within three days it was suppressed. The ringleaders were tried and executed. It was the last "direct action" by the radical right in prewar Japan.

The military continued interfering in the formation of cabinets. From 1936 on, moderate prime ministers gave way to more outspokenly militaristic figures. Opposition to militarism remained substantial nonetheless. In the 1937 election, the two major centrist parties won 354 Diet seats. The Japanese people were more level-headed than their leaders. But the Diet could not oppose a government in wartime, and by summer, Japan was at war in China.

There were three critical junctures between the outbreak of war with China and the World War II campaign in the Pacific. The first was the decision in January 1938 to strike a knockout blow at the Nationalist Party (GMD) government. The war had begun as an unplanned skirmish between Chinese and Japanese troops in the Beijing area but had spread quickly. The general staff argued that the only way to end the war was to convince the nationalists that fighting was hopeless. The Japanese army occupied most of the cities and railroads of eastern China, but Jiang Jieshi refused to give in. A stalemate ensued that lasted until 1945. China was never a major theater of the war in the Pacific.

The second critical decision was the signing of the **Tripartite Pact** with Germany and Italy in September 1940. In 1936, Japan had joined Germany in the Anti-Comintern Pact directed against international communism. It also wanted an alliance with Germany against the Soviet Union, but Germany insisted that any alliance would also have to be directed against the United States and Britain. The Japanese disagreed. When Japanese troops skirmished with Russian troops on the Mongolian border in the summer of 1939, sentiment rose in favor of an alliance with Germany, but then Germany "betrayed" Japan by signing a nonaggression pact with the Soviet Union. Japan tried to improve its relations with the United States, but America insisted that Japan get out of China. By the late spring of 1940, German victories in Europe again led military leaders in Japan to favor an alliance with Germany.

Tripartite Pact   The alliance between Japan and Nazi Germany and Fascist Italy that was signed in 1940.

Four Years Before Pearl Harbor, the Japanese invaded and occupied most of eastern China. Early in 1937, Japanese troops captured Nanjing, entering the city through its triple-arched gate. Chinese resistance led to a breakdown of military discipline and the "rape of Nanjing," an event still alive in Chinese memory many decades later.

How did the United States react to Japan's occupation of Nanjing?

Japan signed the Tripartite Pact with three objectives in mind: to isolate the United States, to take over the Southeast Asian colonies of the countries defeated by Germany in Europe, and to improve its relations with the Soviet Union. The last objective was reached when Japan signed a neutrality pact with the Soviet Union in April 1941. Two months later, Germany attacked the Soviet Union without consulting Japan and then asked Japan to attack the Soviet Union in the east. Japan waited and, when the German advance was stopped short of Moscow, decided to honor its neutrality pact with the Soviet Union and turn south. This effectively ended Japan's participation in the Axis. Yet instead of deflecting American criticism as intended, the pact, by linking Japan to Germany, led to a hardening of America's position on China.

The third fateful decision was to go to war with the United States. In June 1940, following Germany's defeat of France, Japanese troops had moved into northern French Indochina. When Japanese troops took southern Indochina in July 1941, the United States embargoed all exports to Japan; this cut Japanese oil imports by 90 percent. Japan's military argued that oil reserves would last only two years and pressed for the capture of the oil-rich Dutch East Indies. But it was too dangerous to move against Dutch and British colonies in Southeast Asia with the United States in the Philippines. The navy, therefore, planned a preemptive strike against the United States, and on December 7, 1941, it bombed Pearl Harbor. The Japanese decision for war wagered Japan's land-based airpower, shorter supply lines, and what it saw as greater willpower against American productivity. The war left Japan defeated and in ruins.

JAPANESE MILITARISM AND GERMAN NAZISM

HOW WAS Japan similar to and different from Germany during this period?

The growths of militarism in Japan and Nazi Germany had some similarities. Both countries were late developers with elitist, academic bureaucracies and strong military traditions. Both had patriarchal family traditions and relatively new parliamentary systems. Both tried to solve the economic problems created by the Great Depression with territorial expansion. Both had modernized their military services, schools, governments, and communications to support authoritarian regimes, but their values were not sufficiently modern or democratic to resist antiparliamentary forces.

The differences between the two countries are also striking. Japan was more homogeneous than Germany. It had no Catholic–Protestant split, no Junker class, and no significant socialist movement. Japan did not suffer from inflation and the Depression did not decimate its middle class. In Germany, parliament ruled, and the Nazis had to win an election to come to power. Japan's Diet was weaker. Control of the government was taken away from the Seiyūkai and Minseitō even while they continued to win elections.

The process by which the two countries went to war was also different. The Nazis created a mass party and a totalitarian state and then declared war. In Japan, there was neither a mass party nor a single group of leaders in continuous control of the government. It was not the totalitarian state that made war as much as it was war that made the state totalitarian—creating a nationalism so intense that university students became suicide (*kamikaze*) pilots after the outbreak of hostilities.

The Allies compared General Tōjō Hideki (1884–1948), Japan's prime minister, with Hitler. However, although Nazi authority survived until Hitler died in a Berlin bunker, General Tōjō was removed from office when American planes began to bomb Japan in 1944. The military continued to prosecute the war, but when the Imperial Conference on August 14, 1945, divided three-to-three over the Allied ultimatum demanding unconditional surrender, the emperor broke the deadlock, saying that the unendurable must be endured. It was the only important decision that he had ever been allowed to make.

Tōjō Hideki (1884–1948), prime minister at the time of the attack on Pearl Harbor in 1941 and one of the chief figures in the rise of Japanese militarism.
What happened to Tōjō Hideki after Pearl Harbor?

CHRONOLOGY

MODERN JAPAN

Overthrow of Tokugawa *Bakufu*

1853–1854	Perry obtains Treaty of Friendship
1858	*Bakufu* signs commercial treaty
1861–1863	Chōshū and Satsuma emerge
1866	Chōshū defeats *bakufu* army
1868	Meiji Restoration

Nation Building

1868–1871	Shaping a new state
1871–1873	Iwakura mission
1873–1878	Social revolution from above
1877	Satsuma Rebellion
1881	Promise of constitution
1889	Meiji Constitution promulgated
1890	First Diet session

Imperial Japan

1894–1895	Sino-Japanese War
1900	Seiyūkai formed
1904–1905	Russo-Japanese War
1910	Korea annexed

Era of Party Government

1918	Hara becomes prime minister
1924	Katō becomes prime minister
1925	Universal manhood suffrage passed

Militarism

1931	Japan takes Manchuria
1937	War with China
1941	Japan attacks Pearl Harbor
1945	Japan surrenders

SUMMARY

MODERN CHINA (1839–1949)

WHAT WERE the most serious threats to Manchu rule in the nineteenth century?

Close of Manchu Rule. The Opium War (1839–1842) posed little threat to the Qing heartland. Far more serious were the Taiping and other rebellions. Gentry armies succeeded in suppressing these rebellions. Not until the very end of the century did the Chinese begin substantial westernizing reforms—and by then it was too late for the dynasty. *page 697*

WHO WERE the key figures in the revolution of 1911?

From Dynasty to Warlordism (1895–1926). The Boxer Rebellion convinced even conservatives that fundamental reforms were needed. The gentry and military commanders were early leaders in rebellion. After the Qing fell in 1912, China was ruled by regional warlords. *page 702*

WHY WAS Marxism-Leninism so appealing to Chinese intellectuals?

Cultural and Ideological Ferment: The May Fourth Movement. The newly entering flood of Western ideas fed a growing nationalism. The Marxist critique of capitalism did not apply to China, but Marxism-Leninism gained adherents. *page 703*

WHO WAS Jiang Jieshi?

Nationalist China. Nationalism permeated the Guomindang (or Nationalist) army under Jiang Jieshi; it lent legitimacy to the army's march north and to the establishment of the Nanjing government. Then Japan invaded and occupied areas on which the Guomindang had depended. The Communists built up their army, extended their influence, and won the civil war that ended in 1949. *page 704*

MODERN JAPAN (1853–1945)

WHAT ROLE did Chōshū and Satsuma play in the overthrow of Tokugawa rule?

Overthrow of the Tokugawa Bakufu (1853–1868). The Toku-gawa regime collapsed only fifteen years after the arrival of Perry in 1853. Chōshū and Satsuma led diplomatic efforts to unify the *bakufu* and the court between 1861 and 1863; the two domains fought against each other until 1866. Then they united and led the overthrow of the *bakufu.* *page 708*

WHAT POWERS did the Meiji Constitution give to the emperor?

Building the Meiji State (1868–1890). The new Meiji government began sweeping westernizing reforms in every field. Power was centralized, land taxes were reformed, political parties were created, and the Meiji Constitution was promulgated. *page 709*

WHY DID Japan set out to build a modern economy?

Growth of a Modern Economy. The Japanese government hoped a modern economy would help it build militry strength. Reforms spurred economic growth. *page 711*

HOW DID political parties develop in Japan?

The Politics of Imperial Japan (1890–1945). The emperor became the unifying symbol for traditional and conservative thinkers. The Diet (Japan's parliament) became the focus for progressives and liberals. A shifting balance between conservatives and liberals ensued, with parliamentary democracy making gains into the 1920s. But then the Great Depression and a crisis in Manchuria opened the way for the rise of militarism in the 1930s. *page 713*

HOW WAS Japan similar to and different from Germany during this period?

Japanese Militarism and German Nazism. There were notable similarities between Japan and Germany, particularly after the Great Depression as each expanded its territory. But there were also differences, beginning with Japan's greater homogeneity. *page 720*

REVIEW QUESTIONS

1. Which had the greater impact on China, the Opium War or the Taiping Rebellion?

2. How did the Qing (Manchu) dynasty recover from the Taiping Rebellion? Why was the recovery inadequate to prevent the overthrow of the dynasty in 1912?

3. Did the May Fourth Movement prepare the way for the Nationalist revolution? the Communist revolution? Or was it incidental to both?

4. How did Marxism gain adherents in China?

5. What were Jiang Jieshi's strengths and weaknesses as a leader?

6. How did the Chōshū and Satsuma domains become instrumental in the development of Japan's government?

7. How did political parties develop in Japan?

8. After the Meiji Restoration, what steps did Japan's leaders take to achieve their goal of "wealth and power"?

9. What were some social costs of economic development in Japan?

10. What were the strengths and weaknesses of Japan's prewar parliamentary institutions? What led to the sudden rise of militarism during the 1930s?

11. Compare and contrast the process of modernization in Japan and China in the twentieth century. Which country was more successful? Why?

KEY TERMS

Boxers (p. 702)
Diet (p. 710)
Guomindang (GMD) (GWO-MIHN-DONG) (p. 704)
Long March (p. 706)
Meiji Restoration (MAY-JEE) (p. 709)

self-strengthening (p. 700)
Taiping Rebellion (TEYE-PIHNG) (p. 698)
treaty ports (p. 700)
Tripartite Pact (p. 719)
zaibatsu (zeye-BAHT-soo) (p. 712)

Note: To learn more about the topics in this chapter, please turn to the Suggested Readings at the end of the book.

INTERPRETING THE PAST

East Asia in the Modern Era: Westernization, Assimilation, and Resistance

Sources from MyHistoryLab for Chapter 28

myhistorylab

1) President Fillmore, *Letter to the Emperor of Japan* (1852)

2) Feng Guifen on *Western Strength* (circa 1860)

Sources from Chapter 28

1) Natsume Sōseki, from *The Civilization of Modern Japan* and *Passers-By*, page 714

The process of modernization in East Asia during the nineteenth and early twentieth centuries was inevitably linked to contact with the West—either through cooperation, trade, diplomatic and technological exchanges, or more coercive methods characterized by outright military intimidation and colonial subjugation. China and Japan, as the most populous and prosperous nations in East Asia, possessed many of the preconditions required for modernization but had quite different experiences in adapting Western technology, ideas, and values to their own society.

In this exercise you will read brief primary sources that focus on the encounters between East Asian nations and the West and the process of modernization.

The first source is the letter that American president Millard Fillmore sent to the Japanese emperor with the naval squadron led by Commodore Matthew Perry in 1854. In this diplomatic but firm dispatch, Fillmore outlines what the Americans would like to obtain from Japan in the short term, as well as his longer-term goal of opening trade relations with the almost totally isolated island nation. The second document is written by Feng Guifen, a Chinese teacher and official whose ideas were central to the "Self-Strengthening Movement" that attempted to rapidly adopt Western technology and armaments beginning in the 1860s. The final documents, excerpts from works by Japanese novelist Natsume Sōseki, highlight the social and psychological impacts of modernization.

Questions

What is Natsume Sōseki's point? How do you think his readers in Japan would have responded? How might President Fillmore have responded?

How do Sōseki's arguments differ from Feng Guifen's effort to begin a "Self-Strengthening" movement in China?

What types of suggestions and guidance does the American president offer the Japanese emperor? Why was it necessary for him to forcefully advocate such major changes to isolationist Japan?

29
Imperialism and World War I

Queen Victoria's Golden Jubilee. By the late nineteenth century, British manufacturers were commonly printing commemorative wallpapers to celebrate special events. This wallpaper, celebrating Queen Victoria's Golden Jubilee in 1887, uses exotic images of the empire to demonstrate the power of the Queen. It probably would have been displayed in hotels and inns rather than in private homes. The flora and fauna of the empire—a kangaroo (Australia), an ostrich (Africa), a tiger (India)—as well as a couple skating on a frozen pond (Canada) surround the monarch. The distant lands of the empire have been tamed and absorbed into domestic British culture.

Why did empires become attractive to European powers in the late nineteenth century?

WHAT WAS the New Imperialism?

WHAT WERE Bismarck's goals for Germany?

WHAT CAUSED the outbreak of World War I in 1914?

WHY WERE the Bolsheviks able to
seize power in Russia?

WHY DID the Versailles settlement leave Germany bitter?

GLOBAL PERSPECTIVE

IMPERIALISM AND THE GREAT WAR

The outburst of European imperialism in the last part of the nineteenth century brought Western countries into contact with almost all the inhabited areas of the world and intensified their activity in places where they had already been interested. The growth of industry, the increased ease of transportation and communication, and the development of a world economic system all tended to bring previously remote and isolated places into the orbit of the West. By the time of the outbreak of World War I, European nations had divided Africa among themselves for exploitation, as the advent of steamships and railroads in the late nineteenth century allowed them to penetrate the African interior for the first time. The vast subcontinent of India had long been a British colony, producing primary products such as raw cotton that fed British industry. Much of China had fallen under European control after American "gunboat diplomacy" and the "Opium War" destabilized Chinese imperial rule in the nineteenth century. Indochina was under French rule. The islands of the Pacific had been divided among Western powers. Much of the Middle East was under the nominal control of the Ottoman

Empire, which was in its death throes and under European influence. The Monroe Doctrine made Latin America a protectorate of the United States. Japan, pushed out of its isolation, had itself become an imperial power at the expense of China and Korea. What all of the Western imperial powers, as well as Japan, had in common was a need to extract raw materials from their colonies to feed their industries. Their colonies in turn were to serve as markets for Western manufactured goods, even at the expense of indigenous manufactures, as in the case of India's ancient cloth weaving industry. This, as well as the prestige that colonies afforded, helps explain why nations were so determined to obtain and retain colonies.

The emergence of a new, powerful German state at the center of Europe upset the old balance of power and threatened the peace established in 1815. Germany's Chancellor Bismarck, however, created a new system of alliances that preserved the peace for as long as he remained in power. The new German emperor, William II, abandoned this policy of restraint and sought greater power and influence for his country. The result was a system of

D uring the second half of the nineteenth century, Europe exercised unprecedented control over the rest of the world. The Americas, Australia, and New Zealand almost became part of the European world as streams of European immigrants populated these areas. Africa was divided among European nations (see Chapter 27), and Europe imposed its power across Asia (see Map 29–1 and Chapter 28). By 1900, European dominance had brought every part of the globe into a single world economy.

These developments helped to foster competition and hostility among the great powers of Europe and to bring on a terrible war. The frenzy for imperial expansion that seized Europeans in the late nineteenth century did much to destroy its peace, prosperity, and dominant place in the world. ▪

EXPANSION OF EUROPEAN POWER AND THE NEW IMPERIALISM

WHAT WAS the New Imperialism?

Explosive developments in nineteenth-century science, technology, industry, agriculture, transportation, communication, and military weapons enabled a few Europeans (and Americans) to impose their will on other peoples many times their number. Westerners had institutional as well as material advantages—particularly the mobilizing power of national states and a belief in the superiority of their civilization.

The expansion of European influence was not new. Spain, Portugal, France, Holland, and Britain had controlled territories overseas for centuries. By the mid-nineteenth century, only Great Britain retained extensive overseas holdings, and there was general hostility to territorial expansion. The dominant doctrine of free trade opposed political interference in other lands. But after 1870, European states swiftly exerted control over about a fifth of the world's land area and a tenth of its population in a movement called the **New Imperialism** (see Map 29–1).

New Imperialism The extension in the late nineteenth and early twentieth centuries of Western political and economic dominance to Asia, the Middle East, and Africa.

alliances that divided Europe into two armed camps and greatly increased the chances of a general war. What began as yet another Balkan war involving the European powers became a world war that profoundly influenced the rest of the globe. As the terrible war of 1914–1918 dragged on, the real motives that had driven the European powers to fight gave way to public affirmations of the principles of nationalism and self-determination. Peoples under colonial rule took seriously the public statements, and sometimes the private promises, made to secure their cooperation in supplying the war effort and sought to win their independence and nationhood. For the most part they were disappointed by the peace settlement. The establishment of the League of Nations and the system of mandates in place of open colonial rule did not change much. The British Empire inherited vast territories from the defeated German and the defunct Ottoman Empires and was larger than ever. The French retained and expanded their holdings in Africa, the Pacific, and the Middle East. The Americans added to the islands they controlled in the Pacific. Japanese imperial ambitions were rewarded at the expense of China.

A glance at the new map of the world could give the impression that the old imperial nations, especially Britain and France, were more powerful than ever. However, that impression would be superficial and misleading. The great western European powers paid an enormous price in lives, money, and will for their victory in the war. Colonial peoples pressed for the rights that Western nations proclaimed as universal but denied to their colonies; influential minorities in the countries that ruled them sympathized with colonial aspirations for independence. Tension between colonies and their ruling nations was one cause of the instability in the world created by the Paris treaties of 1919.

Focus Questions

◆ Why were Western powers eager to obtain colonies?

◆ Why is World War I a turning point in history?

◆ How did World War I alter the relationship between imperial powers and colonized peoples?

THE NEW IMPERIALISM

Imperialism can be defined as extending a nation's influence by some form of power over foreign peoples. The usual pattern of the New Imperialism was for the European nation to invest capital in the "backward" country and thereby to transform its economy and culture. To guarantee their investments, European states would establish different degrees of political control ranging from full annexation as a colony, to protectorate status (whereby the local ruler was controlled by the dominant European state), to "spheres-of-influence" status (whereby the European state received special privileges without direct political involvement).

MOTIVES FOR THE NEW IMPERIALISM

The predominant interpretation of the motives for the New Imperialism has been economic, in the form given by the English radical economist J. A. Hobson (1858–1928) and later adapted by Lenin. Lenin saw imperialism as the final stage in capitalism's development—the pursuit of monopoly. Competition inevitably eliminates inefficient capitalists and therefore leads to monopoly. Powerful industrial and financial capitalists soon run out of profitable areas of investment in their own countries and persuade their governments to gain colonies in "less developed" countries. Here they can find higher profits from their investments, new markets for their products, and safe sources of raw materials.

The facts, however, do not support this thesis. Only a small part of European investments overseas went to the colonies acquired by the New Imperialism. Most of it went to older, established areas like the United States, Canada, and Australia. Colonies were not usually important markets for the great imperial nations, and it is not even clear that control of the new colonies was particularly profitable. A full understanding of the New Imperialism requires a search for other motives.

At the time, advocates of imperialism gave various justifications for it. Some argued that the advanced European nations had a duty to bring the benefits of their

Knitting the World. The New Imperialism was not restricted to Europe. An advertisement for the Singer Sewing Machine Company, based in New York, shows a seamstress sewing together the two halves of the Western Hemisphere. By the late nineteenth century, U.S. firms like Singer created a global demand for their goods. Singer sewing machines came with instruction booklets printed in fifty-four languages. Of the fifteen factories making the machines, only seven were in the United States.
What was the role of the United States in the New Imperialism?

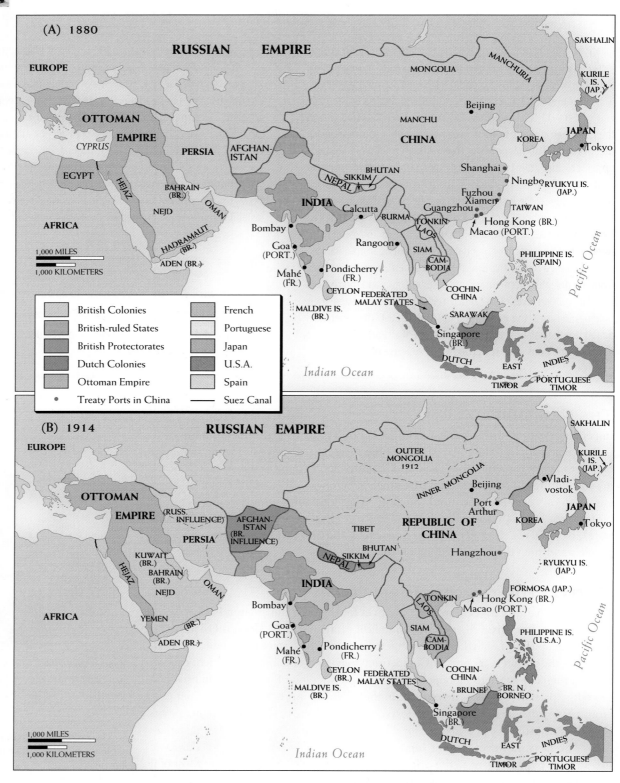

MAP 29–1   Asia, 1880–1914.   As in Africa (see Map 27–4), the late nineteenth century saw imperialism spread widely and rapidly in Asia. Two new powers, Japan and the United States, joined the British, French, and Dutch in extending control both to islands and to the mainland and in exploiting an enfeebled China.

How did the new Japanese empire affect the balance of power in Asia?

higher culture and superior civilization to so-called backward peoples. Religious groups demanded that Western governments support Christian missionaries politically and even militarily. Some politicians and diplomats supported imperialism as a tool of social policy. In Germany, for instance, some people suggested that imperial expansion would deflect public interest away from domestic politics and social reform. Yet Germany acquired few colonies, and such considerations played little, if any, role in its colonial policy. In Britain, Joseph Chamberlain (1836–1914), the colonial secretary from 1895 to 1903, argued for the empire as a source of profit and economic security that would finance a great program of domestic reform and welfare, but these arguments were made well after Britain had acquired most of its empire. Another apparently plausible justification for imperialism was that colonies would attract a European country's surplus population. In fact, most European emigrants went to areas their countries did not control, chiefly the Americas and Australia.

The "Scramble for Africa"

Strategic and prestige considerations seem to have been more important in bringing on the New Imperialism in the late nineteenth century, when European imperial powers expanded their economic and political control of Africa. During the "scramble for Africa," which occurred between the late 1870s and about 1900, the European powers sought to maximize their control of African territory and raw materials. Motivated by intense economic and political competition, they rationalized their expansionary policies on both religious and cultural grounds. The imperial powers divided almost all the continent among themselves. The short- and long-term consequences were complex and in most cases devastating for Africans. Among the long-term effects was that European control forcibly integrated African societies into the modern world economy. In the process, new forms of social organizations emerged and new market economies and political structures developed that would later form the basis for the modern, postcolonial African nations.

For centuries, European slave-trading bases had dotted the African coastline, but few Europeans had penetrated the interior. This changed in the late 1870s. (See Chapter 27). The Congress of Vienna had prohibited the Atlantic slave trade in 1815. Africa was no longer a source for slave labor except in Central and East Africa, where Arab slave traders continued to export slaves to the Muslim world until at least the 1890s. Instead, Africa became an important supplier of raw materials, such as ivory, rubber, minerals, and, notably, diamonds and gold to the West. The British, French, Belgians, Germans, Italians, and Portuguese sought to maximize their access to these resources. The competition was so fierce and the scramble for African territories so frantic that the imperial powers worried about how to parcel Africa among them without the contest leading to war. To set the rules, the German chancellor Otto von Bismarck called a conference in Berlin in 1884 to 1885 that mapped out a European-controlled Africa. African colonies had become both trophies for European powers and possible bargaining chips in their economic and political competition with each other.

The imperial scramble for Africa was not based on a universal policy, and each power acquired and administered its new possessions in different ways. Their goal, however, was the same: to gain control, or at least dominance, through diplomacy or superior force and then either to place Europeans directly in charge of administering the territories or, in some cases, to compel local rulers to accept European "advisers" who would exercise the real authority. The Europeans justified their activities by claiming that this was a civilizing mission—that they were bringing civilization to "savage" and "backward" natives. In fact, the European powers ran Africa primarily for their own benefit.

British Fort at Alexandria, Egypt.   The opening of the Suez Canal in 1869 sharply reduced the time needed for travel from Europe to the Far East and, for Great Britain, from England to its colony in India. Britain acquired a financial interest in the canal, giving it a strategic interest in Egypt. In 1882 Britain made Egypt a protectorate in order to secure the canal.

Why was the Suez Canal so strategically important for Britain?

In North Africa, the experience of European imperialism was slightly different from that in sub-Saharan Africa. Because much of North Africa was still technically part of the Ottoman Empire, the European powers secured their interests primarily through economic penetration (investments and loans) and diplomatic pressure. Force, however, was always an option. By 1914, European powers controlled all of North Africa. France had begun the conquest of Algeria in 1830 (see Chapter 27). The French also took control of Tunisia in the early 1880s and of Morocco between 1901 and 1912. Italy seized Libya from Turkey in 1911 to 1912. Egypt, the richest North African country, fell under the control of Britain.

Egypt was an unusual case. For most of the nineteenth century, it had been a semi-independent province of the Ottoman Empire under the hereditary rule of a Muslim dynasty. The Khedives, as these rulers were titled, had tried to modernize the country by building new harbors, roads, and a European-style army. To pay for these projects, the Egyptian government borrowed money from European creditors. To earn the money to repay these loans, it forced farmers to plant cash crops. Ultimately, the Egyptian government became utterly dependent on European creditors. The construction of the Suez Canal, which opened in 1869, was the final blow to Egypt's finances. Built by French engineers with European capital, the canal connected the Mediterranean to the Red Sea, which meant that ships from Europe no longer had to sail around Africa to reach Asia. Yet the tangible benefits to Egypt were not immediately clear. By 1876, the Khedive was bankrupt; most of his shares in the company that ran the canal were sold to Britain. Egypt's European creditors took more than 50 percent of Egyptian revenue each year to repay their loans and forced the Egyptian government to increase taxes. This provoked a rebellion, and in 1881 the Egyptian army took over the government to defend Egypt from foreign exploitation. Then Britain easily defeated the Egyptians and established seventy years of British supremacy in the country.

Egypt never became an official part of the British Empire, but the British exercised control through a relatively small number of British administrators and soldiers. Their primary goal was stability and control of the Suez Canal, which the British regarded as their "lifeline" to their empire in India and the Far East. They also prevented the Egyptians from establishing a textile industry that would compete with Britain's own textile mills. While the Egyptian economy grew and tax revenues increased, per capita income actually declined among Egyptians, most of whom were peasant farmers who owned little or no land. This led to the growth of Egyptian nationalism and to increasing demands that the British leave Egypt.

Perhaps the most remarkable story in the European scramble for Africa was the acquisition of the Belgian Congo. In the 1880s, the lands drained by the vast Congo River became the personal property of King Leopold II of Belgium (r. 1865–1909). The Belgian government, however, had no interest in acquiring colonies. So despite being a constitutional monarch, Leopold used his own wealth and political guile to realize his colonial ambitions under the guise of humanitarian concern for Africans. He recruited the English-born journalist and explorer Henry Morton Stanley (1841–1904) to undertake a major expedition into the Congo. Between 1879 and 1884, Stanley made "treaties" on Leopold's behalf with local rulers who had no idea what they were signing.

Leopold became the personal ruler of an African domain that was over seventy times the size of Belgium itself. Leopold's administration used slave labor, intimidation, torture, mutilation, and mass murder to extract rubber and ivory from what became known as the Congo Free State. Eventually Leopold's crimes were exposed, and he formally turned the Congo over to Belgium in 1908.

The cruelties in the Congo, which became the basis for Joseph Conrad's classic novel *Heart of Darkness* (1902), were recorded for posterity in photographs, eyewitness accounts, newspaper articles, and by an official Belgian commission. The most responsible historical estimates suggest that the exploitation Leopold's administration carried out halved the population of the Congo in about thirty years.

In South Africa, fertile pastures and farmland and vast deposits of coal, iron ore, gold, diamonds, and copper made the land appealing to a host of people. The Afrikaners or Boers, descendants of seventeenth- and eighteenth-century Dutch settlers, had long inhabited the area around the Cape of Good Hope, and the British started to settle there after Britain took over from the Dutch during the Napoleonic wars. Though the British met with considerable resistance from the Zulu, Shona, and Ndebele peoples, they eventually established colonies in what is now South Africa, Botswana, Zambia, and Zimbabwe. In 1910, after a series of bloody wars with the white Afrikaners, the British formed a pact with them that guaranteed the rule of the European minority over the majority black and nonwhite population. Africans and people of mixed race were forbidden to own land, denied the right to vote, and excluded from positions of power. To preserve their political power and economic privileges, the white elite of South Africa eventually enforced a policy of racial apartheid—"separateness"—that turned the country into a totally segregated land. The result was decades of oppression, racial tensions, and economic exploitation.

Cruelty in the Belgian Congo. A naked slave, tied to the ground, is whipped by an overseer.

Why were there so many atrocities in the Belgian Congo?

THE NEW IMPERIALISM IN ASIA AND THE PACIFIC

The emergence of Japan as a great power frightened the other powers that were interested in China (see Chapter 28). The Russians were building a railroad across Siberia to Vladivostok and were afraid of any threat to Manchuria. Together with France and Germany, they applied diplomatic pressure that forced Japan out of the Liaotung Peninsula in northern China and its harbor, Port Arthur. All pressed feverishly for concessions in China. Fearing that China, its markets, and its investment opportunities would soon be closed to U.S. citizens, the United States proposed the open-door policy in 1899. This policy opposed foreign annexations in China and allowed entrepreneurs of all nations to trade there on equal terms. British support helped win acceptance of the policy by all the powers except Russia.

The United States had only recently emerged as a force in international affairs. The Monroe Doctrine of 1823 had, in effect, made the entire Western Hemisphere an American protectorate. Cuba's attempt to gain independence from Spain was the spark for the new U.S. involvement in international affairs. Sympathy for the Cuban cause, U.S. investments on the island, the desire for Cuban sugar, and concern over the island's strategic importance in the Caribbean all helped persuade the United States to fight Spain.

CHRONOLOGY

EXPANSION OF EUROPEAN POWER AND THE NEW IMPERIALISM

1869	Suez Canal completed
1875	Britain gains control of the Suez Canal
1879–1884	Leopold II establishes his personal rule in the Congo
1880s	Britain establishes protectorate over Egypt
1882	France controls Algeria and Tunisia
1884–1885	Germany establishes protectorate over Southwest Africa (Namibia), Togoland, the Cameroons, and East Africa (Tanzania)
1898	Spanish-American War: United States acquires Puerto Rico, Philippines, and Guam, annexes Hawaiian Islands, and establishes protectorate over Cuba
1899	United States proposes open-door policy in Far East
1899–1902	Boer War in South Africa
1908	Belgium takes over the Congo from Leopold II

Victory in the Spanish-American War of 1898 brought the United States an informal protectorate over Cuba and the annexation of Puerto Rico and drove Spain completely out of the Western Hemisphere. The United States forced Spain to sell the Philippine Islands and Guam, and Germany bought the other Spanish islands in the Pacific. The United States and Germany also divided Samoa between them. France and Britain took the remaining Pacific islands. The United States had dominated Hawaii for some time and annexed it in 1898, five years after an American-backed coup had overthrown the native Hawaiian monarchy. This burst of activity after the Spanish-American War made the United States an imperial and Pacific power.

Thus, by the turn of the century, most of the world had come under the control of the industrialized West. The one remaining area of great vulnerability was the Ottoman Empire. Its fate, however, was closely tied up with European developments.

WHAT WERE
Bismarck's goals
for Germany?

QUICK REVIEW

Bismark's Goals

◆ No additional territorial expansion

◆ Tried to cultivate friendship with France

◆ Sought to prevent alliance between France and any other European power that would threaten Germany on two fronts

EMERGENCE OF THE GERMAN EMPIRE

FORMATION OF THE TRIPLE ALLIANCE (1873–1890)

Prussia's victories over Austria and France and its creation of the German Empire in 1871 revolutionized European diplomacy. The sudden appearance of a powerful new state posed problems.

The balance of power created at the Congress of Vienna was altered radically. Britain and Russia retained their positions. Austria, however, had lost ground and was threatened by nationalism within the Austro-Hungarian Empire. French power and prestige were badly damaged by the Franco-Prussian War and the German annexation of Alsace-Lorraine. The French were both afraid of Germany and resentful of their loss of territory and traditional dominance in western Europe.

BISMARCK'S LEADERSHIP (1873–1890)

Until 1890 Otto von Bismarck (1815–1898) continued to guide German policy. He insisted after 1871 that Germany wanted no further territorial gains, and he meant it. He wanted to avoid a war that might lead to Germany's disintegration. He tried to assuage French resentment by cultivating friendly relations and by supporting French colonial aspirations. He also prepared for the worst. If France could not be conciliated, it must be isolated. Bismarck sought to prevent an alliance between France and any other European power—especially Austria or Russia—that would threaten Germany with a war on two fronts.

Bismarck's first move was to establish the Three Emperors' League in 1873. The league brought together the three great conservative empires of Germany, Austria, and Russia. It collapsed when Russia went to war with Turkey in 1877. The tottering Ottoman Empire was preserved chiefly by the competing aims of those powers that awaited its demise. Ottoman weakness encouraged its Slavic subjects in the Balkans to rebel.

When Russia entered the fray, it created an international crisis. The Russians hoped to gain control of Constantinople. Russian intervention also reflected the influence of the **pan-Slavic movement**, which sought to bring all the Slavs, even those under Austrian or Ottoman rule, under the protection of Holy Mother Russia.

The Ottoman Empire was forced to sue for peace. The Treaty of San Stefano of March 1878 was a Russian triumph. The Slavic states in the Balkans were freed of Ottoman rule, and Russia obtained territory and an indemnity. But the terms of the Russian victory alarmed the other great powers. Austria feared that the new Slav states and the increase in Russian influence would threaten its own Balkan provinces. The British were alarmed by the possible Russian control of Constantinople. Disraeli (1804–1881) was determined to resist, and British public opinion supported him.

Disraeli sent a fleet to Constantinople, and Britain and Austria forced Russia to agree to an international conference at which the provisions of San Stefano would be reviewed by the other great powers. The resulting Congress of Berlin met in June and July of 1878 under the presidency of Bismarck. The Congress's decisions were a blow to Russian ambitions. Bulgaria lost two thirds of its territory. Austria-Hungary was given Bosnia and Herzegovina to "occupy and administer" under formal Ottoman rule. Britain received Cyprus, and France gained permission to occupy Tunisia. These were compensations for the gains that Russia was permitted to keep. Germany asked for nothing, but the Russians were angry. The Three Emperors' League was dead.

The major trouble spot now was in the south Slavic states of Serbia and Montenegro. They deeply resented the Austrian occupation of Bosnia and Herzegovina, as did many of the natives of those provinces. The south Slavic question, as well as the estrangement between Russia and Germany, was a threat to the peace of Europe.

Bismarck could ignore the Balkans but not the breach in his eastern alliance system. With Russia alienated, he concluded a secret treaty with Austria in 1879. The resulting Dual Alliance provided that if either Germany or Austria was attacked by Russia, the ally would help the attacked party. If either was attacked by someone else, each promised at least to maintain neutrality. The treaty was renewed every five years until 1918. As the central point in German policy, it was criticized at the time; some have judged it mistaken in retrospect. It appeared to tie the German fortunes to those of the troubled Austro-Hungarian Empire and thus to borrow trouble. It also isolated the Russians and pushed them to alliances in the West.

Bismarck was aware of these dangers but discounted them. He never allowed the alliance to drag Germany into Austria's Balkan quarrels. He made it clear to the Austrians that Germany would never attack Russia. Bismarck expected the Austro-German negotiations to frighten Russia into seeking closer relations with Germany, and he was right. By 1881, he had renewed the Three Emperors' League on a firmer basis.

In 1882, Italy, annoyed by the French preemption of Tunisia, asked to join the Dual Alliance. Bismarck was now allied with three of the great powers and friendly with Great Britain, which held aloof from all alliances. France was isolated. Although the Three Emperors' League was allowed to lapse, the Triple Alliance (Germany, Austria, and Italy) was renewed for another five years in 1887. To restore German

pan-Slavic movement The movement to create a nation or federation that would embrace all the Slavic peoples of Eastern Europe.

Bismarck and the Kaiser. Bismarck and a young Kaiser William II meet in 1888. The two disagreed over many issues, and in 1890 William dismissed the aged chancellor.

Why did Kaiser William II disagree with Bismarck?

DOCUMENT

Bismarck Explains His Foreign Policy

Otto von Bismarck, chancellor of the new German Empire, guided German foreign policy in the years from its establishment of the empire in 1871 until his dismissal from office in 1890. In that period and for another quarter century, Europe was free of war among the great powers. The system of alliances Bismarck took the lead in creating is often given credit for preserving that peace. The following passage from his memoirs, written in his retirement, sets forth in retrospect his intentions in creating this system.

- **What** alliances made up Bismarck's systems? How were they meant to preserve the peace? What is

Bismarck's stated purpose for avoiding a war in Europe? Were there other reasons too?

The Triple Alliance which I originally sought to conclude after the peace of Frankfurt, and about which I had already sounded Vienna and St. Petersburg, from Meaux, in September 1870, was an alliance of the three emperors with the further idea of bringing into it monarchical Italy. It was designed for the struggle which, as I feared, was before us, between the two European tendencies which Napoleon called Republican and Cossack, and which I, according to our present ideas, should designate on the one side as the system of order on a monarchical basis, and on

relations with Russia, Bismarck negotiated the Reinsurance Treaty that same year, in which both powers promised to remain neutral if either was attacked. However, a change in the German monarchy overturned Bismarck's system (see Document, "Bismarck Explains His Foreign Policy").

In 1888, William II (r. 1888–1918) came to the German throne. Like many Germans of his generation, he was filled with a sense of Germany's destiny as the leading power of Europe. To achieve a "place in the sun," he wanted a navy and colonies like Britain's. These aims, of course, ran counter to Bismarck's policy. In 1890, William dismissed Bismarck. During Bismarck's time, Germany was a force for European peace. This position would not have been possible without its great military power. But it also required a statesman who could exercise restraint and understand what his country needed and what was possible.

FORGING THE TRIPLE ENTENTE (1890–1907)

Almost immediately after Bismarck's retirement, his system of alliances collapsed. His successor, General Leo von Caprivi (1831–1899), refused the Russian request to renew the Reinsurance Treaty, which he considered incompatible with the Austrian alliance. Political isolation and the need for foreign capital drove the Russians toward France. The French, who were even more isolated, were glad to pour capital into Russia if it would help produce security against Germany. In 1894 the Franco-Russian alliance was signed.

Britain now became the key to the international situation. Colonial rivalries pitted the British against the Russians in Central Asia and against the French in Africa. Traditionally, Britain had also opposed Russian control of Constantinople and French control of the Low Countries. There was no reason to think that Britain would soon become friendly to its traditional rivals or abandon its friendliness toward the Germans. Yet within a decade of William II's accession, Germany had become the enemy in the minds of the British because of Germany's foreign and naval policies.

At first Germany tried to win over the British to the Triple Alliance, but when Britain clung to "splendid isolation," Germany sought to demonstrate its worth as an ally by making trouble for Britain. The Germans began to exert pressure against Britain in Africa by barring British attempts to build a railroad from Cape Town to Cairo.

the other as the social republic to the level of which the antimonarchical development is wont to sink, either slowly or by leaps and bounds, until the conditions thus created become intolerable, and the disappointed populace are ready for a violent return to monarchical institutions in a Cæsarean form, I consider that the task of escaping from this *circulus vitiosus,* or, if possible, of sparing the present generation and their children an entrance into it, ought to be more closely incumbent on the strong existing monarchies, those monarchies which still have a vigorous life, than any rivalry over the fragments of nations which people the Balkan peninsula. If the monarchical governments have no understanding of the necessity for holding together in the interests of political and social order, but make themselves subservient to the chauvinistic impulses of their subjects, I fear that the international revolutionary and social struggles which will have to be fought out will be all the more dangerous, and take such a form that the victory on the part of monarchical order will be more difficult. Since 1871 I have sought for the most certain assurance against those struggles in the alliance of the three emperors, and also in the effort to impart to the monarchical principle in Italy a firm support in that alliance.

Source: Otto von Bismarck, *Reflections and Reminiscences,* ed. by Theodore S. Hamerow (New York: Harper Torchbooks, 1968), pp. 236–237.

They also openly sympathized with the Boers of South Africa in their resistance to British expansion.

In 1898, William's dream of a German navy began to achieve reality with the passage of a naval law providing for nineteen battleships. In 1900, a second law doubled that figure. The architect of the new navy, Admiral Alfred von Tirpitz (1849–1930), proclaimed that Germany's naval policy was aimed at Britain. As the German navy grew and German policies seemed more threatening, the British abandoned their traditional policies (see Figure 29–1).

The first breach in Britain's isolation came in 1902 when an alliance was concluded with Japan to help defend British interests in the Far East against Russia. Next, Britain in 1904 concluded a series of agreements with the French, collectively called the Entente Cordiale. It was not a formal treaty and had no military provisions, but it settled all outstanding colonial differences between the two nations. The Entente Cordiale was a big step toward aligning the British with Germany's great potential enemy.

In March 1905, William II landed at Tangier and challenged the French predominance there in a speech in favor of Moroccan independence. Germany's chancellor, Prince Bernhard von Bülow (1849–1929), intended to show France how weak it was and how little it could expect from Britain; he also hoped to gain colonial concessions. The Germans might

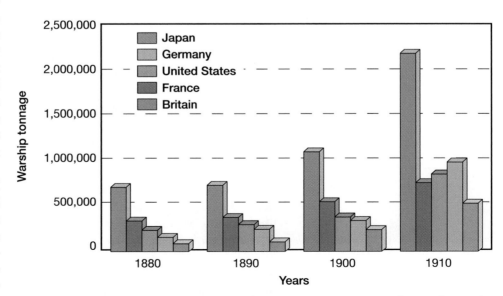

FIGURE 29–1 **Warship Tonnage of the World's Navies, 1880–1910.** Naval strength was the primary index of power before World War I. Paul Kennedy, *Rise and Fall of the Great Powers* (New York: Random House, 1987), p. 203.

Which countries experienced dramatic change in warship tonnage?

have achieved their aims, but they demanded an international conference to exhibit their power. The conference met in 1906 at Algeciras in Spain. Austria sided with its German ally, but Spain, Italy, and the United States voted with Britain and France. The French were confirmed in their position in Morocco, and German bullying had driven Britain and France closer together. Sir Edward Grey (1862–1933), the British foreign secretary, authorized conversations between the British and French general staffs. By 1914, French and British military and naval plans were so mutually dependent that the two countries were effectively allies.

Britain's new relationship with France was surprising enough. Hardly anyone believed that Britain and Russia could ever be allies. The 1904–1905 Russo-Japanese War made such a development seem even less likely because Britain was allied with Russia's enemy. But defeat and the Russian Revolution of 1905 left Russia weak and reduced British apprehensions. The British were also concerned that Russia might drift into the German orbit. With French support, in 1907 an agreement settled Russo-British quarrels in Central Asia and Persia and opened the door for wider cooperation. The Triple Entente, an informal but powerful association of Britain, France, and Russia, was now ranged against the Triple Alliance. Because Italy was unreliable, Germany and Austria-Hungary stood surrounded by two great land powers and Great Britain.

William II and his ministers had turned Bismarck's nightmare of the prospect of a two-front war with France and Russia into a reality and had added Britain to the hostile coalition. Bismarck's alliance system had been intended to maintain peace, but the new one increased the risk of war and made the Balkans, where Austrian and Russian ambitions clashed, a likely spot for it.

WORLD WAR I

WHAT CAUSED the outbreak of World War I in 1914?

THE ROAD TO WAR (1908–1914)

Except for the Greeks and the Romanians, most of the inhabitants of the Balkans were Slavs and felt a kinship with one another and with Russia. For centuries they had been ruled by Austrians, Hungarians, or Turks, and the nationalism that characterized late-nineteenth-century Europe made many Slavs eager for liberty or at least autonomy. The more radical among them longed for a union of the south Slavic, or Yugoslav, peoples in a single nation led by independent Serbia. They hoped to detach all the Slavic provinces (especially Bosnia, which bordered on Serbia) from Austria. Serbia was to unite the Slavs at the expense of Austria, as Piedmont had united the Italians and Prussia the Germans.

In 1908, modernizing reformers called the Young Turks overthrew the Ottoman government. This threatened to revive the empire and precipitated a series of Balkan crises that would lead to world war. Austria and Russia decided to act before Turkey became stronger. They agreed to call an international conference in which each of them would support the other's demands. Russia would agree to the Austrian annexation of Bosnia and Herzegovina, and Austria would support Russia's request to open the Dardanelles to Russian warships.

Austria, however, declared the annexation unilaterally before any conference was called. The British, concerned about their own position in the Mediterranean, rejected the Russian demand. The Russians were furious. The Serbs were enraged by the annexation of Bosnia. The Russians were too weak to do anything but accept the new situation. The Germans were unhappy because Austria's action threatened their relations with Russia. But Germany felt so dependent on the Dual Alliance that it assured Austria of its support. To an extent, German policy was being made in Vienna. It was a dangerous precedent. At the same time, the failure of Britain and France to support Russia strained the Triple Entente and made it harder for them to oppose Russian interests again if they wanted to retain Russian friendship.

The second Moroccan crisis, in 1911, emphasized the French and British need for mutual support. When France sent an army to Morocco to put down a rebellion, Germany took the opportunity to extort colonial concessions in the French Congo by sending the gunboat *Panther* to the port of Agadir in Morocco, allegedly to protect German citizens there. As in 1905, the Germans went too far.

Anglo-German relations had already been deteriorating, chiefly because of the naval race. The British now mistakenly believed that the Germans meant to turn Agadir into a naval base on the Atlantic. The crisis passed when France yielded bits of the Congo and Germany withdrew from Morocco. The main result was to draw Britain closer to France. Plans were formulated for a British expeditionary force to help defend France against German attack, and the British and French navies agreed to cooperate.

After the second Moroccan crisis, Italy feared that France would move into Ottoman Libya. Consequently, in 1911 Italy attacked the Ottoman Empire to forestall the French and obtained Libya and the Dodecanese Islands in the Aegean. The Italian victory encouraged the Balkan states to try their luck. In 1912, Bulgaria, Greece, Montenegro, and Serbia attacked the Ottoman Empire and won easily. The Serbs and the Bulgarians then quarreled about the division of Macedonia, and in 1913, Turkey and Romania joined Greece and Serbia against Bulgaria, which lost much of what it had gained since 1878.

The Austrians were determined to limit Serbian gains and prevent the Serbs from obtaining a port in Albania on the Adriatic. An international conference sponsored by Britain in early 1913 resolved the matter in Austria's favor and called for an independent kingdom of Albania. But Austria felt humiliated by the public airing of Serbian demands and in October unilaterally forced Serbia to withdraw from Albania. Russia again let Austria have its way.

The lessons learned from this affair influenced behavior in the final crisis of 1914. The Russians had, as in 1908, been embarrassed by their passivity, and their allies were now more reluctant to restrain them. The Austrians were determined not to accept an international conference again. They and their German allies had seen that better results might be obtained from a threat of force.

SARAJEVO AND THE OUTBREAK OF WAR (JUNE–AUGUST 1914)

On June 28, 1914, a Bosnian nationalist killed the Austrian Archduke Francis Ferdinand (1863–1914), heir to the throne, and his wife in the Bosnian capital of Sarajevo. The assassin was a member of a conspiracy hatched by a political terrorist society. The chief of intelligence of the Serbian army had helped plan the crime. Even though his role was unknown at the time, it was generally believed that Serbian officials were involved.

The assassination was condemned throughout Europe. To those Austrians who had long favored an attack on Serbia as a solution to the empire's Slavic problem, the opportunity seemed

Assassination of the Archduke.   Above: The Austrian Archduke Franz Ferdinand and his wife in Sarajevo on June 28, 1914. Later in the day the royal couple was assassinated by young revolutionaries trained and supplied in Serbia, igniting the crisis that led to World War I. Below: Moments after the assassination the Austrian police captured one of the assassins.

Why did this assassination trigger World War I?

CHRONOLOGY

COMING OF WORLD WAR I

1871	End of the Franco-Prussian War; creation of the German Empire; German annexation of Alsace-Lorraine
1873	Three Emperors' League (Germany, Russia, and Austria-Hungary)
1875	Russo-Turkish War
1878	Congress of Berlin
1879	Dual Alliance between Germany and Austria
1881	Three Emperors' League is renewed
1882	Italy joins Germany and Austria in Triple Alliance
1888	William II becomes German emperor
1890	Bismarck dismissed
1894	Franco-Russian alliance
1898	Germany begins to build battleship navy
1902	British alliance with Japan
1904	Entente Cordiale between Britain and France
1904–1905	Russo-Japanese War
1905	First Moroccan crisis
1907	British agreement with Russia
1908–1909	Bosnian crisis
1911	Second Moroccan crisis; Italy attacks Turkey
1912–1913	First and second Balkan wars
1914	Outbreak of World War I

mobilization The placing of a country's military forces on a war footing.

Schlieffen Plan Germany's plan for achieving a quick victory in the West at the outbreak of World War I by invading France through Belgium and Luxembourg.

irresistible. But Count Stefan Tisza (1861–1918), speaking for Hungary, resisted. Count Leopold Berchtold (1863–1942), the Austro-Hungarian foreign minister, knew that German support would be required if Russia should decide to protect Serbia and to persuade the Hungarians to go to war. The question of peace or war, therefore, had to be answered in Berlin.

William II and Chancellor Theobald von Bethmann-Hollweg (1856–1921) readily promised German support for an attack on Serbia. It has often been said that they gave the Austrians a "blank check," but their message was firmer than that. They urged the Austrians to move swiftly while the other powers were still angry at Serbia. They also indicated that a failure to act would be evidence of Austria-Hungary's uselessness as an ally. The Austrians hoped, with the protection of Germany, to avoid a general European conflict but were prepared to risk one. The Germans also knew that they risked a general war but hoped to "localize" the fight between Austria and Serbia. Bethmann-Hollweg hoped that German support would deter Russian involvement. Failing that, he believed that rapid victory over France would allow a full-scale attack on the Russians, who were slow to bring their strength into action. This policy depended on British neutrality, and the German chancellor convinced himself that the British could be persuaded to stand aloof. But all these hopes were futile.

The Austrians were slow to act. They did not even deliver their deliberately unacceptable ultimatum to Serbia until July 24, when the general hostility toward Serbia had begun to subside. Serbia returned an embarrasingly conciliatory answer, but the Austrians were determined to fight. On July 28, they declared war on Serbia, even though they could not field an army until mid-August.

The Russians responded angrily. Nationalists, pan-Slavs, and most of the politically conscious classes demanded action. The government ordered partial **mobilization** against Austria only. This policy was militarily impossible, but its purpose was diplomatic: to pressure Austria to hold back its attack on Serbia.

Mobilization of any kind, however, was generally understood to be equivalent to an act of war. It was especially alarming to German General Helmuth von Moltke (1848–1916). Russian mobilization could upset the delicate timing of Germany's battle plan—the **Schlieffen Plan**, which required an attack on France first—and would endanger Germany. From this point on, Moltke pressed for war. The pressure of military necessity became irresistible (see Map 29–2).

The western European powers were not eager for war. The French gave the Russians the same assurances that Germany had given its ally. The British worked hard for another conference of the powers, but Austria would not hear of it. The Germans privately supported the Austrians but were publicly conciliatory in the hope of keeping the British neutral.

Soon, however, Bethmann-Hollweg realized what he should have known all along: If Germany attacked France, Britain must fight. While Bethmann-Hollweg was urging restraint on the Austrians, Moltke was pressing them to act. In any case, it was too late for the Austrians to back down.

On July 30, Austria ordered mobilization against Russia. Russia and Germany then ordered general mobilization. The Schlieffen Plan went into effect. The Germans invaded Belgium on August 3. The British had guaranteed Belgian neutrality, so Britain was now united against Germany. Germany then invaded France. On August 4, Britain declared war on Germany. The Great War had begun; Europe would never be the same.

The Western Front.   French troops advancing on the western front. This scene of trench warfare characterizes the twentieth century's first great international conflict. The trenches were protected by barbed wire and machine guns, which gave defenders the advantage.

How did military tactics change in World War I?

STRATEGIES AND STALEMATE (1914–1917)

Jubilation greeted the outbreak of war throughout Europe. No general war had been fought since Napoleon, and the horrors of modern warfare were not yet understood. The dominant memory was of Bismarck's swift and decisive campaigns in which costs and casualties were light and the rewards great. Both sides expected quick victory. The Triple Entente powers—or the Allies, as they came to be called—had superior numbers and financial resources as well as command of the sea. Germany and Austria, the Central Powers, had the advantages of internal lines of communication and of having launched their attack first.

After 1905 Germany's only war plan was the one developed by Count Alfred von Schlieffen (1833–1913), chief of the German general staff from 1891 to 1906 (see Map 29–2). It aimed to outflank the French defenses by sweeping through Belgium to the Channel, then wheeling to the south and east to envelop the French and crush them against the German fortresses in Lorraine. In the east the Germans planned to stand on the defensive against Russia until France had been beaten, a task they thought would take only six weeks.

The execution of his plan, however, was left to Helmuth von Moltke, a gloomy and nervous man, who made enough tactical mistakes to cause it to fail by a narrow margin. As a result, the French and British were able to stop the Germans at the Battle of the Marne in September 1914. Thereafter, the war in the west became one of position. Both sides dug in behind a wall of trenches protected by barbed wire that stretched from the North Sea to Switzerland. Machine-gun nests made assaults dangerous. Both sides, nonetheless, attempted massive attacks initiated by artillery bombardments of unprecedented force and duration. Still, the defense always prevented a breakthrough.

In the east, the Russians advanced into Austrian territory and inflicted heavy casualties, but Russian incompetence and German energy soon reversed the situation. General Erich Ludendorff

MAP 29–2 **The Schlieffen Plan of 1905.** Germany's grand strategy for quickly winning the war against France in 1914 is shown by the wheeling arrows on the map. The crushing blows at France were, in the original plan, to be followed by the release of troops for use against Russia on Germany's eastern front. But the plan was not adequately implemented, and the war on the western front became a long contest instead.

Why did the Schlieffen Plan fail?

(1865–1937), under the command of the elderly Paul von Hindenburg (1847–1934), destroyed or captured an entire Russian army at the Battle of Tannenberg. In 1915, the Central Powers drove into the Baltic states and western Russia, inflicting more than 2 million casualties. Russian confidence was shaken (see Map 29–3).

Both sides sought new allies. Turkey and Bulgaria joined the Central Powers. Italy joined the Allies in 1915, after they agreed to give it **Italia Irredenta** (i.e., the Trentino, the South Tyrol, Trieste, and some of the Dalmatian Islands) from Austria after victory. Romania joined the Allies in 1916 but was quickly defeated and driven

Italia Irredenta Meaning "unredeemed Italy." Italian-speaking areas that had been left under Austrian rule at the time of the unification of Italy.

MAP 29–3 **World War I in Europe.** Despite the importance of military action in the Far East, in the Middle East, and at sea, the main theaters of activity in World War I were in the European areas shown here.

Which regions were most affected by military action?

from the war. In the Far East, Japan honored its alliance with Britain and overran the German colonies in China and the Pacific.

In 1915, the Allies undertook to break the deadlock in the fighting by going around it. The idea came chiefly from Winston Churchill (1874–1965), First Lord of the British Admiralty. He proposed to attack the Dardanelles and capture Constantinople. This policy would knock Turkey from the war and ease communication with Russia. Success depended on daring leadership, which was lacking. Before the campaign was abandoned, the Allies lost almost 150,000 men.

Both sides turned back to the west in 1916. Erich von Falkenhayn (1861–1922), who had succeeded Moltke in September 1914, sought success by an attack on the French stronghold of Verdun. It failed. The Allies, in turn, launched a major offensive along the River Somme in July, resulting in enormous casualties on both sides. The land war dragged on with no end in sight.

Control of the sea gained importance. In spite of international law, the British imposed a strict blockade to starve out the enemy. The Germans responded with submarine warfare to destroy British shipping. They declared the waters around the British Isles a war zone, where even neutral ships would not be safe. Both policies were unwelcome to neutrals, especially the United States, but the sinking of neutral ships by German submarines was both more dramatic and offensive than Britain's blockade.

In 1915, the British *Lusitania* was torpedoed by a German submarine. Among the 1,200 drowned were 118 Americans. President Woodrow Wilson (1856–1924) protested, and the Germans desisted rather than further anger the United States. This development gave the Allies a considerable advantage. The German fleet that had cost so much money played no significant part in the war.

In December 1916, President Wilson attempted to bring about a negotiated peace. But neither side would give up its hopes for total victory. The war seemed likely to continue until one or both sides reached exhaustion. Two events early in 1917 changed the situation. One was the February 1 announcement by the Germans of the resumption of unrestricted submarine warfare. This led the United States to declare war on Germany on April 6.

Another factor was the overthrow of Russia's tsarist government in March 1917. Since Wilson conceived of the war as an idealistic crusade "to make the world safe for democracy," the presence of autocratic tsarist Russia among the Allies had been a deterrent to earlier American intervention.

A German U-Boat. By the time this U-Boat was photographed moored in its harbor in 1917, German submarine warfare had been severely curtailed.

How did submarines transform naval warfare?

Petrograd Munitions Workers Demonstrating in 1917. The barely legible slogan at the top of the banner reads, "Victory to the Petrograd Workers!"

Who benefited from the Russian Revolution?

THE RUSSIAN REVOLUTION

WHY WERE the Bolsheviks able to seize power in Russia?

The March revolution in Russia was neither planned nor led by any political faction. It was the result of the collapse of the monarchy's ability to govern. Military and domestic failures produced massive casualties, widespread hunger, worker strikes, and disorganization. All political factions were discontented.

In early March 1917, strikes and demonstrations erupted in Petrograd, as St. Petersburg had been renamed. The ill-disciplined troops in the city refused to fire on the demonstrators, and the tsar abdicated on March 15. The Duma formed a provisional government composed chiefly of Constitutional Democrats with Western sympathies. Various socialists also began to organize the workers into councils called **soviets.** They became estranged as the Constitutional Democrats failed to control the army or purge "reactionaries" from the government.

soviets Workers' and soldiers' councils formed in Russia during the Revolution.

The provisional government decided to continue the war against Germany, but a new offensive in the summer of 1917 collapsed. Disillusionment with the war, shortages of food and other necessities, and the demand for land reform undermined the government, even after its leadership had been taken over by the moderate socialist Alexander Kerensky (1881–1970).

The Bolsheviks had been working against the provisional government since April. The Germans had rushed V. I. Lenin (1870–1924) in a sealed train from his exile in Switzerland to Petrograd in the hope that he would cause trouble for the revolutionary government. The Bolsheviks demanded that all political power go to the soviets, which they controlled. They attempted a coup, but it failed. Lenin fled to Finland, and his chief collaborator, Leon Trotsky (1877–1940), was imprisoned. An abortive right-wing countercoup gave the Bolsheviks another chance. Trotsky, released from prison, led the powerful Petrograd Soviet. Lenin returned in October, and by the extraordinary force of his personality persuaded his colleagues to act. Trotsky organized the November 6 coup that concluded with an armed assault on the provisional government. The Bolsheviks seized power.

QUICK REVIEW

The Russian Revolution

- March 1917: tsar abdicates, formation of provisional government
- November 1917: Bolsheviks seize power
- Bolsheviks withdrew from World War I
- Bolsheviks defeated "White" Russians in civil war

The victors moved to fulfill their promises and to assure their own security. The provisional government had decreed an election for late November to select a Constituent Assembly. The Social Revolutionaries won a large majority over the Bolsheviks. When the assembly gathered in January, the Red Army, controlled by the Bolsheviks, dispersed it. All other political parties ceased to function in any meaningful fashion. The Bolshevik government nationalized the land and turned it over to its peasant proprietors. Factory workers were put in charge of their plants. Banks were seized for the state, and the debt of the tsarist government was repudiated. The property of the church was also seized.

The Bolsheviks believed the war benefited only capitalism. They signed an armistice with Germany in December 1917. On March 3, 1918, they accepted the Treaty of Brest-Litovsk, by which Russia yielded Finland, Poland, the Baltic states, the Ukraine, and Georgian territory in the Transcaucasus. The Bolsheviks also agreed to pay an indemnity. These terms were a high price to pay for peace, but the Bolsheviks needed time to impose their rule on a devastated and chaotic Russia.

"White" Russians Those Russians who opposed the Bolsheviks (the "Reds") in the Russian Civil War of 1918–1921.

The Bolsheviks confronted massive domestic resistance. A civil war erupted between the "Red" Russians supporting the revolution and the **"White" Russians**, who opposed the Bolsheviks and received aid from the Allies. In the summer of 1918, the tsar and his family were murdered. Led by Trotsky, the Red Army overcame the opposition. By 1921, Lenin and his supporters were in firm control.

OVERVIEW   Casualties of the Major Belligerents in World War I

COUNTRY	KILLED	WOUNDED
Austria-Hungary	1.1 million	3.62 million
Belgium	38,000	44,000
Britain	723,000	1.16 million
Bulgaria	88,000	152,000
France	1.4 million	2 million
Germany	2 million	4.2 million
Italy	578,000	947,000
Ottoman Empire	804,000	400,000
Romania	250,000	120,000
Russia	1.8 million	1.45 million
Serbia	278,000	138,000
United States	114,000	205,000
Total	**9,173,000**	**14,436,000**

END OF WORLD WAR I

MILITARY RESOLUTION

The Treaty of Brest-Litovsk brought Germany to the peak of its success. In 1918, it decided to gamble everything on a last offensive. But the German army could not get beyond the Marne. Germany was exhausted. The Allies, on the other hand, were bolstered by the arrival of American troops in ever-increasing numbers. They launched a counteroffensive that was irresistible. As the Austrian fronts in the Balkans and Italy collapsed, the German high command knew that the end was imminent but wanted peace to be made before the army could be thoroughly defeated in the field, so that responsibility would fall on civilians. The army allowed a new government to be established on democratic principles to seek peace. The new government, under Prince Max of Baden (1867–1928), asked for peace on the basis of the **Fourteen Points** that President Wilson had declared as the American war aims. These were idealistic principles, but Wilson insisted that he would deal only with a democratic German government that spoke for the German people.

The disintegration of the German army forced William II to abdicate on November 9, 1918. The Social Democratic Party proclaimed a republic to prevent the establishment of a soviet government. Two days later this republican, socialist-led government signed an armistice and accepted German defeat. The German people were, in general, unaware that their army had been defeated. No foreign soldier stood on German soil. Many Germans expected a mild settlement. The real peace embittered the German people, many of whom came to believe that Germany had been betrayed by republicans and socialists at home.

Casualties on all sides came to about 10 million dead and twice as many wounded. The financial resources of the European states were badly strained. The victorious Allies, formerly creditors to the world, became debtors to the new American colossus.

WHY DID the Versailles settlement leave Germany bitter?

Fourteen Points   President Woodrow Wilson's (1856–1924) idealistic war aims.

John Singer Sargent, *Gassed*, 1918–1919.
Many new weapons were used extensively for the first time in the Great War of 1914–1918, including machine guns, barbed wire, tanks, airplanes, and several kinds of poison gas. The Germans were the first to employ gas as a weapon, firing a nonlethal kind of tear gas at the Russians on the eastern front in January 1915. By April, they had learned how to use the poison gas chlorine against the Allies on the western front. *Gassed*, by the American painter John Singer Sargent, can be compared to ancient Greek friezes depicting mythical battles. There is, however, an important difference in treatment: While Greek sculptures always portray an element of heroism along with death and suffering, Sargent's painting reveals only the horror of battle.

John Singer Sargent (1856–1925), "Gassed, an Oil Study". 1918–19 Oil on Canvas. Private Collection. Imperial War Museum, Negative Number Q1460

Why did World War I alter European attitudes toward warfare?

QUICK REVIEW

The Big Four at Versailles

- ◆ Woodrow Wilson, United States
- ◆ David Lloyd George, Britain
- ◆ Georges Clemenceau, France
- ◆ Vittorio Emanuele Orlando, Italy
- ◆ Significant role for Japan
- ◆ The Soviet Union and Germany excluded

The old international order was dead. Russia was ruled by a Bolshevik dictatorship that preached world revolution. Germany was in chaos. Austria-Hungary had disintegrated. These changes also stirred the colonial empires ruled by the European powers. Europe was no longer the center of the world, free to interfere when it wished or to ignore the outer regions if it chose. Its easy confidence in progress was shattered. The memory of war shook the nerve of the victorious Western powers in the postwar world.

SETTLEMENT AT PARIS

Representatives of the victorious states gathered at Versailles and other Parisian suburbs in the first half of 1919. Wilson speaking for the United States, David Lloyd George (1863–1945) for Britain, Georges Clemenceau (1841–1929) for France, and Vittorio Emanuele Orlando (1860–1952) for Italy made up the Big Four. Japan, recognized for the first time as a great power, also participated.

Wilson's idealism came into conflict with the war aims of the victorious powers and with the secret treaties that had been made before and during the war. The British and French people had been told that Germany would be made to pay for the war. Romania had been promised Transylvania at the expense of Hungary. Italy and Serbia had competing claims in the Adriatic. During the war, the British had encouraged Arab hopes of an independent Arab state carved out of the Ottoman Empire; those plans conflicted with the Balfour Declaration (1917), in which the British also seemed to accept Zionism and to promise the Jews a national home in Palestine. Both of these plans conflicted with an Anglo-French agreement to divide the Near East between themselves.

The national goals of the victors presented further obstacles to an idealistic "peace without victors." France was eager to achieve a settlement that would permanently weaken Germany and preserve French political and military superiority. Italy sought to acquire *Italia Irredenta*; Britain looked to its imperial interests; Japan pursued its own advantage in Asia; and the United States insisted on freedom of the seas, which favored American commerce, and on its right to maintain the Monroe Doctrine.

Finally, the peacemakers of 1919 faced a world in turmoil. The greatest immediate threat appeared to be Bolshevism. While Lenin and his colleagues were distracted by civil war, the Allies landed small armies in Russia to help overthrow the Bolshevik regime. Communist governments were established in Bavaria and Hungary. Berlin also experienced an abortive communist uprising. The Allies were so worried that they supported the suppression of these communist movements by right-wing forces. They even permitted an army of German volunteers to fight the Bolsheviks in the Baltic states. But fear of Germany remained the chief concern for France, and traditional interests governed the policies of the other Allies.

The Paris settlement consisted of five separate treaties. The Soviet Union (as Russia was now called) and Germany were excluded from the peace conference. The Germans were simply presented with a treaty and compelled to accept it. The principle of national self-determination was, unavoidably, violated often. The undeserved adulation accorded Wilson on his arrival turned into equally undeserved scorn. He had not abandoned his ideals, simply given way to the irresistible force of reality.

Wilson put great faith in the new **League of Nations**. Its covenant was an essential part of the peace treaty. The league was not intended as an international government but as a body of sovereign states that agreed to pursue common policies. If war threatened, the members promised to submit the matter to an international court or the League Council. Refusal to abide by this agreement would justify league intervention in the form of economic or military sanctions. But the league was to have no armed forces. Action would require the unanimous consent of its council, which was to consist of Britain, France, Italy, the United States, Japan, and four other states with temporary seats. The league was generally seen as a device to ensure the security of the victorious powers, and the exclusion of Germany and the Soviet Union undermined the league's claim to even-handedness.

Provisions of the covenant that dealt with colonial areas and disarmament were ineffective. Members of the league remained fully sovereign and continued to pursue their national interests. In the West, the main territorial issue was the fate of Germany. The French would have liked to set up the Rhineland as a buffer state, but Lloyd George and Wilson would not permit that. But France did receive Alsace-Lorraine and the right to work the coal mines of the Saar for fifteen years. Germany west of the Rhine, and 50 kilometers east of it, was to be a demilitarized zone; Allied troops could stay on the west bank for fifteen years. The treaty also provided that Britain and the United States would guarantee to aid France if it were attacked by Germany. Such an attack was made more unlikely by the permanent disarmament of Germany. Its army was limited to 100,000 men; its fleet was all but eliminated; and it was forbidden to have war planes, submarines, tanks, heavy artillery, or poison gas. As long as these provisions were observed, France would be safe (see Map 29–4).

The settlement in the East ratified the collapse of the empires that had ruled it for centuries. Germany lost part of Silesia, and East Prussia was cut off from the rest of Germany by a corridor carved out to give the revived state of Poland access to the sea. The Austro-Hungarian Empire disappeared. Most of its German-speaking people in the small Republic of Austria were forbidden to unite with Germany. The Magyars occupied the much-reduced kingdom of Hungary.

The Czechs of Bohemia and Moravia joined with the Slovaks and Ruthenians to form Czechoslovakia, which also included several million dissatisfied Germans. The southern Slavs were united in the kingdom of Serbs, Croats, and Slovenes, or Yugoslavia. Italy gained the Trentino and Trieste. Romania gained Transylvania from Hungary and

Versailles.   The German delegation signs the peace treaty ending the First World War in the Hall of Mirrors of the Palace of Versailles on June 28, 1919. This painting by Sir William Orpen, completed in 1921, now hangs in the Imperial War Museum in London. U.S. President Woodrow Wilson is seated in the center, holding a clutch of papers.

What were the major defects of the Versailles settlement?

League of Nations   The association of sovereign states set up after World War I to pursue common policies and avert international aggression.

MAP 29–4   World War I Peace Settlement in Europe and the Middle East.   The map of central and eastern Europe, as well as that of the Middle East, underwent drastic revision after World War I. The enormous territorial losses suffered by Germany, Austria-Hungary, the Ottoman Empire, Bulgaria, and Russia were the other side of the coin represented by gains for France, Italy, Greece, and Romania and by the appearance, or reappearance, of at least eight new independent states, from Finland in the north to Yugoslavia in the south. The mandate system for former Ottoman territories outside Turkey proper laid foundations for several new, mostly Arab, states in the Middle East.

How did the creation of new countries in central and eastern Europe set the stage for future conflicts?

Bessarabia from Russia. Bulgaria lost territory to Greece and Yugoslavia. Finland, Estonia, Latvia, and Lithuania became independent states, and much of Poland was carved out of formerly Russian soil. In the Caucasus, the new nations of Georgia, Armenia, and Azerbaijan took advantage of the turmoil following the Russian revolution to enjoy a period of independence (1918–1921). Ukraine and Russia were also autonomous during this brief period.

The old Ottoman Empire disappeared. The new republic of Turkey was limited to little more than Constantinople and Asia Minor. Palestine and Iraq came under British control and Syria and Lebanon under French control as mandates under the purely theoretical authority of the League of Nations. Germany's former colonies in Africa and the Pacific were divided among the victors. In practice, mandated territories were treated as colonies, and colonialism remained a problem.

Perhaps the most debated part of the peace settlement dealt with reparations. Before the armistice, the Germans promised to pay compensation "for all damages done to the civilian population of the Allies and their property." France and Britain, however, wanted Germany to pay the full cost of the war. No sum was fixed at the conference; Germany was to pay $5 billion annually until 1921, when a final figure would be set, which Germany would have to pay within thirty years. The French calculated that either Germany would be bled into impotence or refuse to pay and justify French intervention.

To justify these huge reparation payments, the Allies inserted the notorious **war guilt clause** into the treaty, which placed the responsibility for the war solely on Germany. The Germans bitterly resented the charges but were given no opportunity to negotiate. The German government led by the Social Democrats and the Catholic Center Party signed the treaty. These parties formed the backbone of the German Republic, but they never overcame the stigma of accepting the treaty.

Peacemakers.   The Allies promoted Arab efforts to secure independence from Turkey in an effort to remove Turkey from the war. Delegates to the peace conference of 1919 in Paris included British Colonel T. E. Lawrence, who helped lead the rebellion against Turkey, and representatives from the Middle East. Prince Feisal, the third son of King Hussein, stands in the foreground of this picture; Lawrence is in the middle row, second from the right; and Brigadier General Nuri Pasha Said of Baghdad is second from the left.

What happened to the Ottoman Empire?

EVALUATION OF THE PEACE

Few peace settlements have been more attacked than the Treaty of Versailles, but many of the attacks on it are unjustified. Germany was neither dismembered nor ruined. Reparations were scaled down, and until the Great Depression of the 1930s, the German economy recovered. The attempt at achieving self-determination for nationalities was less than perfect, but it was the best Europe had ever accomplished.

The peace, nevertheless, was unsatisfactory. The elimination of the Austro-Hungarian Empire, however inevitable, created serious problems. Economically it was disastrous, for it separated raw materials from manufacturing areas and producers from their markets. Poland and especially Czechoslovakia contained unhappy German minorities. Disputes over territories in eastern Europe promoted further tension. The peace also rested on a defeat that Germany did not admit. Germans believed they had been cheated.

Finally, the peace failed to accept reality. Germany and Russia must inevitably play an important part in European affairs, yet they were excluded from the settlement and from the League of Nations. Given the many discontented parties, the peace was not self-enforcing; yet no satisfactory machinery for enforcing it was established. The League of Nations was never a serious force for this purpose, particularly after Wilson's political mistakes helped prevent American ratification of the treaty. It was left to France, with no guarantee of support from Britain and no hope of help from the United States, to defend the new arrangements. France was simply not strong enough for the task if Germany were to rearm. The Treaty of Versailles was neither conciliatory enough to remove the desire for change nor harsh enough to make another war impossible.

war guilt clause Clause of the Versailles Treaty that assigned responsibility for World War I solely to Germany.

SUMMARY

WHAT WAS the New Imperialism?

Expansion of European Power and the New Imperialism. Economic and social factors—especially the pursuit of prestige—seem to have driven the New Imperialism. By 1914, European nations had divided Africa among themselves and controlled large parts of Asia and the islands of the Pacific. Much of the Middle East was under the nominal control of the Ottoman Empire, which was itself under European influence. The Monroe Doctrine made Latin America a protectorate of the United States. Japan had become an imperial power at the expense of China and Korea. *page 726*

WHAT WERE Bismarck's goals for Germany?

Emergence of the German Empire. Bismarck masterminded the creation of the German empire and created a system of treaties and alliances to ensure that Germany would not be threatened on two fronts simultaneously. In 1890, the young Kaiser William II dismissed Bismarck, and soon Russia and France were allied against Germany. By 1914, Britain too was enmeshed in military partnership with France against Germany. *page 732*

WHAT CAUSED the outbreak of World War I in 1914?

World War I. The alliance system divided Europe into two armed camps. What began as yet another Balkan war involving the European powers became a world war that influenced the rest of the world. As the terrible war of 1914 to 1918 dragged on, the real motives that had driven the European powers to fight gave way to public affirmations of the principles of nationalism and self-determination. *page 736*

WHY WERE the Bolsheviks able to seize power in Russia?

The Russian Revolution. Russia suffered during the war, and many groups blamed the government. In March 1917, the tsar was overthrown. The provisional government was overturned by the Bolsheviks in November, largely thanks to Lenin's Persuasive Powers. Russia withdrew from the war soon thereafter. *page 742*

WHY DID the Versailles settlement leave Germany bitter?

End of World War I. Europe's imperial nations, especially Britain and France, paid an enormous price in lives, money, and will for their victory in the war. The peace settlement at Versailles has been criticized for many reasons, both fair and unfair. Certainly it left many tensions unresolved. Germany was given many obligations to fulfill, without being given any change to negotiate. Tension between colonies and their ruling nations was a cause of instability in the world created by the Paris treaties of 1919. *page 743*

INTERPRETING THE PAST

The New Imperialism: Motives, Justifications, and Costs

Sources from MyHistoryLab for Chapter 29

myhistorylab

1) Jules Ferry, *Le Tonkin et la Mère-Patrie* (1896)

2) Charles Seignobos, *The Great African Hunt* (1909)

3) Rudyard Kipling, *The White Man's Burden* (1899)

4) Edward D. Morel, *The Black Man's Burden* (1920)

Visual Sources from MyHistoryLab

1) *Pygmies, 1904 World's Fair*

2) *Pears' Soap Advertisement*

The New Imperialism was characterized by European acquisition of new territories and the establishment of economic and political hegemony over other nations. More than a century later, it is still a hot topic for debate. While it is clear that imperialism brought some economic benefits to Western nations in the form of inex-

REVIEW QUESTIONS

1. Which explanation, or combination of explanations, for the New Imperialism seems most plausible and why?

2. Summarize the experiences of three regions in Africa with the New Imperialism.

3. What role did Bismarck envisage for the new Germany after 1871? How successful was he in carrying out his vision? Was he wise to tie Germany to Austria-Hungary?

4. Why and in what stages did Britain abandon "splendid isolation" at the turn of the century? Were the policies it pursued instead wise ones, or should Britain have followed a different course?

5. How did developments in the Balkans lead to the outbreak of World War I? What was the role of Serbia? of Austria? of Russia? What was the aim of German policy in July 1914? Did Germany want a general war?

6. Why did the United States enter World War I? Were there good reasons for it to enter the war when it did, or would it have been better for the United States to enter earlier, later, or not at all?

7. Why did Germany lose World War I? Could Germany have won, or was victory never a possibility?

8. Why was Lenin successful in establishing Bolshevik rule in Russia? What role did Trotsky play? Was it wise policy for Lenin to take Russia out of the war?

9. Assess the settlement of Versailles. What were its benefits to Europe, and what were its drawbacks? Was the settlement too harsh or too conciliatory? Could it have secured lasting peace in Europe? How might it have been improved?

10. How did World War I alter the relationship between imperial powers and colonized peoples?

KEY TERMS

Fourteen Points (p. 743)
Italia Irredenta (ih-TAL-ee-yuh IHR-ih-DENT-ah) (p. 740)
League of Nations (p. 745)
mobilization (p. 738)
New Imperialism (p. 726)
pan-Slavic movement (p. 733)
Schlieffen Plan (SHLEE-fehn) (p. 738)
soviets (p. 742)
war guilt clause (p. 747)
"White" Russians (p. 742)

Note: To learn more about the topics in this chapter, please turn to the Suggested Readings at the end of the book.

pensive commodities extracted by low-cost (or slave) labor and captive markets for their products, the overall profitability is still in doubt. Just as important, Western nations sought strategic and political advantages through their extensive overseas holdings. Yet basic questions remain: What were the primary motives of European imperialists? What are the lasting historical and cultural impacts on the West and non-Western nations?

In this exercise you will read four primary sources from the late nineteenth and early twentieth centuries and examine two images that illustrate the political, military, economic, and cultural impacts of imperialism.

The first document is written by Jules Ferry (1832–1893), a French statesman who advocated aggressive colonial expansion for France. The second source, by Charles Seignobos, describes "the scramble for Africa" in which European nations raced to obtain territories and influence after the Berlin Conference of 1885. The third source is the classic poem "The White Man's Burden," by Rudyard Kipling, that communicates the then widely held view (among Westerners) that colonization benefited African and Asian peoples. The fourth primary source was written by Edward D. Morel, a British journalist and reformer who forcefully refutes

"The White Man's Burden" by illustrating the effects of Western exploitation on the people and culture of Africa.

The two accompanying images offer evidence of how Africans were viewed by Westerners a century ago—the first shows members of a tribe of African pygmies who were displayed at the St. Louis World's Fair of 1904, and the second is an advertisement for Pear's soap, graphically illustrating the negative associations of "darkness."

Questions

What are Ferry's chief reasons for promoting colonial expansion? What consequences does Ferry predict for European countries should they not expand their markets?

How does *The Great African Hunt* by Charles Seignobos depict African culture and history? What might explain this view from an eminent French scholar?

What is the "White Man's Burden," according to Kipling? What is the "Black Man's Burden," according to Morel? How does Morel view capitalism in the African colonial context?

30

Depression, European Dictators, and the American New Deal

Nazi Party Rally.   Young women among an enthusiastic crowd extend the Nazi salute at a party rally in 1938. Note the gender divisions in this photograph. Nazi ideology encouraged women to favor traditional domestic roles over employment in the workplace and to bear many children. The men are portrayed as defenders of the homeland.

Bildarchiv Preussischer Kulturbesitz.

How did the Nazis come to power?

AFTER VERSAILLES: DEMANDS FOR REVISION AND ENFORCEMENT *page 752*

WHICH GROUPS were dissatisfied with the Versailles settlement?

TOWARD THE GREAT DEPRESSION IN EUROPE *page 753*

WHAT FACTORS made the Great Depression so severe and long lasting?

THE SOVIET EXPERIMENT *page 755*

HOW DID Stalin gain and keep power in the Soviet Union?

THE FASCIST EXPERIMENT IN ITALY *page 760*

WHY DID the Fascists achieve power in Italy?

GERMAN DEMOCRACY AND DICTATORSHIP *page 761*

WHAT ROLE did terror play in Nazi Germany?

THE GREAT DEPRESSION AND THE NEW DEAL IN THE UNITED STATES *page 769*

HOW DID FDR's policies affect the role of the federal government?

THE INTERWAR PERIOD IN EUROPE AND THE UNITED STATES

The two decades between the great wars marked a period of immense political and economic transition around the globe. Many regions endured political turmoil and economic instability, followed by the establishment of militaristic authoritarian regimes. In Italy, it was the Fascists; in Germany, the Nazis; in the Soviet Union, Stalin's regime. Spain too came under the rule of a military dictator who rose to power with the assistance of the Nazis. Many Europeans, battered by the global economic crisis of the 1930s and, in the case of Germany, the harsh terms of the Treaty of Versailles, believed that only strong leaders could lead their countries to prosperity again in the global competition for resources and territory. In East Asia, Japan came into the grip of a right-wing militaristic government. China saw more than twenty years of civil war and revolution that would culminate with the rise to power of the Communists under Mao. Most of Latin America came under the sway of dictators or governments heavily influenced by the military.

With the exception of Russia (and later China), all of these governments were right wing. In fact, the Russian Revolution was a pivotal factor in the rise of right-wing and Fascist dictators, who often justified their power on the basis of their firm opposition to the "Red Menace" and the growing popularity enjoyed by socialism and communism in many European countries during the economic crisis of the 1930s.

To many observers in the late 1930s, the day of liberal parliamentary democracy appeared to be ending. The disruptions arising from World War I and the social and economic turmoil of the depression seemed to pose problems that liberal governments could not address. Only the radical medicine of socialism, communism, or right-wing dictatorships seemed capable of resolving the crisis. Some countries, such as France in the mid-1930s, were brought to the brink of civil war by the deep divisions between the right and left in their populations. Spain became engulfed in the civil war that brought General Francisco Franco (1892–1975) to power in 1939.

The interwar period also departed from the nineteenth-century ideal of laissez-faire economics, in which central governments assumed little responsibility for guiding the economies of their countries. The German inflation of the early 1920s, the worldwide financial collapse of the late 1920s, the vast unemployment of the early 1930s, and the agricultural crisis of both decades roused demands for government action as millions of

I n the two decades that followed the conclusion of the Paris settlement, the Western world saw a number of experiments in politics and economic life. Two broad factors accounted for these experiments. First, the war, the Russian Revolution, and the peace treaty had transformed the political face of Europe. The new regimes that emerged in the wake of the collapse of the monarchies of Germany, Austria-Hungary, and Russia faced economic dislocation and nationalistic resentments.

Second, the Great Depression caused political instability and economic crisis. In Europe this often produced authoritarian regimes. In the United States it led to an increased role for the federal government. ▪

AFTER VERSAILLES: DEMANDS FOR REVISION AND ENFORCEMENT

WHICH GROUPS were dissatisfied with the Versailles settlement?

The Paris settlement fostered resentments that sullied European politics for the next two decades. The arrangements for reparations led to endless haggling. National groups in eastern Europe felt that injustice had been done to them and demanded border adjustments. The victorious powers, especially France, often believed that the treaty was being inadequately enforced. Too many political figures were willing to exploit these discontents for domestic votes.

people experienced very real, and often sudden, economic hardship and suffering. One reason for these demands was simply that more governments throughout the world were responsible to mass democratic electorates. Governments that failed to adequately address the problems were put out of office. This happened to the Republicans in the United States, the Socialist and Liberal parties in Germany, the left-wing parties in Japan, and various political parties in Latin America that failed to deal with the depression. Paradoxically, many democratic electorates actually turned themselves over to politically authoritarian regimes as they searched for social and economic stability.

Extreme forms of nationalism in both Europe and Japan also spawned authoritarianism. The authoritarian governments of Germany, Italy, and Japan all had agendas of nationalistic aggression. They shared the nineteenth-century conviction that territorial expansion was essential to national prestige and economic security. As a result they were prepared to move wherever they saw fellow nationals living outside their borders (a legacy of the creation of nation-states in the eighteenth and nineteenth centuries) or where they could establish dominance over other peoples and thus become imperial powers. Japan moved against

Manchuria and later other parts of Asia. Italy invaded Ethiopia. Germany sought union with German-speaking peoples in Austria and Czechoslovakia and then sought to expand throughout eastern Europe. In turn, those actions challenged the dominance of Great Britain and the vital security interests of the United States. By the end of the 1930s the authoritarian regimes and the liberal democracies stood on the brink of a major confrontation.

Focus Questions

◆ Why did many people in the 1930s lose faith in liberal democracy and laissez-faire economics?

◆ What led many countries to adopt authoritarian regimes during this period? Why did authoritarian governments seem to pose a solution to economic hardship and social instabililty?

◆ What was the relationship between extreme nationalism and the outbreak of World War II?

TOWARD THE GREAT DEPRESSION IN EUROPE

Three factors combined to bring about the severity and the extended length of the **Great Depression**. First, a financial crisis stemmed directly from the war and the peace settlement. In addition, a crisis erupted in the production and distribution of goods in the world market. Finally, these difficulties were exacerbated because no major western European country or the United States provided responsible economic leadership.

WHAT FACTORS made the Great Depression so severe and long lasting?

FINANCIAL TAILSPIN

France was determined to collect reparations from Germany. The United States was no less determined that its allies repay the wartime loans it had extended to them. German reparations were to provide the means of repaying these debts.

The quest for payment of German reparations caused one of the major diplomatic crises of the 1920s; the crisis itself resulted in further economic upheaval. In early 1923, the Allies—France in particular—declared Germany to be in default of its reparation payments. On January 11, French troops occupied Germany's Ruhr mining and manufacturing district. The **Weimar Republic** ordered passive resistance. Confronted with this tactic, the French ran the German mines and railroads. The Germans paid, but Britain became more sympathetic to Germany. The cost of the Ruhr occupation, moreover, damaged the French economy.

The political and economic turmoil of the Ruhr invasion led to international attempts to ease German payment of reparations. The most famous were the Dawes

Great Depression A prolonged worldwide economic downturn that began in 1929 with the collapse of the New York Stock Exchange.

Weimar Republic The German democratic regime that existed between the end of World War I and Hitler's coming to power in 1933.

Jarrow Crusade.   In what was known as the "Jarrow Crusade" during the autumn of 1936 a group of approximately two hundred protesters marched from the town of Jarrow in northeastern England to London to demonstrate their need for employment and the plight of their town, where the previous year the shipyard had been closed.

Why was unemployment so widespread in Europe in the 1930s?

QUICK REVIEW

Commodity Market Collapse

◆ Grain production increased, prices fell

◆ Farm debt crisis in Europe

◆ Non-European farmers unable to afford European manufactured goods

◆ Cycle of unemployment, economic depression created

Plan of 1924 and the Young Plan of 1929, both devised by Americans. At the same time, American investment capital was pouring into Europe. However, the crash of Wall Street in October 1929—the result of unregulated speculation—saw the loss of large amounts of money. Thereafter, little American capital was available for investment in Europe.

In May 1931, the Kreditanstalt—a primary lending institution for much of central and eastern Europe—collapsed. The German banking system then came under severe pressure. As German difficulties increased, U.S. President Herbert Hoover (1874–1964) announced in June 1931 a one-year moratorium on all payments of international debts. The Hoover moratorium was a prelude to the end of reparations. In the summer of 1932, the Lausanne Conference, in effect, ended the era of reparations.

PROBLEMS IN AGRICULTURAL COMMODITIES

The 1920s witnessed a contraction in the market demand for European goods. The difficulty arose from agriculture. Better methods of farming and more extensive transport facilities all over the globe vastly increased the quantity of grain. Wheat prices fell to record lows, decreasing the income of European farmers while increasing the cost of the industrial goods they used. Consequently, farmers had great difficulty paying off their debts. These problems were especially acute in central and eastern Europe and abetted farmers' disillusionment with liberal politics. German farmers, for example, would become prime supporters of the National Socialist Workers Party (Nazis).

Outside Europe similar problems affected wheat, sugar, coffee, rubber, wool, and lard producers. The people who produced these goods in underdeveloped nations could no longer make enough money to buy finished goods from industrial Europe. Commodity production had outstripped world demand.

The result was stagnation and depression for European industry. Coal, iron, and textiles had depended largely on international markets. Unemployment spread from these industries to those producing consumer goods. Unemployment in Britain and Germany during the 1920s had created "soft" domestic markets. The policies of reduced spending, with which the governments confronted the depression, further weakened domestic demand. By the early 1930s, the depression was feeding on itself.

DEPRESSION AND GOVERNMENT POLICY

The depression did not mean absolute economic decline or total unemployment. However, the economic downturn made people insecure. Even the employed often seemed to make no progress, and their anxieties created discontent.

The governments of the late 1920s and the early 1930s were not well suited to confront these problems. The electorates demanded action. Government response depended largely on the severity of the depression in a particular country and on the self-confidence of its political system.

Great Britain and France undertook moderate political experiments. In 1924, the Labour Party in Great Britain established itself as a viable governing entity.

Under the pressure of the depression, Labour prime minister Ramsay MacDonald (1866–1937) organized a National Government, which was a coalition of the Labour, Conservative, and Liberal parties. It remained in power until 1935, when a Conservative ministry led by Stanley Baldwin (1867–1947) replaced it.

The most important French political experiment was the **Popular Front** Ministry, which came to office in 1936. This government was composed of socialists, radicals, and communists—the first time that socialists and communists had cooperated in a ministry. The Popular Front addressed major labor problems in the French economy, but by 1938 it came to an end.

The political experiments of the 1920s and 1930s that reshaped world history involved a Soviet government in Russia, a Fascist regime in Italy, and a Nazi dictatorship in Germany.

Lenin.   Anxiety over the spread of the Bolshevik Revolution was a fundamental factor of European politics during the 1920s and 1930s. Images like this Soviet portrait of Lenin as a heroic revolutionary conjured fears among people in the rest of Europe of a political force determined to overturn their social, political, and economic institutions.

Gemalde von A. M. Gerassimow, "Lenin as Agitator"/Bildarchiv Preussischer Kulturbesitz.

Compare this painting of Lenin with the image of Stalin on page 759. What are the similarities and differences in how the two men are portrayed?

Popular Front   A government of all left-wing parties that took power in France in 1936 to enact social and economic reforms.

THE SOVIET EXPERIMENT

The Bolshevik Revolution in Russia led to the most durable of all twentieth-century authoritarian governments. The Communist Party of the Soviet Union retained power from 1917 until the end of 1991, and it influenced the history of much of the world. Unlike the Italian Fascists or the German National Socialists, the Bolsheviks seized power violently through revolution. Their leaders long felt insecure about their hold on the country. The Communist Party was neither a mass party nor a nationalistic one. The Bolsheviks confronted a much less industrialized economy than that in Italy or Germany. They believed in and practiced the collectivization of economic life attacked by right-wing dictatorships. The Marxist-Leninist ideology was broader than the nationalism of the Fascists and the racism of the Nazis. Communism was an exportable commodity. Communists regarded their government and their revolution as epoch-making events in the development of humanity. (See Document, "A Communist Woman Demands a New Family Life.") Fear of communism and determination to stop its spread were leading political forces in Western Europe and the United States for most of the rest of the century and would influence global political relationships.

HOW DID Stalin gain and keep power in the Soviet Union?

WAR COMMUNISM

Within months of the revolution, a new secret police, known as *Cheka*, appeared. Throughout the Russian civil war Lenin had declared that the Bolshevik Party, as the vanguard of the revolution, was imposing the dictatorship of the proletariat. Under the economic policy of **War Communism**, the revolutionary government confiscated banks, transport facilities, and heavy industry. The state also requisitioned grain and shipped it from the countryside to feed the army and the cities.

War Communism   The economic policy adopted by the Bolsheviks during the Russian Civil War to seize the banks, heavy industry, railroads, and grain.

A Communist Woman Demands a New Family Life

While Lenin sought to consolidate the Bolshevik Revolution against internal and external enemies, there existed within the young Soviet Union a vast utopian impulse to change and reform virtually every social institution that had existed before the revolution or that Communists associated with capitalist society. Alexandra Kollontai (1872–1952) was a spokesperson of the extreme political left within the early Soviet Union. There had been much speculation on how the end of bourgeois society might change the structure of the family and the position of women. In this passage written in 1920 Kollontai proposes a radically utopian vision of this change. After the revolution, extreme rumors circulated in both Europe and America about sexual and family experimentation in the Soviet Union. Statements such as this raised profound moral anxieties about the possible spread of communism beyond the borders of the Soviet Union. Kollontai herself later became a supporter of Stalin and a Soviet diplomat.

- **Why** did Kollontai see the restructuring of the family as essential to the establishment of a new kind of

communist society? Would these changes make people loyal to that society? What changes in society does the kind of economic independence she seeks for women presuppose? What might childhood be like in this society?

There is no escaping the fact: the old type of family has seen its day. It is not the fault of the Communist State, it is the result of the changed conditions of life. The family is ceasing to be a necessity of the State, as it was in the past; on the contrary, it is worse than useless, since it needlessly holds back the female workers from more productive and far more serious work. ... But on the ruins of the former family we shall soon see a new form rising which will involve altogether different relations between men and women, and which will be a union of affection and comradeship, a union of two equal members of the Communist society, both of them free, both of them independent, both of them workers. No more domestic "servitude" of women. No more inequality within the family. No more

War Communism helped the Red Army defeat its opponents, but it generated domestic opposition. Many Russians were no longer willing to make the sacrifices demanded by central party bureaucrats. In 1920 and 1921, strikes occurred. Peasants resisted the requisition of grain. In March 1921, the navy mutinied. Each of these incidents suggested that the proletariat itself was opposing the dictatorship of the proletariat. Also, by late 1920, it had become clear that revolution would not sweep across the rest of Europe. The Soviet Union was a vast island of revolutionary socialism in a sea of worldwide capitalism.

THE NEW ECONOMIC POLICY

New Economic Policy (NEP) A limited revival of capitalism, especially in light industry and agriculture, introduced by Lenin in 1921 to repair the damage inflicted on the Russian economy by the Civil War and War Communism.

Lenin made a strategic retreat. In March 1921, he outlined the **New Economic Policy**, or NEP. Apart from "the commanding heights" of banking, heavy industry, transportation, and international commerce, private economic enterprise was allowed and peasants could farm for a profit. The countryside became more stable, and a secure food supply seemed assured for the cities. Similar free enterprise flourished within light industry and retail trade. The revolution seemed to have transformed Russia into a land of small farms and private shops and businesses.

STALIN VERSUS TROTSKY

The NEP had caused sharp disputes within the Politburo, the highest governing committee of the Communist Party. These frictions increased when Lenin suffered a stroke in 1922 and died in 1924. Two factions emerged from an intense struggle for leadership of the party. One was led by Trotsky, the other by Joseph Stalin (1879–1953), who had become general secretary of the party in 1922.

fear on the part of the woman lest she remain without support or aid with little ones in her arms if her husband should desert her. The woman in the Communist city no longer depends on her husband but on her work. It is not her husband but her robust arms which will support her. There will be no more anxiety as to the fate of her children. The State of the Workers will assume responsibility for these. Marriage will be purified of all its material elements, of all money calculations, which constitute a hideous blemish on family life in our days. ...

The woman who is called upon to struggle in the great cause of the liberation of the workers—such a woman should know that in the new State there will be no more room for such petty divisions as were formerly understood: "These are my own children, to them I owe all my maternal solicitude, all my affection; those are your children, my neighbour's children; I am not concerned with them. I have enough to do with my own." Henceforth the worker-mother, who is conscious of her social function, will rise to a point where she no longer differentiates between yours and mine; she must remember that there are henceforth only our children, those of the Communist State, the common possession of all the workers.

The Worker's State has need of a new form of relation between the sexes. The narrow and exclusive affection of the mother for her own children must expand until it embraces all the children of the great proletarian family. In place of the indissoluble marriage based on the servitude of woman, we shall see rise the free union, fortified by the love and mutual respect of the two members of the Workers' State, equal in their rights and in their obligations. In place of the individual and egotistic family there will arise a great universal family of workers, in which all the workers, men and women, will be, above all, workers, comrades.

Source: From Alexandra Kollontai, *Communism and the Family*, as reprinted in Rudolf Schlesinger, ed. and trans., *The Family in the USSR* (London: Routledge and Kegan Paul, 1949), pp. 67–69. Reprinted by permission.

The power struggle was fought over the question of Russia's path toward industrialization and the future of the Communist revolutionary movement. Trotsky, speaking for what became known as the left wing, urged rapid industrialization and looked to voluntary collectivization of farming by poor peasants as a means of increasing agricultural production. Trotsky further argued that the revolution in Russia could succeed only if new revolutions took place elsewhere. A right-wing faction manipulated by Stalin opposed Trotsky. This group pressed for the continuation of Lenin's NEP and a policy of relatively slow industrialization. Stalin was the ultimate victor. Unlike the other early Bolshevik leaders, he had not spent a long exile in western Europe. He was much less an intellectual and internationalist. He was also much more brutal. His power lay in his command of bureaucratic and administrative methods. He mastered the crucial details of party structure, including admission and promotion. He had the support of the lower levels of the party when he clashed with other leaders.

In 1924, Stalin enunciated, in opposition to Trotsky, the doctrine of "socialism in one country." Russian success did not depend on the fate of the revolution elsewhere. Stalin thus nationalized the previously international scope of the Marxist revolution. By 1927, Trotsky had been ousted from the party. In 1929, he was expelled from Russia and was eventually murdered in 1940 in Mexico by one of Stalin's agents. Stalin was firmly in control of the Soviet state.

DECISION FOR RAPID INDUSTRIALIZATION

During the depression, the Soviet Union registered tremendous industrial advance. As usual in Russia, the direction and impetus came from the top. Stalin far exceeded the tsars in the coercion and terror he brought to the task. Russia achieved its economic growth during the 1930s only at the cost of millions of human lives. Stalin's

QUICK REVIEW

Stalin's Rise to Power

- Sided with the opposition to Trotsky in the 1920s
- Used control of the Central Committee to marginalize Trotsky and his supporters
- Emerged from struggle with Trotsky with unchallenged control of the Soviet state

Kulaks. During Stalin's drive to collectivize agriculture, wealthy peasants known as kulaks become the object of his wrath. Here a group of mostly peasant women demonstrate against the kulaks.

What happened to the kulaks?

collectivization The bedrock of Stalinist agriculture, which forced Russian peasants to give up their private farms and work as members of collectives, large agricultural units controlled by the state.

economic policy clearly proved that his earlier rivalry with Trotsky had been a matter of political power, not ideological difference.

Through 1928, Lenin's NEP steered Soviet economic development. A few farmers, the *kulaks*, became prosperous. During 1928 and 1929, the kulaks and other farmers withheld grain from the market because prices were too low. Food shortages in the cities caused unrest. Stalin came to a momentous decision. Russia must industrialize rapidly to match the power of the West. Agriculture must be collectivized to produce sufficient grain for food and export and to free peasant labor for the factories. This program unleashed a second Russian revolution.

In 1929, Stalin ordered party agents to confiscate hoarded wheat. As part of the general plan to collectivize farming, the government undertook to eliminate the kulaks as a class. A kulak, however, soon came to mean any peasant who opposed Stalin's policy. In the countryside, peasants at all levels of wealth resisted stubbornly. They wreaked their vengeance on the policy of **collectivization** by slaughtering more than 100 million horses and cattle between 1929 and 1933. The situation in the countryside amounted to open warfare. Peasant resistance caused Stalin to call a brief halt to the process in March 1930.

As many as 10 million peasants were killed, and millions of others were sent to labor camps. Because of the turmoil, famine persisted in 1932 and 1933. Yet Stalin persevered. Peasants had their lands incorporated into large collective farms. The state controlled the machinery for these units.

The government now had primary direction over the food supply. Peasants could no longer determine whether there would be stability or unrest in the cities. Stalin and the Communist Party had won the battle of the wheat fields, but the problem of producing enough grain still plagues the former Soviet Union.

The revolution in agriculture had been undertaken for the sake of industrialization. The increased grain supply was to feed the labor force and provide exports to finance the imports required for industrial development. The industrial achievement of the Soviet Union between 1928 and World War II was one of the most striking accomplishments of the twentieth century. Russia made a more rapid advance toward economic growth than any other nation in the Western world has ever achieved during a similar period of time. Soviet industrial production rose approximately 400 percent between 1928 and 1940. Few consumer goods were produced. Labor for this development was supplied internally. Capital was raised from the export of grain, even at the cost of internal shortage. Technology was borrowed from industrialized nations.

The organizational vehicle for industrialization was a series of five-year plans that began in 1928. The State Planning Commission, or Gosplan, set goals of production and organized the economy to meet them. Coordinating all facets of production was difficult and complicated. A vast program of propaganda was undertaken to sell the five-year plans to the Russian people. The industrial labor force became subject to regimentation similar to that being imposed on the peasants. The accomplishment of the three five-year plans probably allowed the Soviet Union to survive the German invasion.

Many non-Russian contemporaries admired the Soviet economic experiment. While the capitalist world lay in the throes of the depression, the Soviet economy had grown at an unprecedented pace. These observers seemed to have had little idea of the social cost of the Soviet achievement. Millions had been killed or uprooted. The suffering and human loss during those years will probably never be known; it far exceeded anything described by Marx and Engels in relation to nineteenth-century industrialization in western Europe.

THE PURGES

Stalin's decisions to industrialize rapidly and to move against the peasants aroused internal political opposition because they were departures from the policies of Lenin. In 1933, Stalin began to fear that he would lose control over the party apparatus. These fears were probably paranoid. Nevertheless, they resulted in the **Great Purges**, among the most mysterious and horrendous political events of this century.

On December 1, 1934, Sergei Kirov (1888–1934), the popular party chief of Leningrad (formerly St. Petersburg), was assassinated. In the wake of the shooting, thousands of people were arrested, and still more were expelled from the party and sent to labor camps. It now seems certain that Stalin himself authorized Kirov's assassination to forestall any threat from him.

The purges after Kirov's death were just the beginning. Between 1936 and 1938, spectacular show trials were held in Moscow. Previous high Soviet leaders publicly confessed political crimes and were executed. Their confessions were palpably false. Other leaders and party members were tried in private and shot. Thousands of people received no trial at all. It is inexplicable why some were executed, others sent to labor camps, and still others left unmolested. After the civilian party members had been purged, important officers, including heroes of the civil war, were killed. The exact numbers of executions and imprisonments are unknown but ran into the millions.

The scale of the political turmoil was unprecedented. The Russians themselves did not comprehend what was occurring. Political murders and executions were not new, but the absurd confessions were novel. The only rational explanation is found in Stalin's concern for his own power. The purges created a new party structure absolutely loyal to him.

Despite the violence and repression, the Soviet experiment found many sympathizers. The Soviet Union after the Bolshevik seizure of power had fostered Communist parties subservient to Moscow throughout the world. Others who were not members of these parties sympathized with what they believed were the goals of the Soviet Union. During at least the first fifty years of its existence, the Soviet Union managed to capture the imagination of some intellectuals

Propaganda.   Stalin used intimidation and propaganda to support his drive to collectivize Soviet agriculture. The poster shows an idealized Soviet collective farm on which tractors owned by the state have replaced peasant labor. In reality, collectivization provoked fierce resistance and caused famines in which millions of peasants died.

Poster concerning the 1st 5 Year Plan with a photograph of Joseph Stalin (1879–1953), 'At the end of the Plan, the basis of collectivisation must be completed', 1932 (colour litho) by Klutchis (fl.1932). Deutsches Plakat Museum, Essen, Germany/Archives Charmet/The Bridgeman Art Library.

Why might collages such as this, which mixed printed slogans with portions of multiple photographs, have been effective propaganda?

Great Purges   The imprisonment and execution of millions of Soviet citizens by Stalin between 1934 and 1939.

Party Congress, 1936.   By the mid-1930s Stalin's purges had eliminated many leaders and other members from the Soviet Communist Party. This photograph of a meeting of a party congress in 1936 shows a number of the surviving leaders with Stalin, who sits fourth from the right in the front row. To his left is Vyacheslav Molotov, longtime foreign minister. The first person on the left in the front row is Nikita Khrushchev, who headed the Soviet Union in the late 1950s and early 1960s.

Compare this photograph with the one on page 761. Do you see any similarities? What are the differences?

around the globe who hoped for a utopian egalitarian transformation of society. During much of the 1930s, the Soviet Union also appeared as an enemy to the fascist experiments in Italy and Germany. The Marxist ideology championed by the Soviet Union appealed to many people living in the European colonial empires as a vehicle for freeing themselves. The Soviet Union welcomed and trained many anticolonial leaders. With what is now known about Soviet repression, it is difficult to understand the power the nation exercised over many people's political imaginations, but that attraction was a factor in world politics from the 1920s through at least the early 1970s.

THE FASCIST EXPERIMENT IN ITALY

WHY DID the Fascists achieve power in Italy?

The first authoritarian political experiment in western Europe that arose in part from fears of the spread of bolshevism occurred in Italy. The general term *fascist*, which has been used to describe the various right-wing dictatorships that arose between the wars, was derived from the Italian Fascist movement of Benito Mussolini (1883–1945).

Governments regarded as fascist were antidemocratic, anti-Marxist, antiparliamentary, and frequently anti-Semitic. They hoped to hold back the spread of bolshevism, which seemed a real threat at the time. They sought a world that would be safe for the middle class and small farmers. **Fascism** rejected the political ideas of the French Revolution and of liberalism. Facist adherents believed that parliamentary politics and parties sacrificed national greatness to petty party disputes. They wanted to overcome the class conflict of Marxism and the party conflict of liberalism by consolidating all classes within the nation for great national purposes. Fascist governments were usually single-party dictatorships rooted in mass political parties and characterized by terrorism and police surveillance.

fascism Political movements that tend to be antidemocratic, anti-Marxist, antiparliamentary, and often anti-Semitic. Fascists were invariably nationalists and exhalted the nation over the individual. They supported the interests of the middle class and rejected the ideas of the French Revolution and nineteenth-century liberalism. The first fascist regime was founded by Benito Mussolini (1883–1945) in Italy in the 1920s.

RISE OF MUSSOLINI

The Italian *Fasci di Combattimento* ("Band of Combat") was founded in 1919 in Milan. Most of its members were war veterans who felt that the sacrifices of World War I had been in vain. They resented Italy's failure to gain the city of Fiume at the Paris conference. They feared socialism, inflation, and labor unrest.

Their leader or **Duce**, Benito Mussolini, had been active in Italian socialist politics but broke with the socialists in 1914 and supported Italian entry into the war. He then established his own paper, *Il Popolo d'Italia*, and was wounded in the army. As a politician, Mussolini was an opportunist. He could change his ideas and principles to suit any occasion. Action for him was always more important than thought.

Duce Meaning "leader." Mussolini's title as head of the Fascist Party.

Postwar Italian politics was a muddle. Many Italians were dissatisfied with the parliamentary system. They felt that Italy had not been treated as a great power at the peace conference and had not received the territories it deserved. The main spokesman for this discontent was the extreme nationalist writer Gabriele D'Annunzio (1863–1938). In 1919, he captured Fiume with a force of patriotic Italians. The Italian army drove him out, but this made the parliamentary ministry seem unpatriotic.

Between 1919 and 1921, Italy was also wracked by social turmoil. Numerous strikes occurred, and workers occupied factories. Peasants seized land. Parliamentary government seemed incapable of dealing with this unrest. Many Italians believed that a Communist revolution might break out.

Mussolini first supported the factory occupations and land seizures but soon reversed himself. He had discovered that many upper- and middle-class Italians who were pressured by inflation and feared property loss had no sympathy for the workers or peasants. They wanted order. Consequently, Mussolini and his Fascists took direct action in the face of the government inaction. They terrorized socialists, attacked strikers and farm workers, and protected strikebreakers. Conservative land and factory owners were grateful. The government ignored these crimes. By early 1922, the Fascists controlled the local government in much of northern Italy.

In 1921, Mussolini and thirty-four of his followers had been elected to the Chamber of Deputies. The Fascist movement now had hundreds of thousands of supporters. In October 1922, the Fascists, dressed in their characteristic black shirts, began a march on Rome. King Victor Emmanuel III (r. 1900–1946) refused to authorize using the army against them, which ensured a Fascist seizure of power. The cabinet resigned. On October 29, the king telegraphed Mussolini in Milan and asked him to become prime minister. The next day Mussolini arrived in Rome by train and, as head of the government, greeted his followers when they entered the city.

Technically, Mussolini had come into office by legal means. The monarch had the power to appoint the prime minister. Mussolini, however, had no majority in the Chamber of Deputies. Behind the legal facade lay the months of terrorist intimidation and the threat of the Fascists' October march.

Mussolini and the Black Shirts.   Mussolini poses with supporters the day after the Black Shirt March on Rome intimidated the king of Italy into making him prime minister.

Why did many Italians support Mussolini?

THE FASCISTS IN POWER

Mussolini, who had not expected to be appointed prime minister, succeeded because of the impotence of his rivals, his use of his office, his power over the masses, and his ruthlessness. On November 23, 1922, the king and Parliament granted Mussolini dictatorial authority for one year to restore order. Wherever possible, Mussolini appointed Fascists to office. In 1924, Parliament changed the election law so that the party that gained the largest popular vote (with at least 25 percent) received two thirds of the seats in the chamber. Coalition government, with all its compromises and hesitations, would no longer be necessary. In the election of 1924, the Fascists won complete control of the Chamber of Deputies. They used that majority to end legitimate parliamentary life. Laws permitted Mussolini to rule by decree. In 1926, Italy was transformed into a single-party, dictatorial state.

One domestic initiative brought Mussolini significant political dividends and respectability. Through the Lateran Accord of February 1929, the Roman Catholic Church and the Italian state made peace with each other. The agreement recognized the pope as the temporal ruler of Vatican City. The Italian government agreed to pay an indemnity to the papacy for confiscated land. The state also recognized Catholicism as the religion of the nation, exempted church property from taxes, and allowed church law to govern marriage.

GERMAN DEMOCRACY AND DICTATORSHIP

THE WEIMAR REPUBLIC

The Weimar Republic was born from the defeat of the imperial army, the revolution of 1918, and the hopes of German Liberals and Social Democrats. Its name derived from the city of Weimar, where its constitution was written in August 1919. While the constitution was being debated, the republic, headed by the Social Democrats,

WHAT ROLE did terror play in Nazi Germany?

Inflation in Germany. During the German inflation of 1923, currency literally was not worth the paper on which it was printed. Here German children play with batches of worthless banknotes.

What led to such extreme inflation in postwar Germany?

Reichstag The German parliament, which existed in various forms until 1945.

QUICK REVIEW

National Socialism

- Hitler became associated with the National Socialist German Workers Party (Nazis) in 1920

- Party goals included repudiation of Treaty of Versailles, unification of Austria and Germany, and the exclusion of Jews from German citizenship

- Nazi "socialism" meant the subordination of economic enterprises to the welfare of the nation

Nazis The German Nationalist Socialist Party.

accepted the humiliating Versailles Treaty. Although its officials had signed only under duress, the republic was permanently associated with the national disgrace. Throughout the 1920s, the government was required to fulfill the economic and military provisions imposed by the Paris settlement. Nationalists and military figures whose policies had brought on the tragedy and defeat of the war blamed the young republic and the socialists for its results. In Germany, the desire to revise the treaty was related to a desire to change the form of government.

The Weimar Constitution was an enlightened document. It guaranteed civil liberties and provided for direct election, by universal suffrage, of the **Reichstag** and the president. It also, however, contained structural flaws that eventually allowed it to be overthrown. A complicated system of proportional representation made it relatively easy for small political parties to gain seats in the Reichstag, creating instability. The president appointed and removed the chancellor, the head of the cabinet. Article 48 allowed the president, in an emergency, to rule by decree. This permitted a possible presidential dictatorship.

Violence was the hallmark of the first five years of the republic. In March 1920, a right-wing putsch, or armed insurrection, erupted in Berlin. It failed, but only after government officials had fled the city. In the same month, strikes took place in the Ruhr, and the government sent in troops. Such extremism from both the left and the right haunted the republic. In May 1921, the Allies presented a reparations bill for 132 billion gold marks. The German government accepted this preposterous demand only after new Allied threats. Throughout the early 1920s, there were assassinations or attempted assassinations of republican leaders.

Inflation brought on the major crisis of this period. The value of German currency fell due to war and postwar deficit spending. By early 1921, the German mark traded against the American dollar at a ratio of 64 to 1, compared with a ratio of 4.2 to 1 in 1914. The German financial community contended that the mark could not be stabilized until the reparations issue had been solved. Meanwhile, the government kept issuing paper money, which it used to redeem government bonds.

The French invasion of the Ruhr in January 1923, to secure the payment of reparations, and the German response of passive economic resistance produced cataclysmic inflation. Unemployment spread, creating a drain on the treasury and reducing tax revenues. The printing presses had difficulty providing enough paper currency to keep up with the daily rise in prices. Money was literally not worth the paper it was printed on. Stores were unwilling to exchange goods for the worthless currency, and farmers hoarded produce.

The values of thrift and prudence were undermined. Middle-class savings, pensions, insurance policies, and investments in government bonds were wiped out. Debts and mortgages could not be paid off. Speculators made fortunes, but to the middle and lower-middle classes, inflation was another trauma coming hard on the heels of military defeat and the peace treaty. This social and economic upheaval laid the groundwork for the later German desire for order and security at almost any cost.

In 1923, Adolf Hitler (1889–1945) made his first significant appearance on the German political scene. The son of a minor Austrian customs official, his hopes of becoming an artist had been dashed in Vienna. Hitler absorbed the rabid German nationalism and extreme anti-Semitism that flourished there. He came to hate Marxism, which he associated with Jews. During World War I, Hitler fought in the

German army, was wounded, rose to the rank of corporal, and won the Iron Cross for bravery. The war gave him his first sense of purpose.

After the conflict, Hitler settled in Munich and became associated with a small nationalistic, anti-Semitic party that in 1920 adopted the name of National Socialist German Workers Party, better known as the **Nazis**. The group paraded under a red banner with a black swastika. Its program called for the repudiation of the Versailles Treaty, the unification of Austria and Germany, the exclusion of Jews from German citizenship, agrarian reform, the prohibition of land speculation, the confiscation of war profits, state administration of the giant cartels, and the replacement of department stores with small retail shops.

The "socialism" that Hitler and the Nazis had in mind had nothing to do with traditional German socialism. It meant not state ownership of the means of production but instead the subordination of all economic enterprise to the welfare of the nation. It often implied protection for small economic enterprises. The Nazis discovered their party appealed to economic groups that were at risk and under pressure. They often tailored their messages to the particular local problems these groups confronted in different parts of Germany. The Nazis also found considerable support among war veterans, who faced economic and social displacement in Weimar society. The ongoing Nazi demand for revision of the Versailles Treaty appealed to a broad spectrum of economic groups as well as the disaffected war veterans.

Nazi stormtroopers, or SA (*Sturm Abteilung*), were organized under the leadership of Captain Ernst Roehm (1887–1934). The stormtroopers were the chief Nazi instrument for terror and intimidation before the party controlled the government. The organization constituted a means of preserving military discipline and values outside the small army permitted by the Paris settlement. The existence of such a private party army was a sign of the potential for violence in the Weimar Republic and of contempt for the republic.

The social and economic turmoil following the French occupation of the Ruhr and the German inflation gave the Nazis an opportunity for direct action against the Weimar Republic. By this time, Hitler dominated the Nazi Party. On November 9, 1923, Hitler and a band of followers, accompanied by General Erich Ludendorff (1865–1937), attempted an unsuccessful putsch at a beer hall in Munich. Local authorities crushed the rising, and sixteen Nazis were killed. Hitler and Ludendorff were tried for treason. The general was acquitted. Hitler made himself into a national figure. In his defense, he condemned the republic, the Versailles Treaty, and the Jews. He was sentenced to five years in prison but spent only a few months in jail before being paroled. During this time, he dictated **Mein Kampf** (My *Struggle*). Another result of the brief imprisonment was his decision to seize political power by legal methods.

Gustav Stresemann (1878–1929) was primarily responsible for the reconstruction of the republic and its achievement of a sense of self-confidence. Stresemann abandoned the policy of passive resistance in the Ruhr. With the aid of banker Hjalmar Schacht (1877–1970), he introduced a new German currency. The rate of exchange was 1 trillion of the old German marks for one new Rentenmark. Stresemann also moved against challenges from both the left and the right. He supported the crushing of both Hitler's abortive putsch and smaller communist disturbances. In late November 1923, after four months as chancellor, he became foreign minister, a post he held until his death in 1929.

Weimar Germany.   In this painting, which reflects the mood of social and political disillusionment that prevailed in much of Europe in the 1920s, George Grosz satirized conservative and right-wing groups in Weimar Germany, including the army, the courts, the newspapers, and the Nazi Party.

What references to violence can you find in this painting?

Mein Kampf   Meaning "My Struggle." Hitler's statement of his political program, published in 1924.

QUICK REVIEW

Locarno Agreements

- October 1925: Britain and France accept revision of the Treaty of Versailles
- Agreements brought new hope to Europe
- Many people in both Germany and France were unhappy with Locarno

CHRONOLOGY

MAJOR POLITICAL EVENTS OF THE 1920s AND 1930s

1919	August	Constitution of the Weimar Republic promulgated
1920		Kapp Putsch in Berlin
1921	March	Kronstadt mutiny leads Lenin to initiate his New Economic Policy
1922	October	Fascist march on Rome leads to Mussolini's assumption of power
1923	January	France invades the Ruhr
	November	Hitler's Beer Hall Putsch
1924		Death of Lenin
1925		Locarno Agreements
1928		Kellogg-Briand Pact; first Five-Year Plan launched in USSR
1929	January	Trotsky expelled from USSR
	February	Lateran Accord between the Vatican and the Italian state
	October	New York stock market crash
	November	Stalin's central position in the USSR affirmed
1930	March	Brüning government begins in Germany
		Stalin calls for moderation in his policy of agricultural collectivization because of "dizziness from success"
	September	Nazis capture 107 seats in German Reichstag
1931	August	National Government formed in Britain
1932	March 13	Hindenburg defeats Hitler for German presidency
	May 31	Franz von Papen forms German Cabinet
	July 31	German Reichstag election
	November 6	German Reichstag election
	December 2	Kurt von Schleicher forms German Cabinet
1933	January 30	Hitler made German chancellor
	February 27	Reichstag fire
	March 5	Reichstag election
	March 23	Enabling Act consolidates Nazi power
1934	June 30	Blood purge of the Nazi Party
	August 2	Death of Hindenburg
	December 1	Assassination of Kirov leads to the beginning of Stalin's purges
1936	May	Popular Front government in France
	July–August	Most famous of public purge trials in Russia

In 1924 the Weimar Republic and the Allies renegotiated the reparation payments. The Dawes Plan lowered the annual payments and allowed them to fluctuate according to the fortunes of the German economy. The last French troops left the Ruhr in 1925. The same year, Field Marshal Paul von Hindenburg (1847–1934), a military hero and a conservative monarchist, was elected president of the republic. He governed in strict accordance with the constitution, and conservative Germans seemed reconciled to the republic. The latter 1920s were prosperous, and prosperity helped to establish broader acceptance and appreciation of the republic.

In foreign affairs, Stresemann pursued a conciliatory course. He fulfilled the provisions of the Versailles Treaty but attempted to revise it by diplomacy. He accepted the settlement in the west but aimed to recover German-speaking territories lost to Poland and Czechoslovakia and possibly to unite with Austria, chiefly by diplomatic means.

These developments gave rise to the Locarno Agreements of October 1925. Foreign ministers Austen Chamberlain (1863–1937) for Britain and Aristide Briand (1862–1932) for France accepted Stresemann's proposal for a fresh start. France and Germany accepted the western frontier established at Versailles. Britain and Italy agreed to intervene if either side violated the frontier or if Germany sent troops into the demilitarized Rhineland. No such agreement was made about Germany's eastern frontier, but the Germans made treaties with Poland and Czechoslovakia, and France strengthened its alliances with those countries. France supported German membership in the League of Nations and agreed to withdraw its occupation troops from the Rhineland in 1930, five years earlier than specified at Versailles.

Germany was pleased to have achieved respectability and a guarantee against another Ruhr occupation, as well as the possibility of revision in the east. Britain enjoyed playing a more evenhanded role. Italy was glad to be recognized as a great power. The French were happy, too, because the Germans voluntarily accepted the permanence of their western frontier, which was also guaranteed by Britain and Italy, and France maintained its allies in the east.

The Locarno Agreements brought new hope to Europe. Chamberlain, Briand, and Stresemann received the Nobel Peace Prize. The spirit of Locarno was carried even further when the leading European states, Japan, and the United States signed the Kellogg-Briand Pact in 1928, renouncing "war as an instrument of national policy." The joy and optimism were not justified. France had merely recognized its inability to coerce Germany without help. Britain had shown its unwillingness to uphold the settlement in the east. Germany was not reconciled to the eastern settlement.

In both France and Germany, moreover, the conciliatory politicians represented only a part of the populace. In Germany especially, most people continued to reject Versailles and regarded Locarno as an extension of it. Despite these problems, war was by no means inevitable. Europe, aided by American loans, was returning to prosperity. German leaders like Stresemann would certainly have continued to press for change but not through warfare. Continued prosperity and diplomatic success might have won the loyalty of the German people for the Weimar Republic and moderate revisionism, but the Great Depression of the 1930s brought new forces to power.

DEPRESSION AND POLITICAL DEADLOCK

The outflow of foreign, and especially American, capital from Germany that began in 1928 undermined the prosperity of the Weimar Republic. The resulting economic crisis brought parliamentary government to a halt. In 1928, a coalition of center parties and the Social Democrats governed. When the depression struck, the coalition partners differed sharply on economic policy, and the coalition dissolved in March 1930. President von Hindenburg appointed Heinrich Brüning (1885–1970) as chancellor. Lacking a majority in the Reichstag, the new chancellor governed through emergency presidential decrees. The Weimar Republic had become a presidential dictatorship.

German unemployment rose from 2,258,000 in March 1930 to more than 6,000,000 in March 1932. The economic downturn and the parliamentary deadlock worked to the advantage of extremists. In the election of 1928, the Nazis had won only 12 seats in the Reichstag and the Communists won 54. In the election of 1930, the Nazis won 107 seats and the Communists won 77.

The power of the Nazis in the streets also rose. Unemployment brought thousands of men into the stormtroopers, which had almost 1 million members in 1933. The SA attacked Communists and Social Democrats. For the Nazis, politics meant the capture of power through terror and intimidation as well as through elections. Decency and civility in political life vanished. Nazi rallies resembled religious revivals. They paraded through the streets and the countryside. They gained powerful supporters in the business, military, and newspaper communities. Some intellectuals were also sympathetic. The Nazis transformed the discipline and enthusiasm born of economic despair and nationalistic frustration into electoral results.

HITLER COMES TO POWER

For two years, Brüning governed with the confidence of Hindenburg. The economy did not improve, and the political situation deteriorated. In 1932, the 83-year-old president stood for reelection. Hitler ran against him and Hindenburg won. But Hitler got 36.8 percent of the final vote, convincing Hindenburg that Brüning had lost the confidence of conservative Germans. In May 1932, he appointed Franz von Papen (1878–1969) chancellor. Papen was one of a small group of extremely conservative advisers on whom Hindenburg had become dependent. With the continued paralysis in the Reichstag, the advisers' influence over the president amounted to control of the government.

Papen and the circle around the president wanted to draw the Nazis into cooperation with them without giving Hitler effective power. The government needed the popular support on the right that only the Nazis seemed able to generate. The Hindenburg circle decided to convince Hitler that the Nazis could not come to power on their own. Papen removed the ban on Nazi meetings that Brüning had imposed and called a Reichstag election for July 1932. The Nazis won 230 seats and polled 37.2 percent of the vote. Hitler would enter the cabinet only if he were made chancellor. Hindenburg refused. Another election was called in November. The Nazis gained only 196 seats, and their percentage of the popular vote dipped to 33.1 percent. Hindenberg's advisers still refused to appoint Hitler to office.

In early December 1932, Papen resigned and General Kurt von Schleicher (1882–1934) became chancellor. People were now afraid of civil war between the extreme left and the far right. Schleicher tried to fashion a coalition of conservatives and trade unionists. The Hindenburg circle did not trust Schleicher's motives, which have never been clear. They persuaded Hindenburg to appoint Hitler chancellor. To control him, Papen was named vice chancellor, and other traditional conservatives were appointed to the cabinet. On January 30, 1933, Adolf Hitler became the chancellor of Germany.

Hitler had come into office by legal means. The proper procedures had been observed, so the civil service, courts, and other government agencies were able to support him in good conscience. He had forged a rigidly disciplined party structure and had mastered the techniques of mass politics and propaganda. His support appears to have come from across the social spectrum. Pockets of resistance appeared among Roman Catholic voters in the country and small towns. Support for Hitler was strong among farmers, veterans, and the young, who had suffered from the insecurity of the 1920s and the depression. Hitler promised them security, effective government in place of petty politics, and a strong, restored Germany.

There is little evidence that business contributions made any crucial difference to the Nazis' success. Hitler's supporters were frequently suspicious of business and giant capitalism. They wanted a simpler world in which small property would be safe from both socialism and large-scale capitalist consolidation. These people looked to Hitler and the Nazis rather than to the Social Democrats because the latter never appeared sufficiently nationalistic. The Nazis won out over other conservative nationalistic parties because only the Nazis addressed the problem of social insecurities.

HITLER'S CONSOLIDATION OF POWER

Once in office, Hitler moved swiftly to consolidate his control. This process had three facets: the capture of full legal authority, the crushing of alternative political groups, and the purging of rivals within the Nazi Party itself. On February 27, 1933, a mentally ill Dutch Communist set fire to the Reichstag building in Berlin. The Nazis turned the incident to their own advantage by claiming that the fire proved the existence of a Communist threat to the government. To the public, this seemed plausible. Hitler suspended civil liberties and arrested Communists or alleged Communists under a decree that was not revoked for as long as Hitler ruled Germany.

In early March another Reichstag election took place. The Nazis received only 43.9 percent of the vote, but the arrest of the newly elected communist deputies and the political fear aroused by the fire meant that Hitler could control the Reichstag. On March 23, 1933, the Reichstag passed an Enabling Act that permitted Hitler to rule by decree. Thereafter, there were no legal limits on his power. The Weimar Constitution was never formally repealed—it was simply supplanted.

Hitler understood that he and his party had come to power because his potential opponents had stood divided between 1929 and 1933. To prevent them from regrouping, Hitler outlawed or undermined any German institutions that might have served as rallying points for opposition. By the close of 1933, all major institutions of potential

Hitler.   Hitler's mastery of the techniques of mass politics and propaganda—including huge staged rallies like this one in 1938—was an important factor in his rise to power.

Why do you think people participated in mass events such as this rally?

opposition—trade unions, other political parties, the federal state governments—had been eliminated.

The final element in Hitler's personal consolidation of power involved the Nazi Party itself. Ernst Roehm, the commander of the SA, was a possible rival to Hitler. The German officer corps, whom Hitler needed to rebuild the army, were jealous of the SA. To protect his own position and to shore up support with the army, Hitler ordered the murder of key SA officers, including Roehm. Between June 30 and July 2, 1934, more than 800 people were killed, including the former chancellor Kurt von Schleicher and his wife. The German army, which might have prevented the murders, did nothing. On August 2, 1934, President Hindenburg died, and the offices of chancellor and president were combined. Hitler was now the sole ruler, or **Führer**, of Germany and of the Nazi Party.

Führer   Meaning "leader." The title taken by Hitler when he became dictator of Germany.

THE POLICE STATE

Terror and intimidation had helped propel the Nazis to office. As Hitler consolidated his power, he oversaw the organization of a police state. The chief vehicle of police surveillance was the SS (*Schutzstaffel*), or security units, commanded by Heinrich Himmler (1900–1945). This group was a more elite paramilitary organization than the larger SA. In 1933, the SS had approximately 52,000 members. It was the instrument that carried out the blood purges of the party in 1934. By 1936, Himmler had become head of all police matters in Germany.

The police character of the Nazi regime permeated society, but the people who most consistently experienced its terror were the Jews. Anti-Semitism had been a key plank of the Nazi program, an anti-Semitism based on biological racial theories stemming from late-nineteenth-century thought rather than from religious discrimination. Before World War II, the Nazi attack on the Jews went through three stages. In 1933, the Nazis excluded Jews from the civil service and attempted to enforce boycotts of Jewish businesses. The boycotts won little public support. In 1935, the Nuremberg Laws robbed German Jews of their citizenship. All persons with at least one Jewish grandparent were defined as Jews. The professions and major occupations were closed to Jews. Marriage and sexual intercourse between Jews and non-Jews were prohibited. Legal exclusion and humiliation of the Jews became the norm.

Anti-Jewish Policies.   Soon after seizing power, the Nazi government began harassing German Jewish businesses. Non-Jewish German citizens were urged not to buy merchandise from shops owned by Jews.

Why did the Nazis target Jews?

Kristallnacht   Meaning "crystal night" because of the broken glass that littered German streets after the looting and destruction of Jewish homes, businesses, and synagogues across Germany on the orders of the Nazi Party in November 1938.

The persecution of the Jews increased again in 1938. In November, under orders from the Nazi Party, thousands of Jewish stores and synagogues were destroyed. The Jewish community itself had to pay for the damage that occurred on this **Kristallnacht** because the government confiscated the insurance money. In both large and petty ways, the German Jews were harassed. This persecution allowed the Nazis to inculcate the rest of the population with the concept of a master race of pure German "Aryans" and also to display their own contempt for civil liberties.

After the war broke out, Hitler decided in 1942 to destroy the Jews in Europe. It is thought that over 6 million Jews, mostly from eastern European nations, died as a result of that decision, unprecedented in its scope and implementation.

WOMEN IN NAZI GERMANY

The Nazis believed in separate social spheres for men and women. Men belonged in the world of action, women in the home. Women who sought to liberate themselves and to adopt roles traditionally followed by men in public life were considered symptoms of cultural decline. Respect for women should arise from their function as wives and mothers.

These attitudes conflicted with the social changes that German women, like women elsewhere in Europe, had experienced during the first three decades of the twentieth century. German women had become much more active and assertive. They worked in factories or were independently employed and had begun to enter the professions. Under the Weimar Constitution, they voted. Throughout the Weimar period, there was also a lively discussion of women's emancipation. For the Nazis, these developments were signs of cultural weakness.

The Nazis' point of view was supported by women of a conservative outlook and women who followed traditional roles as housewives. In a period of high unemployment, the Nazi attitude also appealed to many men because it discouraged women from competing with them in the workplace. Such competition had begun during World War I, and many Nazis considered it symptomatic of the social confusion that had followed the German defeat.

The Nazi discussion of the role of women was also rooted in Nazi racism. It was the special task of German mothers to preserve racial purity. Hitler championed the view that women were to breed strong sons and daughters for the German nation. Nazi journalists often compared the role of women in childbirth to that of men in battle. Each served the state in particular gender roles. In both cases, the good of the nation was superior to that of the individual. The Nazis attacked feminist outlooks. Women were encouraged to bear

---

OVERVIEW   Characteristics Shared by Fascist, Nazi, and Soviet Communist Regimes of the 1920s and 1930s

1. Well-organized, highly disciplined political parties
2. Intense nationalism
3. Programs that promised to cure social, political, and economic malaise
4. A monopoly over mass communications and propaganda
5. Highly effective instruments of terror and police power
6. Real or imagined national, class, or racial enemies who could be demonized to whip up mass support
7. Command over modern technology and its capacity for immense destruction

many children because the Nazis believed the declining German birthrate was the result of emancipated women who had spurned their natural roles as mothers. The Nazis sponsored schools that taught women how to rear children. The Nazis saw women as educators of the young and thus the protectors of German cultural values. Through cooking, dress, music, and stories, mothers were to instill a love for the nation. As consumers for the home, women were to buy German goods and avoid Jewish merchants.

The Nazis realized that in the midst of the depression many women would need to work, but the party urged them to pursue employment that the Nazis considered natural to their character. These tasks included agriculture, teaching, nursing, social work, and domestic service. Nonetheless, the percentage of women employed in Germany changed little from the Weimar to the Hitler years: 37 percent in 1928 and the same again in 1939. Thereafter, because of the war, many more women were recruited into the German workforce.

THE GREAT DEPRESSION AND THE NEW DEAL IN THE UNITED STATES

The United States emerged from World War I as a world power. It retreated from that role when the Senate refused to ratify the Versailles Treaty and failed to join the League of Nations. In 1920, Warren Harding (1865–1923) became president and urged a return to what he termed "normalcy," which meant minimal involvement abroad and conservative economic policies at home. Business interests remained in the ascendant, and the federal government took a relatively inactive role in national life, especially under Harding's successor, Calvin Coolidge (1872–1933).

HOW DID FDR's policies affect the role of the federal government?

The first seven or eight years of the decade witnessed remarkable American prosperity. New electrical appliances such as the radio, phonograph, washing machine, and vacuum cleaner appeared on the market. Real wages rose for many workers. Industry grew at a robust rate. Automobile manufacturers assumed a major role in national economic life. Factories became mechanized. Engineers and efficiency experts were the heroes of the business world. The stock market boomed. This activity stood in marked contrast to the economic dislocations of Europe.

This material prosperity emerged in a divided society. Segregation remained a basic fact of life for black Americans. The Ku Klux Klan, which sought to terrorize blacks, Roman Catholics, and Jews, enjoyed a resurgence. The Prohibition Amendment of 1919 (repealed in 1933) forbade the manufacture and transport of alcoholic beverages. In the wake of this divisive national policy, major criminal operations arose to supply liquor and disrupt civic life. Many immigrants came from Mexico and Puerto Rico. They settled in cities where their labor was desired but where they were often not welcomed or assimilated. Finally, the wealth of the nation was concentrated in few hands.

Women Members of the Ku Klux Klan in New Castle, Indiana, August 1, 1923.
The revived Klan was a powerful presence in scores of American communities during the early 1920s, especially among native-born white Protestants, who feared cultural and political change. In addition to preaching "100 percent Americanism," local Klan chapters also served a social function for members and their families.

Does the fact that these Klu Klux Klan members are from Indiana complicate commonly-held notions about racial tolerance in the United States?

Unemployed Workers. The Great Depression brought unprecedented unemployment to the United States. In 1930 unemployed workers were photographed standing outside the Municipal Lodging House in New York City.

What were the effects of widespread unemployment on American society?

ECONOMIC COLLAPSE

In March 1929 Herbert Hoover became president, the third Republican in as many elections. On October 29, 1929, the New York stock market crashed. The other financial markets also went into a tailspin. During the next year the stock market continued to fall. The banks that had loaned people money with which to speculate in the market suffered great losses.

The financial collapse of 1929 triggered the Great Depression in America, although there were other underlying domestic causes. Manufacturing firms had not made sufficient capital investment. The disproportionate amount of profits going to about 5 percent of the U.S. population had begun to undermine the purchasing power of other consumers. Agriculture had been in trouble for years. Finally, the economic difficulties in Europe and Latin America, which predated those in the United States, meant foreigners were less able to purchase U.S.-made products.

The most pervasive problem of the Great Depression was unemployment. Joblessness hit unskilled workers first but then worked its way up the job ladder to touch factory and white-collar workers. As unemployment spread, small retail businesses suffered. In the major American manufacturing cities, hundreds of thousands of workers could not find jobs. The price of corn fell so low in some areas that it was not profitable to harvest it. By the early 1930s, banks began to fail, and people lost their savings.

The federal government was not equipped to address the emergency. There was no tradition of federal action to alleviate economic distress. President Hoover organized economic conferences and encouraged the Federal Reserve to make borrowing easier. He supported the ill-advised Hawley-Smoot Tariff Act of 1930, which hoped to protect American industry by a high tariff barrier. Hoover believed relief was a matter for local government and voluntary organizations; however, many local relief agencies had run out of money by 1931.

NEW ROLE FOR GOVERNMENT

The election of 1932 was one of the most crucial in American history. The Democratic Party's candidate, Franklin Delano Roosevelt (1882–1945), promised "a new deal for the American people." He overwhelmingly defeated Hoover and quickly redirected federal policy toward the depression.

Roosevelt had been born into a moderately wealthy New York family and was a distant cousin of Theodore Roosevelt (1858–1919). After serving in World War I as Assistant Secretary of the Navy, in 1920 he ran as the Democratic vice presidential candidate. The next year, however, he was struck with polio and his legs became paralyzed, but he went on to be elected governor of New York in 1928. As president, he attempted to convey to the nation the same kind of optimistic spirit that had informed his personal struggle in the 1920s.

Roosevelt's first goal was to give the nation a sense that the federal government was meeting the economic challenge. The first hundred days of his administration became legendary. He immediately closed all the banks and permitted only sound institutions to reopen. Congress rapidly passed a new banking act and then enacted the Agricultural Adjustment Act and the Farm Credit Act to aid farmers. To provide jobs, Roosevelt sponsored the Civilian Conservation Corps. The Federal Emergency Relief Act funded state and local relief agencies. To restore confidence, Roosevelt began making speeches, known as "fireside chats," to the American people.

Roosevelt's most ambitious program was the National Industrial Recovery Act (NIRA), which established the National Recovery Administration (NRA). This agency attempted to foster codes written by various industries to regulate wages and prices, in hopes that regulated competition might protect jobs and assure production.

The NIRA and other New Deal legislation, such as the Wagner Act of 1935, which established the National Labor Relations Board and the Fair Labor Standards Act of 1938, provided a larger role in the American economy for organized labor. It became easier for unions to organize. Union membership grew steadily, and American unionism took on a new character. Previously, most unions had organized by craft and had been affiliated with the American Federation of Labor. In the 1930s, however, whole industries composed of workers in various crafts were organized in a single union. The most important of these organizations were the United Mine Workers and United Automobile Workers. These new unions organized themselves into the Congress of Industrial Organizations. The CIO and the AFL were rivals until they merged in the 1950s. These new strong industrial labor organizations introduced a powerful new force into the American economic scene.

In 1935 the U.S. Supreme Court declared the NRA unconstitutional. Thereafter, Roosevelt deemphasized centralized economic planning. The number of federal agencies increased, but they operated in general independence from each other.

Through New Deal legislation, the federal government was far more active in the economy than it had ever been. The government itself attempted to provide relief for the unemployed in the industrial sector. The major institution of the relief effort was the **Works Progress Administration (WPA)**. Created in 1935, the WPA began a massive program of public works.

Programs of the New Deal years also involved the federal government directly in economic development rather than turning such development over to private enterprise. Through the Tennessee Valley Authority (TVA), the government became directly involved in the economy of the four states of the Tennessee River valley. The TVA built dams and then produced and sold hydroelectricity. Never had the government undertaken so extensive an economic role. Another major new function for the government was providing security for the elderly through the establishment of the Social Security Administration in 1935.

In one area of American life after another, it was decided that the government must provide personal economic security. These actions established a mixed economy in the United States—that is, one in which the federal government would play an ongoing active role alongside the private sector. The New Deal changed much of American life, but it did not solve the unemployment problem. In the late 1930s, the economy began to falter again. Only the entry of the nation into World War II brought the U.S. economy to full employment.

The experience of the United States under the New Deal stood in marked contrast to the economic and political experiments in Europe. Many businesspeople found Roosevelt too liberal and his policies too activist. Nonetheless, the New Deal preserved capitalism in a democratic setting where, again in contrast to Europe, there was free political debate—much of it critical of the administration. The United States had demonstrated that a nation with a vast industrial economy could confront its gravest economic crisis and still preserve democracy.

QUICK REVIEW

New Deal

◆ Legislated extensive government involvement in economy

◆ Did not end unemployment

◆ Demonstrated flexibility and strength of democracy and capitalism

Works Progress Administration (WPA) New Deal program created by the Roosevelt administration in 1935 that provided relief for the unemployed in the industrial sector during the Great Depression in the United States.

The Works Progress Administration.   This group of men repairing a street worked for the Works Progress Administration, one of the chief New Deal agencies designed to create public works projects that would generate employment.

What was the New Deal?

SUMMARY

WHICH GROUPS were dissatisfied with the Versailles settlement?

After Versailles: Demands for Revision and Enforcement. The Versailles settlement bred political discontent and resentment throughout Europe among both victors and the defeated. Wrangles over reparations between Germany and the Allied powers persisted through the 1920s. *page 752*

WHAT FACTORS made the Great Depression so severe and long lasting?

Toward the Great Depression in Europe. After World War I, Europe never recovered its prewar prosperity or stability. The Great Depression was triggered by a financial crisis relating to German reparations and a commodity crisis caused by overproduction. It caused severe economic, social, and political problems throughout Europe, and no government offered responsible financial leadership. *page 753*

HOW DID Stalin gain and keep power in the Soviet Union?

The Soviet Experiment. The Bolsheviks were forced to consolidate their regime within Russia. Lenin's New Economic Policy gave the state control over heavy industry, transportation, and international commerce but allowed for small-scale private enterprise and peasant farms. Stalin abandoned this policy to push for rapid industrialization. He abolished private enterprise, collectivized agriculture, and eliminated his opponents in a series of purges in which millions were imprisoned or killed. Despite the violence and oppression, Marxist parties around the world were subservient to the Soviet Union as the world's only communist state and the enemy of fascism. *page 755*

WHY DID the Fascists achieve power in Italy?

The Fascist Experiment in Italy. Many Italians were dissatisfied with the terms of the Versailles Treaty and frightened by the social unrest that followed World War I. Benito Mussolini promised order and a strong state. Although he achieved power by legal means, he soon transformed Italy into a single-party dictatorship. In 1929 he came to terms with the Catholic Church by negotiating the Lateran Accord, which recognized the pope as the independent ruler of Vatican City. *page 760*

WHAT ROLE did terror play in Nazi Germany?

German Democracy and Dictatorship. The Weimar Republic was buffeted by social, political, and financial instability. Many Germans refused to accept Germany's defeat in World War I or the terms of the Versailles Treaty. Rampant inflation destroyed middle-class savings, and the Great Depression brought financial collapse and massive unemployment. Once Adolf Hitler came to power in 1933, he established a one-party dictatorship based on police terror, propaganda, racial anti-Semitism, and the cult of Hitler as supreme leader. Jews, in particular, were persecuted. *page 761*

HOW DID FDR's policies affect the role of the federal government?

The Great Depression and the New Deal in the United States. The United States emerged from World War I as a world power but retreated into isolation during the 1920s. The prosperity of the 1920s ended in the Great Depression. Franklin Delano Roosevelt's New Deal greatly expanded the power of the federal government in social and economic affairs and preserved capitalism in a democratic setting. *page 769*

INTERPRETING THE PAST

Fascism, Collective Action, and Women's Rights

Sources from MyHistoryLab for Chapter 30

myhistorylab

1) Benito Mussolini, *The Political and Social Doctrine of Fascism*

2) John Maynard Keynes, *The End of Laissez-Faire*

Source from Chapter 30

1) *A Communist Woman Demands a New Family Life* (pages 756–757)

The authoritarian ideologies that developed in the 1920s and 1930s did so as a result of the failure of traditional governing philosophies and institutions to cope with financial collapse, agricultural crisis, and political uncertainties in Europe after World War I. Fascism and one of its variants, Nazism, were each

REVIEW QUESTIONS

1. Were there any groups that supported the Versailles settlement?

2. Explain the causes of the Great Depression. Why was it more severe, and why did it last longer, than previous economic downturns? Could it have been avoided?

3. What was the cause of disagreement between Trotsky and Stalin? What was the outcome of their disagreement?

4. How did Stalin achieve supreme power in the Soviet Union? Why did he decide that Russia had to industrialize rapidly? Why did this require the collectivization of agriculture? Was the policy a success? How did it affect the Russian people? What were the causes of the Great Purges?

5. What influence did the Soviet Union exert on other parts of Europe during this period?

6. Why was Italy dissatisfied and unstable after World War I? How did Mussolini achieve power?

7. What were the characteristics of the fascist state?

8. Why did the Weimar Republic collapse in Germany? Discuss Hitler's rise to power. Which groups in Germany supported Hitler, and why were they pro-Nazi? How did he consolidate his power?

9. Compare the authoritarian regimes in the Soviet Union, Italy, and Germany. What characteristics did they have in common? What role did terror play in each?

10. Why did the U.S. economy collapse in 1929? What policies did Roosevelt use to combat the depression? How did his policies affect the role of the federal government in national life?

KEY TERMS

collectivization (p. 758)
Duce (DOO-chay) (p. 760)
fascism (p. 760)
Führer (p. 767)
Great Depression (p. 753)
Great Purges (p. 759)
Kristallnacht (p. 768)
Mein Kampf (p. 763)
Nazis (p. 762)

New Economic Policy (NEP) (p. 756)
Popular Front (p. 755)
Reichstag (REYEKS-tahg) (p. 762)
War Communism (p. 755)
Weimar Republic (p. 753)
Works Progress Administration (p. 771)

Note: To learn more about the topics in this chapter, please turn to the Suggested Readings at the end of the book.

associated with fervent and aggressive nationalism, combined with a contempt for liberal principles of individual liberty and the democratic political system. Communism, an ideology that first developed in the nineteenth century, was refined by Russian Bolsheviks in the early twentieth century and also disdained individual freedoms and democratic principles.

In this exercise you will read three primary sources from the early twentieth century that focus on fascism, the role of the government in the economy, and women's rights.

The first document is written by Benito Mussolini, the leader of the Italian state from 1922 to 1943, and fascism's most articulate spokesman. In this explanation of the movement, he outlines the roles of an all-powerful state and the individual citizen in the modern era. The second document, from 1926, is by British economist John Maynard Keynes, who advocated government of the economy to protect individuals from capitalism's down cycle. The third document details how the Communist Party

(and the state) could assist in restructuring family life and the role of women in pursuit of a shared common goal.

Questions

How does Mussolini justify the lack of individual freedom under a fascist state? What are the primary doctrines of fascism? How does he explain the development of the fascist ideology?

What does Keynes mean when he advocates "collective action" to improve the "technique of modern capitalism"? How does Keynes's views on the role of government contrast with Mussolini's?

The Kollontai document focuses on women and their role in society. What changes in their traditional role does she envision as desirable?

31
World War II

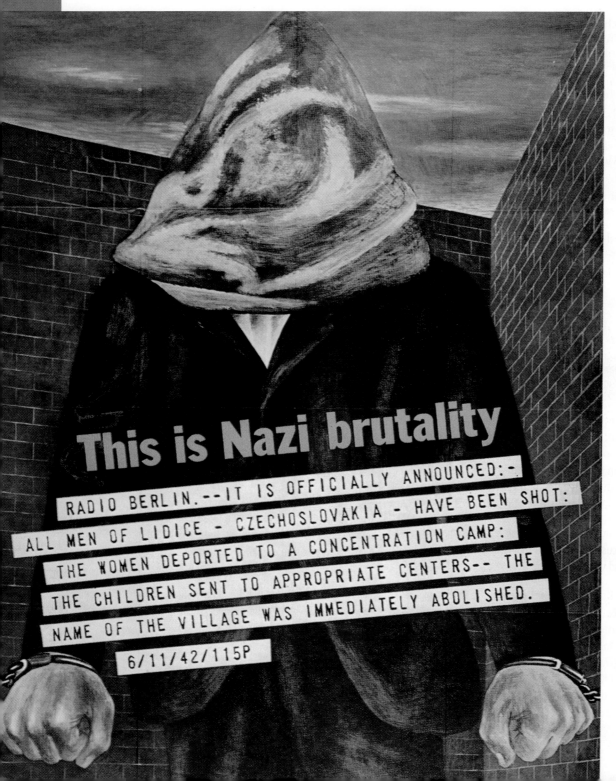

This is Nazi brutality

RADIO BERLIN.--IT IS OFFICIALLY ANNOUNCED:-
ALL MEN OF LIDICE - CZECHOSLOVAKIA - HAVE BEEN SHOT:
THE WOMEN DEPORTED TO A CONCENTRATION CAMP:
THE CHILDREN SENT TO APPROPRIATE CENTERS-- THE
NAME OF THE VILLAGE WAS IMMEDIATELY ABOLISHED.
6/11/42/115P

Nazi Terror. In this vivid poster, the artist Ben Shahn (1898–1969) memorialized the destruction of Lidice. The Czechoslovakian town was obliterated by the Nazis on June 11, 1942, in vengeance for the resistance by Czechs against their Nazi rulers.

How did the Nazis gain control of Czechoslovakia?

GLOBAL PERSPECTIVE

WORLD WAR II

The second great war of the twentieth century (1939–1945) grew out of the unsatisfactory resolution of the first. In retrospect, the two wars appear to some people to be one continuous conflict—a kind of twentieth-century Thirty Years' War—with the two main periods of fighting separated by an uneasy truce. To others, that point of view distorts the situation by implying that the second war was the inevitable result of the first and its inadequate peace treaties.

The latter opinion seems more sound. Whatever the flaws of the treaties of Paris, the world suffered an even more terrible war than the first as a result of failures of judgment and will on the part of the victorious democratic powers. The United States, which had become the wealthiest and potentially the strongest nation in the world, disarmed almost entirely and withdrew into a shortsighted and foolish isolation; it could play no important part in restraining the angry and ambitious dictators who brought on the war. Britain and France refused to face the reality of the threat the Axis powers posed until the most deadly war in history was required to put it down. If the victorious democracies had remained strong, responsible, and realistic, they could have

remedied whatever injustices or mistakes arose from the treaties without endangering the peace.

Equally important, however, was the unwillingness of the victorious powers to adjust the peace treaties from World War I, especially to lessen the burden on the devastated German economy, even in the face of the obvious inability of Germany to pay the enormous war reparations the victors demanded. Here too, the isolationism of the United States played a pivotal role, as the government insisted that its allies in World War I, France and Britain, whose economies were also struggling after the war, repay their debts to the United States. France and Britain, in turn, sought to fund their war debts using reparations extracted primarily from Germany, whose economy was also burdened by the occupation of the Ruhr valley and the ensuing loss of some of its best industrial infrastructure and resources. A vicious cycle ensued, which the advent of the Great Depression only exacerbated. The inability of the democratic German government of the Weimar Republic to negotiate a better deal from the inflexible victors of World War I added to the perception of ordinary Germans that it was weak and inept and thus contributed to its

T*he more idealistic survivors of the First World War, especially in the United States and Great Britain, thought of it as "the war to end all wars" and "a war to make the world safe for democracy." Only thus could they justify that war's awful slaughter, expense, and upheaval. They could not have imagined that only twenty years after the peace treaties a second great war would break out that would be more truly global than the first. In this war the democracies would be fighting for their lives against militaristic, nationalistic, authoritarian, and totalitarian states in Europe and Asia. Great Britain and the United States would be allied with the communist Soviet Union. The defeat of the militarists and dictators would not bring the longed-for peace, but rather a cold war in which the European states became second-class powers, subordinate to the Soviet Union and the United States.* ■

WHAT WERE the main events between 1933 and 1939 that led to World War II?

AGAIN THE ROAD TO WAR (1933–1939)

World War I and the Versailles Treaty had only a marginal relationship to the world depression of the 1930s. But in Germany, where the reparations settlement had contributed to the vast inflation of 1923, economic and social discontent focused on the Versailles settlement as the cause of all ills. Throughout the late 1920s, Adolf Hitler and the Nazi Party had never ceased denouncing Versailles as the source of all Germany's trouble; the economic woes of the early 1930s seemed to bear them out. This, in addition to Nazi Party discipline and a message of fervent nationalism, helped Hitler overthrow the Weimar Republic and take control of Germany.

downfall. One of the legacies of World War II was a realization on the part of the Western world of the dangers excessively high foreign debts can pose to the world order, as poor countries, unable to repay or renegotiate their debt structures, can be tempted to secede from international institutions and invade their neighbors in an effort to salvage their economies and shore up their governments.

The second war itself was plainly a global war. The Japanese occupation of Manchuria in 1931, while not technically a part of that war, was a significant precursor. Italy attacked Ethiopia in 1935. Italy, Germany, and the Soviet Union intervened in the Spanish Civil War (1936–1939). Japan attacked China in 1937. European colonies or former colonies, such as Australia and other South Pacific islands, the Philippines, and regions of the Middle East and North Africa became theaters of war or, like India, were drawn into the conflict by helping to supply the combatants. Men and women from all the inhabited continents thus took part. The use of atomic weapons brought the frightful struggle to a close, but what are called conventional weapons did almost all the damage while state-sponsored genocide, such as

the Holocaust, killed millions of civilians. The world reached a level of destructiveness that threatened the very survival of civilization, even without the use of atomic or nuclear devices.

The aftermath of World War II, and the analysis on the part of the victors of the causes of the conflict, led to the creation of the United Nations, an international organization designed to forestall future conflict through improved international diplomacy. Imperfect as the United Nations is, most scholars agree that it has helped preserve world peace.

Focus Questions

◆ What was the relationship between World War I and World War II? Why was the isolationism of the United States after World War I such an important factor in the advent of World War II?

◆ Why was World War II truly a global war?

◆ What lessons did the world learn from the experiences of World War I and World War II?

HITLER'S GOALS

From first to last, Hitler's racial theories and goals held the central place in his thought. He meant to go far beyond Germany's 1914 boundaries in order to bring together the entire German people (*Volk*), understood as a racial group, into a single nation. The new Germany would include all the Germanic parts of the old Habsburg Empire, including Austria. This virile nation would need more space to live (*Lebensraum*), which would be taken from the Slavs, a lesser race. The new Germany would be purified by the removal of the Jews, the most inferior race in Nazi theory. The plan required the conquest of Poland and the Ukraine as the primary areas for the settlement of Germans and for the provision of badly needed food. However, neither *Mein Kampf* nor later statements of policy were blueprints for action. Hitler was a brilliant improviser who exploited opportunities as they arose. But he never lost sight of his goal, which would almost certainly require a major war (see Document, "Hitler Describes His Goals").

Lebensraum Meaning "living space," the Nazi plan to colonize and exploit Eastern Europe.

DESTRUCTION OF VERSAILLES

When Hitler came to power, Germany was weak. The first problem was to shake off the fetters of Versailles and make Germany a formidable military power. In October 1933, Germany withdrew from an international disarmament conference and from the League of Nations. These acts were merely symbolic, but in March 1935, Hitler renounced the disarmament provisions of the Versailles Treaty with the formation of a German air force. Soon he reinstated conscription, which aimed at an army of half a million men.

DOCUMENT

Hitler Describes His Goals

From his early career, Hitler had certain long-term general views and goals. They were set forth in Mein Kampf, which appeared in 1925, and included consolidation of the German Volk ("people"), provision of more land for the Germans, and contempt for such "races" as Slavs and Jews. Here are some of Hitler's views.

- **What** is the basic principle on which Hitler's policy is founded? How does he justify his plans for expansion? What reasons does he give for hostility to France and Russia? What is the basis for Hitler's claim of a right of every man to own farmland? Was that a practical goal for Germany in the 1930s? Was there any way for Hitler to achieve his goals without a major war?

The National Socialist movement must strive to eliminate the disproportion between our population and our area—viewing this latter as a source of food as well as a basis for power politics—between our historical past and the hopelessness of our present impotence. ...

The demand for restoration of the frontiers of 1914 is a political absurdity of such proportions and consequences as to make it seem a crime. Quite aside from the fact that the Reich's frontiers in 1914 were anything but logical. For in reality they were neither complete in the sense of embracing the people of German nationality, nor sensible with regard to geomilitary expediency. ...

As opposed to this, we National Socialists must hold unflinchingly to our aim in foreign policy, namely, to

His path was made easier because the League of Nations was ineffective. In September 1931, Japan occupied Manchuria. China appealed to the league, which condemned the Japanese for resorting to force. But the powers would not impose sanctions. Japan withdrew from the league and kept Manchuria.

The league formally condemned Hitler's decision to rearm Germany, but it took no steps to prevent it. France and Britain felt unable to object because they had not carried out their own promises to disarm. Instead, they met with Mussolini (1883–1945) in June 1935 to form the so-called Stresa Front and agreed to maintain the status quo in Europe by force if necessary. But Britain was desperate to maintain superiority at sea. Britain soon made a separate naval agreement with Hitler, allowing him to rebuild the German fleet to 35 percent of the British navy.

QUICK REVIEW

Discrediting the League of Nations

- Germany withdrew from league to pursue rearmament
- Japan withdrew from league to keep Manchuria
- League sanctions against Italy for invading Ethiopia were ineffective

ITALY ATTACKS ETHIOPIA

Using a border incident as an excuse, Mussolini attacked Ethiopia in October 1935. Mussolini's real intent was to avenge a humiliating defeat that the Italians had suffered in 1896 and perhaps to divert Italians from Fascist corruption and Italy's economic troubles.

The international response underscored the impotence of the League of Nations and the timidity of the Allies. The League of Nations voted economic sanctions and imposed an arms embargo. But Britain and France were afraid of alienating Mussolini, so they refused to place an embargo on oil, the one economic sanction that could have prevented Italian victory. Nor did the British prevent the movement of Italian troops and munitions through the Suez Canal. This wavering policy was disastrous. The League of Nations and collective security were discredited, and Mussolini turned to Germany. By November 1, 1936, he could speak publicly of a Rome-Berlin "Axis."

REMILITARIZATION OF THE RHINELAND

The Ethiopian invasion influenced Hitler's evaluation of the strength and determination of the Western powers. On March 7, 1936, Hitler took his greatest risk yet, sending a small armed force into the demilitarized Rhineland. This was a breach of the Versailles Treaty and of the Locarno Agreements. It also removed an important secure for the German people the land and soil to which they are entitled on this earth. ...

... The soil on which some day German generations of peasants can beget powerful sons will sanction the investment of the sons of today, and will some day acquit the responsible statesmen of blood-guilt and sacrifice of the people, even if they are persecuted by their contemporaries. ...

Much as all of us today recognize the necessity of a reckoning with France, it would remain ineffectual in the long run if it represented the whole of our aim in foreign policy. It can and will achieve meaning only if it offers the rear cover for an enlargement of our people's living space in Europe. ...

If we speak of soil in Europe today, we can primarily have in mind only Russia and her vassal border states. ...

... See to it that the strength of our nation is founded, not on colonies, but on the soil of our European homeland. Never regard the Reich as secure unless for centuries to come it can give every scion of our people his own parcel of soil. Never forget that the most sacred right on this earth is a man's right to have earth to till with his own hands, and the most sacred sacrifice the blood that a man sheds for this earth.

Source: Excerpts from Adolf Hitler, *Mein Kampf*, trans. by Ralph Manheim. Published by Pimlico. Copyright © 1943, renewed 1971 by Houghton Mifflin Company. Reprinted by permission of Houghton Mifflin Company, the Estate of Ralph Manheim, and Random House UK Limited. All rights reserved.

element of French security. Yet Britain and France, both weakened by growing pacifism, made only feeble protests.

A Germany that was rapidly rearming and had a defensible western frontier presented a new problem to the Western powers. Their response was the policy of **appeasement**. It was based on the assumption that Germany had real grievances, that Hitler's goals were limited, and that the wise thing to do was to make concessions before a crisis could lead to war. Behind this approach was the horror of another war. As Germany armed, the French huddled behind their defensive wall, the Maginot Line, and the British hoped for the best.

appeasement The Anglo-French policy of making concessions to Germany in the 1930s to avoid a crisis that would lead to war. It assumed that Germany had real grievances and Hitler's aims were limited and ultimately acceptable.

THE SPANISH CIVIL WAR

The new European alignment that found the Western democracies on one side and the Fascist states on the other was made clearer by the Spanish Civil War, which broke out in July 1936. In 1931, the Spaniards had established a republic. Elections in February 1936 brought to power a government of the left. The defeated groups, especially the Falangists (Spanish Fascists), would not accept defeat at the polls. In July, General Francisco Franco (1892–1975) led an army against the republic.

Thus began a civil war that lasted almost three years, killed hundreds of thousands, and provided a training ground for World War II. Germany and Italy aided Franco with troops and supplies. The Soviet Union sent equipment and advisers

Pablo Picasso, *Guernica*, 1937. The Spanish Civil War divided Europe, with Fascist Italy and Nazi Germany assisting Franco and Soviet Russia aiding the republic. Before its end in 1939, the war in Spain took some 500,000 lives. On April 26, 1937, planes from the German Condor Legion bombed the Basque town of Guernica, killing a thousand men, women, and children and destroying about 70 percent of the buildings. It was the most effective aerial bombardment of a city up to that time, and its purpose was simply to create terror.

Pablo Picasso , "Guernica" 1937, Oil on canvas. 11'5 1/2 x 25'5 3/4. Museo Nacional Centro de Arte Reina Sofía/© 2007 Estate of Pablo Picasso/Artists Rights Society (ARS), New York.

Why is the Spanish Civil War sometimes described as a rehearsal for World War II?

Axis The alliance between Nazi Germany and fascist Italy. Also called the Pact of Steel.

Anschluss Meaning "union." The annexation of Austria by Germany in March 1938.

QUICK REVIEW

The Occupation of the Sudetenland

♦ May 1938: Czechs mobilize their army in response to rumors of German invasion

♦ September 1938: Neville Chamberlain forces Czechs to separate the Sudetenland from Czechoslovakia

♦ September 29, 1938: Sudetenland is given to Germany at Munich conference

Agreement at Munich. On September 29–30, 1938, Hitler met with the leaders of Britain and France at Munich to decide the fate of Czechoslovakia. The Allied leaders abandoned the small democratic nation in a vain attempt to appease Hitler and avoid war. Hitler sits in the center of the picture. To his right is British Prime Minister Neville Chamberlain.

What is appeasement?

to the Republicans. Liberals and leftists from Europe and America volunteered to fight in the Republican ranks against fascism.

The civil war, fought on blatantly ideological lines, profoundly affected world politics. It brought Germany and Italy closer together, leading to the Rome-Berlin **Axis** Pact. The Axis powers were joined in the same year by Japan in the Anti-Comintern Pact, ostensibly against communism but really a new and powerful diplomatic alliance. In western Europe and the United States, the appeasement mentality reigned. By early 1939 the Fascists effectively controlled Spain.

AUSTRIA AND CZECHOSLOVAKIA

Hitler made good use of his new friendship with Mussolini. In 1934 Mussolini, not yet allied with Hitler, had frustrated a Nazi coup in Austria by threatening military intervention. In 1938 the new diplomatic situation encouraged Hitler to try again. Mussolini made no objection, and Hitler marched into Vienna to the cheers of his Austrian sympathizers.

The *Anschluss*, or union of Germany and Austria, had great strategic significance. Czechoslovakia was now surrounded by Germany on three sides. It was allied both to France and the Soviet Union but contained about 3.5 million ethnic Germans who lived in the Sudetenland, a portion of Czechoslovakia near the German border. Supported by Hitler, they agitated for privileges and autonomy within the Czech state. The Czechs made concessions, but Hitler's true intent was to destroy Czechoslovakia (see Map 31–1).

The French deferred to British leadership. The British prime minister Neville Chamberlain (1869–1940) was determined not to allow Britain to go to war again. In September 1938, German intervention seemed imminent. Chamberlain sought to appease Hitler by compelling the Czechs to grant the Sudetenland separate status. But Hitler then increased his demands and insisted on immediate German military occupation of the Sudetenland.

MUNICH

France and Britain prepared for war. At the last moment, Mussolini proposed a conference of Germany, Italy, France, and Britain. The group met on September 29 at Munich. Hitler received almost everything he had demanded. The Sudetenland became part of Germany, thus depriving the Czechs of any chance of self-defense. In return, the rest of Czechoslovakia was spared. Hitler promised, "I have no more territorial demands to make in Europe." Chamberlain told a cheering crowd, "I believe it is peace for our time."

Even in the short run, the appeasement of Hitler at Munich was a failure. Soon Poland and Hungary also tore bits of territory from Czechoslovakia, and the Slovaks

demanded autonomy. Finally, on March 15, 1939, Hitler broke his promise and occupied Prague, putting an end to Czech independence and to illusions that his only goal was to restore Germans to the Reich. Munich remains an example of short-sighted policy that helped bring on a war in disadvantageous circumstances as a result of the very fear of war and the failure to prepare for it.

MAP EXPLORATION

To explore this map further go to **http://www.prenhall.com/craig_maps**

MAP 31–1   Partitions of Czechoslovakia and Poland, 1938–1939.   The immediate background of World War II is found in the complex international drama unfolding on Germany's eastern frontier in 1938 and 1939. Germany's expansion inevitably meant the victimization of Austria, Czechoslovakia, and Poland. With the failure of the Western powers' appeasement policy and the signing of a German-Soviet pact, the stage for the war was set.

How did the failure of appeasement lead to war?

Hitler's occupation of Prague discredited appeasement in Britain. Poland was the next target of German expansion. In the spring of 1939, the Germans put pressure on Poland to restore the formerly German city of Danzig and allow a railroad and a highway through the Polish corridor to connect East Prussia with the rest of Germany. When the Poles would not yield, the pressure mounted. On March 31, Chamberlain announced a Franco-British guarantee of Polish independence. Hitler did not take the guarantee seriously. He knew that both countries were unprepared for war and that much of their populations opposed war for Poland.

Belief in the Polish guarantee was further undermined by the inability of France and Britain to get effective help to the Poles. The only way to defend Poland was to bring Russia into the alliance against Hitler, but a Russian alliance posed problems. Each side was suspicious of the other. The French and British were hostile to communism, and since Stalin's (1879–1953) purge of the officer corps of the Red Army, they questioned Russia's military abilities. Besides, both Poland and Romania were suspicious of Russian intentions—with good reason. As a result, Western negotiations with Russia were slow and cautious.

THE NAZI-SOVIET PACT

The Russians resented being left out of the Munich agreement and were annoyed by the low priority that the West seemed to give to negotiations with Russia. They rightly feared that the Western powers meant for them to bear the burden of the war against Germany. As a result, they opened negotiations with Hitler, and on August 23, 1939, the world was shocked to learn of a Nazi-Soviet nonaggression pact. Its secret provisions divided Poland between them and allowed Russia to annex the Baltic states and take Bessarabia from Romania. Communist parties in the West changed their line overnight from advocating resistance to Hitler to a policy of peace and quiet.

The Nazi-Soviet Pact sealed the fate of Poland. On September 1, 1939, the Germans invaded Poland. Two days later, Britain and France declared war on Germany. World War II had begun.

WORLD WAR II (1939–1945)

WHY WAS 1942 the turning point in World War II?

World War II was truly global. Fighting took place in Europe and Asia, the Atlantic and the Pacific Oceans, the Northern and Southern Hemispheres. The demand for the fullest exploitation of material and human resources for increased production, the use of blockades, and the intensive bombing of civilian targets made the war of 1939 even more "total"—that is, comprehensive and intense—than that of 1914.

CHRONOLOGY

EVENTS LEADING TO WORLD WAR II

1919	June	Versailles Treaty
1923	January	France occupies the Ruhr
1925	October	Locarno Agreements
1931	Spring	Onset of Great Depression in Europe
1933	January	Hitler comes to power
	October	Germany withdraws from League of Nations
1935	March	Hitler renounces disarmament, starts an air force, and begins conscription
	October	Mussolini attacks Ethiopia
1936	March	Germany reoccupies and remilitarizes the Rhineland
	July	Outbreak of Spanish Civil War
	October	Formation of the Rome-Berlin Axis
1938	March	Anschluss with Austria
	September	Munich Conference and partition of Czechoslovakia
1939	March	Hitler occupies Prague; France and Great Britain guarantee Polish independence
	August	Nazi-Soviet pact
	September 1	Germany invades Poland
	September 3	Britain and France declare war on Germany

GERMAN CONQUEST OF EUROPE

The speed of the German victory over Poland astonished everyone, and the Russians hastened to collect their share of the booty before Hitler could deprive them of it. On September 17, Russia invaded Poland from the east, dividing the country with the Germans. The Russians then absorbed Estonia, Latvia, and Lithuania. In November 1940, the Russians invaded Finland, but the Finns fought back and retained their independence.

Meanwhile, the western front was quiet. The French remained behind the Maginot Line. Britain imposed the traditional naval blockade. Cynics in the west called it the phony war, but in April 1940, the Germans invaded Denmark and Norway. A month later, a combined land and air attack struck the Low Countries. The Dutch surrendered in a few days, and the Belgians less than two weeks later. British and French armies in Belgium were forced to flee to the English Channel to seek escape from the beaches of Dunkirk. More than 200,000 British and 100,000 French soldiers were saved, but valuable equipment was abandoned.

The Maginot Line ran from Switzerland to the Belgian frontier. Hitler's swift advance through Belgium therefore circumvented France's main line of defense. The French army, poorly led, collapsed. Mussolini attacked France on June 10, though without success. Less than a week later, the French government, under the ancient hero of Verdun, Henri Philippe Pétain (1856–1951), asked for an armistice.

The terms of the armistice, signed on June 22, 1940, allowed the Germans to occupy more than half of France, including the Atlantic and English Channel coasts. To prevent the French from fleeing to North Africa to continue the fight, Hitler left southern France unoccupied. Pétain set up a dictatorial regime at the resort city of Vichy and collaborated with the Germans to preserve as much autonomy as possible. The French were too stunned to resist. Many thought that Hitler's victory was certain and saw no alternative to collaboration. A few, notably General Charles de Gaulle (1890–1969), fled to Britain and organized the French National Committee of Liberation, or "Free French." As expectations of a quick German victory faded, French resistance arose.

BATTLE OF BRITAIN

Hitler expected to make a deal with the British. He was prepared to allow Britain to retain its empire in return for a free hand for Germany in Europe. If there was ever a chance that the British would consider such terms, it disappeared when Winston Churchill (1874–1965) replaced Chamberlain as prime minister in May 1940.

One of Churchill's greatest achievements was establishing a close relationship with the American president Franklin D. Roosevelt (1882–1945). In 1940 and 1941, before the United States was at war, America sent military supplies, traded destroyers for leases on British naval bases, and even convoyed ships across the Atlantic to help the British survive. As Britain remained defiant, Hitler was forced to contemplate an invasion, which required control of the air. The German air force (**Luftwaffe**) destroyed much of London, and about 15,000 people were killed. But theories of victory through airpower alone proved vain; casualties were much less than expected, and the bombings made the British people more resolute. Moreover, the Royal Air Force (RAF), aided by the newly developed technology of radar, inflicted heavy losses on the *Luftwaffe*. Hitler lost the Battle of Britain in the air and was forced to abandon his plans for invasion.

GERMAN ATTACK ON RUSSIA

Operation Barbarossa, the code name for the invasion of Russia, was aimed at knocking Russia out of the war before winter could set in. Success depended in part on an early start, but here Hitler's Italian alliance proved costly. Mussolini had launched an attack against the British in Egypt and also invaded Greece. But in North Africa the British counterattacked and drove into Libya, and the Greeks repulsed the Italians. In March 1941, the British sent help to the Greeks, and Hitler was forced to divert his attention to the Balkans and to Africa. General Erwin Rommel (1891–1944) soon drove the British back into Egypt. In the Balkans, the German

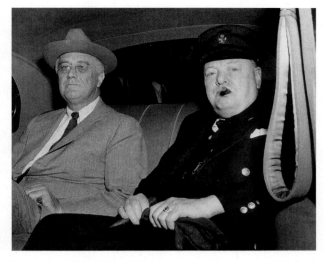

Roosevelt and Churchill. The close cooperation between Prime Minister Winston Churchill of Britain and President Franklin Roosevelt of the United States helped to assure the effective alliance of their two countries in World War II.

How were the ties of friendship between Britain and the United States critical to the success of the Allies?

Luftwaffe The German air force in World War II.

Battle of Britain. A rubble-strewn street in London after the city had experienced a night of German bombing. Despite many casualties and widespread devastation, the German bombing of London did not break British morale or prevent the city from functioning.

What did Hitler hope to accomplish by the aerial bombing of Britain?

army occupied Yugoslavia and crushed Greek resistance, but the price was a delay of six weeks for Barbarossa (see Map 31–2). This proved to be costly the following winter.

Operation Barbarossa was launched against Russia on June 22, 1941, and it almost succeeded. Stalin panicked. By November, the German army stood at the gates of Leningrad, on the outskirts of Moscow, and on the Don River. Of the 4.5 million troops with which the Russians had begun the fighting, they had lost 2.5 million; of their 15,000 tanks, only 700 were left.

A German victory seemed imminent, but Hitler at that point diverted significant forces to the south. By the time he decided to march on Moscow, winter was setting in.

MAP 31–2 **Axis Europe, 1941.** On the eve of the German invasion of the Soviet Union, the Germany-Italy Axis bestrode most of western Europe by annexation, occupation, or alliance—from Norway and Finland in the north to Greece in the south and from Poland to France. Britain, the Soviets, a number of insurgent groups, and, finally, the United States had before them the long struggle of conquering this Axis "fortress Europe."

What were the strengths and weaknesses of Germany's territorial position in 1941?

The German army lacked appropriate equipment, and Stalin had reorganized, fortified the city, and brought in troops from Siberia. In November and December, the Russians counterattacked. Hitler's *blitzkrieg* ("war by lightning strokes") turned into a war of attrition.

HITLER'S EUROPE

The demands of war and Hitler's defeat prevented him from fully carrying out his plans, so no one can be sure precisely what he intended. But the measures he took before his death suggest a regime unmatched in history for planned terror and inhumanity. Hitler regarded the conquered lands merely as a source of plunder and slave labor. He stripped them of entire industries and their peoples of basic necessities. He intended ultimately to displace their inhabitants and appropriate their lands to provide *Lebensraum* for Germans. Regions such as Scandinavia and the Low Countries, inhabited by people Hitler considered racially akin to the Germans, were to be absorbed into Germany.

RACISM AND THE HOLOCAUST

The most horrible aspect of the Nazi rule in Europe arose from the inhumanity inherent in Hitler's racial doctrines. He considered the Slavs *Untermenschen*, subhuman creatures like beasts who need not be treated as people. In Poland the upper and professional classes were either jailed, deported, or killed. Schools and churches were closed; marriage was controlled to keep down the Polish birthrate; and harsh living conditions were imposed. In Russia things were even worse. Hitler spoke of his Russian campaign as a war of extermination. Heinrich Himmler (1900–1945), head of Hitler's elite SS guard, formed extermination squads to eliminate 30 million Slavs to make room for the Germans. Some 6 million Russian prisoners of war and deported civilian workers may have died under Nazi rule.

Hitler had special plans for the Jews. He meant to make all Europe *Judenrein* ("free of Jews"). For a time he thought of sending them to Madagascar but later decided on the "final solution of the Jewish problem": extermination. The Nazis built

blitzkrieg Meaning "lightning war." The German tactic early in World War II of employing fast-moving, massed armored columns supported by airpower to overwhelm the enemy.

QUICK REVIEW

Operation Barbarossa

◆ June 22, 1941: Surprise invasion of Soviet Union by Germany (Operation Barbarossa) launched

◆ Germany advanced rapidly in the early stages of the campaign

◆ German failure to deliver a decisive blow delayed victory until winter set in, turning the tide in Soviet favor

Roundup of Warsaw Jews. World War II resulted in the near-total destruction of the Jews of Europe, victims of the Holocaust spawned by Hitler's racial theories of the superiority and inferiority of particular ethnic groups. Hitler placed special emphasis on the need to exterminate the Jews, to whom he attributed particular wickedness. This picture shows a roundup of Jews in Warsaw, where there was a large Jewish population, ultimately on their way to concentration or death camps.

How did the Holocaust fundamentally transform European society?

Holocaust The Nazi extermination of millions of European Jews between 1940 and 1945. Nazis called it the "final solution to the Jewish problem."

extermination camps in Germany and Poland and used the latest technology to kill millions of men, women, and children just because they were Jews. Before the war was over, 6 million Jews had died in what has come to be called the **Holocaust**. Only about a million remained alive, mostly in pitiable condition (see Map 31–3).

THE ROAD TO PEARL HARBOR AND AMERICA'S ENTRY INTO THE WAR

The war took on truly global proportions in December 1941. The Japanese were already at war with China, and between the outbreak of that war in 1937 and the opening of the World War II campaign in the Pacific, there were three critical junctures. The first was Japan's January 1938 invasion of China to overthrow the Chinese Nationalist Party government in Nanjing. The Japanese army occupied most of the cities and railroads of eastern China, killing more than 300,000 people and brutally raping 7,000 women. Chinese Nationalist leader Jiang Jieshi (Chiang Kai-shek) refused to surrender, however, and a stalemate ensued until the end of the global conflict in 1945.

The second critical decision was the Tripartite Pact that Japan signed with Germany and Italy in September 1940. Germany's European victories in late spring 1940 seemed a prelude to German victory, and Japan hoped that the pact would help it achieve three objectives: to isolate the United States (which was demanding that Japan withdraw from China); to take over the Southeast Asian colonies of Britain, France, and the Netherlands; and to improve its relations with the Soviet Union through Germany's help. This last objective was reached when Japan signed a neutrality pact with the Soviet Union in April 1941. Japan remained neutral when Germany attacked the Soviet Union and ceased at that point to work with the Axis powers. But its association with them hardened America's demands that it leave China.

The third and fateful decision was to go to war with the United States. In June 1941, following Germany's defeat of France, Japanese troops had occupied northern French Indochina. The United States retaliated by limiting strategic exports to Japan. In July 1941 Japanese troops took southern Indochina, and the United States embargoed all exports to Japan, cutting Japanese oil imports by 90 percent. The Japanese navy urged seizure of the oil-rich Dutch East Indies, but this was dangerous as long as the United States held the Philippines. Japan's navy, therefore, planned a preemptive strike against the United States.

MAP 31–3   The Holocaust. The Nazi policy of ethnic cleansing—targeting Jews, Gypsies, political dissidents, and "social deviants"—began with imprisoning them in concentration camps, but by 1943 the *Endlösung*, or Final Solution, called for the systematic extermination of "undesirables."

Which countries were most severely affected by the Holocaust?

Pearl Harbor. The successful Japanese attack on the American base at Pearl Harbor in Hawaii on December 7, 1941, together with simultaneous attacks on other Pacific bases, brought the United States into war against the Axis powers. For Japan, it was the opening phase of a campaign to capture European and American colonies in Southeast Asia.

How was Japan's attack on Pearl Harbor the beginning of its ultimate demise?

On Sunday morning, December 7, 1941, even while Japanese representatives were discussing a settlement in Washington, Japan launched an air attack on Pearl Harbor, Hawaii, the chief American naval base in the Pacific. The next day, the United States and Britain declared war on Japan. Three days later, Germany and Italy declared war on the United States.

THE TIDE TURNS

The potential power of the United States was enormous, but America was ill prepared for war. Although conscription had been introduced in 1940, the army was tiny, inexperienced, and poorly supplied. American industry was not ready for war. The Japanese swiftly captured Guam, Wake Island, and the Philippines (see Map 31–4). They also attacked Hong Kong, Malaya, Burma, and Indonesia. By the summer of 1942, the Japanese Empire stretched from the western Aleutian Islands south almost to Australia, and from Burma east to the Gilbert Islands in the mid-Pacific.

In the same year, the Germans almost reached the Caspian Sea in their drive for Russia's oil fields. In Africa, Rommel drove the British back toward the Suez Canal and was finally stopped at El Alamein, only seventy miles from Alexandria. Relations between the democracies and their Soviet ally were not close; German submarines were threatening British supplies; the Allies were being thrown back on every front, and the future looked bleak.

The tide turned at the Battle of Midway in June 1942. A month earlier, both sides had suffered massive losses in the Battle of the Coral Sea, but greater U.S. ship production made such trade-offs unprofitable for Japan. At Midway, American planes destroyed four Japanese aircraft carriers. Soon American Marines landed on Guadalcanal in the Solomon Islands and began to reverse the momentum of the war. The war in the Pacific was far from over, but Japan was checked sufficiently to allow the Allies to concentrate their efforts first in the West.

In November 1942, an Allied force landed in French North Africa. Already, the British Field Marshal Bernard Montgomery (1887–1976), after stopping Rommel at

MAP 31–4   **The War in the Pacific.**   As in Europe, the Allies initially had trouble recapturing areas that had been seized quickly early in the war, in this case by the Japanese. The map shows the initial expansion of the Japanese and the long struggle of the Allies to push them back to their homeland and defeat them.

What was the American strategy for defeating Japan in World War II?

El Alamein, had begun a drive to the west. The American General Dwight D. Eisenhower (1890–1969) had pushed eastward through Morocco and Algeria. The German army was trapped in Tunisia and crushed. The Mediterranean was now under Allied control, and southern Europe was exposed. In July and August 1943 the Allies took Sicily. Mussolini was driven from power, the Allies landed in Italy, and Marshal Pietro Badoglio (1871–1956), the leader of the new Italian government, declared war on Germany. Churchill had spoken of Italy as the "soft underbelly" of the Axis, but German resistance was tough and determined. Still, the need to defend Italy strained the Germans' energy and resources and left them vulnerable on other fronts.

The Russian campaign became especially demanding. In the summer of 1942 the Germans resumed the offensive on all fronts. In the south, their goal was the oil fields near the Caspian Sea, and they got as far as Stalingrad on the Volga, a key point for protecting the flank of their southern army. Hitler was determined to take the city and Stalin to hold it. The Battle of Stalingrad raged for months with unexampled ferocity.

Stalingrad. Russian soldiers, in their heroic defense of Stalingrad, dug trenches from building to building in the city. The German defeat at Stalingrad in February 1943 marked the turning point of the Russian campaign. Thereafter the Russians advanced inexorably westward.

Why was Hitler committed to victory at Stalingrad?

The Russians lost more men than the Americans lost in combat during the entire war, but their heroic defenses prevailed. Because Hitler again overruled his generals and would not allow a retreat, an entire German army was lost. Stalingrad marked the turning point of the Russian campaign. Thereafter, as the German military and material resources dwindled, the Russians advanced westward inexorably.

In 1943 the Allies also gained ground in production and logistics. The industrial might of the United States neared full force. New technology and tactics made great strides in eliminating the submarine menace. The American and British air forces began a series of massive bombardments of Germany by night and day. This bombing did not have much effect on the war until 1944. Then the Americans introduced long-range fighters that could protect the bombers and allow accurate missions by day. By 1945 the Allies could bomb at will.

DEFEAT OF NAZI GERMANY

On June 6, 1944 (D-day), in one of greatest amphibious assaults ever attempted, Allied troops landed in force on the coast of Normandy (see Map 31–5). By the beginning of September France had been liberated.

All went smoothly until December, when the Germans launched a counterattack called the Battle of the Bulge through the Forest of Ardennes. It was their last gasp. The Allies recovered the momentum and pushed eastward. They crossed the Rhine in March 1945, and German resistance crumbled. This time there could be no doubt that the Germans had lost the war on the battlefield.

In the east, the Russians were within reach of Berlin by March 1945. Because the Allies insisted on unconditional surrender, the Germans fought on until May. Hitler

MAP 31–5 **Defeat of the Axis in Europe, 1942–1945.** Here we see some major steps in the progress toward Allied victory against Axis Europe. From the south through Italy, the west through France, and the east through Russia, the Allies gradually conquered the continent to bring the war in Europe to a close.

Why was it important for the Allies to force the Germans to fight on more than one front?

committed suicide in an underground hideaway in Berlin on May 1, 1945. The Russians occupied Berlin by agreement with their Western allies. The Third Reich had lasted a dozen years instead of the millennium predicted by Hitler.

FALL OF THE JAPANESE EMPIRE

The war in Europe ended on May 8, 1945, and by then victory over Japan was in sight (see also Chapter 28). The original Japanese attack on the United States had been a calculated risk against the odds. The longer the war lasted, the greater the impact of American superiority in industrial production and human resources. Beginning in 1943 American forces began a campaign of "island hopping," selecting major bases and places strategically located along the enemy supply line. Starting from the Solomons, they moved northeast toward the Japanese homeland. American bombers launched a terrible wave of bombings that destroyed Japanese industry and disabled the Japanese navy. But still the Japanese government, dominated by a military clique, refused to surrender.

D-Day. Allied troops landed in Normandy on D-day, June 6, 1944. This photograph, taken two days later, shows long lines of men and equipment moving inland from the beach to reinforce the troops leading the invasion.

The Allied invasion of Normandy was the greatest amphibian assault in history. Does this photo capture the scale and size of the invasion?

Confronted with Japan's determination, the Americans made plans for a frontal assault on the Japanese homeland. They calculated it would cost unacceptable American casualties and even greater losses for the Japanese. At this point, science and technology presented the Americans with another choice. Since early in the war a secret program had been in progress. Its staff was working to use atomic energy for military purposes.

On August 6, 1945, an American plane dropped an atomic bomb on the city of Hiroshima. More than 70,000 of its 200,000 residents were killed. Two days later the Soviet Union declared war on Japan and invaded Manchuria. The next day a second atomic bomb fell, this time on Nagasaki. Even then the Japanese were prepared to face

an invasion rather than give up. It was only the unprecedented intervention of Emperor Hirohito (r. 1926–1989) that forced the government to surrender on August 14. Even then, the Cabinet made the condition that Japan could keep its emperor. President Harry Truman (1884–1972), who had come to office on April 12, 1945, on the death of Franklin D. Roosevelt, accepted the condition. Peace was formally signed on September 2, 1945.

THE COST OF WAR

World War II was the most terrible war in history. Military deaths are estimated at 15 million, and at least as many civilians were killed. If deaths linked indirectly to the war are included, as many as 40 million may have died. Most of Europe and significant parts of Asia were devastated. Yet the end of so terrible a war brought little opportunity for relaxation. The dawn of the Atomic Age that brought a dramatic end to the war made people conscious that another major war might destroy humanity. Everything depended on the conclusion of a stable peace, but even as the fighting ended, the victors began to quarrel.

Hiroshima. This photo, taken a few days after an atomic bomb was dropped, poignantly captures the total devastation wreaked on the city.

Why did the United States use nuclear weapons against Japan?

THE DOMESTIC FRONTS

HOW DID war affect civilians in Germany, France, Britain, the United States, and the Soviet Union?

World War II represented an effort of total war by all the belligerents. Never before in world history had so many men and women and so many resources been devoted to military effort. One result was the carnage that occurred on the battlefields and at sea. Another was an unprecedented organization of civilians on the various home fronts. Each domestic effort and experience was different, but almost no one escaped the impact of the conflict. Shortages, propaganda campaigns, and new political developments were ubiquitous.

GERMANY: FROM APPARENT VICTORY TO DEFEAT

Hitler had expected to defeat all his enemies by rapid strokes, or *blitzkrieg*. Such campaigns would scarcely have affected Germany's society and economy. During the first two years of the war, Hitler demanded few important sacrifices from the German people. Spending on domestic projects continued, and food was plentiful; the economy was not on a full wartime footing. The failure to knock out the Soviet Union changed everything. Because food could no longer be imported from the east, Germany had to mobilize for total war, and the government demanded major sacrifices.

A great expansion of the army and military production began in 1942. As minister for armaments and munitions, Albert Speer (1905–1981) guided the economy, and Germany met its military needs instead of making consumer goods. Major German business enterprises aided the growth of wartime production. Between 1942 and late 1944 the output of military products tripled, but as the war went on the army absorbed more men from industry, hurting the production of even military goods.

Beginning in 1942 everyday products became scarce. Prices and wages were controlled, but the standard of living of German workers fell. Burdensome food rationing began in April 1942, and shortages were severe until the Nazi government seized food from occupied Europe. To preserve their own home front, the Nazis passed on the suffering to their defeated neighbors.

By 1943 there were serious labor shortages. The Nazis required German teenagers and retired workers to work in the factories, and increasing numbers of women joined them. To achieve total mobilization the Germans closed retail businesses, raised the maximum age of women eligible for compulsory service, shifted non-German domestic workers to wartime industry, moved artists and entertainers into military service, closed theaters, and reduced such basic public services as mail and railways. Finally, the Nazis forced thousands of people from conquered lands to labor in Germany.

Hitler assigned women a special place in the war effort. The celebration of motherhood continued, with an emphasis on women who were the mothers of important military figures. Films portrayed ordinary women who became especially brave and patriotic during the war and remained faithful to their husbands who were at the front. The government portrayed other wartime activities as the natural fulfillment of women's maternal roles. As air raid wardens they protected their families; as factory workers in munitions plants they aided their sons on the front lines. Women working on farms were providing for their soldier sons and husbands; as housewives they were helping to win the war by conserving food and managing their households frugally. Finally, by their faithful chastity, German women were protecting racial purity. German women thus demonstrated the kind of service and courage required by the war.

There was an intensification of political propaganda beyond what occurred in other countries. Hitler and other Nazis believed that weak domestic support had led to Germany's defeat in World War I, and they were determined that this would not happen again. Nazi propaganda blamed the outbreak of the war on the British and its prolongation on the policies of Germany's opponents. It also stressed the might of Germany and the inferiority of its foes. Propaganda Minister Josef Goebbels (1897–1945) used radio and films to boost the Nazi cause. Movies of the collapse of Poland, Belgium, Holland, and France demonstrated German military might. Later in the war the ministry broadcast exaggerated claims of Nazi victories. As the German armies were checked on the battlefield, propaganda became a substitute for victory. To stiffen German resolve, the propaganda also aimed to frighten the German population about the consequences of defeat.

After May 1943, when the Allies began their major bombing offensive over Germany, the German people had much to fear. One German city after another endured heavy bombing, fires, and destruction. But the bombing did not undermine German morale—on the contrary, it may have confirmed the general fear of defeat at the hands of such savage opponents and increased German resistance.

World War II brought increased power to the Nazi Party. Every area of the economy and society came under its direct influence or control. The Nazis were determined that they, rather than the traditionally honored German officer corps, would profit from the new authority flowing to the central government because of the war effort. Throughout the war years there was virtually no serious opposition to Hitler or his ministers. In 1944 a small group of army officers made an attempt to assassinate Hitler, but the effort failed, and it had no significant popular support.

Youth Rally. Members of the Nazi German Women's Youth Movement perform calisthenics.

What roles did the Nazis encourage for women?

The war brought great changes to Germany, but what transformed the country afterward was the experience of defeat accompanied by vast physical destruction, invasion, and occupation. Hitler and the Nazis had brought the nation to such a complete and disastrous end that only a new kind of state with new political structures could emerge.

FRANCE: DEFEAT, COLLABORATION, AND RESISTANCE

In France the Vichy government cooperated closely with the Germans for a variety of reasons. Some of the collaborators believed that the Germans were sure to win and wanted to be on the victorious side. A few sympathized with the ideas and plans of the Nazis. Many conservatives regarded the French defeat as a judgment on what they saw as the corrupt, secularized, liberal Third Republic. But most of the French were not active collaborators and remained demoralized by defeat.

Many conservatives and extreme rightists saw the Vichy government as a device to reshape the French national character and halt the decadence they associated with political and religious liberalism. The Roman Catholic clergy, who had lost power and influence under the Third Republic, gained status under Vichy. The church supported Pétain; his government supported religious education. Vichy adopted the church's views of the importance of family and spiritual values. Divorce was made difficult, and large families were rewarded.

The Vichy regime embraced an intense, chauvinistic nationalism. It encouraged the long-standing prejudice against foreigners working in France and persecuted those who were not regarded as genuinely and thoroughly French. The chief victims were French Jews. Anti-Semitism was not new in France. Even before Germany undertook Hitler's "final solution" in 1942, the French had begun to remove Jews from

Bombing of Cologne. The Allied campaign of aerial bombardment did terrible damage to German cities. This photograph shows the devastation it delivered to the city of Cologne on the Rhine.

What was the overall effect of Allied aerial bombing?

government, education, and publishing. In 1941 the Germans began to intern Jews living in occupied France; soon they carried out killings and imposed large fines collectively on the Jews of the occupied zone. In the spring of 1942 the Germans began deporting Jews, ultimately over 60,000, to the extermination camps of eastern Europe. The Vichy government had no part in these decisions, but it made no protest, and its own anti-Semitic policies facilitated the process.

A few Frenchmen had fled to join de Gaulle's Free French forces soon after the defeat of 1940. Serious internal resistance to the German occupiers and to the Vichy government, however, developed only late in 1942. The Germans attempted to force young people in occupied France to work in German factories; some of them fled and joined the Resistance, but the total number of resisters was small. Many were deterred by fear. Some disliked the violence that resistance inevitably entailed. As long as it appeared that the Germans would win the war, moreover, resistance seemed imprudent and futile. In all, less than 5 percent of the adult French population appear to have been involved.

By early 1944 the tide of battle had shifted. An Allied victory appeared inevitable, and the Vichy government was clearly doomed. Only then did an active Resistance assert itself. From Algiers on August 9, 1944, the Committee of National Liberation declared the authority of Vichy illegitimate. Soon French soldiers joined in the liberation of Paris and established a government for Free France. On October 21, 1945, France voted to adopt a new constitution as the basis of the Fourth Republic. Bitter quarrels over who had done what during the occupation and the Vichy period divided the French for decades to come.

GREAT BRITAIN: ORGANIZATION FOR VICTORY

On May 22, 1940, the British Parliament gave the government emergency powers. The government could now institute compulsory military service, food rationing, and various controls over the economy. Churchill and the British war cabinet quickly mobilized the nation. By the end of 1941 British production had surpassed Germany's. To meet the heavy demands on the labor force, factory hours were extended, and women were brought into the workforce in great numbers. Unemployment disappeared, and the working classes had more money to spend than they had enjoyed for many years. To avoid inflation, savings were encouraged, and taxes were raised to absorb excess purchasing power.

The bombing "blitz" conducted by the German *Luftwaffe* against British targets in the winter and spring of 1940 to 1941 was the most immediate and dramatic experience of the war for the British people. The German air raids killed thousands and destroyed the homes of many more. Many families removed their children to the countryside. Gas masks were issued to thousands of city dwellers, who were frequently compelled to take shelter from the bombs in the London subways. After the spring of 1941 Hitler needed most of his air force for the Russian front, but the bombing of Britain continued. In England as in Germany, however, bombing did not break the people's spirit but seems to have made them more determined.

During the worst months of the "blitz" the remarkable speeches of Winston Churchill cheered and encouraged the British people. He united them with a sense of common suffering and purpose. They were called on to make many sacrifices: Transportation facilities were strained, food and clothing for civilians were in short supply, and the government adopted strict rationing to achieve a fair distribution. Every scrap of land was farmed, increasing the productive portion by almost 4 million acres. Gasoline was in short supply, so private vehicles almost disappeared.

The British established their own propaganda machine. The British Broadcasting Company (BBC) sent programs to every country in Europe in the local language to encourage resistance against the Nazis. At home the government used the radio to unify the nation. Soldiers at the front heard the same programs as their families at home.

For most of the population the standard of living actually improved over the course of the war, as did the general health of the nation. These gains should not be exaggerated, but many connected them with the active involvement of the government in the economy and the lives of the citizens. This wartime experience may have contributed to the Labour Party's victory in 1945; many feared that a return to Conservative rule would bring a return to the economic misery of the 1930s.

THE UNITED STATES: WOMEN AND AFRICAN AMERICANS IN THE WAR EFFORT

In the United States, the induction of millions of men into the armed forces created a demand for new workers, especially in the burgeoning defense industries. It was filled in part by women, some of them taking jobs in defense plants doing work usually done only by men. Economic pressures caused by the Great Depression of the 1930s had already brought many more women into the workforce than had been common before. Most came from poor families and worked in white-collar jobs to support themselves or to help their families eke out a living. Even so, the heavy burden of housework and the widespread hostility to the idea of women working outside the home kept the vast majority of women at home.

America's entry into the war changed things quickly. The need for vast amounts of equipment to wage the war called for and attracted new groups to seek work in the many enlarged and newly created factories. African Americans from the South came to northern and western cities to seek well-paying jobs, and women, too, came forward in greater numbers than ever before. Prejudices of various kinds had kept them from many opportunities, but in October 1942, President Roosevelt made the new situation clear: "In some communities employers dislike to hire women. In others they are reluctant to hire Negroes. We can no longer afford to indulge such prejudice."

Rosie the Riveter. Norman Rockwell's famous image of Rosie the Riveter that appeared on the cover of the May 29, 1943, edition of the *Saturday Evening Post* was based on real people, such as these two women working in a munitions plant.

Why did women and African Americans gain access to jobs from which they previously would have been discouraged?

Many women already working moved over to jobs in the defense industries; others entered the workforce for the first time, lured less by wages than by patriotism. Their brothers and boyfriends were risking their lives for their country and its ideals of freedom and democracy. They were eager to do their part to support them, to be, in the words of a current song, the woman "behind the man behind the gun." Another popular song, "Rosie the Riveter," told of a young woman working in an aircraft factory to provide protection for her boyfriend in the Marines. Rosie came to be one of the best-known symbols of the war effort when she appeared on the cover of the *Saturday Evening Post*.

THE SOVIET UNION: "THE GREAT PATRIOTIC WAR"

No nation suffered greater loss of life or more extensive physical destruction during World War II than the Soviet Union. Perhaps as many as 16 million people were killed, and vast numbers of Soviet troops were taken prisoner. Hundreds of cities and towns and well over half the industrial and transportation facilities of the country were devastated. The Germans sent thousands of Soviet prisoners to work as forced labor in factories in Germany. The Germans also confiscated grain supplies and drew mineral resources and oil from the Soviet Union to serve their own war effort.

Stalin (1879–1953) conducted the war as virtual chief of the armed forces, and the State Committee for Defense provided strong central coordination. In the decade before the war, Stalin had already made the Soviet Union a highly centralized nation; he had attempted to manage the entire economy centrally through the five-year plans, the collectivization of agriculture, and the purges. The country was thus on what amounted to a wartime footing long before the conflict erupted. When the war began, millions of citizens entered the army, but the army did not grow in influence at the expense of the state and the Communist Party—that is, Stalin.

Soviet propaganda differed from that of other nations. Because the Soviet government distrusted the loyalty of its citizens, it confiscated radios to prevent the people from listening to German propaganda. In major cities the government erected large loudspeakers to broadcast to the people in place of radios. Soviet propaganda emphasized Russian patriotism, not Marxist class conflict. The struggle was called "The Great Patriotic War." As in other countries, writers and playwrights helped sustain public support for the war. Sometimes they drew on communist themes, but they also portrayed the common Soviet citizen as contributing to a patriotic struggle.

Great Russian novels of the past reappeared; more than half a million copies of Tolstoy's *War and Peace* were published during the siege of Leningrad. Other authors wrote straightforward propaganda fostering hatred of the Germans. The great filmmaker Sergei Eisenstein (1898–1948) produced a vast epic entitled *Ivan the Terrible*, which glorified one of the most brutal tsars of Russia's past. Musicians, such as Dimitri Shostakovich (1906–1975), wrote scores that sought to contribute to the struggle and evoke heroic emotions. The most important of these was Shostakovich's Seventh Symphony, also known as the "Leningrad Symphony."

Stalin even made peace with the Russian Orthodox Church. He pursued friendly relations with church leaders and allowed them to enter the Kremlin. Stalin hoped that this new policy would give him more support at home and permit the Soviet Union to be viewed more favorably in those parts of eastern Europe where the Orthodox Church predominated.

Within occupied portions of the western Soviet Union, an active resistance movement arose against the Germans. The swiftness of the German invasion had stranded thousands of Soviet troops, some of whom escaped and carried on irregular resistance warfare behind enemy lines. Stalin supported partisan forces in lands held by the enemy for two reasons: He wanted to cause as much difficulty as possible for the Germans; and the Soviet-sponsored resistance reminded the peasants in the conquered regions that the Soviet government, with its policies of collectivization, had not disappeared. Stalin feared that the peasants' hatred of the communist government might lead them to collaborate with the invaders. When the Soviet army moved westward toward the end of the war, it incorporated the partisans into the regular army.

Home Front. Russian women apply grease to howitzer shells at a munitions plant during World War II.

How was the entire Russian society mobilized for war during World War II?

As the Soviet armies reclaimed the occupied areas and then moved across eastern and central Europe, the Soviet Union established itself as a world power second only to the United States. Stalin had been a reluctant belligerent, but he emerged a major victor. In that respect, the war and the extraordinary patriotic effort and sacrifice it generated consolidated the power of Stalin and the party more effectively than had the political and social policies of the previous decade.

OVERVIEW Allied Summits during World War II

Allied leaders met repeatedly during the war in various configurations and to various ends. Suspicion between the leaders of Britain and the United States and the Soviet leader, Stalin was a recurring theme; antipathy was kept in check for the duration of the war but reemerged quickly and set the stage for the Cold War.

August 1941	Atlantic Charter	Roosevelt and Churchill agree on principles for peace.
January 1942	Military alliance	The Soviet Union, Britain, and the United States agree only to fight together; all political decisions are postponed.
October 1943	Foreign ministers meeting	Foreign ministers of the Soviet Union, Britain, and the United States (the "Big Three") meet in Moscow, agreeing to fight until unconditional surrender of enemy and to cooperate later in a united-nations organization.
November–December 1943	Tehran Conference	Stalin, Churchill, and Roosevelt planned attacks on Germany—the U.S.S.R. from the east, Britain and the United States from the west (not the south).
February 1945	Yalta Conference	Stalin, Churchill, and Roosevelt continued to agree on the importance of founding a united-nations organization; Stalin won concessions in Asia, where Roosevelt was hoping to avoid heavy U.S. casualties.
July 1945	Potsdam Conference	Stalin, Churchill (and his successor Attlee), and Truman alter Poland's borders and create occupation zones in defeated Germany; Truman learns of the successful experimental explosion of an atomic device like the ones dropped on Japan weeks later to end the war.

PREPARATIONS FOR PEACE

WHY DID the cooperation between the Soviet Union and the Western powers break down in 1945?

The split between the Soviet Union and its wartime allies that followed the war should cause no surprise. As the self-proclaimed center of world communism, the Soviet Union was openly dedicated to the overthrow of the capitalist nations, although this message was muted when the occasion demanded. The Western allies were equally open about their hostility to communism and its chief purveyor, the Soviet Union.

Although cooperation against a common enemy and strenuous propaganda efforts in the West helped improve Western feeling toward the Soviet ally, Stalin remained suspicious and critical of the Western war effort. Likewise, Churchill never ceased planning to contain the Soviet advance into Europe. For some time Roosevelt seems to have hoped that the Allies could continue to work together after the war, but even he was losing faith by 1945. Differences in historical development and ideology, as well as traditional conflicts over political power and influence, soon dashed hopes of a mutually satisfactory peace settlement and continued cooperation.

THE ATLANTIC CHARTER

In August 1941, even before America entered the war, Roosevelt and Churchill had agreed to the Atlantic Charter. A broad set of principles in the spirit of Wilson's Fourteen Points, it provided a theoretical basis for the peace they sought. When Russia and the United States joined Britain in the war, the three powers entered a purely military alliance in January 1942, leaving all political questions aside. The first political conference was the meeting of foreign ministers in Moscow in October 1943. The ministers reaffirmed earlier agreements to fight on until the enemy surrendered unconditionally and to continue cooperating after the war in a united-nations organization.

TEHRAN

The first meeting of the three leaders took place at Tehran, the capital of Iran, in 1943. Western promises to open a second front in France the next summer (1944) and Stalin's agreement to join in the war against Japan (when Germany was defeated) created an atmosphere of goodwill in which to discuss a postwar settlement. Stalin wanted to retain what he had gained in his pact with Hitler and to dismember Germany. Roosevelt and Churchill made no firm commitments.

The most important decision was for the Western Allies to attack Germany from Europe's west coast instead of from southern Europe by way of the Mediterranean. This decision meant, in retrospect, that Soviet forces would occupy eastern Europe and control its destiny. At Tehran in 1943 the Western Allies did not foresee this clearly, for the Russians were still fighting deep within their own frontiers, and military considerations were paramount everywhere.

By 1944 the situation was different. In August, Soviet armies were in sight of Warsaw, which had risen in expectation of liberation. But the Russians turned south into the Balkans, allowing the Polish rebels to be annihilated. The Russians gained control of Romania and Hungary, gaining advances of which centuries of expansionist tsars had only dreamed. Alarmed by these developments, Churchill went to Moscow and met with Stalin in October. They agreed to share power in the Balkans on the basis of Soviet predominance in Romania and Bulgaria, Western predominance in Greece, and equality of influence in Yugoslavia and Hungary. These agreements were not enforceable without American approval, and the Americans were known to be hostile to such un-Wilsonian devices as "spheres of influence."

The three powers easily agreed on Germany's disarmament and denazification and on its division into four zones of occupation by France and the Big Three (the USSR, Britain, and the United States). Churchill, however, began to balk at Stalin's plan to dismember Germany and objected to his demand for reparations in the amount of $20 billion as well as for forced labor from all the zones, with Russia to get half of everything. These matters were left to fester and cause dissension in the future.

The settlement of eastern Europe remained a problem. Everyone agreed that the Soviet Union deserved neighboring governments that were friendly, but the West insisted that they also be independent, autonomous, and democratic. The Western leaders, and especially Churchill, were not eager to see eastern Europe fall under Russian domination. Roosevelt in particular was truly committed to democracy and self-determination. However, Stalin knew that independent, freely elected governments in Poland and Romania might not be friendly to Russia. He had already established a subservient government in Poland at Lublin in competition with the Polish government in exile in London. Under pressure from the Western leaders, Stalin agreed to reorganize the government and to include some Poles friendly to the West. He also signed a Declaration on Liberated Europe, promising self-determination and free democratic elections. Stalin feared that the Allies might still make an arrangement with Germany and betray him. Yet he appeared eager to avoid conflict before the war with Germany was over, and he probably thought it worth endorsing some meaningless principles as the price of continued harmony. In any case, he wasted little time violating these agreements.

YALTA

The next meeting of the Big Three was at Yalta in the Crimea in February 1945. The Western armies had not yet crossed the Rhine, and the Soviet army was within a hundred miles of Berlin. The war with Japan continued, and no atomic explosion had yet taken place. Roosevelt, faced with an invasion of Japan and prospective heavy losses, was eager to bring the Russians into the Pacific war as soon as possible.

As a true Wilsonian, Roosevelt also suspected Churchill's determination to maintain the British Empire and Britain's colonial advantages. The Americans thought that Churchill's plan to set up British spheres of influence in Europe would encourage the Russians to do the same and lead to friction and war. To encourage Russian participation in the war against Japan, Roosevelt and Churchill made extensive concessions to Russia in Asia. Again in the tradition of Wilson, Roosevelt stressed a united nations organization. Soviet participation in this venture seemed well worth concessions elsewhere.

POTSDAM

The Big Three met for the last time in the Berlin suburb of Potsdam in July 1945. Much had changed by then. Germany was defeated, and news of the successful experimental explosion of an atomic weapon reached the American president during the meetings. The cast of characters was also different: President Truman replaced Roosevelt; Clement Attlee (1883–1967), leader of the Labour Party, replaced Churchill during the conference. Previous agreements were reaffirmed, but progress on undecided questions was slow.

Russia's western frontier was moved far into what had been Poland and included part of German East Prussia. In compensation, Poland was allowed "temporary administration" over the rest of East Prussia and Germany east of the Oder-Neisse river line, a condition that became permanent. In effect, Poland was moved about a hundred miles west, at the expense of Germany, to accommodate the Soviet Union. The Allies agreed that Germany would be divided into occupation zones until the final peace treaty was signed. The country remained divided until the end of the Cold War more than forty years later.

A Council of Foreign Ministers was established to draft peace treaties for Germany's allies. Growing disagreements made the job difficult, and it was not until February 1947 that Italy, Romania, Hungary, Bulgaria, and Finland signed treaties. The Russians signed their own agreements with the Japanese in 1956.

Big Three at Potsdam. This photograph shows the "Big Three" at Potsdam. By the summer of 1945 only Stalin remained of the original leaders of the major Allies. Roosevelt and Churchill had been replaced by Harry Truman and Clement Attlee.

What agreements did the Allied leaders reach at the end of the war?

SUMMARY

WHAT WERE the main events between 1933 and 1939 that led to World War II?

Again the Road to War (1933–1939). The second great war of the twentieth century (1939–1945) grew out of the unsatisfactory resolution of the first. But whatever the flaws of the treaties of Paris, the world suffered an even more terrible war than the first as a result of failures of judgment and will on the part of the victorious democratic powers. Italy attacked Ethiopia in 1935. Italy, Germany, and the Soviet Union intervened in the Spanish Civil War (1936–1939). Japan attacked China in 1937. Aggressive forces were on the march around the globe, and the defenders of the world order lacked the will to stop them. Britain and France refused to face the threat posed by the Axis powers until the most deadly war in history was required to put it down. *page 776*

WHY WAS 1942 the turning point in World War II?

World War II (1939–1945). The formation of the Axis among Germany, Italy, and Japan guaranteed that a second war would be fought around the world with fighting and suffering in Asia, Africa, the islands of the Pacific, and Europe. Hitler's demented racial theories combined with preexisting anti-Semitism to create the concentration camps where millions of Jews and other "undesirables" were killed. In 1942, the United States won the Battle of Midway, Allied forces controlled North Africa, and the Russians went on the offensive. The use of atomic weapons brought the struggle to a close. *page 782*

HOW DID war affect civilians in Germany, France, Britain, the United States, and the Soviet Union?

The Domestic Fronts. All the belligerents strove for total war. Economic mobilization and propaganda campaigns were noteworthy features of involvement on the home front. Other experiences varied: Hitler restructured German society, but these changes largely disappeared with the Reich; France was largely passive, until the Resistance became a significant force near the end of the conflict; the British government was more involved in citizens' lives than ever; the United States relied on the labor of women, African Americans, and others who previously had been discouraged from seeking high-paying jobs; and the Soviet Union united around Russian nationalism. *page 792*

WHY DID cooperation between the Soviet Union and the Western powers break down in 1945?

Preparations for Peace. A series of conferences and meetings among the victors brought the war to a close without a formal peace treaty in Europe. The world quickly split into two unfriendly camps, led by the United States and the Soviet Union, as the ideological opposition between communism and capitalism reemerged. *page 798*

INTERPRETING THE PAST

Totalitarian States and Total War

Sources from MyHistoryLab for Chapter 31

myhistorylab

1) Kita Ikki, *Outline for the Reconstruction of Japan*
2) Franklin Delano Roosevelt, *The Four Freedoms*
3) Nadezhda Mandelstam, from *Hope Against Hope: A Memoir*

Text Source from Chapter 31

1) *Hitler Describes His Goals* (pages 778–779)

Visual Sources from MyHistoryLab

1) *The Warsaw Ghetto*
2) *German Civilian Refugees in Europe*

Militarism and nationalism, along with the authoritarian ideologies that grew popular in the 1920s and 1930s, were significant contributing factors to the start of World War II. Economic crises and the high debts and repayments required of Western nations allowed leaders who offered simplistic and forceful answers to gain power. Hitler in Germany, Mussolini in Italy, Franco in

REVIEW QUESTIONS

1. What was the relationship between World War I and World War II? Why was the isolationism of the United States after World War I such an important factor in the advent of World War II?

2. Why was World War II truly a global war?

3. What were Hitler's foreign policy aims? Was he bent on conquest in the East and dominance in the West, or did he simply want to return Germany to its 1914 boundaries?

4. What was Hitler's "final solution" to the "Jewish problem"? Why did Hitler want to eliminate Slavs as well?

5. Why did Britain and France adopt a policy of appeasement in the 1930s? What were its main features? Did the appeasers buy the West valuable time to prepare for war by their actions at Munich in 1938?

6. How was Hitler able to defeat France so easily in 1940? Why was the air war against Britain a failure? Why did Hitler invade Russia? Why did the invasion ultimately fail? Could it have succeeded?

7. Why did Japan attack the United States at Pearl Harbor? What was the significance of American intervention in the war?

8. Why did the United States drop atomic bombs on Japan? Did President Truman make the right decision when he ordered the bombs used?

9. What impact did World War II have on the civilian population of Europe? How did experiences on the domestic front of Great Britain differ from those of Germany and France? What impact did "The Great Patriotic War" have on the people of the Soviet Union? Did participation in World War II solidify Stalin's hold on power?

10. Some historians have looked at the twentieth century and have seen a period of great destruction as well as of great progress. Can the twentieth century be described as a "century of Holocaust"? Discuss.

KEY TERMS

Anschluss (AHN-shloos) (p. 780)

appeasement (p. 779)

Axis (p. 780)

blitzkrieg (BLIHTZ-kreeg) (p. 785)

Holocaust (p. 786)

Lebensraum (LAY-behnz-ROWM) (p. 777)

Luftwaffe (LOOFT-vah-fah) (p. 783)

Note: To learn more about the topics in this chapter, please turn to the Suggested Readings at the end of the book.

Spain, as well as the military-dominated government in Japan advocated aggressive military action, extreme social regimentation, and the demonization of specific ethnic and racial groups to restore their countries to a mythical age of virtuous unity.

In this exercise you will read four primary sources from the early twentieth century—two propounding extreme nationalism, one describing its effects, and one response from a Western democratic leader—and examine two images that focus on authoritarian nationalism.

The first document is written by Kita Ikki, who outlines the policies of the militaristic nationalists responsible for Japan's entry in World War II and its invasion of China in the 1930s. The second source is a speech given by U.S. president Franklin Roosevelt almost a year before Japan attacked American forces at Pearl Harbor. The president defines American policy as diametrically opposed to the authoritarian dictatorships of Germany and Japan. The third document offers graphic evidence of the impact of Russian dictator Josef Stalin's authoritarian methods on the behavior of the country's citizens. The final document is an excerpt from Adolf Hitler's book *Mein Kampf*, which describes the principles upon which the Nazi Party would later rule Germany.

The two accompanying visual sources illustrate the impact on civilians of the policies of the militaristic ultranationalists in Europe during World War II.

Questions

What are Kita Ikki's primary goals in reorganizing Japan? How would you characterize the rights of individuals versus the rights of the state in Ikki's view?

How do the programs and policies advocated by Ikki differ from those proposed by Adolf Hitler? How are they similar? Are there any similarities between Ikki's and Mussolini's beliefs about war?

What is the basic principle of Hitler's vision of his party's role in German political life?

What are Roosevelt's "four freedoms"? How do the national polices he announces differ from those that Hitler and Ikki promote?

How did the authoritarian policies of the Russian state affect those who were arrested? How did the state create the "terror" and fear throughout society?

32
The West Since World War II

The **"Beautiful Game" by Way of Europe.** In the twentieth century the sport of soccer became the most popular game in the world. The World Cup, which takes place every four years, is a truly global event. The 2006 Cup attracted over 28 billion television viewers—the most-watched event in history. Here Florent Malouda from France is taken down by two Italian players in the final in Berlin on July 10, 2006. Like several other players from the French squad, Malouda was an emigré. Indeed, the captain of the French team, Zinedine Zidane, who was ejected in a controversial call late in the game, has been quoted as saying, "First I am an Algerian from Marseille, and then a Frenchman." Italy went on to the win the match 5–3 in penalty kicks.

Why has immigration changed European society?

THE COLD WAR ERA *page 805*

WHAT WERE the causes of the Cold War?

EUROPEAN SOCIETY IN THE SECOND HALF OF
THE TWENTIETH CENTURY AND BEYOND *page 811*

WHAT MAJOR trends have marked European
society since World War II?

AMERICAN DOMESTIC SCENE SINCE WORLD WAR II *page 817*

WHAT ARE the main themes that have characterized
postwar America?

THE SOVIET UNION TO 1989 *page 820*

HOW DID leaders after Stalin attempt to reform
Soviet government?

1989: YEAR OF REVOLUTIONS IN EASTERN EUROPE *page 823*

WHY DID communist regimes collapse so easily in Eastern
Europe in 1989?

THE COLLAPSE OF THE SOVIET UNION *page 824*

WHO WERE the leaders in the period surrounding the
collapse of the Soviet Union?

THE COLLAPSE OF YUGOSLAVIA AND CIVIL WAR *page 827*

HOW DID the West respond to the collapse
of Yugoslavia?

CHALLENGES TO THE ATLANTIC ALLIANCE *page 828*

IS NATO still a viable alliance in the post-Cold War era?

GLOBAL PERSPECTIVE

THE WEST SINCE 1945

The history of the West since the end of World War II has been full of paradoxes. Europe, which gave birth to Western civilization and remained its center from the eighteenth century until the war, declined in world influence. During the four decades immediately after the war, the United States and the Soviet Union rose to predominance and replaced Western Europe as the major powers on the world scene. Consequently, while the traditional center of Western influence exerted little power, both new great Western powers came to exert more political and military power than any other previous nation of continental Europe. But they did so in conflict with each other.

Immediately after 1945 the nations of the West entered the Cold War. That ideological, economic, and military rivalry between the United States and the Soviet Union dominated political struggles throughout the world for roughly half a century. It divided Europe between NATO and Warsaw Pact military forces and forced nations outside of Europe, in Asia, Africa, and Latin America, to side with one or the other of the superpowers. Hence the Cold War too became a world war that had an important impact on non-Western nations. At times these other nations became theaters of conflict in which indigenous civil wars melded into the struggle between the United States and the Soviet

Union, as in the case of Cuba, Angola, Korea, and Vietnam. A neutral stance in this conflict became extremely difficult for any nation to sustain.

In the later 1980s, however, the Cold War unexpectedly ended as the Soviet Union and the nations of Eastern Europe, their economies exhausted from failed experiments in central planning and repression, experienced enormous internal political changes and began the difficult transition to democracy and capitalism. These changes have clearly opened a new epoch of Western history. The United States has emerged from the Cold War as the single remaining superpower. Western Europe has achieved a new level of economic and political unity under the auspices of the European Union (EU), although its peoples and governments are hesitant to press the process too far too rapidly. The economic success of the European Union has inspired other regional global treaties to promote free markets, including NAFTA (North Atlantic Free Trade Association), as well as the global WTO (World Trade Organization). Europe has also been more ambitious than the United States in promoting international organizations such as the World Court designed to discipline countries that oppress their neighbors or threaten world peace. Eastern Europe and the former Soviet Union are experiencing economic turmoil and

Cold War The ideological and geographical struggle between the United States and its allies, and the USSR and its allies that began after World War II and lasted until the dissolution of the USSR in 1989.

ince the conclusion of World War II, Europe's influence on the world has been transformed. The destruction of the war itself left Europe incapable of exercising the kind of power it had formerly exerted. The **Cold War** between the United States and the Soviet Union made Europe a divided and contested territory. Furthermore, Europeans soon began to lose control of their overseas empires.

The decision by the United States to take an activist role in world affairs touched every aspect of the postwar world. American domestic politics and foreign policy became intertwined as in no previous period of American history.

Like virtually every other part of the world, Europe experienced the impact of American culture through military alliances, trade, tourism, and popular entertainment. Europeans also began to build structures for greater economic cooperation.

While Western Europe enjoyed increased democratization and unprecedented prosperity, Eastern Europe experienced economic stagnation and Soviet domination. Yet from the late 1970s onward, there were political stirrings in the East. These culminated in 1989 with revolutions throughout Eastern Europe and in 1991 with the collapse of Communist government in the Soviet Union itself. Since then, Europeans have sought new political direction. The movement toward unification, particularly economic, continues in Western Europe. Political confusion and economic stagnation afflict some of the nations that emerged from the Soviet Union, and the attacks of September 11, 2001, on the United States led to events that have challenged the post–World War II Western alliance. ■

political uncertainty. Although some Eastern European countries such as Poland, the Czech Republic, and Hungary are better prepared than others to join the European Union, the shared aspiration of all Eastern European nations to become EU members bodes well for the future of this region. Except for Latvia, Estonia, and Lithuania, newly independent former regions of the Soviet Union such as Ukraine, Georgia, and Belarus have an even more difficult path ahead of them in developing their economies and societies. Together with the Islamic countries, such as Uzbekistan, Turkmenistan, and Kazakhstan, these countries face added difficulties from the legacy of repressive authoritarian government and centrally planned economies. The security of Europe's eastern borders will depend on the success of these Eastern European nations and former Soviet republics in making the transition to democracy.

Another important factor in the history of both the United States and Europe since World War II has been the rising immigration from the rest of the world. Germany has seen the influx of significant numbers of *gastarbeiters* (guest workers) from Turkey, while France, Italy, and Spain receive more immigrants from North Africa and the Middle East, many from their former colonies. The United States, with its long history as an immigrant nation, has been more comfortable dealing with the influx of non-European immigrants, but struggles persist over language, cultural identity, and assimilation. Europe, less accustomed to non-European immigration, has found it even more difficult to accommodate immigrants whose religions, languages, and appearance differ from those of Europeans.

Focus Questions

◆ What was the Cold War, and why can we rightly call it a world war?

◆ How has the relationship between the United States and Europe changed since World War II? How might it develop in the future?

◆ What immediate and long-term factors accounted for the collapse of the Soviet Union?

◆ How has immigration changed the face of Europe since 1945?

THE COLD WAR ERA

INITIAL CAUSES

WHAT WERE the causes of the Cold War?

The tense relationship between the United States and the Soviet Union that dominated world history during the second half of the twentieth century originated in the closing months of World War II.

The split arose from basic differences of ideology and interest. The Soviet Union's attempt to extend its control westward into Europe and southward into the Middle East was a continuation of the policy of tsarist Russia. It had been Britain's traditional role to restrain Russian expansion into these areas; the United States inherited that task as Britain's power waned. The alternative was to permit a major increase in power by a huge, traditionally hostile state. That state, dedicated in its official ideology to the overthrow of nations like the United States, was governed by Stalin (1879–1953), an absolute dictator with a proven record of horrible cruelties.

The United States made no attempt to roll back Soviet power where it already existed, even though American military forces were the greatest in its history, American industrial power was unmatched, and America had a monopoly on atomic weapons. In less than a year from the war's end, the United States reduced its forces in Europe from 3.5 million to half a million. The speedy withdrawal was in accord with America's peacetime goals, which included support for self-determination, autonomy, and democracy in the political sphere; and free trade, freedom of the seas, no barriers to

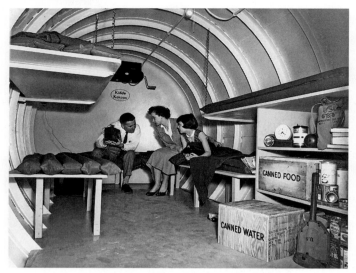

H-Bomb Shelter. In 1950 Albert Einstein wrote that "Radioactive poisoning of the atmosphere and hence annihilation of any life on earth has been brought within the range of technical possibilities. . . . In the end, there beckons more and more clearly general annihilation." The U.S. government, however, fostered belief in manageable atomic warfare in spite of the evidence from Japan, and backyard bomb shelters were a 1950s fad. This one could house a small family for up to five days. Standard features included canned food and water, sterno stove, battery-powered radio, chemical toilet, flashlight, blankets, and first-aid kit. During peacetime, the shelter could be used as a spare bedroom, for storage space, or even to cultivate mushrooms.

Why does this family appear to be at ease even though it is sitting inside a bomb shelter?

Marshall Plan The U.S. program, named after Secretary of State George C. Marshall, that provided economic aid to Europe after World War II.

investment, and an open-door policy in the economic sphere. As the strongest, richest nation in the world, the United States would benefit from an international order based on such goals.

American hostility to colonial empires created tensions with France and Britain, but these stresses were minor. The main conflict was with the Soviet Union. From the Soviet perspective, extending the borders of the USSR and dominating the formerly independent states of Eastern Europe would provide needed security and would compensate the Soviet people for the fearful losses they had endured in the war. American objections over Poland and other states could be seen as attempts to undermine regimes friendly to Russia and to encircle the Soviet Union with hostile neighbors.

The growth in France and Italy of communist parties taking orders from Moscow led the Americans to believe that Stalin was engaged in a great worldwide plot to subvert capitalism and democracy. In the absence of reliable evidence about Stalin's intentions, it is impossible to know whether these suspicions were justified, but most people in the West considered them plausible.

AREAS OF EARLY COLD WAR CONFLICT

Signs of hostility among the former allies appeared quickly. In February 1946, both Stalin and his foreign minister, Vyacheslav Molotov (1890–1986), publicly spoke of the Western democracies as enemies. A month later, Churchill (1874–1965) delivered a speech in Fulton, Missouri, in which he spoke of an Iron Curtain dividing a free and democratic West from an East under totalitarian rule. In this atmosphere, difficulties grew.

The attempt to deal cooperatively with the problem of atomic energy was an early victim of the Cold War. The United States continued to develop its own atomic weapons in secrecy, and the Russians did the same. By 1949, the Soviet Union had exploded its own atomic bomb, and the race for nuclear weapons was on.

The resistance of Westerners to what they perceived as Soviet intransigence and Communist subversion took clearer form in 1947. Since 1944, civil war had been raging in Greece between the royalist government restored by Britain and insurgents supported by the Communist countries. In 1947, Britain informed the United States that it was financially no longer able to support the Greeks. On March 12, President Truman (1884–1972) asked Congress to provide funds to support Greece and Turkey, which was also under Soviet pressure. Congress complied. In what became known as the Truman Doctrine, the American president advocated a policy of supporting "free people who are resisting attempted subjugation by armed minorities or by outside pressures," by implication anywhere in the world.

American aid to Greece and Turkey took the form of military equipment and advisers. For Western Europe, where the menacing growth of Communist parties was fueled by postwar poverty and hunger, the Americans devised the European Recovery Program. Named the **Marshall Plan** after George C. Marshall (1880–1959), the secretary of state who introduced it, this program provided broad economic aid to European states only on condition that they work together. The Soviet Union forbade its satellites to take part. The Marshall Plan helped restore prosperity to Western Europe, setting the stage for its unprecedented economic growth, and led to the establishment of solid democratic regimes in Western Europe.

From the Western viewpoint, this policy of "containment" was a new and successful response to the Soviet and communist challenge. Stalin may have considered it a renewal of the old Western attempt to isolate and encircle the USSR. Stalin's answer was to replace all multiparty governments behind the Iron Curtain with thoroughly Communist regimes under his control. In 1947, he organized the Communist Information Bureau (Cominform), dedicated to spreading revolutionary communism throughout the world. In February 1948 a brutal display of Stalin's new policy took place in Prague. The Communists expelled the democratic members of what had been a coalition government, murdered the foreign minister, and forced the president to resign. Czechoslovakia was brought fully under Soviet rule.

These Soviet actions increased America's determination to make its own arrangements in Germany. The Russians dismantled German industry in the eastern zone, but the Americans tried to make Germany self-sufficient, which meant restoring its industrial capacity. To the Soviets the restoration of a powerful industrial Germany was unacceptable.

Disagreement over Germany produced the most heated postwar debate. When the Western powers agreed to go forward with a separate constitution for the western sectors of Germany in February 1948, the Soviets walked out of the joint Allied Control Commission. Berlin, although well within the Soviet zone, was governed by all four powers. The Soviets sealed off the city by closing all railroads and highways to West Germany. Their purpose was to drive the Western powers out of Berlin. The Western allies responded to the Berlin Blockade with an airlift of supplies that lasted almost a year. In May 1949, the Russians were forced to reopen access to Berlin. The incident greatly increased tensions and suspicions between the two powers and hastened the separation of Germany into two states, which prevailed for forty years. West Germany became the German Federal Republic in September 1949, and the eastern region became the German Democratic Republic a month later.

Berlin Airlift.   The Allied airlift in action during the Berlin Blockade. Every day for almost a year Western planes supplied the city until Stalin lifted the blockade in May 1949.

Why was the lifting of the Berlin blockade a major victory for the West?

NATO AND THE WARSAW PACT

Meanwhile, the nations of Western Europe were coming closer together. The Marshall Plan encouraged international cooperation. In April 1949, Belgium, Britain, Denmark, France, Iceland, Italy, Luxembourg, the Netherlands, Norway, and Portugal signed a treaty with Canada and the United States that formed the North Atlantic Treaty Organization (NATO) for mutual assistance in case of attack. NATO formed the West into a bloc. A few years later Greece, Turkey, and West Germany joined the alliance (see Map 32–1).

The states of Eastern Europe were under direct Soviet domination through local Communist parties controlled from Moscow and overawed by the Red Army. The Warsaw Pact of May 1955, which included Albania, Bulgaria, Czechoslovakia, East Germany, Hungary, Poland, Romania, and the Soviet Union, merely gave formal recognition to the existing system: Europe stood divided into two unfriendly blocs.

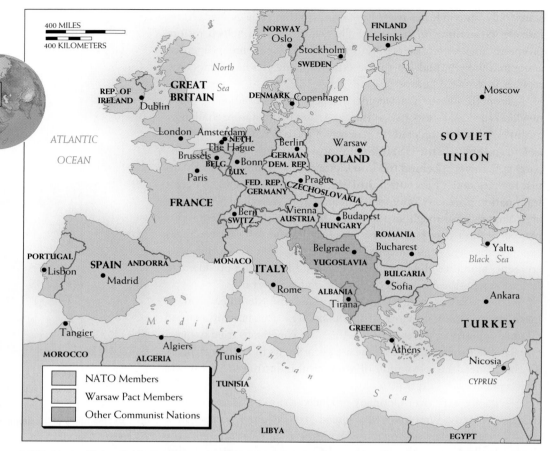

MAP 32–1   Major Cold War European Alliance Systems.   The North Atlantic Treaty Organization, which includes both Canada and the United States, stretches as far east as Turkey. By contrast, the Warsaw Pact nations were the contiguous communist states of Eastern Europe with the Soviet Union, of course, as the dominant member.

Why did NATO and the Warsaw Pact emerge and become rivals after World War II?

Stalin died in 1953; later that year an armistice was concluded in Korea (see Chapter 33). Both events produced hope that international tensions might lessen, but the rivalry of power and polemics soon resumed.

CRISES OF 1956

The events of 1956 had considerable significance both for the Cold War and for what they implied about the realities of European power in the postwar era.

In July 1956, President Gamal Abdel Nasser (1918–1970) of Egypt nationalized the Suez Canal. Britain and France feared that this action would imperil their supplies of oil in the Persian Gulf. In October 1956, war broke out between Egypt and Israel. The British and French intervened. The United States, however, refused to support them, and the Soviet Union protested vehemently. The Anglo-French forces had to be withdrawn, and control of the canal remained with Egypt. The Suez intervention proved that without the support of the United States, the nations of Western Europe could no longer impose their will on the rest of the world.

Developments in Eastern Europe demonstrated similar limitations on independent action among the Soviet bloc nations. When the prime minister of Poland died, the Polish Communist Party refused to ratify the successor selected by Moscow. Considerable tension developed. In the end, Wladyslaw Gomulka (1905–1982) emerged as the new communist leader of Poland. He proved acceptable to the Soviets because he promised to keep Poland in the Warsaw Pact. However, he halted the collectivization of Polish agriculture and improved relations with the Polish Roman Catholic Church.

Hungary provided the second trouble spot for the Soviet Union. In late October, fighting erupted in Budapest. A new ministry headed by Imre Nagy (1896–1958) was installed. Nagy was a Communist who sought an independent position for Hungary. Unlike Gomulka, he called for Hungarian withdrawal from the Warsaw Pact, a position unacceptable to the Soviet Union. Soviet troops deposed Nagy, who was later executed, and imposed Janos Kadar (1912–1989) as premier.

THE COLD WAR INTENSIFIED

The events of 1956 ended the era of fully autonomous action by the European nation-states. The two superpowers had demonstrated the new political realities. After 1956 the Soviet Union began to talk about "peaceful coexistence" with the United States. In 1959 tensions relaxed sufficiently for Soviet Premier Nikita Khrushchev (1894–1971) to tour the United States. A summit meeting was scheduled for May 1960 in Paris, and American President Dwight D. Eisenhower (1890–1969) was to go to Moscow.

Just before the gathering, however, the Soviet Union shot down an American U-2 aircraft that was flying reconnaissance over Soviet territory. Khrushchev refused to take part in the summit conference, and Eisenhower's trip was canceled. In fact, the Soviets had long been aware of the American flights. They chose to protest at this time for two reasons. Khrushchev had hoped that the leaders of Britain, France, and the United States would be so divided over the future of Germany that a united Allied

Soviet Invasion of Czechoslovakia. In the summer of 1968 Soviet tanks rolled into Czechoslovakia, ending that country's experiment in liberalized communism, known as the Prague spring. This picture shows defiant, flag-waving Czechs passing a Soviet tank in the immediate aftermath of the invasion.

When did the Czechs regain their freedom?

CHRONOLOGY

MAJOR DATES IN THE ERA OF THE COLD WAR

1948		Berlin Blockade
1949		Formation of the North Atlantic Treaty Organization (NATO)
1950		Outbreak of the Korean War
1953		Death of Stalin
1956	July	Egypt seizes the Suez Canal
	October	Anglo-French attack on the Suez Canal; Hungarian Revolution
1957		Treaty of Rome establishes the European Economic Community (EEC)
1960		Paris Summit Conference collapses
1961		Berlin Wall erected
1962		Cuban Missile Crisis
1963		Russian-American Test Ban Treaty
1968		Russian invasion of Czechoslovakia
1975		Helsinki Accords
1979		Russian invasion of Afghanistan
1981		Military crackdown on Solidarity movement in Poland
1985		Reagan-Gorbachev summit
1987		Major American-Soviet Arms Limitation Treaty
1989		Berlin Wall comes down
1991		Soviet Union dissolves

front would be impossible. These divisions did not arise. Second, by 1960 the Communist world had become split between the Soviets and the Chinese, who accused the Russians of lacking revolutionary zeal. Khrushchev's action was an attempt to prove the Soviet Union's hard-line credentials.

The abortive Paris conference opened the most difficult period of the Cold War. Throughout 1961, thousands of refugees from East Germany had fled to West Berlin. To stop this outflow, in August 1961 the East Germans erected a concrete barrier—the Berlin Wall—allong the border between East and West sectors that remained until November 1989. A year later the Cuban Missile Crisis brought the most dangerous days of the Cold War. The Soviet Union placed missiles in Cuba, a nation friendly to Soviet aims lying less than a hundred miles from the United States. The United States blockaded Cuba, halted the shipment of new missiles, and demanded the removal of existing installations. After a tense week the Soviets backed down.

QUICK REVIEW

The Cuban Missile Crisis

- 1959: Fidel Castro comes to power as a result of the Cuban revolution
- 1962: Khrushchev orders construction of missile bases in Cuba
- Tense negotiations resulted in the Soviets backing down and removing the missiles

Cuban Missile Crisis of 1962. The American ambassador to the United Nations displayed photographs to persuade the world of the threat to the United States less than one hundred miles from its own shores.

How did the crisis bring the world to the brink of war?

DÉTENTE AND AFTERWARD

In 1963 the two powers concluded a Nuclear Test Ban Treaty. This agreement marked the start of a détente, or lessening in tensions, between the United States and the Soviet Union that intensified during the presidency of Richard Nixon (1913–1994). This policy involved trade agreements and mutual reduction of strategic armaments. But the Soviet invasion of Afghanistan in 1979 hardened relations between Washington and Moscow, and the U.S. Senate refused to ratify the Strategic Arms Limitation Treaty of 1979.

Later, President Ronald Reagan (1911–2004) and Soviet leader Mikhail S. Gorbachev (b. 1931) held a friendly summit meeting in 1985, the first East–West summit in six years. Other meetings followed. In December 1987, the United States and the Soviet Union agreed to dismantle more than two thousand medium- and shorter-range missiles. The treaty provided for mutual inspection. This action represented the most significant agreement since World War II between the two superpowers.

The political upheavals in Eastern Europe and the Soviet Union soon overwhelmed the issues of the Cold War. The Soviet Union abandoned its support for Communist governments in Eastern Europe. By the close of 1991, the Soviet Union itself had collapsed. The Cold War was over.

President Ronald Reagan and Premier Mikhail Gorbachev.   The two leaders confer at a summit meeting in December 1989.

Why are the missile agreements signed by Gorbachev and Reagan among their most important accomplishments?

EUROPEAN SOCIETY IN THE SECOND HALF OF THE TWENTIETH CENTURY AND BEYOND

The sharp division of Europe into a democratic West and communist East for most of the second half of the twentieth century makes generalizations about social and economic developments difficult. Prosperity in the West contrasted with shortages in the Eastern economies, which were managed to benefit the Soviet Union. Most of the developments discussed in this chapter took place in Western Europe.

WHAT MAJOR trends have marked European society since World War II?

TOWARD WESTERN EUROPEAN UNIFICATION

Since 1945, the nations of Western Europe have taken unprecedented steps toward economic cooperation. The process is not complete and has been complicated by the collapse of the Soviet Union and the emergence of new free governments in Eastern Europe.

The Marshall Plan and NATO gave the countries involved new experience in working with each other and demonstrated the productivity, efficiency, and simple possibility of cooperative action. In 1950 France, West Germany, Italy, and the Benelux countries (Belgium, the Netherlands, and Luxembourg) organized the European Coal and Steel Community. Its success reduced the suspicions of government and business groups about the concept of coordination and economic integration.

In 1957, through the Treaty of Rome, the six members of the Coal and Steel Community agreed to form a new organization: the **European Economic Community (EEC)**, or Common Market. The members sought to achieve the eventual elimination of tariffs, a free flow of capital and labor, and similar wage and social benefits in all the

European Economic Community (EEC) The economic association formed by France, Germany, Italy, Belgium, the Netherlands, and Luxembourg in 1957. Also known as the Common Market.

The Euro.   Some thousand people stand around a huge euro symbol in a park in Frankfurt's banking district in Germany on January 1, 1997.

How has the euro given Europeans a new identity?

European Union (EU)   The new name given to the EEC in 1993. It included most of the states of Western Europe.

euro   The common currency created by the EEC in the late 1990s.

participating countries. The Common Market was a stunning success. By 1968, all tariffs among the six members had been abolished. Trade and labor migration among the members grew steadily. Moreover, nonmember states began to seek membership. In 1973, Denmark, Great Britain, and Ireland became members, and Austria, Finland, Greece, Portugal, Spain, and Sweden were eventually admitted.

In 1988, the leaders of the EEC decided to create a virtual free-trade zone throughout the member community. In 1991, the Treaty of Maastricht called for a unified currency and a strong central bank. The European Community was renamed the **European Union (EU)**. The most striking instance of expanding economic cooperation was the adoption of a common currency, the **euro.** In January 2002 the national currencies of twelve nations—mostly in Western Europe—were replaced by new coins and notes denominated in the euro. Such a widespread common currency is unprecedented in European history. In 2004, the EU accepted ten new members (see Map 32–2). This expansion poses enormous challenges, because the economies of the new members (mostly former states from the Eastern Soviet bloc) are much less developed than those of the former members. They will be permitted to adopt the euro only when their economies have become sufficiently strong.

Ongoing debate over the possible admission of Turkey serves as a proxy for debate over the cultural and religious character of the EU itself. Religion has not been a major topic of discussion within the EU, but the possible admission of a nation with an overwhelmingly Islamic population has brought the issue to the fore.

TOWARD A WELFARE STATE SOCIETY

The Great Depression, the rise of authoritarian states, and the experiences of World War II changed how many Europeans thought about social welfare. Governments began to spend more on social welfare than they did on the military. This reallocation of funds was a reaction to the state violence of the first half of the century and was possible because the NATO defense umbrella, which the United States primarily staffed and funded, protected Western Europe.

The modern European welfare state was broadly similar across the Continent. Before World War II, except in Scandinavia, the two basic models for social legislation were the German and the British. Bismarck had introduced social insurance in Germany during the 1880s to undermine the German Social Democratic Party. In effect, the imperial German government provided workers with social insurance and, thus, some sense of social security while denying them significant political participation. In early-twentieth-century Britain, where all classes had access to the political system, social insurance was targeted toward the poor. In both the German and British systems, workers were insured only against the risks from disease, injury on the job, and old age. Unemployment was assumed to be only a short-term problem and often one that workers brought on themselves. People higher in the social structure could look out for themselves and did not need government help.

After World War II, the concept emerged that social insurance against predictable risks was a social right and should be available to all citizens. The first major European nation to begin to create a welfare state was Britain in 1945 to 1951. The

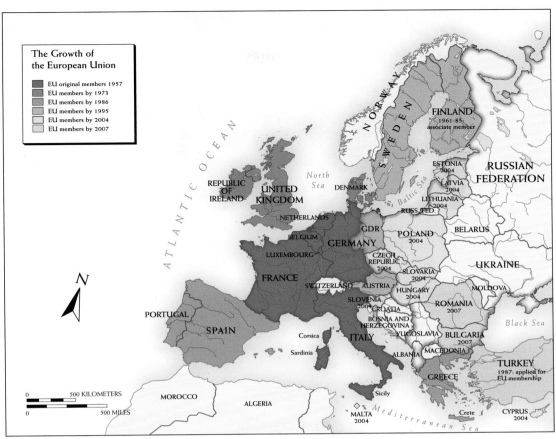

MAP 32–2 The Growth of the European Union.   This map traces the growth of membership in the European Union from its founding in 1957 through the introduction of its newest members in 2004. Note that Turkey has applied for membership but has not yet been admitted.

What are the advantages and disadvantages of European Union membership?

spread of welfare legislation (including unemployment insurance) within Western Europe was related to both the Cold War and domestic political and economic policy. The communist states of Eastern Europe were promising their people social security as well as full employment. The capitalist states came to believe they had to provide similar security for their people, but, in fact, the social security of the communist states was often more rhetoric than reality.

RESISTANCE TO THE EXPANSION OF THE WELFARE STATE

Western European attitudes toward the welfare state have reflected three periods that have marked economic life since the end of the war. The first period was one of reconstruction from 1945 through the early 1950s. It was followed by twenty-five years of generally steady and expanding economic growth. The third period brought first an era of inflation in the late 1970s and then one of relatively low growth and high unemployment from the 1990s to the present. During each of the first two periods, a general conviction existed that the foundation of economic policy was government involvement in a mixed economy. From the late 1970s, more people came to believe the market should be allowed to regulate itself and that government should be less involved in the economy.

The March of Pain. Under the banner "The March of Pain," a crowd of angry protesters from the southern Italian city of Bari, members of an association for the handicapped, lobby for more government assistance. The demands of special interest groups on the welfare state increased dramatically in the sixties and seventies.

What has happened to the welfare state since the 1970s?

QUICK REVIEW

Western Europe's Consumer Society

- ◆ Western Europe's economy emphasized consumer goods in the second half of the twentieth century

- ◆ Soviet bloc economies focused on capital investments and the military

- ◆ Discrepancy in Western and Eastern European standards of living caused resentment in the East

The most influential political figure in reasserting the importance of markets was Margaret Thatcher (b. 1925) of the British Conservative Party who served as Prime Minister from 1979 to 1990. Her goal was to make the British economy more efficient and competitive. Although her administration roused enormous controversy, over time the British Labour Party itself largely came to accept what was at the time known as the Thatcher Revolution.

While Thatcher redirected the British economy, the continental Europe's government-furnished welfare services began to encounter resistance. The leveling off of population growth in Europe has imperiled the benefits of the welfare state. The next working generation will have fewer people to support the retired elderly population. Middle-class taxpayers have also become reluctant to support existing systems. Europeans in the next few decades may look at the second half of the twentieth century as the golden age of welfare states and may find their own societies dealing with social welfare differently.

THE MOVEMENT OF PEOPLES

Many people migrated from, to, and within Europe during the half century following World War II. In the decade and a half after 1945, approximately a half million Europeans each year settled elsewhere in the world. Many of these migrants were educated city dwellers. Decolonization in the postwar period contributed to an inward flow of European colonials and non-European inhabitants of the former colonies to Europe. This influx has caused social tension and conflict. In Great Britain, for example, during the 1980s clashes arose between the police and non-European immigrants. France has had similar difficulties. Moreover, large Islamic populations now exist in several European nations and have become political factors in France and Germany.

World War II and its aftermath created millions of refugees. Once the Cold War set in, Soviet domination made it impossible for Eastern Europeans to migrate to other parts of Europe. The major motivation for internal migration from the late 1950s onward has been economic opportunity. The prosperous nations of northern and Western Europe offered jobs that paid good wages and provided excellent benefits. There was a flow of workers from the poorer countries of Greece, Italy, Portugal, Spain, Turkey, and Yugoslavia into the wealthier countries of the Benelux nations, France, Switzerland, and West Germany. The establishment of the EEC in 1957 facilitated this movement. Migrant workers were usually welcomed during years of prosperity and resented when economies began to slow in the mid-1980s. In Germany during the early 1990s, migrant workers were attacked.

In the late 1980s politics again became a major factor in European migration. With the collapse of the Communist governments, people from all over Eastern Europe migrated to the West. Civil war in the former Yugoslavia also created many refugees. These new migrants generated some resentment, and several nations have taken steps to restrict migration.

THE NEW MUSLIM POPULATION

Well into the twentieth century Europeans encountered Muslims, if at all, as subjects in their colonies. With the exception of a few minority communities in the Balkans and the former Soviet Empire, Europeans saw themselves and their national cultures as Christian or secular.

European indifference toward Islam had dissolved by the end of the twentieth century as a sizable Muslim population settled in Europe. This highly diverse immigrant community had become an issue in Europe even before the events of September 11, 2001, discussed later in this chapter.

Europe's economic growth and decolonization encouraged Muslim emigration to Western Europe. As Western economies recovered in the wake of World War II, a labor shortage developed in Europe, and laborers ("guest workers"), many of whom came from Muslim nations, were imported to fill it. The aftermath of decolonization and the quest for a better life led Muslims from East Africa and the Indian subcontinent to Great Britain and others from North Africa to France. Smaller but significant numbers settled in Denmark, Italy, the Netherlands, Spain, and Sweden, nations that had previously had homogeneous populations.

These Muslim immigrant communities share some characteristics. Many Muslims came to Europe expecting eventually to return to their homelands, an expectation their host countries shared. Unlike the United States, few European countries had any experience in dealing with large-scale immigration, and many Muslim communities have remained unassimilated. Most of the Muslim immigrants to Europe were neither highly skilled nor professionally educated, and many of the unskilled jobs that they originally filled have disappeared. As European economic growth has slowed, Muslims have been blamed for a host of problems, from crime to unemployment.

The radicalization of parts of the Islamic world has also affected Europe's Muslim communities. Muslims in both Germany and Great Britain have been involved in radical Islamic groups, and some belonged to organizations involved in the September 11, 2001, attacks on the United States. The French government has exerted more control over its Muslim community. Despite the fact that Europe's Muslims are not a homogeneous group—they come from different countries, have different class backgrounds, and espouse different Islamic traditions—their communities are often plagued by poverty and unemployment.

NEW PATTERNS IN THE WORK AND EXPECTATIONS OF WOMEN

The work patterns and social expectations of women have changed markedly since World War II. In all social ranks, women have begun to assume larger economic and political roles. They have entered the professions and are filling major managerial positions.

Despite enormous gains, gender inequality remained a major characteristic of European societies at the opening of the twenty-first century. After World War II, Simone de Beauvoir's (1908–1986) book, *The Second Sex* (1949), was a major influence on European feminism (see Document, "Simone de Beauvoir Urges Economic Freedom for Women"). She and other feminists documented the social, legal, and economic disadvantages of their gender, challenged discrimination against women in family law, and called attention to social problems such as spousal abuse.

Muslim Women Wearing Headscarves, France. The presence of foreign-born Muslims whose labor is necessary for the prosperity of the European economy is a major issue in contemporary Europe. Many of these Muslims, such as these women, live in self-contained communities.

Why do some non-Muslim Europeans find headscarves threatening?

QUICK REVIEW

Muslims in Europe

- Many Muslims immigrated to Europe as "guest workers"
- Assimilation rates are low
- Unemployment rates are high
- Islamic radicalization affects Muslim immigrant communities

Simone de Beauvoir. Shown here with her companion, the philosopher Jean-Paul Sartre, Simone de Beauvoir was the major feminist writer in postwar Europe.

How have women's roles changed in postwar Europe?

DOCUMENT

Simone de Beauvoir Urges Economic Freedom for Women

Simone de Beauvoir was the single most important feminist voice of mid-twentieth-century Europe. In The Second Sex, published in France in 1949, she explored the experience of women coming of age in a world of ideas, institutions, and social expectations shaped historically by men. Much of the book discusses the psychological strategies that modern European women had developed to deal with their status as "the second sex." Toward the end of her book, de Beauvoir argues strongly that economic freedom and advancement for women are fundamental to their personal fulfillment.

- **Why** does de Beauvoir argue that the achievement of civic rights must be accompanied by economic freedom for women? Why does the example of the small number of professional women illustrate issues for European women in general? How does she indicate that even professional women must overcome a culture in which the experience of women is fundamentally different from that of men? Do de Beauvoir's comments seem relevant for women at the opening of the twenty-first century?

According to French law, obedience is no longer included among the duties of a wife, and each woman citizen has the right to vote; but these civil liberties remain theoretical as long as they are unaccompanied by economic freedom. ... It is through gainful employment that woman has traversed most of the distance that separated her from the male; and nothing else can guarantee her liberty in practice. Once she ceases to be a parasite, the system based on her dependence crumbles; between her and the universe there is no longer any need for a masculine mediator. ...

When she is productive, active, she regains her transcendence; in her projects she concretely affirms her

Both middle- and working-class women have increasingly sought employment outside the home, and the number of married women in the workforce has risen sharply. Some employers adjust hours to accommodate women workers, and consumer conveniences and child care make it easier for women to work. Children, now compelled to spend much of their time in school, are no longer expected to contribute to the support of their families. If additional income is needed, their mothers work outside the home. But even when there is no financial necessity, both parents are now likely to pursue careers.

The work patterns of European women display much more continuity than they did in the nineteenth century. Single women enter the workforce after their schooling and continue to work after marriage. The number of married women in the workforce has risen sharply. Both middle- and working-class married women have sought jobs outside the home. They might withdraw from the workforce to care for young children but return when the children begin school.

Women's increasing life expectancy is one of the most important factors in these changes. The lengthening life span has meant that child rearing occupies relatively less of women's lives. Women throughout the Western world have new concerns about how they will spend the years when they are not rearing children. The age at which women bear children has risen; in urban areas, childbearing occurs later and the birthrate is lower than elsewhere. Many women have begun to limit the number of children they bear or to forgo childbearing altogether. Both men and women continue to expect to marry, but the new careers open to women and the desire of couples for a higher standard of living have contributed to a declining birthrate.

Many paradoxes surround the situation of women in post-Communist Eastern Europe. Under communism women generally enjoyed social equality as well as a broad spectrum of government benefits. Well over 50 percent of women worked in these societies, though there were no significant women's movements since they, like all status as subject; in connection with the aims she pursues, with the money and the rights she takes possession of, she makes trial of and senses her responsibility. ...

There are... a fairly large number of privileged women who find in their professions a means of economic and social autonomy. These come to mind when one considers woman's possibilities and her future. ... [E]ven though they constitute as yet only a minority; they continue to be the subject of debate between feminists and antifeminists. The latter assert that the emancipated women of today succeed in doing nothing of importance in the world and that furthermore they have difficulty in achieving their own inner equilibrium. The former exaggerate the results obtained by professional women and are blind to their inner confusion. There is no good reason... to say they are on the wrong road; and still it is certain that they are not tranquilly installed in their new realm: as yet they are only halfway there. The woman who is economically emancipated from man is not for all that in a moral, social, and psychological situation identical with that of man. The way she carried on her profession and her devotion to it depends on the context supplied by the total pattern of her life. For when she begins her adult life she does not have behind her the same past as does a boy; she is not viewed by society in the same way; the universe presents itself to her in a different perspective. The fact of being a woman today poses peculiar problems for an independent human individual.

Source: Simone de Beauvoir, *The Second Sex*, trans. by H. M. Parshley. Copyright © 1952 and renewed 1980 by Alfred A. Knopf, Inc. Reprinted by permission of Alfred A. Knopf, a division of Random House Inc.

independent associations, were frowned on. The new governments of the region have shown little concern toward women's issues. Economic difficulties endanger the funding of various health and welfare programs that benefit women and children, such as extensive maternity benefits.

AMERICAN DOMESTIC SCENE SINCE WORLD WAR II

Three major themes have characterized the postwar American experience—an opposition to the spread of communism, an expansion of civil rights to blacks and other minorities at home, and a determination to achieve ongoing economic growth.

WHAT ARE the main themes that have characterized postwar America?

TRUMAN AND EISENHOWER ADMINISTRATIONS

The foreign policy of President Harry Truman was directed against Communist expansion in Europe and East Asia. Domestically, the Truman administration tried to continue the New Deal. However, Truman encountered opposition from conservative Republicans, who in 1947 passed the Taft-Hartley Act limiting labor union activity. Truman won the 1948 election against great odds. Through policies he called the Fair Deal, he sought to extend economic security. Those efforts were frustrated by fears of a domestic Communist menace fanned by Senator Joseph McCarthy (1909–1957) of Wisconsin.

War hero Dwight D. Eisenhower (1890–1969) was elected in 1952. In retrospect, his presidency seems a period of calm. Eisenhower ended the Korean War. The country was generally prosperous. The president was less activist than either Roosevelt or Truman had been. Beneath the apparent quiet stirred forces that would lead to the disruptions of the 1960s.

CIVIL RIGHTS AND NEW SOCIAL PROGRAMS

In 1954, the U.S. Supreme Court, in *Brown v. Board of Education of Topeka*, declared racial segregation unconstitutional. Shortly thereafter, the Court ordered the desegregation of schools. In 1957, President Eisenhower had to send troops into Little Rock, Arkansas, to integrate the schools, and for the next ten years, the struggle over school integration and civil rights for black Americans stirred the nation. Southern states attempted to resist desegregation. American blacks began to protest it. In 1955, Reverend Martin Luther King Jr. (1929–1968) organized a boycott in Montgomery, Alabama, against segregated buses that marked the beginning of the use of civil disobedience to fight racial discrimination in the United States. The civil rights struggle continued well into the 1960s. The greatest achievements of the movement were the Civil Rights Act of 1964, which desegregated public accommodations, and the Voting Rights Act of 1965, which cleared the way for blacks to vote. Black citizens were brought nearer to the mainstream of American life than they had ever been.

Much remained undone. In 1967, there were race riots in American cities. Those riots, followed by the assassination of Martin Luther King Jr. in 1968, weakened the Civil Rights Movement. A new leader did not emerge until the late 1980s, when Reverend Jesse Jackson (b. 1941) spearheaded a move to register black voters. In 1992, a court decision involving treatment of black Americans by police sparked one of the most destructive riots in American history in Los Angeles. Furthermore, as other groups, particularly Latino Americans, began to raise issues on behalf of their own communities, racial relations became more complicated. Black Americans and other minorities continue to lag behind white Americans economically.

The advance of the Civil Rights Movement in the late 1950s and early 1960s was part of a new advance of political liberalism. In 1960, John F. Kennedy (1917–1963) narrowly won the presidential election. He attempted unsuccessfully to expand medical care under the Social Security program, but the reaction to his assassination in 1963 allowed his successor, Lyndon Johnson (1908–1973), to press for activist legislation. Johnson's domestic program, known as the War on Poverty, established major federal programs to create jobs and provide job training. It also added new entitlements to the Social Security program, including Medicare, which provides medical services for the elderly and disabled. Johnson's drive for what he called the Great Society ended the era of major federal initiatives that had begun under Franklin Roosevelt. By the late 1960s, the electorate had become more conservative.

THE VIETNAM WAR, DOMESTIC TURMOIL, AND WATERGATE

Johnson's activist domestic vision was overshadowed by the U.S. involvement in Vietnam (see Chapter 33). By 1965, Johnson had decided to send American troops to Vietnam. This policy led to the longest of American wars. At home, the war and the military draft provoked large-scale protests; the Vietnam War divided the nation as had no conflict since the Civil War.

QUICK REVIEW

Desegregation Landmarks

- *Brown v. Board of Education of Topeka*, 1954
- Montgomery bus boycott, 1955
- Little Rock schools integrated, 1957
- Civil Rights Act, 1964

Martin Luther King Jr.   King, pictured here with his wife Coretta, was the most prominent civil rights leader in the United States. Here he leads a protest march in 1965.

What did the Civil Rights Movement accomplish in the United States? Is its work complete?

Johnson decided not to seek reelection in 1968. Richard Nixon led the Republicans to victory. His election marked the beginning of an era of American politics dominated by conservative policies. Perhaps the most important act of his administration was to establish diplomatic relations with the People's Republic of China. Although half of the casualties in the Vietnam War occurred under Nixon's administration, he concluded the war in 1972. That same year he was reelected, but the Watergate scandal began to erode his administration.

On the surface, the Watergate scandal involved only the burglary of the Democratic Party national headquarters by White House operatives in 1972. The deeper issues related to presidential authority and the right of the government to intrude into the lives of citizens. In 1974, audiotapes revealed that Nixon had ordered federal agencies to try to cover up White House participation in the burglary. Nixon became the first American president to resign from office.

Kent State Protest.   The clash between protesting students and the Ohio National Guard at Kent State University was the most violent moment in the protests against the U.S. involvement in Vietnam.

What makes a photograph such as this one disturbing to so many people?

Watergate shook public confidence in the government. It was also a distraction from the major problems facing the country, especially inflation, which had resulted from fighting the war in Vietnam while expanding domestic expenditures. The administrations of Gerald Ford (1974–1977; 1913–2006) and Jimmy Carter (1977–1981; b. 1924) battled inflation and high interest rates without success.

THE TRIUMPH OF POLITICAL CONSERVATISM

In 1980 Ronald Reagan (1911–2004) was elected president by a large majority and reelected four years later. Reagan was the first fully ideological conservative to be elected in the postwar era. He sought to reduce the role of the federal government in American life through major tax cuts. This plus vastly increased defense spending produced the largest fiscal deficit in American history, but inflation was controlled, and the economy expanded.

In 1988, George H. W. Bush (b. 1924) was elected to succeed Reagan. In the summer of 1990, in response to the invasion of Kuwait by Iraq, he forged a worldwide coalition that forced Iraq out of Kuwait in 1991. But Bush stumbled in the face of serious economic problems. In 1992, the Democratic nominee, Governor William (Bill) Clinton (b. 1946) of Arkansas, won the election. In 1994, the Republican Party won majorities in both houses of Congress in an election that marked a major conservative departure in American political life. This Congress continued the conservative redirection of federal policy that had begun under Reagan. President Clinton and a Republican-dominated Congress were reelected in 1996, but scandals plagued both parties. Because of a personal sexual scandal and allegations of perjury, President Clinton was impeached in 1998 but acquitted. In terms of policy, Clinton moved the Democractic Party into a more conservative stance.

The presidential election of 2000 between Texas governor George W. Bush (son of the former president) and Vice President Al Gore was the closest in modern American history. Gore won a majority of the popular vote but failed to win a majority in the electoral college. The pivotal electoral votes depended on which candidate carried Florida, where the final vote count was disputed for more than a month after the November election. After complicated legal disputes, the U.S. Supreme Court voted 5 to 4 to halt Florida's recount, which resulted in Bush being declared the winner.

On September 11, 2001, surprise terrorist attacks on New York City and Washington, D.C., transformed the political life of the United States. In October 2001, the United States began a war against the extremist Islamic Taliban regime in Afghanistan, which had tolerated the presence of Islamic terrorists. In 2003 the United States invaded Iraq, an event fully discussed in the last section of this chapter and in Chapter 34.

In 2004 President Bush overcame Democratic challenger John Kerry and was reelected, this time with a popular and electoral college majority vote. In the congressional elections of 2006 the Democratic Party regained control of both houses of Congress in an election fought largely over the American intervention in Iraq.

THE SOVIET UNION TO 1989

HOW DID leaders after Stalin attempt to reform Soviet government?

The Soviet Union emerged from World War II as a major world power, but Stalin did little or nothing to modify the repressive regime he had fostered. The police remained ever present. The cult of personality around Stalin expanded, and the central bureaucracy continued to grow. Heavy industry was still favored in place of production for consumers. Agriculture continued to be troubled. Stalin's personal authority over the party and the nation remained unchallenged. In foreign policy he solidified Soviet control over Eastern Europe for the purposes of both Communist expansion and Soviet national security. The Soviet army assured subservience to the goals of the Soviet Union. This continued until Stalin died on March 6, 1953.

THE KHRUSHCHEV AND BREZHNEV YEARS

No single leader immediately replaced Stalin. By 1956 Nikita Khrushchev became premier, but without the extraordinary powers of Stalin.

In 1956, at the Twentieth Congress of the Communist Party, Khrushchev denounced Stalin and his crimes. This "Secret Speech" shocked party circles and opened the way for limited internal criticism of the Soviet government. Under Khrushchev, intellectuals were somewhat freer to express their opinions. In economic policy, Khrushchev made moderate efforts to decentralize economic planning, but the consumer sector improved only marginally. The ever-growing defense budget and the space program made major demands on the nation's productive resources. Khrushchev redirected Stalin's agricultural policy, removing the most restrictive regulations on private cultivation, but the agricultural problem continued to grow. The Soviet Union could not feed its own people; by the 1970s the Soviet Union imported vast quantities of grain from the United States and other countries.

By 1964 Communist Party leaders had concluded that Khrushchev had tried to do too much too soon and had done it too poorly. His foreign policy, culminating in the backdown over the Cuban Missile Crisis, appeared a failure. On October 16, 1964, Khrushchev was forced to resign. Leonid Brezhnev (1906–1982) emerged as his successor.

The Soviet government became more repressive after 1964. Intellectuals enjoyed less freedom, and Jewish citizens were harassed. The internal repression gave rise to a dissident movement. A few Soviet citizens dared to criticize the

The Kitchen Debate. One of the most famous incidents of the Cold War was a spontaneous debate between Nikita Khrushchev and Vice President Richard Nixon at a trade fair in Moscow. Because it took place at a display of kitchen appliances, it was sometimes called the Kitchen Debate.

Did either Nixon or Kruschev "win" the Kitchen Debate?

regime for violating the human rights provisions of the 1975 Helsinki Accords. The Soviet government responded with further repression.

In foreign policy the Brezhnev years witnessed attempts both to reach accommodation with the United States and to continue to expand Soviet influence and maintain Soviet leadership of the communist movement. Growing spending on defense squeezed the consumer side of the economy.

In December 1979, the Soviet Union invaded Afghanistan for reasons that remain unclear. The Afghanistan invasion exacerbated tensions with the United States and tied the hands of the Soviet government in Eastern Europe. Soviet hesitation to react to events in Poland during the 1980s stemmed in part from the military commitment in Afghanistan and from the condemnation the invasion provoked from many governments. The Soviet government also lost support at home as its army became bogged down and suffered steady losses.

COMMUNISM AND SOLIDARITY IN POLAND

In July 1980 the Polish government raised meat prices, causing strikes across the country. In August, a strike at the Lenin shipyard at Gdansk spread to other shipyards, transport facilities, and factories. The Gdansk strike, led by Lech Walesa (b. 1944), ended on August 31 after the government promised the workers the right to organize an independent union, called Solidarity. Less than a week later the Polish Communist head of state was replaced; later that year the state-controlled radio—for the first time in thirty years—broadcast a Roman Catholic Mass.

In the summer of 1981, for the first time in any European Communist state, secret elections for the Polish party congress permitted choices among the candidates. Poland remained a Communist state, but real debate was temporarily permitted within the party congress. This experiment ended in December 1981, when General Wojciech Jaruzelski (b. 1923) became head of the party. Martial law was declared and continued until late in the 1980s.

"Solidarity." In 1989, the Polish trade union successfully forced the Polish Communist government to hold free elections. In June of that year Solidarity, whose members here are collecting funds for their campaign, won overwhelmingly.

Which members of Polish society belonged to Solidarity?

GORBACHEV ATTEMPTS TO REDIRECT THE SOVIET UNION

By the time of Brezhnev's death in 1982, the Soviet system seemed incapable of meeting the needs of its people or pursuing a successful foreign policy. But no observers expected rapid change in the Soviet Union or its satellites. Both of Brezhnev's immediate successors, Yuri Andropov (1914–1984) and Constantin Chernenko (1911–1985), died after holding office for short periods. However, in 1985, Mikhail S. Gorbachev (b. 1931) came to power and immediately set about making the most remarkable changes that the Soviet Union had witnessed since the 1920s. His reforms unleashed forces that within seven years would force him to retire and end both Communist rule and the Soviet Union itself.

Initially, Gorbachev and his supporters challenged the way the party and bureaucracy managed the Soviet government and economy. Under the policy of *perestroika,* or "restructuring," they proposed major economic and political reforms. The centralized economic ministries were streamlined. By early 1990, Gorbachev had even begun to advocate private ownership of property. He and his advisers considered policies to move the economy rapidly toward a free market. However, the Soviet economy,

perestroika Meaning "restructuring." The attempt in the 1980s to reform the Soviet government and economy.

Statue of Lenin.   The collapse of Communist Party governments in Eastern Europe and the Soviet Union was the most important political event of the closing years of the twentieth century. It was accompanied by the destruction of the public symbols of those governments. Throughout the region gigantic statues of Communist Party leaders were torn down. Here, Hungarians explore a toppled statue of Lenin.

Why were most Eastern European revolutions peaceful?

instead of growing, stagnated and even declined. Shortages of food, consumer goods, and housing became chronic. Old-fashioned Communists blamed these results on the abandonment of centralized planning, while democratic critics blamed them on overly slow reform.

Gorbachev also allowed public criticism of Soviet history and Soviet Communist Party policy. This development was termed **glasnost,** or "openness." In factories, workers were permitted to criticize party officials and the economic plans of the party and the government. Censorship was relaxed and free expression encouraged. Dissidents were released from prison. In 1988, a new constitution permitted contested elections. After real political campaigning, the Congress of People's Deputies was elected in 1989 and then formally elected Gorbachev as president.

The Soviet Union was a vast empire of diverse nationalities. Some had been conquered under the tsars; others had been seized by Stalin. *Glasnost* quickly brought to the fore the discontents of all such peoples. Gorbachev proved inept in addressing these ethnic complaints.

OVERVIEW Leaving the Soviet Bloc

Various Eastern bloc nations tried to escape Soviet domination. Most attempts ended in intensified repression, until 1989, when a cluster of successful revolutions contributed to the 1991 collapse of the Soviet Union itself.

POLAND

In 1956, Polish Communist Party leaders rejected the prime minister selected for them by the Soviet Union; Moscow went along with the Poles' choice because he pledged to stay in the Warsaw Pact. Strikes at the Gdansk shipyard in the summer of 1980 led to reforms and liberalization until 1981, when martial law was imposed. Strikes in 1988 suggested a loosening of Soviet control, and Communist candidates were defeated in 1989 elections.

HUNGARY

Hungary's premier tried to leave the Warsaw Pact in 1956; he was executed, and Hungary was occupied by the Soviets. By the 1980s, it had established a relatively independent economy. In 1989 Parliament deposed the Soviet puppet premier and announced open elections.

CZECHOSLOVAKIA

"Prague Spring," a brief period of liberalization in 1968, ended with a Soviet invasion. In 1989, street demonstrations coupled with political pressure from Civic Forum and other groups drove the Communists from office. Vaclev Havel was elected president.

ROMANIA

Dictator Nicolae Ceaucescu and his cronies were driven from office by violent street demonstrations in December 1989. The aggressive tactics of Ceaucescu's security forces inflamed passions, and Ceaucescu and his wife were executed.

YUGOSLAVIA

Marshal Tito led Yugoslavia from the 1940s until his death in 1980. He unified ethnic groups through a cult of personality and adept power-sharing; he also managed to maintain significant independence from Stalin and Soviet policies. Ethnic conflict emerged after 1980, leading to civil war and the breakup of the state.

1989: YEAR OF REVOLUTIONS IN EASTERN EUROPE

In 1989 Soviet domination and communist rule in Eastern Europe came to an abrupt end. None of these revolutions could have taken place without the refusal of the Soviet Union to intervene militarily as it had done in 1956 and 1968. For the first time since the end of World War II, the peoples of Eastern Europe could shape their own political destiny. Once they realized the Soviets would stand back, thousands of citizens denounced Communist Party domination and asserted their desire for democracy.

The generally peaceful character of most of these revolutions may have resulted from the shock with which the world responded to the violent repression of prodemocracy protesters in Beijing's Tienanmen Square in May 1989. The Communist Party officials of Eastern Europe and the Soviet Union clearly decided that they could not offend world opinion with a similar attack.

WHY DID communist regimes collapse so easily in Eastern Europe in 1989?

glasnost Meaning "openness." The policy initiated by Mikhail Gorbachev in the 1980s of permitting open criticism of the policies of the Soviet Communist Party.

SOLIDARITY REEMERGES IN POLAND

During the mid-1980s, Poland's government relaxed martial law. By 1984, leaders of Solidarity began again to work for free trade unions and democratic government. New dissenting organizations emerged. Poland's economy continued to deteriorate. In 1988, new strikes occurred. This time the communist government failed to reimpose control. Solidarity was legalized.

Jaruzelski, with the tacit consent of the Soviet Union, promised free elections to Parliament. When elections were held in 1989, the Communists lost overwhelmingly to Solidarity candidates. On August 24, 1989, after negotiating with Lech Walesa and getting Gorbachev's approval, Jaruzelski named Tadeusz Mazowiecki (b. 1927) the first non-Communist prime minister of Poland since 1945.

HUNGARY MOVES TOWARD INDEPENDENCE

Hungary had for some time shown the greatest economic independence from the Soviet Union in Eastern Europe. The Hungarian government had emphasized the production of food and consumer goods. In early 1989, the Hungarian Communist government permitted independent political parties and free travel between Hungary and Austria, opening the first breach in the Iron Curtain. Thousands of East Germans then moved through Hungary and Austria to West Germany.

In May 1989, Premier Janos Kadar (1912–1989) was voted from office by the Parliament. In October, Hungary promised free elections. By 1990, a coalition of democratic parties governed the country.

THE BREACH OF THE BERLIN WALL AND GERMAN REUNIFICATION

In the autumn of 1989 demonstrations erupted in East German cities. The streets filled with people demanding an end to Communist Party rule.

Gorbachev told the leaders of the East German Communist Party that the Soviet Union would no longer support

The Fall of the Berlin Wall.   The most dramatic moment in the weeks of the collapse of communist regimes in Eastern Europe occurred in November 1989 when crowds destroyed the Berlin Wall, the most prominent symbol of the Cold War divisions in Europe.

Why did East Germany not interfere with the breaching of the Berlin Wall?

them. They resigned, making way for a younger generation of Communist Party leaders who promised reforms. Few East Germans were convinced, however. In November 1989, the government of East Germany ordered the opening of the Berlin Wall, and thousands of East Berliners crossed into West Berlin. By early 1990, the Communist government of East Germany had been swept away.

The citizens of the two Germanys were determined to reunify. By February 1990, reunification had become a foregone conclusion, accepted by France, Great Britain, the Soviet Union, and the United States.

THE VELVET REVOLUTION IN CZECHOSLOVAKIA

Late in 1989, in "the velvet revolution," Communist rule in Czechoslovakia unraveled. In November, under popular pressure from street demonstrations and well-organized political opposition, the Communist Party began to retreat from office. The patterns were similar to those occurring elsewhere: Old leadership resigned, and younger Communists replaced them, but the changes they offered were inadequate.

The popular new Czech leader was Václav Havel (b. 1936), a renowned playwright whom the government had imprisoned. Havel and his group, called Civic Forum, negotiated changes with the government that included an end to the political dominance of the Communist Party and the inclusion of non-Communists in the government. In late December 1989, Havel was elected president.

VIOLENT REVOLUTION IN ROMANIA

The most violent upheaval of 1989 occurred in Romania, where President Nicolae Ceausescu (1918–1989) had governed without opposition for almost a quarter century. Romania was a corrupt, one-party state with total centralized economic planning. Ceausescu, who had long been at odds with the Soviet government, maintained his Stalinist regime in the face of Gorbachev's reforms. He was supported by a loyal security force.

On December 15, troubles erupted in the city of Timisoara in western Romania. The security forces fired on demonstrators, and casualties ran into the hundreds. By December 22, Bucharest was in full revolt. Fighting broke out between the army, which supported the revolution, and the security forces. Ceausescu and his wife attempted to flee the country but were captured and executed on December 25. His death ended the fighting. The provisional government in Bucharest announced the first free elections since the end of World War II.

THE COLLAPSE OF THE SOVIET UNION

WHO WERE the leaders in the period surrounding the collapse of the Soviet Union?

Gorbachev believed that the Soviet Union could no longer afford to support Communist governments in Eastern Europe. He also saw that the Communist Party within the Soviet Union was losing power.

RENUNCIATION OF COMMUNIST POLITICAL MONOPOLY

In early 1990, Gorbachev formally proposed that the Soviet Communist Party abandon its monopoly of power. After intense debate, the Central Committee abandoned the Leninist position that only a single elite party could act as the vanguard of the revolution and forge a new Soviet society.

Gorbachev confronted challenges from three major political forces by 1990. One group—considered conservative in the Soviet context—wanted to maintain the influence of the Communist Party and the Soviet army. They were disturbed by the country's economic stagnation and disorder. They appeared to have significant support. During late 1990 and early 1991, Gorbachev, who himself seems to have been disturbed by the nation's turmoil, began to appoint members of this group to government posts. In other words, Gorbachev seemed to be making a strategic retreat. He apparently believed that these more conservative forces could give him the support he needed against opposition from a second group, led by Boris Yeltsin (b. 1931), who wanted to move quickly to a market economy and a more democratic government. In 1990, Yeltsin was elected president of the Russian Republic, the most important of the Soviet Union's constituent republics. That position gave him a firm political base from which to challenge Gorbachev's authority and increase his own.

The third force was regional unrest, especially from the three Baltic republics of Estonia, Latvia, and Lithuania. During 1989 and 1990, the parliaments of the Baltic republics tried to increase their independence, and Lithuania actually declared itself independent. Discontent also arose in the Soviet Islamic republics in Central Asia. Gorbachev sought to negotiate new constitutional arrangements between the republics and the central government but failed. This may have been the most important reason for the rapid collapse of the Soviet Union.

AUGUST 1991 COUP AND THE YELTSIN YEARS

The turning point came in August 1991 when the conservative forces that Gorbachev had brought into the government attempted a coup. Armed forces occupied Moscow, and Gorbachev himself was placed under house arrest in the Crimea. Yeltsin denounced the coup and asked the world for help.

Within two days the coup collapsed. Gorbachev returned to Moscow, but in humiliation, having been victimized by the groups he had turned to for support. From that point on, Yeltsin steadily became the dominant political figure in the nation. The Communist Party, compromised by its participation in the coup, collapsed. On December 25, 1991, the Soviet Union ceased to exist, Gorbachev left office, and the Commonwealth of Independent States came into being (see Map 32–3).

As president of Russia, Yeltsin was head of the largest and most powerful of the new states, but by 1993 he faced serious problems. Opposition to Yeltsin personally and to his economic and political reforms grew in the Russian Parliament, whose members were mostly former Communists. In September 1993, Yeltsin suspended Parliament, which responded by deposing him. The military, however, backed Yeltsin and surrounded the Parliament building. On October 4, 1993, after pro-Parliament rioters rampaged through Moscow, Yeltsin ordered tanks to attack the Parliament building, crushing the revolt.

These actions temporarily consolidated Yeltsin's position and authority. The major Western powers supported him. But the crushing of Parliament left Yeltsin highly dependent on the military, and the country's continuing economic problems bred unrest. In the December 1993 parlimentary elections, radical nationalists made an uncomfortably strong showing. In 1994 and again after 1999, the central government faced war in the province of Chechnya. In December 1999, Yeltsin, who suffered from poor health, resigned and was succeeded as president by Vladimir Putin (b. 1952), who promised strong leadership.

Putin renewed the war against the rebels in Chechnya, which resulted in heavy casualties and enormous destruction there, but also strengthened Putin's political support within Russia. After the 2001 terrorist attacks on the United States, Putin cooperated with the American assault on Afghanistan largely because the Russian government fears the spread of Islamic extremism beyond Chechnya.

MAP 32–3 The Commonwealth of Independent States. In December 1991 the Soviet Union broke up into its fifteen constituent republics. Eleven of these were loosely joined in the Commonwealth of Independent States. Also shown is the autonomous region of Chechnya, which has waged two bloody wars with Russia in the last decade.

What does the breakup of the Soviet Union say about the importance of nationalism in the modern world?

The Chechen war spawned an appalling terrorist act. In September 2004, a group of Chechens captured an elementary school in Beslan, in the north Caucasus. Approximately 1,200 students, teachers, and parents were held hostage for several days. When government troops stormed the school, approximately 330 of the hostages were killed.

Putin pursued policies of strong governmental centralization, taking power from local political units and also moving against citizens who have accumulated great wealth in the past decade. Democratic processes face great difficulties in Russia. Tensions have developed between Russia and the United States over the growth of NATO on the eastern borders of Russia and the rise of American influence on nations that were once part of the Soviet Union. Conflict in the Middle East, particularly in relationship to Iraq and Iran, presents another arena of tension between the United States and Russia.

Chechnya.   A Chechen fighter points his rifle at the head of a Russian prisoner of war outside the Chechen capital Grozny in August 1996.

Which other Caucasian regions have experienced conflict with Russia in recent years? Why?

THE COLLAPSE OF YUGOSLAVIA AND CIVIL WAR

Yugoslavia was created after World War I. It included six major national groups— Serbs, Croats, Slovenes, Montenegrins, Macedonians, and Bosnians (Muslims)— among whom there have been ethnic disputes for centuries (see Map 32–4). The Croats and Slovenes are Roman Catholic and use the Latin alphabet. The Serbs, Montenegrins, and Macedonians are Eastern Orthodox and use the Cyrillic alphabet. The Bosnians are Islamic. Most members of each group reside in a region with which they are associated historically and these regions constituted individual republics within Yugoslavia. Many Serbs, however, lived outside Serbia proper.

HOW DID the West respond to the collapse of Yugoslavia?

Yugoslavia's first Communist leader, Marshal Tito (1892–1980) held Yugoslavia together largely through a cult of personality. After his death, ethnic differences came to the fore. Nationalist leaders—most notably Slobodan Milošević (b. 1941) in Serbia and Franjo Tudjman (b. 1922) in Croatia—gained increasing authority. Ethnic tension and violence soon resulted.

During the summer of 1990, in the wake of the changes in the former Soviet bloc nations, Slovenia and Croatia declared independence from the central Yugoslav government. By June 1991, full-fledged war had erupted between Serbia and Croatia. In 1992, Croatian and Serbian forces divided Bosnia-Herzegovina. The Muslims in Bosnia—who had lived alongside Serbs and Croats for generations—were soon crushed between the opposing forces. The Serbs in particular, pursuing a policy called "ethnic cleansing," killed or forcibly moved many Bosnian Muslims.

The United Nations attempted unsuccessfully to intervene. In 1995, NATO forces carried out strategic air strikes. Later that year, under the leadership of the United States, the leaders of the warring forces completed a peace agreement in Dayton, Ohio, which recognized an independent Bosnia. The terms of the agreement were enforced by the presence of NATO troops.

MAP EXPLORATION

To explore this map further, go to http://www.prenhall.com/craig_maps

MAP 32–4 **Ethnic Composition in the Former Yugoslavia.** The rapid changes in Eastern Europe during the close of the 1980s intensified long-standing ethnic tensions in the former Yugoslavia. This map shows where Yugoslavia's ethnic population lived in 1991 before internal conflicts escalated.

How does the Balkans conflict illustrate the importance of ethnic identity in the modern world?

In the late 1990s Serbian aggression against ethnic Albanians in the province of Kosovo again provoked a NATO response. In early 1999 NATO launched an air attack against the Serbian forces. The Serbian army withdrew from Kosovo, and NATO ground forces protected ethnic Albanians. In 2000 a revolution overthrew the regime of Slobodan Milošević.

CHALLENGES TO THE ATLANTIC ALLIANCE

IS NATO still a viable alliance in the post-Cold War era?

CHALLENGES ON THE INTERNATIONAL SECURITY FRONT

After the collapse of the Soviet Union, NATO has expanded its membership to include Poland, the Czech Republic, and Hungary. Yet the present purpose of NATO remains ill defined. NATO attempted to assume the role of internal peacekeeper in the new Europe, but some members and European publics disapproved.

Destruction of Sarajevo.   An elderly parishioner walks through the ruins of St. Mary's Roman Catholic Church in Sarajevo. The church was destroyed by Serb shelling in May 1992.

Which other regions of the world have experienced "ethnic cleansing" in recent years?

NATO's uncertain mission and continental Europe's inward-looking tendency shaped reactions to the September 11, 2001, attack by al-Qaeda on the United States. Initially, Europeans sympathized deeply with Americans, but a significant split soon developed over President George W. Bush's response to the terrorist assault. In what Bush termed "a war on terrorism," the United States overthrew the Taliban government of Afghanistan in late 2001. This destroyed some of al-Qaeda's bases but not its leadership.

The Bush administration then set forth a new policy of preemptive strikes and intervention against potential enemies of the United States, which aroused controversy both at home and abroad. The American invasion of Iraq in 2003, which will be discussed more fully in Chapter 34, received the support of numerous European

CHRONOLOGY

THE BREAKUP OF YUGOSLAVIA

1991	June	Slovenia declares independence
		Croatia declares independence
1992	January	Macedonia declares independence
	April	Serbia and Montenegro proclaim a new Federal Republic of Yugoslavia; war erupts in Bosnia and Herzegovina after Muslims and Croats vote for independence
1995	November	Peace agreement reached in Dayton, Ohio
1998	March	War breaks out in Kosovo, a province of Serbia
1999	March	NATO bombing of Serbia begins
2000		Milošević regime overthrown

Protesters at the UN Climate Change Conference, Montreal. Thousands of people march through the streets of Montreal on December 3, 2005, as part of a worldwide day of protest against global warming. The demonstration coincided with a United Nations Climate Change Conference.

Why are most of the demonstrators in this photograph young people?

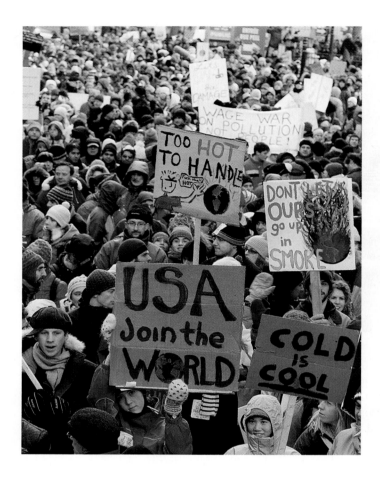

governments, but some traditional European allies of the United States—particularly France and Germany—sharply criticized American decision making and actions. Popular political opinon across Europe dissented vocally from American policy.

Terrorists have struck in Europe and have shown how al-Qaeda–sponsored attacks can influence European politics. On March 11, 2004, at least 190 people were killed in commuter train bombings in Madrid, Spain, and on July 7, 2005, more than 50 were killed by a similar attack in London. The Spanish attack occurred just before an election, and the Spanish government that had supported the American invasion of Iraq was voted from office.

Profound divisions have arisen between the United States and many of its post-war allies. Many Europeans see their values and their emerging political community as different from those of Americans. Over time, external events and the wider conflict between the West and radical political Islam will most likely determine the character of the Atlantic alliance, just as the division between a democratic West and a communist East did in the past.

STRAINS OVER ENVIRONMENTAL POLICY

The impact of economic development on the environment has been a growing concern. Politically active environmental movements have developed around the world. Some have worked within the existing political system; others have taken more radical courses of action including ecological terrorism, sabotage, and confrontation with police at major meetings of world leaders.

Environmental issues have proved divisive within the industrial democracies. During the past decade the political tensions arising from environmentalism have begun to impinge upon international relations, too. The chief issue has been the emission of what are termed *greenhouse gases*, which the scientific community has concluded is raising the temperature of the planet.

In 1997 various members of the United Nations signed the Kyoto Protocol on Climate Change. This treaty set specific mandatory goals for the reduction of the emission of greenhouse gases in the most developed industrial countries against 1990 benchmarks. Those gases include carbon dioxide, methane, hydrofluorocarbons, and sulphur hexafluoride, among others. The Kyoto Protocol received the support of numerous major nations including Japan, Russia, and the European Union and became binding on its signatories in 2005. But the United States, along with Australia, has not ratified the protocol. The Bush administration indicated that it feared implementation would harm economic growth in the United States. The administration also criticized those parts of the treaty that permit developing nations such as China and India not to reduce their emissions, contending this would disadvantage the United States in world trade.

This stance put the United States at odds with traditional European allies as well as Japan. Moreover, as the United States pursued its intervention in Iraq, numerous European governments criticized the American government for pressing unilateral policies on a number of fronts. In the spring of 2007 the United States sought to modify its position, offering to enter negotiations with all nations that are major contributors to greenhouse emissions including India and China, and to negotiate specific targets for elimination of emissions. Germany and other nations, meanwhile, have proposed ambitious goals for the reduction of greenhouse emissions.

Numerous factors account for recent shifts in environmental policy. The American National Academy of Sciences has determined the rate of worldwide greenhouse emissions is growing faster than anyone predicted. Many industrial and commercial companies have found it to their advantage to embrace the environmental cause. Across the globe, environmental activists have been making great strides in publicizing their case.

Two trends clearly lie ahead. First, environmental pollution will continue to grow. Second, a period of protracted negotiations will ensue. Those negotiations will contribute to the ongoing tension between the United States and its traditional Atlantic partners.

SUMMARY

WHAT WERE the causes of the Cold War?

The Cold War Era. U.S.–Soviet cooperation did not survive World War II. After 1945 Europe was divided into a Soviet-dominated zone in the East (the Warsaw Pact) and a U.S.-led zone in the West (NATO). U.S.–Soviet rivalry played itself out around the world from the 1950s to the 1980s, although gradually a spirit of détente arose between the two powers, especially under President Ronald Reagan and Soviet leader Mikhail Gorbachev. The Cold War ended with the disappearance of the Soviet Union in 1991. *page 805*

WHAT MAJOR trends have marked European Society since World War II?

European Society in the Second Half of the Twentieth Century and Beyond. Since World War II, European society has been marked by a rise in prosperity and consumerism, more rights and opportunities for women, and moves toward political and economic unification symbolized by the adoption of a common currency, the euro, in 2002. *page 811*

WHAT ARE the main themes that have characterized postwar America?

American Domestic Scene Since World War II. The major themes in postwar American history were opposition to communism at home and abroad, the expansion of civil rights to African Americans, and economic prosperity. Politically, the relatively liberal years from the late 1950s through the 1970s were succeeded by a growing conservatism, especially under the presidencies of Ronald Reagan, George Bush, and George W. Bush. Even the democratic President Bill Clinton was more a centrist than a liberal. After the terrorist attacks of September 11, 2001, the United States embarked on a war on terrorism that led to wars in Afghanistan and Iraq. *page 817*

HOW DID leaders after Stalin attempt to reform Soviet government?

The Soviet Union to 1989. Khrushchev loosened the grip of the Stalinist state, but his foreign policy failures—notably the Cuban Missile Crisis—led to his resignation in 1964. The Brezhnev era saw both increased repression at home and attempts to reach accommodations with the West. Poland's Solidarity movement was temporarily suppressed. Gorbachev's reformist policies were based around the concepts of *perestroika* (restructuring) and *glasnost* (openness). *page 820*

WHY DID communist regimes collapse so easily in Eastern Europe in 1989?

1989: Year of Revolutions in Eastern Europe. Solidarity reemerged in Poland, and in 1989 Gorbachev approved Poland's first postwar non-Communist prime minister. In Hungary in 1990, open elections displaced Communist rule. East Germany opened the Berlin Wall in late 1989, and soon Germany reunified. Vaclev Havel, a playwright, led the "velvet revolution" in Czechoslovakia. In Romania, however, the overturn of Communist rule was violent, ending with the execution of dictatorial President Ceausescu. *page 823*

WHO WERE the leaders in the period surrounding the collapse of the Soviet Union?

The Collapse of the Soviet Union. The failure of the communist regimes in Eastern Europe and the Soviet Union to produce economic prosperity or political liberalization led to their growing unpopularity. Soviet economic difficulties led Mikhail Gorbachev to institute liberal reforms that led to the collapse of communist rule first in Eastern Europe, then in the Soviet Union itself. The disappearance of the Soviet Union led to independence for much of the former Soviet empire. Russia itself has experienced social, economic, and political turmoil under presidents Boris Yeltsin and Vladimir Putin. *page 824*

HOW DID the West respond to the collapse of Yugoslavia?

The Collapse of Yugoslavia and Civil War. In the former Yugoslavia, the end of communist rule led to dismemberment and civil war. In the 1990s the NATO powers, led by the United States, intervened to halt the fighting and end a pattern of ethnic atrocities. *page 827*

IS NATO still a viable alliance in the post-Cold War era?

Challenges to the Atlantic Alliance. NATO has endured and grown, but its mission is unclear. The Bush administration's unilateralism has alienated traditional American allies. Environmental policy is another area of disagreement between Europe and the United States. *page 828*

REVIEW QUESTIONS

1. What were the causes of the Cold War? What was the effect of the Cold War on Europe?

2. How did the outcome of World War II affect Europe's position in the world? What prompted European unification? How successful has it been?

3. What were the chief characteristics of Western European society in the decades since 1945? What was the experience of Eastern Europe during the same period and why was it different? Be sure to discuss women's roles.

4. How has immigration changed the face of Europe since 1945?

5. What were the most important developments in the domestic history of the United States between 1945 and 1968? How did the Vietnam War affect American society? When did the shift to political conservatism occur in the United States? What did it mean for the role of the federal government?

6. Describe the Soviet economy between 1945 and 1990. Did it meet the needs of the Soviet people? What were the causes of the collapse of the Soviet Union? What role did Gorbachev play in that process?

7. Describe the collapse of communist rule in Eastern Europe. Why was it a relatively bloodless revolution? What problems have ensued?

8. Why did Yugoslavia break apart and slide into civil war? How did the West respond to this crisis?

9. How did the American response to the attacks of September 11, 2001, cause significant rifts in the NATO alliance? Why do some European nations dissent from the U.S. position in the Middle East?

10. What aspects of environmental policy have divided the United States and Europes?

KEY TERMS

Cold War (p. 804)
euro (p. 812)
European Economic Community (EEC) (p. 811)
European Union (EU) (p. 812)

glasnost (GLAZ-nohst) (p. 823)
Marshall Plan (p. 806)
perestroika (PAYR-uhs-TROY-kuh) (p. 821)

Note: To learn more about the topics in this chapter, please turn to the Suggested Readings at the end of the book.

INTERPRETING THE PAST

Feminism and Civil Rights after World War II

Sources from MyHistoryLab for Chapter 32

myhistorylab

1) *Ladies' Home Journal*, "Young Mother," 1956
2) Martin Luther King Jr., *Letter from Birmingham Jail*, 1963

Source from Chapter 32

1) *Simone de Beauvoir Urges Economic Freedom for Women* (pages 816-817)

As the global economy and society changed in the years after World War II, women assumed larger roles in the workforce and in politics. Married women were no longer relegated to the domestic sphere, and increasing numbers of younger women entered college, slowly gaining a foothold in the higher-paid professions. Yet gender inequality persisted throughout the second half of the twentieth century. As a result, the feminist movement gained influence.

The Civil Rights Movement in the United States grew out of continuing efforts of African Americans to gain their full rights as citizens. During the 1950s and 1960s, black World War II veterans and their families joined with clergymen such as Martin Luther King, Jr., and younger supporters to engage in strikes and demonstrations to end restrictive laws and traditions.

In this exercise you will read three primary sources relating to feminism and the Civil Rights Movement. Then answer the following questions to complete the assignment.

The first document is an excerpt from *The Second Sex*, by Simone de Beauvoir, one of the pioneering feminists of the post–World War II era. The second source is a 1956 article from *Ladies' Home Journal*, a popular magazine for American women, exploring the world of a suburban housewife. The third source is Martin Luther King, Jr.'s *Letter from Birmingham Jail*, written to a group of white Alabama clergyman who stated their support of King's cause while disagreeing with his tactics.

Questions

What are de Beauvoir's arguments on behalf of economic rights for women? How does she link them to women's civil rights?

How does the *Ladies' Home Journal* article depict suburban life for the young mother being profiled? What is her role? How does it differ from the roles envisioned by de Beauvoir?

How does King justify breaking laws and demonstrating peacefully against injustice? What is his response to those who urge him to wait for court action? How does he invoke an economic dimension to racial injustice?

33

East Asia: The Recent Decades

The Price of Growth. A coal-powered plant in Hebei province, northern China, February 2006. According to the Worldwatch Institute, sixteen of the world's twenty most polluted cities are in China. On average, China builds one coal-fired plant a week.

What are the costs of China's economic expansion?

JAPAN *page 837*

HOW DID the postwar occupation change Japan politically?

CHINA *page 843*

WHY DID Mao launch the Cultural Revolution?

TAIWAN *page 849*

HOW DO U.S. and Chinese policies toward Taiwan differ?

KOREA *page 851*

HOW DID South Korean and North Korean postwar developments differ?

VIETNAM *page 854*

HOW DOES the recent history of Vietnam illustrate the legacies of both colonialism and the Cold War?

GLOBAL PERSPECTIVE

MODERN EAST ASIA

Before World War II, only Europe, the United States, and Japan had successfully combined the ingredients needed for modern economic growth. It was as though these countries had a magic potion that the rest of the world lacked. Industrialization in East Asia during the second half of the twentieth century made clear that there was no magic potion: The West and Japan just got there first. The industrialization of East Asia raises issues that powerfully affect relations among nations.

One question is whether high-wage nations will be able to compete with those low-wage nations that have found the formula for growth. Until recently, advanced nations were satisfied with their share of world trade. They sold the products of their heavy industries and advanced technologies and bought raw materials and the labor-intensive products of light industries. They assumed that their technological advantage was permanent and that they could always stay sufficiently ahead of the less-developed nations to maintain high wages for their workers. This assumption has now been challenged. Since the 1960s, Taiwan, South Korea, Hong Kong, and Singapore have not only achieved modern economic growth but have also moved rapidly into high technology—well before their wages reached Western levels. This has made them formidable competitors in precisely those areas in which the West has

considered itself preeminent. Since the late 1980s, China has done the same. The United States, by keeping its market open, regained competitiveness during the 1990s, but at the cost of holding down wages, drastic corporate restructuring, relocating jobs abroad, and accumulating huge trade deficits. Will it be willing to continue paying this price? Will competition, combined with runaway immigration, create a permanent two-tier system of wages? China, the most recent East Asian industrializer, will possess the economic advantages of cheap labor for decades. If it succeeds in its development goals, the impact on high-wage nations will be massive.

A second issue raised by East Asian economic growth concerns natural resources. An oil crisis occurred in the early 1970s when demand outran supply. There were shortages at the pumps, a steep rise in the price of oil, and a transfer of wealth from industrial to oil-rich nations. Experts pointed out that the world's reserves were dwindling. Market forces, however, uncovered new sources of supply and the crisis faded, yet oil reserves are still being used up faster than ever as demand rises. At some point demand, including new demand from China and India, will again outstrip supply. Soaring gas prices suggest the point is near at hand. Will struggles over scarce resources become a central feature in future international relations?

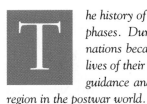

T he history of East Asia since the end of World War II may be divided into two phases. During the first phase, from 1945 to 1980, several East Asian nations became communist. They achieved only a small improvement in the lives of their peoples. In stark contrast, the nations that used a mixture of state guidance and market-oriented economies made East Asia the most dynamic region in the postwar world.

Japan led the way economically and also developed into a robust parliamentary democracy with freedoms comparable to those of Western Europe or the United States. Taiwan and South Korea began their economic development later and from a lower level. Though lacking the political freedom of Japan, they attained stunning economic growth, as did Hong Kong and Singapore. Viewing the progress of these countries, it would appear that the values of the East Asian heritage—hard work, frugality, family orientation, thirst for education, and concern for getting ahead—lead to economic development if given half a chance.

The communist nations—China, Vietnam, and North Korea—did poorly. China was wracked by continuous political convulsions. The contrast between the low productivity of the Chinese in China and the high productivity of the same people in Hong Kong and Taiwan was remarkable. Vietnam, plagued by wars during these early decades, did not develop at all. North Korea did slightly better during the decade after the Korean War but then plummeted to a state of misery.

The second phase of postwar East Asian history began during the 1980s. Those nations that had prospered earlier continued to grow. Japan's per capita product zoomed to European

A third issue is population. Japan's population quadrupled in the course of its industrialization and then began to level off without a need for draconian measures. Its pattern resembled that of the advanced nations of the West. China, in contrast, already had a huge population when it began its recent industrialization. Since it could ill afford a further quadrupling, it adopted extremely tough policies to limit births. Its population may peak at 1.6 billion in 2030. Whether other less-developed nations in the world follow the Japanese or Chinese pattern will depend on their particular circumstances, but for many, the Chinese model may be unavoidable. More people are no blessing.

A fourth issue concerns the political consequences of economic growth. The recent history of Taiwan and South Korea suggests that East Asian dictatorships can evolve toward democracy as standards of living rise. Will this happen in China? China is prospering, and its people are caught up in consumerism, but the Chinese Communist Party, so far, shows no signs of relaxing its monopoly on government. Also, postwar Taiwan and South Korea were less thoroughly authoritarian to begin with and were strongly influenced by the United States. It is too early to speak with any confidence.

A final issue, the dark companion of industrial and population growth, is pollution. As long as most of the world remained underdeveloped, the industrial nations assumed that their wastes would harmlessly vanish into the vast reaches of surrounding lands and seas. But as populations encroach on forested lands, and Eastern Europe, India, Russia, South America, and East Asia industrialize, pollution becomes more threatening. Even apart from disasters such as Minamata and Chernobyl, automobile fumes, industrial effluents, chimney gases, pesticides, garbage, and sewage cause lakes to die, forests to wither, and levels of toxins to rise.

Focus Questions

◆ What is the impact of East Asian economic growth on the world's natural resources? On international relations?

◆ Does recent history suggest that the Chinese government will become more democratic as its citizens become more prosperous?

levels. *Taiwan, South Korea, Hong Kong, and Singapore (sometimes referred to as the "tiger" economies) also achieved amazing advances. Growth went hand in hand with social stability and an increasingly varied cultural life. Especially notable were advances in democracy in Taiwan and South Korea (see Map 33–1).*

The most notable positive changes occurred in China, which in 1978 launched a market economy within a communist dictatorship. Explosive growth and an export boom resulted. As the economy grew, the society was also transformed. Vietnam adopted a weaker version of the same policy. Only North Korea resisted the changes sweeping the rest of the communist world. The rigidities of its singular brand of communism took their toll: In the early years of the twenty-first century, its people suffered hunger and misery, and its government pursued desperate policies. ■

JAPAN

HOW DID postwar occupation change Japan politically?

By early 1945, most Japanese were poor, hungry, and ill-clothed. Cities were burnt out, factories scarred by bombings; ships had been sunk, railways were dilapidated, and trucks and cars were scarce. On August 15, 1945, the emperor broadcast Japan's surrender to the Japanese people. They expected a harsh and vindictive occupation, but when they found it constructive, their receptivity to new democratic ideas and their repudiation of militarism led one Japanese writer to label the era "the second opening of Japan."

MAP 33–1   Contemporary East Asia.

Which nations in East Asia are Communist today?

THE OCCUPATION

General Douglas MacArthur was the Supreme Commander for the Allied powers in Japan, and the occupation forces were mostly American. The chief concern of the first phase of the occupation was demilitarization and democratization. Civilians and soldiers abroad were returned to Japan and the military was demobilized. Wartime leaders were brought to trial for "crimes against humanity." Shinto was disestablished as the state religion, labor unions were encouraged, and the holding companies of *zaibatsu* combines were dissolved. Land reform expropriated landlord holdings and sold them to landless tenants at a fractional cost.

zaibatsu Large industrial combines that came to dominate Japanese industry in the late nineteenth century.

The new constitution, written by MacArthur's headquarters and passed into law by the Japanese Diet, fundamentally changed Japan's polity in five respects:

1. A British-style parliamentary state was established along with an American-style independent judiciary and a federal system of prefectures with elected governors.

2. Women were given the right to vote.

3. The rights to life, liberty, the pursuit of happiness, a free press, and free assembly were guaranteed. These were joined by newer rights, such as academic freedom, collective bargaining, sexual equality in marriage, and minimal standards of wholesome and cultural living.

4. **Article 9,** the no-war clause, stipulated: "The Japanese people forever renounce war as a sovereign right of the nation" and will never maintain "land, sea, and air forces" or "other war potential." This article would make Japan into something unique in the world: a major power without commensurate military strength.

5. The constitution defined a new role for the emperor as "the symbol of the state deriving his position from the will of the people with whom resides sovereign power."

The Japanese people accepted the new constitution and embraced democracy with uncritical enthusiasm. To create a climate in which the new democracy could flourish, the occupation in its second phase turned to Japan's economic recovery. It dropped plans to deconcentrate big business further, encouraged the Japanese government to curb inflation, and cracked down on Communist unions. The United States also gave Japan $2 billion in economic aid.

The outbreak of the Korean War in 1950 marked the start of the third and final phase of the Occupation. The American military had little time for Japan, and the Japanese cabinet and Diet began to assume more responsibility for the country. When Japan regained its sovereignty in April 1952, the changeover was hardly noticeable in the daily life of the Japanese people. On the same day as the peace treaty, Japan signed a security treaty with the United States, which became the cornerstone of Japan's minimalist defense policy.

Emperor Hirohito and General MacArthur. The two men met at the U.S. Embassy in Tokyo in 1945. MacArthur felt the emperor contributed to the stability of Japan and made the work of the Occupation easier. The emperor was glad to be of use and relieved he was not hanged as a war criminal.

What was the Occupation?

Article 9 of the No-War Constitution
Article 9 of the Japanese Constitution forbids not only the use of force as a means to settling international disputes but also the maintenance of an army, navy, or air force.

PARLIAMENTARY POLITICS

Japan's postwar politics can be divided into three periods. The first, from 1945 to 1955, was the continuation of prewar party politics as modified to fit the new political environment. Two conservative parties, the Liberals and the Democrats, and the Japanese Socialist Party emerged. For most of this first decade, the Liberals held power.

In the long second period from 1955 to 1993, the Liberal Democratic Party **(LDP),** which was formed by a merger of the two conservative parties, held power and the Japanese Socialist Party was the permanent opposition. The LDP became identified as the party that was rebuilding Japan and maintaining Japan's security through close ties with the United States. Despite the cozy relationships that developed between the LDP and business, periodic scandals, and a widespread distrust of

LDP The Liberal Democratic Party. A conservative party that has dominated postwar Japanese politics.

CHRONOLOGY

JAPAN SINCE 1945

1948–1954	Yoshida ministries
1950–1953	Korean War
1952	Peace and security treaties
1955	Liberal and Democratic Parties merge to form the LDP
1955–1973	Double-digit economic growth
1972	Japan recognizes the People's Republic of China
1973–1989	Economic growth continues at slower pace
1990	Bubble bursts and recession begins
1993	Socialists lose half of their Diet seats
1994–1996	Non-LDP coalitions govern; LDP-led coalitions reestablished
2001–2006	Koizumi Junichirō of the LDP as prime minister
2003	Japan sends troops to Iraq
2006	Abe Shinzō of the LDP becomes prime minister
2007	Fukuda Yasuo of the LDP becomes prime minister

QUICK REVIEW

Factors in Japan's Postwar Growth

◆ Survival of pre-war service and skills infrastructure

◆ High savings rate facilitated reinvestment

◆ Growing, well-educated labor force

◆ Pro-business government policies

Opening the Olympics. In the 1964 Tokyo Olympics Japan stepped back onto the international stage after the disasters of the war years. Holding the Olympic torch was Yoshinori Sakai, who was born in Hiroshima on August 6, 1945, when the atomic bomb was dropped on the city.

Why was Japan so open to Western influence after World War II?

politicians, the Japanese people voted to keep it in power. Rule by a single party for such a long period provided an unusual continuity in government policies.

A third era of politics began with the 1993 election. The notable feature of this era was the decline and fall of the left. The end of the Cold War and the worldwide rejection of Marxism contributed to the demise of socialism in Japan, and the Communist Party also slumped. The collapse of the left inaugurated an era of multiparty conservative politics, but the LDP remained the largest party. Japanese politics were plagued by scandals and factional strife during the 1990s, but the major issue was the economy. Concern for the economy strengthened opposition to the LDP and raised the possibility that a two-party system might emerge. After the turn of the millennium, the economy strengthened and with it the fortunes of the LDP. From 2001 to 2006, the popular Koizumi Junichirō was party president and prime minister. He was followed as prime minister by the belligerent and less popular Abe Shinzō and, in 2007, by the dovish Fukuda Yasuo. For the time being the LDP maintains its popular hegemony.

ECONOMIC GROWTH

The extraordinary story of the economic rise of East Asia after World War II began with Japan. Several factors explain this growth. An infrastructure of banking, marketing, and manufacturing skills had carried over from prewar Japan. The international situation was also favorable: Oil was cheap, access to raw materials and export markets was easy, and American sponsorship gained Japan early entry into international financing organizations. A tradition of frugality created a rate of savings close to 20 percent, which helped reinvestment.

A revolution in education contributed as well. By the early 1980s, almost all middle school graduates went on to high school, and a rising percentage went on to higher education. By the early 1980s, Japan was graduating more engineers than the United States. (The annual output of law schools in the United States equals the total number of lawyers in Japan.) This upgrading of human capital and channeling of its best minds into productive careers let Japan tap the huge backlog of technology that had developed in the United States during and after the war years. After "improvement engineering," Japan sold its products to the world.

Another factor was an abundance of high-quality, cheap labor provided by a postwar baby boom. Workers quickly moved from agriculture to industry, and labor organizations proved no bar to economic growth. (In 2005, only about one fifth of the labor force belonged to unions.) The government also aided manufacturers with tariff protection, foreign exchange, and special depreciation allowances. Industries engaged in advanced technologies benefited from cheap loans, subsidies, and research products of government laboratories. Critics who spoke of "Japan Inc." as though Japan were a single gigantic corporation overstated the case, but government was more supportive of business than it was regulative.

By 1973, the Japanese economy had become "mature." Double-digit growth gave way to 4 percent growth. Smokestack industries declined while service industries, pharmaceuticals, specialty chemicals, scientific equipment, computers, and robots grew. Japan's trade began to generate huge surpluses. The surpluses were generated mainly by the appetite of world markets for Japanese products, but they were also a result of protectionist policies that the United States and Europe insisted be abolished.

Sluggish growth, at best, characterized the nineties. Japanese had bid up the price of corporate shares and land to unrealistic levels. In 1991 the "bubble" burst: The price of land and stocks plummeted. As banks and individuals retrenched, the economy slowed and unemployment rose. In 2002 an export-led recovery began. The reviving American economy and the soaring Chinese economy were critical. Japanese economists began to speak of the "complementarity" of Japanese and Chinese markets. In 2004 consumers began to spend, and stock valuations also rose. Banks still carried many bad debts. Public debt was high, but the Japanese, protected by lifetime employment, were unwilling to shoulder new taxes. As in the developed economies of the United States and Europe, industrial production continued to move abroad in pursuit of cheap, skilled labor. But Japanese strengths were also formidable: Industry was restructured with greater rewards for talent. Japanese automobiles were coveted throughout the world, and the Japanese export surplus grew. Even Japan's redoubtable management skills seemed exportable: Nissan's Tennessee plant took 17.37 hours to assemble an automobile, while at General Motors the average was 26.75. Equally notable was Japan's determination to maintain its lead in flat screens, fermentation chemistry, robotics, and materials research and to become a world force in biotechnology, medical instruments, and airplanes.

At the dawn of the third millennium Japan's economy loomed large. It was second only to the United States, larger than the other East Asian economies combined, or almost as large as the economies of Germany and France combined. (See the comparative data in Figure 33–1 and in the Overview table on p. 842.) Japan achieved a near-European level of affluence through the peaceful development of human resources in a free society.

Nissan Motors Assembly Line. An almost completely automated assembly line at Nissan Motors' Zama factory. The high cost of labor in Japan makes such robot-intensive production economical.

Why are labor costs high in Japan?

A Comparison of Japan with Germany and France in the Year 2006 (IMF Estimates)		
GDP (in billions)	Population (in millions)	Per Capita GDP
Germany $2,872	82	$35,024
France $2,149	64	$33,578
Total $5,021	146	$34,390 (average)
Japan $4,883	127	$38,449

FIGURE 33–1. A comparison of recent Gross Domestic Product and population statistics for Japan, Germany, and France help put Japan's economy in perspective.

What is remarkable about Japan's recent economic growth?

Middle School Students in a Japanese Literature Class. Girls and boys wear school uniforms and study together. Desks are pushed together to accommodate large classes. The teacher is dressed like a businessman.

What role has education played in Japan's development?

SOCIETY AND CULTURE

The triple engines of change—Occupation reforms, economic growth, and rapid expansion of higher education—transformed Japanese society. In 1945, almost half of the population lived in villages rooted in the past; half a century later most Japanese lived in cities, and a tiny portion of the population raised the food that fed the rest. In 1945, arranged marriages and three-generation extended families were common. Now nuclear families and "love matches" are the rule. Consumerism was constrained only by the small size of living units. Reforms imposed during the American occupation gave women the right to vote, legal equality, and equal inheritance rights. As women were admitted to prestigious universities and embarked on careers, the average age of marriage rose and more wives worked outside the home. Divorce rates also tripled. Prospering in the new Japan depended on education, and a rigorous system of examinations determined admission at every level. The enormous prewar gap between the tiny educated elite and the masses disappeared as 90 percent of Japanese came to see themselves as middle class. This fostered democracy, while a new respect for personal autonomy helped diminish some traditional ethnic prejudices. The highly disciplined lifestyle encouraged by the educational system and corporate culture, however, created a phenomenon called *karōshi*, or death from overwork.

The most serious social problem facing Japan today is the aging of its population. By 2010, there will be fewer than two workers for every retired person. A

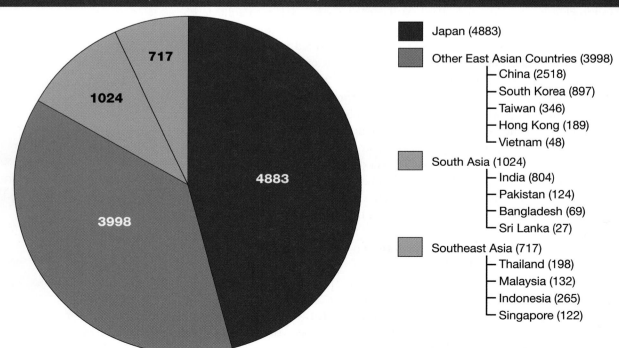

OVERVIEW — Gross Domestic Products (GDP) of Japan, Other East Asian Nations, and Other Asian Nations in 2006 (in billions of dollars)

- Japan (4883)
- Other East Asian Countries (3998)
  - China (2518)
  - South Korea (897)
  - Taiwan (346)
  - Hong Kong (189)
  - Vietnam (48)
- South Asia (1024)
  - India (804)
  - Pakistan (124)
  - Bangladesh (69)
  - Sri Lanka (27)
- Southeast Asia (717)
  - Thailand (198)
  - Malaysia (132)
  - Indonesia (265)
  - Singapore (122)

recurring question is how the old will be supported and how they will vote in elections. All developed nations have experienced a comparable shift in demographics, but the imbalance is particularly severe in Germany, Italy, and Japan. Japan is crowded, and some see its current low birthrate as an opportunity to reduce population. Many illegal immigrants, however, come from other parts of Asia to take lowly jobs that the Japanese despise.

The cultural strains produced by Japan's rapid transformation have dislocated some people and created followings for new religions. One aberrant apocalyptic cult released nerve gas in a Tokyo subway in 1995. Yet traditions of lifetime employment, a low crime rate, stable families, and a flourishing artistic culture (which excels at Western as well as traditional Japanese arts) testify to Japan's remarkable success at recovering from the devastation of World War II.

JAPAN AND THE WORLD

At the start of the new millennium, Japan had three sets of critical international relationships: with the world, East Asia, and the United States. With the world, Japan was a trading partner and, as it described itself, a "UN nation." It gave generous foreign aid to developing countries and was a member of major international economic organizations. A second set was with its East Asian neighbors. For reasons of history and proximity, Japan was extraordinarily alert to developments in Korea, Taiwan, China, and the Russian Far East. China's growing military strength was a concern. The third critical relationship was with the United States. The two countries were political allies, major trading partners, and linked by mutual security concerns. The 1952 security treaty remained the cornerstone of Japanese defense planning. When terrorists struck at the United States in September 2001, Prime Minister Koizumi spoke out in support of the United States and against terrorism, and in 2003 Japan sent troops to Iraq. Japan feels increasingly vulnerable in light of the nuclear arsenals of its neighbors, and should its trust in the U.S. "nuclear umbrella" waver, it would quickly become a nuclear power.

Comic Book. Raised from childhood in the arts of *ninja*, the young heroine Azumi slays evil men. The popularity of this *Bigu Komikku* (Big Comic) led to a movie (*anime*, or animated) version. Was this the Japanese model for *Kill Bill?* Japan has specialized comics for every demographic group—for children, teenage boys, teenage girls, and adults.

Why might the escapism of comic books be particularly appealing for the Japanese?

CHINA

The story of China after 1949 is rooted in theories about economics and population. Marx rejected the Malthusian hypothesis that population growth tends to outstrip food production as a myth of capitalist societies, and Mao Zedong agreed. From 1949 until 1981, China's population increased from 550 million to nearly 1 billion. Growth in the Chinese economy was eaten up by all the new mouths, and in 1981 China adopted a policy of one child per family. This policy runs contrary to the deep-rooted Chinese sense of family, but the government argued that without it, China's future would be bleak. Thereafter population growth slowed dramatically, but the population still crossed the 1.3 billion mark in 2005. The median age in China in 2007 is thirty-three. Consequently, the birthrate remains high, despite the one-child policy. Population will continue to grow until sometime before the middle of the century.

WHY DID Mao launch the Cultural Revolution?

SOVIET PERIOD (1950–1960)

Civil war in China ended in 1949 as the last of Jiang Jieshi's troops fled to Taiwan. The People's Republic of China was proclaimed in October. The following year, China entered into an alliance with the Soviet Union. The decade that followed is often called the "Soviet period" because the Soviet model was adopted for the government, the army, the economy, and higher education.

Trial of a Landlord. The judges, seated at tables with their hats beneath, are former tenants and Communist Party cadres. The accused, bound and guarded by PRC soldiers, is a former landlord or village head. During the land reform of the early 1950s, the sentence was often death.

What has happened in China's rural areas since the Communists came to power?

brainwashing Attempting to "re-educate" or alter a person's thoughts and beliefs to create behavior desired by the state, regardless of the individual's wishes.

Great Leap Forward Mao's disastrous attempt to modernize the Chinese economy in 1958.

Cultural Revolution A movement launched by Mao between 1965 and 1976 against the Soviet-style bureaucracy that had taken hold in China. It involved widespread disorder and violence.

The first step taken by the communist government was military consolidation. Areas inhabited by Tibetans, Uighur Turks, Mongols, and other minorities were occupied by the Chinese army and settled by Chinese immigrants. Political consolidation then followed. The Communist Party held the key levers of power in the government, army, and security forces. Mao was chairman of the party and head of state. He ruled through the Politboro and a system of regional, provincial, and district committees with party cells in every village, factory, school, and government office. Party members were exhorted to enforce the local enactment of government policies. Economic reconstruction was attempted on a massive scale, with the help of the Soviet Union, which sent financial aid as well as engineers and planners.

During the early 1950s, intellectuals and universities also became a target for thought reform; the Chinese slang term was **brainwashing**. This involved study and indoctrination in Marxism, group pressures to produce an atmosphere of insecurity and fear, followed by confession, repentance, and reacceptance by society. The indoctrination was intended to strengthen party control and mobilize human energies on behalf of the state. By the late 1950s, Mao was disappointed with the results of collectivization, and in 1958, he resorted to mass mobilization to unleash the productive energies of the people, a policy called the **Great Leap Forward**. Campaigns were organized to accomplish vast projects, and village-based collective farms gave way to communes of 30,000 persons or more. The results were disastrous. Between 1958 and 1962, 20 to 30 million Chinese reportedly starved to death. Policies were modified, but agricultural production continued to fall, plagued by the ills of low incentives and collective responsibility.

Sino-Soviet relations also deteriorated. Disputes arose over borders. China was dissatisfied with Soviet aid. The Soviet Union condemned the Great Leap Forward as "leftist fanaticism" and resented Mao's view of himself, after Stalin's death, as the foremost exponent of world communism. In 1960, the Soviet Union halted economic aid and withdrew its engineers from China. Each country deployed about a million troops along their mutual border. The Sino-Soviet split was arguably the single most important development in postwar international politics.

The years between 1960 and 1965 saw conflicting trends. The failure of the Great Leap Forward led some Chinese leaders to turn away from Mao's reckless radicalism toward more moderate policies. Mao remained head of the party but had to give up his post as head of state. Yet even as the government moved toward realistic goals and stable bureaucratic management, a new mass movement was begun to promote ideological indoctrination.

THE GREAT PROLETARIAN CULTURAL REVOLUTION (1965–1976)

In 1965, Mao once again emerged to dominate Chinese politics. He feared that the Chinese revolution—his revolution—would end up as a Soviet-style bureaucratic communism run for the benefit of officials. So he called for a new revolution to create a truly egalitarian culture.

Obtaining army support, Mao urged students and teenagers to form bands of Red Guards to carry out a new **Cultural Revolution**. Mao's sayings, the "Little Red Book," assumed the status of scripture. Universities were shut down as student factions fought. Teachers were beaten, imprisoned, and humiliated. Books were burned and art destroyed. Homes were ransacked for foreign books and Chinese who had studied abroad were persecuted. Red Guards beat to death those viewed as reactionaries. High officials were purged. Chinese today recall these events as a species of mass hysteria that defies understanding.

Eventually Mao tired of the violence and near anarchy. In 1968 and 1969 he called in the army. Millions of students and intellectuals were sent to the countryside to work on farms. Worsening relations with the Soviet Union also made China's leaders desire greater stability at home. When President Richard Nixon proposed a renewal of ties, China responded. Nixon visited Beijing in 1972, opening a new era of diplomatic relations.

The second phase of the Cultural Revolution between 1969 and 1976 was moderate only in comparison with what had gone before. On farms and in factories, ideology was still substituted for economic incentives. Universities reopened, but students were admitted by class background, not examination. In 1971, the so-called Gang of Four, which included Mao's wife and was abetted by the aging Mao, came to power.

CHRONOLOGY

CHINA SINCE 1949

1949	Communist victory; People's Republic of China established
1950	Sino-Soviet alliance; China invades Tibet
1953	First five-year Plan
1958	Great Leap Forward
1960–1963	Sino-Soviet split
1965–1976	Cultural Revolution
1972	Nixon visits Beijing
1976	Mao Zedong dies
1978–1997	Deng Xiaoping in power
1980–2007	China's economy grows at double-digit rate
1989	Tienanmen Square incident
2003	Hu Jintao becomes premier

QUICK REVIEW

Sino-Soviet Relations

- 1958: Mao abandons Soviet economic model in favor of Great Leap Forward
- Disputes over borders and Chinese dissatisfaction with Soviet aid leads to deteriorating relations
- 1960: Soviet Union halts economic aid and withdraws engineers

Performance During Cultural Revolution. Members of the Xiangyang Commune in Jiangsu Province take part in the campaign to "Criticize Lin Biao and Confucius," one of the last large "campaigns" dictated by members of Chinese government in charge of the Cultural Revolution. Here, the commune's amateur art troupe performs a ballad criticizing Confucius. The campaign began after the death of Lin Biao, who, though for a time was Mao Zedong's chosen successor, was accused of attempting to seize power.

What was the Cultural Revolution?

CHINA AFTER MAO

Mao's death in 1976 brought immediate changes. The Gang of Four and their radical supporters were arrested. In their place, Deng Xiaoping (1904–1997) emerged as the dominant figure in Chinese politics. Deng ousted his enemies, rehabilitated those purged during the Cultural Revolution, and put his supporters in power. After the lunacy of the Cultural Revolution, a "normal" Communist Party dictatorship was a relief. The people could now enjoy a measure of security and material improvement. There continued, however, a tension between the determination of the ruling party to maintain its grip on power and its desire to obtain the benefits of liberalization.

Universities returned to normal in 1977. Entrance examinations were reinstituted, purged teachers returned to their classrooms, and scholars were sent to study in Japan and the West. Students began to demand still greater freedoms with the hope that they would lead to political democracy.

In April and May 1989, hundreds of thousands of students, workers, and people from all walks of life demonstrated for democracy in Tienanmen Square in Beijing and in dozens of other cities. The government sent in tanks and troops. Hundreds of students were killed, and leaders who did not escape abroad were jailed. The event defined the political climate in China for the decades that followed: Freedom was allowed in most areas of life, but no challenge to Communist Party rule was tolerated.

In the economic sphere, China's leaders repudiated the policies of Mao. Deng's great achievement in the years after 1978 was to demonstrate in China the superiority of market incentives to central planning. In China's villages, as the family farm once again became the basic unit of production, grain production rose. State-operated enterprises, which often ran at a loss and employed twice the labor needed to run them efficiently, were a constant drain on China's state-owned banks. As the free market sector grew faster, their share of production declined. Finally, the government announced that "state ownership" would give way. The costs of privatization would be high—defaulted loans, bankruptcies, unemployed workers, and a sudden rise in pensioners, but the drain on the state budget would end. The contribution of state-owned enterprises to total industrial production declined from 40 to 31 percent from 1997 to 2003, but much of this was due to rapid growth in the market sector of the economy.

The main driver of the economy has been the free market sector. After 1980, the Chinese economy grew faster than any other Asian economy. Exports skyrocketed. New enterprises surged in special economic zones along the coasts, and the tide of enterprise swept inland. Yet in the hinterlands large regions lagged behind. To achieve growth, the government was willing to tolerate personal and regional inequities.

The factors that fueled this growth were clear: China used tariffs to shield its markets while making use of cheap labor to flood foreign markets with goods and build up its currency reserves, which in 2003 were second only to those of Japan. China joined the World Trade Organization in 2001; since then its protectionism has become less blatant.

During the Mao years, farmers had been tied to their collective or village. Cities were closed to those without residence

Goddess of Democracy and Freedom.   Student activists construct a "Goddess of Democracy and Freedom," taking the Statue of Liberty as their model. The goddess was in place in Tienanmen Square shortly before tanks drove students from the square in June 1989.

What happened in Tienanmen Square?

permits. City dwellers were members of "units" that provided their members with jobs, housing, food, child care, medical services, and pensions. Party cadres exercised near total control over the unit's members. Block organizations reported any infractions of "socialist morality" to the authorities.

Under Deng, controls were loosened. The police became less active (except against political dissidents), censorship was reduced, and ties with the outside world were allowed to develop. The "unit" also diminished in importance as food became widely available in free markets, and apartments were sold to their inhabitants on easy terms. Private housing brought with it the freedom to change jobs. As workers with higher salaries began to provide for their own needs, life became freer and more enjoyable. The market economy placed a premium on individual decisions and initiatives.

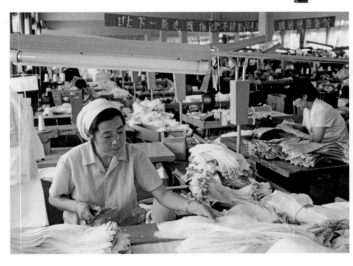

Cheap Labor. Wages at this Beijing shirt factory are low by Western standards but high by Chinese standards. This is not a sweatshop but a modern factory.

Should Western nations leave the production of textiles to low-wage nations? What about steel or microelectronics?

The new prosperity and changing mores became increasingly visible. The blue Mao uniforms of the 1960s were followed by suits, however ill-fitting, and later, for the young, blue jeans, sneakers, and colorful jackets. By the 1990s, innovative Chinese designers were holding fashion shows in Shanghai and Beijing. Young people associated freely, and in urban areas earlier taboos against public displays of affection were relaxed. The household treasures of the 1960s, radios and bicycles, gave way to stoves and refrigerators, and then to washing machines and color televisions. By the early nineties, motorbikes and privately owned cars competed in crowded streets with the ceaseless flow of bicycles. Private restaurants opened, and travel for pleasure became commonplace. In 1988, most passengers on domestic airline flights were foreign; ten years later, most were Chinese. The estimated Chinese per capita GDP, as measured by the exchange value of its currency, was about $1,902 in 2006. Although this is low, in purchasing power the figure is closer to $7,600. Chinese are keenly aware that their living standard has improved sharply over the past two decades and expect similar improvements in the future.

The new wealth was unevenly distributed. The more successful entrepreneurs bought houses, cars, microwaves, computers, and cell phones. As their lifestyle became more Western, they were sometimes called China's new middle class, but in fact they constituted an upper class. Many barely scraped by, and in the hinterlands, poverty and hardship remained the rule. In the West envy is green. In China the envy and resentment of have-nots toward the newly affluent is called the "red-eye disease."

The Cold War largely defined foreign relations in the China of Mao. It was amicable toward its communist neighbors—the Soviet Union, North Korea, and North Vietnam—and hostile toward South Korea, Japan, U.S.-protected Taiwan, and the United States. It sent troops to rescue North Korea during the latter phase of the Korean War (1950–1953), and it sent material aid to the North Vietnamese during the Vietnam War (1959–1975). However, its rupture with the Soviet Union in 1960 isolated it from the other major communist power in East Asia. China's fear of the Soviet Union and America's despair over its war in Vietnam opened the way for President Nixon's visit to China in 1972. The visit notwithstanding, China's foreign relations until after Mao's death in 1976 were largely a reflection of the revolutionary tumult within.

Deng Xiaoping's embrace of market capitalism after 1978 was, necessarily, coupled with an about-face in foreign relations, since world trade was critical

DOCUMENT

U.S. Foreign Policy: A Chinese Dissident's View

*W**ei Jingsheng, a Chinese advocate of democratic rights, was deported to the United States in late 1997. A year later, in an op-ed page essay in The New York Times, he criticized U.S. policy as pandering to Chinese tyranny.***

- **Should** U.S. foreign policy be used to promote human rights even in poor countries with cultural traditions different from those in the West? Or should the United States avoid interference in the domestic politics of other nations and aim primarily at furthering American economic and security goals? What can foreign policy achieve? Where should the balance be struck?

CHINA'S DIVERSIONARY TACTICS

One year ago, after 18 years in a Chinese prison, I was "released" and sent here. A Chinese official said that if I ever set foot in China again, I would immediately be returned to prison... .

The State Department, in a report last January, used my forced exile as evidence that China was taking "positive steps in human rights" and that "Chinese society continued to become more open." These "positive steps" led the United States and its allies to oppose condemnation of China at a meeting of the United Nations Commission on Human Rights in April. In the months that followed, President Clinton and other Western leaders

Chinese Affluence. Shoppers at Pacific Place in Hong Kong, one of the many new upscale shopping malls found throughout China.

How has consumerism affected Chinese society?

QUICK REVIEW

Sino-American Relations

- ◆ 1979: United States recognized China
- ◆ China resents U.S. military alliances in region
- ◆ United States criticizes China's human rights record, nuclear testing, and arms sales
- ◆ Immense imbalance in U.S.-China trade

for export-led economic growth. China reestablished relations with the Soviet Union. It welcomed increased trade and investments from Japan, South Korea, and Taiwan. It developed a growing trade with the European Economic Community.

Relations with the United States were complicated, despite the U.S. recognition of China in 1979. American military alliances with Japan and South Korea, its unofficial support of Taiwan, and its ties to the noncommunist nations of Southeast Asia continued to act as the main countervailing force to Chinese hegemony in the region. China resented the U.S. presence in what it considered its own sphere of influence. The United States was appreciative of the benefits of trade with China but was critical of the extreme imbalance: China's exports to the United States increased from $62 billion in 1997 to $288 billion in 2006 and still rise; its imports from the United States during the same period increased from $13 to $55 billion. The United States protested the continuing Chinese piracy of hundreds of millions of dollars' worth of U.S. movies, computer software, and CDs each year. It also criticized human rights abuses, nuclear testing, and arms sales to Iran and Pakistan. (See Document, "U.S. Foreign Policy: A Chinese Dissident's View.")

A third phase of Chinese foreign policy—of China as a great power—began to take form at the turn of the century. As Japan had earlier, China moved to establish relations with Africa, South America, and the Middle East to secure stable sources of raw materials. It also stepped up the transformation of its military forces from a mass army to a smaller but more powerful, hi-tech, modern military. Unlike Japan, it possessed an arsenal of atomic and hydrogen bombs. The rapid growth of its military budget will soon enable China to project its military strength beyond its borders.

U.S. policy toward the new China rested on the assumption that a wider Chinese engagement with the world would lead to better relations. The Chinese premier visited the United States in 1997, and the U.S. president returned the visit the following year. In 2000, the U.S. House of Representatives accorded China a traveled to China, trumpeting increased economic ties and muting criticism on human rights.

Thus, without fear of sanction, the Chinese Government intensified its repression in 1998. Once the leaders achieved their diplomatic victories, they turned to their main objective: the preservation of tyrannical power. This year, about 70 people are known to have been arrested... .

Li Peng, the speaker of the National People's Party Congress, declared recently, "If an organization's purpose is to promote a multiparty system in China and to negate the leadership prerogatives of the Chinese Communist Party, then it will not be permitted to exist."

This statement clearly shows that the Communist Party's primary objective is to sustain its tyranny, and to do so it must deny the people basic rights and freedoms. We must measure the leaders' progress on human rights not by the "release" of individuals but by the people's ability to speak, worship and assemble without official interference and persecution.

Source: Wei Jingsheng, *The New York Times,* 24 December 1998. Copyright © 1998 by *The New York Times.* Reprinted by permission.

most-favored nation trade status; the following year China was admitted to the World Trade Organization. When terrorists destroyed the World Trade Center in September 2001, China saw this as an opportunity to move against pro-independence Muslim groups in its own western provinces and gave verbal backing to the U.S. campaign against terrorism. Since 2003, China has cooperated with the United States, Japan, Russia, and South Korea to end the development of nuclear weapons by North Korea. A generational change in Chinese leadership occurred when Hu Jintao became general secretary of the CCP in 2002 and premier in 2003. He introduced a more open style of administration but did not relinquish the CCP's monopoly on government. In 2005, Hu visited Washington and Seattle, where he had dinner with Bill Gates.

TAIWAN

Taiwan is a mountainous island less than a hundred miles off the coast of central China. A little larger than Massachusetts, it has a population of 22.9 million. It was part of the Qing empire before becoming a Japanese colony in 1895. The Japanese colonial government suppressed opium and bandits, eradicated epidemic diseases, built roads and railroads, reformed the land system, and improved agriculture. It also introduced mass education and light industries.

HOW DO U.S. and Chinese policies toward Taiwan differ?

Anticolonial feelings rose slowly, but the Taiwanese were happy to see the Japanese leave in 1945. Kuomintang (Guomindang) officials, however, looted the economy and ruled harshly. By the time Jiang Jieshi and 2 million other military and civilian mainlanders fled to the island in 1949, its economy and society were in disarray. Taiwanese hated their new rulers and even compared them unfavorably to the Japanese.

From the 1950s onward three interdependent developments occurred: the growth of the economy, the rise of democratic politics, and a changing relation to the mainland of China.

The GMD, which had failed in China, succeeded in Taiwan. Part of the reason is that its control of the island was complete and the times were peaceful. It had restored order by the mid-fifties, and rapid growth followed. Heavy industries were put under state control; other former Japanese industries were sold to private parties. With the outbreak

Reviewing the Troops in Hong Kong.
Chinese President Hu Jintao inspects the People's Liberation Army garrison during a three-day visit to the Stonecutter's Naval Base in Hong Kong in 2007. Hu was on a three-day visit to celebrate the tenth anniversary of Hong Kong's handover to Chinese rule.

What is the significance of Hong Kong?

of the Korean War in 1950, U.S. aid became substantial. Foreign investment was welcomed. Light industries were followed by consumer electronics, steel, and petrochemicals and then by computers and semiconductors. Private industries led the way. During the late eighties, substantial Taiwanese investments in China began. By the late nineties, Taiwan was the world's largest producer of monitors, keyboards, motherboards, and computer mice. Many of these were actually manufactured in Taiwanese-owned plants in mainland China. Estimated Taiwanese per capita product in 2006 was $12,500 (or nearer to $29,000 in actual purchasing power), several times that of mainland China.

For the first twenty years, the GMD government of Taiwan was a dictatorship. It maintained that it was the government of all of China. Social changes began during the 1960s. Education advanced, with rising numbers entering universities. As the economy advanced, a new middle class emerged. Jiang Jieshi died in 1975. In 1987, opposition parties were allowed to form and martial law was lifted.

The next advance occurred in 1988, when Li Denghui, a Taiwanese who had risen within the GMD, became president. This ended the pattern of mainlander rule. In 1996, in what he billed as "the first free election in 5,000 years of Chinese history," Li became the first "elected" president of Taiwan. In 2000, opposition leader Chen Shuibian was elected as Li's successor. His election, which ended fifty years of GMD rule, was hailed by one scholar as "the first peaceful transition of power from one political party to another in Taiwanese history, and probably in all of Chinese history." Chen was reelected in 2004.

Since 1949, the Communist government in Beijing had claimed that Taiwan was a province of China controlled by a "bandit" government. It did not rule out taking Taiwan by force and refused diplomatic relations with any nation maintaining such ties with Taiwan. From the outbreak of the Korean War in 1950 until 1979, Taiwan was a protégé of the United States. In 1979, however, the United States broke off relations with Taipei and recognized Beijing as the sole government of a China that included Taiwan. But the United States continued to trade with Taiwan and to sell it arms, and curiously, it was during the years of diplomatic limbo after the 1979 break that Taiwan's economy grew and its society became democratic.

At the onset of the twenty-first century, both China and the United States were apprehensive about Taiwan. China was concerned that a democratically elected government would give Taiwan a claim to legitimacy, and that Taiwan's prosperity would make its peoples less willing to rejoin the mainland—a view supported by public opinion polls in Taiwan. It spoke anew of using force to retake the island. The United States feared that China would soon have the military power to attempt the conquest and cautioned Taiwan's president not to speak of independence. Some in the U.S. Congress felt that the United States could not stand by and see this prosperous and democratic state, which it had helped to create, be forcibly taken over by China.

KOREA

Korea and Vietnam, the other two countries in the East Asian zone of civilization, both became colonies: Vietnam became a part of French Indochina in 1883; Korea was annexed by Japan in 1910. In both countries, the imposition of colonialism on a people with a high indigenous culture and a strong sense of national identity engendered a powerful anticolonial nationalism. After World War II, both were divided into a communist north and a noncommunist south, Korea immediately and Vietnam years later. Both experienced civil war. In each instance the United States entered the conflicts to stem the spread of communism. Never before had the United States fought in countries about which it knew so little.

HOW DID South Korean and North Korean postwar developments differ?

QUICK REVIEW

Two Koreas

- After defeat of Japan in 1945, U.S. troops occupied the south and Soviet troops occupied the north
- U.S. supported government of Syngman Rhee in the south
- Soviets supported government of Kim Il-Sung in the north

KOREA AS A JAPANESE COLONY

The social ills and political and economic weaknesses that had plagued the Choson dynasty in 1800 continued through the nineteenth century. As the century drew to a close, a three-cornered, imperialist rivalry arose among China, Japan, and Russia, with Korea as the prize. Japan won. Defeating China in the Sino-Japanese War (1894–1895) and Russia in the Russo-Japanese War (1904–1905), Japan made Korea a protectorate in 1905 and annexed it in 1910.

Japan introduced measures designed to make Korea into a model colony. A land survey and land tax reform clarified land ownership. Infectious diseases dropped, and the population grew from 14 million in 1910 to 24 million in 1940. Attendance at schools became widespread. New money was issued and banks established. A huge investment was made in roads, railways, telegraph lines, hydroelectric power, nitrogenous fertilizer plants, and mining. Koreans who studied at Japanese universities brought new knowledge back to Korea. By the 1930s a modern culture was forming in Korea's cities.

Being a Japanese colony was a hard road to modernity, for the colonial government was authoritarian. The government's goal was to make Korea a subordinate part of imperial Japan. Any benefits to the Koreans were incidental. Education was given in Japanese. In government, banking, or industry, Koreans were relegated to the lower echelons. The colonial regime suppressed all nationalist movements and political opposition. The police were brutal. Koreans were pressured to adopt Japanese names, drafted to fight in Japan's wars, and sent to labor in Japan. "Comfort women" were recruited, sometimes forcibly, to service Japanese troops. Only in recent years has this bitter colonial legacy begun to subside.

NORTH AND SOUTH

Immediately upon Japan's defeat in 1945, Soviet troops entered the north; a month later U.S. forces occupied Korea south of the 38th parallel. There had been a promise of unification, but two separate states developed. In the south, the United States initially aimed at the formation of a democratic, self-governing nation but settled for the anticommunist and somewhat authoritarian government of Syngman Rhee (1875–1965), a longtime nationalist leader whose party won the 1948 election. Many of Rhee's officials and officers had served the Japanese. His government was strongly supported by conservative Koreans and those who had fled the north.

In the north, the Russians established a Communist government under Kim Il-Sung (1912–1994) in 1948 and withdrew its troops from North Korea—now the Democratic People's Republic of Korea. During 1949 and early 1950, the United States also withdrew most of its troops from the south, part of a general disengagement from continental Asia that followed the Communist victory in China.

Comfort Women. South Korean women who were forced to become sex slaves by the Japanese during World War II protest near the Japanese embassy in Seoul, January 2003.

What is the relationship between Japan and South Korea today?

chaebol Large family-owned business conglomerates with strong ties to the South Korean government.

CIVIL WAR AND U.S. INVOLVEMENT

On June 25, 1950, North Korea invaded South Korea in an attempt to reunite the Korean peninsula. Kim Il-Sung, the North Korean leader, had received Stalin's permission for the invasion and a promise from Mao to send Chinese troops in case the United States entered the war. Kim planned for a quick victory, before the United States had time to intervene, but the United States saw the invasion as an act of aggression by world communism. It rushed troops from Japan to South Korea and obtained UN backing. The Korean War was a catalyst for a major turn in postwar American foreign policy.

During the first months of the war, the unprepared American and South Korean forces were driven southward into a small area around Pusan (see Map 33–2). But then amphibious units landed at Inchon and drove deep into North Korea. American policy shifted from containment of communism to a rollback. China then sent in "volunteers" to rescue the beleaguered North Koreans and pushed the overextended UN forces back to a line close to the 38th parallel. The war ended with an armistice on July 27, 1953. Thereafter, the two Koreas maintained a hostile peace. The 142,000 American casualties made the war the fourth largest in U.S. history.

SOUTH KOREA: DEMOCRACY AND GROWTH

After the armistice, two remarkable and intertwined stories unfolded in South Korea: stunning economic growth and the rise of a democratic polity.

Rhee remained in office until 1960, when he was forced to retire in the wake of massive student demonstrations. There followed twenty-seven years of rule by two generals and then twenty years of democratic government. The first general, Park Chung-hee, seized power in a military *coup d'état* in 1961. Shedding his uniform, he then won a controlled election and became a civilian president. His rule was semiauthoritarian: Opposition parties were legal and active but their leaders were often jailed. In time, even Koreans who approved of Park's economic policies came to resent his use of police and intelligence agencies to sustain his rule. Park was assassinated by his intelligence chief in 1979. Another general seized power the following year, transformed himself into a civilian president, and ruled until 1987 in the pattern established by his predecessor.

At the inception of Park's rule, unemployment had been rife and poverty widespread. Park and his successor were determined to promote economic growth. Emphasizing science and technology, they supported business and swiftly expanded higher education. Management drew on skills learned during the colonial era; labor was disciplined, hardworking, and cheap. The United States gave large amounts of aid and provided an open market for Korean exports. The result was double-digit growth. Especially notable was the growth of ***chaebol*** such as Hyundai or Daewoo, which resembled the Mitsui or Mitsubishi *zaibatsu* of prewar Japan. The policies of the two leaders, and of their successors after 1987, were successful beyond their expectations. Korea's gross national product rose dramatically (see Figure 33–2). With

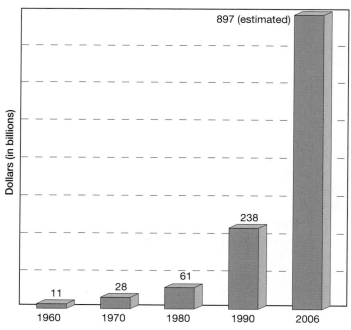

FIGURE 33–2. South Korean Gross Domestic Product, 1960–2006.
What enabled South Korea's economy to grow so dramatically?

an estimated per capita product in 2006 of $17,720 (and a purchasing power considerably higher), South Korea moved into the ranks of developed nations and became the world's tenth largest economy. The country's voice in world affairs grew with its economy.

Ironically, the industrialization and urbanization wrought by the two generals created an affluent and educated middle class that was no longer willing to tolerate authoritarian rule. In 1987, an era of increasingly democratic politics began. In the election of that year a former general was elected as president. Five years later, a moderate, conservative party politician with no ties to the military was voted into office. He purged the generals who had supported the two previous presidents and launched investigations of his predecessors' finances. The hundreds of millions of dollars in secret bank accounts uncovered by investigators astonished even the Koreans. In 1995, the previous presidents and several top *chaebol* leaders were arrested, found guilty, and sent to prison, though they were later released.

In the election of 1997, in which the leader of an opposition party, Kim Dae-jung, became president. A longtime pro-democracy campaigner, Kim was pro-labor, a populist, a Catholic, and an idealist. He took office with high hopes but encountered difficulties that proved insurmountable. The economy sagged; layoffs and fear of further job losses left public opinion unsettled. Kim also adopted a "sunshine policy" of openness, reconciliation, and material aid toward North Korea. His efforts to reduce tensions on the peninsula earned him a Nobel Peace Prize in 1998, but it later came out that North Korea had agreed to a summit only after receiving a bribe from South Korea. When North Korea failed to reciprocate Kim's overtures, Kim's popularity fell.

The underlying trend continued, however: In 2002 a younger, more liberal opposition politician, Roh Moo-hyun, was elected president. Critical of the United States and open to closer relations with China and the government in North Korea, Roh's presidency suggested a change in South Korea's international stance. By the end of his term, however, Roh had lost his popularity, and some predicted that conservative politicians would be returned to power.

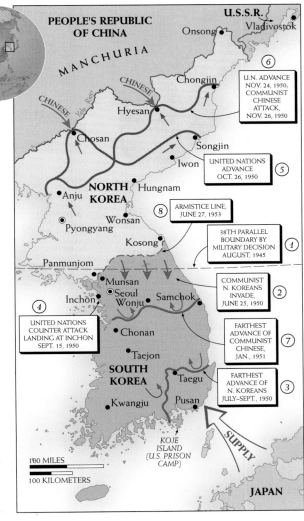

MAP 33–2 The Korean War, 1950–1953.

Why did the Korean War end in stalemate?

NORTH KOREA

Before 1945, most Japanese industries in Korea were located in the north, giving its industrialization an early edge. But North Korea's planned economy was enclosed within a tightly sealed, authoritarian state, which stressed heavy industry, organized its farmers in collectives, and totally controlled education and the media. By the 1970s, its economy became sluggish, and shortages of food, clothing, and necessities were chronic. During the 1990s, there were periods in which famines led to a drop in population.

The cult of personality surrounding "the great leader" Kim Il-Sung went beyond that of Stalin or Mao. The Korean Communist Party was Marxist-Leninist, but the kinship terminology used to describe the fatherly leader, the mother party, and the familial North Korean state gave the official state philosophy an almost Confucian coloration. Kim designated his son, "the beloved leader" Kim Jong-Il (b. 1942), as his successor, and when the father died in 1994, the son became the leader of North Korea—the only instance of hereditary succession in a communist state.

The Two Kims. South Korean President Kim Dae-jung traveled to Pyongyang in June 2000 to promote his "sunshine policy." As he departed he hugged Kim Jong-il, the North Korean leader. But when the North Korean leader failed to respond with a visit to Seoul or with an easing of tensions, sunshine turned to rain, and Kim Dae-jung's popularity sagged.

Why is North Korea such a closed society?

INTERNATIONAL RELATIONS

Since the Korean War, South Korea had been allied with the United States, which guaranteed its defense. North Korea was backed by the Soviet Union and China. But after the collapse of the Soviet Union, Russia lost interest in its former ally. China continued to offer aid and trade but was more attracted by the allure of a vibrant South Korea, with which it established diplomatic relations in 1992. Since then, South Koreans have invested billions in China, trade between the two nations has flourished, and in 1995 the Chinese president visited Seoul. North Korea was increasingly an orphan.

North Korea has been a poor global citizen: To obtain hard currency, it engaged in counterfeiting and drug smuggling; it ran prison camps; it kidnapped Japanese citizens, fired missiles into Japanese waters, and threatened Japan. Increasingly isolated, and with a garrison state mentality, it used a Pakistani connection to import nuclear technology. When charged with this in 2003, it first denied and then boasted of the development. The United States, China, Russia, South Korea, and Japan moved to persuade North Korea to abandon its development of such weapons. Even China did not want a nuclear North Korea on its doorstep. But both China and South Korea with its "sunshine policy" were reluctant to apply pressure, fearing a North Korean collapse and a flood of refugees. In October 2006 North Korea exploded its first atomic bomb. This led China, North Korea's principal trading partner, to toughen its stance, and in February 2007 an agreement settling some issues was reached between North Korea and the six powers: food and aid in exchange for an abandonment of nuclear weapons. What kind of final settlement would be reached was still unclear. All that can be said with certainty was that a small, isolated, bankrupt dictatorship had kept the attention of its larger neighbors for more than a decade.

VIETNAM

HOW DOES the recent history of Vietnam illustrate the legacies of both colonialism and the Cold War?

THE COLONIAL BACKDROP

The Nguyen dynasty that reunited Vietnam in 1802 proved no match for France. France completed its conquest of Vietnam and Cambodia by 1883 and added Laos to the Indochinese Union in 1893.

In many ways Indochina was a classic example of colonial rule: a people of one race and culture, for the sake of economic benefits and national glory, controlling and exploiting a people of another race and culture in a far-off land. To obtain access to the country's natural resources, the French built harbors, roads, and a railway linking Saigon, Hanoi, and southern China. They established rubber plantations in the Mekong Delta and tea plantations in the highlands. They introduced modern mining technology for the extraction of coal and built breweries, rice and paper mills, and glass and cement factories. Large industries were dominated by the French, smaller enterprises by Vietnamese-Chinese. Workers were paid poorly. Vietnamese were mainly laborers, except for the few that became landlords. In the south, 3 percent of landowners owned 45 percent of the land and received 60 percent of the crop grown by their tenants. Although new irrigation works in the Mekong Delta quadrupled the area of rice fields, the consumption of rice by peasants declined. The skewed distribution of wealth meant that no indigenous middle class developed, apart from the landlords and Chinese merchants whose commercial acumen was resented by the Vietnamese. The French also did little to educate the Vietnamese: In 1939, over 80 percent of the population was illiterate, possibly a higher percentage than in the early nineteenth century under the Nguyen.

Under the French, only clandestine opposition parties survived. The most skilled organizer of such parties was Ho Chi Minh (1892–1969), who founded the Indochinese

QUICK REVIEW

French Indochina

◆ Transportation infrastructure and extractive industries developed by the French

◆ Most Vietnamese were poorly paid laborers

◆ No indigenous middle class developed

◆ Poor education left majority illiterate

Communist Party in 1930. Shortly before the outbreak of the Pacific War, the Japanese occupied Vietnam. Ho, who in 1941 had formed the **Viet Minh** (League for the Independence of Vietnam) as a popular front organization to resist the Japanese, proclaimed the Democratic Republic of Vietnam in 1945. Since then, the history of Vietnam can be seen in terms of three cycles of war followed by almost three decades of peace.

THE ANTICOLONIAL WAR

The first war lasted from 1946 to 1954. On one side was the Viet Minh led by Ho. It was controlled by Communists but also included representatives of nationalist parties. On the other side were the French and their conservative Vietnamese allies. The French lost a major battle at Dien Bien Phu in 1954 and, with it, the will to continue what critics at home called the "dirty war." They departed in defeat.

A conference at Geneva divided the country into a communist north Vietnam and a noncommunist south. In the south Vietnam, Ngo Dinh Diem, a nationalist leader who had not collaborated with the French, came to power and established the Republic of Vietnam. Much of his political support came from the 900,000 Vietnamese who had fled from the north.

THE VIETNAM WAR

The second cycle of war was from 1959 to 1975 and involved the United States. During the 1940s, the United States, which opposed colonialism, urged the French to reach an accommodation with Ho Chi Minh. But after the rise of Communist China, the United States came to see French actions in Vietnam as an attempt to stem the tide of communism. When the French withdrew, it supported Diem.

Fighting began with guerrilla warfare in the south and eventually became a full-scale war between the north and the south (see Map 33–3). The north received material aid from the Soviet Union and China. The south was supported by the United States, whose forces increased to more than half a million in 1969. Despite such massive assistance, South Vietnam—and the United States—lost the war. The reasons for the defeat were several.

1. South Vietnam was difficult to govern. In comparison to North Vietnam, the region had been less deeply influenced by Chinese culture. It was ethnically diverse, with Chinese, Cambodians, and Chams as well as Vietnamese. In religion, it was divided among several varieties of Buddhism, Catholicism, and two powerful "new religions," the Cao Dai in the eastern provinces and the Hoa Hao in the western provinces. These two millenarian sects possessed private armies, and though opposed to the Communists, they stood apart from the South Vietnamese government, at times warring among themselves. Throughout this era, the inability of successive southern governments to unify their fragmented society was a basic weakness in their struggles with the communist north.

2. The South Vietnamese government, often corrupt, inspired little loyalty in its citizens.

3. Ho Chi Minh was a national hero to many South Vietnamese as well as to those in North Vietnam. Even noncommunists sometimes viewed the United States as the successor to the French—despite its lack of colonial ambitions in Southeast Asia—and supported communist guerrillas as the heirs of the earlier anticolonial struggle.

4. Both the communist guerrillas in South Vietnam and the North Vietnamese troops fought better than the soldiers of the South Vietnamese government.

5. In the jungle terrain of Vietnam, the technological edge of the United States was blunted. A greater tonnage of bombs was dropped on supply trails in Cambodia than on Japan in World War II, yet supplies continued to flow to South Vietnam.

Ho Chi Minh (1892–1969). Ho became a Communist in France in 1920, studied in Moscow, and founded the Indochinese Communist Party in 1930. He fought, in succession, against the Japanese, French, and Americans. He did not live to see the communist victory in 1975.

How did Ho Chi Minh use Western ideas in his fight against Western imperialism?

Viet Minh The Communist-dominated popular front organization formed by Ho Chi Minh to establish an independent Vietnamese republic.

MAP EXPLORATION

To explore this map further, go to
www.prenhall.com/craig_maps

MAP 33–3   **Vietnam and Its Southeast Asian Neighbors.**   The map identifies important locations associated with the war in Vietnam.

Which neighboring countries were most affected by the Vietnam War?

Khmer Rouge   Meaning "Red Cambodia." The radical Communist movement that ruled Cambodia from 1975 to 1978.

At the beginning, the U.S. government saw the war, like the earlier war in Korea, as a part of the broader struggle against world communism. After the gravity of the Sino-Soviet split became apparent, the government saw it more narrowly as a war to halt the spread of Chinese communism. Few in the United States understood the depth of the traditional Vietnamese ambivalence toward China. As the war dragged on and casualties mounted, opposition to the war grew. President Richard Nixon called for the "Vietnamization" of the war and began to withdraw American troops. In January 1973, a cease-fire was arranged in Paris, and two months later the last U.S. troops left. Fighting broke out anew between North and South Vietnam; the South Vietnamese forces collapsed in 1975, and the country was reunited under the Hanoi government in the north. Saigon was renamed Ho Chi Minh City.

In the mid-1970s, few areas of the world were as devastated as Vietnam and its neighbors. After unifying the country, Hanoi sent many thousands of those associated with the former South Vietnamese government to labor camps, collectivized its agricultural lands, and in 1976 began a five-year plan for the economy. Several hundred thousand Vietnamese and ethnic Chinese fled by boat or across the Chinese border.

WAR WITH CAMBODIA

Vietnam's third and briefest cycle of war was with its neighbor, Cambodia. Pol Pot (1926–1998) and the Communist **Khmer Rouge** ("Red Cambodia") had come to power in 1975. His government evacuated cities and towns, abolished money and trade, banned Buddhism, and killed an estimated 1 million people, roughly 15 percent of the total population. Schoolteachers and the educated were singled out as special targets.

Clashes occurred between Khmer Rouge troops and Vietnamese troops along their common border. Vietnam was Cambodia's historical enemy, as China was Vietnam's. When Pol Pot purged the Khmer Rouge of pro-Vietnamese elements, Vietnam retaliated in 1978 by invading and occupying most of Cambodia and setting up a puppet government. Most Cambodians accepted Vietnamese rule: They feared Pol Pot more than they hated Vietnam. But Vietnamese troops were unable to completely suppress Pol Pot's guerrilla forces.

In its international relations, the unified Vietnam of 1975 became an ally of the Soviet Union. Relations with China, never good, worsened. In 1979, China invaded four northern provinces. Seasoned Vietnamese troops repelled the invaders, but losses were heavy on both sides. For years thereafter China supported Pol Pot's guerrillas and maintained pressure on Vietnam's northern border with occasional shellings and attacks.

RECENT DEVELOPMENTS

During the late 1980s, the situation changed abruptly. The collapse of the Soviet Union destroyed Vietnam's primary international relationship. In 1989, Vietnam tired of its costly occupation of Cambodia and withdrew in favor of a UN-sponsored government made up of contending Cambodian factions. One of these factions, led by a pro-Vietnamese communist leader, staged a coup in 1997 and took over the government. His rule was strengthened when Pol Pot died in 1998 and the Khmer Rouge collapsed. This, in turn, opened the way to better relations with China: Cross-border trade began and China's landlocked Yunnan province began to use the Vietnamese port of Haiphong as an outlet for its products. In 1995, Vietnam joined ASEAN (Association of Southeast Asian Nations)—an important advance in its relations with its closest and richer neighbors—and reestablished diplomatic relations with the United States. It moved toward "normal" relations with the rest of the world. Europeans and Americans began to take package tours to Vietnam, visiting scenic spots that only two decades earlier had been the battle zones of a bitter war.

By the late 1990s, a "Chinese pattern" had emerged in Vietnam. On the one hand, the communist government in Hanoi monopolized political power and controlled the army, police, and media. On the other, the leaders, aware that victories in wars were hollow as long as their people remained destitute, embraced capitalism as the road to growth. In place of collective agriculture, farmers were allowed to keep the rice they grew; as a result Vietnam went from near starvation to become the world's second largest exporter of rice. Stock markets were established in Hanoi and Ho Chi Minh City. Taxes were kept low and a premium was put on education. Garment manufacturing, food processing, and the production of other consumer goods grew apace. Between 1991 and 2007, the economy averaged over 8 percent growth and received more offers of foreign investment than it could absorb. Taiwan and Singapore were the largest investors, but Intel, Nike, and other American companies were not far behind. Vietnam's exports to the United States in 2006 were nine times greater than its imports, a problem for relations between the two nations. By the turn of the millennium, shops in Vietnam were full of food and goods, when only a decade or so earlier there had been regional famine. During the first decade of the millennium, Vietnam was the second fastest growing economy in the world—only China was faster. In this new climate South Vietnam was the engine of the economy. It also served as a model—slightly more open, pluralistic, and cosmopolitan—which even most North Vietnamese saw as attractive.

Population offered a mixed picture. With 86 million persons in 2007, Vietnam was one of the world's most densely populated nations. The government limited families to two children—in contrast to China's one. Hanoi's population increased from 130,000 in the 1930s to about 4 million, while Ho Chi Minh City's (Saigon's) population went from less than a million in the 1970s to 4.5 million. The gap in the standard of living between urban and rural Vietnamese grew wider, an uncomfortable fact for a communist government. More than half of the population was born after the end of the Vietnam War; its youth and low medical costs made labor cheap. In 2007, Vietnam's estimated per capita income was a low $800 but rising (as measured by purchasing power, it was over $3,600). It had begun the trajectory that all East Asian nations but North Korea had in common.

Skulls. A worker cleans a skull excavated from a mass grave in Cambodia. The Khmer Rouge, under Pol Pot, murdered about one sixth of the Cambodian population. Doctors, teachers, and other educated people were especially targeted.

Who were the Khmer Rouge?

SUMMARY

HOW DID the postwar occupation change Japan politically?

Japan. The U.S.-led occupation after World War II established a democratic government and set Japan on the way to its remarkable postwar prosperity. By the twenty-first century, Japan had the second largest economy in the world. Politically, the conservative Liberal Democratic Party has remained dominant, despite occasional electoral losses. Socially, Japan has remained stable with the world's highest longevity rate. *page 837*

WHY DID Mao launch the Cultural Revolution?

China. Communist rule was established in 1949. Until his death in 1976, Mao Zedong controlled China. Mao broke with the Soviet Union in the 1960s and launched the disastrous Cultural Revolution in 1965 in an ill-conceived effort to avoid Soviet-style bureaucratization. After Mao's death, China opened its economy to free-market reforms. The result has been surging economic growth and rising prosperity. Politically, the Communist Party has blocked democratic reform, even using force in 1989 to crush a pro-democracy movement. *page 843*

HOW DO U.S. and Chinese policies toward Taiwan differ?

Taiwan. The Nationalist Party set up a separate state in Taiwan under U.S. protection after its defeat in the Chinese civil war in 1949. Since then Taiwan has moved from poverty to prosperity, from dictatorship to democracy. The Chinese government insists that Taiwan is a province of China. The status of Taiwan is an outstanding issue between the United States and China. *page 849*

HOW DID South Korean and North Korean postwar developments differ?

Korea. The postwar occupation of Korea by the Soviet Union and the United States led to its division into the communist state of North Korea and pro-Western South Korea. This division survived the Korean War of 1950 to 1953. The prosperity of democratic South Korea contrasts with the poverty and hunger of North Korea. Although contacts between the two Koreas have increased, North Korea remains a closed society and now has nuclear capabilities. *page 851*

HOW DOES the recent history of Vietnam illustrate the legacies of both colonialism and the Cold War?

Vietnam. From the end of World War II until the 1970s, Vietnam was almost continuously involved in war, first against the reimposition of French colonial rule, then against the United States and its South Vietnamese allies. North Vietnam's victory over South Vietnam in 1975 reunified the country. Vietnam has recently embraced free market principles. *page 854*

INTERPRETING THE PAST

The Transformation of Postwar East Asia

Sources from MyHistoryLab for Chapter 33
myhist**o**rylab

1) James Schnabel, *The United States Army in the Korean War*
2) Truong Nhu Tang, *Myth of a Liberation*
3) Deng Xiaoping, *On Introducing Capitalism*

Visual Sources from MyHistoryLab

1) *Japanese Election, 1946*
2) *Asian Games, Tokyo, 1958*

East Asia faced numerous challenges in the decades following World War II as economic, political, and social changes engulfed the vast and populous region. After more than a century of being economically dominated and often directly controlled by the West, East Asian nations began to effectively compete with Europe and the United States. Rapid industrialization first occurred in Japan, as it recovered from the devastating bombings of World War II, followed by Taiwan, South Korea, Singapore, Thailand, and China.

Along with economic gains, East Asian nations have had to change their ancient cultures and antiquated bureaucracies and

REVIEW QUESTIONS

1. Is postwar Japan better understood as a return to the relative liberalism of the 1920s or as a fresh start based on Occupation reforms? Why did the Occupation of Japan go so smoothly, in contrast to the American occupation of Iraq?

2. How has Japanese society changed since 1945? In what ways does it seem to be a more fair and open society? Is there a downside to the changes?

3. Compare present-day Chinese and Japanese income levels and standards of living. In Japan, what factors led double-digit growth to turn into single-digit growth? Will the same factors come into play in China?

4. Is China from 1949 until the death of Mao better understood as an outgrowth of its earlier history or as a communist state comparable, say, to the old Soviet Union? And to what country would you compare post-Deng China?

5. Does recent history suggest that the Chinese government will become more democratic as its citizens become more prosperous?

6. How did the precolonial and colonial eras of Korea and Vietnam shape their history after World War II? How did the Cold War shape their history?

7. What factor or factors were most important in the defeat of South Korea (and the United States) in the Vietnam War?

8. Given the failure of South Korea's "sunshine policy" toward North Korea, can you see any way to improve relations between the two Koreas or to improve relations between other countries and North Korea?

9. If you were the U.S. secretary of state, what long-term China policy would you propose to the president?

10. What has been the impact of East Asian economic growth on international relations?

KEY TERMS

Article 9 of the No-War Constitution (p. 839)
brainwashing (p. 844)
chaebol (JHE-buhl) (p. 852)
Cultural Revolution (p. 844)

Great Leap Forward (p. 844)
Khmer Rouge (p. 856)
LDP (p. 839)
Viet Minh (p. 855)
Zaibatsu (p. 838)

Note: To learn more about the topics in this chapter, please turn to the Suggested Readings at the end of the book.

political systems to conform with their citizens' needs and expectations, as well as those of their international business partners. One of the key problems in many countries in East Asia is the need to adapt nationalism to the complicated reality of ethnic, regional, and local differences, in which competing agendas often transcend the ideal of national unity.

In this exercise you will read four primary sources relating to the politics and economies of East Asia, especially focusing on how nationalism has changed since World War II. You will then answer the following questions in the process of completing the assignment below.

The first document is an excerpt from a U.S. Army history detailing the partitioning of the Korean peninsula at the conclusion of World War II. The momentous economic changes that would propel this East Asian nation to the forefront of the global economy were still decades in the future, but the decisions made in 1945 are still being felt in Korea today. The second source is written by Truong Nhu Tang, a South Vietnamese leader of the "National Liberation Front," which fought the French and Americans from the 1950s to the 1970s. The third document is a portion of a speech by Deng Xiaoping, China's leader in the 1980s and early 1990s, in which he justifies the need for capitalism and a market economy in the country's socialist system.

The two accompanying images illustrate similar processes of social and political change: the first depicting the first elections after World War II in Japan, and the second depicting large-scale multinational athletic games in Tokyo in 1958.

Questions

Schnabel's account details the partition of Korea in 1945. What were the main considerations in the decision to partition the country? What were its consequences?

While Truong Nhu Tang was allied with the North Vietnamese in the fight against the French and the Americans, he was a southerner and a founder of the National Liberation Front. What was his attitude toward the North Vietnamese leadership? Had this been understood, might it have affected the outcome of the war?

What are Deng Xiaoping's reasons for introducing capitalism into China's socialist system? How would capitalism affect China's chances of becoming a democracy? What does it mean to build capitalism within socialism?

34

Postcolonialism and Beyond: Latin America, Africa, Asia, and the Middle East

Darfur, Western Sudan.   Sudanese refugees wait at a food and clothing aid distribution point. The conflict, which began in February 2003, has killed as many as 300,000 people through violence, hunger, and disease. Some 2.5 million people have been displaced by the fighting.

Why do you think this photograph shows mostly women and children?

BEYOND THE POSTCOLONIAL ERA *page 862*

WHAT ARE the two main developments that have occurred in the postcolonial world?

LATIN AMERICA SINCE 1945 *page 865*

WHERE IN Latin America did the major attempts to establish revolutionary governments occur?

POSTCOLONIAL AFRICA *page 870*

WHAT ARE the most significant issues that Africa faces in the twenty-first century?

THE ISLAMIC HEARTLANDS FROM NORTH AFRICA TO INDONESIA *page 875*

HOW HAS Islam affected politics in the developing world?

THE POSTCOLONIAL MIDDLE EAST *page 879*

HOW DID the creation of the state of Israel affect the history of the modern Middle East?

GLOBAL PERSPECTIVE

DEMOCRATIZATION, GLOBALIZATION, AND TERRORISM

Two remarkable political and economic developments have shaped our era: democratization and globalization. The apparent progress of these two processes has been challenged, at least symbolically, by acts of terrorism, most dramatically by the al-Qaeda attacks of September 11, 2001.

Since 1970, on one continent or another, democratic political rights have expanded. Authoritarian regimes of both the right and the left have been reformed or collapsed. Democracies have replaced dictatorships, military juntas, or one-party communist autocracies. Progress has not been uniform, but more and more people everywhere aspire to have a voice in how they are governed. This process of political change, usually termed *democratization*, involves expanding the number of people who participate in the political processes and the orderly change in, or confirmation of, executive and legislative leaders through elections and the establishment of viable civil societies. Although there are still many autocracies and authoritarian states, never before have so many nations around the world seen such an extension of democratic government.

An unprecedented series of economic linkages, generally termed *globalization*, has paralleled the spread of democracy. This process has included the forging of new trade and manufacturing agreements, such as NAFTA, among the leading industrial nations. Globalization has reduced trade barriers, including tariffs and other regulations that have hindered the circulation of goods, services, and labor among nations. The emergence of such worldwide trading and investment networks has led to the consolidation of economic enterprises as owners of capital seek to locate their centers of production in the most advantageous labor and resource markets. The giant corporations of the United States, Europe, and Asia now operate in a multinational setting.

Globalization's supporters believe that it will produce more goods and services at a lower cost to consumers than a highly regulated economy could. Its critics argue that globalization will concentrate power in the hands of unregulated corporations and that governments have surrendered too much of their authority to regulate the economy, preserve the environment, and protect workers. The critics also believe that the new economic structures mean that poor nations, many of them the emerging nations discussed in this chapter, become poorer so that rich nations can become richer. Globalization rode the wave of prosperity that seems to have crested in the late 1990s. It remains to be seen what will occur in more difficult times.

The six decades since World War II saw Europe eclipsed by the rise of the two superpowers—the United States and the Soviet Union—and then witnessed the collapse of the Soviet Union (see Chapter 32). Elsewhere in the world, especially in the industrializing regions, the post–World War II decades witnessed the end of Western colonialism and challenges to European and superpower imperialism. New nations emerged in Africa and Asia.

Two developments in non-Western regions have major implications for the future. East Asia, Japan, and China have emerged as major political and economic powers. And radical Islamic movements present a political and military challenge across much of the globe. The period of colonialism that began in earnest in the seventeenth century was a relatively brief episode in world history. The last significant colonial holdings were given their independence in the 1960s, but the legacies of colonialism—positive as well as negative—continue. ■

WHAT ARE the two main developments that have occurred in the postcolonial world?

BEYOND THE POSTCOLONIAL ERA

It could be argued, with the collapse of apartheid in South Africa, the fall of the Berlin Wall, and recent economic growth in India and China, that the postcolonial era has ended. Remnants of colonialism persist in many global regions, however. Industrializing areas are witnessing waves of economic growth, much like those of the early 1990s in East Asia; the forging of new political alignments, both regional and transregional; internal struggles to build political systems that allow the development of civil society and limit the domination of corrupt oligarchic or dictatorial regimes; and, most dramatically, the determination of radical Islamists to confront Western and, in particular, American influence.

The debate over globalization has made both its admirers and detractors more aware of the vast areas of deep poverty that persist around the world, especially in South and Central America, the Caribbean, Africa, and much of Asia—regions that still struggle with the legacy of European colonialism. Most of these regions were impoverished by early stages of globalization in the late nineteenth century before globalization achieved its present momentum, but the enormous and widely advertised prosperity of so much of the Northern Hemisphere has made the poorer regions more conscious of their poverty and, especially in Africa and the Middle East, ripe for political extremism. Among Muslims, such extremism has often come to be associated with political Islamism. As the most prosperous nation and global superpower, the United States has become the target of those suffering from and opposed to globalization.

The economic, military, and diplomatic involvement of the United States in other regions of the globe has led some people to view it as an imperial power and to attack it using terrorist tactics. Its overwhelming support for the state of Israel, the festering Israeli-Palestinian conflict, and, most recently, the U.S. invasion of Iraq have also convinced many peoples, especially those in the Muslim world, that the United States is the enemy of Islam and that using terrorist tactics to attack it is justified. Within the United States, as well as around the world, debate continues over the future role of the United States and whether the United States can best protect the interests of its citizens and the peace and prosperity of the world through unilateral and preemptive invasions such as that of Iraq or through greater cooperation with international bodies such as the United Nations.

Focus Questions

◆ What are the arguments of the proponents and opponents of globalization?

◆ How has the legacy of European colonialism affected the Middle East, Asia, and Africa?

◆ Why has the United States become a prime target for terrorists? What is the debate over how the United States should best respond to this threat?

Since 1945, two distinct developments have occurred in the postcolonial world. The first—in a process that is generally termed *decolonization*—was the emergence of the various parts of Africa and Asia from the direct administration of foreign powers (see Map 34–1). The second was the organization of those previous colonial dependencies into independent states with greater or lesser degrees of stability.

Postcolonial societies have experienced four stages in their relationship to the industrial European and Europeanized nations: the influence of Cold War rivalries on the new states, the economic effects of **globalization**, progress in the spread of the ideals of civil society and participatory government, and finally a resurgence of cultural and religious traditions.

A central question for the present era is whether to see the global variety of social, cultural, and religious traditions as a creative or divisive force in the twenty-first century and beyond. One model for understanding the complex international scene today is that of the "West versus the Rest," in which the European and Europeanized world and its ethos are seen as the hope of the future, while all other social, religious, and cultural traditions are depicted as rallying points for opposition to the spread of European-style "modernity." This analysis pits

decolonization The achievement of political self-determination for former colonies, usually through national independence.

globalization Term used to describe the increasing economic and cultural interdependence of societies around the world.

The End of Empire. A statue of Queen Victoria is removed from the front of the Supreme Court building in Georgetown, former capital of the British colony of Guyana (South America), in February 1970, in preparation for the transition to independence.

Why was there a wave of decolonization in the mid-twentieth century?

OVERVIEW Postcolonial Periods

Each former colony has its own history and occupies its own niche in the world today. There are, however, some common trends and typical progressions that the former colonies in Africa and Asia have tended to follow. These periods sometimes overlap.

DECOLONIZATION

During the period of decolonization, very roughly from 1945 to 1965 in Africa and Asia, colonies prepared for, were granted, and began to exercise political independence. Local people took over most governmental offices and functions, and the new nations were recognized by the international community.

COLD WAR CLIENTAGE

Between 1945 and 1990, the Cold War superpowers—the United States and the Soviet Union—vied for clients among small states all around the world. A few former colonies managed to maintain nonaligned status, in which they could play the two powers (and sometimes also China) off against each other, but most states were under the patronage of either the United States or the Soviet Union.

GLOBALIZATION

Particularly since the 1990s, increasing numbers of transregional and even truly global institutions (from the European Union to McDonald's), coupled with the emergence of ever-larger mass cultures (music and movies, for example), have made it seem possible that local identities might eventually disappear. The economy has become significantly globalized already, but so far at least politics remains mostly local.

EMERGENCE OF CIVIL SOCIETY

Perhaps a more cyclical phenomenon is the emergence of civil society, democratization, and other elements of "people power" as a force that can alter political, social, and economic landscapes.

ENDURANCE OF CULTURAL SPECIFICITY

The terrorist attacks of September 11, 2001, were a stark reminder that not all groups want to merge into a global, democratic, secular, market-driven civilization. Traditional self-conceptions, religious values, nonmonetized economies, and other identities, institutions, and ideas continue to link individuals to particular cultures. This endurance has given rise to the "West versus the Rest" and "clash of civilizations" models of current affairs.

---

clash of civilizations   Political theory, most often identified with Harvard political scientist Samuel P. Huntington, that contends that conflict between the world's religio-cultural traditions or "civilizations" increasingly dominates world affairs.

Islamic, European and Eastern Orthodox Christian, Buddhist, Hindu, Confucian, and other religious, social, and cultural traditions against one another in a **clash of civilizations**. This concept became popular following the attacks of September 11, 2001.

Other observers urge that studying the varied traditions of world culture leads to an understanding of the modern world as a domain in which many cultural and religious and political traditions interact and compete but in which people of all kinds can get along. Our common need for solutions to transnational, planetwide problems must take precedence over wide "civilizational" differences.

In any case, we must recognize the persistent influence of the great religious and moral traditions of humankind. In particular, Buddhist, Christian, and Islamic faith and values continue to claim the allegiance of major sectors of our globe. No longer can we assume that secular rationalism will easily monopolize ideology during the process of material modernization. Rather we can expect a pluralistic global community in which diverse traditions best coexist and learn from one another.

MAP 34–1 **Decolonizaton since World War II.** Europe's rapid retreat from imperialism after World War II is graphically depicted on this map, showing half the globe—from Africa to the Pacific.

How are the effects of colonialism still present in Africa and Asia today?

LATIN AMERICA SINCE 1945

During the last half century, the nations of Latin America have experienced divergent paths of political and economic change. Their leaders have tried to alleviate their people's dependence on the more developed nations. At best, these efforts have had mixed results.

Before World War II, the states of Latin America had been economically dependent on the United States and Western Europe. Beginning in the 1950s, Latin America became an arena for confrontations between the United States and the Soviet Union. During this era, attempts were made to expand the industrial base and agricultural production of the various national economies. Financing came from U.S. and Western European banks or from Soviet subsidies. Enormous debts were contracted that made Latin American economies virtual prisoners to the fluctuations of world interest rates and international banks or to Soviet subsidies. These new relationships did not alter the underlying character of most Latin American economies, which remain exporters of agricultural commodities and mineral resources. Since the 1970s, Latin America has also shipped massive amounts of cocaine to the United States and Europe. This has led to political turmoil and civil war in Colombia.

A culture of poverty continues. Migration into the cities from the countryside has caused urban overcrowding and slums inhabited by the desperately poor (see Figure 34–1). The standards of health and nutrition have often fallen. The growth of service industries in the cities has also fostered the emergence of a professional, educated middle class that has displayed little taste for radical politics, social reform, or revolution. They and the

WHERE IN Latin America did the major attempts to establish revolutionary government occur?

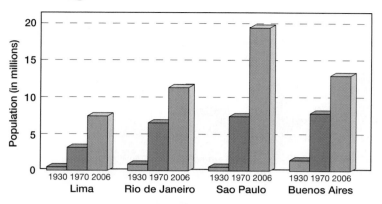

FIGURE 34-1 Population of Major South American Cities, 1930–2006. **What trend is clearly visible?**

more traditional elites were willing, especially during the 1960s and 1970s, to support military governments pledged to maintain the status quo.

Political events in Latin America led to the establishment of authoritarian governments of both the left and the right and to a retreat from the model of parliamentary democracy. Only Mexico, Colombia, Venezuela, and Costa Rica remained parliamentary states throughout this period. Elsewhere, two paths of political development were followed. In Cuba and Nicaragua, and briefly in Chile, revolutionary Socialist governments with close ties to the Soviet Union were established. Elsewhere, often in response to the fear of revolution or communism, military governments held power, sometimes punctuated with brief interludes of civilian rule. Such were the situations in Argentina, Bolivia, Brazil, Chile, Peru, and Uruguay. Governments of both the left and the right engaged in political repression.

These political changes fostered new roles for the military and the Roman Catholic Church. Latin American armies have played key political roles since the wars of independence. But since World War II, they have frequently assumed the direct government of nations rather than using indirect influence. Many Roman Catholic priests and bishops have protested inequalities and attacked political repression. Certain Roman Catholic theologians have combined traditional Christian concern for the poor with Marxist ideology to formulate what is called **liberation theology**, which has been attacked by the Vatican.

liberation theology The effort by certain Roman Catholic theologians to combine Marxism with traditional Christian concern for the poor.

Since the 1980s, several nations have moved toward democratization and free-market economies. Yet in most nations, the military keeps a watchful eye on democratic developments and possible disorder. The end of the Cold War brought to a close one source of external political challenge, but internal social problems continue to raise difficulties. In several nations, drug-producing cartels challenge governmental authority.

REVOLUTIONARY CHALLENGES: CUBA, CHILE, AND NICARAGUA

Cuba had remained a colony until the Spanish-American War of 1898. It achieved independence within a sphere of U.S. influence that took the form of economic domination and military intervention. The governments of the island were ineffective and corrupt. During the 1950s, Fulgencio Batista (1901–1973), a dictator supported by the United States, ruled Cuba. On July 26, 1953, Fidel Castro Ruz (b. 1926), his close associate Ernesto Che Guevara, and others attacked a government army barracks. The revolutionary movement that he thereafter came to lead in exile took its name from that date: the Twenty-Sixth of July Movement. In 1956, Castro and a handful of followers landed in Cuba and attacked Batista's forces. Batista fled Cuba on New Year's Day in 1959. In January, Castro arrived in Havana as the revolutionary victor.

Castro undertook the most extensive political, economic, and social reconstruction seen in recent Latin American history. He rejected parliamentary democracy. The

Fidel Castro. Castro waves to cheering crowds acknowledging his triumph over the Batista regime on January 1, 1959. **What did Castro achieve in Cuba?**

revolutionary government carried out major land redistribution. The Cuban Revolution concentrated on the agricultural sector. Sugar preserved its leading role. The sugar industry depended on large Soviet subsidies and on the Soviet bloc nations for its market.

In foreign affairs, the Cuban Revolution was characterized by a sharp break with the United States. Castro aligned himself with the Cuban Communist Party and with the Soviet bloc. The United States was hostile toward Castro and toward the presence of a Communist state less than a hundred miles from Florida. In 1961, the United States and Cuban exiles launched the unsuccessful Bay of Pigs invasion. The close Cuban relationship to the Soviet Union led to the missile crisis of 1962, the most dangerous incident of the Cold War. Despite the collapse of the Soviet Union, the Castro government continues firmly in charge. Cuba remains the only state closely associated with the former Soviet bloc that has not experienced substantial political or economic reform. Some observers believe Castro's death will lead to a collapse of the government; others believe that the bureaucracy Castro created may endure.

Throughout the Cold War, Cuba assumed an importance far greater than its size might suggest. After 1959, it served as a center for the export of Communist revolution; it sent troops to Angola in the late 1970s. The U.S. government, seeking to prevent the establishment of a second Cuba in Latin America, intervened in other revolutionary situations and supported authoritarian governments in Latin America.

Until the 1970s, Chile was the most enduring model of parliamentary democracy in Latin America. During the 1960s, however, Chilean politics had become polarized. There was high unemployment, labor unrest, and popular resentment of the economic domination of Chile by large U.S. corporations. The situation came to a head in 1970 when Salvador Allende (1908–1973), a Marxist, was elected president. His coalition did not control the Chilean congress, nor did it have the support of the military. Allende nationalized some businesses. Other policies were blocked in the congress, so Allende governed by decree. He began to expropriate foreign property; he frightened Chilean business owners but did not satisfy workers. Inflation ballooned. Harvests were poor. By 1973, Allende had little domestic political support and many foreign enemies. The army became hostile, and the Nixon administration supported the discontent. In mid-September 1973, an army coup overthrew Allende, who was killed.

For the next fifteen years Chile was governed by a military junta under General Augusto Pinochet (1915–2006). The military government pursued a close relationship with the United States and resisted Marxism in the hemisphere. It established a state-directed free-market economy and reversed the expropriations of the Allende years. There was also harsh political repression. In a referendum held in late 1988, Chileans rejected Pinochet's bid for another term as president. Democratization was relatively smooth. Civilian rule has included efforts to investigate the political repression of the Pinochet years. Thousands of cases of torture and murder have been revealed. During the past two decades Chile has moved toward a more liberal constitutional government.

In the summer of 1979, a Marxist guerrilla force, the **Sandinistas**, overthrew the corrupt dictatorship of the Somoza family in Nicaragua. The Sandinistas established a collective government that pursued social and economic reform and reconstruction. The movement, with Roman Catholic priests on its leadership council, epitomized the new political and social forces in Latin America. However, the revolutionary government confronted significant domestic political opposition and military challenge from the contra guerrilla movement.

The government of the United States, particularly under the Reagan administration (1981–1989), was hostile to the Sandinistas. It provided both direct and indirect aid to the opposition guerrillas. The U.S. government feared the spread of Marxist

QUICK REVIEW

Salvador Allende

- Elected president of Chile in 1970
- Lacked support in congress and military
- Marxist policies led to economic crisis
- Assassinated in 1973 army coup

Sandinistas The Marxist guerrilla force that overthrew the Somoza dictatorship in Nicaragua in 1979.

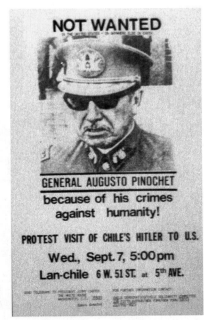

Pariah. A 1977 poster from a New York protest highlights the enormous international opposition to the policies of General Pinochet.

Which other political leaders have been accused of "crimes against humanity" in recent times?

revolutionary activity in Central America, a fear reinforced by the close ties between the Sandinistas and the Soviet Union.

Sandinista rule came to a relatively quick end. In early 1990, after a negotiated peace settlement with the contras, they lost the presidential election to an opposition coalition and relinquished power peacefully. A democratic government supported by the United States has remained in control despite persistent economic weaknesses.

PURSUIT OF STABILITY UNDER THE THREAT OF REVOLUTION: ARGENTINA, BRAZIL, AND MEXICO

In 1955, the Argentine army revolted against the Perón dictatorship and Juan Perón (1895–1974) went into exile. Two decades of economic stagnation and social unrest followed. By 1976, the army had undertaken direct rule. There was widespread repression; thousands of citizens disappeared, never to be heard of again. In April 1982, General Leopoldo Galtieri (b. 1926) launched a disastrous invasion of the Islas Malvinas (Falkland Islands). Argentina was defeated by Britain.

In 1983 civilian rule was restored, and Argentina set out on the road to democratization. Under President Raul Alfonsín (b. 1927), many of the figures responsible for repression received prison sentences. Argentina has provided the most extensive example in Latin America of the restoration of democracy after military rule. Peaceful elections and transitions of governments have occurred for two decades despite serious economic difficulties. In 2001, rising unemployment, a currency devaluation, and drastic cuts in basic government services led to political turmoil. Significant economic growth has occurred for the past several years, however.

In Brazil, the military assumed direct government in 1964 and held it until 1985, stressing order and using repression to maintain it. Non-Brazilian corporations were invited to spearhead the drive toward industrialization. One result was a massive foreign debt, the servicing and repayment of which have become perhaps Brazil's most important national problem. Brazil also became the major industrialized nation in Latin America, which has had a huge impact on the Brazilian rain forest. By 1998, large landowners, encouraged by subsidies and tax incentives, had cleared 12 percent of Brazil's rain forest. The question now is how growing urbanization and other social changes wrought by industrialism will receive political accommodation. In 2003, in the wake of economic turmoil, Luiz Inácio Lula da Silva became the first person from a working-class background to be elected president of Brazil. He was reelected in 2006. His administration has combined socialist concern for social services with an austere economic policy.

Institutionally, Mexico has undergone few political changes since World War II. In theory, the government continued to pursue the goals of the revolution. Power remained in the control of the Partido Revolucionario Institucional (PRI). Yet shifts had occurred. In the early 1950s, certain large landowners were exempted from the expropriation and redistrib-

Deforestation in the Amazon.   A cut and burned section of trees on federal land in Brazil's Amazonian state of Para. The problems of deforestation, wood trafficking, habitat destruction, slave labor, land grabbing, and violence are all intertwined as colonization of the region accelerates.

What is the global impact of deforestation in the Amazon?

ution of land. The Mexican government maintained relations with Cuba and the other revolutionary regimes of Latin America but also resisted Marxist doctrines within Mexico. It arrested malcontents.

Mexico experienced an oil boom from 1977 to 1983, but the aftermath revealed the absence of stable growth. Like so many other states in the region, Mexico amassed large foreign debts and thus surrendered real economic independence.

In 1988, opposition candidates received much of the vote in a hotly contested election. The PRI leadership began to decentralize the party. President Carlos Salinas moved to privatize economic enterprise. He also favored free-trade agreements. The most important of these was the North American Free Trade Agreement (NAFTA), which created a vast free-trade area including Mexico, Canada, and the United States. In 1991, Salinas made new accommodations with the Roman Catholic Church, thus moving away from the traditional anticlericalism of Mexican politics. By 1991, the PRI appeared to have regained its former political ascendancy.

However, in 1994 Mexico underwent political shocks. Troops had to quell armed rebellion in Chiapas. During the election that year, the leading candidate was assassinated and party members were charged with complicity in the deed. Party corruption received increased publicity. Early in 1995, Mexico suffered a major economic downturn, and only loans from the United States saved the economy. Ernesto Zedillo, elected president in 1994, blamed Salinas and his family for the situation, and the corruption of the Salinas government became public. The government faced further unrest in Chiapas, growing power among drug lords, and turmoil within the governing party itself. In 2000 the PRI candidate for president lost to Vicente Fox of the National Action Party (PAN). Fox's term ended in late 2006 with a sharply contested election in which Felipe Calderon, also a candidate of PAN, came into office with a very narrow electoral win.

CONTINUITY AND CHANGE IN RECENT LATIN AMERICAN HISTORY

The most striking aspect of the history of the past six decades in Latin America is its tragic continuity with the region's previous history. Revolution has brought moderate social change, but at the price of authoritarian government, economic stagnation, and dependence on different foreign powers. Real independence has not been achieved.

The recent trends toward democratization and market economics may mark a break in that pattern. The region might well enjoy healthy economic growth if inflation can be contained and investment fostered. The challenge will be to see that the fruits of any new prosperity are shared in a way that prevents new political resentment and turmoil.

Zapatistas.   Named after the revolutionary hero Emiliano Zapata (depicted on the banner, see Chapter 26), the Zapatistas demanded rights for the impoverished Native American population of Mexico, especially in the southern state of Chiapas, where this photograph was taken in 1997.
Why have the indigenous peoples of Latin America been politically and socially repressed?

Latin American Politics.   The turn to the left in Latin American politics is represented by Hugo Chavez, who has oil wealth to fund his ambitions, and Evo Morales, the first indigenous president of Bolivia. Chavez assumed power in 1999, Morales in 2006.
Why have Latin American politics generally been dominated by conservative leaders?

POSTCOLONIAL AFRICA

WHAT ARE the most significant issues that Africa faces in the twenty-first century?

Most of Africa's modern nations follow colonial boundaries; colonial capitals have typically become national capitals. Africa provides striking examples of how attractive nationalism can be as a motive for supratribal and transregional state formation. In World War II the important roles that Africa was called on to play with its natural and human resources, as well as the experience of thousands of Africans who were conscripted or volunteered to fight or labor abroad, proved a catalyst for African nationalism. After the war, Europe was largely disposed to give up its colonial empires (see Chapter 32).

Kenyan Independence. President Jomo Kenyatta is congratulated on Kenya's independence as England's Queen Elizabeth II looks on, December 12, 1963. **Why were most African transitions to independence initially peaceful?**

THE TRANSITION TO INDEPENDENCE

In 1950, only Egypt, Liberia, Ethiopia, and white-controlled South Africa were sovereign states. By 1980 no sizable African territory was ruled by a European state, although South Africa and Namibia continued to be white-dominated. African leaders, such as Kwame Nkrumah (1909–1972) in the Gold Coast (modern Ghana), Jomo Kenyatta (1893–1978) in Kenya, Julius Nyerere (1922–1999) in Tanganyika (later Tanzania), and Patrice Lumumba (1925–1961) in the Congo became symbols of African self-determination.

The actual transition from colonial administrative territories to independent national states was generally peaceful. Violence was more likely in colonies with large populations of European settlers (such as Algeria) or lucrative exports of minerals or other resources (Congo, for example). The internal conflicts that arose in some newly independent states were intense. Much of the instability in African states has been a legacy of both the colonial powers' generally minimal efforts to prepare their colonial subjects for self-government and the haphazard nineteenth-century division of the continent into arbitrary colonial units.

Few African states had the numbers of educated and experienced native citizens needed to staff the apparatuses of a sovereign country. Corruption and military coups were rife; the attempt to implement planned economies on a socialist model often brought economic catastrophe; and tribal and regional revolts at times led to civil war. Most dangerous and costly were the separatist struggles, civil wars, and border clashes between new states that grew out of the independence struggles. However, these conflicts tended to ratify the postcolonial state divisions (instead of regional or tribal/linguistic divisions).

NIGERIA, SOUTH AFRICA, CONGO, AND RWANDA

The modern Republic of Nigeria is the most populous state in Africa with about 120 million inhabitants in 2005. Nigeria achieved independence from Britain in 1960 as arguably the most powerful and potentially successful state in independent Africa. The republican constitution of 1964 federated three provincial regions—the Eastern, Western, and Northern—under a national government based in Lagos, the former British administrative capital. Nigeria's largest ethnic and linguistic groups are the major ones of the same three regions: Igbo in the Eastern, Yoruba in the Western, and Hausa and Fulani in the Northern province.

A 1966 *coup d'état* brought a military government into power. Its leader was soon assassinated, and Lieutenant Colonel Yakubu Gawon (b. 1934) took over amid ethnic unrest. In May 1967, the Eastern Province's assembly empowered its leader, Lieutenant Colonel Chukwuemeka Odumegwu Ojukwu (b. 1933), to form a new, independent state of Biafra. Biafra gained recognition from several African states; secured arms and support from France, South Africa, and Portugal; and developed successful worldwide propaganda depicting itself as a small, brave, Christian country fighting for its survival against a hostile, oppressive, Muslim central government. The ensuing two and a half years saw a tragic civil war. The larger federal forces slowly chipped away at the Biafran state. The estimated death toll soared above a million—the overwhelming majority of whom were Igbo civilians, mostly refugees who died of starvation—before the Biafrans surrendered in January 1970.

Gawon was overthrown by another military commander in 1975. In the ensuing years Nigeria was plagued by political instability at the top, with its leadership passing usually from one military ruler to another.

Nobel laureate author Wole Soyinka (b. 1934) led protest demonstrations against the military government in 1994. Novelist and environmental activist Kenule "Ken" Saro-Wiwa (1941–1995) was executed by the military in 1995. Military rule was replaced in 1999 by civilian government under an elected president, Olusegun Obasanjo, and a new constitution was implemented. Umaru Musa Yar'Adua succeeded Obasanjo as president after a flawed election in April 2007. Problems of religious animosities and ethnic divisions remain. Despite the nation's wealth, corruption and mismanagement have hindered Nigeria's development.

The Union of South Africa was governed under the racist policy of **apartheid** ("apartness") from the time the Afrikaner-led National Party (NP) came to power in 1948 until 1991. The white minority (in 1991, 5.4 million persons) ran the country, maintaining economic and political control and privilege. Its 31 million blacks, 3.7 million "coloreds" (people with dual ancestry), and 1 million Indians were kept strictly segregated—treated, at best, as second-class citizens. This system was maintained chiefly by repression.

In part as a result of worldwide opposition to apartheid, South Africa was increasingly isolated. In the 1960s and 1970s the government created three tiny "independent homelands" for blacks inside the country, allowing the white minority to treat blacks as immigrant "foreigners" in the parts of South Africa where most had to work. The international community refused to recognize the homelands, or "Bantustans." Zulu chief Albert Luthuli (1898?–1967) and Anglican bishop Desmond Tutu (b. 1931) were awarded Nobel Prizes in 1969 and 1984, respectively, for their work against apartheid.

By 1978, as Pieter Botha (1916–2006) came to power, apartheid was failing: The homelands were economic and political catastrophes; the country was in an inflationary recession; skilled whites were emigrating; and South Africa was becoming a pariah state. Beginning in 1986, many nations responded to Tutu's call and imposed economic sanctions against the government. Strikes by black workers in 1987 led the government to declare a state of emergency: Western nations embargoed trade. In 1988 more than 2 million black workers went on strike to protest new repressive labor laws and political bans. Botha resigned in 1989.

In 1990 president F. W. de Klerk (b. 1936) began a series of landmark actions: lifting the ban on the African National Congress (ANC), the main anti-apartheid organization; releasing ANC leader Nelson Mandela after twenty-seven years of imprisonment; and repealing the Separate Amenities Act, the legal basis for segregation in public places. In early 1991 de Klerk announced plans to end all apartheid laws. De Klerk and Mandela led the endorsement of a new interim constitution, for which they shared the Nobel Peace Prize for 1993.

Multiracial elections were held in April 1994. The ANC won 63 percent of the vote. Nelson Mandela was elected president of what Tutu called the Rainbow Nation,

QUICK REVIEW

Nigeria
- Achieved independence in 1960
- Collapse of three-province federation led to dictatorship and civil war
- Brutality, instability, and corruption have marked Nigerian government since 1975

apartheid "Apartness," the term referring to racist policies enforced by the white-dominated regime that existed in South Africa from 1948 to 1992.

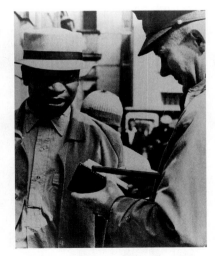

Apartheid. A police officer checks a black African's identification card, under the apartheid system's hated pass laws.

Can apartheid be compared to segregation in the United States? How were they similar? How were they different?

Nelson Mandela. The anti-apartheid hero campaigning for the presidency of postapartheid South Africa.

Why is Mandela so widely admired?

Truth and Reconciliation Commission
A quasi-judicial body that investigated apartheid-era human rights abuses. The TRC emphasized disclosure over punishment, and often offered amnesty in exchange for testimony.

in honor of South Africa's racial and political diversity. The **Truth and Reconciliation Commission** (TRC), established in 1995, offered an unprecedented way to come to terms with the country's past: Rather than attempting to bring to justice the many perpetrators of human rights abuses during the apartheid era, the TRC offered amnesty in exchange for testimony and provided victims a platform for detailing their losses. The TRC's premises were controversial—some victims of apartheid atrocities protested that their persecutors were evading punishment—but it is unlikely that any other mechanism could have generated a more comprehensive account of apartheid's abuses.

The government of Thabo Mbeki, who succeeded Mandela in 1999 and was reelected in 2004, is striving to deal with the challenges that the majority of the population face. Despite substantial mineral resources, and the highest GNP in Africa, South Africa still faces huge problems: one of the world's highest rates of HIV/AIDS infection; high unemployment, poverty, and crime rates; extreme income inequality; inadequate public services and infrastructure; and water shortages.

European rule in Africa may have reached its nadir in the Congo Free State. In this personal fiefdom of Belgium's King Leopold II between 1885 and 1908, Africans were routinely mutilated or killed for offenses such as failing to meet local officials' quotas for rubber collection. As a Belgian colony, Congo fared slightly better, but from independence onward Congo's history has had more than its share of atrocities.

The Republic of Congo gained independence on June 30, 1960, with Patrice Lumumba (1925–1961) as prime minister and Joseph Kasavubu (1910–1969) as president. Lumumba and Kasavubu belonged to different parties. Kasavubu dismissed Lumumba from office; Lumumba resisted. In the ensuing crisis the Congolese Army's chief of staff, Joseph-Désiré Mobutu (1930–1997), overthrew them both. Lumumba was assassinated in 1961. Various presidents served brief terms until 1965, when Mobutu again seized power. This time he had the backing of the U.S. Central Intelligence Agency, and he kept power for more than thirty years. Mobutu outlawed all political parties except his own, the Popular Movement of the Revolution, from 1967 to 1990. He launched the Authenticité campaign to celebrate African culture, and re-named the country Zaire. Mobutu developed a powerful cult of personality. Corruption made his rule a kleptocracy.

The combination of the end of the Cold War and Mobutu's failing health created an opening for opposition leaders, which they were quick to seize. Refugees from Rwanda's genocide (see below) further destabilized the country, and, starting in 1996, insurgents supported by Rwanda, Uganda, Zambia, and Angola captured much of eastern Zaire. Most of these outsiders backed Laurent Kabila (1939–2001) when he was sworn in as president on May 29, 1997. The country was again renamed the Democratic Republic of the Congo (DRC). Since then, what has been called the Second Congo War (the revolt against Mobutu being the first) or even the African World War has roiled the DRC. In 2001, Kabila was assassinated; his son, Joseph Kabila, took office. In 2006, in disputed elections, he defeated other candidates for the presidency.

The DRC is immense and has a wealth of natural resources. Nonetheless its future is uncertain; fighting continues, much infra-

Aftermath of Genocide. Rwandan refugees carry their belongings as they stream out of the Mugunga refugee camp in Zaire (Congo) back toward Rwanda in the aftermath of the 1994 genocide.

How did events in Zaire and Rwanda become interconnected?

structure has been destroyed, and most citizens have little reason to trust their government. Estimates vary wildly, but probably close to 4 million people have died as a result of fighting there since the mid-1990s.

Rwanda is roughly one one-hundredth the size of the Democratic Republic of the Congo, but during and after the Rwandan genocide of 1994 the two countries' histories became intertwined. Under Belgian administration, ethnicity in Ruanda-Urundi (now, Rwanda and Burundi) was determined by wealth: Since the minority Tutsi tribe already constituted the elite, anyone deemed wealthy by the Belgians became a "Tutsi" and most others were designated as belonging to the largest preexisting ethnic group, the "Hutu." At independence in 1961, Rwanda and Burundi separated, and Rwanda became a republic with Hutu leadership.

Over the following decades, there were many crossborder clashes between Rwanda, Burundi, and Uganda. Although this violence was usually labeled as Tutsi versus Hutu, there is no way to determine the extent to which ethnic animosity actually drove these conflicts. On April 6, 1994, when a helicopter carrying the (Hutu) presidents of both Rwanda and Burundi was shot down over Rwanda's capital, killing both presidents, Tutsis were blamed. The groundwork had been laid for interethnic civil war. Over the following months, approximately 800,000 Tutsis and moderate Hutus were killed in a massive genocide. The Uganda-based, Tutsi-led Rwandan Patriotic Front (RPF) under Paul Kagame (b. 1957), meanwhile, gradually took control of the country, and millions of Hutu refugees fled to Zaire. RPF and Ugandan forces pursued them into Zaire, creating one of the triggers for Mobutu's overthrow.

United Nations peacekeepers were on the ground in Rwanda when the genocide began, but under the terms of their deployment they were unable to intervene. United States President Bill Clinton was harshly criticized for failing to take action.

Following a period under a transitional government, a new constitution was approved and Kagame was elected president in 2003. Rwanda is undergoing a remarkable recovery.

HIV/AIDS Collection of symptoms and infections resulting from the specific damage to the immune system caused by the human immunodeficiency virus (HIV). The late stage of the condition leaves individuals susceptible to opportunistic infections and tumors. Although treatments for AIDS and HIV exist to decelerate the virus's progression, there is currently no known cure.

THE AFRICAN FUTURE

The last half century has seen radical change and development. Overall, the prospects for future government stability are stronger than ever. Economic problems still loom, but progress is being made after decades of failed schemes. The burdens of the past—be they regional rivalries and hatreds, religious and linguistic divisions, major economic and social policy mistakes in early independence, or the crippling experience of apartheid—still present hurdles. Probably even more serious are the newer problems with which almost all of Africa's nations have to contend as they strive to build civil societies and achieve economic health. Each African state faces unique problems and must draw on its unique resources if it is to be successful in the present century.

There is a variety of health and environmental challenges facing Africa, the most notorious of which is **HIV/AIDS**. In late 2005, nearly 25 million people in sub-Saharan Africa were infected with HIV. There are significant regional variations in HIV infection rates: In general, rates are highest (over 20 percent of the adult population) in southern African nations, followed by East and Central Africa, while rates are generally relatively low (often under 5 percent) in West African nations (see Map 34–2). Governments have also varied tremendously in their responses to HIV/AIDS. Uganda, for example, embarked on an aggressive public education campaign in the 1990s, which seems to have helped reduce infection rates there. In contrast, in early 2000, South African President Thabo Mbeki publicly questioned whether HIV causes AIDS, contributing to an atmosphere of denial and shame surrounding HIV/AIDS.

Ellen Sirleaf-Johnson. Sirleaf-Johnson was elected president of Liberia in 2005. She is the first woman elected to lead an African nation.
What are some significant issues facing African nations today?

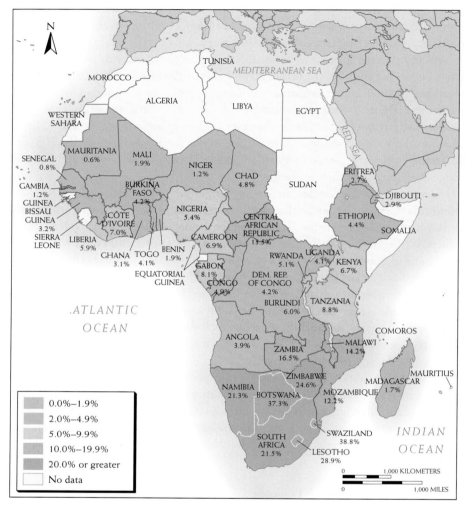

MAP 34–2   Distribution of HIV Infection Rates in Africa.

What general trends do you notice in HIV infection rates in Africa?

Other diseases sicken or kill millions of Africans every year. The World Health Organization declared the prevalence of tuberculosis an emergency in Africa in 2005. Malaria and other primarily tropical diseases reduce life expectancy, increase absenteeism from school and work, and reduce economic productivity in almost all parts of Africa. Only very recently have significant global health initiatives, such as the Global Network for Neglected Tropical Diseases (established in 2006), begun to target Africa's interrelated health challenges.

African environmental challenges run the gamut from wildlife poaching to soil erosion to improper disposal of hazardous waste. Africans have been in the forefront of the environmental justice movement with activists including Ken Saro-Wiwa (see p. 871) and Nobel laureate Wangari Maathai, leader of Kenya's Green Belt Movement, building grassroots environmental campaigns.

African society has changed rapidly during the postcolonial period, though many traditions endure. Rapid urbanization is a trend that began in the colonial period and has continued to the present. The explosive growth of new urban centers at the expense of rural areas has disrupted the continent's traditionally agrarian-based societies, age-old family and tribal allegiances, religious values, and sociopolitical systems. Migrants come to cities in search of wage labor, but African urban economies have never grown as quickly as their populations; many African cities include large slum areas where masses of people live in substandard housing. Men have been more likely to migrate from rural to urban areas than women, so there are often gender imbalances in both rural and urban areas.

In a significant discontinuity with the colonial era, African women have been elected to many national offices. Women were active in anticolonial and anti-apartheid movements and took leadership roles in some postindependence rebellions (for example, in Uganda), but it is only since the mid-1990s that large numbers of women have been elected to national parliaments and other high offices. Ellen Sirleaf-Johnson, the first woman elected to lead an African nation, won the presidency of Liberia in 2005.

Demography and religion help shape African societies. Population growth has been rapid throughout Africa, while deaths from HIV/AIDS have created new population trends, such as the large numbers of "AIDS orphans." Christianity and Islam both continue to gain converts. Evangelical Christianity, in particular, is growing rapidly.

TRADE AND DEVELOPMENT

During the Cold War, one of the areas in which the West and the Soviet bloc competed was in dispensing development aid in Africa. Starting in the 1990s, trade has been emphasized as the best mechanism for growing African economies and improving standards of living. Under President Bill Clinton the United States encouraged private-sector trade and investment through the Partnership for Economic Growth and Opportunity in Africa. President Bush supported the African Global Competitiveness Initiative (AGCI) to build sub-Saharan Africa's capacity for trade and competitiveness. A factor of rapidly growing importance is trade with, and direct investment by, China. African economies still need to grow tremendously to meet their populations' needs.

THE ISLAMIC HEARTLANDS FROM NORTH AFRICA TO INDONESIA

HOW HAS Islam affected politics in the developing world?

The lands today dominated or significantly marked by Islamic culture and containing either Muslim majority populations or sizable Muslim minorities are found in the Arab world from Morocco to Iraq and the Gulf, in West and East Africa, in the Balkans and the Turkish-speaking world of Turkey and the former Soviet Central Asian republics, in Persian-speaking Iran and parts of Central Asia, in western China, and in South and Southeast Asia. India, Bangladesh, Pakistan, and Indonesia have the four largest Muslim populations in the world. The nations of this huge region illustrate the different ways Islamic faith and practice may manifest themselves and affect political life.

TURKEY

Turkey represents a modernist republican experiment that has attempted to create a civil society and a democratically elected government despite struggles over the roles of the military, ethnicity, culture, and religion in society. However, the Turkish military has repeatedly deposed elected governments and supervised the selection of new leadership. Economically, Turkey has certainly had its difficulties, but along with Israel it is still the most economically advanced Middle Eastern country. With the creation of new Turkic-language-speaking states in Central Asia after the breakup of the Soviet Union, Turkey may strengthen its ties with this underdeveloped part of the world. (See Document, "A Modernist Muslim Poet's Eulogy for His Mother.")

DOCUMENT

A Modernist Muslim Poet's Eulogy for His Mother

The following is a poem drawn from the autobiography of Aziz Nesin, *That's How It Was but Not How It's Going to Be* (1966). Nesin (b. 1915) is a prolific Turkish writer, political commentator, and social critic whose writing career began in 1946 with his publication of a satirical weekly paper. The following poem is a eulogy for his long-dead mother, a reflection on the deprivations she endured, and a determined promise to ensure women a better life in the future. It reflects the widespread feeling among secular modernists in Turkey and elsewhere that one of the hallmarks of modernity is the emancipation of women. The final two lines repeat the original Turkish title of Nesin's book.

- **What** is the impact of addressing the poem to his own mother rather than to some other female figure? What specific things is Nesin criticizing in the poem?

VOW TO MY MOTHER'S MEMORY

All mothers, the most beautiful of mothers,
You are the most beautiful of the beautiful,
At thirteen you married;
At fifteen you gave me birth.

Khomeini. The bearded ayatollah waves to a cheering throng in Tehran, Iran, in February 1979.

Who supported the Iranian Revolution that brought Khomeini to power?

QUICK REVIEW

Islamic Revolution in Iran

- 1978: Shi'ites and secularists joined to overthrow shah
- 1979: Republican constitution is Islamic, not secular
- Shi'ite leader Ayatollah Ruhollah Khomeini takes power

Geographically and culturally Turkey is part of both Europe and Asia. Istanbul, its main commercial and cultural center, is located in continental Europe. Turkey is a member of NATO and is seeking admission into the European Union. Many Europeans are skeptical about admitting an overwhelmingly Muslim nation into the Union. Persecution of Turkey's Kurdish minority and other human rights violations, as well as indebtedness to the International Money Fund, have worked against Turkey's case for EU admission. Islamist parties have emerged in Turkey, complicating the political landscape. It remains to be seen whether Turkey will align itself more with Europe, the Middle East, or Central Asia in the years ahead.

IRAN AND ITS ISLAMIC REVOLUTION

Iran, the most important state of west Asia, was ruled from 1925 to 1941 as a monarchy by a former army commander, Reza Khan, who had come to power by military takeover and the support of the British. He attempted to introduce modernist economic, educational, and governmental reforms. His goal was to create a highly centralized autocratic monarchy. Russian and British forces deposed him in 1941 and installed his son, Muhammad Reza, as shah. He sought legitimacy through linkage with the imperial dynasties of pre-Islamic Persia and continued his father's secular and industrial state building. From 1951 to 1953, Iran's most popular Prime Minister Muhammad Mosaddeq (1881–1967) served at the head of a broad coalition. He was ousted by the U.S. Central Intelligence Agency and British Military Intelligence, earning the United States and Britain several generations of deep hatred and distrust by Iran.

In the 1960s Muhammad Reza Shah's heavy-handed repression stoked opposition. Finally in 1978 Shi'ite religious leaders (the *ulama*) and secularist professional revolutionaries joined forces to end the shah's long regime with a revolution filled with a wide spectrum of emotion, ideology, and symbolism. What had begun as an "Iranian Revolution" ended up as an "Islamic Revolution," so that in 1979 the constitution of a new postshah republic was not a secular but an Islamic one adapted under the guidance of the Shi'ite religious leader Ayatollah Ruhollah Khomeini (1902–1989). A protracted war with Iraq (1980–1988) and new repression followed. Still, the new state—with religious leaders exercising a degree of influence over politics not seen since early Safavid times in the sixteenth century—has survived. Khomeini and his successors struggled to find a new formula for combining Muslim values and norms with twentieth-century *realpolitik*.

You were twenty-six,
You died before you lived.
I owe you this heart overflowing with love.
I don't even have your picture;
It was a sin to have a photograph taken.
You saw neither movie, nor play.
Electricity, gas, water, stove,
Nor even a bedstead was found in your home.
You could never bathe in the sea,
You couldn't read nor write.
Your lovely eyes

Looked at the world from behind a black veil.
When you were twenty-six
You died, before you lived.
Henceforward, mothers will not die before they live.
That's how it was,
But not how it's going to be!

Mohammad Khatami was elected president in 1997 by a resounding majority in the first real national leadership election since the 1979 revolution. Khatami tried to steer Iran on a more moderate, liberal course. Wide-ranging reforms failed to materialize, however. In 2003, Iranian lawyer Shirin Ebadi won the Nobel Peace Prize for her work to improve the status of women and children in Iran; Iran's leadership paid no attention. In 2005, Mahmud Ahmadinejad (b. 1956), a veteran of the Iraq-Iran war, won the presidential election. The United States and its allies (particularly Israel) oppose his policies on nuclear energy and military involvement in Iraq. The future is very uncertain.

AFGHANISTAN AND THE FORMER SOVIET REPUBLICS

North of Iran, 70 million or more Central Asian Muslims of the former Soviet Union and China have had to sustain their religious and intellectual traditions in the face of Russian and Chinese cultural, linguistic, and political imperialism.

The Soviet invasion of Afghanistan had unexpected results. Thousands of Muslims, mostly fundamentalists, had arrived in Afghanistan to oust the Soviets and their Afghan puppets. Conservative Arab states and the United States supported this effort, which succeeded by the late 1980s. The conservative Arab states saw the Afghan War as an opportunity both to resist the expansion of Soviet influence and to divert the energies of their own religious extremists. The United States saw the Afghan War as another round in the Cold War. The militant Muslim fundamentalists saw it as a religious struggle against an impious non-Muslim power.

After the Soviets withdrew, a power vacuum in Afghanistan lasted almost a decade. By 1998, however, rigorist Muslims known as the *Taliban* had seized control of the country. They imposed their own version of Islamic law, which involved strict regimentation of women and public executions and mutilations for criminal offenses. The Taliban also allowed groups of Muslim terrorists known as *al-Qaeda*, which means "base," to establish training camps in their country. The terrorists who attacked the United States on September 11, 2001, came from these camps. As will be seen later in the chapter, one response of the United States to those attacks was a military campaign against the Taliban government of Afghanistan.

Iranian Nobel Prize Winner Shirin Ebadi at the Street Children's Home That She Founded in Tehran. Ebadi was awarded the prestigious prize for her work in defending human rights. She was the first Muslim woman to be awarded a Nobel Prize.

Does Ebadi's accomplishment contradict widely-held views in the West on the status of women in the Muslim world?

QUICK REVIEW

Nehru Dynasty

- Jawaharal Nehru (1889–1964): First prime minister of India
- Indira Gandhi (1917–1984): Daughter of Nehru, prime minister of India (1966–1977)
- Rajiv Gandhi (1944–1991): Son of Indira Gandhi, prime minister of India (1984–1989)

Hindu Militants. Hindu militants attack a Muslim mosque in Ayodhya, India, December 6, 1992. The razing of this mosque at the hands of a mob led by Hindu communalist extremists touched off a wave of Hindu-Muslim violence in India. The Hindus claimed the mosque, built some five hundred years ago, occupied the site of what had originally been a Hindu temple and sought to have a new temple built once the mosque was cleared away.

Why have Hindus and Muslims been in conflict in India?

INDIA

India, a largely Hindu state, and Pakistan, a largely Muslim state, gained independence in 1947 after the British agreed to a partition of the subcontinent. Much of their subsequent history has been one of mutual antagonism. About 8 million Muslims were displaced from the new India, and another 8 million Hindus and Sikhs were displaced from the new Pakistan. The two states still have not resolved their major differences, including their conflicting claims to Kashmir. Their rivalry has been exacerbated by Indian underground nuclear tests in 1998, which were closely followed by similar Pakistani tests.

After the assassination of Mohandas Gandhi (1869–1948) by a Hindu fanatic, India has been directed for most of its existence by the leaders of Gandhi's Congress Party. Jawaharlal Nehru (1889–1964) developed India's famous theory of political neutrality vis-à-vis world alignments. His secularist, reconciliatory policies reduced the communal hatreds, religious zealotry, and regional tensions of the postpartition era, and he also made progress in the huge task of economic development of the overpopulated, underdeveloped new nation. Nehru's resolute opposition to caste privilege also helped improve equality of citizenship beyond universal suffrage.

Indira Gandhi (1917–1984; no familial relation to Mohandas Gandhi) similarly managed to steer a tricky course of neutralism during the Cold War. India's 1971 victory over Pakistan and the subsequent creation of Bangladesh to replace East Pakistan strengthened her political control, but the failure of her efforts to reduce national poverty overcame her postwar popularity. Her resolute efforts to quell Sikh separatism brought about her assassination in 1984 by two Sikhs from her own palace guard.

Indira Gandhi's son, Rajiv Gandhi (1944–1991), was elected prime minister after her, and his handling of the thorny Sikh issue was generally applauded. Indications that he and Pakistan's Prime Minister Benazir Bhutto (1953–2007) might work together to resolve some India-Pakistan hostilities were also promising. But he was assassinated by a Sri Lankan Tamil suicide bomber in 1991.

India's problems remain large. Poverty and disease, including plague outbursts, remain serious. Separatist movements based on regional linguistic affinity, such as that of the Tamil peoples of the south, or religious affinity, such as that of the Sikhs of the Punjab, have pulled at the unity of the Indian state. Industrialization and agricultural modernization have recently made great strides. Yet India's population is now at about 1 billion and growing at nearly 2 percent per year. New outbreaks of communal violence between Hindus and India's large Muslim minority threaten political stability. As the world's largest functioning democracy, India will be an important model of representative government and pluralistic society if it succeeds in staying together.

PAKISTAN AND BANGLADESH

The first president of Pakistan, Muhammad Ali Jinnah (1876–1948), oversaw the creation of a Muslim state comprising the widely separated East and West Pakistan in the two predominantly Muslim areas of northwest India and East Bengal. In 1971 East Pakistan seceded and became the new Islamic nation of Bangladesh. Pakistan's groping efforts to create a fully Islamic society and to solve its massive economic problems have been hampered by periodic lapses into dictatorship.

The elections of 1988 opened the door to the possible success of parliamentary government rule. The new prime minister, Benazir Bhutto, was the first female leader of a major Islamic state in the twentieth century. She was in and out of office before being assassinated in 2007. In 1999, General Parviz Musharraf took over as chief executive of Pakistan and has continued to govern, despite increasing protest, since that time. Of all Central Asian governments, Pakistan's has confronted the most direct challenge from radical Islam.

INDONESIA AND MALAYSIA

The new East Indies state of Indonesia came into being in 1949. Indonesia, the largest Muslim country in the world (about 216 million of its estimated 245 million people are Muslim), is trying to achieve a consensus among its disparate and scattered parts. It must determine how Muslim religious faith is to be reconciled with secularist government.

Malaya received its independence from British colonial rule in 1957 as a federation under a rotating monarch; it was later joined by the states of Sarawak and Sabah in northern Borneo, forming the federation of Malaysia. The overriding problem for Malaysia (population 20 million) has been the cleft between the largely Chinese (32 percent) and partly Indian (9 percent) non-Muslim minority on the one hand, and the largely Muslim majority of Malay and other indigenous peoples (59 percent) on the other.

Both nations have rich cultural traditions and natural resources; it remains to be seen how each will preserve them while meeting the demands of modern global politics and participation in the global economy. An important part of the future of Islam as a global religious and cultural tradition is at stake.

THE POSTCOLONIAL MIDDLE EAST

POSTCOLONIAL NATIONS IN THE MIDDLE EAST

The modern Middle East arose from the fall of the Ottoman Empire and the intervention in the region by Western powers, which carved out new nations and protectorates. Egypt, Iraq, and Saudi Arabia became sovereign states after World War I; Lebanon and Syria were given independence by France during World War II. In 1948, Great Britain abandoned its protectorate over Palestine, and the United Nations recognized the state of Israel. Subsequently, other Arab states gained independence: Jordan, 1946; Libya, 1951; Morocco and Tunisia, 1956; Algeria, 1962; and, by 1971, Yemen, Oman, and the small Arabian Gulf states (see Map 34–3).

These states all share the classical Arabic written language (*fusha*), but the spoken colloquial language (*'amiyya*) varies. Attempts to create pan-Arab alliances or federations have failed primarily because of regional differences and political interests, but appeals to Arab nationalism remain powerful.

In the wake of World War II, many of the leaders of Arab nationalism, such as Gamal Abdul Nasser of Egypt (1918–1970), were sympathetic to socialism or to the Soviet Union. Popular among both secular and religious middle-class supporters, "Islamic socialism" had gained considerable support in the 1980s until discredited by the contradictory actions of Arab, Turkish, Iranian, and Kurdish leaders. Soviet-style communism, however, was so overtly secular and antireligious that many Arab, Turkish, and Iranian Muslims tended to be tentative if not hostile to their secular-minded contemporaries who embraced communist parties and trade union politics so readily.

Nationalism in the basic sense of "patriotism to the homeland" remains the most important ideology from Morocco to India. Arab governments, defining themselves according to the values of nationalism, have worked out arrangements with local Muslim authorities. For example, the Saudi royal family turned over its educational system to adherents of a rigorist, puritanical form of Islam called *Wahhabism* (see Chapter 27) while modernizing the country's infrastructure. The Egyptian government attempted to play different Islamic militant and professional groups off against one another. These governments retained the support of prosperous, devout middle-class Muslims while doing little about the plight of the poor.

HOW DID the creation of the state of Israel affect the history of the modern Middle East?

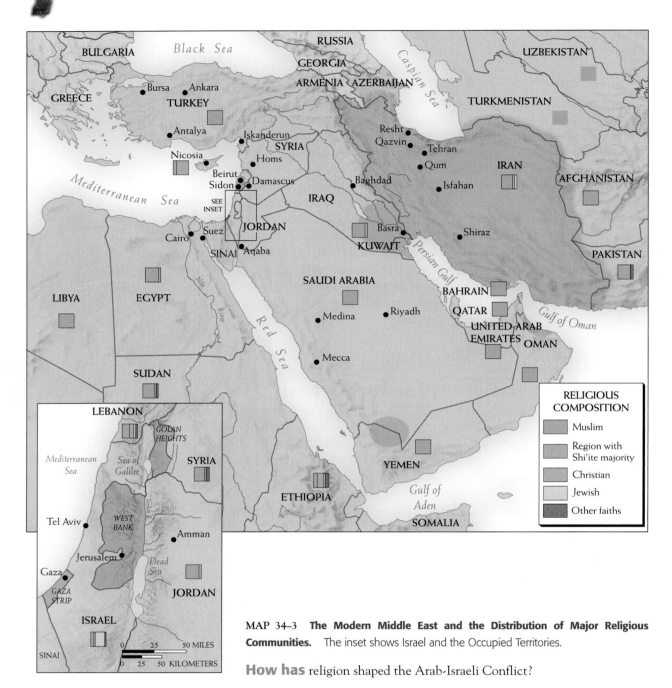

MAP 34–3   **The Modern Middle East and the Distribution of Major Religious Communities.**   The inset shows Israel and the Occupied Territories.

How has religion shaped the Arab-Israeli Conflict?

THE ARAB-ISRAELI CONFLICT

Nowhere have the effects of the West's interventions in the Middle East been more sharply felt than in the creation of the state of Israel in the former British mandate territory of Palestine (1948). The British Balfour Declaration of 1917 supported establishment of a national homeland for the Jews in Palestine, but by 1920 there were only about 60,000 Jews (one-tenth the number of Arabs) in Palestine.

The interwar years saw increasing Jewish settlement and growing communal conflict. Immigration of Jews, largely from eastern Europe, increased in the 1920s and 1930s. Britain's efforts to restrict it in 1936 tragically prevented many Jews from escaping the Nazi Holocaust. After the war, the Zionist movement received a tremendous boost from Jews worldwide and the Allied nations, which felt the need to atone for the

intifadah   Literally, "shaking." Uprisings by the Palestinians against Israeli occupation.

occupied territories   Land occupied by Israel as a result of wars with its Arab neighbors in 1948–1949, 1967, and 1973.

Holocaust by securing a refuge for Jews. The dream of return to the Holy Land had a long history in Judaism.

Under the Ottomans, the Holy Land had been the home of Arabic-speaking Palestinians, primarily Muslims, but also Christians and Jews. None of these had a hand in determining the fate of their land. The Palestinians understandably do not see why they should be displaced, either because of another people's historic religious attachment to the land or as reparation for Europe's sins against the Jews. Jews, however, felt a desperate need for a homeland where they might be safe from future persecutions.

In 1947, the British turned the issue over to the United Nations. The UN called for partition of the mandate territory into a Jewish and an Arab state. The Arab states refused to accept the UN resolution, but in May 1948, Jews in Palestine proclaimed the independent state of Israel. Egypt, Iraq, Jordan, Lebanon, Saudi Arabia, and Syria promptly attacked Israel but lost to the better-armed, better-trained, and more resolute Israelis. The Israeli-Arab war of 1948 to 1949 won the Jews not only the UN-proposed territory but also a substantial portion of that proposed for a Palestinian state. The creation of Israel subjected some Palestinians to Israeli rule or occupation and produced a massive Palestinian refugee problem. Another war in 1967 and the aftermaths of two subsequent *intifadahs* (uprisings: literally, "shaking off") further swelled refugee ranks.

Since 1948 there has been, at best, an armed truce between Israel and its neighbors. The Arab nations and the Palestinian people have generally not accepted Israel's right to exist as a state, and to ensure its survival. Israel (with the support of the United States) has taken aggressive measures, often in defiance of world opinion and international law regarding **occupied territories**. The most serious military confrontations have been the Suez Crisis of 1956, when Israel (and briefly France and England) invaded the Sinai; the 1967 June war (the "Six Day War"), when Israel occupied the Sinai, the Golan Heights, and the West Bank (of the Jordan River); the October (Yom Kippur) war of 1973, when the Egyptians and Syrians staged a surprise attack on Israel; and the Israeli invasions of Lebanon in 1978 and 1982 to extricate anti-Israeli terrorist refuges. Since the fall of 2000, regional violence has worsened, with repeated Israeli military assaults on towns and refugee camps in the West Bank and Gaza and regular Palestinian extremist suicide attacks on mainly civilian targets. The highly provocative construction by Israel of a massive "separation wall" through the West Bank impinges on more Palestinian territory as an effort to protect Israelis from suicide bombings. The United States has pulled back from serious efforts to mediate.

Arab and some non-Arab states have been equally intransigent about recognizing Israel's right to exist. Egypt was the first notable exception to this policy. Egypt's President Anwar Sadat (1918–1981) and Israel's prime minister Menachem Begin (1913–1994), with the mediation of U.S. President Jimmy Carter (b. 1924), reached an agreement—the Camp David Accords—in 1978 and in 1979 signed a formal peace treaty. Sadat was assassinated in 1981 by Egyptian Muslim extremists, but the treaty has held up.

Holy City. Jews pray at the Wailing Wall in Jerusalem during Passover, immediately below the Dome of the Rock, Islam's third holiest site.

How has the concentration of holy sites for multiple religions within a small area affected Israel's history?

CHRONOLOGY

ISRAEL: A HISTORY OF CONFLICT

1917	Britain's Balfour Declaration supports creation of Jewish state in Palestine
1947	United Nations Partition Plan calls for creation of two states, one Jewish and one Muslim/Christian/Arab, in Palestine
1948	Israel created
1948–1949	Arab-Israeli war
1956	Suez Crisis, Israel invades the Sinai
1967	Six Day War
1973	Yom Kippur War
1978	Israel invades Lebanon
1979	Camp David Accords signed by Israel and Egypt
1982	Israel invades Lebanon
1993	Oslo Agreement

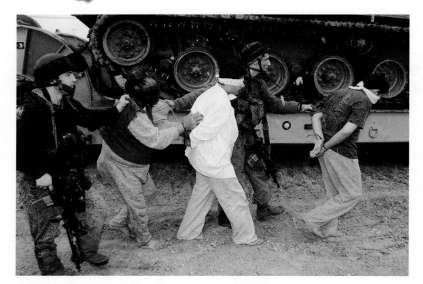

Confrontation. Israeli soldiers guard blindfolded Palestinian militants at the Herez border crossing in February 2004.

Why is there so much distrust between Israelis and Palestinians?

Recent Israeli military actions in the occupied territories were provoked by, and in turn have brought on, more Palestinian terrorist bombings in Israel and abroad. Arabs and many Muslims outside the Arab world have come to view Jews, without distinction, as oppressors and enemies, and similarly many Jews around the world have vilified all Arabs and Muslims.

The 1993 Middle East Peace Agreement, also known as the Oslo Agreement, raised hopes for a negotiated settlement and the creation of an independent Palestinian state alongside the Jewish state of Israel. There has been little substantive progress since then. Jordan and Egypt did agree in 1994 to a peace treaty with Israel, but some other Arab states—foremost among them Syria—have still not been willing to negotiate with Israel, and Israel has preferred to keep developing settlements and roads in such a way as to preclude any contiguous territory with which to form a viable state. Extremists on both sides have put up obstacles to the success of the peace initiative.

The Palestinian Authority created by the 1993 peace agreement, under the leadership of Yasser Arafat (1929–2004), grew steadily more corrupt, ineffective, and out of touch with its constituencies. Despite the efforts of the Palestinian and Israeli security forces, Palestinian guerrillas of the extremist wing of the resistance organization Hamas found ways to kill Israelis in a sustained effort to torpedo the already shaky **peace process**. These terrorist attacks led Israel to seal its borders, resulting in the additional loss of 11 percent of West Bank Palestinian farmlands, a source of livelihood for thousands of Arabs in the occupied territories who normally work in Israel proper. This has exacerbated Gaza's dire plight and in turn feeding the extremist resistance groups.

peace process Efforts, chiefly by the United States, to broker a peace between the State of Israel and the PLO.

In March 2000, Ariel Sharon became Israel's prime minister. His administration has been marked by an escalation of violence on both sides. Sharon has proposed that Israel withdraw from Gaza and close Israeli settlements in that region, a proposal that has proved controversial on both sides. His government erected a fence separating Israeli and Palestinian territory. Arafat died in late 2004. His passing may present a new opportunity for negotiations, with the Palestinians now led by Mahmoud Abbas (Abu Mazen), elected to the Palestinian presidency in January 2005.

MIDDLE EASTERN OIL

The oil wealth of the Arab and Iranian world has been both a blessing and a curse for the people and countries of the Middle East. Ever since the discovery of oil in Iran in 1908, the world demand for oil has surged. In the mid-1970s, oil became a major bargaining chip in international diplomacy, one the Arab and other oil-rich Third World states—such as Venezuela, Nigeria, Iran, and Indonesia—have used to their advantage. In the Arab countries of North Africa and especially of Arabia and the Gulf, oil production and wealth have changed every aspect of life. Oil has propelled formerly peripheral and virtually unknown countries of the Sahara or the Arabian deserts into major roles in the world of international banking and finance. Oil has also boosted the damaged self-confidence of the Arab world after a century and a half of European domination. A testimony to the global importance of Middle Eastern oil was the willingness of the United States and European nations to form a coalition with some Arab countries and to commit massive forces to the region to expel Iraq from Kuwait after Iraq's invasion of its neighbor in 1990. Though the economic benefits of oil are all too obvious, this resource has not necessarily had the corresponding political remuneration for people in the Middle East. Because of its importance to the world economy, the Middle East has been subject to considerable foreign involvement, whether from Europe, the United States, or the former Soviet Union.

THE RISE OF MILITANT ISLAMISM

The increase in the global importance of the oil-producing states of the Middle East has coincided with a surging movement there and elsewhere for the revival of pristine Muslim values and reformation of Muslim societies. Many Muslims have sought to return to the "fundamentals" of Islam, which they see as a means for rejuvenating societies corrupted by Western secularist and materialist values. A major new element in Muslim revivalism is a consciousness of being a viable response to the destructive influence of Western-style "modernity."

Much of the appeal of Islamist groups everywhere is their willingness and ability to address the needs of the underclasses in Middle Eastern, North African, and Asian cities and countries. Where governments of Muslim-majority countries have failed to provide social services such as housing, medical care, education, and jobs, the Islamist groups have succeeded. Although the world press reports only on the relatively small fringe groups of Islamist extremists, Muslims at the grassroots level have watched while the major Islamist groups in the dictatorships or military regimes under which most of them live provide services for which the state has long abdicated responsibility.

Such Muslim fundamentalism—or more correctly, "Islamist reformism"—motivated the overthrow of the shah of Iran in 1978, the Muslim Brethren movement in Egypt and elsewhere, the Welfare Party in Turkey, and many other groups, from Morocco to the Persian Gulf and beyond the Middle East. All such Islamist groups see themselves as traditionalist, as true to basic Muslim values and norms. Whether these movements will bring lasting change to Islamic societies is an open issue, but there is no question about their current attraction and influence.

The background to modern Islamist reform lies in the European expansion over much of the globe in just a few centuries. This expansion brought far more social and political change than religious or even cultural change to the Islamic world. It saw the emergence globally of European-style nationalism and the idea of the nation-state; of post-Enlightenment ideals of individual liberties and rights and representative government; and of the concept of one's religious faith and affiliation as a strictly private, "religious" matter and one's citizenship as a public, "secular" matter. Such ideas proved disruptive in the Islamic world, especially in this century.

Parts of the Islamic world today have a checkered history of autocratic governments that are as far removed from their citizenries as any medieval or premodern dynasty. Experiments with European-style parliamentary government have only rarely taken hold; nor have either liberal democratic or Marxist-socialist ideals proven viable for the long term. Until recently, however, little of the political discourse in Islamic lands has given serious thought to *Islamic* alternatives.

The postcolonial independence of many national states divorced politics from Islamic religious traditions and norms. Where leaders had previously claimed Muslim faith and allegiance, some espoused secular ideologies and ignored religion except to use it as a political weapon. In the late twentieth and early twenty-first centuries, Islamic religious allegiance has commonly been invoked to bolster a ruler's claim to

theocracy A state ruled by religious leaders who claim to govern by divine authority.

legitimacy and to cloak mundane objectives and programs in pious garb. In short, the recent past has seen no realization of an "ideal" Islamic state in which religious authority and political authority are conjoined. Even in the postrevolutionary Islamic Republic of Iran a clear division exists between political realities and religious standards. However sincerely the latter are claimed as the basis of state policy, no one can miss the frequent stretching of norms to justify pragmatic political decisions. When we look at the Islamist movements of recent decades, we find that the calls for a congruence of religion and politics in the Islamic world trace less to some kind of ideal model of a religious state or so-called **theocracy** than to a sorely felt need for simple social and political justice. The cries for a *jihad* of Muslims are aimed less often outward than inward, less at foreign "devils" and more at domestic tyrants, corruption, and social and economic injustice. The most international and widely influential of all contemporary Islamic revivalist or reform movements, the Tabligh-i Jama'at, is explicitly apolitical. It aims to convert the individual to true submission *(islam)*, not lip service, on the principle that reform of the world begins with oneself.

As for those reform movements that are avowedly political, be they activist but nonviolent (the majority) or extremist and violent (the minority), they feed on the deep sense of socioeconomic and political injustice that citizens of most Islamic countries rightfully feel. When such feelings go over the edge, the result is extremism and terrorism. Osama bin Laden, the dispossessed Saudi millionaire who founded and has led al-Qaeda from the 1990s to the present, stunned the world by using U.S. civilian airliners to destroy the World Trade Center towers and part of the Pentagon building on September 11, 2001. His motive was revenge for the American military presence in Saudi Arabia, the American-led blockade of Iraq, and the American support of Israel against the Palestinians.

These carefully executed and massively destructive attacks have involved the U.S. military ever more deeply in the Middle East and Central Asia. In October 2001, the United States attacked the Taliban government of Afghanistan, rapidly overthrew it, and dispersed, but did not destroy, al-Qaeda's organization. Whether this military response to the threat of terrorism will be successful remains to be seen. Certainly the ongoing war on terrorism is radically changing the security needs of the United States. The U.S. military is transferring many of its troops and bases, previously located in Western Europe and East Asia, closer to the Middle East. American troops will not soon leave this part of the world. Further United States intervention followed in 2003 with the invasion of Iraq.

IRAQ AND UNITED STATES: INTERVENTION AND OCCUPATION

The modern nation of Iraq was established after World War I. Iraq as such had never been a distinct political unit and until 1921 was primarily a geographic term, referring to today's southern Iraq. Postwar imperial concern and the potential of oil under Iraqi soil motivated the British government to oversee the creation of an Iraq that they felt would best protect their interests in the region. Given the disparate ethnic and religious groups in the country, the British could not find a suitable native leader. They imported a politician from Arabia, Faysal ibn Husayn, and crowned him first king of the Hashemite monarchy. The dynasty ruled with British help until 1958.

Iraqis developed a sense of national identity that led them to resent the foreign presence in their country, and in 1958 a bloody coup, led by Abd al-Karim Qasem, terminated the monarchy. By 1979, the Ba'ath party had become the dominant force in Iraq politics, bringing Saddam Hussein to the start of his tyrannical reign. Following a

QUICK REVIEW

Iraq in the Early Twentieth Century

- Territory controlled by Britain after World War I
- Competing ethnic and religious groups
- Ruled by Arab Hashemite dynasty, 1921–1958

long, bloody, and unsuccessful war with Iran (1980–1988), Saddam Hussein invaded and occupied Kuwait (1990). After an international military coalition under the leadership of the United States (in Operation Desert Storm) expelled the Iraqi army from Kuwait, Iraq became an international pariah. It was subject to economic sanctions monitored by the United Nations until 1998, when the Iraqi government expelled the UN inspectors; the United Nations was unable to reinsert them for almost five years.

In the wake of the September 11, 2001, terrorist attacks the Bush administration decided that Saddam Hussein had to be overthrown to remove the threat of Iraqi weapons of mass destruction. During late 2002 and early 2003, the U.S. and British governments sought to obtain passage of the UN Security Council resolutions that would require Iraq to disarm on its own or to face disarmament by military force. When opposition from France and Russia blocked the resolution, Australia, Great Britain, and the United States, with more than forty other nations (the "Coalition of the Willing") invaded Iraq. After three weeks of fighting that began in mid-March 2003, the coalition removed Saddam Hussein from power. The announced goals of the invasion, in addition to toppling the Iraqi regime, were to destroy Iraq's capacity to manufacture or deploy weapons of mass destruction and to bring consensual government to the Iraqi people.

The invasion of Iraq occasioned considerable international opposition, most notably from France, Germany, and Russia, and provoked large antiwar demonstrations in the United States and other parts of the world. The war has created strains within the European Union and NATO and begun a new era in international relations.

Currently, it is immensely difficult to ensure peace and stability in Iraq. Many Iraqis have resisted occupation by foreign forces and historical factors militate against formation of a new unified government. The unpreparedness of the Americans and their allies to deal with the chaos of postwar Iraq has exacerbated matters, and the failure to find weapons of mass destruction in Iraq led to wide questioning of the rationale for the war. Throughout Iraq an insurgency has been launched against the coalition forces and against Iraqi collaborators. President George W. Bush, who was reelected in 2004, has vowed to continue to pursue his existing policies in the Middle East. In late January 2005, an election was held in Iraq under conditions of insurgent attacks to elect the assembly that wrote a new constitution; in October 2005 the constitution was ratified. The challenges of securing internal support for democratic processes now confront the emerging Iraqi government and American policy makers. Internal violence and effective civil war continue.

Suicide Car Bomb Explosion, Iraq, 2007. An Iraqi woman reacts at the site of a car bomb explosion in Baghdad that killed more than eighty-five civilians and wounded dozens of others.

How is violence in Iraq transforming the relations between Sunni and Shi'ites

SUMMARY

WHAT ARE the two main developments that have occurred in the postcolonial world?

Beyond the Postcolonial Era. Since 1945, independent states have emerged from the European colonies of Africa and Asia. These states have had to adjust their political and economic relations first to the superpowers during the Cold War and, more recently, to the globalized economy and political structures. *page 862*

WHERE IN Latin America did the major attempts to establish revolutionary governments occur?

Latin America Since 1945. Most Latin American countries remain politically and economically dependent. Cuba was the only revolutionary movement to overturn the traditional structure of Latin American society, though Socialist revolution was also attempted in Chile and Nicaragua. Despite social and economic problems, Argentina and Brazil have managed to move from military rule to stable democratic, civilian government. In Mexico, the long dominance of the PRI ended in 2000. *page 865*

WHAT ARE the most significant issues that Africa faces in the twenty-first century?

Postcolonial Africa. Independent Africa has faced arbitrary boundaries, disease, economic dependence, and political instability. While Nigeria has experienced ethnic and religious strife under a succession of military dictatorships, South Africa has emerged as a stable, multiethnic democracy. The challenge for Africa as a whole is to build a truly civil society and achieve economic health and political stability despite health, environmental, and other hurdles. *page 870*

HOW HAS Islam affected politics in the developing world?

The Islamic Heartlands from North Africa to Indonesia. The vast area encompassing countries with large Muslim populations includes diverse national stories. Turkey straddles Europe and Central Asia geographically and culturally. India's politics have been significantly shaped by relations—generally antagonistic—with Muslim Pakistan. Indonesia has the world's largest population of Muslims. *page 875*

HOW DID the creation of the state of Israel affect the history of the modern Middle East?

The Postcolonial Middle East. Controversy surrounding the creation of the state of Israel has dominated the politics of the Middle East since the 1940s. Although efforts to negotiate an Israeli-Palestinian peace have sometimes progressed, the cycle of terror and retaliatory violence has persisted. Although vast deposits of oil have made some Middle Eastern governments wealthy, they have not led to the creation of prosperous democratic societies. In the wake of the terrorist attacks of September 11, 2001, the United States overthrew Saddam Hussein in Iraq and has become increasingly embroiled in a chaotic and unstable region of the world. *page 879*

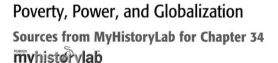

INTERPRETING THE PAST

Poverty, Power, and Globalization

Sources from MyHistoryLab for Chapter 34

myhistorylab

1) *United Nations Universal Declaration of Human Rights*
2) Frantz Fanon, *The Wretched of the Earth*
3) Juan Perón, *The Voices of Perón*

Visual Sources from MyHistoryLab

1) *Indonesian Guerillas*
2) *Cocoa Harvesting, Ghana*

Source from Chapter 34

1) "A Modernist Muslim Poet's Eulogy for His Mother" (pp. 876–877)

Democracy and globalization have transformed societies around the world in the six decades since the end of World War II. The decline of authoritarian regimes, and the spread of economic linkages among the United States, Europe, Asia, Africa, and Latin America led to more efficient and global trade networks. As a

REVIEW QUESTIONS

1. Are the nations of Latin America still economically dependent on the United States and Western Europe? If so, why? How did the superpower rivalry of the Cold War affect Latin America? How successful has the worldwide trend toward democratization been in Latin America? Describe the transition from military rule to civilian democracy in Brazil, Argentina, and Chile. Has Mexico made a similar transition?

2. What challenges did many newly independent states in Africa share? Has postcolonial Nigeria lived up to its potential? Why is Nigeria's record significant for Africa as a whole? Describe the apartheid regime in South Africa. Why was it dismantled in the 1990s? What problems does the Democratic Republic of the Congo face? What factors contributed to the 1994 genocide in Rwanda?

3. Compare and contrast the roles of social change, religion, and economics in Turkey, Iran, Pakistan, and Malaysia. How does the profound influence of Islam in this and other regions of the world suggest the power of religious tradition in modern politics and society? Compare the nationalization process and results in 1951 Iran and in 1956 Egypt.

4. What have been the major factors in the creation of the modern Middle East? How have interventions by European powers and the United States affected this region? Compare and contrast the roles of religion and nationalism in the Middle East.

5. Explain the origin and course of the Israeli-Palestinian conflict. What have been the major turning points?

Have there been moments when the conflict might have reached a peaceful resolution?

6. Describe the origins and character of political and militant Islam. Why has it taken so radical a political course in the post–Iranian Revolution era (1979)? Why was the Soviet invasion of Afghanistan an important event in its development? Why has the United States become the primary target of militant Islamists?

7. What is *globalization*? What are its costs and its benefits?

8. How has the legacy of European colonialism affected the Middle East, Asia, and Africa?

9. How and why was Iraq created? What influence does this early-twentieth-century history have on current events in the region? What has happened in Iraq in the twenty-first century?

KEY TERMS

apartheid (uh-PAHRT-heyed) (p. 871)
clash of civilizations (p. 864)
decolonization (p. 863)
globalization (p. 863)
HIV/AIDS (p. 873)
intifadah (IN-tuh-FAH-duh) (p. 880)

liberation theology (p. 866)
occupied territories (p. 880)
peace process (p. 882)
Sandinistas (sahn-dihn-EES-tahs) (p. 867)
theocracy (p. 884)
Truth and Reconciliation Commission (TRC) (p. 872)

Note: To learn more about the topics in this chapter, please turn to the Suggested Readings at the end of the book.

result, large-scale demographic changes have occurred in emerging economies as millions have migrated to cities from the countryside. Staggering poverty still exists side by side with great prosperity, exacerbated by the availability of relatively inexpensive communication technologies: cable and satellite television, cell phones, movies, and radio. As a result, developing countries in Latin America, the Caribbean, Africa, and Asia are again vulnerable to those who promise an end to poverty and exploitation by offering extremist policies.

In this exercise you will read four primary sources relating to the problems of poverty and powerlessness in non-Western regions. The first document is taken from the 1948 United Nations *Universal Declaration of Human Rights*, which links and updates many principles of the American and French Revolutions. The second primary source is written by Frantz Fanon, an author, psychiatrist, and revolutionary who describes the effect of colonialism and oppression, economic and otherwise, on colonized peoples. The third source comprises several excerpts of speeches delivered by Juan Perón, the president and dictator of Argentina from 1946 to 1956. Perón's philosophy is characterized

by extreme nationalism and authoritarianism, as well as astute coalition-building and an emphasis on economic revitalization. The fourth document is Turkish poet Aziz Nesin's commentary on his mother's life and women's roles more generally.

The two accompanying images show peasants engaged in agriculture and in political protests.

Questions

What rights in the Declaration are universal? Are all of the rights listed important? Would the application of these rights help marginalized women such as Nesin's mother? Why or why not?

What are the similarities and differences in the approaches of Fanon and Perón to help the marginalized and powerless? Compare Fanon's observations of the effects of colonization with Nesin's discussion of women's roles.

Are the effects of colonization observed by Fanon comparable to the exploitation of peoples in developing nations by multinational corporations in the postcolonial era? Explain.

CHAPTER 15

J. ABUN-NASR, A History of the Maghrib in the Islamic Period (1987). The most recent North African survey. Pages 59–247 are relevant to this chapter.

E.K. AKYEAMPYONG, ed., Themes in West Africa's History (2006). A wide-ranging collection of essays by leading scholars.

I. BATTUTA, N. KING, S. HAMDUN, Ibn Battuta in Black Africa rev. ed. (2005). Well-selected excerpts from Battuta's extensive journals.

P. BEN-AMOS, Art, Innovation and Politics in Eighteenth-Century Benin (1999). Offers insights into the many levels of meaning and authority in Benin's artworks.

I. BERGER, E.F. WHITE, C. SKIDMORE-HESS, Women in Sub-Saharan Africa: Restoring Women to History (1999). A valuable resource on the role of women in African history.

D. BIRMINHAM, Central Africa to 1870 (1981). Chapters from the Cambridge History of Africa that give a brief, lucid overview of developments in this region.

P. BOHANNAN and P. CURTIN, Africa and Africans, rev. ed. (1995). Accessible, topical approach to African history, culture, society, politics, and economics.

P.D. CURTIN, S. FEIERMANN, L. THOMPSON, and J. VANSINA, African History, rev. ed. (1995). An older, but masterly survey. The relevant portions are Chapters 6–9.

B. DAVIDSON, West Africa Before the Colonial Era (1998). A typically readable survey by one of the great popularizers of African history.

R. ELPHICK, Kraal and Castle: Khoikhoi and the Founding of White South Africa (1977). An incisive, informative interpretation of the history of the Khoikhoi and their fateful interaction with European colonization.

R. ELPHICK and H. GILIOMEE, The Shaping of South African Society, 1652–1820 (1979). A superb, synthetic history of this crucial period.

J.D. FAGE, A History of Africa, rev. ed., (2001). Still a readable survey history.

E. GILBERT and J. REYNOLDS, Africa in World History (2004). The best new survey of African history, placing it in a global context. See especially chapters six and seven on Islam, and chapters nine through twelve for the period leading to European colonization.

M. HISKETT, The Development of Islam in West Africa (1984). The standard survey study of the subject. Of the relevant sections (Chapters 1–1, 12, 15), that on Hausaland, which is treated only in passing in this text, is noteworthy.

M. HORTON and J. MIDDLETON, The Swahili (2000).

R.W. JULY, A History of the African People, 3rd ed. (1980). Chapters 3–6 treat Africa before about 1800 area by area; Chapter 7 deals with "The Coming of Europe."

N. LEVTZION, R. POUWELS, eds. History of Islam in Africa (2000). A wide-ranging collection of essays.

N. LEVTZION, D.T. NIANI, eds., Africa from the Twelfth to the Sixteenth Century, UNESCO General History of Africa, Vol. IV (1984). Many survey articles cover the various regions and major states of Africa in the centuries noted in the title.

R. OLIVER, The African Experience (1991). A masterly, balanced, and engaging survey, with outstanding syntheses and summaries of recent research.

C.A. QUINN and F. QUINN, Pride, Faith, and Fear: Islam in Sub-Saharan Africa (2005). A readable account of Islam in Africa, bringing the story up to the present.

A.F.C. RYDER, Benin and the Europeans: 1485–1897 (1969). A basic study.

D. ROBINSON, Muslim Societies in African History (2004). A comprehensive overview.

JOHN K. THORNTON, The Kingdom of Kongo: Civil War and Transition, 1641–1718 (1983). A detailed and perceptive analysis for those who wish to delve into Kongo state and society in the seventeenth century.

M. WILSON and L. THOMPSON, eds., The Oxford History of South Africa, Vol. I., South Africa to 1870 (1969). Relatively detailed, if occasionally dated, treatment.

CHAPTER 16

M. BRECHT, Martin Luther: His Road to Reformation, 1483–1521 (1985). Best on young Luther.

C. BROWN, ET AL., Rembrandt: The Master and His Workshop (1991). A great master's art and influence.

R. BRIGGS, Witches and Neighbors: A History of European Witchcraft (1996). A readable introduction.

E. DUFFY, The Stripping of the Altars (1992). Strongest argument yet that there was no deep reformation in England.

H.O. EVENNETT, The Spirit of the Counter Reformation (1968). The continuity and independence of Catholic reform.

HANS-JÜRGEN GOERTZ, The Anabaptists (1996). Best treatment of minority Protestants.

O.P. GRELL and A. CUNNINGHAM, Health Care and Poor Relief in Protestant Europe (1997) The civic side of the Reformation.

M. HOLT, The French Wars of Religion, 1562–1629 (1995). Scholarly appreciation of religious side of the story.

J.C. HUTCHISON, Albrecht Dürer (1990). The life behind the art.

H. JEDIN, A History of the Council of Trent, Vols. 1, 2 (1957–1961). Comprehensive, detailed, and authoritative.

M. KITCHEN, The Cambridge Illustrated History of Germany (1996). Comprehensive and accessible.

A. KORS and E. PETERS, eds., European Witchcraft, 1100–1700 (1972). Classics of witch belief.

W. MACCAFFREY, Elizabeth I (1993). Magisterial study.

G. MATTINGLY, The Armada (1959). A masterpiece, novel-like in style.

D. MCCOLLOCH, The Reformation (2004). No stone unturned, with English emphasis.

H.A. OBERMAN, Luther: Man Between God and Devil (1989). Authoritative biography.

J.W. O'MALLEY, The First Jesuits (1993). Extremely detailed account of the creation of the Society of Jesus and its original purposes.

S. OZMENT, The Age of Reform, 1250–1550: An Intellectual and Religious History of Late Medieval and Reformation Europe (1980). Broad, lucid survey.

S. OZMENT, When Fathers Ruled: Family Life in Reformation Europe (1983). Effort to portray the constructive side of Protestant thinking about family relationships.

S. OZMENT, The Bürgermeister's Daughter: Scandal in a Sixteenth-Century German Town (1996). What a woman could do at law in the sixteenth century.

G. PARKER, The Thirty Years' War (1984). Large, lucid survey.

J.H. PARRY, The Age of Reconnaissance (1964). A comprehensive account of explorations from 1450 to 1650.

W. PRINZ, Dürer (1998). Latest biography of Germany's greatest painter.

J.J. SCARISBRICK, Henry VIII (1968). The best account of Henry's reign.

G. STRAUSS, ed. and trans., Manifestations of Discontent in Germany on the Eve of the Reformation (1971). A rich collection of sources for both rural and urban scenes.

H. WUNDER, He Is the Sun, She Is the Moon: Women in Early Modern Germany (1998). Best study of early modern women.

CHAPTER 17

J. ABUN-NASR, A History of the Maghrib in the Islamic Period (1987). The most recent North African survey. Pages 59–247 are relevant to this chapter.

D. BIRMINHAM, Central Africa to 1870 (1981). Chapters from the Cambridge History of Africa that give a brief, lucid overview of developments in this region.

P. BOHANNAN and P. CURTIN, Africa and Africans, rev. ed. (1971). Accessible, topical approach to African history, culture, society, politics, and economics.

P.D. CURTIN, S. FEIERMANN, L. THOMPSON, and J. VANSINA, African History (1978). An older, but masterly survey. The relevant portions are Chapters 6–9.

R. ELPHICK, Kraal and Castle: Khoikhoi and the Founding of White South Africa (1977). An incisive, informative interpretation of the history of the Khoikhoi and their fateful interaction with European colonization.

R. ELPHICK and H. GILIOMEE, The Shaping of South African Society, 1652–1820 (1979). A superb, synthetic history of this crucial period.

J.D. FAGE, A History of Africa (1978). Still a readable survey history.

M. HISKETT, The Development of Islam in West Africa (1984). The standard survey study of the subject. Of the relevant sections (Chapters 1–10, 12, 15), that on Hausaland, which is treated only in passing in this text, is noteworthy.

R.W. JULY, Precolonial Africa: An Economic and Social History (1975). Chapter 10 gives an interesting overall picture of slaving in African history.

R.W. JULY, A History of the African People, 3rd ed. (1980). Chapters 3–6 treat Africa before about 1800 area by area; Chapter 7 deals with "The Coming of Europe."

I.M. LEWIS, ed., Islam in Tropical Africa (1966), pp. 4–96. Lewis's introduction is one of the best brief summaries of the role of Islam in West Africa and the Sudan.

D.T. NIANI, ed., Africa from the Twelfth to the Sixteenth Century, UNESCO General History of Africa, Vol. IV (1984). Many survey articles cover the various regions and major states of Africa in the centuries noted in the title.

R. OLIVER, The African Experience (1991). A masterly, balanced, and engaging survey, with outstanding syntheses and summaries of recent research.

J.A. RAWLEY, The Transatlantic Slave Trade: A History (1981). Impressively documented, detailed, and well-presented survey history of the Atlantic trade; little focus on African dimensions.

A.F.C. RYDER, Benin and the Europeans: 1485–1897 (1969). A basic study.

JOHN K. THORNTON, The Kingdom of Kongo: Civil War and Transition, 1641–1718 (1983). A detailed and perceptive analysis for those who wish to delve into Kongo state and society in the seventeenth century.

M. WILSON and L. THOMPSON, eds., The Oxford History of South Africa, Vol. I., South Africa to 1870 (1969). Relatively detailed, if occasionally dated, treatment.

CHAPTER 18

B. BAILYN, Atlantic History: Concepts and Contours (2005). An essential overview to this burgeoning area of historical inquiry, written by a leader in the field.

I. BERLIN, Many Thousands Gone: The First Two Centuries of Slavery in North America (1998); Generations of Captivity: A History of African American Slaves (2003). Two volumes representing the most extensive and important recent treatment of slavery in North America; highlights the diversity of slave experiences.

R. BLACKBURN, The Making of New World Slavery from the Baroque to the Modern 1492–1800 (1997). An extraordinary work.

V. CARRETTA, Equiano, the African: The Biography of a Self-Made Man (reprint 2007). Provides context and analysis of the renowned accounts of one-time slave Olaudah Equiano.

B. COBO and R. HAMILTON, History of the Inca Empire, rev. ed. (1983). A seventeenth-century account, with a modern translation and interpretation.

N.D. COOK, Born to Die: Disease and New World Conquest, 1492–1650 (1998). A survey of the devastating impact of previously unknown diseases on the native populations of the Americas.

M.S. CREIGHTON and L. NORLING, eds. Iron Men, Wooden Women: Gender and Seafaring in the Atlantic World, 1700–1920 (2006). Eye-opening accounts of life at sea, and how gender-roles were shaped and challenged on the Atlantic.

P.D. CURTIN, The Atlantic Slave Trade: A Census (1969). Remains a basic work.

P.D. CURTIN, The Rise and Fall of the Plantation Complex (1998). Places the plantation economy in the context of world history.

D.B. DAVIS, The Problem of Slavery in Western Culture (1966). A brilliant and far-ranging discussion.

D. ELTIS, The Rise of African Slavery in the Americas (1999). Detailed discussion of the size and scope of the Atlantic market, with attention to the role of Africans on both sides of the Atlantic.

H.L. GATES JR. and W.L. ANDREWS, eds., Pioneers of the Black Atlantic: Five Slave Narratives from the Enlightenment, 1772–1815 (1998). An anthology of autobiographical accounts.

S. GRUZINSKI, The Conquest of Mexico: The Incorporation of Indian Societies into the Western World, 16th–18th Centuries (1993). Interprets the experience of Native Americans, from their own point of view, during the time of the Spanish conquest.

L. HANKE, Bartolomé de Las Casas: An Interpretation of His Life and Writings (1951). A classic work.

R. HARMS, The Diligent: A Voyage through the Worlds of the Slave Trade (2002). A powerful narrative of the voyage of a French slave trader.

J. HEMMING, The Conquest of the Incas, rev. ed., (2003). A lucid account of the conquest of the Inca Empire and its aftermath.

J. HEMMING, Red Gold: The Conquest of the Brazilian Native Americans, 1500–1760 (1978). A careful account with excellent bibliography.

H. KLEIN, The Atlantic Slave Trade (1999). A synthesis of scholarly knowledge.

W. KLOOSTER and A. PADULA, The Atlantic World: Essays on Slavery, Migration, and Imagination (2004). Essays by leading scholars examine important aspects of the creation of a new way of living—and a new way of thinking about the world.

P.E. LOVEJOY, Transformations in Slavery: A History of Slavery in Africa (2000). An important new evaluation of slavery as it was practiced within Africa, and its relation to the Islamic and trans-Atlantic slave trades.

K. MANN, Rethinking the African Diaspora: The Making of a Black Atlantic World in the Bight of Benin and Brazil (2005). This analysis of the dynamics of human and cultural migration and exchange on the busiest route of the slave trade is a significant addition to Atlantic World scholarship.

P. MANNING, Slavery and African Life: Occidental, Oriental, and African Slave Trades (1990). An admirably concise economic-historical synthesis of the evidence, with multiple tables and statistics to supplement the magisterial analysis.

A. PAGDEN, Lords of All the World: Ideologies of Empire in Spain, Britain, and France, c. 1500–c. 1800 (1995). An effort to explain the imperial thinking of the major European powers.

S. PEABODY and K. GRINBERG, Slavery, Freedom, and the Law in the Atlantic World: A Brief History with Documents (2007). Examines the legal frameworks through which slavery was institutionalized, and documents the many ways people challenged slavery.

D.K. RICHTER, Facing East from Indian Country: A Native History of Early America (new ed. 2003). Uses the biographies of three Native Americans to offer a fresh perspective on North American history from the time of Columbus to the American Revolution.

S.B. SCHWARTZ, ed., Tropical Babylons: Sugar and the Making of the Atlantic World, 1450–1680 (2003). A comprehensive examination of the role of sugar in the plantation economy.

I.K. STEELE, The English Atlantic, 1675–1740s: An Exploration of Communication and Community (1986). An exploration of culture and commerce in the transatlantic world.

H. THOMAS, Conquest: Montezuma, Cortés, and the Fall of Old Mexico (1993). A splendid modern narrative of the event, with careful attention to the character of the participants.

H. THOMAS, The Slave Trade: The Story of the Atlantic Slave Trade, 1440–1870 (1999). A sweeping narrative overview.

J. THORNTON, Africa and Africans in the Making of the Atlantic World, 1400–1680 (1992). A discussion of the role of Africans in the emergence of the transatlantic economy.

J. THORNTON, The Kongolese Saint Anthony: Dona Beatriz Kimpa Vita and the Antonian Movement, 1684–1706 (1998). Describes a fascinating period in Kongolese history, when Beatriz Kimpa Vita led a Christian movement during a time of political and social turmoil.

N. WACHTEL, The Vision of the Vanquished: The Spanish Conquest of Peru Through Indian Eyes, 1530–1570 (1977). A presentation of Incan experience of conquest.

CHAPTER 19

China

D. BODDE and C. MORRIS, Law in Imperial China (1967). Focuses on the Qing dynasty (1644–1911).

T. BROOK, The Confusions of Pleasure: Commerce and Culture in Ming China (1988).

C.S. CHANG and S.L.H. CHANG, Crisis and Transformation in Seventeenth-century China: Society, Culture, and Modernity (1992).

P. CROSSLEY, Translucent Mirror: History and Identity in Qing Imperial Ideology (1999).

W.T. DE BARY, Learning for One's Self: Essays on the Individual in Neo-Confucian Thought (1991). A useful corrective to the view that Confucianism is simply a social ideology.

M.C. ELLIOTT, The Manchu Way: The Eight Banners and Ethnic Identity in Late Imperial China (2001). The latest word; compare to Crossley above.

M. ELVIN, The Pattern of the Chinese Past: A Social and Economic Interpretation (1973). A controversial but stimulating interpretation of Chinese economic history in terms of technology. It brings in earlier periods as well as the Ming, Qing, and modern China.

J.K. FAIRBANK, ed., The Chinese World Order: Traditional China's Foreign Relations (1968). An examination of the Chinese tribute system and its varying applications.

H.L. KAHN, Monarchy in the Emperor's Eyes: Image and Reality in the Ch'ien-lung Reign (1971). A study of the Chinese court during the mid-Qing period.

P. KUHN, Soulstealers: The Chinese Sorcery Scare of 1768 (1990).

LI YU, The Carnal Prayer Mat, trans. by P. Hanan (1990).

F. MOTE and D. TWITCHETT, eds., The Cambridge History of China: The Ming Dynasty 1368–1644, Vols. VI (1988) and VII (1998).

S. NAQUIN, Peking Temples and City Life, 1400–1900 (2000).

S. NAQUIN and E.S. RAWSKI, Chinese Society in the Eighteenth Century (1987).

J.B. PARSONS, The Peasant Rebellions of the Late Ming Dynasty (1970).

P.C. PERDUE, Exhausting the Earth, State and Peasant in Hunan, 1500–1850 (1987).

D.H. PERKINS, Agricultural Development in China, 1368–1968 (1969).

E. RAWSKI, The Last Emperors: A Social History of Qing Imperial Institutions (1998).

M. RICCI, China in the Sixteenth Century: The Journals of Matthew Ricci, 1583–1610 (1953).

W. ROWE, Hankow (1984). A study of a city in late imperial China.

G.W. SKINNER, The City in Late Imperial China (1977).

J.D. SPENCE, Ts'ao Yin and the K'ang-hsi Emperor: Bondservant and Master (1966). An excellent study of the early Qing court.

J.D. SPENCE, Emperor of China: A Self-Portrait of K'ang-hsi (1974). The title of this readable book does not adequately convey the extent of the author's contribution to the study of the early Qing emperor.

J.D. SPENCE, Treason by the Book (2001). An account of the legal workings of the authoritarian Qing state that reads like a detective story.

L.A. STRUVE, trans. and ed., Voices from the Ming-Qing Cataclysm (1993). A reader with translations of Chinese sources.

F. WAKEMAN, The Great Enterprise (1985). On the founding of the Manchu dynasty.

Japan

M.E. BERRY, Hideyoshi (1982). A study of the sixteenth-century unifier of Japan.

M.E. BERRY, The Culture of Civil War in Kyoto (1994). On the Warring States era.

H. BOLITHO, Treasures Among Men: The Fudai Daimyo in Tokugawa Japan (1974). A study in depth.

H. BOLITHO, Bereavement and Consolation: Testimonies from Tokugawa Japan (2003). Instances of how Tokugawa Japanese handled the death of a child.

C.R. BOXER, The Christian Century in Japan, 1549–1650 (1951).

The Cambridge History of Japan; Vol. 4 J.W. Hall (ed.), Early Modern Japan (1991). A multi-author work.

M. CHIKAMATSU, Major Plays of Chikamatsu, trans. by D. Keene (1961).

R.P. DORE, Education in Tokugawa Japan (1965).

G.S. ELISON, Deus Destroyed: The Image of Christianity in Early Modern Japan (1973). A brilliant study of the persecutions of Christianity during the early Tokugawa period.

J.W. HALL and M. JANSEN, eds., Studies in the Institutional History of Early Modern Japan (1968). A collection of articles on Tokugawa institutions.

J.W. HALL, K. NAGAHARA, and K. YAMAMURA, eds., Japan Before Tokugawa (1981).

S. HANLEY, Everyday Things in Premodern Japan: The Hidden Legacy of Material Culture (1997).

H.S. HIBBETT, The Floating World in Japanese Fiction (1959). An eminently readable study of early Tokugawa literature.

M. JANSEN, ed., The Nineteenth Century, Vol. 5 in The Cambridge History of Japan (1989).

K. KATSU, Musui's Story (1988). The life and adventures of a boisterous, no-good samurai of the early nineteenth century. Eminently readable.

D. KEENE, trans., Chushingura, the Treasury of Loyal Retainers (1971). The puppet play about the forty-seven men who took revenge on the enemy of their former lord.

O.G. LIDIN, Tanegashima: The Arrival of Europe in Japan (2002). The impact of the musket and Europeans on sixteenth-century Japan.

M. MARUYAMA, Studies in the Intellectual History of Tokugawa Japan, trans. by M. Hane (1974). A seminal work in this field by one of modern Japan's greatest scholars.

J.L. MCCLAIN, ET AL., Edo and Paris: Urban Life and the State in the Early Modern Era (1994). Comparison of city life and government role in capitals of Tokugawa Japan and France.

K.W. NAKAI, Shogunal Politics (1988). A brilliant study of Arai Hakuseki's conceptualization of Tokugawa government.

P. NOSCO, ed., Confucianism and Tokugawa Culture (1984). A lively collection of essays.

H. OOMS, Tokugawa Village Practice: Class, Status, Power, Law (1996).

A. RAVINA, Land and Lordship in Early Modern Japan (1999). A sociopolitical study of three Tokugawa domains.

I. SAIKAKU, The Japanese Family Storehouse, trans. by G.W. Sargent (1959). A lively novel about merchant life in seventeenth-century Japan.

G.B. SANSOM, The Western World and Japan (1950).

J.A. SAWADA, Confucian Values and Popular Zen (1993). A study of Shingaku, a popular Tokugawa religious sect.

C.D. SHELDON, The Rise of the Merchant Class in Tokugawa Japan (1958).

T.C. SMITH, The Agrarian Origins of Modern Japan (1959). On the evolution of farming and rural social organization in Tokugawa Japan.

P.F. SOUYRI, The World Turned Upside Down: Medieval Japanese Society (2001). After a running start from the late Heian period, an analysis of the overthrow of lords by their vassals.

R.P. TOBY, State and Diplomacy in Early Modern Japan: Asia in the Development of the Tokugawa Bakufu (1984).

C. TOTMAN, Tokugawa Ieyasu: Shōgun (1983).

C. TOTMAN, Green Archipelago, Forestry in Preindustrial Japan (1989).

H.P. VARLEY, The 'nin War: History of Its Origins and Background with a Selective Translation of the Chronicle of 'nin (1967).

K. YAMAMURA and S.B. HANLEY, Economic and Demographic Change in Preindustrial Japan, 1600–1868 (1977).

Korea

T. HATADA, A History of Korea (1969).

W.E. HENTHORN, A History of Korea (1971).

KI-BAIK LEE, A New History of Korea (1984).

P. LEE, Sourcebook of Korean Civilization, Vol. I (1993).

Vietnam

J. BUTTINGER, A Dragon Defiant, a Short History of Vietnam (1972).

NGUYEN DU, The Tale of Kieu (1983).

N. TARLING, ed., The Cambridge History of Southeast Asia (1992).

K. TAYLOR, The Birth of Vietnam (1983).

A.B. WOODSIDE, Vietnam and the Chinese Model (1988).

CHAPTER 20

F. ANDERSON, The Crucible of War: The Seven Years' War and the Fate of Empire in British North America, 1754–1766 (2000). A splendid narrative and analysis.

J. BLUM, Lord and Peasant in Russia from the Ninth to the Nineteenth Century (1961). Remains a thorough and wide-ranging discussion.

P. BURKE, The Fabrication of Louis XIV (1992). Examines the manner in which the public image of Louis XIV was forged in art.

P. BUSHKOVITCH, Peter the Great: The Struggle for Power, 1671–1725 (2001). Replaces previous studies.

L. COLLEY, Britons: Forging the Nation, 1707–1837 (1992) A major study of the making of British nationhood.

P. DEANE, The First Industrial Revolution (1999). A well-balanced and systematic treatment.

J. DE VRIES, European Urbanization, 1500–1800 (1984). The most important and far-ranging of recent treatments of the subject.

W. DOYLE, The Old European Order, 1660–1800 (1992). The most thoughtful treatment of the subject.

R.J.W. EVANS, The Making of the Habsburg Monarchy, 1550–1700: An Interpretation (1979). Places much emphasis on intellectual factors and the role of religion.

D. FRASER, Frederick the Great: King of Prussia (2001). Excellent on both Frederick and eighteenth-century Prussia.

E. HOBSBAWM, Industry and Empire: The Birth of the Industrial Revolution (1999). A survey by a major historian of the subject.

K. HONEYMAN, Women, Gender and Industrialization in England, 1700–1850 (2000). Emphasizes how certain work or economic roles became associated with either men or women.

O.H. HUFTON, The Poor of Eighteenth-Century France, 1750–1789 (1975). A brilliant study of poverty and the family economy.

L. HUGHES, Russia in the Age of Peter the Great (1998). An excellent account.

D.I. KERTZER and M. BARBAGLI, The History of the European Family: Family Life in Early Modern Times, 1500–1709 (2001). A series of broad-ranging essays covering the entire Continent.

S. KING and G. TIMMONS, Making Sense of the Industrial Revolution: English Economy and Society, 1700–1850 (2001). Examines the Industrial Revolution through the social institutions that brought it about and were changed by it.

M. KISHLANSKY, A Monarchy Transformed: Britain 1603–1714 (1996). An excellent synthesis.

P.L ANGFORD, A Polite and Commercial People: England 1717–1783 (1989). An excellent survey of mid-eighteenth-century Britain covering social history as well as politics, the overseas wars, and the American Revolution.

A. LOSSKY, Louis XIV and the French Monarchy (1994). The most recent major analysis.

F.E. MANUEL, The Broken Staff: Judaism Through Christian Eyes (1992). An important discussion of Christian interpretations of Judaism.

M.A. MEYER, The Origins of the Modern Jew: Jewish Identity and European Culture in Germany, 1749–1824 (1967). A general introduction organized around individual case studies.

D. UNDERDOWN, Fire from Heaven: Life in an English Town in the Seventeenth Century (1992). A lively account of how a single English town experienced the religious and political turmoil of the century.

D. VALENZE, The First Industrial Woman (1995). An elegant work exploring the manner in which industrialization transformed the work of women.

J. WEST, Gunpower, Government, and War in the Mid–Eighteenth Century (1991). A study of how warfare touched much government of the day.

CHAPTER 21

S.S. BLAIR and J. BLOOM, The Art and Architecture of Islam, 1250–1800 (1994). A fine survey of the period for all parts of the Islamic world.

R. CANFIELD, ed., Turko-Persia in Historical Perspective (1991). A good general collection of essays.

K. CHELEBI, The Balance of Truth (1957). A marvelous volume of essays and reflections by probably the major intellectual of Ottoman times.

W.T. DE BARY ET AL., comp., Sources of Indian Tradition, 2nd ed. (1958),Vol. I, From the Beginning to 1800, ed. and rev. by Ainslie T. Embree (1988). Excellent selections from a wide variety of Indian texts, with good introductions to chapters and individual selections.

S. FAROQI, Towns and Townsmen of Ottoman Anatolia (1984). Examines the changing balances of economic power between the urban and rural areas.

C.H. FLEISCHER, Bureaucrat and Intellectual in the Ottoman Empire: The Historian Mustafa Ali (1541–1600) (1986). A major study of Ottoman intellectual history.

G. HAMBLY, Central Asia (1966). Excellent survey chapters (9–13) on the Chaghatay and Uzbek (Shaybanid) Turks.

R.S. HATTOX, Coffee and Coffee-Houses: The Origins of a Social Beverage in the Medieval Near East (1985). A fascinating piece of social history.

M.G.S. HODGSON, The Gunpowder Empires and Modern Times, Vol. 3 of The Venture of Islam, 3 vols. (1974). Less ample than Vols. 1 and 2 of Hodgson's monumental history, but a thoughtful survey of the great post-1500 empires.

S.M. IKRAM, Muslim Civilization in India (1964). Still the best short survey history, covering the period from 711 to 1857.

H. INALCIK, The Ottoman Empire: The Classical Age, 1300–1600 (1973). An excellent, if dated, survey with solid treatment of Ottoman social, religious, and political institutions.

H. INALCIK, An Economic and Social History of the Ottoman Empire, 1300–1914 (1994). A masterly survey by the dean of Ottoman studies today.

C. KAFADAR, Between Two Worlds: The Construction of the Ottoman State (1995). A readable analysis of theories of Ottoman origins and early development.

N.R. KEDDIE, ed., Scholars, Saints, and Sufis: Muslim Religious Institutions in the Middle East Since 1500 (1972). A collection of interesting articles well worth reading.

M. MUJEEB, The Indian Muslims (1967). The best cultural study of Islamic civilization in India as a whole, from its origins onward.

G. NECIPOGLU, Architecture, Ceremonial, and Power: The Topkapi Palace in the Fifteenth and Sixteenth Centuries (1991). A superb analysis of the symbolism of Ottoman power and authority.

L. PIERCE, The Imperial Harem: Women and Sex in the Ottoman Empire (1993). Ground-breaking study on the role of women in the Ottoman Empire.

D. QUATARERT, An Economic and Social History of the Ottoman Empire, 1300–1914 (1994). The authoritative account of Ottoman economy and society.

J. RICHARDS, The Mughal Empire, Vol. 5 of The New Cambridge History of India (1993). An impressive synthesis of the varying interpretations of Mughal India.

S.A.A. RIZVI, The Wonder That Was India, Vol. II (1987). A sequel to Basham's original The Wonder That Was India; treats Mughal life, culture, and history from 1200 to 1700.

F. ROBINSON, Atlas of the Islamic World Since 1500 (1982). Brief, excellent historical essays, color illustra-tions with detailed accompanying text, and chronological tables, as well as precise maps, make this a refreshing general reference work.

R. SAVORY, Iran Under the Safavids (1980). A solid and readable survey.

S.J. SHAW, Empire of the Gazis: The Rise and Decline of the Ottoman Empire, 1280–1808, Vol. I of History of the Ottoman Empire and Modern Turkey (1976). A solid historical survey with excellent bibliographic essays for each chapter and a good index.

CHAPTER 22

D. BEALES, Joseph II: In the Shadow of Maria Theresa, 1741–1780 (1987). The best treatment in English of the early political life of Joseph II.

M. BIAGIOLI, Galileo Courtier: The Practice of Science in the Culture of Absolutism (1993). A major revision-ist work that emphasizes the role of the political set-ting on Galileo's career and thought.

D.D. BIEN, The Calas Affair: Persecution, Toleration, and Heresy in Eighteenth-Century Toulouse (1960). Classic treatment of the famous case.

T.C.W. BLANNING, The Culture of Power and the Power of Culture: Old Regime Europe 1660–1789 (2002). The strongest treatment of the relationship of eighteenth-century cultural changes and politics.

R. DARNTON, The Literary Underground of the Old Regime (1982). Classic essays on the world of printers, publishers, and booksellers.

P. DEAR, Revolutionizing the Sciences: European Knowledge and Its Ambitions, 1500–1700 (2001). A broad-ranging study of both the ideas and institutions of the new science.

I. DE MADARIAGA, Catherine the Great: A Short History (1990). A good brief biography.

S. GAUKROGER, Francis Bacon and the Transformation of Early-Modern Philosophy (2001). An excellent, accessible introduction.

J. GLEIXK, Isaac Newton (2003) The best brief biography.

D. GOODMAN, The Republic of Letters: A Cultural His-tory of the French Enlightenment (1994). Concen-trates on the role of salons.

I. HARRIS, The Mind of John Locke: A Study of Political Theory in Its Intellectual Setting (1994). The most comprehensive recent treatment.

J.L. HEILBRON, The Sun in the Church: Cathedrals as Solar Observatories (2000). A remarkable study of the manner in which Roman Catholic cathedrals were used to make astronomical observations and calculations.

K.J. HOWELL, God's Two Books: Copernican Cosmology and Biblical Interpretation in Early Modern Science (2003). Best introduction to early modern issues of science and religion.

J. MELTON, The Rise of the Public in Enlightenment Europe (2001). A superb overview of the emergence of new institutions that made the expression of a broad public opinion possible in Europe.

T. MUNCK, The Enlightenment: A Comparative Social History 1721–1794 (2000). A clear introduction to the social background that made possible the spread of Enlightenment thought.

S. MUTHU, Enlightenment against Empire (2003). A study of *philosophes* who criticized the European empires of their day.

D. OUTRAM, The Enlightenment (1995). An excellent brief introduction.

R. PORTER, The Creation of the Modern World: The Untold Story of the British Enlightenment (2001). A superb, lively overview.

P. RILEY, The Cambridge Companion to Rousseau (2001). Excellent accessible essays by major scholars.

E. ROTHCHILD, Economic Sentiments: Adam Smith, Condorcet, and the Enlightenment (2001). A sensitive account of Smith's thought and its relationship to the social questions of the day.

S. SHAPIN, The Scientific Revolution (1996). An important revisionist survey emphasizing social factors.

L. STEINBRÜGGE, The Moral Sex: Woman's Nature in the French Enlightenment (1995). Emphasizes the conservative nature of Enlightenment thought on women.

P. ZAGORIN, How the Idea of Religious Toleration Came to the West (2003). An excellent exploration of the rise of toleration.

CHAPTER 23

R. ANSTEY, The Atlantic Slave Trade and British Abolition, 1760–1810 (1975). A standard overview that emphasizes the role of religious factors.

B. BAILYN, The Ideological Origins of the American Revolution (1967). An important work illustrating the role of English radical thought in the perceptions of the American colonists.

K.M. BAKER, Inventing the French Revolution: Essays on French Political Culture in the Eighteenth Century (1990). Important essays on political thought before and during the revolution.

K.M. BAKER and C. LUCAS, eds., The French Revolution and the Creation of Modern Political Culture, 3 vols. (1987). A splendid collection of important original articles on all aspects of politics during the revolution.

R.J. BARMAN, Brazil: The Forging of a Nation, 1798–1852 (1988). The best coverage of this period.

C. BECKER, The Declaration of Independence: A Study in the History of Political Ideas (1922). Remains an important examination of the political and imperial theory of the Declaration.

J.F. BERNARD, Talleyrand: A Biography (1973). A useful account.

L. BETHELL, The Cambridge History of Latin America, Vol. 3 (1985). Contains an extensive treatment of independence.

R. BLACKBURN, The Overthrow of Colonial Slavery, 1776–1848 (1988). A major discussion quite skeptical of the humanitarian interpretation.

T.C.W. BLANNING, ed., The Rise and Fall of the French Revolution (1996). A wide-ranging collection of essays illustrating the debates over the French Revolution.

J. BROOKE, King George III (1972). The best biography.

R. COBB, The People's Armies (1987). The major treatment in English of the revolutionary army.

O. CONNELLY, Napoleon's Satellite Kingdoms (1965). The rule of Napoleon and his family in Europe.

E.V. DA COSTA, The Brazilian Empire (1985). Excellent coverage of the entire nineteenth-century experience of Brazil.

D.B. DAVIS, The Problem of Slavery in the Age of Revolution, 1770–1823 (1975). A transatlantic perspective on the issue.

F. FEHÉR, The French Revolution and the Birth of Modernity (1990). A wide-ranging collection of essays on political and cultural facets of the revolution.

A. FORREST, The French Revolution and the Poor (1981). A study that expands consideration of the revolution beyond the standard social boundaries.

M. GLOVER, The Peninsular War, 1807–1814: A Concise Military History (1974). An interesting account of the military campaign that so drained Napoleon's resources in western Europe.

J. GODECHOT, The Counter-Revolution: Doctrine and Action, 1789–1804 (1971). An examination of opposition to the revolution.

A. GOODWIN, The Friends of Liberty: The English Democratic Movement in the Age of the French Revolution (1979). A major work that explores the impact of the French Revolution on English radicalism.

L. HUNT, Politics, Culture, and Class in the French Revolution (1986). A series of essays that focus on the modes of expression of the revolutionary values and political ideas.

W.W. KAUFMANN, British Policy and the Independence of Latin America, 1802–1828 (1951). A standard discussion of an important relationship.

E. KENNEDY, A Cultural History of the French Revolution (1989). An important examination of the role of the arts, schools, clubs, and intellectual institutions.

M. KENNEDY, The Jacobin Clubs in the French Revolution: The First Years (1982). A careful scrutiny of the organizations chiefly responsible for the radicalizing of the revolution.

M. KENNEDY, The Jacobin Clubs in the French Revolution: The Middle Years (1988). A continuation of the previously listed study.

H. KISSINGER, A World Restored: Metternich, Castlereagh and the Problems of Peace, 1812–1822 (1957). A provocative study by an author who became an American secretary of state.

G. LEFEBVRE, The Coming of the French Revolution (trans. 1947). A classic examination of the crisis of the French monarchy and the events of 1789.

G. LEFEBVRE, Napoleon, 2 vols., trans. by H. Stockhold (1969). The fullest and finest biography.

J. LYNCH, The Spanish American Revolutions, 1808–1826 (1986). An excellent one-volume treatment.

P. MAIER, American Scripture: Making the Declaration of Independence (1997). Stands as a major revision of our understanding of the Declaration.

G. MASUR, Simón Bolívar (1969). The standard biography in English.

S.E. MELZER and L.W. RABINE, eds., Rebel Daughters: Women and the French Revolution (1992). A collection of essays exploring various aspects of the role and image of women in the French Revolution.

M. MORRIS, The British Monarchy and the French Revolution (1998). Explores the manner in which the British monarchy saved itself from possible revolution.

R. MUIR, Tactics and the Experience of Battle in the Age of Napoleon (1998). Examines the wars from the standpoint of the soldiers in combat.

H. NICOLSON, The Congress of Vienna (1946). A good, readable account.

T.O. OTT, The Haitian Revolution, 1789–1804 (1973). An account that clearly relates the events in Haiti to those in France.

R.R. PALMER, Twelve Who Ruled: The Committee of Public Safety During the Terror (1941). A clear narrative and analysis of the policies and problems of the committee.

R.R. PALMER, The Age of the Democratic Revolution: A Political History of Europe and America, 1760–1800, 2 vols. (1959, 1964). An impressive survey of the political turmoil in the transatlantic world.

C. PROCTOR, Women, Equality, and the French Revolution (1990). An examination of how the ideas of the Enlightenment and the attitudes of revolutionaries affected the legal status of women.

A.J. RUSSELL-WOOD, ed., From Colony to Nation: Essays on the Independence of Brazil (1975). A series of important essays.

P. SCHROEDER, The Transformation of European Politics, 1763–1848 (1994). A fundamental treatment of the diplomacy of the era.

T.E. SKIDMORE and P.H. SMITH, Modern Latin America, 4th ed. (1997). A very useful survey.

A. SOBOUL, The Parisian Sans-Culottes and the French Revolution, 1793–94 (1964). The best work on the subject.

A. SOBOUL, The French Revolution (trans. 1975). An important work by a Marxist scholar.

D.G. SUTHERLAND, France, 1789–1825: Revolution and Counter revolution (1986). A major synthesis based on recent scholarship in social history.

T. TACKETT, Religion, Revolution, and Regional Culture in Eighteenth-Century France: The Ecclesiastical Oath of 1791 (1986). The most important study of this topic.

T. TACKETT, Becoming a Revolutionary: The Deputies of the French National Assembly and the Emergence of a Revolutionary Culture (1789–1790) (1996). The best study of the early months of the revolution.

J.M. THOMPSON, Robespierre, 2 vols. (1935). The best biography.

D.K. VAN KEY, The Religious Origins of the French Revolution: From Calvin to the Civil Constitution, 1560–1791 (1996). Examines the manner in which debates within French Catholicism influenced the coming of the revolution.

M. WALZER, ed., Regicide and Revolution: Speeches at the Trial of Louis XVI (1974). An important and exceedingly interesting collection of documents with a useful introduction.

I. WOLOCH, The New Regime: Transformations of the French Civic Order, 1789–1820s (1994). An important overview of just what had and had not changed in France after the quarter century of revolution and war.

G. WOOD, The Radicalism of the American Revolution (1991). A major interpretation.

CHAPTER 24

I. BERLIN, Generations of Captivity: A History of African-American Slaves (2003). A major work.

D. BLACKBOURN, The Long Nineteenth Century: A History of Germany, 1780–1918 (1998). An outstanding survey.

D.G. CREIGHTON, John A. MacDonald (1952, 1955). A major biography of the first Canadian prime minister.

D. DONALD, Lincoln (1995). Now the standard biography.

R.B. EDGERTON, Death or Glory: The Legacy of the Crimean War (2000). Multifaceted study of a badly mismanaged war that transformed many aspects of European domestic politics.

M. HOLT, The Rise and Fall of the American Whig Party: Jacksonian Politics and the Onset of the Civil War (2003). An extensive survey of the Jacksonian era.

R. KEE, The Green Flag: A History of Irish Nationalism (2001). A vast survey.

W. LACQUER, A History of Zionism (1989). The most extensive one-volume treatment.

M.B. LEVINGER, Enlightened Nationalism: The Transformation of Prussian Political Culture, 1806–1848 (2002). A major work based on the most recent scholarship.

J.M. MCPHERSON, The Battle Cry of Freedom: The Civil War Era (1988). An excellent one-volume treatment.

D. MORTON, A Short History of Canada (2001). Useful popular history.

J.P. PARRY, The Rise and Fall of Liberal Government in Victorian Britain (1994). An outstanding study.

A. PLESSIS, The Rise and Fall of the Second Empire, 1852–1871 (1985). A useful survey of France under Napoleon III.

D.M. POTTER, The Impending Crisis, 1848–1861 (1976). A penetrating study of the coming of the American Civil War.

A. SKED, Decline and Fall of the Habsburg Empire, 1815–1918 (2001). A major, accessible survey of a difficult subject.

D.M. SMITH, Cavour (1984). An excellent biography.

C.P. STACEY, Canada and the Age of Conflict (1977, 1981). A study of Canadian foreign relations.

D. WETZEL, A Duel of Giants: Bismarck, Napoleon III, and the Origins of the Franco-Prussian War (2001). Broad study based on most recent scholarship.

CHAPTER 25

M. ADAS, Machines as the Measure of Men: Science, Technology, and Ideologies of Western Dominance (1989). The best single volume on racial thinking and technological advances as forming ideologies of European colonial dominance.

A. ASCHER and P.A. STOLYPIN, The Search for Stability in Late Imperial Russia (2000). A broad-ranging biography based on extensive research.

I. BERLIN, Karl Marx: His Life and Environment, 4th ed. (1996). A classic volume that remains an excellent introduction.

JANET BROWNE, Charles Darwin, 2 vols. (2002). An eloquent, accessible biography.

J. BURROW, The Crisis of Reason: European Thought, 1848–1914 (2000). The best overview available.

A.D. CHANDLER JR., The Visible Hand: Managerial Revolution in American Business (1977). Remains the best discussion of the innovative role of American business.

A. CLARKE, The Struggle for the Breeches: Gender and the Making of the British Working Class (1995). An examination of the manner in which industrialization made problematical the relationships between men and women.

W. CRONIN, Nature's Metropolis: Chicago and the Great West, 1848–1893 (1991) The best examination of any major American nineteenth-century city.

P. GAY, Freud: A Life for Our Time (1988). The new standard biography.

R.F. HAMILTON, Marxism, Revisionism, and Leninism: Explication, Assessment, and Commentary (2000). A contribution from the perspective of a historically minded sociologist.

S. HAHN, A Nation under Our Feet: Black Political Struggles in the Rural South from Slavey to the Great Migration (2003). A major synthesis.

A. HOURANI, Arab Thought in the Liberal Age 1789–1939 (1967). A classic account, clearly written and accessible to the nonspecialist.

D.I. KERTZER and M. BARBAGLI, eds., Family Life in the Long Nineteenth Century, 1789–1913: The History of the European Family (2002). Wide-ranging collection of essays.

J.T. KLOPPENBERG, Uncertain Victory: Social Democracy and Progressivism in European and American Thought (1986). An extremely important comparative study.

J. KÖHLER, Zarathustra's Secret: The Interior Life of Friedrich Nietzsche (2002). A controversial new biography.

L. KOLAKOWSKI, Main Currents of Marxism: Its Rise, Growth, and Dissolution, 3 vols. (1978). Especially good on the last years of the nineteenth century and the early years of the twentieth.

P. KRAUSE, The Battle for Homestead, 1880–1892 (1992). Examines labor relations in the steel industry.

D. LANDES, The Wealth and Poverty of Nations: Why Some Are So Rich and Some So Poor (1998). A major international discussion of the subject.

M. MCGERR, A Fierce Discontent: The Rise and Fall of the Progressive Movement in America, 1870–1920 (2003). The best recent synthesis.

E. MORRIS, Theodore Rex (2002). Major survey of Theodore Roosevelt's presidency and personality.

A. PAIS, Subtle Is the Lord: The Science and Life of Albert Einstein (1983). Remains the most accessible scientific biography.

J. RENDALL, The Origins of Modern Feminism: Women in Britain, France and the United States, 1780–1860 (1985). A well-informed introduction.

R. SERVICE, Lenin: A Biography (2002). Based on new sources and will no doubt become the standard biography.

R.M. UTLEY, The Indian Frontier and the American West, 1846–1890 (1984). A broad survey of the pressures of white civilization against Native Americans.

D. VITAL, A People Apart: The Jews in Modern Europe, 1789–1939 (1999). A deeply informed survey.

CHAPTER 26

S. ARROM, The Women of Mexico City, 1790–1857 (1985). A pioneering study.

E. BERMAN, ed., Women, Culture, and Politics in Latin America (1990). Useful essays.

L. BETHELL, ed., The Cambridge History of Latin America, 8 vols. (1992). The single most authoritative coverage, with extensive bibliographical essays.

V. BULMER-THOMAS, The Economic History of Latin America Since Independence (1994). A major study in every respect.

E.B. BURNS, The Poverty of Progress: Latin America in the Nineteenth Century (1980). Argues that the elites suppressed alternative modes of cultural and economic development.

E.B. BURNS, A History of Brazil (1993). The most useful one-volume treatment.

D. BUSHNELL and N. MACAULAY, The Emergence of Latin America in the Nineteenth Century (1994). A survey that examines the internal development of Latin America during the period.

R. CONRAD, The Destruction of Brazilian Slavery, 1850–1889 (1971). A good survey of the most important problem in Brazil in the second half of the nineteenth century.

R. CONRAD, World of Sorrow: The African Slave Trade to Brazil (1986). An excellent survey of the subject.

E.V. DA COSTA, The Brazilian Empire: Myths and Histories (1985). Essays that provide a thorough introduction to Brazil during the period of empire.

H.S. FERNS, Britain and Argentina in the Nineteenth Century (1968). Explains clearly the intermeshing of the two economies.

M. FONT, Coffee, Contention, and Change in the Making of Modern Brazil (1990). Extensive discussion of the problems of a single-commodity economy.

R. GRAHAM, Britain and the Onset of Modernization in Brazil (1968). Another study of British economic dominance.

S.H. HABER, Industry and Underdevelopment: The Industrialization of Mexico, 1890–1940 (1989). Examines the problem of industrialization before and after the revolution.

G. HAHNER, Emancipating the Female Sex: The Struggle for Women's Rights in Brazil, 1850–1940 (1990). An extensive examination of a relatively understudied issue in Latin America.

C.H. HARING, Empire in Brazil: A New World Experiment with Monarchy (1958). Remains a useful overview.

J. HEMMING, Amazon Frontier: The Defeat of the Brazilian Indians (1987). A brilliant survey of the experience of Native Americans in modern Brazil.

R.A. HUMPHREYS, Latin America and the Second World War, 2 vols. (1981–1982). The standard work on the topic.

F. KATZ, ed., Riot, Rebellion, and Revolution in Mexico: Social Base of Agrarian Violence, 1750–1940 (1988). Essays that put the violence of the revolution in a longer context.

A. KNIGHT, The Mexican Revolution, 2 vols. (1986). The best treatment of the subject.

S. MAINWARING, The Catholic Church and Politics in Brazil, 1916–1985 (1986). An examination of a key institution in Brazilian life.

M.C. MEYER and W.L. SHERMAN, The Course of Mexican History (1995). An excellent survey.

M. MORNER, Adventurers and Proletarians: The Story of Migrants in Latin America (1985). Examines immigration to Latin America and migration within it.

J. PAGE, Perón: A Biography (1983). The standard English treatment.

D. ROCK, Politics in Argentina, 1890–1930: The Rise and Fall of Radicalism (1975). The major discussion of the Argentine Radical Party.

D. ROCK, Argentina, 1516–1987: From Spanish Colonization to Alfonsin (1987). Now the standard survey.

D. ROCK, ed., Latin America in the 1940s: War and Postwar Transitions (1994). Essays examining a very difficult decade for the continent.

R.M. SCHNEIDER, "Order and Progress": A Political History of Brazil (1991). A straightforward narrative with helpful notes for further reading.

T.E. SKIDMORE, Black into White: Race and Nationality in Brazilian Thought (1993). Examines the role of racial theory in Brazil.

P.H. SMITH, Argentina and the Failure of Democracy: Conflict Among Political Elites. 1904–1955 (1974). An examination of one of the major political puzzles of Latin American history.

S.J. STEIN and B.H. STEIN, The Colonial Heritage of Latin America: Essays on Economic Dependence in Perspective (1970). A major statement of the dependence interpretation.

D. TAMARIN, The Argentine Labor Movement, 1930–1945: A Study in the Origins of Perónism (1985). A useful introduction to a complex subject.

H.J. WIARDA, Politics and Social Change in Latin America: The Distinct Tradition (1974). Excellent essays that stress the ongoing role of Iberian traditions.

J.D. WIRTH, ed., Latin American Oil Companies and the Politics of Energy (1985). A series of case studies.

J. WOLFE, Working Women, Working Men: São Paulo and the Rise of Brazil's Industrial Working Class, 1900–1955 (1993). Pays particular attention to the role of women.

J. WOMACK, Zapata and the Mexican Revolution (1968). A classic study.

CHAPTER 27

General Works

S. COOK, Colonial Encounters in the Age of High Imperialism (1996). A good introduction to the imperial enterprise in Africa and Asia.

D.K. FIELDHOUSE, The West and the Third World. Trade: Colonialism, Depedence and Development (1999). Addresses whether colonialism was detrimental or beneficial to colonized peoples.

D. HEADRICK, The Tentacles of Progress: Technology Transfer in the Age of Imperialism, 1850–1940 (1988). Discusses the roles of new methods of transportation (railroads, steamships), forms of expertise (doctors, botanists), and other types of "technology transfer" in European colonization, and post-independence development.

P. HOPKIRK, The Great Game: The Struggle for Empire in Central Asia (1992). Focuses on the political and economic rivalries of the imperial powers.

India

A. AHMAD, Islamic Modernism in India and Pakistan, 1857–1964 (1967). The standard survey of Muslim thinkers and movements in India during the period.

C.A. BAYLY, Indian Society and the Making of the British Empire, The New Cambridge History of India, II. 1 (1988). One of several major contributions of this author to the ongoing revision of our picture of modern Indian history since the eighteenth century.

A. GHOSH, In an Antique Land: History in the Guise of a Traveler's Tale (1992). An anthropologist traces the footsteps of a premodern slave traveling with his master from North Africa to India. A gripping tale of premodern life in the India Ocean basin and also of contemporary Egypt.

R. GUHA, ed., Subaltern Studies: Writings on South Asian History and Society (1982). Essays on the colonial period that focus on the social, political, and economic history of "subaltern" groups and classes (hill tribes, peasants, etc.) rather than only the elites of India.

S.N. HAY, ed., "Modern India and Pakistan," Part VI of Wm. Theodore de Bary et al., eds., Sources of Indian Tradition, 2nd ed. (1988). A superb selection of primary-source documents, with brief introductions and helpful notes.

F. ROBINSON, ed., The Cambridge Encyclopedia of India, Pakistan, Bangladesh, Sri Lanka, Nepal, Bhutan, and the Maldives (1989). A fine collection of survey articles by various scholars, organized into topical chapters ranging from "Economies" to "Cultures."

Central Islamic Lands

J.J. DONAHUE and J.L. ESPOSITO, eds., Islam in Transition: Muslim Perspectives (1982). An interesting selection of primary-source materials on Islamic thinking in this century.

W. CLEVELAND, A History of the Modern Middle East, 3rd ed. (2004). A balanced and well-organized overview of modern Middle Eastern history.

A. DAWISHA, Arab Nationalism in the Twentieth Century, From Triumph to Despair (2003). A good overview of the development of Arab nationalism.

S. DERINGIL, The Well-Protected Domains: Ideology and the Legitimation of Power in the Ottoman Empire, 1876–1909 (1998). An impressive study on nationalism and reform in the Ottoman Empire.

D.F. EICKELMAN, Knowledge and Power in Morocco: The Education of a Twentieth-Century Notable (1985). A fascinating study of traditional Islamic education and society in the twentieth century through a social biography of a Moroccan religious scholar and judge.

A. HOURANI, Arabic Thought in the Liberal Age, 1798–1939 (1967). The standard work, by which all subsequent scholarship on the topic is to be judged.

N.R. KEDDIE, An Islamic Response to Imperialism (1968). A brief study of al-Afghani, the great Muslim reformer, with translations of a number of his writings.

B. Lewis, The Emergence of Modern Turkey, 2nd ed. (1968). A concise but thorough history of the creation of the Turkish state, including nineteenth-century background.

J.O. Voll, Islam: Continuity and Change in the Modern World (1982). Chapters 1–6. An interpretive survey of the Islamic world since the eighteenth century. Its emphasis on eighteenth-century reform movements is especially noteworthy.

Africa

C. Achebe, Things Fall Apart (1959). Reading this classic novel may be the best way to get a profound sense of the ways African and European cultures interacted in the early colonial period.

D. Anderson, Histories of the Hanged: The Dirty War in Kenya and the End of Empire (2005). This account of the Kikuyu-led Mau Mau movement in Kenya emphasizes the way Mau Mau activities, and the British response, shaped and distorted Kenya's independence movement. (See also C. Elkins' Imperial Reckoning..., below.)

A.A. Boahen, Africa Under Colonial Domination, 1880–1935 (1985). Vol. VII of the UNESCO General History of Africa. Excellent chapters on various regions of Africa in the period. Chapters 3–10 detail African resistance to European colonial intrusion in diverse regions.

W. Cartey and M. Kilson, eds., The Africa Reader: Colonial Africa (1970). Original source materials give a vivid picture of African resistance to colonial powers, adaptation to foreign rule, and the emergence of the African masses as a political force.

P. Curtin, S. Feiermann, L. Thompson, and J. Vansina, African History (1978). The relevant portions are Chapters 10–20.

B. Davidson, Modern Africa: A Social and Political History (1989). A very useful survey of African history.

C. Elkins, Imperial Reckoning: The Untold Story of Britain's Gulag in Kenya (2004). The Pulitzer Prize–winning account of Britain's appalling response to the Mau Mau movement in colonial Kenya; while Elkins focuses on the British, D. Anderson in Histories of the Hanged (see above) emphasizes the Kenyan side of the story.

J.D. Fage, A History of Africa (1978). The relevant chapters, which give a particularly clear overview of the colonial period, are 12–16.

B. Freund, The Making of Contemporary Africa: The Development of African Society Since 1800 (1984). A refreshingly direct synthetic discussion and survey that take an avowedly, but not reductive, materialist approach to interpretation.

E. Gilbert and J.T. Reynolds, Africa in World History: From Prehistory to the Present (2004). An engaging overview of the period, with attention to technology, economics, and ideologies, among other factors. See especially chapters 13–15.

D. Headrick, Tools of Empire (1982). A provocative evaluation of the roles played by technology in the imperial venture.

A. Hochschild, King Leopood's Ghost: A Story of Greed, Terror, and Heroism in Colonial Africa (1998). A compelling, well-documented narrative of the atrocities committed in turn-of-the-twentieth-century Congo when it was held as the personal fiefdom of Belgium's monarch.

T. Pakenham, The Scramble for Africa (1991). An excellent analysis of the imperialist age in Africa.

A.D. Roberts, ed., The Colonial Moment in Africa: Essays on the Movement of Minds and Materials, 1900–1940 (1986). Chapters from The Cambridge History of Africa treating various aspects of the colonial period in Africa, including economics, politics, and religion.

CHAPTER 28

China

P.M. Coble, The Shanghai Capitalists and the Nationalist Government, 1927–1937 (1980).

L.E. Eastman, The Abortive Revolution: China Under Nationalist Rule, 1927–1937 (1974).

L.E. Eastman, Seeds of Destruction: Nationalist China in War and Revolution, 1937–1949 (1984).

M. Elvin and G.W. Skinner, The Chinese City Between Two Worlds (1974). A study of the late Qing and Republican eras.

J.W. Esherick, The Origins of the Boxer Rebellion (1987).

S. Et, China's Republican Revolution (1994).

J.K. FAIRBANK and M. GOLDMAN, China, a New History (1998). A survey of the entire sweep of Chinese history; especially strong on the modern period.

J.K. FAIRBANK and D. TWITCHETT, eds., The Cambridge History of China. Like the premodern volumes in the same series, the volumes on modern China represent a survey of what is known. Volumes 10–15, which cover the history from the late Qing to the People's Republic, have been published, and the others will be available soon. The series is substantial. Each volume contains a comprehensive bibliography.

J. FITZGERALD, Awakening China: Politics, Culture, and Class in the Nationalist Revolution (1996).

C. HAO, Chinese Intellectuals in Crisis: Search for Order and Meaning, 1890–1911 (1987).

W.C. KIRBY, ed., State and Economy in Republican China (2001).

P.A. KUHN, Rebellion and Its Enemies in Late Imperial China: Militarization and Social Structure, 1796–1864 (1980). A study of how the Confucian gentry saved the Manchu dynasty after the Taiping Rebellion.

P. KUHN, Origins of the Modern Chinese State (2002).

J. LEVENSON, Liang Ch'i-ch'ao and the Mind of Modern China (1953). A classic study of a major Chinese reformer and thinker.

LU XUN, Selected Works (1960). Novels, stories, and other writings by modern China's greatest writer.

S. NAQUIN, Peking: Temples and City Life, 1400–1900 (2000).

E.O. REISCHAUER, J.K. FAIRBANK, and A.M. CRAIG, East Asia: Tradition and Transformation (1989). A detailed text on East Asian history. Contains ample chapters on Japan and China and shorter chapters on Korea and Vietnam.

H.Z. SCHIFFRIN, Sun Yat-sen, Reluctant Revolutionary (1980). A biography.

B.I. SCHWARTZ, Chinese Communism and the Rise of Mao (1951). A classic study of Mao, his thought, and the Chinese Communist Party before 1949.

B.I. SCHWARTZ, In Search of Wealth and Power: Yen Fu and the West (1964). A fine study of a late-nineteenth-century thinker who introduced Western ideas into China.

J.D. SPENCE, The Gate of Heavenly Peace: The Chinese and Their Revolution, 1895–1980 (1981). Historical reflections on twentieth-century China.

J.D. SPENCE, The Search for Modern China (1990). A thick text but well written.

M. SZONYI, Practicing Kinship: Lineage and Descent in Late Imperial China (2002).

S.Y. TENG and J.K. FAIRBANK, China's Response to the West (1954). A superb collection of translations from Chinese thinkers and political figures, with commentaries.

T.H. WHITE and A. JACOBY, Thunder Out of China (1946). A view of China during World War II by two who were there.

Japan

G. AKITA, Foundations of Constitutional Government in Modern Japan (1967). A study of It Hirobumi in the political process leading to the Meiji constitution.

G.C. ALLEN, A Short Economic History of Modern Japan (1958).

A.E. BARSHAY, The Social Sciences in Modern Japan: the Marxian and Modernist Traditions (2004). Different interpretations of history.

J.R. BARTHOLOMEW, The Formation of Science in Japan (1989). The pioneering English-language work on the subject.

W.G. BEASLEY, Japanese Imperialism, 1894–1945 (1987). Excellent short book on the subject.

G.M. BERGER, Parties Out of Power in Japan, 1931–1941 (1977). An analysis of the condition of political parties during the militarist era.

G.L. BERNSTEIN, Recreating Japanese Women, 1600–1945 (1991).

The Cambridge History of Japan, The Nineteenth Century, M.B. Jansen, ed. (1989); The Twentieth Century, P. Duus, ed. (1988). Multi-author works.

A.M. CRAIG, Chsh in the Meiji Restoration (2000). A study of the Chsh domain, a Prussia of Japan, during the period 1840–1868.

A.M. CRAIG and D.H. SHIVELY, eds., Personality in Japanese History (1970). An attempt to gauge the role of individuals and their personalities as factors explaining history.

P. Duus, Party Rivalry and Political Change in Taisho Japan (1968). A study of political change in Japan during the 1910s and 1920s.

P. Duus, The Abacus and the Sword: The Japanese Penetration of Korea, 1895–1910 (1995). A thoughtful analysis.

S. Ericson, The Sound of the Whistle: Railroads and the State in Meiji Japan (1996). An economic and social history of railroads, an engine of growth and popular symbol.

Y. Fukuzawa, Autobiography (1966). Japan's leading nineteenth-century thinker tells of his life and of the birth of modern Japan.

A. Garon, The State and Labor in Modern Japan (1987). A fine study of the subject.

C.N. Gluck, Japan's Modern Myths: Ideology in the Late Meiji Period (1988). A brilliant study of the complex weave of late Meiji thought.

A. Gordon, The Evolution of Labor Relations in Japan: Heavy Industry, 1853–1955 (1985). A seminal work.

B.R. Hackett, Yamagata Aritomo in the Rise of Modern Japan, 1932–1922 (1973). History as seen through the biography of a central figure.

I. Hall, Mori Arinori (1973). A biography of Japan's first minister of education.

T.R.H. Havens, The Valley of Darkness: The Japanese People and World War II (1978). Wartime society.

C. Iriye, After Imperialism: The Search for a New Order in the Far East, 1921–1931 (1965). (Also see other studies by this author.)

D.M.B. Jansen and G. Rozman, eds., Japan in Transition from Tokugawa to Meiji (1986). Contains fine essays.

W. Johnston, The Modern Epidemic: A History of Tuberculosis in Japan (1995). A social history of a disease.

E. Keene, ed., Modern Japanese Literature, An Anthology (1960). A collection of modern Japanese short stories and excerpts from novels.

F.Y.T. Matsusaka, The Making of Japanese Manchuria, 1904–1932 (2001). On railroad strategies in empire building.

J.W. Morley, ed., The China Quagmire (1983). A study of Japan's expansion on the continent between 1933 and 1941. (For diplomatic history, see also the many other works by this author.)

R.H. Myers and M.R. Peattie, eds., The Japanese Colonial Empire, 1895–1945 (1984).

T. Najita, Hara Kei in the Politics of Compromise, 1905–1915 (1967). A study of one of Japan's greatest party leaders.

K. Ohkawa and H. Rosovsky, Japanese Economic Growth: Trend Acceleration in the Twentieth Century (1973).

M. Ravina, The Last Samurai: The Life and Battles of Saigo Takamori (2004). Unlike the movie, this account of the Satsuma uprising is historical.

G. Shiba, Remembering Aizu (1999). A stirring autobiographical account of a samurai youth whose domain lost in the Meiji Restoration.

K. Smith, A Time of Crisis: The Great Depression and Rural Revitalization (2001). An intellectual history of village movements during the 1930s.

J.J. Stephan, Hawaii Under the Rising Sun (1984). Japan's plans for rule in Hawaii.

R.H. Spector, Eagle Against the Sun: The American War with Japan (1985). A narrative of World War II in the Pacific.

E.P. Tsurumi, Factory Girls: Women in the Thread Mills of Meiji Japan (1990). A sympathetic analysis of the key component of the Meiji labor force.

W. Wray, Mitsubishi and the N. Y. K., 1870–1914 (1984). The growth of a shipping zaibatsu, with analysis of business strategies, the role of government and imperialist involvements.

CHAPTER 29

L. Albertini, The Origins of the War of 1914, 3 vols. (1952, 1957). Discursive but invaluable.

V.R. Berghahn, Germany and the Approach of War in 1914 (1973). A work similar in spirit to both of Fischer's (see below) but stressing the importance of Germany's naval program.

S.B. FAY, The Origins of the World War; 2 vols. (1928). The most influential of the revisionist accounts.

F. FISCHER, Germany's Aims in the First World War (1967). An influential interpretation that stirred a great controversy in Germany and around the world by emphasizing Germany's role in bringing on the war.

D. FROMKIN, Europe's Last Summer: Who Started the Great War in 1914? (2004). A lively account that fixes on the final crisis in July 1914.

J.N. HORNE, Labour at War: France and Britain, 1914–1918 (1991). An examination of a major issue on the home fronts.

J. KEEGAN, The First World War (1999). A vivid and readable narrative.

P. KENNEDY, The Rise of the Anglo-German Antagonism, 1860–1914 (1980). An unusual and thorough analysis of the political, economic, and cultural roots of important diplomatic developments.

D.C.B. LIEVEN, Russia and the Origins of the First World War (1983). A good account of the forces that shaped Russian policy.

A. MOMBAUER, The Origins of the First World War: Controversies and Consensus (2002). A fascinating survey of the debate over the decades and the current state of the question.

R. PIPES, A Concise History of the Russian Revolution (1996). A one-volume version of a scholarly masterpiece.

Z. STEINER, Britain and the Origins of the First World War (1977). A perceptive and informed account of the way British foreign policy was made in the years before the war.

H. STRACHAN, The First World War (2004). A fine one-volume account of the war.

A.J.P. TAYLOR, The Struggle for Mastery in Europe, 1848–1918 (1954). Clever but controversial.

S.R. WILLIAMSON JR., Austria-Hungary and the Origins of the First World War (1991). A valuable study of a complex subject.

CHAPTER 30

W.S. ALLEN, The Nazi Seizure of Power: The Experience of a Single German Town, 1930–1935, rev. ed. (1984). A classic treatment of Nazism in a microcosmic setting.

J. BARNARD, Walter Reuther and the Rise of the Auto Workers (1983). A major introduction to the new American unions of the 1930s.

K.D. BRACHER, The German Dictatorship (1970). A comprehensive treatment of both the origins and the functioning of the Nazi movement and government.

A. BULLOCK, Hitler: A Study in Tyranny, rev. ed. (1964). The best biography.

M. BURLEIGH and W. WIPPERMAN, The Racial State: Germany 1933–1945 (1991). Emphasizes the manner in which racial theory influenced numerous areas of policy.

R. CONQUEST, The Great Terror: Stalin's Purges of the Thirties (1968). The best treatment of the subject to this date.

G. CRAIG, Germany, 1866–1945 (1978). A major survey.

I. DEUTSCHER, The Prophet Armed (1954), The Prophet Unarmed (1959), and The Prophet Outcast (1963). Remains the major biography of Trotsky.

I. DEUTSCHER, Stalin: A Political Biography, 2nd ed. (1967). The best biography in English.

B. EICHENGREEN, Golden Fetters: The Gold Standard and the Great Depression, 1919–1939 (1992). A remarkable study of the role of the gold standard in the economic policies of the interwar years.

E. EYCK, A History of the Weimar Republic, 2 vols. (trans. 1963). The story as narrated by a liberal.

M.S. FAUSOLD, The Presidency of Herbert Hoover (1985). An important treatment.

G. FELDMAN, The Great Disorder: Politics, Economics, and Society in the German Inflation, 1914–1924 (1993). The best work on the subject.

S. FITZPATRICK, Stalin's Peasants: Resistance and Survival in the Russian Village After Collectivization (1994). A pioneering study.

P. FUSSELL, The Great War and Modern Memory (1975). A brilliant account of the literature arising from World War I during the 1920s.

J.K. GALBRAITH, The Great Crash (1979). A well-known account by a leading economist.

R. GELLATELY, The Gestapo and German Society: Enforcing Racial Policy, 1933–1945 (1990). A discussion of how the police state supported Nazi racial policies.

H.J. GORDON, Hitler and the Beer Hall Putsch (1972). An excellent account of the event and the political situation in the early Weimar Republic.

R. HAMILTON, Who Voted for Hitler? (1982). An examination of voting patterns and sources of Nazi support.

J. HELD, ed., The Columbia History of Eastern Europe in the Twentieth Century (1992). Individual essays on each country.

P. KENEZ, The Birth of the Propaganda State: Soviet Methods of Mass Mobilization, 1917–1929 (1985). An examination of the manner in which the Communist government inculcated popular support.

B. KENT, The Spoils of War: The Politics, Economics, and Diplomacy of Reparations, 1918–1932 (1993). A comprehensive account of the intricacies of the reparations problem of the 1920s.

D. LANDES, The Unbound Prometheus: Technological Change and Industrial Development in Western Europe from 1750 to the Present (1969). Includes an excellent analysis of both the Great Depression and the few areas of economic growth.

B. LINCOLN, Red Victory: A History of the Russian Civil War (1989). An excellent narrative account.

M. McAULEY, Bread and Justice: State and Society in Petrograd, 1917–1922 (1991). A study that examines the impact of the Russian Revolution and Leninist policies on a major Russian city.

D.J.K. PEUKERT, Inside Nazi Germany: Conformity, Opposition, and Racism in Everyday Life (1987). An excellent discussion of life under Nazi rule.

R. PIPES, The Unknown Lenin: From the Secret Archives (1996). A collection of previously unpublished documents that indicated the repressive character of Lenin's government.

P. PULZER, Jews and the German State: The Political History of a Minority, 1848–1933 (1992). A detailed history by a major historian of European minorities.

L.J. RUPP, Mobilizing Women for War: German and America Propaganda, 1939–1945 (1978). Although concentrating on a later period, it includes an excellent discussion of general Nazi attitudes toward women.

A.M. SCHLESINGER JR., The Age of Roosevelt, 3 vols. (1957–1960). The most important overview.

D.M. SMITH, Mussolini's Roman Empire (1976). A general description of the Fascist regime in Italy.

D.M. SMITH, Italy and Its Monarchy (1989). A major treatment of an important neglected subject.

A. SOLZHENITSYN, The Gulag Archipelago, 3 vols. (1974–1979). A major examination of the labor camps under Stalin by one of the most important contemporary Russian writers.

R.J. SONTAG, A Broken World, 1919–1939 (1971). An exceptionally thoughtful and well-organized survey.

A.J.P. TAYLOR, English History, 1914–1945 (1965). Lively and opinionated.

H.A. TURNER JR., German Big Business and the Rise of Hitler (1985). An important major study of the subject.

H.A. TURNER JR., Hitler's Thirty Days to Power (1996). A narrative of the events leading directly to the Nazi seizure of power.

L. YAHIL, The Holocaust: The Fate of European Jewry, 1932–1945 (1990). A major study of this fundamental subject in twentieth-century history.

CHAPTER 31

A. ADAMTHWAITE, France and the Coming of the Second World War, 1936–1939 (1977). A careful account making good use of the French archives.

O. BARTOV, Mirrors of Destruction: War, Genocide, and Modern Identity (2001). Remarkably penetrating essays.

E.R. BECK, Under the Bombs: The German Home Front, 1942–1945 (1986). An interesting examination of a generally unstudied subject.

P.M.H. BELL, The Origins of the Second World War in Europe, 3rd ed. (2007). A comprehensive study of the period and debates surrounding the European origins of the Second World War.

A. BEEVOR, The Spanish Civil War (2001). Particularly strong on the political issues.

C. BROWNING, The Origins of the Final Solution: The Evolution of the Nazi Jewish Policy (2004). The story of how Hitler's policy developed from discrimination to annihilation

A. BULLOCK, Hitler: A Study in Tyranny, rev. ed. (1964). A brilliant biography.

W.S. CHURCHILL, The Second World War, 6 vols. (1948–1954). The memoirs of the great British leader.

A. CROZIER, The Causes of the Second World War, 1997. An examination of what brought on the war.

R.B. FRANK, Downfall: The End of the Imperial Japanese Empire (1998). A thorough, well-documented account of the last months of the Japanese empire and the reasons for its surrender.

J.L. GADDIS, We Now Know: Rethinking Cold War History (1998). A fine account of the early years of the Cold War, making use of new evidence emerging since the collapse of the Soviet Union.

J.L. GADDIS, P.H. GORDON, E. MAY, eds., Cold War Statesmen Confront the Bomb: Nuclear Diplomacy Since 1945 (1999). A collection of essays discussing the effect of atomic and nuclear weapons on diplomacy since WWII.

M. GILBERT, The Holocaust: A History of the Jews of Europe During the Second World War (1985). The best and most comprehensive treatment.

A. IRIYE, Pearl Harbor and the Coming of the Pacific War (1999). Essays on how the Pacific war came about, including a selection of documents.

J. KEEGAN, The Second World War (1990). A lively and penetrating account by a master military historian.

I. KERSHAW, Hitler: 1889–1936: Hubris (1999) and Hitler, 1936–1945: Nemesis (2001). An outstanding two-volume biography.

W.F. KIMBALL, Forged in War: Roosevelt, Churchill, and the Second World War (1998). A study of the collaboration between the two great leaders of the West based on a thorough knowledge of their correspondence.

W. MURRAY and A.R. MILLETT, A War to Be Won: Fighting the Second World War (2000). A splendid account of the military operations in the war.

P. NEVILLE, Hitler and Appeasement: The British Attempt to Prevent the Second World War (2005). A defense of the British appeasers of Hitler.

R. OVERY, Why the Allies Won (1997). An anlysis of the reasons for the victory of the Allies, with special emphasis on technology.

N. RICH, Hitler War Aims, 2 vols. (1973–1974). The best study of the subject in English.

P. WANDYCZ, The Twilight of French Eastern Alliances, 1926–1936 (1988). A well-documented account of the diplomacy of central and eastern Europe in a crucial period.

G.L. WEINBERG, A World at Arms: A Global History of World War II (1994). A thorough and excellent narrative account.

CHAPTER 32

B.S. ANDERSON and J.P. PINSSER, A History of Their Own: Women in Europe from Prehistory to the Present, Vol. 2 (1988). A broad-ranging survey.

R. BERNSTEIN, Out of the Blue: The Story of September 11, 2001, from Jihad to Ground Zero (2002). An excellent account by a gifted journalist.

A. BROWN, The Gorbachev Factor (1996). An important commentary by an English observer.

D. CALLEO, Rethinking Europe's Future (2003). A daring book by an experienced commentator.

J.L. GADDIS, What We Know Now (1997). Examines the Cold War in light of newly released documents.

D.J. GARROW, Bearing the Cross: Martin Luther King Jr. and the Southern Leadership Conference, 1955–1968 (1986). The best work on the subject.

W. HITCHCOCK, Struggle for Europe: The Turbulent History of a Divided Continent, 1945–2002 (2003). The best overall narrative now available.

D. KEARNS, Lyndon Johnson and the American Dream (1976). A useful biography.

J. KEEP, The Last of the Empires: A History of the Soviet Union, 1956–1991 (1995). A clear narrative.

M. MANDELBAUM, The Ideas That Conquered the World: Peace, Democracy, and Free Markets (2002). An important analysis by a major commentator on international affairs.

J. MANN, The Rise of the Vulcans: The History of Bush's War Cabinet (2004). An account of the major foreign policy advisors behind the invasion of Iraq.

R. MANN, A Grand Delusion: America's Descent into Vietnam (2001). The best recent narrative.

J. McCORMICK, Understanding the European Union: A Concise Introduction (2002). Outlines the major features.

N. NAIMARK, Fires of Hatred: Ethnic Cleansing in Twentieth-Century Europe (2002). A remarkably sensitive treatment of a tragic subject.

R. SAWKA and ANNE STEVENS, eds., Contemporary Europe (2000). A collection of essays on major topics.

G. STOKES, ed., From Stalinism to Pluralism: A Documentary History of Eastern Europe Since 1945 (1996). An important collection of documents that are not easily accessible elsewhere.

M. WALKER, The Cold War and the Making of the Modern World (1994). A major survey.

CHAPTER 33

China

R. BAUM, Burying Mao: Chinese Politics in the Age of Deng Xiaoping (1996).

A. CHAN, R. MADSEN, J. UNGER, Chen Village Under Mao and Deng (1992).

J. CHANG, Wild Swans: Three Daughters of China (1991). An intimate look at recent Chinese society through three generations of women. Immensely readable.

J. FENG, Ten Years of Madness: Oral Histories of China's Cultural Revolution (1996).

J. FEWSMITH, China Since Tiananmen: The Politics of Transition (2001). Focus is on the rise to power of Jiang Zemin and Chinese politics during the nineties.

B.M. FROLIC, Mao's People: Sixteen Portraits of Life in Revolutionary China (1987).

T. GOLD, State and Society in the Taiwan Miracle (1986). The story of economic growth in postwar Taiwan.

M. GOLDMAN, Sowing the Seeds of Democracy in China: Political Reform in the Deng Xiaoping Era (1994).

A. IRIYE, China and Japan in the Global Setting (1992).

D.M. LAMPTON, Same Bed, Different Dreams: Managing U.S.–China Relations, 1989–2000 (2001).

H. LIANG, Son of the Revolution (1983). An autobiographical account of a young man growing up in Mao's China.

K. LIEBERTHAL, Governing China, from Revolution Through Reform (2004).

B. LIU, People or Monsters? and Other Stories and Reportage from China After Mao (1983). Literary reflections on China.

R. MACFARQUHAR and J.K. FAIRBANK, eds., The Cambridge History of China, Vol. 14, Emergence of Revolutionary China (1987), and Vol. 15, Revolutions Within the Chinese Revolution, 1966–1982 (1991).

L. PAN, Sons of the Yellow Emperor: A History of the Chinese Diaspora (1990). A pioneer study that treats not only Southeast Asia but the rest of the world as well.

M.R. RISTAINO, Port of Last Resort: The Diaspora Communities of Shanghai (2001).

T. SAICH, Governance and Politics of China (2004).

H. WANG, China's New Order (2003). Translation of a work by a Qinghua University professor, a liberal within the boundaries of what is permissable in China.

G. WHITE, ed., In Search of Civil Society: Market Reform and Social Change in Contemporary China (1996).

M. WOLF, Revolution Postponed: Women in Contemporary China (1985).

ZHANG X. and SANG Y., Chinese Lives: An Oral History of Contemporary China (1987).

Japan

G.L. BERNSTEIN, Haruko's World: A Japanese Farm Woman and Her Community (1983). A study of the changing life of a village woman in postwar Japan.

T. BESTOR, Neighborhood Tokyo (1989). A portrait of contemporary urban life in Japan.

G.L. CURTIS, The Logic of Japanese Politics: Leaders, Institutions, and the Limits of Change (1999).

G.L. CURTIS, Policymaking in Japan: Defining the Role of Politicians (2002).

M.H. CUSUMANO, The Japanese Automobile Industry (1985). A neat study of the postwar business strategies of Toyota and Nissan.

R.P. DORE, City Life in Japan (1999). A classic, reissued.

R.P. DORE, Land Reform in Japan (1959). Another classic.

S. GARON, Molding Japanese Minds: The State in Everyday Life (1997).

S.M. GARON, The Evolution of Civil Society from Meiji to Heisei (2002). That is to say, from the mid-nineteenth century to the present day.

A. GORDON, ed., Postwar Japan as History (1993).

H. HIBBETT, ed., Contemporary Japanese Literature: An Anthology of Fiction, Film, and Other Writing Since 1945 (1977). Translations of postwar short stories.

Y. KAWABATA, The Sound of the Mountain (1970). Sensitive, moving novel by a Nobel author.

J. NATHAN, Sony, the Private Life (1999). A lively account of the human side of growth in the Sony Corporation.

D. OKIMOTO, Between MITI and the Market (1989). A discussion of the respective roles of government and private enterprise in Japan's postwar growth.

S. PHARR, Losing Face: Status Politics in Japan (1996).

E.F. VOGEL, Japan as Number One: Lessons for America (1979). While dated and somewhat sanguine, this remains an insightful classic.

Korea and Vietnam

B. CUMINGS, Korea: The Unknown War (1988).

B. CUMINGS, The Origins of the Korean War (Vol. 1, 1981; Vol. 2, 1991).

B. CUMINGS, The Two Koreas: On the Road to Reunification? (1990).

C.J. ECKERT, Korea Old and New, A History (1990). The best short history of Korea, with extensive coverage of the postwar era.

C.J. ECKERT, Offspring of Empire: The Koch'ang Kims and the Colonial Origins of Korean Capitalism, 1876–1945 (1991).

G.M.T. KAHIN, Intervention: How America Became Involved in Vietnam (1986).

S. KARNOW, Vietnam: A History, rev. ed. (1996).

L. KENDALL, Shamans, Housewives, and Other Restless Spirits: Women in Korean Ritual and Life (1985).

K.B. LEE, A New History of Korea (1984). A translation by E. Wagner and others of an outstanding Korean work covering the full sweep of Korean history.

T. LI, Nguyen Cochinchina: South Vietnam in the Seventeenth and Eighteenth Centuries (1998).

D. MARR, Vietnam 1945: The Quest for Power (1995).

C.W. SORENSEN, Over the Mountains Are Mountains (1988). How peasant households in Korea adapted to rapid industrialization.

A. WOODSIDE, Vietnam and the Chinese Model (1988). Provides the background for Vietnam's relationship to China.

CHAPTER 34

General Works

P. FARMER, Pathologies of Power: Health, Human Rights, and the New War on the Poor (2003). Farmer, a physician, uses his experiences at Harvard and in the Caribbean to argue that inadequate healthcare in the third world violates human rights, and imperils us all.

J.H. LATHAM, Africa, Asia, and South America Since 1800: A Bibliographic Guide (1995). A valuable tool for finding materials on the topics in this chapter.

S. POWER, A Problem from Hell: America and the Age of Genocide (2002). A masterful analysis of genocides in the twentieth century (in Armenia, the Holocaust, the Khmer Rouge, Kurds, Rwanda, and Bosnia) and the U.S. response.

J.D. SACHS, The End of Poverty: Economic Possibilities for Our Time (2005). A renowned economist's plan to end extreme poverty around the world by 2025.

Latin America

P. BAKEWELL, A History of Latin America: c. 1450 to the Present (2003). An up-to-date survey.

A. CHOMSKY ET AL., The Cuba Reader: History, Culture, Politics (2004). Very useful, broad-ranging anthology.

J. DOMINGUEZ and M. SHIFTER, Constructing Democratic Governance in Latin America (2003). Contains individual country studies.

G. JOSEPH ET AL., The Mexico Reader: History, Culture, Politics (2003). Excellent introduction to major issues.

P. LOWDEN, Moral Opposition to Authoritarian Rule in Chile (1996). A discussion of Chilean politics from the standpoint of human rights.

J. PRESTON and S. DILLON, Opening Mexico: The Making of a Democracy (2004). Excellent analysis of recent developments in Mexico.

H. WIRARDA, Democracy and Its Discontents: Development, Interdependence, and U.S. Policy in Latin America (1995). A useful overview.

Africa

B. DAVIDSON, Let Freedom Come (1978). Remains a thoughtful commentary of African independence.

P. GOUREVITCH, We Wish to Inform You that Tomorrow We Will Be Killed with Our Families (1999). An account of the Rwandan genocide that is beautifully written, and almost unbearable to read.

J. HERBST, States and Power in Africa (2000). Relates current issues of African state-building to those before the colonial era.

R.W. JULY, A History of the African People, 5th ed. (1995). Provides a careful and clear survey of post–World War I history and consideration of nationalism.

N. MANDELA, Long Walk to Freedom: The Autobiography of Nelson Mandela (1995). Autobiography of the African leader who transformed South Africa.

L. THOMPSON, A History of South Africa (2001). The best survey.

N. VAN DE WALLE, African Economies and the Politics of Permanent Crisis, 1979–1999 (2001). Exploration of difficulties of African economic development.

India and Pakistan

O.B. JONES, Pakistan: Eye of the Storm (2003). Best recent introduction.

R. RASHID, Taliban: Militant Islam, Oil and Fundamentalism in Central Asia (2001). Analysis of radical Isalmist regime in Afghanistan.

R.W. STERN, Changing India: Bourgeois Revolution on the Subcontinent (2003). Overview of forces now changing Indian society.

S. WOLPERT, A New History of India (2003). The closing chapters of this fine survey history are particularly helpful in orienting the reader in postwar Indian history until the mid-1980s.

Islam and the Middle East

A. AHMED, Discovering Islam: Making Sense of Muslim History and Society, rev. ed. (2003). An excellent and readable overiew of Islamic–Western relations.

J. ESPOSITO, The Islamic Threat: Myth or Reality, 2nd ed. (1992). A useful corrective to some of the polemics against Islam and Muslims today.

J.J. ESPOSITO, ed., The Oxford Encyclopedia of Islam (1999). A thematic survey of Islamic history, particularly strong in the Modern Era.

D. FROMKIN, A Peace to End All Peace: The Fall of the Ottoman Empire and the Creation of the Modern Middle East (2001). Very good on the impact of World War I on the region.

G. FULLER, The Future of Political Islam (2003). A very good overview of Islamist ideology by a former CIA staff member.

J. KEAY, Sowing the Wind: The Seeds of Conflict in the Middle East (2003). A balanced account.

N.R. KEDDIE, Modern Iran: Roots and Results of Revolution (2003). Chapters 6–12 focus on Iran from 1941 through the first years of the 1978 revolution and provide a solid overview of history in this era.

G. KEPEL, Jihad: The Trail of Political Islam (2002). An extensive treatment by a leading French scholar of the subject.